The WPA Guide to 1930s Kansas

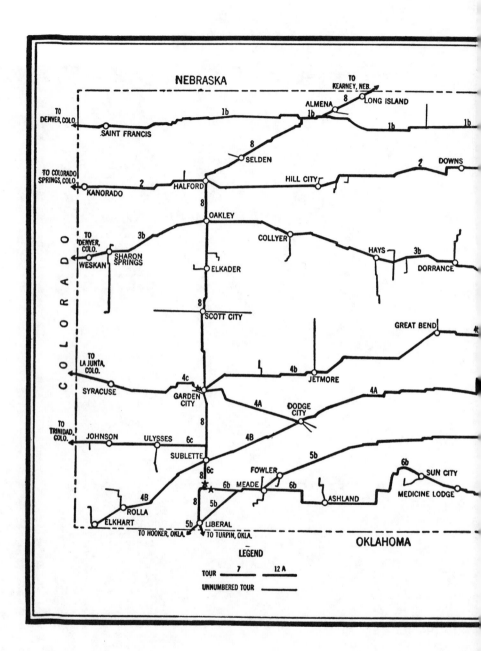

KEY TO KANSAS TOURS

The
WPA GUIDE
to 1930s Kansas

Compiled and Written by the Federal Writers'
Project of the Work Projects Administration
for the State of Kansas
with a New Introduction by James R. Shortridge

UNIVERSITY PRESS OF KANSAS

Introduction © 1984 by the University Press of Kansas
Copyright 1939 by the Kansas Department of Education
All rights reserved

First paperback edition, with a new introduction, published in 1984
Originally published by Viking Press in 1939 under the title
Kansas: A Guide to the Sunflower State

Published by the University Press of Kansas (Lawrence,
Kansas 66049), which was organized by the Kansas Board of Regents
and is operated and funded by Emporia State University,
Fort Hays State University, Kansas State University, Pittsburg State
University, the University of Kansas, and Wichita State University

Library of Congress Catalog Card Number 84-51694
ISBN 0-7006-0249-6

Printed in the United States of America
10   9   8   7   6   5   4

Introduction to the Paperback Edition

AMERICANS are inveterate travelers. We have made explorers such as Daniel Boone and John Wesley Powell into mythic figures and currently are such itinerants that we support a special weekly travel section in nearly every major newspaper. This predilection is full of positive features. Seeing, feeling, and gradually coming to acquire a more complete understanding of peoples and places are marvelous experiences for mind and emotions. Travel brings lessons of cultural appreciation, tolerance, and, often, increased self-knowledge.

Exploration can be undertaken blindly, simply by pointing a car in an arbitrary direction or by boarding the next available bus. If such a traveler is sensitive and takes enough time, the spirit of the places visited can be absorbed and the exploration be deemed a success. William Least Heat Moon's desultory wanderings published as *Blue Highways* (1982) are a recent case in point. For the majority of us, however, with limited time for our travel, a good guide book is of inestimable value. The volume before you is from a series that, quite simply, is the best ever produced for this country.

Serious explorers of America sooner or later hear about this American Guide Series. Once the books are known, no trip is made without them, for they are literate, complete, and thoroughly entertaining companions for the road. Each State has one, and separate volumes exist for selected cities, including Leavenworth in Kansas. They are a legacy of the Federal Writers' Project, a New Deal enterprise begun in 1935 to employ needy writers and research workers.

The Kansas volume, like the others, was truly a group effort. Field workers interviewed older residents and local experts in many fields. Others checked data sources, photographed, and took mileages. Finally Harold Evans and his staff edited the mass into a coherent whole, and the completed book appeared in 1939.

It is one thing to praise a forty-five-year-old book, but quite another matter to recommend it as a travel companion for the 1980's. Still, I make the recommendation without hesitation and know that I am not alone in doing so. Despite the unprecedented changes in landscape of recent decades—interstate highways, suburbanization, and specialized agriculture to name only a few—this old guide continues in demand. Used book stores cannot keep it in stock, and library copies still circulate at a brisk pace. Other State guides have experienced similar demand, and this Kansas reissuance is but one of many occurring nation-wide.

Certainly quality is a major factor in the continuing popularity of the WPA guides. Most other travel books on the market show precious little evidence of real familiarity with their subject region. Often they are little more than a combined listing of motels, State parks, and commercialized "tourist attractions." Like the brochures put out by State tourism bureaus, they ignore the commonplace interplay of land and life that truly characterizes a place. Industries and cities that have fallen on hard times rarely are discussed. The result is a rosy but superficial and highly distorted regional view.

It is easy to criticize the modern books that pass for "guides" to Kansas and other States, but as one who has tried to understand the complex web of circumstances that gives character to a place, I can assure you that the task is not easy. The WPA guides were able to bring together field workers and writers in both a quantity and quality that may never be duplicated again. They truly are classics. Like its companions, the Kansas guide book captures well the elusive sense of place that was the State in 1939. To overhaul paragraphs here and there in light of modern changes, as any reader will be tempted to do, is to harm the mood and tone of the original. Although several States have tried to revise the guides, I think the product ultimately is unsatisfactory. The possibility of a completely new companion volume for the 1939 Kansas guide is an appealing option that will be pursued in years to come.

Evolving Images of Kansas

Beyond the issues of quality and the lack of a modern alternative, the guide book merits attention today precisely because of its age. It is as much a guide to 1939 as it is to Kansas, and 1939 constitutes an excellent cultural baseline from which to measure change. The state was then still in depression times, but it nevertheless saw itself and was seen by others in relatively positive terms. Kansas was the epitome of Thomas Jefferson's pastoral America, and the Nation idealized this as the best kind of life. Big cities still were things to be distrusted, particularly after the Depression had thrown so many people out of urban jobs. Kansans saw themselves as moral leaders. They had been active in the abolitionist and prohibition struggles, in populism, and in progressive social issues generally. William Allen White, from his editorial desk in Emporia, had become essentially the nation's spokesman in the period between the world wars.

Belief in Jeffersonian democracy probably reached a zenith about 1920.

The "back to the land" movement of the Depression prolonged the idealization somewhat, but by 1939 Karl Menninger could discern a collective inferiority complex among the State's people (*Kansas Magazine,* pp. 3–6). Most modern observers agree with his assessment. Political writer Neal Pierce called Kansas "the eclipsed state" in 1972, for example, "scarcely the place where things happen 'first' " (*The Great Plains States of America,* p. 221). Progressivism somehow gave way to conservatism, leadership to cultural backwater. Interpretations of Kansas appearing in the popular literature now routinely begin with a statement of the State's poor image. Although some authors proceed to justify the image and others to challenge it, the important point is that virtually all, at least through the 1970's, recognized that it existed.

Two examples from the mass media should clarify the perceptions. Superman, after coming to Earth as a baby, was raised by a Kansas farm couple named Kent. From them and the rural utopian surroundings, he presumably acquired his notions of "truth, justice, and the American way." A villain from the James Bond adventure "Diamonds Are Forever" epitomizes the other view of Kansas. He wanted to destroy part of the country with a satellite laser, but rejected Kansas as a target because "nobody would notice."

It is possible that another image shift for Kansas is occurring in the 1980's. The glamour of urban life in New York and California, a factor partly responsible for the Kansas "eclipse," has lessened. Americans disenchanted with the stress and alienation seemingly integral to our technological urban society are attracted anew to pastoral settings. Kansans, their rural image firmly intact, are now being touted for their sense of community and harmony with the environment.

Place images are always distorted, and perhaps one of the basic allures of travel is to match our perceptions with the reality of a place. Exploring Kansas today with the 1939 guide in hand gives one the opportunity to examine a whole series of images. Was Kansas in 1939 a rural utopia? Is modern Kansas better described as backwater or as a vanguard for the society as a whole? What has and has not changed on the landscape? Answers are not easy; but the fun, of course, is in the quest. Test the guide's descriptions against the utopian stereotype. Test your personal observations against newspaper sobriquets.

Virtues and Limitations of the Guide

The Kansas guide is sufficiently varied to be both satisfying and disappointing to every reader, depending on individual biases. I think nearly everyone would agree, though, that the former points far outweigh the latter. Good, thorough field interviews and observation top the list of virtues. The writers provide a vivid sense of how places looked and how local economies worked. For example, in consecutive paragraphs describing Route 160 in extreme southwestern Kansas, the reader is given an assessment of agricultural recovery after the Dust Bowl, an explanation of tumbleweeds, and a description of a local tradition of building houses half underground (p. 437).

Part of the power of the descriptions comes from an excellent grasp of local history. We are told the locations of former Indian villages, springs important to early travelers, the inside story on various county seat "wars," and the atmosphere and impact of cattle drives and rain-making schemes. Traditional political and economic history is related in an introductory chapter, and the tours provide almost countless examples of incidents that fit into the larger scheme. In this way, history comes alive for the reader-traveler. Incidents that border on folklore—such as the Moreland "treasure box," Houdini's visit to Garnett, and the naming of Liberal—heighten this feeling. Much of this information came from field interviews with original homesteaders and other pioneers. Guide writers in the 1930's could still find such people; we in the 1980's have an invaluable and vivid picture of evolving Kansas society because they did.

Another virtue of the guide is its honest assessment of the characteristics of a place. This may seem a modest claim, but it is rare in travel literature. Tourism is now big business, and because of it, everyone from major State agencies through chambers of commerce to small-town entrepreneurs tries to make themselves attractive. A *Wall Street Journal* article a few years ago made fun of Cawker City's "largest ball of string" and Greensburg's "deepest hand-dug well," but these promotional efforts are no different in spirit from those undertaken throughout our modern society. Increasingly, hyperbole has replaced frank appraisal, and promotional schemes abound. The guide is a breath of fresh air.

The absence of a promotional tone was partially the result of a Federal Writers' Project policy, but it also was a product of the era. Tourism was not a major industry in 1939; people traveled more slowly and not as frequently. Consider the significance of the simple statement introducing Tour 1, US 36 across the state: "hard-surfaced roadbed over half the route, remainder graveled" (p. 307). Perhaps as a result of such conditions, interesting places on private land are routinely described as "open" or by the phrase "visitors welcome." The unmistakable sense is of neighbors sharing their heritage with neighbors; there are here no "locals" trying to protect themselves from invading hordes of "outsiders" or to exploit these hordes with giant statues of "jackalopes" or a fantasized version of Dorothy and Toto's house. Each city, for example, is described in terms of its historical background, economic base, notable buildings, important events, and the like, but nothing beyond. Ratings (and even listings) of restaurants, lodgings, and the like are avoided. Growth and progress are described where they have occurred, but so is decline. Two of the most interesting discussions, in fact, are on the aftermath of the Dust Bowl in the southwestern part of the State and the status of Iola, Independence, and other towns following the collapse of an industrial boom that ended about 1920.

Most of the limitations of the guide for the modern traveler are unavoidable consequences of forty-five years of change. These changes are more intriguing than frustrating, however, leading to speculation on the nature and pace of our alterations of the State. To undertake the thirteen rural tours that constitute the last two-fifths of the guide, for example, one needs to understand only several major changes in highway numbering. On Tour 3, US 40 has been relocated in two places: between Topeka and Manhattan the road is now called US 24, while between Salina and Dorrance it is Kansas 140. The confusion of having a US 50N and a US 50S on Tour 4 has been rectified: old 50N from Olathe to Larned is now US 56; from Larned to Garden City the old road is currently US 156. Tour 4A's route 50S has become simply US 50. On Tour 4B, Kansas 45 between Dodge City and Elkhart is now US 56. More modest changes affect Tours 8 and 12. Between the Nebraska State line and Selden, US 83 has become US 383. South of Garnett, US 59 has been relocated. The old route is now called US 169 to just south of Chanute, and then becomes a county road eastward to Erie.

William Allen White, in the introductory essay for this guide, emphasized a much-debated issue of Kansas culture that the writers proper failed to probe. Are eastern and western Kansans different breeds of people? White suggested that the harsher western land led not only to a changed economy but to a distinctive cast of mind as well. The characters in Robert Day's novel *The Last Cattle Drive* (1977) seem to feel similarly. Recent cultural studies are inconclusive, but note that western Kansans belong to churches in larger percentages, subscribe to more periodicals per capita, and are more traditional in their choice of names for their children than their eastern counterparts. Young people from the west may be ''go-getters,'' as White suggested, but they are also more apt than others to see their home region in negative terms. What all this means is uncertain, but the subject is a fascinating one to ponder while traveling the state and getting to know its people.

The major weakness of the WPA guides is their treatment of physical geography. The Kansas writers note terrain differences in simple descriptive phrases, but they discuss Doniphan County's orchards without reference to the glacial silt deposits that make them possible and ignore such singular Kansas phenomena as Cheyenne Bottoms in Barton County and the Post Rock country. With some background information, the physical landscape can become as interesting to the traveler as the human scene. I will try to touch some high points in the next few paragraphs; for a more comprehensive but still very readable treatment, see *Kansas Geology* (1984), listed at the end of this introduction.

The rock layers of eastern Kansas are mostly limestones and shales, dipping slightly toward the west. Limestones, because they are relatively resistant to erosion, are the more prominent rocks, and commonly form bluffs up to two hundred feet high. One of these bluff sites is occupied by the University of Kansas campus. The Flint Hills are a continuation of the limestone topography, with a little greater relief. Actually, the distinctiveness of the Flint Hills is more a product of its grass cover and ranching economy than of unique land forms. Sandstone replaces limestone occasionally in eastern Kansas, producing soils of lower fertility. The largest region of this type is called the Chautauqua Hills, a zone about ten miles wide extending along the border between Elk and Chautauqua Counties on the west and Wilson and Montgomery Counties on the east. Even today, these hills remain timbered, a point made several times in the guide.

North of the Kansas River and east of the Big Blue and Tuttle Creek Lake the bedrock has been covered by debris brought to Kansas by glaciation. The result is a strikingly different physical world. Stone houses and fences disappear, for example, as does coal mining, for the limestones and other rocks lie several tens of feet beneath the surface. The terrain is gently rolling in appearance, and the soil is generally deep and rich. Hard reddish rocks called quartzite are scattered about the landscape. These provide clear evidence of the ice's presence, for quartzite does not occur as a surface rock anywhere else in the state. The nearest outcrops are in South Dakota. Terraces are another legacy of the ice important in human affairs. During major glacial advances so much of the world's water supply is frozen that sea levels fall several hundred feet. This drop induces rivers to cut new, deeper channels. Terraces, remnants of the old flood plain, are a by-product of this cutting, left high above the new channel. These terraces have fertile soil, but no flood hazard, and are preferred sites for towns, railroads, highways, and most other valley activities. Tour 4 between Topeka and Junction City follows one of these terraces, usually about seven feet above the flood plain proper.

West of the Flint Hills, dipping limestones and shales continue to be important landscape components. One limestone, the Greenhorn, that appears in a thirty-mile-wide band extending from Republic to Hodgeman County, is the source for the stone fence posts that have come to rival the sunflower as a State symbol. Several of the tours intercept this region. For details on quarrying procedures and a guide to folk architecture using the stone, stop at the Post Rock Museum in LaCrosse or see *Land of the Post Rock* (1975), listed below.

Just to the east of the Greenhorn is another distinctive rock band. Sandstones dominate here, creating the Smoky Hills. Several of the landmarks mentioned in the guide are outcrops of this sandstone, including Rock City, Coronado Heights, and Pawnee Rock. The sandstone formerly was widely used as a building material. Its dark color gives a distinctive, almost ''non-Kansas'' appearance to local structures, including the old bank building now incorporated as part of the famous Brookville Hotel. Because the sandstone fractures and erodes in a pattern different from the dominant Kansas limestones, the topography of the Smoky Hills is also distinctive. Kanapolis Lake in Ellsworth County is an excellent place for inspection.

The High Plains of western Kansas are a remnant of rock and soil debris washed eastward following the uplift of the Rocky Mountains. Beneath the surface these outwash gravels, known as the Ogallala Formation, hold vast amounts of water and are the source for the irrigation boom that began in the 1960's. The land surface iself is mantled by several feet of windblown silt, called loess, which produces a stone-free, fertile soil. Here and there on the High Plains are depressions, or sinks, where the surface material has collapsed into a sub-surface void. St. Jacob's Well, Big Basin, and Old Maid's Pool are examples noted in the guide, although the most famous one, Cheyenne Bottoms, was somehow overlooked. New sinks, caused usually by ground water dissolving beds of rock salt or gypsum, occur regularly, including several in 1984 that threatened the Interstate 70 pavement just west of Russell. Sand deposits along the Arkansas River are a final physical feature worthy of note. A major dune field exists just south of Garden City, now stabilized by irrigation. Stafford County is the core of a vast sand plain with the ''great bend'' of the river. Here wind erosion is such a problem that nearly all farmers resort to planting crops in alternate bands (strip cropping). For similar reasons, shelter belts are more common here than elsewhere in the state.

Kansas Now and Then

Perhaps the greatest pleasure the WPA guide affords modern Kansans is the chance to contemplate a half-century of man-made changes in the landscape. What things have disappeared? What is new? And possibly most important of all, what has remained constant on the scene? The most obvious changes to travelers are probably the roads themselves. The guide was published only fourteen years after the federal government created a uniform system of numbered highways. Interstate systems, a product of the 1956 Federal Aid Highway Act, were far in the future. Many observers have noted the isolating effect created by the high speeds and town by-passes of interstate highways, removing travelers from close contact with local life. Standardization of signs, restaurants, and motels produced an unvarying roadside landscape. Interstates also concentrate travel, so that most visitors to Kansas never see physical or human sites off the I-35, I-70 corridor. It is pointless to try to characterize this change as good or bad. Roadside businesses along US 36 were hurt as I-70 came to dominate east-west travel in the State, for example; but one could also argue that towns along Route 36 have retained a certain integrity and sense of community now lost in towns serving I-70. By concentrating traffic on a few routes, the interstates have left other highways for those who wish to travel and observe at a more leisurely pace.

Because people have continued to move from rural to urban areas in recent decades, it is not surprising that the ''cities and towns'' section of the guide is the most dated. The descriptive sketch for each place is still worth reading, since the focus is mostly on the historical evolution of the local economy, but much else has changed. Comparing city populations given in the guide with 1980 numbers provides some insights. Kansas City, Wichita, and Topeka were the most populous places in 1939, and they continue so today. Wichita has replaced Kansas City at the top spot if one looks strictly at city figures, but if suburban Johnson County is added to the Kansas City total, the old rankings are retained.

The growth of Johnson County is easily the major urban change in the State. This county is remarkable in many ways, but perhaps most notably in the contrast it presents with Kansas City's neighboring Wyandotte County. This county line, in fact, is the sharpest cultural divide in the State. Wyandotte County is a blue-collar, industrial area. It votes Democratic and contains large ethnic and black populations. Because its realtors rarely advertise in the *Kansas City* (Missouri) *Star* and *Times,* newcomers to the metropolitan area seldom locate there. The Kansas City, Kansas, population is thus more stable than that of other cities of comparable size, and its residents have deeper historical ''roots'' in the area. Johnson County is the antithesis of all this, exemplifying a well-to-do suburbia. Outside observers contrast a superiority complex on the part of Johnson Countians with an inferiority complex in Wyandotte County. A recent poll of college students from the two places reinforces this contrast: many Wyandotte students saw their home as ''the slums,'' many Johnson Countians labeled their home as ''snob hill.''

Beyond suburban developments, major growth has occurred in two other types of cities. Lawrence and Manhattan, the leading university towns, each has more than tripled its population since 1939. Both have excellent rail and highway connections, but their "college atmosphere" is probably more responsible for the growth. A group of western cities, Garden City, Great Bend, Hays, and Liberal also have grown threefold. These towns have extended their trade areas far beyond their county borders and are now dominant regional centers. The reasons for growth are unclear in many cases, but the whole northwestern quarter of Kansas is now tributary to Hays. Garden City, a major meat-packing center, has surpassed Dodge City as "the metropolis of southwest Kansas" (p. 177), and Great Bend is expanding into the traditional trade area of Pratt. Liberal's growth is tied to the extremely large Hugoton natural gas field that was just starting to be developed in 1939.

Population stagnation or decline since the 1930's has been concentrated in eastern, especially southeastern, cities. The declines have not been precipitous, never more than 2,500 people, but even stagnation in a generally growing state and nation is worthy of note. The city list includes Arkansas City, Atchison, Chanute, Coffeyville, Fort Scott, Independence, Iola, Parsons, and Pittsburg. Atchison, in the northeast, continues the slow decline it has endured since the last century. It lost a bid to become a major transportation center and is now sandwiched between larger cities, its Victorian architecture a reminder of past dreams. The other cities include every place of size south and east of Emporia. These cities were among the most industrialized in Kansas early in this century, when one of the Nation's first natural gas fields was harnessed. Zinc from the nearby Tri-State mines was smelted, and glass, cement, bricks, and other products were manufactured. The boom peaked from 1900 to 1910, and decline had begun for the guide writers to see in the 1930's. None of the major towns collapsed altogether; capital and good railroad connections accumulated in the boom were used to attract other industries not so dependent on cheap power. The results, however, have been mixed. Pittsburg, the largest city in southeastern Kansas, was east of the natural gas area. Its stagnation has been the result of a balance between declining employment in the coal and zinc mines and increasing employment at the local university and in the service industries.

Travelers who prefer rural to urban areas will also find Kansas changed in many ways from the 1930's. The guide makes much of county lakes, for example, many of them newly built with New Deal money, and lauds Lake McKinney in Kearny County as the "largest body of water" in the State (p. 389). These features are now dwarfed by a series of vast reservoirs built by the Army Corps of Engineers. Major flooding in 1951 led to a call for better flood protection and eventually to the construction of over twenty major dams. Several problems exist with this "big dam" approach to flood control, including the amount of valuable farmland lost to the lakes, the high rates of siltation and consequent short life span of the reservoirs, and the encouragement such dams give to indiscriminate industrial development on flood plains. Since most of the construction money comes from federal sources, however, and since the reservoirs provide recreation for many and economic boosts for surrounding towns, the public generally seems happy with the projects. One wonders, though, if these dams will still be around in another forty-five years for a third issuance of this guide.

Farming in the 1980's remains a mainstay of the Kansas economy, but changes since 1939 have been as great here as in any other aspect of the State. General farms were then the standard in eastern Kansas, places where a variety of crops and animals were raised and the surpluses of each marketed. Specialization is now the rule. Once-common sidelines such as raising chickens have been abandoned; rural Kansas today is littered with falling-down brooder houses. Flax and broomcorn, two crops mentioned in the guide, have fallen victim to competition from synthetic products. Crops planted in increasing acreage include soybeans in eastern Kansas and grain sorghums (milo) all over the State. The increase in soybeans, grown for their oil, has occurred unhampered by government acreage restrictions. Grain sorghums, with a rare ability to withstand moderate periods of drought, have become a viable feed-grain alternative to corn. The crop has spread eastward across the State after hybridization work produced high-yielding varieties.

Center-pivot irrigation in western Kansas is the most spectacular agricultural change in recent decades. These giant sprinkler systems irrigate 160 acres apiece and do not require expensive land leveling. They came on the scene in the 1960's wherever ground-water supplies were adequate, especially in the southwest and the northwest where the Ogallala aquifer was easily tapped. Farmers switched from wheat to higher-yielding corn and alfalfa, with the result that western Kansas now produces more corn than does the east. Cattle formerly shipped east for fattening can now be fed locally, and the feedlots, in turn, have tempted meat packers to move their industry westward. One upshot is the near abandonment of the famous Kansas City stockyards and that city's "eleven packing houses" (p. 210). In recent years, falling water tables have led to questions about the longevity of the irrigation boom; other experts think that the energy costs of pumping may be the limiting factor. For the present, though, much of western Kansas is a sea of green. Irrigation plus the revenues from natural gas wells have made southwest Kansas, per capita, the richest section of the State.

It is tempting to extend this discussion of old and new in Kansas indefinitely. Perhaps enough has been said, though, to make you an active explorer of the State. Look, for example, at the effects on cities of declining oil and coal fields, or the impact on the landscape of the trend toward grazing cattle on Flint Hills pastures year-round instead of only seasonally. See what school closings and consolidations have done to community vitality. Among the many specific points of interest added to the local scene since 1939, let me mention only four located off the main traveled roads: the Dane Hansen Museum, a major institution in tiny Logan (Phillips County); an excavated Pawnee Indian lodge in Republic County, now part of the State park system; the Pioneer Adobe House in Hillsboro, stocked with Mennonite culture materials; and the Safari Museum in Chanute, a major collection of artifacts from central Africa.

Kansas and the other Great Plains States, being gateways to the spectacular Rocky Mountain region, have always suffered an image problem. The prevailing view, as summarized in an article from the *New York Times Magazine* is "the type of changeless life depicted in the movie 'Picnic' with its opening longshot of mammoth Hutchinson grain elevators looming beside the Santa Fe tracks that stretch endlessly away into an all-pervading flatness, moral, cultural, social, topographical, political" (October 20, 1974, p. 36). The material in the WPA guide challenges all of these stereotypes. At the core of the region called the Middle West, Kansas possesses the "characteristic landscape" of the country, to use Walt Whitman's phrase. Many seasoned travelers agree with the poet's further observations that the prairie scenes, "while less stunning at first sight [than the Rockies], last longer, [and] fill the esthetic sense fuller" (*Specimen Days,* 1882, p. 94).

Because the Kansas landscape is subtle, a traveler needs preparation. This guide book is the best single beginning point that I know. Beyond it, I recommend a slow pace and some time spent with large-scale topographic maps of the region in question. Finally, the following books are useful for special interests and topics.

Bonnifield, Paul. *The Dust Bowl: Men, Dirt and Depression* (Albuquerque: University of New Mexico Press, 1979).

Buchanan, Rex, ed. *Kansas Geology: An Introduction to Landscapes, Rocks, Minerals, and Fossils* (Lawrence: University Press of Kansas, 1984).

Carman, J. Neale. *Foreign-Language Units of Kansas, I. Historical Atlas and Statistics* (Lawrence: University of Kansas Press, 1962).

Clark, John G. *Towns and Minerals in Southeastern Kansas: A Study in Regional Industrialization 1890–1930* (Lawrence: Kansas Geological Survey, 1970).

Collins, Joe, ed. *Natural Kansas* (Lawrence: University Press of Kansas, 1984).

Franzwa, Gregory. *The Oregon Trail Revisited* and *Maps of the Oregon Trail* (Gerald, Mo.: Patrice Press, 1978, 1982).

Madson, John. *Where the Sky Began: Land of the Tallgrass Prairie* (Houghton Mifflin, 1982).

Miner, H. Craig. *The Fire in the Rock: A History of the Oil and Gas Industry in Kansas 1855–1976* (Wichita: Kansas Independent Oil & Gas Association, 1976).

Muilenberg, Grace, and Ada Swineford. *Land of the Post Rock* (Lawrence: University Press of Kansas, 1975).

Peirce, Neal R. *The Great Plains States of America* (New York: W. W. Norton & Co., 1972).

Richmond, Robert. *Kansas, a Land of Contrast,* rev. ed. (Arlington Heights, Ill.: Forum Press, 1979).

Rydjord, John. *Kansas Place Names* (Norman: University of Oklahoma Press, 1973).

Shortridge, James R. *Kaw Valley Landscapes: A Guide to Eastern Kansas* (Lawrence: Coronado Press, 1977).

Socolofsky, Homer E., and Huber Self. *Historical Atlas of Kansas* (Norman: University of Oklahoma Press, 1972).

Stewart, George R. *U.S. 40: Cross Section of the United States* (Boston: Houghton Mifflin Co., 1953).

Vale, Thomas R., and Geraldine R. Vale. *U.S. 40 Today: Thirty Years of Landscape Change in America* (Madison: University of Wisconsin Press, 1983).

JAMES R. SHORTRIDGE

Preface

ALTHOUGH men and women have been writing books about Kansas for almost a century, this is the State's first guide book. To residents of other States it will open new vistas. And the Kansan who wants to know more about his own State—its history, its industrial background, its vast agricultural and mineral resources, its numerous points of historical interest and scenic beauty, as well as its many recreation spots—will find that this volume is comprehensive and informative.

The Federal Writers' Project was designed to give employment to needy writers and research workers in compiling information directly from the field and from research through various sources. The Kansas guide is, to date, the State's major contribution to the project's American Guide Series, which will include a guide to each of the forty-eight States, Puerto Rico, and Alaska, as well as numerous city and regional guides.

Many Kansans have had a part in making this book. Consultants have rendered valuable voluntary assistance in providing factual material and verifying information obtained from other sources. Federal, State, and local governmental agencies have given appreciated help. Thanks are especially due to Mr. Kirke Mechem, secretary of the State Historical Society; and his assistants, Mr. George A. Root and Mr. Nyle Miller, for the use of the Society's library, archives, and newspapers and photograph files. The gratitude of the Kansas Writers' Project also is extended to Professor Kenneth K. Landes, assistant State geologist; Professor James Malin, of the State University; J. C. Mohler, State secretary of agriculture; Professor Paul Weigel, Professor John Helm, Jr., and Professor Charles E. Rogers of Kansas State College.

HAROLD C. EVANS, Chief Editor

Federal Works Agency

WORK PROJECTS ADMINISTRATION

F. C. HARRINGTON, *Commissioner*

FLORENCE KERR, *Assistant Commissioner*

HENRY G. ALSBERG, *Director of the Federal Writers' Project*

Contents

III. Highways and Byways

CONTENTS

IV. Appendices

Maps

Illustrations

ILLUSTRATIONS

ILLUSTRATIONS

General Information

Railroads: Atchison, Topeka & Santa Fe Ry. (Santa Fe); Chicago, Burlington & Quincy R.R. (Burlington); Chicago, Great Western R.R. (Corn Belt); Chicago, Rock Island & Pacific Ry. (Rock Island); Kansas City Southern Ry.; Kansas, Oklahoma & Gulf Ry. (KO&G); Missouri-Kansas-Texas Lines (Katy); Missouri Pacific R.R. (MOP); Midland Valley R.R.; Northeast Oklahoma R.R. (NO); St. Louis-San Francisco Ry. (Frisco); St. Joseph & Grand Island Ry. (GI); Union Pacific R.R. (UP); Joplin-Pittsburg R.R.; Kansas City, Kaw Valley & Western R.R.; Arkansas Valley Interurban Ry. (Arkansas Valley); Missouri & Kansas R.R. (M&K); Southwest Missouri R.R. (Electric). *(See TRANSPORTATION map.)*

Highways: Nineteen Federal highways, all with transcontinental or international connections. No motorcar inspection. Gasoline tax 3¢. Highway patrol. Bus lines follow most Federal highways. *(See STATE map for routes.)*

Air Lines: Transcontinental & Western Airlines (TWA) and Braniff Airlines (BA), from Kansas City, Mo. to western and southwestern points, stop at Wichita.

Motor Vehicle Laws (digest): No speed limit except on certain stretches of road where warnings and limits are posted. Spotlights prohibited. No licenses required for non-residents. Minimum age for drivers, 16 yrs. Personal injury or property damage (over $50) must be reported to some civil authority. Parking on highway prohibited. Interstate transport trucks must register at port of entry stations; these are situated within short distance of border on all routes.

Radio: Sixteen stations now operate within the State: at Abilene, Coffeyville, Dodge City, Emporia, Salina, Garden City, Hutchinson, Kansas City, Great Bend, Lawrence (two), Manhattan, Topeka, Pittsburg and Wichita (two).

Accommodations: In east and central part of State: hotels chiefly in cities; ample tourist accommodations in well-furnished tourist cabins and modern lodging houses in rural communities and small towns. In western part: hotels in larger towns; accommodations in rural districts scattered and limited to small tourist cabins and private homes.

Liquor Regulation: Beer of 3.2 percent alcoholic content sold legally. Sale or possession of spirituous liquors prohibited.

Climate and Equipment: Slight variation in temperature within the State. Extremes of temperature in summer and winter with sudden changes in winter and early spring. Daily newspaper and radio reports on highway conditions and weather. Topcoats and overcoats necessary September 1 to June 1.

Poisonous Snakes and Plants: Copperheads and rattlesnakes, while not common, are found occasionally in rocky wooded areas. Water moccasins found infrequently in muddy streams and ponds. Poison-ivy common in wooded areas, but may be easily recognized by its three-petaled leaf.

Fish and Game Laws (digest): Unlawful to hunt or fish without license on person, or to trespass upon property without first obtaining consent of owner. Hunting and fishing license required for men and women between ages of 18 and 70. Shooting from cars, airplanes, or motorboats or upon a public highway prohibited. Killing of migratory birds prohibited, except on the wing. Commercial fishing in Missouri River only.

Licenses: Non-resident: hunting, $7; fishing, $3.

Open Season for Fishing: Year round except during spawning season (Apr. 15 to May 15) for bass, crappie, rock bass, or channel cat.

Limits: Daily catch not to exceed more than 15 total of all species; 30 in possession. No bass less than 10 in.; crappie, less than 7 in.; ring perch, less than 6 in.; catfish (not including bullheads), less than 12 in.; drum, less than 10 in.

Prohibited: Use of more than two poles and lines, one trotline having 25 hooks, or 6 banklines with 2 hooks each. Trapping, seining, spearing, dynamiting, poisoning, ice fishing, or any manner of taking fish except with artificial lures or baited hooks.

Open Season for Hunting (inclusive): Fur-bearing animals, Dec. 1-Jan. 31; quail, Nov. 20-30; doves, Sept. 1-Oct. 15; fox-squirrels, Aug. 1-Jan. 1.

Limits: Quail, daily bag 10, season bag 25; doves, daily bag 20. No season or limit on rabbits.

Prohibited: Killing pheasants, trapping or killing beaver and otter, molesting any wild songbird or insectivorous bird, or destroying its nest or eggs. Season bag limits and other regulations on ducks, geese, brant, coot, jack-snipe, rails, turkeys, grouse and partridges, are established by the U.S. Department of Agriculture Biological Survey, and vary. Information published shortly before the season opens; available on application from county clerk.

General Information and Service: State Chamber of Commerce, National Reserve Bldg., Topeka. See also general information under cities.

Calendar of Events

(nfd means no fixed date)

Jan. 29	Topeka	Kansas Day Club Banquet
nfd	Kickapoo Reservation	New Years' Dance
nfd	Manhattan	Farm and Home Week
Feb. 22	Topeka	Washington Day Club Banquet
nfd	Wichita	State Choir and Orchestra Concerts
Mar. 1	Emporia	St. David's Day Celebration
nfd	Wichita	Girls' National Basketball Tournament
3d week	Topeka	State High School Basketball Tournament
last Sun.	Fort Scott	Holy City Sacred Cantata
4th week	Emporia	County School Music Festivals
Apr. 1st week after Easter	Kansas City	Music Week
2d or 3d week	Emporia	College of Emporia Music Festival
3d week	Lawrence	Kansas Relays
nfd	Emporia	State High School Music Festival, State Teachers' College
nfd	Leavenworth	Competitive ROTC drill
nfd	Lindsborg	Music Festival, *The Messiah*
nfd	Lindsborg	Art Exhibit
nfd	Kickapoo Reservation	Spring Dance
nfd	Pittsburg	Hi-school Music Festival
nfd	Troy	Apple Blossom Festival
May 5	Kansas City	Mexican Fiesta
4th week	Fort Riley	Cavalry School Horse Show and Race Meet
nfd	Abilene	National Coursing Association Spring Meeting
nfd	Emporia	State-wide Scholarship Contest, State Teachers' College

	nfd	Hays	Academic Music Festival
	nfd	Lawrence	Music Week
	nfd	Fort Leavenworth	Horse Show
	nfd	Newton	Mennonite Music Festival
	nfd	Wichita	Spring Concerts, Singing Quakers of Friends University
June	nfd	Newton	Institute of International Relations
July	4	Hutchinson	Fourth of July Fiesta and Athletic Carnival
	nfd	Topeka	Mexican Fiesta
	nfd	Kickapoo Reservation	Corn Dance
	nfd	Pottawatomie Reservation	Pottawatomie Fair
Aug.	4	Nicodemus	Emancipation Celebration
	1st week	Phillipsburg	Rodeo
	4th week	Stockton	Western Kansas-Nebraska Fair
	4th week	Goodland	Northwest District Free Fair
	4th week	Iola	Southeastern Kansas Exposition
	4th week	Hanover	Days of Forty-Nine
	nfd	Salina	Salina Race Meeting
	nfd	Wichita	National Semi-Pro Baseball Tournament
	nfd	Winfield	Winfield Race Meet
Sept.	1st week	Coffeyville	Montgomery County Fair
	1st week	Ottawa	Franklin County Fair
	1st week	Belleville	North-Central Kansas Free Fair
	1st week	Horton	Tri-County Fair
	2d week	Topeka	Kansas Free Fair
	15 and 16	Kansas City	Mexican Fiesta
	3d week	Dodge City	Great Southwest Free Fair
	3d week	Hutchinson	Kansas State Fair
	nfd	Fort Scott	Dairy Show
	nfd	Dodge City	Pioneer Picnic
	nfd	Troy	Apple Harvest Festival
	nfd	Abilene	Central Kansas Free Fair
	nfd	Hiawatha	Fall Festival
Oct.	31	Arkansas City	Arkalalah
	31	Independence	Neewollah (Hallowe'en)

4th week of Oct. or 1st week of Nov.	Kansas City	American Royal Live Stock and Horse Show
nfd	Leavenworth	Horse Show
nfd	Kickapoo Reservation	Harvest Dance
nfd	Abilene	National Coursing Association Fall Meeting
nfd		State Corn Husking Contest
Nov. 1st week	Dodge City, Hays, Pittsburg, Salina, Topeka, Wichita	State Teachers' Convention
11	Oberlin	Annual Armistice Day Celebration and Athletic Carnival
nfd	Lawrence	University Home-Coming
nfd	Manhattan	Kansas State College Home-Coming
nfd	Manhattan	Kansas State High School Band Contest
nfd	Wichita	Stock Show
Dec. Christmas Season	Atchison	Music Festival

PART I

The State and Its People

THE PRAIRIE

Contemporary Scene

By WILLIAM ALLEN WHITE

ON THE continental map, Kansas is in the exact center of the United States, a parallelogram with one corner nibbled off by the Missouri River. The State on this map looks flat and uninteresting topographically, for within its boundaries are no lakes, no mountains, no really navigable rivers. It seems to be a rectangle of prairie grass with no more need for a guide book than is met by its highway junction signs.

Yet this Kansas rectangle has its distinguishing features. These come not from rivers, mountains, or inland seas, but from the fact that this grass plot rises nearly 3,000 feet in 400 miles. In that slanting slab of prairie sod which begins descending eastward just beyond the foothills and rough country of the Rockies, lie at least two separate economic units. They amount to two different States. First, they have different soil. The eastern part of Kansas is a rich, deep, alluvial loam. The western part of Kansas is a sandy soil made by grinding down the glacial boulders of the Rocky Mountains in the waters of an ancient inland sea and by great rushing rivers that rolled along those latitudes. In the second place, not only is the soil different but the climate somewhat varies in each of these units. Eastern Kansas is a corn State. We have rainfall three years out of five, generally eight years out of ten, which will produce corn in most of the counties east of Hutchinson and Salina. The grass is lush and in central Kansas is highly charged with lime from those heavily rolling prairies that are called the Flint Hills, our bluestem pastures. In western Kansas the grass is short, but shot full of nourishment. Its short fuzz fools strangers into thinking the land is barren and useless. Yet that short fuzzy will nourish range cattle adequately and, when the soil is turned over, that sod is rich in those chemicals which make wheat. We like to say "Kansas grows the best wheat in the world." This is not exactly true, but it is true that Kansas grows splendid wheat, that it grades high, probably on the whole higher than the wheat of any other State which grows winter wheat. Further north they grow spring wheat, that is to say in the Dakotas and Manitoba. There they plant their wheat in the spring and harvest it in the autumn. In western Kansas they plant their wheat in the autumn and harvest it in the late spring and early summer. The rainfall is so distributed and the heat of summer is so devastating on these high plains that spring wheat will not prosper.

So there abide here two States: the grazing, farming corn land of eastern Kansas and the short grass pasture land and great wheat fields of western Kansas. Eastern Kansas is divided into small farms from 100 to 200 acres. Large-scale farming does not pay except in cattle growing where the bluestem pastures nourish flocks larger than Abraham ever drove out of the Land of Ur when he had "cattle on a thousand hills." But mostly in eastern Kansas the farmer is a barnyard stockman who grows his own corn, has his own pasture lot, cuts and bales his own alfalfa and hay, puts up his own fodder in the silo, and is economically sufficient to himself in the manufacture of the world's beefsteak, ham and eggs, fried chicken, and butter. In western Kansas, the tendency is to large farms. It is a one crop country, a statement which needs quick modification, for alfalfa and buffalo grass pasture and in certain northwest counties of the State an occasional corn crop makes it possible for the farmer to live on a 200-acre farm. But speaking rather broadly, western Kansas is a wheat bin. Farms are profitable when they pass 200 acres. Large agricultural units requiring a heavy endowment of machinery are fairly profitable in western Kansas. The people tend to live in towns and villages. They do their farming in August and September when the great motor plows furrow the fields, and again the farmers get busy in July when the combines reap and thresh the grain. The little farm with its garden, its diversified crop, its chickens, its calves, its pigs, is not found so often in western Kansas, indeed it is found rarely there. But in eastern Kansas the diversified crop is the normal type.

These geographical, indeed geological, differences between eastern and western Kansas make different economic interests and different kinds of people. The eastern Kansas farmer is a thrifty, cautious, diligent descendant of the New England Puritan, physically and spiritually. The western Kansas farmer is a gambler, a go-getter. In western Kansas are many strains that did not come out of New England. The Mennonites live on the eastern fringe of western Kansas. They were Germans who lived a hundred years in Russia before coming to America and they have brought their own culture, their own civilization, which has persisted through all the 60 years of their Kansas exile!

So in our politics, eastern and western Kansas often find antagonistic interests, honest and deeply divisory differences. Western Kansas, in politics, is inclined to be clannish. Western Kansans form blocs in the legislature. They throw their votes in the ballot box to men who best represent their interests, which are somewhat different from the interests of eastern Kansas. Problems of taxes, of education, of transportation are not the same in the rolling prairie country, four or five tiers of counties in from the Missouri Line, as they are in that flat, lovely plains country, four or five tiers east of the Colorado Line.

So the parallelogram 400 by 200 in the center of our Nation is something different in reality from its appearance on the map. Every State is unique, but Kansas is visibly so, because of its geography and geology. In these latter days of the mid-third of the century, oil is coming into western Kansas to transform its civilization entirely. Oil will modify its politics. It will change the social outlook of its people. We shall have a kingdom of oil and wheat out of the high plains west of Newton and Abilene, the old cow towns of the cattle days, a State which will be rich in spots, polka-dotted with well-to-do farms and highly civilized country towns. Three times in the history of Kansas, western Kansas has completely changed. It had its energized vision in its pioneer days of the 1880's; its discouraging and desolate days just before the discovery of winter wheat in the 1890's; its days of high prosperity in the first two decades of the century, climaxing in the wheat bonanza days of the War. And now comes oil to change it again. In the meanwhile eastern Kansas goes on with a distinctly evolutionary line of progress from the days of the Civil War until today. Nothing has ever changed radically in eastern Kansas in economics or in agriculture. Within 70 years prosperity has come in waves, slowly but steadily.

These words of preface are necessary before one reads the Guide Book to this midcontinental rectangle of grass prairie and high plains that is known to her neighbors and the world as Kansas: "First in freedom, first in wheat!"

Natural Setting
and Conservation

A GREAT rectangle in form, with the northeast corner cut off by the
Missouri River, Kansas is bounded on the north by Nebraska, on
the east by Missouri, on the south by Oklahoma, and on the west by Colorado. It contains both the geodetic and the geographic centers of continental United States. The geodetic center, from which the U. S. Coast and
Geodetic Survey calculates latitude and longitude is on Meade's ranch in
Osborne County; the geographic center is commonly accepted as being on
the Fort Riley Reservation in Geary County. Kansas extends 410 miles
east and west, and 210 miles north and south. It has a total area of
82,158 square miles, of which 384 are water surface.

Topography and Climate

Contrary to popular belief, the State is not a flat, featureless plain. The
surface slopes eastward from an elevation of 4,135 feet along the western
boundary to 734 feet in the southeastern corner, and is drained by two
main watersheds. The Kansas River with its tributaries flows eastward
through the northern half of the State, and the Arkansas with its tributaries flows in a general southeast direction through the southern part.
Between these two river basins a small area is drained by the Marais des
Cygnes, and in the extreme northeast the streams flow into the Missouri.

Topographically, Kansas may be divided into three sections: the High
Plains, constituting approximately the western third; a large area of nearly
flat land, called the Low Plains or the Great Bend Prairie in the center;
and the Flint Hills region—or, as it has been more recently called, the
Bluestem Belt—occupying the eastern third.

In this section the broad river valleys, cutting through the uplands and
affording picturesque vistas, are covered with rich silt deposits, and the
soil permits a more diversified agriculture than is found in the central and

western sections of the State. The uplands are rolling, interspersed with limestone cliffs. The most prominent of these are the Flint Hills which extend from the Oklahoma to the Nebraska lines and include the greater part of ten counties and the lesser part of three additional ones. Here grow bluestem grasses, making a grazing region unlike any other in the country, excepting the Osage section of Oklahoma which is, in reality, an extension of the Bluestem Belt. Rainfall is sufficient to permit the growth of timber in the plains and valley slopes, and even the hills in the northeastern part are heavily wooded.

In the central portion of the State, north of the Great Bend Prairie, lie the Smoky Hills Upland and the Blue Hills Upland. South of the prairie area are the Cimarron Breaks, heavily eroded cliffs and terraces bordering the Cimarron River.

Only in the western third of the State is the terrain comparatively monotonous and treeless. Professor Kenneth K. Landes, assistant State geologist, has pointed out that, though the Great Plains are undistinguished from a scenic standpoint, they have an interesting geological history. "They were made by ancient streams," he writes, "that flowed eastward from the Rocky Mountains carrying an enormous load of gravel, sand, and silt which was deposited to a depth of many feet along a wide belt extending from Canada to Texas. . . . Two streams that cross the High Plains of Kansas, the Arkansas and the Smoky Hill, have excavated their valleys below the base of the prehistoric river deposits, thereby exposing the older and underlying rock."

The Smoky Hill River, cutting through the sand and silt deposits which floor the High Plains in Logan and Gove Counties, has laid bare expanses of white, yellow, and orange chalk formations. These are considered the outstanding natural wonders in the State. Water and wind erosion have exposed fossil beds here containing many specimens of extinct species of fish, flying reptiles, and prehistoric birds. Castle Rock, a chalk spire in western Gove County, rises to seventy feet and is visible for miles. Also in this section are the Monument Rocks or "Pyramids," and a chalk pile which wind and water have carved into a likeness of the Sphinx.

Other unusual formations are Kansas' natural bridge and a cave cut through gypsum rock, both in Barber County. The mesas and buttes found in this area are not unlike those that dot the landscape in New Mexico. The cap rock is of white gypsum and the slopes are of red shale or sandstone. Nearby, in Comanche County, is Hell's Half Acre, a spot of unique beauty; and in Clark County is the Little Basin, one of Kansas' sink holes or sinks, as they are more commonly called.

These are depressions in the land surface which occur, geologists explain, when the soluble rock layers are dissolved by underground water. The roofs of the subterranean caves, thus formed, crumble and the overlying rocks sink down below the normal level of the terrain. The Little Basin is believed to be many centuries old, judging by the evidence of large trees which grow along its inner walls. One-half mile west of Little Basin is Big Basin, a crater-like depression a mile in diameter and 100 feet deep. Formerly considered the crater of an extinct volcano, it is now regarded as a sink of similar origin to others in the State.

The largest of these depressions developed with dramatic speed in September 1937 on a wheat farm near Potwin in Butler County. Shortly after the completion of fall plowing, the farmer noticed a large depression in his field. Twenty-four hours later the earth caved in, leaving a hole 300 feet long and 250 feet wide, which later partially filled with water. In 1930 an unusual sink hole developed in Hamilton County. Beginning as a small circular hollow near the Colorado line, this depression deepened until whole sections of a county road were engulfed. When last measured this sink was 100 feet across and nearly 50 feet deep.

The climate is unusually variable with extremes of temperature and an unusual abundance of sunshine, conditions resulting in great measure from the State's location. Almost midway between the Atlantic and Pacific Oceans and approximately 600 miles distant from any large body of water, Kansas lies in the path of air currents moving north from the tropics and south from the Arctic Circle.

The yearly mean temperature is 54 degrees; January is the coldest month, and July the hottest. The term "sunny" is well deserved, for no other part of the country receiving as much rain has so many clear days. A 38-year record shows that there have never been more than 104 cloudy days in any year. The amount of cloudiness is greatest in the eastern part of the State, but even here the record for sun is high. At Lawrence in northeast Kansas the sky is overcast 59 per cent of the time in April, the cloudiest month, while in August, the sunniest month, it is overcast only 35 per cent of the time.

The average rainfall is approximately 26 inches, but it is very unevenly distributed. In the southeast section, where rainfall is heaviest, the annual average is 40 inches; this decreases to 15 inches at the western border. Precipitation in the form of snow is common during the winter months—December through March—although the ground is rarely covered with snow for more than a few days at a time.

Differences in wind velocities in the eastern and western sections are

Painting by John Steuart Curry

almost as marked as the differences in rainfall. In the eastern third the winds are not noticeably higher than those in the eastern part of the country as a whole; the western third of the State, however, is one of the windiest inland spots in the Nation. Winds of high velocity in this section blow loose soil into "dust storms" and lead to wind erosion during the dry season in winter or early spring.

Though Kansas has acquired the reputation of being a tornado State, records show that these storms do not occur here with any greater frequency than in other Plains States. Tornadoes strike the eastern part of Kansas oftener than the western, and are more likely to occur in late spring or early summer than at other times of the year.

What is believed to be the first fixed schedule of radio transmissions of weather reports in the United States was inaugurated by the physics department of the State college at Manhattan in 1912 when station 9YV began a daily broadcast of weather conditions.

Recent years of almost unprecedented drought have led to the often expressed belief that the climate of Kansas is changing. Geologists and meteorologists, however, point out that weather runs in cycles, the most pronounced being about a third of a century in length. Conditions during a cycle are easily mistaken by laymen for permanent changes. Despite year by year fluctuations in temperature and precipitation, recorded evidence shows that general climatic conditions remain unchanged.

Glacial Deposits

In the Mississippi Valley the ice cap of the glacial age extended as far south as the present sites of Lawrence, Topeka, Manhattan, and Kansas City in Kansas. The great ice sheets passed over hills and valleys, carrying with them great loads of rock, gravel, sand, and clay which they ground and scraped from the surface. Rocks and boulders, frozen into the bottom of the glacier, scratched and grooved the solid rock beneath. As the ice sheets melted, the accumulated materials were left behind, either spread over the surface or piled into ranges of irregular hills, known as moraines.

The second of the four great ice sheets was the only one that invaded the region, but it left an indelible mark on northeastern Kansas—the area lying north and east of the Kaw and Big Blue Rivers. As a result, this section differs in many respects from the rest of the State. The surface is covered by glacial drift or till, a confused mixture of clay, sand, gravel, and boulders that is found on hilltops as well as in valleys. The pebbles and boulders are of varying shapes and colors. South and southwest of Atchison the drift is unusually stony. In many places, however, it is composed of clay with few pebbles and boulders. The heaviest deposits are found in Nemaha and in portions of Brown and Jackson Counties, where the drift is from thirty to one hundred feet in thickness. From this central area of heavy deposit the drift thins to less than five feet in thickness on the borders of the glaciated region.

Numerous boulders lie scattered over the pastures in this section of the State, most of them red or pinkish in color and hard as flint. These boulders of red quartzite have been used to some extent in building construction and are locally known as "niggerheads." Boulders of granite and other types of rock are also found. They are most abundant south of the Kaw River in the vicinity of Wamego, a few miles south of Topeka, and near Westmoreland in Pottawatomie County. None of these belong to the rock systems of the region; their nearest ledges are in southeastern Minnesota and South Dakota.

The influence of the ice sheet on northeastern Kansas was, on the whole, beneficial. The glacier brought vast quantities of rich fertile soil, filled depressions and valleys, and produced large areas suitable for farming. The heart of the glacial section in Brown and Nemaha Counties is perhaps the finest agricultural land in Kansas. The glacier also deposited great quantities of sands and gravels that have been utilized in road and building construction.

Fossil Remains

The vast deposits of fossils found in the chalk beds of Gove and Trego Counties have long attracted the attention of scientists. Since their discovery in the 1860's these beds have been visited by distinguished scientists from all parts of the world, and many specimens have been removed and placed in museums. The majority of these remains of ancient animals have been petrified. In some instances only an imprint has been left; in others, part or all of the original skeletal structures are preserved.

"The medieval age of geology," writes Professor Norman D. Newell, of the University of Kansas geology department, "is sometimes called the age of reptiles; the rocks of this age are distinguished by the skeletons of scores of kinds of reptiles, ranging from huge ones a hundred feet in length with a weight of several tons, down to lizards the size of a mouse . . . The conclusion is unavoidable that where now stands Kansas, the driest of dry land, was formerly a mighty sea in which lived the thousands of sea denizens now found buried in the rocks beneath the soil."

Shark teeth and fossil remains of huge whale-like reptiles and of large turtles, of the type found only in the sea, have been discovered in the rocks of western Kansas. The deposits also yielded many specimens of birds with teeth, belonging to the medieval geologic age. Two distinct types are found, both adapted to swimming. One was a small shore bird with powerful wings; the other a small-winged diving bird about six feet in length. Prehistoric oyster beds have also been uncovered in this part of the State.

At the time of the earliest Spanish explorations in America there were no horses in either North or South America. The wild herds that roamed the Western plains in later years were descended from those brought by Coronado and other explorers. The horse, however, is known to have existed in prehistoric Kansas, and is preserved in the rocks of these western counties. The skeleton of what is believed to be the oldest horse was found in these rock strata—a small animal, scarcely a foot high, with three toes on its hind feet and four toes on its front feet. Specimens of miniature horses, found in each successive stratum, show the evolution of the modern horse. A progressive loss of toes and an increase in size may be traced, until a horse quite similar to the modern animal was developed.

Dinosaurs have not as yet been discovered in Kansas, but geologists are almost certain that they once existed here, because their remains are found in the adjoining State of Colorado.

Coal and other types of rock formation known to have been formed on land rather than in the sea, and evidences of erosion by rivers within the sequences of rocks, have led geologists to conclude that prehistoric Kansas was inundated by the sea at least fifty times. An ancient mountain range of granite peaks and ridges that traversed eastern Kansas from north to south—known to geologists as the Nemaha Mountains—was buried beneath the floor of the prehistoric sea by the accumulation of sediment. Some of the deepest wells drilled in Kansas have passed through more than 5,000 feet of rocks before reaching the granite which underlies the entire State. This mile deep layer of rock, according to geologists, is the hardened mud that accumulated in the sea bed during the long period of advancing and retreating waters.

Natural Resources and Their Conservation

Minerals: The mineral industry is second in importance to agriculture in Kansas. The value of its mineral products has increased from $58,471,000 in 1932 to $121,723,000 in 1936. For the latter year the principal mineral products in order of value were petroleum, natural gas, zinc, and stone. Kansas ranked second among all the States in quantity and value of zinc and zinc-lead ores, third in quantity and value of chats, and third in value of salt. For the past twenty years it has taken the lead in the production of pumice or pumicite (volcanic ash). Other mineral products include cement, clay products, coal, and gypsum.

Coal, lead, and zinc are mined in the southeastern counties, Crawford and Cherokee. Here coal stripping operations have created large expanses of waste land, which have recently been transformed into the Crawford County State Park by the State forestry, fish and game commission, with the aid of the WPA. Coal is also mined in Osage and Leavenworth Counties, and large clay deposits are found in Cherokee County.

The first oil prospecting in Kansas was near Paola in Miami County. Though oil is now produced in nearly every section of the State, the largest fields have been developed from the pools in the central counties of Butler, Cowley, McPherson, Marion, Rice, and Sedgwick. Oil development has been moving westward in recent years, however, and new fields have been opened in Russell, Reno, Barton, Ellis, Stafford, and Clark counties. The principal gas fields are in Allen County in the eastern section of the State and in Stevens County in the southwest; gas has also been discovered in many other parts of the State. Salt is found in Republic, Reno, Rice, Ellsworth, and Harper counties. Gypsum is mined in Marshall, Barber, and Comanche counties. There are large deposits of volcanic ash in Meade, Sheridan, Rawlins, Wallace, and Comanche counties. Meade County, which leads the State in the production of volcanic ash, has at least twelve separate deposits.

Plant Life: Native grasses, which cover about one-third of Kansas, are its most valuable form of plant life, protecting the soil from erosion and depletion, and forming the basis for the State's enormous livestock industry. There are 60 different groups of grasses, subdivided into 194 species. Bluestem has the greatest forage value, and both species—big and little bluestem, also known as bluejoint turkeyfoot and prairie beardgrass— grow in almost all parts of the State.

The tall grasses are confined to east Kansas. Indian grass thrives in the valleys, little bluestem on the uplands, and sideoat grama on the hillsides. Prairie dropseed and sand dropseed are found in the drier sections, while sloughgrass commonly borders the streams.

In western Kansas the short grasses dominate. Buffalo, blue grama, and hairy grama are, in the order named, the chief forage grasses. Sand reed and turkeyfoot grow in the semi-arid southwest, and saltgrass and alkali sacaton in the alkaline soils.

With a few exceptions the short grasses grow in practically every part of the State. Also ubiquitous, but of little or no grazing value, are tumblegrass, green bristle, tickle and love grasses, switch grass and western wheatgrass, which thrives best in the north central section.

The early settlers found few trees in Kansas. The soil and climate of the western area precluded the natural growth of forests, while the woods in the central and eastern parts of the State had been repeatedly damaged by prairie fires. These were set by the Indians to induce early pasturage for game animals and to prevent invasion by hostile tribes.

Extensive tree planting was begun immediately after the Civil War, and was stimulated by the Federal timber culture act which gave 160 acres of free land to anyone who agreed to grow 10 acres of timber on it. In 1887 the State legislature established two agencies which propagated and distributed many thousand seedling trees during the next twenty years. This work was taken over by the State nursery at Hays in 1907, in cooperation with the forest service of the U. S. Department of Agriculture. The

MONUMENT ROCKS, NEAR GOVE

State forestry, fish and game commission, established in 1925, has chiefly limited its forestation activities to plantings in State parks, but a broader program will probably be undertaken eventually. About 3,000 acres of strip-pit land, given to the commission for reforestation in 1934, were placed under the management of the U. S. Forest Service. This agency, aided by the Civilian Conservation Corps, leveled the area and planted it, chiefly with walnut trees.

Today, Kansas has about 225,000,000 trees, not counting its fruit and street trees. One native conifer, red cedar, is found pretty generally throughout the State. Hackberry, linden, oak, willow, and sycamore grow in east Kansas. Black walnut also thrives here and is economically valuable for furniture and other manufactured products. In western Kansas box elder and cottonwood predominate; the latter is used for excelsior, berry boxes and other soft wood commercial containers. A wide variety of other trees now grow in the State, particularly in the southeast corner. Many regions, once treeless, are now well wooded with orchards, shelterbelts, and woodlots; trees shade the highways and border the fences.

The sunflower's glowing head is seen everywhere in Kansas, and it has been fittingly chosen as the official State flower. A succession of wild flower blooms dot the prairies—delicate yellow, lavender, and white in the spring; orange and purple in summer, when the hot sun turns the grass gray-green. Botanists list 80 flower families, and about 450 species of wild flowers. Among the most widely distributed are the wild daisy, aster, goldenrod, columbine, prairie phlox, clover, and thistle. Many species adapt themselves to different growing conditions. Thus the tall sunflower of the eastern farmlands becomes knee high further west; the spotted evening primrose, ivyleaved morning glory, and large-flowered verbena of eastern Kansas have western counterparts in the white evening primrose, bush morning glory, and small-flowered verbena.

Wild Life: In the 1860's Kansas was known as a hunter's paradise, and shooting parties from as far away as Europe bagged huge quantities of game. The timbered sections of eastern Kansas abounded with bear and panther, with timber wolf, deer, otter, beaver, and smaller fur-bearing animals. Farther west, prairie wolves, wild horses and vast herds of buffalo ranged the High Plains. There were quail, wild turkeys, and other game birds, and migratory waterfowl in great numbers.

The destruction of the buffalo may be taken as an example of what happened to most of this teeming wild life. Hunters ruthlessly slaughtered thousands of buffalo, ripping off the hides and leaving the carcasses to rot on the prairie. One huntsman boasted that he killed 120 buffalo in 40 minutes. By the early 1880's, scarcely a decade after settlement was begun in western Kansas, the buffalo was extinct. Antelope, bear, and deer met with similar fate. The wild horse, because of its greater sagacity, survived and migrated west to more inaccessible regions.

Except for isolated county regulations to protect small game and control crop-damaging animals, no attempt was made to conserve wild life until the State forestry, fish and game commission was established by the State legislature in 1925. By this time grouse and wild turkey had been exterminated, prairie chicken and quail were diminishing rapidly. The central flyways of migratory birds, which once crossed Kansas, had shifted and many species of ducks and geese, formerly abundant, were nesting farther north.

The legislature gave the commission authority over fish and game, which were declared to be the property of the State. Subsequent legislative action has strengthened the original law, until Kansas has, today, conservation measures which compare favorably with those of other States. The commission's budget, derived from the sale of hunting and fishing licenses, has never exceeded $250,000 biennially. But despite inadequate funds, progress in conservation has been steady. The chukar partridge, an Asiatic species, and several hardy species of quail have been introduced into the State, and a method of propagating prairie chickens has been developed. Approximately 10,500 pheasants and 52,000 quail were distributed in the decade 1926–36. An important phase of the commission's work is the development of recreational areas, chiefly in connection with the construction of artificial lakes. These are stocked with fish from the State hatchery at Pratt.

Though the abundant wild life of early Kansas can, obviously, not be restored, game and other animal and bird life is plentiful. Rabbit, muskrat, opossum, coyote, and raccoon are relatively abundant. There are twelve species of bat, two of shrew and of mole, and three of pocket gopher. The State's native birds include the American goldfinch, American robin, blue jay, cardinal, Carolina wren, hairy woodpecker, western meadowlark, and several species of hawk. In winter, tree sparrows, longspurs, and slate-colored juncos sojourn in Kansas; among the summer residents are catbird, brown thrasher, ruby-throated hummingbird, and scarlet tanager.

The Nathaniel Stickeny Goss ornithological collection in the State Historical Museum at Topeka contains mounted specimens of nearly every variety of bird found in Kansas. Goss (1826–1891), known as the "Kansas Audubon," spent more than thirty years gathering material for his *History of the Birds of Kansas,* completed shortly before his death.

In addition to the State and Federal conservation agencies, private citizens take an active interest in the restoration and preservation of the State's plant and wild life through the Kansas Fish and Game Protective Association, Kansas State Game Preservation Association, State division of the Isaak Walton League of America, and Audubon Society of Kansas.

Soil and Water: The future welfare of the State depends largely upon the effectiveness with which its two greatest natural resources—water and soil—are conserved. There is very little soil in Kansas unfit for cultivation; smooth topography, abundant sunshine, and length of growing season are all favorable. The one disadvantageous factor is the scarcity of water. The destructive forces of drought and flood were not unknown in the State in the nineteenth century; there were 6 droughts and 16 floods between 1860 and 1900. But in recent years these related problems have been alarmingly aggravated. Increasing crop failures and flood losses testify to the fact that droughts have become more severe and destructive overflow more frequent. Decades of soil-destroying farming methods have

FIELD PLOWED BY DAMMING LISTER, A FLOOD CONTROL FEATURE

stripped the land of its water-retention properties. The resultant rapid runoff of rain leads, in turn, to three evils—flood, erosion, and a lowered groundwater supply.

Fifty-seven lives and property damage estimated at $36,000,000 resulted from the floods of 1903. Spurred by this disaster, the legislature passed a law providing for the organization of drainage districts by cities and counties; this plan superseded flood control work based on the township unit. Eighty-five drainage districts were set up, protecting only 265,000 of the 1,200,000 acres subject to overflow. These districts were widely separated; they adhered to no uniform plan, safeguarded no area except their immediate region, ignored the necessity of water conservation. In short, they relied on hit-or-miss methods to cope with a problem that called for long range and State-wide planning.

Between 1900 and 1917 Kansas suffered four severe droughts and 55 destructive floods. These apparently unrelated disasters were gradually diagnosed as symptoms of a disease that affected the whole State rather than isolated localities. The legislature consequently established the Kansas Water Commission in 1917 "to secure the most advantageous adjustment of interests involved in floods, drainage, irrigation, water power and navigation." A division of irrigation was organized in 1919 under the supervision of the State board of agriculture. Later these two agencies were consolidated as the division of water resources.

At a general conference held in Topeka in 1927 the division of water resources appointed the so-called Paulen Committee to study the flood control systems of Kansas. The committee's report showed that the drainage districts were merely inadequate makeshifts. As a result of these findings the legislature passed a conservancy act in 1929, patterned after the excellent Ohio conservancy act, which provided for a State-wide program of irrigation and flood control.

The Kansas supreme court shortly declared the Conservancy Act unconstitutional, thus leaving the problem unsolved. Water erosion continued to gnaw at Kansas farmlands; the unharnessed rivers continued to wash away millions of cubic yards of silt; and the ground water level continued to fall, thereby jeopardizing the water supply of 80 per cent of the population.

The various agencies that surveyed the Kansas water problem from time to time were agreed on two points: that rainfall should be retained where it fell by means of land terracing, cover crops, contour farming, and similar devices; and that runoff at the sources of sub-tributaries should be prevented by the construction of reservoirs and pasture ponds. None but the last of these recommendations was acted upon by the legislature. A law passed in 1929, and amended four years later, provided for the reduction of taxes on farmlands whose owners constructed pasture ponds.

Engineers estimated that 50,000 pasture ponds, exclusive of five large reservoirs in each county, would be required to assure adequate flood control and water conservation. That this number would not be built by private capital was a foregone conclusion and the aid of the Federal Government was accordingly enlisted. The Kansas Emergency Relief Administration undertook a program of reservoir construction and completed 27 lakes and 3,000 farm and garden ponds. The WPA later built 15 lakes and 256 ponds. But these, together with 125 State lakes and an unknown number of privately built ponds, fell far short of the required number. Some distress has been alleviated, however, and the ultimate, adequate conservation of water has been given a measure of certainty.

About forty million acres, or three-fourths of the area of Kansas, have been damaged in varying degree by erosion. Water erosion has scarred the land in eastern and northern Kansas, while wind erosion has worked great loss in the western part of the State. The general productivity of the soil has been lowered, in some instances, as much as twenty per cent.

In the period between 1933 and 1937 western Kansas suffered an acute shortage of rainfall. Crop failures in fields prepared for wheat left the land without a protective mantle of vegetation, and top soil was lifted by

"DUST BOWL" FARM AFTER THE STORMS, NEAR LIBERAL

the wind and carried away. By 1935 almost nine million acres of once green farmlands had been scraped and gouged by wind erosion.

Their land made waste by the wind, their reserve capital depleted by repeated crop failures, the wheat farmers clamored for aid to prevent their fields from turning into deserts. The extension service of Kansas State College began to instruct farmers in tillage methods that resisted wind erosion. The Kansas Emergency Relief Committee appropriated $364,136 which was used in 1935 to buy fuel for tractors and feed for horses. Soil listing, strip chiseling, basin listing, strip cropping, and similar measures were applied to 3,350,000 acres.

Under the direction of the U. S. Forest Service, the Prairie States Forestry Project of the WPA has planted shelter belts in 20 counties in south-central Kansas. These belts, established on 16,400 acres of farm land, are now three years old and have proved their worth not only in halting wind erosion but in protecting crops. A total of 1,500 miles have been planted with 5,500,000 trees.

About 5,500,000 acres in western Kansas suffered from wind erosion in 1936. An extensive tillage project was carried on throughout the year with funds obtained from the U. S. Department of Agriculture. About 2,546,-834 acres were tilled through Government aid, and 120,000 acres were tilled at private expense. Funds that remained from the original grant of the U. S. Department of Agriculture were expended in further tillage projects in 1937.

The Kansas legislature enacted a law in 1937 which empowered the board of commissioners in each county to conduct an annual survey of farmlands to determine the areas damaged by wind erosion; "to order that the land be disked, or listed, or chiseled, or cultivated in any particular manner," and to create a "soil drifting fund" by tax levy. The law also provided that the cost of cultivation be assessed against the farm owner in cases which involved deliberate failure to comply with certain erosion-prevention measures.

The Land Utilization Administration of the Federal Government purchased 100,000 acres of sub-marginal Kansas land in 1938 on which experiments in terracing, contour tillage, and basin listing were conducted. Several varieties of drought-resistant crops were successively grown, while wind-eroded hills in the area were planted with cover crops. To enable impoverished wheat farmers to benefit from the methods developed by experimentation in tillage and crop growing, the Farm Security Administration has made loans to 18,868 Kansas applicants.

The adoption of a subsistence farming irrigation plan for southwest Kansas was advocated by Dodge City conservationists, who met with representatives of the Farm Security Administration in September 1938. Officials of this agency and of the Soil Conservation Service had previously announced that a project had been authorized for a ground water survey of western Kansas under the direction of these two agencies. Farm operators may receive assistance in developing stock ponds, pumping plants for irrigation purposes, and other water resources on a long term loan basis. The plan is to supplement the rainfall by irrigation in dry years, thus assuring a crop under unfavorable conditions and enabling the farmer to raise livestock feed and seed to tide him over until a favorable year. Commercial irrigation projects are discouraged. A preliminary survey, which began in the late fall of 1938, was conducted for the purpose of determining water facilities best adapted for the individual farm. All information is tabulated for future use and additional data is obtained by drilling, when necessary. Experimental projects have been developed on the Solomon River in northwest Kansas and in the Walnut Creek Valley in Ness and Lane Counties. Similar projects are planned for the Crooked Creek area in Ford County and the Arkansas Valley near Larned.

Land and water economy must be adjusted to "the State's scant and unreliable water supply," Professor Harlan M. Barrows, of the Water Committee of the National Resources Committee, has pointed out. "No more is possible. Harmonious adjustment to the ways of nature in the Plains must take the place of attempts to 'conquer' her. To hope that she may change her ways is futile."

Archeology

NO EXHAUSTIVE study has yet been made of the prehistoric past of Kansas, though the State is rich in archeological remains. Ancient village sites, mounds, battle fields, stone and clay workshops, and artifacts have been found in nearly every county. Relics range from the most primitive stone implements to artifacts and pottery showing skilled workmanship. One of the most important archeological finds in the State was the "Lansing Man" exhumed at Lansing, Leavenworth County, in 1902 and now in the National Museum, Washington, D. C. The discovery, consisting of a skull and some other skeletal parts of a human male, was found in an undisturbed loess drift under a stratum of carboniferous limestone twenty feet below the surface.

In Douglas, Potawatomi, Riley, Dickinson, Ellsworth, Marion, and Lincoln counties potsherds, bone and flint artifacts, and other relics have been found at depths of twenty to thirty feet. In Morris County, on Clark's Creek near Skiddy, a sort of oven or fireplace of matched stones was uncovered at a depth of sixteen feet. It rested on a solid ledge of rock several feet below the present channel of the stream and was surrounded with ashes, charcoal, bones, and flint artifacts. Of special significance is a small coin-shaped disk of some brass-like metal found nearby. Seven or eight feet above the fireplace and at about the same depth from the surface was the stump of an oak tree in the place of its growth, indicating the great age of the find and pointing to early occupancy of the region by Stone Age Americans.

Archeological remains show that both sedentary people and hunting tribes occupied Kansas in prehistoric times. The sedentary folk were agriculturists who constructed mounds of stone and earth, made and used earthen vessels and exquisitely wrought flint implements. The hunters were probably nomadic, making little pottery and relying upon the chase to supply them with food. There is evidence that both types of aborigines alternately occupied some of the village sites.

Although Kansas lacks the impressive earthworks characteristic of the mound builder sites of the Mississippi Valley, there are numerous earthen remains within the State, particularly in the eastern part along the river bottoms. Waterways served the mound builders as highways for travel, and the distribution of the several groups or subareas correspond to and were determined by the water systems. According to the classification adopted by archeologists Kansas mound remains are included in the cultural division known as the Upper Mississippi area. They form a marginal district, since the mound-building practice reached its western limit among the Kansas tribes. It is possible that these tribes were akin to the Mississippi people but were culturally different. They seem to have been more migratory than the advanced eastern tribes, and therefore left less pretentious remains and fewer walled defenses. But their many sites scattered over the State, indicate that they were a numerous people.

Most of the Kansas earthworks appear to be the remains of domiciliary sites. The common type of mounds are circular in form, twenty to twenty-five feet in diameter, and from two to three feet high. Some of them are apparently the caved-in ruins of timber-framed lodges, domeshaped and covered with earth; they were perhaps built and occupied by the ancestors of the present-day Caddoan peoples who left many such remains in the adjoining states. Those that have been excavated contained the bones of animals, broken catlinite pipes, metates of sandstone, grooved hammers, charcoal and ashes, as well as the usual collection of potsherds, arrowheads, scrapers, and flint knives. In one of them was also found a piece of chain mail in an advanced state of disintegration, indicating that these Indians were in contact with early European explorers, possibly Coronado or some of his party.

Exploration of Kansas mounds was begun in the 1880's when Professor J. A. Udden of Bethany College, Lindsborg, explored a series of fifteen mounds along Paint Creek, a tributary to the Smoky Hill River. His discoveries attracted outside authorities, and in the nineties Jacob V. Brower of St. Paul, Minnesota, made an extensive survey in Geary, Riley, and Wabaunsee counties, resulting in the exploration of more than 100 village sites and the accumulation of nearly 10,000 specimens. This collection, considered one of the best and most extensive in the country, is now in the museum of the Kansas State Historical Society at Topeka. It shows the entire range of aboriginal artifacts, from grindstones to bone fishhooks, from bird bone and shell beads to ornamented pottery.

Following Brower's discoveries, George J. Remsburg, of Potter, and Mark E. Zimmerman, of White Cloud, instituted a series of explorations in Atchison, Doniphan, and Leavenworth counties, which also yielded a large collection of relics. On a bluff along the Missouri River near Atchison they found a dozen skeletons and a quantity of bone, flint, and pottery articles. They also discovered an unusually large and ancient cemetery at Oak Mills, containing hundreds of flint and stone weapons, implements, and potsherds buried with the skeletal remains.

During this exploration, Remsburg discovered the site of "Quans," the grand village of the Kansa Indians, a tribe of Siouan stock. It had been described by the early French explorers but was not found for so long a time that men began to think of it as another fabled city. Remsburg proves that the town of Doniphan, six miles north of Atchison, occupies the ancient site.

Zimmerman unearthed two villages near the mouth of the Nemaha River, containing sixty skulls, and the shell tempered pottery and cist graves characteristic of the Tennessee-Cumberland area. From this evidence is deduced that the sites marked the western limit of mound-building people in Kansas.

Other mounds have been explored, and many have not yet been touched. Among the latter are the five or more—probably the largest in Kansas— near Edwardsville in Wyandotte County. These mounds are about five feet high, twenty-five feet in diameter, and stand fifty feet apart. Their great age is indicated by the heavy growth of oak timber which hid them before the ground was cleared. Many stone and flint implements have been found in the vicinity.

The mound-building trait apparently died out in Kansas in early historic times, but the mound builders must have exerted cultural influence upon the later tribes, or were, some contend, their actual ancestors. The Caddoan Pawnee, who had many towns along the Smoky Hill River, were the most distinctly agricultural tribe of the plains in modern times. Among the Pawnee peoples there survived even in recent years, many customs found among the Aztec when the Spaniards first met them. The story of these later tribes—the Pawnee of Caddoan stock and the Kansa or Kaw of the Siouan group—is written in the old lodge rings and village sites scattered in moderate profusion throughout the State and found usually a foot or so below the surface. Gathering of these data was begun in the 1860's when Professor Benjamin F. Mudge, first State geologist, made surveys of certain portions of the State. Goodnow's survey was in the vicinity of Manhattan, where he accumulated a considerable collection of flint implements, bone heads, pottery, and other artifacts. Operating principally in Rice, Riley, Cloud, and Geary counties, Mudge discovered the first of the clay workshops in Cloud County, on the Solomon River. It contains fragments of the bake ovens, partly moulded clay, and bits of finished pottery.

About three miles north of Neodesha on the Verdigris River an extensive fort and village site were found, probably a center of considerable importance. The fort, formed somewhat like a horseshoe with opening toward the east, was made up of two parallel lines of pits with an elevated ridge in the center formed from the dirt taken from the pits. Many specimens of pottery and buffalo bones have been taken from this site, indicating that the inhabitants were skilled in pottery making and subsisted to a considerable extent on the flesh of the buffalo. Other village sites found along the creeks in McPherson, Saline, Dickinson, Morris, and Geary counties, have yielded large numbers of flint hoes, spades, and other digging implements, from which it is presumed that their owners engaged, at least to some degree, in agriculture.

Big Springs in southwestern Morris County is another location rich in relics. This site was discovered in the 1860's on the David Rude farm and had furnished bushels of artifacts from the ancient flint workshop found near the spring. A half-mile from the village in an open river bottom has been found evidence of a battle between the villagers and an attacking party. Numerous arrow and broken spear points of two distinct types were scattered about. One type, also found in the town itself, was fashioned from the ordinary blue flint common in that locality. The other type, obviously used by the invaders, was much superior in quality and workmanship, being sharper, better pointed and made of varieties of agate, and of gray, white, and red flint. Since none of these superior points have been found in the town it is concluded that the invaders were defeated.

The floor of an Indian lodge and a prehistoric burial ground were excavated in the summer and fall of 1936 in Saline County, about four miles east of Salina. They are considered among the most important archeological finds of recent years. The lodge floor, thirty by thirty-two feet, was uncovered at a depth of eighteen inches. A central fireplace was found filled with ashes, and the earth beneath was burned a deep red. Post holes around the outer side of the floor and near the center indicate that the lodge was constructed of upright and crossed poles, probably chinked and roofed with clay and bluestem grass. The clay plainly showed finger marks of the builders who evidently used their hands as trowels. Five caches of different sizes and depths were sunk in the floor; in two of them were found clam shells, hoes, pipes, beads, pendants, and some charred corn. Bone needles, awls, scrapers, and flint arrows were on the floor. Two interesting pieces of clay modeling, a war club and a screech owl, were also found. In the two weeks following this discovery, hundreds of people visited the site; it was then covered over, and the soil sown to wheat.

Of even greater interest is the burial pit near the lodge floor, discovered in October 1936 on the farm of George E. Kohr. Subsequent investigations have proved it to be the largest Indian ossuary that has been unearthed in this part of the United States. More than one hundred skeletons of men, women and children lie buried four layers deep, in what careful observation shows to be a definite arrangement. The first layer is close to the surface; the lowest one is about forty inches below. Practically all of the skeletons lie on their right sides in a flexed position, heads to the south and facing east. Measurements indicate a race remarkable for size, strength, and endurance—many of the adult males being well over six feet in height. These remains have been expertly exposed and left in the places and positions of their burial. Near them have been found the remains of ceremonial pots, necklaces of shell beads, flint knives, and arrowheads. Several of the individual remains excite unusual interest and speculation. One small skull—evidently that of a child—shows double rows of teeth in each jaw. Near an adult male are the remains of two land turtles. Another adult male is a pronounced hunchback, and he lies on his left side with his head to the west. Almost without exception the skulls are long with low foreheads, although there is one skeleton of small stature with a round head and high forehead. The pit is now protected by a small frame building, which contains Indian artifacts found on the spot and in the vicinity.

An important relic of historic times is the ruin of an old pueblo twelve miles north of Scott City in Scott County. This had been identified as the long lost El Quartelejo, established about 1700, or perhaps earlier, by Picurie Indians from New Mexico, who abandoned the settlement to escape Spanish oppression. It was originally a stone and adobe building, thirty-two by fifty feet, divided into seven rooms, and was probably the first walled house ever constructed in Kansas. In it were found stone, flint, and bone implements; mealing stones, potsherds, charred corn, and other relics characteristic of the Pueblo Indians.

Indians

TWO groups of Indians have lived in Kansas, the native tribes—found by the first white men who entered the Territory—and the emigrant tribes. The latter were from the East, settled on reservations in Kansas by treaties with the Federal Government.

Wandering tribes like the Cheyenne and Arapahoe inhabited sections of the Kansas region, but their culture is not as representative of Indian life in the State as that of the Kansa (Kaw), Osage, and Pawnee. These tribes lived in villages of large and semi-permanent earth lodges, and cultivated maize, beans, and squash. There were significant differences in their social organization, religious ideas, and mode of life, but the Kansa may be taken as an example, since it is from them that the State derived its name.

The Kansa belonged to the Siouan linguistic group and were closely related to the Osage. Their economy was based upon the cultivation of crops and hunting of buffalo or other game. Agriculture was women's work, while hunting was that of the men. Each lodge was a self-contained economic unit providing all its own material needs.

The tribe was governed by five hereditary chiefs. Each office was controlled by a gens—a group of kin related only through the male line. A chief was generally succeeded by his eldest son, but it was possible for a woman to hold office if no son were living. In recognition of an outstanding achievement, a man could be elected chief, and the new chieftainship thus created became hereditary in his gens.

The Kansa lived in earth lodges in permanent villages, which they left periodically on organized buffalo hunts. Because of its great economic importance the buffalo hunt was carefully controlled and the hunters were restricted in many ways. They were divided into three bands, each of which lived as a unit for the duration of the hunt. An announcer informed the village of the day of departure and, as soon as the place for the hunt had been agreed upon, each band chose a prominent warrior as leader. He paid for a feast and was thanked by the chiefs for his services. Then, for police, twenty men were chosen from those who had proved their courage in war by taking a scalp, or slaying an enemy, or in other ways. They were in charge of the hunt, prevented any individual from attacking before the signal was given, policed the camp, and punished offenders by whipping them. When the hunters returned to camp, the police shared the meat as payment for their services.

The most sacred objects possessed by the tribe were the medicine bundles, which contained many objects believed to be imbued with magical powers. The bundles used in war were the most prominent because warfare held the most important role in tribal life. Each gens had its war bundle, and among its number were certain men privileged in its ownership and use. These privileges were obtained by acquiring the proper vision through fasting and prayer. Once a man had been granted his vision, he went to a former owner of the bundle and paid him for instruction in its uses. Thereafter he was a potential war chief.

The custom of scalp taking, which was regarded by the whites as a mere act of savagery, was practiced primarily as a memorial of victory and was an outgrowth of the more ancient form of head hunting. But it also had a ritualistic significance as the scalp-lock was held to be the seat of life, or the spirit of the warrior. It was believed that the scalped victim, being physically incomplete, could not enter the Happy Hunting Ground and consequently could have no rest in the hereafter, but must continue as a spirit-servant to the victor. Therefore, the more scalps a warrior took, the better; he would have more spirit-assistants and fewer enemies when he himself entered the future life.

Boys began about the age of twelve to fast in order to obtain dreams and guardian spirits. A father painted his son's face with clay and sent him to a lonely spot so that he might receive power to do a brave deed. Warrior ancestors appeared to the boy and prophesied his future exploits, and from them he generally acquired war powers. His dreams were primarily concerned with future acts of greatness in war, and were recited whenever he joined a war party. Although this was the fundamental type of vision, others were peopled with the spirits of bear, buffalo, or thunder, one of which became his special protector throughout life. When the boy returned he received a new name, usually based on his vision, and became a member of the tribe.

The great interest of the Kansa and other tribes of the Plains area was warfare, and only by his achievements in war could an individual attain social position. The warrior's preëminence was shown upon every possible social occasion. He was permitted to sit upon a stuffed hide pillow at a feast, to ride ahead of the police to the buffalo herd, and hunt without fear of punishment. He acted as an intermediary in marriage, took charge of dances, and functioned in the naming ceremony. The greatest honor that could be bestowed on a warrior was to have his breast tattooed; and this was accorded only to those who had slain seven enemies and stolen six of their horses.

When a marriage was being arranged, the boy's parents asked a tattooed warrior to be the intermediary. With three other braves of his choosing, he visited the girl's parents and made the proposal. If the parents consented to the marriage, all the warriors recited their exploits in war, and recounted them again on the way back to the boy's lodge. (If they returned in silence, the boy knew that his request had been refused.) At the lodge they announced the result of their mission. Then the boy, if accepted, formally presented a number of horses to the girl's father. On the date set for the marriage the girl, dressed in her finest clothes, went to the groom's lodge, taking many presents. Here the boy's parents dressed her again in a costume they had provided, and seated her upon the ground inside the lodge. Seated back-to-back, the boy and girl partook of a marriage feast. Relatives and friends were then admitted to a general feast, presents were delivered, and the ceremony was ended.

As a tribe, the Kansa were aloof and independent, having little friendly intercourse with any of the neighboring tribes, except the Osage, with whom they were closely related by linguistic ties and intermarriage. They did not penetrate far into what is now Kansas. At the time of the coming of the Spanish in the sixteenth century, they occupied narrow strips of territory on both sides of the Missouri River, approximately from the mouth of the Kansas to the Nebraska line. Two hundred years later they were in virtually the same location. In 1724 de Bourgmont reported two Kansa villages on the Missouri—one a few leagues above the mouth of the Kansas, the other at the mouth of Independence Creek in Doniphan County. It is thought that the latter point was the limit of their ascent up the Missouri, and that they were driven back from there by the Pawnee. Lewis and Clark, in 1804, found no trace of the lower village and only the remains of the upper; the Kansa were at that time established on the Kansas River, with one village in the vicinity of the present Topeka, the other at the mouth of the Big Blue (see MANHATTAN). By 1806 the former village had been deserted, and all the Kansa were collected at the Big Blue.

In 1815 they made their first treaty with the Government, one of peace and good will and involving no land transaction. But at St. Louis on June 3, 1825, they relinquished claim to all land in Missouri, southeast Nebraska, and northeast Kansas, accepting instead a reservation beginning twenty leagues up the Kansas. By 1830 the settlement on the Big Blue had been abandoned, and three villages established near Mission Creek in Shawnee County. These villages were occupied until 1846, when, by a treaty signed January 14, the reservation was diminished, and the Kansa were removed to Council Grove. On October 5, 1859, another treaty reduced their lands to a small tract nine miles wide and fourteen miles long, which was appraised and sold for the benefit of the tribe, when the Kansa were moved to a reservation in Oklahoma about 1873.

Never very numerous, they were reduced by smallpox and liquor introduced by traders. In 1835 they were estimated at 1,606 and in 1872 at hardly more than 200. From a once proud tribe, they had degenerated to a poverty-stricken handful. Yet from these people, through the Pappan family at Topeka (see TOPEKA), was descended one of Kansas' most distinguished citizens—Charles Curtis, late Vice President of the United States.

The Osage, also of the Siouan family, resembled the Kansa in religious observance, social organization, and tribal customs, as well as in physical appearance. Both have been described as tall and well formed. George Catlin, the painter, visited the western tribes about 1835, and reported that the Osage were the tallest Indians in North America, being from six to six and one-half feet tall and well proportioned. They called themselves Wa-zhe-zhe, which became Osage when French traders attempted to render the name in writing. They were divided into two bands, the Great and the Little Osage, when first known to the whites, and were collected in two villages on the Missouri River, each village having its own chief and local government. Prior to 1796, the trade along the Missouri and all its tributary branches had been competitive, and Pierre Chouteau enjoyed a monopoly with the Osage. Superseded by Manuel Lisa, who obtained an exclusive right to trade in this territory from the Governor of Louisiana, Chouteau laid plans to regain the profitable Osage business. He induced the young men from both divisions to bring their families and follow him south to the Verdigris, and later to the Arkansas River, establishing villages along the latter stream. This migrating band was known as the Arkansas and comprised about one-half of the Osage Nation.

Meanwhile the Great and Little Osage had removed from the Missouri to the Osage River. In 1806 the Pike expedition found them in an upper and lower village on the Little Osage. Two years later the Government erected Fort Osage (afterwards Fort Clark), at the site of Sibley, Missouri, presumably for their protection against neighboring tribes, with whom they were in constant warfare. Within a month, Chouteau appeared at the

CHEYENNE CHIEFS IN CAPTIVITY, FORT DODGE (1878)

fort with a treaty, prepared without consultation, by which the Osage were obliged to relinquish virtually all the land they had in Missouri; and in 1815 they moved into new villages on the Neosho. In 1820 the Great Osage had one village on the Osage River and one on the Neosho, while the Little Osage had three villages on the latter stream. All five villages totaled about 2,600 inhabitants. From then until the close of the Civil War the Osage lived mainly in Kansas, hunting about the Neosho, Osage, and Arkansas rivers.

Partly agrarian, they planted their crops in April, gave them one cultivation and left their villages in May for the summer hunt, from which they did not return until August. Then they harvested the crops—usually from ten to twenty bags of corn and beans, and a quantity of dried pumpkin for each family—and feasted. In September they started on the fall hunt which lasted until Christmas.

On June 2, 1825, preceding the Kansa by one day, the Osage ceded all land in the State south of that claimed by the Kansa to the United States, which thus acquired undisputed title. In return the Osage accepted a diminished reserve, beginning twenty-five miles west of the Missouri Line and extending west fifty miles. This reservation was again reduced by a treaty, signed at the Canville Trading Post in Neosho County on September 29, 1865, which provided that the Osage lands should be sold for their benefit if they agreed to move to the Indian Territory in Oklahoma. They so decided and settled on land bought from the Cherokee in 1870.

The Caddoan family, represented in Kansas by the Pawnee and the Wichita, is believed to have migrated from the southwest at a period so remote that only confused accounts of the migration exist in the family traditions. Unlike the Siouan, the Caddoan family did not come as a whole but in tribal divisions extending over a long period; the general direction of the movement was north and east. Caddoan tribes were distributed in a diagonal belt reaching from Louisiana to North Dakota, where the northernmost division, the Arikara, settled along the banks of the Missouri.

Members of this division called themselves Chahiksichahiks, "men of men." But to the whites they were known as the Pawnee (from the Caddoan word, "pa-rik-i," meaning "horn"), because of their scalp-locks, which were so plastered with grease and paint that they stood erect like horns.

They were a powerful tribe, originally estimated at 25,000, divided into four subtribes: the Grand Pawnee on the Platte River in Nebraska; the Loup on the Loup branch of the Platte; the Republican on the Republican River; and the Tapage, or Noisy Pawnee, on the Smoky Hill River. Each village was ruled by a hereditary chief, whose power was more or less absolute, depending on the personality of the individual; and the villages were held together in a confederacy composed of the reigning chiefs, with a superior chief over all.

Their first contact with white men was in 1541, when the "Turk" led Coronado into Kansas, although not all historians agree that Coronado reached "Harahey," as he called the Pawnee country. It is said that he sent for the Pawnee chief, Tatarrax, and that the chief came to Quivira with 200 warriors, "all naked, with bows, and some sort of things on their heads." They were well-known in the seventeenth and eighteenth centuries to the French traders.

Their numbers were steadily decreased in battle, as they were in constant conflict with surrounding tribes, especially the Kansa and Osage, whom they considered their hereditary enemies. However, as with all other tribes, their most formidable enemies were drink and disease. An epidemic of smallpox carried off nearly one-half the nation in 1831. Writing of that calamity, their agent reported them "dying so fast . . . they had ceased to bury their dead, and bodies were to be seen in every direction, lying in the river, lodged on the sand bars, in the weeds around their villages, and in their old corn caches."

In September 1825 they acknowledged the supremacy of the United States and agreed to submit all grievances to the Government for adjustment. This agreement they faithfully kept, even when the offenses were committed by white men. Their cessions of land were insignificant, as much that was rightfully theirs by prior claim and occupancy was ceded by the Kansa and Osage. In 1876 the Pawnee—their numbers reduced to 2,500—relinquished what was left to them in Kansas by a final treaty and moved to Oklahoma.

Of all the Indians of Kansas, the Pawnee have yielded the greatest bulk of songs and folk tales to ethnologists. The beautiful ceremonial dance, *The Hako,* formerly observed by the Algonquian, Caddoan, and Siouan families, was faithfully preserved by the Pawnee and has been recorded by Alice C. Fletcher in the Twenty-second Annual Report (1900–01) of the Bureau of American Ethnology. This ceremony, observed in the spring at the mating season, was a prayer for children that the tribe might increase and be strong; and the people might have long life, enjoy plenty, and be happy and at peace. It was distinguished by its dignity, rhythmic variety, and symbolic concept.

Although the Wichita spoke a Caddoan language related to Pawnee, little is known about them. Catlin could find no resemblance between the two groups in language, physical feature, or custom. The Wichita he described as dark-skinned, clumsy and ordinary, although excellent horsemen—like the Comanche. Their dress, too, was similar to that of the Comanche; and like them they wore their hair long, while the Pawnee shaved and painted their heads.

The Wichita, it is surmised, originally accompanied the Pawnee to the Platte and Republican Rivers, and later, because of some dissatisfaction, retraced their steps to the Arkansas River where they lived for centuries. Coronado found them there in 1541 and called their land Quivira; and succeeding Spanish explorers visited them in the late sixteenth and early seventeenth centuries. When they left Quivira is not known. Probably they were forced out by the southern advance of the Siouan family, and settled along the Cimarron River and on south into Texas. They returned, however, to the old Quivira region during the Civil War and established a village on the site of the city of Wichita. Before the period of land cession they again retreated south, leaving their land to more aggressive tribes.

The Arapahoe and Cheyenne were of the Algonquian family, which

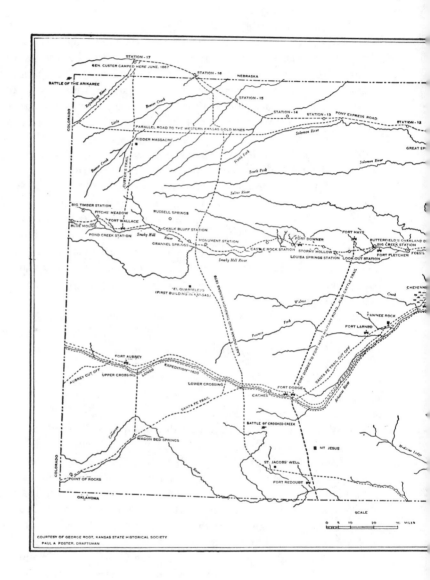

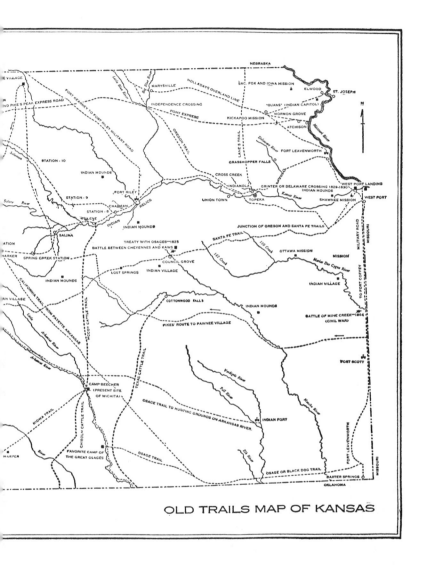

OLD TRAILS MAP OF KANSAS

originally occupied territory about the Red River in northern Minnesota. At some time in their history they had formed an alliance, which has continued to the present time. They were forced west by the northern Siouan movements—the Arapahoe going first into Wyoming; the Cheyenne moving at a later date into the Black Hills of South Dakota, and settling about the Cheyenne River, where they were found in 1804 by the Lewis and Clark expedition.

Divisions of each tribe drifted south and west, forming the Northern and Southern Arapahoe, and the Northern and Southern Cheyenne. But these divisions were only geographical, for they combined forces to carry on warfare against all the neighboring tribes. In 1840 they made peace with the Comanche, Kiowa, and Sioux, but continued hostilities against the Pawnee, Ute, and Shoshoni until all were confined on reservations.

According to their traditions, they were once a sedentary people, living in fixed villages, cultivating the soil, and practicing the arts of pottery and weaving. On the Plains they developed into nomadic hunters, living in portable skin tents *(tipis)* and ranging from the Black Hills to the Arkansas River and into the Rocky Mountains. They were fierce and daring horsemen and the most dreaded foes of the early Mexican traders and California gold-seekers. Although they had many similarities to the Kansa, Osage, and Pawnee, they fit the popular conception of the Plains Indians more exactly.

By a treaty at Fort Laramie, in 1851, the boundaries of the southern divisions were fixed, giving them a large tract in western Kansas and eastern Colorado, which the Government promised to protect. However, the discovery of gold in Colorado in 1858 brought such hordes of white men into the territory that the Indians were forced out of the mountains onto the plains about the Arkansas and Red Rivers. Angered by this breach of faith, and aided by the Sioux in the north and the Kiowa in the south, they began a series of uprisings that lasted until 1878. They figured in the Chivington massacre in Colorado and that of Custer in Wyoming. On February 18, 1861, they ceded all their lands in Kansas, except a small tract lying between the Arkansas and Purgatory Rivers, but continued depredations over all their former territory. The treaty of October 28, 1867, gave them a reservation in Oklahoma, but they refused to accept it until forced to do so by the final treaties of 1874–1875. In 1876 the northern divisions were settled in Wyoming and Montana.

The Arapahoe and Cheyenne participated in the Sun Dance, the annual rite of worship performed by nearly all the Plains tribes and especially by the Siouan, who accompanied it with sacrifices. The Arapahoe were leaders in the Ghost Dance movement, originated about 1888 by Wovoka, a member of the Paviotso tribe in western Nevada. This dance was the ceremonial expression of the "Messiah" religion in which the Indians, realizing the futility of further resistance and resigning themselves to the fate of the conquered, took refuge. It was a mixture of Christianity and Indian mythology, based on the belief that God had sent white people to punish the Indians for their sins. When these sins were fully expiated, it was believed, God would return to destroy the whites and reunite in heaven all Indians, living and dead. To hasten His return, the elaborate ceremony of the Dance, lasting four to five nights, was observed once in every six weeks.

Contrary to popular belief, the Ghost Dance religion did not advocate war on the whites, although it did give indirect impetus to the Sioux outbreak in the spring of 1891. The fundamental teachings of the "Messiah" were "not to tell lies, to harm no one, to do right always, and not to cry when their friends died." It was the most pacific religion ever adopted by an Indian people.

Hopefully the elated converts looked forward to the dates set for the return of their God and the destruction of the whites; when these dates passed without fulfillment of the prophecy, the Indians lost faith and the Ghost Dance faded out.

The Kiowa have the distinction of being the sole representative of their linguistic family. The word, Kiowa, comes from their "Kiowagan," meaning "prominent people." They were a true Plains tribe, having come originally from the upper Yellowstone and Missouri Rivers. Forced out by the Sioux, they drifted south along the base of the Rockies to settle along the Arkansas and Canadian Rivers.

Shortly thereafter they formed an alliance with the Crow, and in 1840 they made a similar agreement with the Arapahoe and Cheyenne, with whom they were associated in border uprisings. They were war-like and predatory and are credited with having killed more white men in proportion to their numbers than any other tribe. They made their first treaty with the United States in 1837 and removed to their present reservation in 1868, although, together with their confederates, they continued depredations until the last outbreak in 1878.

The Comanche, of the Shoshonean family, also ranged across sections of western Kansas. They fought intermittently with the Spanish for 200 years and for nearly half a century with the Texans, who, they felt, had taken their best hunting grounds. They were close confederates of the Kiowa and joined them in all border warfare.

On October 18, 1865, together with the Kiowa, they ceded all land to the Government, that in Kansas being west of the Osage and south of the Arkansas River. By the 1867 treaty at Medicine Lodge they were given a reservation in Oklahoma; but, like the Kiowa, they refused to accept it until general peace was effected. Although covering a great deal of territory, the Comanche were never as numerous as they seemed. In 1904, wasted by war and disease, they numbered only 1,400.

The movement of emigrant tribes into Kansas began with the Shawnee in 1825 and ended with the Wyandot in 1842. At the insistence of the Government these tribes, twenty-eight in number, gave up their ancient lands east of the Mississippi, or land they had acquired by settlement west of the Mississippi, and were given in return small reservations in eastern Kansas, mainly in that portion ceded by the Kansa and Osage. The majority of the emigrant tribes had lived in long association with missionaries and white settlements. They had intermarried with the whites and their leaders were often white men adopted into the tribe, or descendants of mixed blood. Under these combined influences, they had adopted many of the ways of the whites and, to some degree, arrived at their way of thinking.

This was particularly true of the Delaware, Shawnee, and Wyandot. The first printing press in Kansas was brought to the Shawnee; and on it was printed the second newspaper ever published in an Indian language. The code of laws adopted by the Delaware would have compared favorably with that of any group of white people in similar circumstances. The Wyandot—more than three-fourths white, generally educated and in some instances highly cultured—established the first free school in Kansas and played a significant part in the State's territorial history.

But these tribes, brought into the lusty crudeness of a.border country and repeatedly deceived by meaningless promises of the Government, deserted the teachings of missionaries and adopted the worst habits of their conquerors. Drink, supplied by the ubiquitous trader, became a general habit. The Delaware, enticed to the Plains by the buffalo, became embroiled with the Pawnee and burned the Pawnee village on the Republican River in 1832. The Potawatomi also fought with the Pawnee until the latter were defeated.

Eventually these emigrant groups shared the fate of the native families. In 1854, when Kansas was opened to white settlers, a period of land cession was inaugurated and continued until about 1880. At its close virtually all Indian titles had been extinguished. Of the thirty-six tribes, remnants of only six, distributed on small reservations, are now to be found

POTTAWATOMIE AND KICKAPOO HOLY MEN, RESERVATION NEAR HORTON

in Kansas. These are the Chippewa and Munsee in Franklin County; Iowa in Doniphan; Potawatomi in Jackson; and the Sauk and Fox and Kickapoo in Brown County. In 1930 their combined numbers totaled 2,454.

Indian farmers in Kansas today live in much the same manner as their white neighbors. Though there are a few impressive buildings, their houses are usually small; many have telephones and other modern conveniences. It might appear that these people have completely lost their racial heritage, but this is not so. During the summer months, especially, they return to their tribal costumes, not only for festivities but for everyday wear; and few Indians fail to attend the religious dances and games held on Kansas reservations at customary intervals during the year.

In this way they manage to preserve much of their native culture. The Prairie Potawatomi, more than any of the other Kansan Indians, still adhere to their tribal customs and conduct traditional ceremonies on their reservation. The Religious Dance is the most important of these. It represents the fusion of Indian and Christian religious concepts and is held at least five times a year, out-of-doors in spring and summer, and indoors during the winter months. It is conducted by an organization of men and women which functions like a priesthood. Vigorous singing and drumming are sustained for most of the day and night for a period varying from one to eight days, depending on the amount of food available. The entire tribe attends, but only the men dance. Peyote meetings, so named from the stimulant drug, are also held each year for several successive nights and days, for the formal purpose of worship and general thanksgiving. Men and women attend; all eat or drink some peyote and contribute food. Other rituals include the Dance Ceremony for the deceased, the Adoption Ceremony, and the Clan (or Gens) Ceremony.

Games are also played—lacrosse, for men only; woman's ball game, or squaw hockey, for women only; and moccasin game for both men and women. Indian dice, archery and blow-gun games are sometimes played with a neighboring tribe, like the Kickapoo. The promotion of friendship, rather than rivalry, is the objective in these games, for the Indian believes that "All games are gifts from the Good Spirit for the enjoyment of life."

History

PRIOR to the coming of the Spanish in 1541, the Kansas country was known only to the Indians—nomadic bands of hunters and warriors, and the indigenous tribes. Of the latter, Coronado mentions three, the Wichita, Kansa, and Pawnee, and vaguely infers that there may have been more.

For a decade, the "seven cities of Cibola" had been in the minds of Spanish conquistadores; to find and plunder these supposed centers of wealth had been the cherished hope of many adventurers. But only Francisco Vasquez de Coronado, Governor of New Galicia in New Spain, Mexico, comes into the Quivira quest, which grew out of the disappointing Cibola experience and is the colorful prelude to Kansas history.

In 1539 Friar Marcos de Nica, whom Coronado had sent on a preliminary search for the Cibola cities, returned with the good news that he had espied one of these wonderful places of "high houses," though only from a safe distance. An expedition was organized, and 300 Spanish "men of quality" gathered at the rendezvous, Compostela (on the Pacific coast below lower California), by Shrovetide of 1540. With Coronado as captain-general, the army started northward, crossed the mountains, and spent the whole of that year in futile marches through what are now Arizona and New Mexico. Winter overtook them at Tiguex (near Bernalillo, New Mexico). By this time they had found that the cities of Cibola were merely poor pueblo structures; but one of Coronado's captains, Hernando de Alvarado, while on a minor search, had been told by "an Indian slave" whom he called "The Turk," that far beyond "toward Florida" lay the slave's own land, Quivira, which was rich in gold and silver. He could guide the white strangers to it.

In the spring of 1541 (April 23) Coronado and his army left Tiguex, hoping to find in Quivira the precious metals Cibola could not supply. The Turk led them through "the cow country" into western Texas—so far southeastward that at a village on the Colorado River the captain-general called a halt. Their supplies had fallen dangerously low. For 37 days they had followed the Turk and, to conserve their grain supplies, had lived mainly on buffalo meat. Tiguex was "250 leagues" away, and the unknown country beyond might prove barren. Coronado divided his force. Taking with him only "thirty horsemen and six footmen," he headed north to pursue the quest, sending the remainder of his men back to Tiguex to await his return.

With Coronado went the Turk and another guide. Across the panhandles of Texas and Oklahoma Coronado proceeded "until he reached Quivira." His report, October 20, 1541, to his king, reads: "I traveled for forty-two days after I left the force, living all the while solely on the flesh of the bulls and cows which we killed . . . and going many days without water and cooking the food with cow dung, because there is ro other kind of wood in all these plains, away from the gullies and rivers, which are few." The chronicler Suceso placed Quivira as "in the fortieth degree," but another authority, mapping the "Province of Quivira," puts it in the thirty-ninth, between the Arkansas River at Great Bend and the confluence of the Republican and Kansas Rivers, at Junction City.

It was near this place that the Turk was strangled for his treachery, after Coronado had heard that he had tried to incite the Quivira people (Wichita tribe) to kill them. The Turk might have been killed anyway, for by this time one fact was obvious to the angry captain-general: Quivira contained no gold or silver. "These provinces . . ." Coronado wrote, "are a very small affair . . . there is not any gold, nor any metal at all in that country." But he found some satisfaction "on seeing the good appearance of the earth. . . . The province of Quivira . . . 950 leagues from Mexico," he conceded, "is the best I have seen for producing all the products of Spain, for besides the land itself being very fat and black, and being well watered by the rivulets and springs and rivers, I found prunes like those of Spain, and nuts and very sweet grapes and mulberries."

After a stay of 25 days in Quivira, Coronado and his men returned to Tiguex, but by a shorter southwestward route, approximating what later became the Santa Fe Trail. In the summer of 1542, "with less than a hundred men," he reached Mexico City, where he was shorn of his rank and soon died. But the seemingly fruitless journey introduced the horse to the Plains and, by right of discovery, established Spanish claim in the entire western region.

A Franciscan monk, Juan de Padilla, who had been with Coronado in Quivira, returned to that country in 1542, but was killed by the Indians. For a half century Spanish interest in the far north remained inactive. Then, in 1594, Francisco Levya de Bonilla and Antonio Gutierrez de Humaña ventured beyond the Arkansas, traveling northward for twelve days and reaching another river. On their way back they were overtaken and murdered. Don Juan de Oñate, in 1601, was the next Spaniard to traverse Quivira. It is probable that more than a century passed before another Spanish party came so far north.

In the late decades of the seventeenth century, however, the French from Canada began to show active interest in the land west of the Mississippi. In 1673 Louis Jolliet, a trader, accompanied by Father Jacques Marquette, descended the Mississippi River from the mouth of the Wisconsin River to below the mouth of the Arkansas; on the return trip they left the Mississippi at the Illinois. So it hardly seems likely that, as some suppose, Jolliet and Marquette ever reached the Kansas region. Neither did La Salle who, in 1682, descended the Mississippi from the Illinois to its mouth, returning along the same rivers. But there is a Marquette map upon which some Kansas authorities seem to recognize certain topographical features descriptive of Kansas. It was probably drawn from information gained by interrogating Indians with whom the priest came in contact. Marquette in this way learned much about native peoples he never visited. On his map of the Missouri and Kansas region, he marked the names Ouemessourit (Missouri), Kanza (Kaw), Ouchage (Osage), Paneassa (Pawnee), and some others.

In 1694 "Canadian traders were among the Osage and Missouri tribes," and during the next few years the Spanish authorities in New Mexico had several indications that the French traders were on good terms with the Pawnee. By 1706, when Juan de Ulibarri headed a Spanish expedition out of Santa Fé, it was apparent that the French, operating from the north, were becoming rivals of the Spanish of New Mexico for the trade of the interior.

Between 1706 and 1719 the French penetration was steady. In 1708 Canadians explored "three hundred to four hundred leagues" of the Missouri River; and during the next decade the French from the Louisiana capital reached out along other tributaries of the Mississippi. In 1719 Charles Claude du Tisné, sent up the Missouri River by the Governor of Louisiana, visited the Osage villages, near the mouth of the Osage River, and crossed the northeast corner of Kansas to the Pawnee region on the Republican River. The Spanish heard that "he planted the French flag in native villages and even traded in Spanish horses." Don Pedro de Villazur, assigned "to drive the French out of the land," left Santa Fé in 1720 with a Spanish force of 42 soldiers, 3 settlers, 60 Indians, and a priest. The route was "always to the northeast from Santa Fé." Possibly the caravan passed through part of Kansas, but the account mentions only three rivers, the Napestle (Arkansas), the Jesus Maria (south fork of the Platte), and the San Lorenzo (north fork of the Platte). Villazur and most of the Spaniards were killed in a battle, thought to have been fought near the town of North Platte, Nebraska. This defeat ended Spanish operations and left the French in undisputed possession.

The French established themselves more securely in the region in 1722, when Etienne Venyard, Sieur de Bourgmont, erected Fort Orleans near the mouth of the Osage River. Two years later Bourgmont worked among Kansas Indians and penetrated even to the Rocky Mountains. He seemed to have established trading relations with many tribes, but Kansa warriors destroyed Fort Orleans in 1725.

In 1763 French authority, in all America, came to an end. England, victorious in the long French and Indian War, received the Canadian provinces and all French rights to land east of the Mississippi. New Orleans and Louisiana, west of the Mississippi, had already (1762) been ceded by France to Spain.

Spain showed little interest in the Quivira country thus regained, yet the development of Kansas began under its ownership. Pierre Laclède Luguest, with Auguste and Pierre Chouteau of the French fur trading family, established headquarters at St. Louis in 1764, and sent agents from there to the Indians of Missouri, Arkansas, Nebraska, and Kansas. These agents, although few in number, cleared the paths by which Kansas was to emerge from a little-known region into a definite territory.

In 1801, by the Treaty of Madrid, which confirmed the 1800 Treaty of San Ildefonso, Louisiana west of the Mississippi was retroceded to France, which by then had renewed its ambitions for a colonial empire and thereby alarmed the recently formed United States. France, under Napoleon, was at the height of its power—too dominant a neighbor to be viewed placidly. Recognition of this and other considerations led President Thomas Jefferson to propose the purchase by the United States of west Florida and New Orleans. Napoleon's counter proposal, offering the whole of Louisiana, was accepted. On April 30, 1803, Louisiana, including the Kansas region, became the property of the United States.

Explorations sponsored by the United States began immediately. In January 1803, before the Louisiana Purchase was consummated, President Jefferson called the attention of Congress to the land west of the Mississippi, pointing out the possibilities of trade and suggesting an appropriation of $2,500 for the purpose of exploring the country and furthering commerce. The appropriation was made, and an exploring party organized under command of Captain Meriwether Lewis and Lieutenant William Clark.

In March 1804 the Territory was divided into two parts. Land south of the thirty-third parallel was named the Territory of Orleans; that north of the parallel, including Kansas, became the District of Louisiana, attached for legal purposes to the Territory of Indiana.

On June 26, 1804, Lewis and Clark landed at the mouth of the Kansas River on the first lap of their expedition. By July 4 they had reached a stream in the present Doniphan County, which they named "Independence Creek" in honor of the day, firing an evening gun and rationing out an additional gill of whiskey by way of celebration. Two years later, August 5, 1806, they returned to the mouth of the Kansas with the first reliable information on the climate, topography, and general features of the western country.

Before the conclusion of the first expedition, a second was organized by the military commandant of Louisiana, General James Wilkinson, and set out from St. Louis June 24, 1806, under command of Captain Zebulon M. Pike. He visited the Osage in Missouri and the Pawnee on the Republican, arriving among the latter on September 25. Here he found a Spanish flag floating over their council tent. The purchase from Napoleon had no fixed western boundary; the United States claimed territory extending to the Rocky Mountains while Spain fixed the line much farther east. Pike demanded that the Spanish flag be hauled down and the American standard be raised in its place, thus putting an end to all Spanish claim east of the Rockies. He turned south to the Arkansas River and followed it to the present site of Pueblo, Colorado, discovering the mountain now known as Pike's Peak. As this was encroaching on Spanish territory, he was captured and taken to Mexico. During his captivity of some months, Pike gathered considerable information as to the possibilities of trade with the Mexican provinces. The accounts of his travels, published in 1810 on his return to the States, directed an avid interest to these provinces.

Of parts of Kansas he wrote enthusiastically but he saw no possibilities for white settlement in the arid portions of the Louisiana district. "These vast plains of the western hemisphere," his account reads, "may become in time as celebrated as the sandy deserts of Africa; for I saw in my route, in various places, tracts of many leagues where the wind had thrown up the sand in all the fanciful forms of the ocean's rolling wave, on which not a speck of vegetable matter existed."

Maps, presumably based on Pike's report and showing the desert reaching from the west line of Missouri and Arkansas to the Rocky Mountains, from the Platte to the Red River, were incorporated into the school geographies of that period. This misconception gave rise to the legend of a "great American Desert" that included the whole of Kansas.

Meanwhile, March 3, 1805, the District of Louisiana was erected into the Territory of Louisiana, independent of the Territory of Indiana and with its own powers of legislation.

Twelve years elapsed before another expedition was attempted, and during that time a series of events occurred that influenced the future of Kansas. In 1807 Manuel Lisa, a Spanish fur trader, established a number of trading stations about the headwaters of the Missouri River. The Missouri Fur Company was organized the following year by Lisa, together with Auguste and Pierre Chouteau, and a chain of trading posts was established throughout the western country. This company was dissolved in 1812 and was succeeded by the American Fur Company of the Chouteaus, who were beginning to concentrate their activities in Kansas.

On June 4, 1812, the Territory of Missouri, with its western boundary approximating that of the present State of Missouri, was created from the Territory of Louisiana, leaving the remainder without law or official identification for a quarter of a century.

The expedition of Major Stephen H. Long—a scientific exploration sent out by the Government—ascended the Missouri to the present town of Council Bluffs, Iowa, in 1819. Long camped there for the winter, then moved south to the Platte and Red Rivers, entered Colorado, where members of his party made the first ascent of Pike's Peak, and returned to the Mississippi via the Red River. His expedition, following in the path of Pike, accumulated scientific data, and introduced the first steamboat to Kansas waters. The *Western Engineer* entered the mouth of the Kansas on August 10, 1819, and transported his party up the course for one mile. Here the mud left by flood-waters made it necessary to turn back and continue up the Missouri.

A period of still deeper significance for the future of Kansas followed. In 1818 the Missouri Territory asked admission to the Union as a slave State; simultaneously, Alabama, also a slave State, asked admission. Alabama was admitted in 1819, balancing the power of the opposing factions, 11 free and 11 slave States. The debates over Missouri resulted in the Missouri Compromise, passed February 17, 1820, providing that Missouri should be admitted as a slave State, but that all future States west of the Mississippi and north of 36° and 30' should be free. On August 10, 1821, Missouri was admitted under the terms of the compromise and the question of slavery shifted to the territory west of the

Mississippi, where it was to flare anew in Kansas. Two years later the boundary between Missouri and Kansas was definitely fixed.

Thomas Hart Benton, Senator from Missouri, began in Congress his championship of western development in 1824, only to meet with opposition such as the following from Daniel Webster: "What do we want with this vast and worthless area, of this region of savages and wild beasts, of deserts, of shifting sands and whirlwinds, of dust, of cactus and prairie dogs; to what use could we ever hope to put these great deserts, or those endless mountain ranges, impenetrable and covered to their very base with eternal snow? What can we ever hope to do with the western coast, a coast of 3,000 miles, rockbound, cheerless, uninviting and not a harbor in it? Mr. President, I will never vote one cent from the public treasury to place the Pacific Coast one inch nearer Boston than it is now."

The Reverend Isaac McCoy, a missionary to the Indians east of the Mississippi, journeyed to Washington to propose the removal of his charges to western reservations beyond the influence of white settlements. His proposal was favorably received and, in the main, Kansas was selected to provide the reservations, for it was still thought of as desert country and of no value.

In 1825 the Government arranged treaties with the Osage and Kansa, whereby they gave up their lands in eastern Kansas to make way for the emigrant tribes. The first allotment was granted to the Shawnees; then in rapid succession came the Delaware in 1829; the Kickapoo, Potawatomi, Kaskaskia, Peoria, Wea, and Piankeshaw in 1832; the Sauk and Fox and the Iowa in 1836; the Miami in 1840; and the Wyandot in 1843. All were crowded onto small reservations in the eastern part of the State.

With them came the missionaries, who had already taught them the rudiments of civilization. Two Presbyterian missions had been established in 1820 for the Osage, the Union on the Neosho River and the Harmony on the Marais des Cygnes. In the spring of 1827 Daniel Morgan Boone, son of Daniel Boone, was sent by the Government to teach farming to the Kansas Indians occupying the southern part of Jefferson County. There he established his family, the first white family in the Territory; his son, Napoleon, born August 22, 1828, was the first white child to be born within the State. In 1829 the Reverend Thomas Johnson introduced Methodism to the Shawnee, establishing a mission near the present town of Turner in Wyandotte County. Four years later the Reverend Jotham Meeker brought the first printing press to the Shawnee Baptist Mission, and on February 24, 1835, he published the first issue of the *Shawnee Sun,* the first newspaper in Kansas.

By 1830 trading posts were scattered throughout eastern and central Kansas, reaching from the Platte to the Red River. Within a few years, ferries were strung across the Missouri and Kansas Rivers, roads were cut along the ridges, patches of farm land were cleared and planted, and cabin homes fringed the highways. All this was the work of the Indians, under direction of missionaries and Government agents.

Captain William Becknell had made the first successful trade journey to Santa Fé in 1821, establishing the route of the Santa Fé Trail. Twelve months later he led the first wagon train along the trail, beginning the valuable commerce of frontier days. As a midway course between Benton's proposals for western development and the opposing view, Congress authorized the survey and marking of the Santa Fe Trail in 1825. Fort Leavenworth was established as "Cantonment Leavenworth" in May, 1827. Westport (now Kansas City, Missouri) became a depot on the Santa Fe Trail in 1833, and ten years later the city of Wyandot (Kansas City, Kansas) was begun by the Wyandot Indians.

At this time the Government decided to send out another exploration under Lieutenant John C. Frémont. He entered Kansas in 1842, completing his outfit at the trading post of Cyprian Chouteau in Wyandotte County on June 10. With Kit Carson as a guide, Frémont proceeded to explore the Kansas and Platte Rivers, and to survey the South Pass of the Oregon Trail, thereby winning the title of "Pathfinder." He followed this exploration with three more, in 1843, 1845, and 1848. Accounts of these expeditions were published immediately by the Government to direct attention to the West, and in this they were highly successful.

The war between the United States and Mexico ended with the Treaty of Guadelupe-Hidalgo, ratified May 30, 1848. By its terms, the Rio Grande became the boundary between Texas and Mexico, and the international boundary westward, from El Paso to the Pacific, was established almost as it is now. Northward, the ceded territory reached from a league below San Diego, California, to the Oregon country at 42° north latitude; eastward it reached to the Rocky Mountains. This vast region embraced what was then known as New Mexico and Upper California, and what now corresponds to a strip of Texas; the greater parts of New Mexico, Colorado, and Arizona; all of California, Nevada and Utah; and a little of Wyoming. In addition, the treaty of 1846 with Great Britain had established the right of the United States to the Oregon country. Thus in two years the United States cleared from its continental path to the Pacific all conflicting sovereignties as far north as the forty-ninth parallel.

This resulted in a tremendous increase in migration over Kansas trails.

The volume had been swelling since 1843, when the "Great Emigration" to the Oregon country began. Then 900 people in 111 wagons, and 2,000 horses and cattle, had set out from Elm Grove, Kansas. In 1844 four parties, one of 800 and another of 500 to 700 people, had started westward; and 5,000 had left the Missouri border in 1845. The Mormon trek from Nauvoo, Illinois, "to the western wilderness" started in 1846, and by 1848 most of them had safely reached their new homes in the Salt Lake region. These migrations, however, seem small when compared with that of 1849, when the California gold rush brought 90,000 people through Kansas. Although all these emigrants merely swept through the Kansas country with their eyes fixed on the west, they indirectly affected the region. Civilization was now both west and east of Kansas. In 1850 came the overland stagecoach to Utah and the Pacific coast. The myth of the "Great American Desert" was finally dispelled, and Kansas emerged from obscurity.

The first move to organize Kansas into a Territory, made in 1844, was of small consequence, as were all subsequent movements until 1852. In the spring of that year a half-dozen Missourians met at Uniontown, Kansas, framed a set of resolutions, which they presented to the Thirty-second Congress, petitioning that the Platte country, comprising the present States of Kansas and Nebraska, be erected into a territory and styled the Nebraska Territory. The bill was not passed.

The next step was taken by the Wyandot Indians. On July 28, 1853, they met in the council house in Wyandot, organized Kansas-Nebraska into a Provisional Territory and elected a delegate to the Thirty-third Congress. This act was not recognized, nor was the delegate admitted to Congress, but their action precipitated the long debate that resulted in the passage of the Douglas Bill, signed by President Franklin Pierce on May 30, 1854. By this bill the Missouri Compromise was repealed and the Territories of Kansas and Nebraska were organized with the right to determine the question of slavery for themselves.

In creating the two Territories it was tacitly hoped that Kansas would resolve itself into a slave State and that Nebraska would remain free, thus preserving the balance of power between the free and slave factions. This hope was immediately threatened by a movement in the New England States, begun by Eli Thayer of Massachusetts with the organization of the New England Emigrant Aid Company in 1854. The movement proposed to send 20,000 Free Soilers into Kansas each year, but failed to attract emigrants in any such numbers. Still its existence aroused the pro-slavery advocates, who retaliated with counter organizations known as the "Blue

Lodge," "Sons of the South," and others. Both movements proposed a "Squatter Sovereignty."

The Kansas Territory at that time had no more than 1,500 white persons, approximately 700 of whom were in military service and therefore ineligible for the ballot; the others lived in small groups clustered about the trading posts and Indian missions, and along the Oregon and Santa Fe Trails. But across the State line in the western counties of Missouri, were 80,000 citizens who owned approximately 12,000 slaves. It was to their interest to control the policies of the future State, and their resentment of anti-slavery activities was particularly intense. Many immediately crossed the Kansas line to "spot" claims, pending further action by the Government.

In May 1854 treaties were made with the Delaware and Shawnee in eastern Kansas, by which more than two million acres of their reservations were made available to the whites by public auction and preemption. The race for Kansas was on. Settlers poured into the new Territory from Ohio, West Virginia, Indiana, Illinois, Iowa, Pennsylvania, and especially from Missouri. They came in caravans of prairie schooners or Conestoga wagons, by steamboats, on horseback, on foot—in companies and alone. The majority brought their families, their cattle and farm implements, their spinning wheels and looms.

The Territory was then without law. To provide for order until a government could be set up, an association was formed and resolutions were drawn up outlining the rights of the settlers and preparing for the peaceful building of a State.

Towns were established. Leavenworth, adjacent to Fort Leavenworth, was laid out in June 1854. A month later Lawrence was founded by Charles H. Branscomb and Dr. Charles Robinson, agents of the New England Emigrant Aid Company, as a Free State headquarters; and Atchison was established as a rival pro-slavery town. Topeka was platted on December 5 by Cyrus K. Holliday, who designed it for the capital which it later became. Before the year was out Palmyra, Louisiana, and Brooklyn were begun along the Santa Fe Trail, with Prairie City, Baldwin City, and Hickory Point in its close vicinity; on the Oregon Trail (locally known as the California Road) Franklin and Wakarusa appeared.

The first Territorial newspaper, the *Kansas Weekly Herald,* which began publication in Leavenworth, September 15, 1854, supported slavery; and the *Kansas Tribune,* a Free State paper, issued its first number on January 3, 1855, at Lawrence.

The people who ventured into Kansas in the hope of finding peace and well-ordered living were fated to deep and persisting disappointment. It was hardly surprising that the Territory attracted a full complement of desperadoes. But few settlers could have predicted the "bleeding Kansas" of the 1850's and 1860's, with border warfare and violent antagonism among its citizens, most of whom were aggressively committed to one side or the other of the slavery issue.

Andrew H. Reeder of Pennsylvania was named the first Territorial Governor on June 29, 1854, and was inaugurated at Fort Leavenworth on October 7. Under his administration the pro-slavery party, aided by sympathizers from Missouri, gained the ascendancy. At the election of a delegate to Congress on November 29, 1854, Missouri voters dominated the polls; and, at the election of the Territorial legislature on March 30, 1855, abuses were even more flagrant. Four to five thousand armed men from Missouri, inflamed by the speeches of the Southern agitators, Senator David R. Atchison and General B. F. Stringfellow, appeared at the voting places, where they browbeat judges, stuffed ballot boxes, and otherwise transformed the election into a grim farce. Many of the members elected were residents of Missouri, yet Governor Reeder, under threat of his life, was obliged to issue election certificates. Because of the illegality of the election, the body was dubbed the "bogus legislature," by which term it has since been known.

Shortly before the election, Reeder, finding accommodations at Fort Leavenworth inadequate, removed the temporary seat of government to the Shawnee Mission in Johnson County. But partly to further his own land speculations, he convoked the first legislature at Pawnee on July 2, 1855. There the body proceeded to take matters into its own hands. It ousted its few Free State members, and voted, over the Governor's veto, to adjourn to the Shawnee Mission, which it did on July 16. There Reeder refused to recognize its acts, contending that the mission was not the authorized seat of government. The body answered with an appeal to President Pierce, who responded by removing Reeder from office on July 29.

With Daniel Woodson as Acting Governor, the legislature proceeded to adopt the Missouri statutes virtually *in toto,* merely instructing the clerk to strike out "Missouri" and insert the name of the Territory. Only on the subject of slavery did it show originality. Its enactments on this issue, known as the "Black Laws," provided a death penalty for anyone who, by word or deed, should aid in freeing a slave, and a penitentiary sentence for holding an opinion adverse to slavery. Reaction to these measures was widespread, with newspapers of the North and even some of the South protesting. The pro-slavery party prepared to enforce them through the Law and Order Society, which was organized on October 3, 1855, at a meeting in Leavenworth.

Meanwhile Free State advocates countered with a government of their own. In an assembly at Big Springs on September 5, 1855, the acts of the "bogus legislature" were repudiated, the Free State party was formally organized under the leadership of James H. Lane, and delegates were appointed to a constitutional convention which assembled at Topeka on October 23. Here a constitution was drafted and State officers were nominated; at a general election, held December 15, the constitution was ratified, Dr. Charles Robinson was elected Governor, and Lane and Reeder were sent to the United States Senate. They were not seated, the United States Senate refusing to recognize the election.

Nor was this the only move of the Free State party. In April 1855 Dr. Robinson, as agent of the New England Emigrant Aid Company, sent an order to Eli Thayer for 100 Sharp's rifles, which were promptly dispatched and became known as "Beecher's Bibles." These were followed in July by a second shipment which included a small brass cannon. The rifles had a somewhat quieting effect, but it was the quiet before the storm. Through the summer and fall of 1855 animosity smoldered, awaiting only an excuse for an open break. On November 21 Charles W. Dow, a Free State man, was shot and killed by Franklin M. Coleman, a pro-slavery man, in a quarrel over claim boundaries. Coleman surrendered to the sheriff of Douglas County and was released on bond; Dow's friends organized a posse to bring the murderer to justice. A member of this posse was arrested by the sheriff on a trumped-up charge and was promptly rescued by his friends. These events culminated in the threatened invasion of Lawrence, known as the "Wakarusa War." Border ruffians from Missouri gathered on Wakarusa Creek for the purpose of sacking the town and were deterred only by the intervention of Governor Wilson Shannon and United States troops from Fort Leavenworth. But before order was established a second Free State man, Thomas Barber, had been murdered.

Displeased with Governor Shannon's interference and bent on the destruction of Lawrence, the pro-slavery party bided its time until the following May, when a second invasion resulted in a partial destruction of the town. Three days later, May 24, John Brown retaliated with the execution of five pro-slavery men in the Potawatomi Massacre. Brown's action, the first retaliatory move on the part of the Free Staters, unleashed the extremists of both sides. Captain Henry C. Pate, Deputy United States Marshal, under pretext of arresting Brown, instigated fighting on the

PORTRAIT OF JOHN BROWN

south side of the Kansas River, resulting in the battles of Black Jack, Franklin, and Fort Titus, the raiding of Palmyra and Prairie City, and the sacking of Osawatomie. On the north side of the river, at the towns of Atchison, Doniphan, and Leavenworth, Free State families were ejected from their homes and driven out of the Territory. A blockade was established on the Missouri River to prevent further Free State emigration. Lane raised his "Army of the North," and James Montgomery organized reckless young Free Staters into a guerrilla band known as the "Jayhawkers."

For two years a state of open warfare existed. Armed bands of border ruffians from Missouri made forays into Kansas and were answered by retaliatory companies of Jayhawkers. Men were called out into the night and shot down for no other reason than that they supported or were suspected of supporting the opposite cause. Women and children, regardless of age or condition, were driven from their homes with only the clothing on their backs. Fields were laid waste and towns were sacked, all in the name of the cause, but more often to gratify personal revenge or avarice. On May 19, 1858, a band of pro-slavery men, led by Charles A. Hamelton, gathered eleven Free State men of Linn County whom Hamelton wished out of the way, herded them into a ravine near the Marais des Cygnes River in the vicinity of Trading Post, and shot them down.

Under such conditions the gubernatorial office was a hazardous position. In seven years six governors and five acting governors came and went, the Territorial capital was moved about like a chessman, and three State constitutions were written and rejected. Martial law prevailed intermittently, and Free State leaders were indicted and imprisoned for high treason.

Eventually the pro-slavery party was shorn of its power. Although openly approved by the Federal Government under Pierce and again under Buchanan, it was always in the minority and had assumed control only by the high-handed policies of its allies from Missouri. In time the Free State party became too powerful to be bullied. The census of 1860 showed a population of 107,206, of which more than seventy per cent was antislavery.

An election was held March 28, 1859, to decide whether another constitutional convention should be called; an affirmative vote was polled. Delegates convened at Wyandotte on July 5 to frame a fourth constitution, which declared that, "All men are possessed of equal and inalienable natural rights, among which are life, liberty, and the pursuit of happiness." It was ratified by vote of the Territory on October 4, and the bill for admission to the Union was immediately submitted to Congress. The bill was passed by the Senate on January 21, 1861, by the House on January 28, and signed by the President on January 29, making Kansas the thirty-fourth State.

During this period, Kansas entertained some noted visitors. Horace Greeley came to the Territory in May 1859, and on December 1 Abraham Lincoln arrived to make campaign speeches in Elwood, Troy, Doniphan, Atchison, and Leavenworth. Four years later, December 22, 1863, John Wilkes Booth appeared at Leavenworth in *Richard III*.

In June 1859 a drought set in and continued until November 1860. Crops had been neglected because of guerrilla warfare, and no surplus had been accumulated; the result was famine. Many quit their claims in despair and left the Territory. Those who remained were obliged to look to the East for relief. The New York legislature voted $50,000 for that purpose, and other States were equally generous.

But despite tumult and calamity the eastern part of Kansas had made some progress. Forty counties had been set up with a generous sprinkling of frontier towns. A weekly mail schedule linked the Territory with the Pacific Coast by means of stagecoach and pony express, while steamboats on the Missouri and Kansas Rivers connected it with the East. There were more than twenty newspapers, a State Historical Society had been formed, churches were numerous, and a State school system had been organized. Tentative provisions had been made for the University of Lawrence, for a penitentiary, and for other State institutions. Tracks for the first railroad, the Elwood and Marysville (now the Union Pacific), had been laid, and industry and agriculture were developing.

Dr. Charles Robinson was the first Governor of the new State. He at once assembled the legislature and proceeded to inaugurate a State government: establishing courts, organizing additional counties and school systems, and providing for a program of general progress. Before anything could be accomplished, Kansas was called upon to participate in the great national conflict, the Civil War.

On April 15, 1861, President Lincoln issued a call for 75,000 volunteers. Kansas, only three months a State and still suffering from drought and the ravages of internal warfare, responded with 650 men. At the second call, two companies were organized with no promise of pay, since the new State had no money for military service. The total required of Kansas during the four years of war was 16,654 men. This was oversubscribed by more than 3,000, making a total of 20,097—constituting eighteen regiments, three of which were Indian and two Negro. The first regiment was mustered into service June 3, 1861; the last on July 28, 1864. The most important battle in which Kansas troops took part was that of August 10, 1861, at Wilson's Creek, south of Springfield, Missouri, where approximately 10,000 Confederates were engaged by 5,000 Union men under General Nathaniel Lyon. Lyon was killed, and the Unionists retreated with honor. The Eighth Kansas Volunteer Infantry, led by Colonel John A. Martin of Atchison (who later became the State's tenth Governor), after a year of border patrol service, joined the Army of the Cumberland and fought at Chickamaugua, in the Chattanooga campaign, and marched with Sherman to the sea. It was the only Kansas regiment attached to one of the major armies.

The Confederate force of General Sterling Price was the only one of the major armies to cross the Kansas border. In September 1864 General Price conducted the expedition known as "Price's Raid" through Arkansas and Missouri. He entered Kansas through Linn County in an apparent effort to reach Fort Scott, met the Unionists at Mine Creek and again at the crossing of the Osage. Here he was turned back into Missouri, after having caused damage to the extent of one-half million dollars, later to be paid by the Government.

Though it was not in the zone of battle, the young State had its hands full with guerrilla warfare on its eastern border and Indian uprisings in the western part. Bands of bushwhackers—led by William Clarke Quantrill, Bill Anderson, and others—and the "Red Legs," so called from the red morocco leggings they wore, were continually active in burning, pillaging, and murdering. On August 21, 1863, Quantrill raided and sacked the town of Lawrence, slaying about 150 of its citizens. In the west the depredations of the Indians made organized resistance imperative.

National peace closed the conflict in eastern Kansas. Virtually all Indian titles had been extinguished there, and that part of the State was now free to plow its fields, plant orchards and vineyards, develop mines and manufacturing, and extend railroads. By 1870 the agricultural college at Manhattan, the State Teachers' College at Emporia, and the University at Lawrence had been established, as well as various denominational institutions. The first unit of the capital building at Topeka had been completed and was occupied. Coal was being mined in two counties, and gas lights were in use. Meat packing had been established at Wyandotte, and the first beef shipped to New York in refrigerator cars. A cotton gin was in operation at Burlington and woolen mills at Lawrence and Fort Scott. Bridges were spanning the Kansas River at Wyandotte and Topeka, telegraph lines crossed the prairies, and railroad tracks reached a total of

WILD BILL HICKOK, CITY MARSHAL OF ABILENE

1,283 miles. The population had increased to 362,000, and the improved acreage totaled 1,020,610.

Up to the close of the Civil War few settlers had ventured on the Plains in western Kansas, for there was no timber for building, and the Indians were hostile. This section of the State was left to another type of pioneer —the cowboy. When the Union Pacific Railroad reached Abilene in 1867, Joseph G. McCoy conceived the idea of driving long-horned native cattle from Texas to fatten on the convenient buffalo grass before shipping to market. His idea proved profitable and in the next two decades the Plains developed into an immense cow country. Riotous cow towns grew up of which Abilene and Dodge City were typical—with saloons, dance halls, gambling dens, and loose women; and made colorful by the cowboy in broad-brimmed hat, chaps, and kerchief, accoutered with spurs, lariat, and revolver.

Infesting the prairies was another group, the border criminals—cattle thieves, bandits, and desperadoes—who, in turn, called forth such fearless and straight-shooting characters as Wild Bill Hickok, Bat Masterson, and Buffalo Bill Cody. In 1871 "Wild Bill" was installed as marshal at Abilene, where he served so effectively that other towns wanted him to act in the same capacity. About the same time "Buffalo Bill" was employed to provide buffalo meat for the Union Pacific workmen. It is said that in 18 months he killed 4,280 buffaloes for that purpose.

The cattle period was as short as it was lusty. On May 20, 1862, Congress passed the Homestead Law, making it possible to acquire 320 acres of Plains land by homestead and preemption, with special inducements to ex-Union soldiers. On March 3, 1863, it further provided that all Indians should be removed from Kansas, an objective that was gradually accomplished. But the most important factor in populating the range was the railroad.

To encourage road building, large grants of land were made to the railroad companies. As the tracks were extended, these lands were offered for sale and the companies engaged in extensive advertising to speed up purchase. Pamphlets and circulars were broadcast in the East and in Europe, enticing colonists from England, Germany, Russia, Bohemia, and the Scandinavian Peninsula as well as additional emigrants from the eastern States. Distinguished Europeans were invited to come as visitors. One of these was Grand Duke Alexis of Russia who, with his entourage, was entertained at Topeka by Governor James M. Harvey and the State legislature. Twenty years after the passage of the Homestead Law, lines of barbed-wire fence enclosed the range.

Life for the early Plains settlers was filled with hardships. Buffalo chips were the only fuel, and they had to be gathered from wide areas. Money was scarce and crop failures were frequent. Even the possession of dugouts and sod houses often had to be disputed with rattlesnakes and gophers. In lean times the settlers turned, as had the Indians before them, to the buffalo. Thousands were shot for their hides and other thousands for sport from train windows, leaving carcasses to wolves and bones to the weather. This proved fortunate, for the bones could be sold for fertilizer at from six to ten dollars per ton; when crops failed, gathering buffalo bones became a regular occupation. Another source of revenue was provided by the wild horses. Large herds, descended from horses left by the Spanish, roamed the grasslands and needed only to be caught and tamed. This was an arduous task, but the "bronco-busting" settler was undaunted.

In 1874 a partial drought was experienced and following it came the visitation known to Kansans simply as "the grasshoppers." In 1866 and 1867 these insects had appeared in sections of the State, but in 1874 th y came in hordes, filling the air and devouring every particle of vegetation. In the eastern counties sufficient headway had been made to weather the devastation; but in the west, where settlements were new and no surplus had been accumulated, aid again had to come from the East.

In the same year a colony of Mennonite immigrants from Russia arrived, with enough money to buy land and withstand the grasshoppers. Of far greater importance was the bushel or so of hand-picked hard "Turkey Red" wheat carefully stowed away in the baggage of each family. Up to that time attempts to grow wheat on the Plains had not been successful, but the Russian grain was perfectly adapted to these conditions. From this beginning developed the vast wheat fields, which now give Kansas ranking place among the wheat-growing States. Ten years later it was able to reciprocate the aid given in 1874 by shipping carloads of corn to flood victims in Ohio. At the same time, a trainload of grain went to Virginia to help in raising a fund for a home for ex-Confederate soldiers.

The State legislature voted $30,000 in 1876 for the exhibit of native products at the Centennial Exposition in Philadelphia; this created so favorable an impression that it directed new interest to Kansas and resulted in further increase in emigration.

By 1878 the population in the two sections of the State was fairly well-defined. The eastern half was occupied largely by the pro- and anti-slavery emigrants of the ante-bellum period; the western half by latecomers from the East, ex-Union soldiers and Europeans. But it was yet to receive the sudden flow of emancipated Negroes, known as the "exodusters." From the close of the Civil War, freed slaves from the South had trickled into Kansas in small numbers; in 1878 lured by the false promise of "forty acres and a mule," southern Negroes came in such numbers that 20,000 are said to have entered the State in four years. The Negro population in 1870 was 17,108; ten years later it had increased to 43,107. Benjamin (Pap) Singleton, a Negro who styled himself the father of the exodus, induced more than 7,000 Negroes to migrate from Tennessee alone. Most

of those who came in 1876–78 settled in one of his three colonies—
Dunlap in the Neosho Valley, Singleton in Cherokee County, and Nicodemus (the only surviving "Exoduster" community) in Graham County. The
few who had teams and farm implements procured land or found work on
farms; the remainder swelled the growing towns and cities. Subsequent
growth of Negro population was relatively slow, the increase in the next
fifty years being only 23,000.

In 1878 Indian troubles were terminated with the last Cheyenne raid in
western Kansas. The State, finally at peace, had time to consider a long-
vexing problem—prohibition. The control of liquor had always been a
live issue. In 1855 the "bogus legislature" provided for local option with
the Dram Shop Law, copied from the Missouri statutes. This law was
never satisfactory in Kansas and, to improve upon it, such towns as Emporia, Baldwin, and Topeka adopted measures revoking titles to land on
which liquor was sold. The subject of State prohibition was considered at
each constitutional convention. Organizations such as the Good Templars
were created, embodying the temperance pledge in their constitutions. In
1860 the sale of liquor to Indians was prohibited. The State Temperance
Society held its first meeting the following year. The Willard-Murphy
Temperance movement swept the State in 1870; in 1873 the Women's
Crusade was begun, with groups meeting in saloons to smash containers,
spill liquor, and pray with drunken habitués. Through these agencies local
prohibition was effected in various counties and towns, but it was not until
1881, under the administration of the eighth Governor, John P. St. John,
that the State prohibition law was passed.

The decade following "the grasshoppers" was exceptionally prosperous
and the whole State entered into a boom of speculation. Eastern money,
made readily available, was diverted into public and private improvements
with reckless abandon. Land values were boosted, "false front" buildings
erected, "paper" towns were laid out. Then came the drought of 1887,
and the boom collapsed. Demands made for loans could not be met, banks
and business houses failed, and, especially in the western counties, thousands of settlers who faced foreclosure left the State.

In 1889 approximately 50,000 Kansas settlers moved to the newly
opened land in Oklahoma, leaving the Plains virtually abandoned. Four
years later the general panic of 1893, together with another partial crop
failure, brought a second period of "hard times." But the State was then
too well established to be more than temporarily affected. Eastern emigration soon refilled the western counties, and another succession of good

crops restored confidence. Greeley, the last of the State's 105 counties, was organized July 9, 1888, and pioneering days were over.

The year 1889 was distinguished by the largest corn crop in Kansas history and by the first manufacture of beet sugar. To encourage the latter, a bounty was immediately offered by the State, and beet sugar making is now a staple industry in the southwestern counties. In the same year salt making was begun in the central part of the State, and oil and natural gas were added to the list of industries in 1892. Surplus fuel in the gas-producing region brought other manufacturing, such as brickmaking, zinc smelting, glass, and cement. The value of livestock and farm products increased; in seven years, from 1887 to 1894, it aggregated more than $4,000,000,000, making possible the payment of public and private debts to the amount of $100,000,000. From the first experimental orchard planted at the Shawnee Mission (Johnson County) in 1837, patient care and selection had developed fruit raising throughout the eastern part of the State. In 1876 Kansas apples were awarded the gold medal at the exposition in Philadelphia, giving that product a prestige it still maintains.

The State's politics kept pace with its social and industrial development. In 1872 Kansas farmers organized a local grange of the Society of Patrons of Husbandry, which had been formed in Washington, D. C., in 1867, to improve farm life. In 1884 the Women's State Suffrage Association was formed; and three years later the movement secured the admittance of women to school, bond, and municipal elections. In the late 1880's a number of farm and labor parties became active. The Farmers' Alliance was most promising, and within two years it had become a power in the State. In 1890 at a State convention called by Benjamin H. Clover, a Cowley County farmer, it joined with the Grangers, Single Tax Club, Industrial Union, Knights of Labor, and others to form the People's or Populist Party. The party first concentrated its efforts to bring about the defeat of Senator John J. Ingalls and mustered enough votes in the State legislature of 1891 to elect William A. Peffer to the office Ingalls had held for 18 years. Populist orators, led by Mrs. Mary Elizabeth Lease, stumped the State, telling the farmers that the "money power" was conspiring to ruin them. Mrs. Lease is remembered for her advice to Kansas farmers "to raise less corn and more hell." By 1892 Populist strength was sufficient to elect the twelfth Governor, Lorenzo D. Lewelling.

The legislature assembled under Governor Lewelling echoed the turbulence of Territorial days. Both Republicans and Populists claimed the right to organize the house, each holding to its claim with a tenacity that required the presence of the State militia. Speakers from each party occupied the stand, wielding their gavels simultaneously. It is said that, for one night at least, they shared a common blanket back of the rostrum, since neither was willing to yield prerogative to the other. The difference was finally settled by an appeal to the State supreme court, which decided that the Republicans should occupy Representative Hall, the Populists agreeing to meet elsewhere.

Five Populist Congressmen were elected to office during the days of the party's ascendancy, including the brilliant Jerry Simpson of Medicine Lodge, known in Kansas annals as "Sockless Jerry." Simpson, a cattleman who had been ruined by the disastrous blizzard of 1886, was nominated to represent the Seventh Congressional District in 1890; his ability was recognized when he eloquently opposed the platform adopted by the convention, and the platform was revised to conform with his views. He was twice reelected and ably supported all legislation sponsored by his party during his tenure of office.

The Populists repeated their victory with the election of Governor John W. Leedy in 1896—then their power waned. Returning prosperity quieted the political upheaval, and the Populists were eventually reabsorbed by the two main parties, the Democratic and Republican. The latter party, offspring of the Territorial Free Soilers, has, in general, been dominant. Of the 27 Governors to date (1938), only five—including Walter A. Huxman (1937–39)—have been Democrats.

Kansas contributed four regiments to the Spanish-American War. One of them, the 20th under Colonel Frederick Funston, made a remarkable record in the Philippines; the 23rd, composed of Negroes, was sent to Cuba, arriving in time to see the Spanish depart; while the other two, the 21st and 22nd, were trained and held in readiness, but did not leave the States.

In the 1890's another militant leader appeared on the Kansas horizon—a round-faced little woman with a hatchet—Carry Nation. Although "dry" in theory, Kansas was still "wet" in fact. Mrs. Nation, driven by her experiences with a drunken husband, set out to remedy the evil. She smashed saloons with zeal and won for herself a permanent place in history, although her actual accomplishments were little more than a ripple on the pool of the State's "wetness." The problem of liquor is still vexing. In 1937 the State legislature legalized the manufacture and sale of beer of 3.2 per cent alcoholic content. Sterner liquors, although legally banned, are frankly in evidence in many communities.

In other matters the State government has proved competent. In 1883 when the railroads, grown exceedingly wealthy, threatened to become auto-cratic, the State executive council elected a board of railroad commission-ers to curb their power by fixing freight and passenger rates and regulat-ing working conditions. A special session of the legislature was called in 1884 to deal with the foot-and-mouth disease that was scourging Kansas cattle. In 1889 the eight-hour labor law was enacted and the first Monday of September set aside for the observance of "Labor Day." In 1894 a board of irrigation was appointed and an appropriation of $30,000 was made for irrigation experiments.

Other socially progressive action was taken as the need arose. A text book commission and a traveling library commission were established. Laws were passed on compulsory education and child labor, and a juvenile court was created. Pensions were provided for indigent mothers. An ap-propriation of $100,000 was made for the Louisiana Purchase Exposition. Legislation was enacted to regulate the oil industry, and was later made applicable to meat packing, flour milling, and other manufacturing. A blue-sky law, regulating and supervising investment companies, was passed. The public utilities commission was established, weights and measures were standardized. A State highway commission was created and a better roads program was launched. The State printing plant was set up, and the State budget system was started.

In 1913, under the administration of Governor George H. Hodges and preceded only by six other States—Colorado, Idaho, Utah, Wyoming, Washington, and California—Kansas extended complete suffrage to women and increased their number in administrative offices from one to twenty-three. The next administration, under Governor Arthur Capper, waged war on the unfair practices of the natural gas companies and eventually put an end to a litigation that involved thousands of dollars in fees to political lawyers and constituted one of the worst of judicial scandals in the State.

Kansas furnished more than its quota for the World War. Altogether, 80,261 Kansans saw service. The Kansas National Guard became part of the 35th Division. Under the Selective Service Act, Kansans were in the 89th, the 35th and the 42nd (Rainbow) Divisions, and were in action at Saint Mihiel and in the Argonne. But the State perhaps made its greatest contribution through its farmlands and its training camps—Camp Funston and the School of the Line at Fort Leavenworth.

A unique political campaign was conducted in Kansas during the War. Henry J. Allen, although personally engaged in Red Cross Service in France, was nominated and elected Governor by the largest majority ever polled in the State. He resigned from the Red Cross and came home to assume the gubernatorial office on January 13, 1919.

The following autumn Alexander Howat, president of the Kansas district union of the United Mine Workers of America, called a strike of the Kansas coal miners. Reacting to the War, the entire country was then in a state of unrest, and strikes were frequent in many lines of industry. In the preceding three years, 364 strikes had been called in the mines of Kansas, and in the fall of 1919 the coal supply was exhausted. Kansas faced a fuel famine. The Governor obtained a State's receivership for the mines and mined coal with volunteer labor made up of college students, members of the American Legion and others, protected by the Kansas National Guard.

With the crisis over, the Governor sought to prevent recurrence of trouble. In 1920 an extra session of the legislature was called and the Court of Industrial Relations was organized. In this court was vested the power to control strikes and to fix a minimum wage for the miners. Its establishment—the first attempt at compulsory arbitration in the United States—drew the attention of the Nation to Kansas (see INDUSTRY, COMMERCE AND LABOR). The court was abolished by the State legislature in 1925.

Under the administration of Governor Jonathan M. Davis, a bonus of $25,000,000 was distributed to ex-service men in 1923. The following year the Ku Klux Klan, nation-wide in its scope, threatened the political, racial, and religious freedom of the State and brought William Allen White into the race for Governor on an anti-Klan platform, a gesture described by the Kansas City Star as "one of those successful failures through which civilization edges forward."

In 1930, Dr. John R. Brinkley entered the gubernatorial race and, under stress of depression conditions, was almost elected. His candidacy came from a desire for vindication. On September 17, 1930, his license was revoked by the Kansas State Medical Board on charges of quackery and malpractice in his hospital at Milford; five days later he announced his candidacy for Governor. During his campaign, he promised free text books, free medical clinics, hundreds of miles of paved roads, and a free lake in every county, with no increase in taxes.

During Governor Alfred M. Landon's administration a cash basis law was passed in 1933, putting the State on a "pay-as-you-go" policy. Governor Landon's successful administration under this law, and his reelection in 1934 as the only Republican State executive elected west of the Hudson River, led to his nomination as the Republican candidate for the Presidency in 1936. Kansas, however, returned a plurality of more than 60,000 for President Franklin D. Roosevelt and elected its fifth Democratic Governor, Walter A. Huxman, of Hutchinson.

Kansas has weathered many calamities and earned its motto, "To the Stars through Difficulty." Internal strife—at once tragic and fantastic—ravaged the State in its early decades. Blizzards, droughts, floods, and grasshopper plagues brought death and destruction. But progress has been steady. Where once roamed the Indian and the buffalo, there are now orchards and vineyards, dairy farms, and endless fields of wheat, corn, and alfalfa. The vest pocket village, with its lone towering grain elevator and general store, is the meeting place for farmers who live miles apart. The radio and the automobile has rescued him from isolation. Broad ribbons of concrete crisscross the prairies, and the trains of 17 great railway systems steam through the State. Packing plants, flour mills, and mines give employment to thousands of workers. Oil derricks point skyward, and huge power houses churn out electricity. Remedial measures, carried out cooperatively by Federal, State, and local agencies, are solving the three-fold problem of flood, drought, and soil depletion.

WHEAT

Agriculture

ALTHOUGH the first American explorers who passed through the Territory reported that the region was totally unfit for human habitation, history records that the Indians who lived on the Kansas plains before the coming of the white men practiced agriculture after a crude fashion. Thus the first Kansas farmers were Indian squaws who raised small crops of corn and beans to supplement the diet of game. They planted seeds in holes punched in the ground with sharpened sticks, and cultivated the crop with implements fashioned from buffalo bones.

The first white farmers were Frenchmen who settled in the Wolf River country, now Doniphan County, during the latter part of the eighteenth century, and planted fields of corn in the rich glacial soil of this northeastern corner of the State.

In 1827 the Government decided to conduct agricultural experiments in the Territory acquired through the Louisiana Purchase and sent Daniel Morgan Boone to teach farming to the Kansas Indians. This son of the famous Kentucky frontiersman took a farm of one hundred acres on Stonehouse Creek in the present-day Jefferson County, less than fifty miles from the land broken by the Wolf River Frenchmen of the previous century. The early missionaries also engaged in agriculture to some extent; but it did not become the major occupation of the Kansas Plains until the Territory was opened to settlement in 1854.

Many of the early settlers, who turned to agriculture as the only means of livelihood—a precarious means at best—had no natural aptitude or training for it. They were brought into the Territory by the New England Emigrant Aid Company and other organizations solely for the purpose of setting up communities of anti-slavery voters, and were hastily selected with little thought of their fitness as practical farmers. Consequently, it is not strange that Kansas agriculture, hampered from the outset by climatic conditions that were frequently adverse, inexperience on the part of settlers, and bitter political strife, did not prosper.

The pioneer farmers of the 1850's broke the sod with ox teams hitched to crude plows. Many of them planted corn by slitting the sod with an axe, dropping the kernels into the slits, and closing them by stamping. This was in violation of the belief then common that "you can't grow corn on sod." Strangely enough one of the unorthodox corn planters raised a crop that averaged nearly one hundred bushels to the acre. The story of "Sodcorn" Jones was widely circulated, but few of the settlers gave it credence, persisting in the theory that newly broken sod would not grow anything but pumpkins and melons. Corn was cultivated with the hoe; wheat was sown by hand, harvested with a cradle, and threshed with a flail. The first Mennonite wheat farmers separated the grain from the straw by rolling or dragging cogged cylindrical stones over the bundles *(see NEWTON)*.

At the close of the Civil War the Government offered homesteads in Kansas to Union Army veterans and more than 100,000 took advantage of the opportunity. These sturdy young veterans were Kansas' first real pioneer farmers. The majority had been reared on farms in the older semi-prairie States of Illinois, Indiana, and Ohio, and understood the difficulties confronting the farmer who breaks virgin soil in prairie country. Others came from Kentucky, the mountains of Tennessee, and Missouri.

Farming was a year-round occupation in the Kansas of that time. Sod-turning was a tedious process with oxen and a plow not adapted to the task. A team of oxen with one man to drive and one to hold the plow could not break more than an acre in a day, and since this work had to be done between the thawing of the ground in March and corn-planting time in April, a farmer could break only a small amount of land each year. Hand-planting and cultivating consumed all the farmer's time until mid-summer; then he cut prairie hay and stacked it; and after that the corn had to be husked.

Wheat, a minor crop in the early days, and oats were sown broadcast by hand after the sod had rotted long enough to permit the seed to be covered. These grains were harvested by primitive methods precisely like those used by Roman farmers 2,000 years before.

The first radical change in Kansas agriculture occurred in 1874 when a colony of Mennonites came to the plains of central Kansas from southern Russia. Originally German, these bearded farmers had migrated to Russia at the time of Catherine the Great to evade military service, to which they were opposed on religious grounds. During their sojourn in Russia they had developed a variety of hard wheat called Turkey Red because of the color of the grain and because the seed had originally been obtained from Turkey. This variety thrived on the steppes of Russia—a semi-arid plains

A COOPERATIVE ELEVATOR IN SHAWNEE COUNTY

region—and the Mennonites rightly believed it was adapted to Kansas' peculiar conditions of climate and soil.

Turkey Red grew better in Kansas than varieties of the grain brought by earlier settlers from their eastern farms, as it was more drought-resistant and hardy. Observing the success of their oddly dressed neighbors, the American-born farmers bought quantities of Turkey Red seed from them and in turn prospered as wheat growers. Thus began Kansas' greatest industry.

Prior to 1874 Kansas had never produced as much as 5,000,000 bushels of wheat in a year and no one expected it to become a great wheat-raising State. Corn was king in those days and corn bread spread with sorghum molasses was the staple fare of Kansas farm families. Today, thanks to the Mennonites and their imitators, Kansas produces thirty times as much wheat as it did before these immigrants brought their Turkey Red to the State. An average wheat crop today is 170,000,000 bushels. The record yield, in 1931, was 240,000,000 bushels.

The second revolution in Kansas agricultural methods, machine farming, was hailed at its inception as the dawn of an era of everlasting plenty, but it has resulted in near disaster. Prairie agriculture had two elements that encouraged the rapid development of machine farming: the general levelness of the plains and the abundance of horsepower. There were few trees to be cut in clearing the land, no stumps to impede the progress of wheeled implements. There were also thousands of wild horses in Kansas and horse wranglers prospered in the 1880's by roping and breaking these animals for use on farms. At the same time horse breeders began to import heavy European work horses and cross them with the wild horses for the farm market.

Farming in Kansas during the last two decades of the nineteenth century and first decades of the twentieth was a matter of horsepower and wheeled machinery. Corn was still the leading crop; it was in the more highly mechanized age to come that wheat gained the ascendancy. Horse-drawn plows broke out fresh acres of sod, horse-drawn corn planters sowed the grain. During the growing season teams of horses or mules pulled cultivators along the corn rows. Kansas became a great corn State, reaching its peak of corn production in 1889 with a yield of 273,000,000 bushels.

But in these years of apparent prosperity thousands of Kansas farmers were faced with poverty and foreclosure. After the first wave of homesteaders swept across the State following the Civil War, a period of mass development and speculation began. Many Kansas farmers worked under the handicap of a heavy mortgage from the beginning. In the early 1870's the pioneer farmers paid the interest on their mortgages by killing buffalo and selling their hides. After ruthlessly exterminating the buffalo, they paid taxes and interest by gathering buffalo bones and selling them to fertilizer manufacturers.

In Missouri and other States eastward to the Alleghenies a new farm was unmortgagable because no one would lend money on it until it was well improved and showed a profit. In Kansas, however, speculators acquired large areas of land during the frenzied boom days of the 1880's, lured prospective farmers to the treeless plains with promises of wealth, and sold them land on mortgage. The settlers, having acquired the land under this precarious title, were forced to borrow more money to buy material for improvements and for machinery and livestock. Thus mortgaged before the first plow was put to sod, a large proportion of Kansas farms never showed a profit.

Hundreds of farmers were facing foreclosure in 1890. The record-breaking corn crop of 1889 had done little to relieve the situation. Hampered by their heavy mortgages and with the ever-present specter of drought, Kansas farmers needed both a bumper crop and a good price to break even. But a nation-wide depression had lowered the price of farm produce so that corn sold as low as ten cents a bushel, and farmers sold their corn as fast as they husked it to meet interest at the bank. Most of the buyers were speculators who took advantage of the farmers' plight by driving a sharp bargain and holding the grain for a better price. One village banker boasted of buying thousands of bushels of corn at ten cents a bushel and selling it the following year for sixty-five cents. Crop failures in the 1890's brought foreclosures and tax sales. Gradually much of the land reverted to the speculators and farm tenancy began in Kansas, the land of opportunity.

The Farmers' Alliance, which later became the Populist party, appeared at this time, advocating "free silver," a reform of the banking laws, and other measures calculated to enable the farmers to pay off their mortgages. In 1892 the Populists elected a Governor and succeeded in securing a majority in the State legislature. Some benefits resulted but on the whole the speculators and industrialists succeeded in defeating the aims of the Populists.

Accompanied by a steady increase in farm tenancy, Kansas agriculture moved into the twentieth century and the motor age. The use of motorized farm machinery may be thought of as a third cycle in Kansas farming. In 1910 there were 1,150,000 horses and mules on the farms, and these draft animals provided a home market for $50,000,000 worth of Kansas' corn and other feed. But tractors began to replace draft animals in 1915 and the number of all kinds of tractors and motorized harvesters steadily increased. The greater efficiency of large-scale farming led naturally to the introduction of the combine; and the World War, through its enormous consumption of grain, accelerated its use.

This machine, the mechanical answer to the demand for more wheat produced with less labor, harvests the grain in a single operation, threshes it, and pours it into motor trucks for shipment to the elevators. Its introduction materially reduced the number of "harvest hands," those picturesque laborers who crossed the State in an army during every harvest season (see Tour 4). Gone is the Kansas of which Vachel Lindsay wrote:

> And we felt free in Kansas
> From any sort of fear
> And 30,000 tramps like us
> There harvest every year.

Horses also continued to increase in number until 1919, when they reached a peak of 1,300,000 draft animals; thereafter their number began to decline sharply. Seventeen years later (1936) motorized farming was at its height with 63,000 farm tractors and 24,000 combines; in the same year there were only 545,000 draft animals.

As the overproduction of wheat and loss of foreign markets brought prices down, the wheat farmers, by improved technique, increased production in an effort to compensate for price losses. At this time the "suitcase farmers" entered the field. They were non-resident owners who had purchased large areas of land and hired farmers in the neighborhood to plow and seed them to wheat. The term, "suitcase farmer," has also been applied to the small-town bankers and business men in the western Kansas wheat country who bought or leased lands and employed farmers to plant and harvest their crops for them. This practice, defended because it furnished employment for the farmers, was also widely condemned as mere speculation, not farming. It was not unusual for a single suitcase farmer to finance the planting of from 3,000 to 5,000 acres of wheat. With a crop once in five years he could make money, providing he received a good price for his grain.

In 1914 under horse and mule power, Kansas farmers planted 9,000,-000 acres and harvested 181,000,000 bushels of wheat which they sold for $151,500,000. In 1931, at the height of the motorized farming period, they planted 12,000,000 acres and raised 240,000,000 bushels which they sold for $81,500,000. Motorized farming surpassed the older type by a margin of 60,000,000 bushels of wheat in a year; but smaller crops brought greater financial returns. With machines the farmers raised more wheat, by 60,000,000 bushels, and received less money, by $70,000,000. The price per bushel was ninety cents in 1914 and thirty cents in 1931.

Wheat is in some ways a substitute for corn, and the thirty-cent wheat pushed corn down to ten cents a bushel. Feeding this cheap grain to hogs and cattle in an effort to market it in the form of high-priced meat, the unfortunate farmers depressed the market for hogs to two-and-one-half cents a pound. It took a 200-pound porker to bring in a five dollar bill, just as in 1889 the farmers had to load fifty bushels of corn on a single wagon to get five dollars for one trip to market.

It was not until 1914 that wheat acreage exceeded that of corn; there were 9,116,138 acres of wheat and only 5,279,552 acres of corn, the deposed king. This shift represented a sharp increase in wheat acreage rather than a heavy decrease in corn. Wheat reached a peak in 1931 with an acreage of 12,345,596; it dropped in 1933 to 5,755,328 acres, owing partly to the depression price of this grain, which caused many farmers to sow their land to other crops or let them lie fallow, and partly to the

THRESHING

U. S. Agricultural Adjustment Administration program. In that year corn, with an acreage of 7,725,043, briefly regained its former supremacy.

Hot winds and inadequate rainfall during the growing season resulted in a series of corn crop failures in eastern Kansas that brought hundreds of formerly prosperous farmers to the verge of bankruptcy. Desperately in need of a cash crop to meet taxes and interest in the fall of 1936, many of these corn growers tore down their corn field and pasture fences, sawed the hedge fence posts into stove wood lengths, and sowed the fields to wheat. The venture was successful. With a good yield and prices ranging from $1 to $1.10 a bushel, profits were large.

Consequently new wheat fields were planted in 1937 and the State's total wheat acreage leaped to the all-time record of 13,549,000. The purchase of tractors and combines absorbed much of the profits from the 1937 crop, however, and a short crop in 1938 with a much lower price gave the novice wheat growers a severe setback. Agricultural advisers had counseled against turning the fertile river valleys and glacial uplands into a one-crop country; their reasons for advocating diversification and a partial return to the old corn-hog economy were strengthened by weather conditions favorable for production of the traditional crop. Farmers who had stubbornly "stuck to corn" were able to fill their bins for the first time in five years, while their get-rich-quick neighbors were marketing a scanty wheat crop at less than sixty cents a bushel. Grain sorghums and other forage crops were cultivated with success and the replenished supply of grain for livestock feed brought beef and pork "on the hoof" back to deserted pastures and hog lots.

In 1936 there were 174,580 farms in cultivation in the State, averaging 275 acres in area. Of these 96,896 were wholly or partially owned by their occupants, while 76,771 were occupied by tenants. Farms vary in size from 10-acre truck patches in the eastern river valleys to 50,000-acre ranches in some of the western counties. In sections of eastern Kansas, where rainfall is adequate and soil sufficiently fertile to permit intensive farming and wide diversification, 80 to 160 acres is normally a subsistence homestead. On the western plains where wheat is often the only crop, few farmers attempt to make a living on less than 240 acres and many wheat farmers plant several sections.

The northeastern section of the State is regarded as part of the Corn Belt, especially Doniphan, Atchison, Brown, Nemaha, Jackson, Jefferson, Leavenworth, and Shawnee counties, which have large areas of rich glacial drift, and to a lesser degree the remaining counties in the northern tier as far west as Jewell County. Before the drought cycle of 1931–37, more than half of the average homestead of 160 acres was devoted to corn. The remaining portions of the typical Kansas corn-hog farms were pasture, and small fields of wheat, oats, or grain sorghum. The farmer developed the self-sustaining corn-hog economy by feeding his corn to the hogs to fatten them for market and selling the surplus grain.

The river valleys of northeastern Kansas and the major portion of southeastern Kansas are devoted to general farming with diversified cultivation. The Flint Hills region, which is carpeted with bluestem grass, is one of the finest grazing sections of the United States. West of an imaginary line extending north and south through Salina and Wichita to the Oklahoma Line is the winter wheat country, where until recent years, nearly one-half of the hard wheat in the United States was produced.

Efforts at fruit growing, especially in eastern Kansas, met with phenomenal success during the early seventies. The Kansas horticultural exhibit at the Centennial Exposition of 1876 gave the State a widespread reputation. But, as the virgin soil was drained of its productivity, many orchards died and were never successfully replanted. The upland glacial drift in Doniphan County, however, still supports large apple orchards and the cultivation of this fruit is a leading industry in the areas along the great bend of the Missouri River. Strawberries are also grown in the three river counties.

Broom corn is grown extensively in the southwestern corner of the State, in Seward, Stanton, Stevens, and Morton counties. Prior to the dust storms that accompanied the recent drought cycle, the towns of Elkhart and Liberal were among the largest shipping centers of this product in the world. Sugar beets are grown in the Arkansas River Valley near Garden City and Larned where large areas are irrigated. The cultivation of flax, which was an important crop before the introduction of winter wheat, has been revived to a considerable extent in recent years, especially in southeastern Kansas. Experts from the State College are urging farmers to grow flax on a larger scale.

In the fertile valleys of eastern Kansas, particularly the Kaw Valley, potatoes and melons are major crops. In a good season the State produces 2,500,000 bushels of Irish potatoes. Alfalfa, a deep-rooted drought-resistant hay, is important among the lesser crops. Introduced by Charles J. Grosse, of Marion, who planted 90 bushels of seed imported from California in 1869, its first recorded acreage was in 1891, when 34,384 acres were planted. A peak acreage of 1,277,875 was reached in 1918 and the ten-year average since 1927 has been approximately 750,000 acres.

Kansas has never suffered from a lack of transportation from production center to market, owing to the fact that the State, after the first decade of immigration, was settled as part of a great railroad expansion scheme. But farmers during the past fifty years have had to fight ceaselessly against two enemies: land speculation and drought. Through the various agencies of the Federal Government the farmer of the "dust bowl" and semi-arid areas has managed to survive a long period of subnormal rainfall. Economically, central Kansas has weathered adverse climatic conditions better than the eastern and extreme western sections, as crop failures have been less frequent in the central part of the State.

In general, the years of drought have considerably reduced the returns from Kansas agriculture; yet in one of the worst drought years, 1934, the wheat crop was valued at $67,205,989, and the corn crop at $9,183,968. The 1937 wheat crop was valued at $170,000,000. In 1933 Kansas livestock was valued at more than $100,000,000. Prior to the emergency drought programs of 1934 more cattle were raised on Kansas farms than in the days when the western part of the State was an open range. It is

CATTLE FEEDING IN SHELTER OF COTTONWOOD WINDBREAK

estimated (1937) that Kansas has nearly 3,000,000 cattle; 2,500,000 beef cattle, and 500,000 dairy animals. Approximately 2,000,000 hogs and 300,000 sheep are raised for market annually.

In contrast to the reverses from drought and wholesale speculation are the benefits of scientific research carried out by trained workers at Kansas State College of Agriculture and Applied Science. After years of experimentation great improvement in production has been made by selection of the varieties of crops planted. The idea that "rain follows the plow," which grew up during the boom period of the 1880's, has finally been disproved. Farmers are now adjusting their methods to climatic conditions rather than to the futile hope that turning the sod of the arid High Plains will increase the annual rainfall.

Drought-resistant strains of corn and wheat have been developed, and farmers have learned through experience to diversify their crops. In recent years the acreage of grain sorghums, of which many varieties have been produced, has increased, especially in western areas where the rainfall is not adequate for growing corn and the soil has been pulverized to the danger point by a series of unsuccessful attempts to grow wheat.

Nearly every Kansas county is receiving the benefits of the extension

4-H FARMERS ARE VISITED BY THE COUNTY AGENT

service conducted by the United States Department of Agriculture and Kansas State College. The three phases of this service include work with the farmers in agricultural methods, work with farm women in home economics, and work with boys and girls in the 4-H Clubs.

"Through the development of the head, heart, hand, and health," writes M. H. Coe, State club leader, "comes the term '4-H,' which signifies the four-fold educational development or training which 4-H Club boys and girls must receive to insure success in any undertaking." Each club member selects a project designed to show some better practice on the farm or in the home. In 1933 there were 19,353 members in 100 counties with 26,239 completed projects. In the same year 4-H Club members made 4,321 entries at the Topeka and Hutchinson State Fairs and won $4,325 in prize money. The total value of products raised by 4-H Club members was $387,726.

The long succession of abnormally dry seasons turned a considerable area in western Kansas into a near desert. Wheat planting had destroyed the natural coverage of buffalo grass and left the soil exposed to the ravages of drought and wind. By 1934 soil blowing had become a major problem, and by the following year the area affected had increased to 8,871,227 acres. Preventive measures adopted by the Federal Government and the State department of agriculture have largely checked the inroads of wind erosion. Submarginal land has been withdrawn from cultivation and in some areas efforts are being made to revive the buffalo grass pastures. By 1938 the Kansas dust bowl had almost disappeared, and soil drifting was confined to three or four counties in the extreme southwestern corner of the State.

On the recommendation of the U. S. Farm Security Administration, the State department of agriculture, the State planning board, the agricultural extension service, and other conservation agencies, soil-building crops, such as the legumes, are now being planted and a far-reaching program of water conservation and flood control has been adopted.

Transportation

BEFORE the coming of white men, the Indians in Kansas had no beast of burden other than the dog and no means of conveyance save the dugout canoe and the travois, a simple contrivance of two poles between which a dog was hitched, with the packs secured to the dragging ends.

Coronado and the other Spanish explorers who followed him introduced the horse, which the Indians readily adopted for riding and pack-carrying and to replace the dog at the travois. But they attempted no further improvement in transportation.

After the Spanish came the French trappers and fur traders, who explored the country and developed river transportation. They used successively the dugout canoe; the pirogue, two canoes lashed together and floored over to form a raft; the bullboat made by stretching buffalo hides over a circular willow frame; and the bateau or Mackinaw, a clumsy, flat-bottomed boat of from 10 to 20 tons. But there they halted, and no further development took place until after the official explorations of the early nineteenth century.

The expedition of Lewis and Clark to the northwest in 1804 stimulated the fur trade. The great fur companies introduced the keelboat—a large craft of from 20 to 70 tons, so named from the heavy timber that formed its central rib. In 1819 the steamboat, the *Western Engineer,* transported the scientific expedition of Major Stephen H. Long a short distance up the Kansas River and subsequently up the Missouri. Steamboats, however, were not employed commercially in Kansas until 1829, when a steam packet was placed in operation on the Missouri River from St. Louis to Cantonment Leavenworth (now Fort Leavenworth).

Meanwhile, Captain Zebulon M. Pike's second expedition (1806–07) directed interest to the Southwest, particularly to the Spanish town of Santa Fe, which was rich in trading possibilities. In the next few years traders from Missouri attempted to participate in this trade, only to be thrown into Spanish jails for their intrusion. But after Mexican independence had been declared (September 1821), Captain William Becknell opened the trade with a pack train taken from Franklin, Missouri, on the

Missouri River near Booneville, across Kansas to the Arkansas River near Great Bend, up that stream to the Rocky Mountains, then south to Santa Fe, where he disposed of cotton goods at "$3 per yard" and other items in proportion. The next year he returned with three wagons, this time crossing the Arkansas a little west of the present Dodge City, going south over the Cimarron desert, thence west to Santa Fe. Thus Becknell became the "Father of the Santa Fe Trail," establishing its separate courses and introducing wheeled vehicles, the first to cross the Kansas plains.

Other traders were immediately attracted, and the trade flourished. In 1825 Congress authorized the surveying and marking of the trail. Wagons soon outnumbered pack animals; and the light carriers used by Becknell were replaced by heavy Conestogas—huge, ponderous vehicles with a concave bed built high at each end. With their white canvas covers and sway-backed appearance, they became universally known as "prairie schooners." Loaded with cotton and woolen goods, silks, velvets, and hardware to the extent of from 3,000 to 5,000 pounds, and drawn by eight or more oxen or mules, they wended their slow way out of Independence, the eastern terminus, in early spring through incredible herds of northern-bound buffalo, and returned in the fall with horses and mules, blankets, furs, robes, and heavy bags of Spanish gold and silver. By 1843 the annual monetary value of the trade was about $450,000.

Meanwhile the Oregon Trail was being established. In 1830 William Sublette took the first wagons over the Oregon Trail to the head of the Popo Algie River, southwest of Lander, Wyoming. Captain Benjamin L. E. Bonneville succeeded in crossing the Rocky Mountains via the South Pass in 1832, with a train of 20 wagons, paving the way for a few hardy missionaries who settled in the Willamette Valley. Government interest followed, and in 1842 Lieutenant John C. Frémont was sent to locate the South Pass and survey a road into the Territory of Oregon. Before he had completed the task, however, a party of settlers was on the road; and in 1843 the "Great Migration" began.

On May 22 of that year a caravan of 875 persons, including women and children, 111 wagons, and about 2,000 horses and cattle moved out of Independence on the long journey. From Independence they followed the Santa Fe Trail to Gardner, Kansas, where later a crude sign gave the simple direction "Road to Oregon." Here they turned to the northwest, crossing the Kansas River in the vicinity of Topeka, followed the Big Blue to the Platte Valley, and proceeded through the South Pass to their destination.

This was, in effect, the route of the Oregon Trail in Kansas, although, as steamboat traffic increased on the Missouri and created new supply depots, various starting points were selected and eventually numerous roads converged into the main trail. The Santa Fe Trail, too, had starting points all along the western border of Missouri and north Arkansas, with tributary roads branching into it for a considerable distance. One of the better known branches was the Cherokee Trail, which started at Fort Smith, Arkansas, and finally struck the Oregon, California, and Salt Lake trails at Fort Bridger.

Western travel now developed swiftly. In 1844 four parties, independently organized, went to Oregon. One consisted of 800 persons and started from near Bellevue; another started from Independence with 500 to 700 persons. In 1845 the number of travelers increased to between 3,000 and 5,000. At the same time trade, which had been suspended by Mexico in 1843 because of boundary disputes, was resumed with Santa Fe on a much greater scale. In 1846 the United States declared war on Mexico, and the Mormons began their trek to Utah. In 1848 gold was discovered in California.

Ninety thousand persons—chiefly excited gold-seekers and Mormons—are said to have passed over the two trails in 1849–50, employing every manner of vehicle. The more affluent rode in carriages. There was even a wind-wagon, a four-wheeled cart equipped with sails, although it did not pass beyond the experimental stage. But always the bulk of human and inanimate freight was conveyed in the stately, lumbering prairie schooners, arrayed in two to four columns, often miles in length.

Each trail was a natural highway, extending without bridge or grading. Half of the Santa Fe's 800 miles lay across Kansas; the Oregon, 2,000 miles long, had only from 50 to 200 miles in Kansas, depending on the starting point. The Santa Fe Trail was the highway of commerce, and travel was comparatively rapid, six weeks being considered sufficient for the full journey. The Oregon Trail, called by the Indians the "Great Medicine Road of the Whites," was the homesteaders' highway, and all the events of domestic life—courtships, marriages, births, social and religious functions—occurred in the two to five months required for the journey.

One trail was as hazardous as the other. Travel on each was attended by hardship, hunger, disease, and danger. Over both hung the threat of inclement weather, especially on the Oregon Trail, where a late start in the spring meant winter in snowbound mountain passes. The Cimarron cutoff of the Santa Fe Trail shortened the distance, but along that route were 50 miles of desert where men were sometimes forced to drink the blood of their animals.

When the Santa Fe Trail was established, a treaty made with the Osage Indians gave permission to cross their lands. But no treaty was made with the Arapahoe, Comanche, Kiowa, and other Plains tribes, who fiercely resented the invasion of their last hunting grounds. In 1828 two white men were killed on the banks of McNees Creek, a tributary of the Canadian River, and retaliation and counter-retaliations without number followed. Caravans on each trail moved by day in semi-military formation under the leadership of a train captain, and rested at night in guarded stockades formed by their interlocking wagons. Each trail was marked with the scars of raids and massacres, by human graves, bones of mules and oxen, household goods and implements, burned and broken wagons.

Still the tide flowed on. In 1858 gold was discovered in Colorado, bringing a new surge of covered wagons, then emblazoned with "Pike's Peak or Bust!" Many of the prospectors did "bust" and returned disheartened, but for each who returned another always started out.

Meanwhile a new type of travel had appeared on the trails—the organized traffic of the overland freight and mail systems, carrying supplies and news to the settlements in California, Oregon, and Utah. It developed a surprising efficiency. Russell, Majors & Waddell, chief of the Plains freighting companies, accumulated a vast amount of equipment. The firm had a Government contract to transport supplies to the Army in Utah, and during 1858–59 it carried more than 16,000,000 pounds of freight, using 3,500 large wagons, and approximately 40,000 oxen, 1,000 mules, and 4,000 men. The wagons were made up into "bull-trains," which proceeded on the trails at regular intervals, from 10 to 12 miles apart, and were manned by crews of "bullwhackers," who urged the oxen on with picturesque profanity and the pistol-like cracking of long, heavy whips, called bullwhacks.

The first contract mail service across Kansas started on July 1, 1850; two lines originating at Independence connected with Santa Fe and Salt Lake City respectively. Mule-drawn wagons operated on a monthly schedule, but the time was no faster than that of the freighting system. The demand was for news while it was still news, and for more and more speed. Relay stations, stocked with supplies and fresh animals, were erected along the trails at intervals of from 10 to 15 miles; and that most dashing of vehicles, the stagecoach, was introduced. The mail service was increased from monthly to semi-monthly, and then weekly. Running time was cut down—Denver was only six days from St. Joseph, Salt Lake City ten days, and the first through stage from Placerville, California, made the trip in 18 days.

But even this was too slow. Impatient settlers clamored for a daily mail; and in 1860, Russell, Majors & Waddell instituted the Pony Express. A herd of wiry mustang ponies was purchased, and a group of hardy, expert, light-weight riders, was employed. On April 3, mounted riders galloped simultaneously out of Sacramento and St. Joseph on a giant relay arranged in individual stints of from 75 to 100 miles each, with a change of mounts every ten or fifteen miles to assure maximum speed. The pony express from East to West followed the route of the covered wagons from St. Joseph, Missouri, to the present site of Horton, Kansas. Here it struck the military road from Fort Leavenworth and Atchison, and continued by way of Granada and Seneca to Marysville, where it joined the main Oregon Trail. The mail went through in ten days, later shortened to nine in summer, and fifteen days in winter. In March 1861 a daily mail stage was established on the central route, but the Pony Express continued until the completion of the overland telegraph in October of that year made it unnecessary.

By this time the western frontier, long halted at the Missouri River, had advanced to the middle of Kansas. Indian lands, opened to white settlers in 1854, had been taken over; towns, roads, and ferries had been established. The Missouri River, forming the northeastern border of Kansas, was a regular trade route in the 1850's and 1860's, but was comparatively unimportant to Kansas as a transportation route, since it touched only a small portion of its territory.

It did, however, permit the extension of steamboat service up the Kansas River. In April 1854 the *Excel,* a sturdy stern-wheeler of 79 tons, carried a cargo of 1,100 barrels of flour to the newly established Fort Riley; and this was followed by other boats that maintained a more or less regular schedule.

On April 27, 1855 an emigrant company of 75 left Cincinnati on the steamboat *Hartford.* They traveled down the Ohio River, up the Mississippi and west on the Missouri and Kansas Rivers, and grounded near the mouth of the Blue River on June 1, 1855. The company had brought with them ten houses, ready to put up. Three members of the party hired a wagon and drove to the present site of Junction City; the rest joined with some other pioneers to found what is now Manhattan.

The next phase in transportation was the coming of the railroads. In 1845 Asa Whitney, the "Father of Pacific Railroads," memorialized Con-

COAL BARGE ON THE MISSOURI (*c.* 1888)

gress for a charter and land grant to build a line from Chicago to the
Pacific Coast. The feasibility of such a road was then being debated in the
East, but many such petitions were to be presented before Congress took
action. Rival cities each claimed superiority as an eastern terminus; sectional jealousy between the North and South made it impossible for either
to agree to a route that would give advantage to the other. Meanwhile,
Kansas impatiently undertook to build its own railroad to connect with
the Hannibal & St. Joseph line advancing to St. Joseph.

In January 1857 the Elwood & Marysville Railroad was organized and
five miles of track were constructed from Elwood, across the river from
St. Joseph, to Wathena. On April 28, 1860, its first locomotive, the
Albany, was ferried across the Missouri and placed on the tracks. This was
a great occasion. River packets, streaming with bunting, brought hundreds
of visitors; and as the ferry reached the west shore of the river, men and
boys grasped the ropes and pulled the *Albany* up the steep bank. The
track of this road is now a part of the St. Joseph & Western Division of
the Union Pacific Railroad.

Spurred by the same enthusiasm, other lines quickly materialized. In
1857 the Leavenworth, Pawnee & Western was organized and the road

FREIGHT YARDS, KANSAS CITY

graded to Pawnee, but no rails were laid; the Atchison & Topeka (now the Atchison Topeka & Santa Fe) was chartered; the Chicago, Kansas & Nebraska (now the Chicago Rock Island & Pacific) was incorporated; and the Union Pacific Railroad, Eastern Division (which later became the Kansas Pacific and a part of the Union Pacific) was organized.

The outbreak of the Civil War stopped further independent railway development, but it speeded up Federal aid as a war measure. On July 1, 1862, President Lincoln signed an act "to aid in the construction of a Railway and Telegraph line from the Missouri River to the Pacific Ocean," granting alternate odd-numbered sections of land to the amount of five sections a mile within the limits of ten miles, and a loan of $16,000 per mile to the builders. Three companies were formed—the Central Pacific, the Union Pacific, and the Kansas Pacific, each to construct certain portions of the line. But financial difficulties delayed construction; and Congress passed another act, increasing the land granted to the roads to odd-numbered sections within ten miles of either side of the track. As the war was then at its height, the act was designed to bring outlying military posts into closer connection, as well as to promote development of the West.

By 1865 the road was well under way, with the Central Pacific working east over the Sierras, the Union Pacific proceeding west through Nebraska, and the Kansas Pacific completing the connection from the mouth of the Kansas, through Manhattan, Junction City, Salina, and Denver, with the main line at Cheyenne. It took seven years to build the railroad. All materials used by the Union Pacific had to be brought by steamboat and wagon from the East; those for the Central Pacific by water to San Francisco and over the tracks already laid. Virtually every foot of the way was disputed by Indians, fighting to retain their hunting grounds. But at length, on May 10, 1869, at Promontory Point, north of Salt Lake City, a golden spike was driven, and the telegraph signalled to a waiting world, "Done!"

While the line from the Missouri to the Pacific was being built, the Atchison Topeka & Santa Fe Railroad (growing out of the earlier Atchison and Topeka) was chartered and in 1868 began work at Topeka on a route roughly corresponding with the old Santa Fe Trail. By 1872 it had run its tracks to the western border of Kansas and east from Topeka to complete the connection at Atchison.

By 1882 Kansas had 3,855 miles of railroad track, and 23 years later (in 1905) it had 8,905 miles. The present mileage is approximately 9,000. Today, eight main lines (the Atchison Topeka & Santa Fe, Union Pacific, Missouri Pacific, Chicago Rock Island & Pacific, St. Louis & San Fran-

AIRPORT, WICHITA

cisco, Chicago Great Western, Missouri-Kansas-Texas, and Kansas City Southern) converge at its eastern terminals. For 40 years these roads were the autocrats of Kansas transportation.

But the automobile introduced a new element. Considered as a curiosity at its first appearance about 1900, it soon became a commercial and domestic necessity; and with it came the demand for better roads. In 1937 Kansas had 133,063 miles of roads, of which nearly 9,000 were improved highways. The State maintained more than 9,000 miles. In the same year 586,685 motor vehicles of all types were registered in the State.

From motor vehicles the next step was air transport. Kansas now has 43 airports—35 private and municipal fields, six U. S. Department of Commerce fields, and two Army airports. Wichita is a station on the Kansas City-Dallas route and the Kansas stop for transcontinental service between Los Angeles and New York. Coffeyville and Chanute are on the route of the Kansas City-Tulsa line, which is devoted only to mail transportation. Within the State are 242 privately-owned, non-commercial planes, 165 of which are licensed.

In recent years there has been a revival of river transportation. In July 1930, Congress authorized a survey to determine the feasibility of barge navigation on the Missouri and Kansas Rivers. As a result, barges are now in operation on the Missouri along the northeastern edge of the State. It was determined that the Kansas was navigable for barges of as much as 1,000-ton capacity for a distance of nine miles from its mouth. In 1937 a river-rail terminal elevator was completed at Kaw Point above the mouth of the Kansas. Here much of the grain carried by rail to the terminal is transferred to barges and shipped to New Orleans for export. These developments indicate that the rivers, which played so great a part in Indian and pioneer transportation, may regain their importance in the State's transportation system.

Industry, Commerce
and Labor

INDUSTRY was the complement of agriculture during the first fifty
years of settlement in Kansas. This relationship was first evident in
1827 when Daniel Morgan Boone, accompanied by his brother-in-law,
Gabe Phillebert, settled at Stonehouse Creek and tried to introduce the
white man's farming methods to the Indians. Phillebert, a blacksmith, set
up his forge and supplied the crude implements needed by Boone and his
pupils. When not mending or making ring hoes and plowshares, Phillebert hammered out pots and kettles with which the Indians replaced their
primitive utensils.

Flour milling had its Kansas beginning in 1852 when Matthias Splitlog, a Wyandot Indian, established a horsepower mill near the site of
Kansas City. The first waterpower mill was built five years later beside
Mill Creek in what is now Wabaunsee County. The milling industry developed rapidly thereafter, and by 1860, according to census figures, there
were 62 waterpower mills and a larger number of horsepower mills in the
Territory of Kansas.

In point of income flour milling is today the second largest Kansas industry. In the decade 1927–37 Kansas led all other States five times in the
annual production of flour. The yearly output during that period varied
between 12 and 17 million barrels. According to the 1937 report of the
Bureau of the Census, U. S. Department of Commerce, the wheat storage
capacity of Kansas mills (43,000,000 bushels) exceeds that of any other
State. The main milling centers are at Salina, Topeka, Wichita, Atchison,
Hutchinson, and Kansas City.

In the early years of Statehood the minerals of Kansas were not exploited, although the settlers knew of rich deposits of oil and coal. As
early as 1806 explorers had noted that Kansas Indians wore ornaments of
lead. Seventy years later lead and zinc were discovered near the site of
Galena, and 10,000 miners immigrated to the region. Throughout the

1880's the Galena field was known as a "poor man's diggings" because of the many one-acre claims which were worked with windlasses and hand jigs. Large-scale operations were begun in 1899. The ore production of Kansas increased steadily in succeeding years, mounting to 28,463 tons of lead and 126,307 tons of zinc in 1926. A slump set in during the next decade; the ore output for 1936 totalled 11,409 tons of lead and 79,017 tons of zinc.

A similar decline, caused largely by the increasing use of gas and oil for fuel, has been noted in the coal industry. Following the opening of the first mine in 1866, the annual output increased with the population, reaching a peak of 7,561,947 tons in 1917. During 1936 the 77 mines in Kansas produced only 3,147,225 tons; in the following year 61 mines produced about 2,000,000 tons. But the dwindling part played by coal, lead, and zinc in the State's economy has been more than counterbalanced by the development of oil resources. A. D. Searl, a surveyor, found oil oozing from the earth near the site of Paola in 1855. On returning to his home in Conneautville, Pennsylvania, Searl informed Dr. G. W. Brown of his discovery. Dr. Brown came to Kansas in 1859, verified Searl's find, and organized a company which leased thirty thousand acres in Miami County. In 1860 the company drilled three wells. The first two were "dry holes," the last struck oil and salt water at 270 feet.

Throughout the first quarter century of its development, Kansas oil had a small intra-state sale as a lubricant. The wells were shallow and in some instances the oil was obtained by merely skimming it from the surface of streams. By 1889 the annual production of petroleum averaged five hundred barrels. In that year the Kansas legislature recognized the presence of the new industry by enacting a law that required the inspection of petroleum sold as an illuminating agent.

Kansas oil was vigorously exploited during the first decade of the present century. Wells that pumped one thousand barrels a day were "shot" in Montgomery County in 1903. The annual production of the State soon reached 3,000,000 barrels, at which point it hovered for more than a decade. Stimulated by the opening of the Butler County field, the Kansas output for 1916 climbed to 8,000,000 barrels and rose to 36,500,000 barrels the following year.

During 1937 the 18,000 wells in Kansas produced 69,000,000 barrels of oil. The oil fields extend south from Kansas City crescent-wise to the Oklahoma line, and thence northward through the central part of the State. The wells in the eastern part are shallow "strippers" which yield

OIL WELLS NEAR WICHITA

between 10 and 12 barrels daily. Those in central Kansas pump as much as 2,250 barrels per day. Petroleum refining has become the third most important Kansas industry.

Nelson Acres, an oil prospector, struck a pocket of gas near Iola in 1873. His discovery was first utilized in 1889 by the city of Paola, and seven other communities installed gas systems in the following year. By 1925 approximately 27,000,000 cubic feet of gas were consumed annually. This quantity was more than doubled in the next decade, amounting to 57,125,000 cubic feet during 1935.

About two hundred gas wells were drilled in Kansas between 1932–35. Gasoline extraction from natural gas amounted to 36,900,000 gallons during 1936. The largest pocket of natural gas is the Hugoton field at the southwestern corner of Kansas, and smaller pockets exist throughout the oil producing area. One of the three helium plants in the country is at Dexter. When first discovered in 1907, Dexter residents, unaware of the incombustible nature of helium, piped it to their homes and, by reason of the natural gas it contained, managed to ignite it for cooking and illumination.

The total mineral production of Kansas during 1937 was valued at $156,000,000. It included gas, oil, coal, lead, zinc, sand, gravel, stone, chat, pumice, cement, and salt. The latter mineral was discovered near Hutchinson in 1887 by Ben Blanchard, an oil prospector. Exploitation began in 1888 at the rate of 500 barrels per day. At present (1938) Kansas is third among the States in the production of salt. The largest mines are at Hutchinson; others are at Lyons, Anthony, Kanopolis, and Little River.

Several decades before the first oil well was drilled in Kansas, petroleum scooped from the tops of pools was customarily used to grease the wheels of freighters traveling the Santa Fe Trail. Pack trains began to follow this route in the 1820's, and by 1860 about 3,500 men were employed in its commerce.

Following the completion of the Santa Fe Railway in the 1870's, the Santa Fe Trail fell into disuse and its Kansas length was subsequently overgrown with wheat. But the trail left its mark on the economic pattern of the State. According to business analysts, the commerce of Kansas still flows in a southwest direction, and the trade area of a Kansas city generally extends west and south, seldom north and east.

Of later origin than the Santa Fe Trail, but of greater economic importance, was the Chisholm Trail, named for the halfbreed Cherokee who in 1865 marked off its route with the wheels of his trade wagon *(see WICHITA)*. The Chisholm Trail was the main outlet for Texas cattle in the 1870's. During the two decades in which the trail was used, about 5,000,000 longhorns were herded over it to shipping points in Kansas. Meat packing plants were consequently established at Salina, Kansas City, and other communities. The first meat ever transported in refrigerator cars was shipped from Salina in 1872. In point of income meat packing is now the largest Kansas industry. The average output of the packing plants at Wichita and Kansas City is valued annually at more than $125,000,000.

In 1937 Kansas had 36 insurance companies, 104 national farm loan agencies, 140 building and loan associations, and 515 state and private banks. Public utility corporations included 4 in water, 23 in electricity, and 36 in gas. There were 338 Kansas telephone companies.

According to the 1935 *U. S. Census of Manufactures,* Kansas had 1,508 manufacturing plants whose total output that year was valued at $468,690,290. Excluding the three major products already named—meat packing, flour milling, and petroleum refining—the largest items were, in

KANSAS BEEF

the order listed, butter, printing and publishing, railroad repair shops, wholesale poultry dressing and packing, stock and fowl feeds, machinery, cement, salt, ice, and structural and ornamental metal work. The same census enumerated 4,621 wholesale establishments, 9,290 service establishments, and 27,433 retail stores.

Contemporary industries include the manufacture of trailers at Augusta, airplanes at Wichita and Kansas City, strawboard at Hutchinson, garden tractors at Galesburg, snow plows at Wamego, and agrol—a gasoline that contains alcohol extracted from grains—at Atchison. Pipe organs are manufactured at Lawrence, beet sugar at Garden City, paving material at Moline, locomotive parts at Atchison, linseed oil and linseed stock feed at Fredonia, bean-picking machines at Cawker City, carbon black at Hickok, stoves at Leavenworth and Wichita, furniture at Garnett and Leavenworth, soap at Kansas City, steel fixtures at Ottawa and Topeka, ceramic products at Havana, and oil field machinery at Wichita and Independence. Of its raw foodstuffs, Kansas ships wheat in the greatest quantity, one-third of the average annual crop of 170,000,000 bushels going to outer-state markets.

During 1937 about 228,000 part and fulltime industrial workers were employed in Kansas. Of this number an average of 44,000 were employed in trade, 42,000 in manufacturing, 38,000 in transportation, 19,000 in mining and quarrying, 12,000 in service industries, and 11,000 in communication and utilities. The average annual wage in the foregoing industries amounted to $1,233.05.

Kansas industry was, until the second decade of the present century, operated largely on the open shop plan. In the period after the Civil War most of the trade unions in the State reflected the general conditions of the country as a whole, and were mainly local organizations. The formation of national unions was slow.

When the depression of 1873 swept over the country, prices and profits plunged downward. Employers began a tremendous drive to lower wages, which in turn brought about a stiffer resistance on the part of the workers. Labor fought back with the only weapon it had, the strike. This period, therefore, was one of many bitter strikes, among which those of the railroad workers in 1877 were the most outstanding.

The first strike in Kansas occurred in 1877 when employees of the Santa Fe Railway joined a Nation-wide walkout to obtain higher wages. The railroad shops at Topeka, Emporia, and Lawrence were peacefully picketed, but Governor George T. Anthony immediately dispatched militia companies to those cities. The citizens of Emporia termed the use of troops an insult to their persons and their city. The militia was thoroughly discredited when one of their members accidentally shot and killed the Reverend O. J. Shannon, an Emporia minister. Governor Anthony subsequently withdrew the troops and the strike was settled without further disorder.

The first legislation designed to benefit Kansas industrial workers was enacted during the term of Governor John A. Martin (1885–89). The Governor was a member of a typographical union and in sympathy with the general policy of the Knights of Labor, which occupied an outstanding position in the labor movement of that period. In the first year of his governorship the legislature created a bureau of labor and industrial statistics, the establishment of which had been advocated in 1884 by the General Assembly of the Knights of Labor. The same legislature also passed a bill requiring the wage of industrial workers to be paid monthly in "lawful money of the United States." Near the close of the session, however, this bill was all but abrogated by an amendment sponsored by groups that feared to place any restraint on the industrial development of the State.

Two months after Governor Martin had been inaugurated, railroad shopworkers at Parsons and Atchison walked out in response to a strike called in Missouri, Kansas, and Texas to resist wage reductions and increased hours proposed by the Missouri Pacific Railway. The railroad officials immediately telegraphed for troops to guard company property. After a survey of the strikers' picketing methods Governor Martin refused to send the militia, noting, incidentally, that the legal right of a railroad official to request the use of troops had not been established by any Kansas statute.

Governor Martin twice proposed that the strike be arbitrated by a disinterested committee; officials of the railroad company twice declined. On March 13, 1885, however, H. M. Hoxie, vice-president of the Missouri Pacific Railway, asked Governor Martin to confer at St. Louis, Missouri, with the board of railroad commissioners, the Governor of Missouri, and a representative of the railroad company. The Governor promptly assented. The company granted the demands of the workers and the strike ended.

The snags encountered in mediating the railroad strike impelled Governor Martin to propose the creation of legal machinery to expedite the settlement of future industrial disputes. At a special session in January 1886 he asked the legislature to establish a tribunal of voluntary arbitration. A bill was accordingly passed on February 18, empowering the district county courts, upon the petition of employer or employee, to set up a court of voluntary arbitration over which an umpire appointed by the district judge would preside.

Kansas, in common with the Nation, resounded with industrial warfare throughout 1886. Strikes occurred among the coal miners, the railroadmen, and the smelting and refinery workers. Most serious of these was the railroad strike, which began on March 1 in Marshal, Texas, upon the discharge of a foreman of the woodworkers in the Texas and Pacific car shops. It affected Parsons on March 6, Kansas City on March 8, and Atchison on March 10. All traffic on the Missouri Pacific Railway came to a dead halt. Shop machinery was destroyed, several trains were damaged, and one was derailed, resulting in the death of the fireman and a brakeman.

Attempts to have the strike settled in Governor Martin's court of voluntary arbitration failed. The situation took an ugly turn at Parsons, following the issuance of an injunction which enjoined the strikers from interfering with the traffic of the Missouri Pacific Railway. The injunction was generally ignored and Governor Martin was besieged with requests for the militia. Reluctantly, and only after all hope of arbitration had been abandoned, the Governor detailed the First Regiment to Parsons on April 1. A "Law and Order League" was also organized in the city. No further efforts to stop railroad traffic were made, and the strike was lost. In his campaign for re-election in 1887, Governor Martin was censured by industry for his delay in sending the militia, and by industrial workers for having sent the militia. The court of voluntary arbitration, basically a just and democratic principle, was discredited because of its failure to solve the strikes of 1886. The Governor, nevertheless, was re-elected by a considerable majority. At the legislative session of 1887 laws were passed to further the organization of co-operatives, and to insure the wage-payment of miners in "lawful money."

In 1893 the extensive industrial depression throughout the Nation also affected Kansas labor. As in the past, the employers began a general offensive against wages, and the workers fought back with strikes.

The mining area in southeastern Kansas, known as the "little Balkans," was the source of prolonged labor unrest throughout the period. The miners had very real cause for complaint. They mined the so-called "long ton" for a bare subsistence wage that was, until the enforcement of the legislative act of 1887, often paid in company scrip. On July 21, 1893, following the rejection of their demands by the mine operators, the recently formed unit of the United Mine Workers called a strike. The sheriff of Cherokee County telegraphed for the militia. Governor Lewelling, first of Kansas' two Populist governors, assembled ten militia companies on the advice of the attorney general, and held them ready to patrol the strike area. The miners and operators, however, adjusted their difficulties by July 25, and the troops were disbanded.

The larger railroad companies stubbornly resisted the unionization of Kansas railroadmen during the 1890's. Since the open shop preference of the railroad officials was supported by public opinion and the general press, the railroad companies were the more powerful in their disputes with employees. After the 1894 Pullman strike, led by the American Railway Union, one railroad company announced that jobs would not be restored to those who had struck. A number of men thus blacklisted appealed to the United States District Court, the judge of which appointed an investigating committee. The committee subsequently reported that "it is difficult to understand what greater offence an employee could commit than to refuse to work and still insist that no one could take his place." The court thereupon ruled against the blacklisted men, but the effect of the decision was nullified in 1897 when the Populist-Democratic legisla-

COAL MINER

ture passed a law prohibiting discrimination and the publication of black-lists.

The trade union movement was at a low ebb at the beginning of the twentieth century. The American Federation of Labor became active in Kansas in 1907 but, since it operated largely on a craft basis, the masses of unskilled workers were left unorganized. Kansas labor, through the Western Federation of Miners, was also represented in the Industrial Workers of the World, which was organized in 1905 as a protest against the slow progress of the conservative trade unions.

The post-War unrest of industrial workers affected all of Kansas in the autumn of 1919 when the United Mine Workers in the "little Balkans" joined the Nation-wide strike for increased wages and a six-hour day. As the strike lengthened, the weather became very cold and a shortage of fuel seemed imminent. Governor Henry J. Allen threw the mines into a temporary State receivership. About a thousand workers, many of them college students, were hired to mine the Crawford County "strippers" under the protection of National guardsmen.

Governor Allen called a special legislative session at which a criminal syndicalism and sabotage act was passed, and the Court of Industrial Relations was established. The court consisted of three judges, appointed by the Governor, who were empowered to investigate, try, and decide disputes involving "essential industries." The court regulations were presumably intended to safeguard public welfare through the compulsory removal of all obstructions to production. Labor was to be permanently appeased by its right to appeal against low wages, long hours, and discriminatory practices of employers. Industry was to be benefited by Section 15, which forbade picketing and boycotting, and by Section 17, which deprived labor of the right to strike. Violators of Section 17 were to be penalized by a jail sentence of from one to two years and/or fines that ranged from one to five thousand dollars.

Organized labor saw in the Kansas Court of Industrial Relations a crystallization of undemocratic forces. Samuel Gompers, president of the American Federation of Labor, sounded the tocsin with "Kansas cannot legislate men into serfdom. Kansas cannot put upon her statute books a law that will compel men to submit to involuntary servitude." Governor Allen defended the court on all fronts. More than 40,000 persons were turned away, when he and Samuel Gompers debated the issue in Carnegie Hall, New York City, on May 28, 1920.

Since the Court of Industrial Relations was the first and only attempt to enforce compulsory arbitration of labor disputes, its operations were closely followed by the Nation's economists, union leaders, and industrialists. What was publicized as the first case of its kind in America occurred in November 1920 when seven Topeka mill operators were cited to appear before the court and "show cause why men are being laid off . . . and production curtailed without permission of the court." In the previous year the Topeka mill workers had struck for higher pay and lost, their jobs being assumed by non-union men. The case against the mill operators aroused great interest, since many believed that a precedent for industrial stabilization might be established.

The mill operators were not placed under oath, and the "trial" was in the nature of a formal debate. The testimony amounted to the fact that seasonal adjustments of production and employment were required to make flour milling a profitable pursuit. It was further asserted that flour milling was strongly influenced by out-of-State factors. To this the court agreed, dismissing the case as beyond its jurisdiction.

About 6,500 Kansas members of the Federated Shop Crafts walked out in July 1922 in protest against wage cuts proposed by the U. S. Railroad Labor Board. Militia companies were detailed to the strike centers. Strike-breakers were employed in several instances, and the strike was ultimately lost. A large part of the Kansas public, meanwhile, sided with the strikers. Many merchants placed cards in their windows which read: "We are for a living wage and fair working conditions. We are for the striking work-men 100 percent." Attorney General Richard J. Hopkins, in accordance with Section 15 of the regulations of the Court of Industrial Relations, declared that such cards were a form of picketing and therefore punishable by law.

William Allen White, Emporia editor and longtime friend of Governor Allen, placed a sign in the window of his printing shop that read: "We are for the striking workmen 49 percent." White was thereupon signaled out for "picketing" and held for trial, but the case was dismissed on December 8, 1922. "If I was within the law in contending for the right of free utterance for the public wholly outside the controversy," White said, "I should not have been subjected to a shanghied arrest. . . . I was ku kluxed by a court that did not have the guts to pull out their shirt tails and give a ku klux parade."

Employees of the Wolf Packing Company, threatened by a wage cut, appeared before the Court of Industrial Relations, presented their case, and received an order granting an increase in pay. The officials of the packing company appealed to the State supreme court which upheld the decision. They then appealed to the United States Supreme Court which, in a decision written by Chief Justice Taft in 1923, held that the statute creating the Court of Industrial Relations was unconstitutional because it empowered the court to fix a minimum wage, pending the solution of a labor dispute. Two years later it was abolished by the legislature.

Kansas experienced 34 shortlived local strikes throughout the decade ending in 1935. In that year, however, the members of the Mine, Mill and Smelter Workers' International Union ceased work in the lead and zinc fields at the southeast corner of the State. The strikers were replaced by non-union workers who were subsequently organized in a company union known as the Tri-State Metal Mine and Smelter Workers' Union, or, more commonly, the Blue Card Union.

The feud between the striking workers and the Blue Card unionists smoldered for about two years, and then burst into flame when the Committee for Industrial Organization undertook to aid the Mine, Mill and Smelter Workers' International Union. On April 10, 1937, several men distributing leaflets for the CIO at a smelter in Joplin, Missouri, were seized by Blue Card unionists and severely beaten. On the following day about 5,000 members of the Blue Card Union met at Picher, Oklahoma, armed themselves with clubs and pickhandles, dispersed a meeting of CIO organizers and wrecked the local hall of the Mine, Mill and Smelter Workers' International Union.

About 500 Blue Card unionists then traveled by automobile to Treece, Kansas, where they demolished another hall of the CIO union. The caravan of cars continued to Galena, Kansas, where forewarned members of the Mine, Mill and Smelter Workers' International Union had barricaded their meeting hall. The mob formed before the hall, brandishing clubs. Firing broke out, and nine men were shot, one fatally. In the ensuing melee the hall was wrecked and the records of the union stolen. Twenty-five members of the Blue Card Union and ten members of the CIO were arrested and released on bond. A week after the riot occurred, six thousand members of the Blue Card Union voted to join the American Federation of Labor, with which organization they were subsequently affiliated.

The Kansas units of the CIO and A. F. of L. have not generally engaged in inter-union competition. As though a mutual agreement existed between both organizations, they have maintained and respected separate spheres of activity. The A. F. of L. has grown to 500 locals with a membership of about 75,000 in the State. The CIO counts approximately 25,000 members among Kansas workers and has concentrated its membership drive among oil, stove, furniture, packing plant, filling station, soap and glycerine, clay and pottery, paper and box workers. The United Mine Workers of America, which is now affiliated with the CIO has approximately 100 locals in the State. The one strike called in Kansas by the CIO—a five-day sit-down at the Kansas City plant of Armour & Company —was peacefully settled without arbitration. The Kansas Workers' Alliance, an organization of the unemployed, has an estimated membership of 4,500.

During the past few years labor has made considerable gains by the passing of several legislative measures. An industrial hygiene section in the division of sanitation of the State board of health was established in

February 1936. Since its organization this section has been conducting surveys of industries in order to determine what potential exposure hazards, if any, exist in the industries, and to study the means of eliminating such occupational hazards as do exist. Silicosis, an occupational hazard existing in the Tri-State area (parts of Kansas, Oklahoma, and Missouri) is not compensable under Kansas laws, and it is obvious that the organization of an industrial hygiene section means a great deal to the workers of the State.

The 1937 legislature passed laws covering all sections of the Federal social security program; ratified the Federal child-labor amendment, and adopted an unemployment compensation act. The 1938 session of the legislature revived the State's former minimum wage law.

Considerable progress is also to be noted in the relationship between the industrial and agricultural workers. Until comparatively recent years, the average Kansan was little interested in labor relationships unless they directly affected him. Except for the Populist movement of the 1880's, there had been no concerted action on the part of the farmer and industrial worker and Populism in Kansas was largely an agrarian movement.

In the last few years, however, a definite movement for joint action by farmers and industrial workers has been developing. Several meetings of the Farmers Union, the United Cannery, Agricultural Packing, and Allied Workers, and Labor's Non-Partisan League were held recently and programs for concerted action were drawn up. Representatives from Kansas participated. Several other such conferences with representatives of organized labor resulted in a greater understanding of each other's problems and increasing co-operation between the Farmers Union and organized labor. A notable example of such farmer-labor co-operation was the calling off of an impending Colorado beet workers' strike, largely through the efforts of agricultural labor union representatives and National Farmers Union officials. It is also of interest to note that the farm program resolution of the CIO convention, recently held in Pittsburg, cited the agreement recently drawn up and ratified in Colorado, under which the Farmers Union will organize beet growers, and the CIO cannery and agricultural workers will organize the beet workers, both to guarantee mutual recognition and collective bargaining.

Folklore

FOLK tales and folk songs, compounded of dreams, idle imaginings, and wish fulfillment, are usually based on the prosaic doings of men who "earn their living by the sweat of their brow." In Kansas the first workers were the farmer and the cowboy. Within the short span of three decades their not so heroic figures were draped with a spangled mantle of lore and legend.

The present century has not dealt kindly with the farmer. His legends are all but obsolete, and his beliefs have been pared away by the professors at colleges of agriculture. Even the farm-bred bards who twang guitars before radio microphones prefer "I'm Headin' for the Last Roundup" to "Turkey in the Straw" or "Father Put the Cows Away." Agronomists have shown the absurdity of planting crops by the phases of the moon; meteorologists have disproved many hitherto infallible weather omens; and bacteriologists have dispelled the hobgoblins who once merrily soured cream and addled eggs. Nature, in short, has ceased to be mysterious and the farmer has become a mere workman.

The cowboy, however, is well on the way to becoming a figure of magnificent proportions. Bowlegged and gaunt, he stands as the apotheosis of manly perfection. Songs, novels, movies, magazines, and operettas have made the least inquiring of us well acquainted with his extraordinary courage, unfailing gallantry, and uncanny skill with gun or lariat. The farmer, meanwhile, sits stolidly on his tractor, bereft of romance and adventure.

Time was when farming in Kansas was not without perils. The story goes that Lem Blanchard went forth one afternoon in mid-July to inspect his cornfield in the Republic Valley. He scaled a young stalk to overlook the forest-like field and from its top was able to see into the next county. When he turned to descend he was horrified to find that the stalk was growing upward faster than he could scramble down. For two days he made back-breaking efforts to reach the ground. At last, to keep him from starving to death, kind neighbors who had tracked him to the foot of the towering stalk shot Lem dead.

There are those who say that Lem was rescued by a balloonist but that seems improbable. If Lem had not perished on the cornstalk, surely other of his adventures among the gigantic squash, pumpkins, and 'taters on his farm would have been recorded. Lem would have saved himself, if the corn had been mature. Another farmer caught in a similar predicament subsisted on raw ears of corn. When the cornstalk ceased growing, enabling him to descend, he found that forty bushels of corncobs had accumulated below his perch.

The enormous stalks of corn were of course grown on extremely large fields. There was one man whose field was so wide that by the time the mortgage was recorded on the west side, the mortgage on the east side had come due. The hired man and hired girl, following their wedding, went out to milk the cows that grazed on the west side. When they returned they had a child one year old.

The winds that swept across the big farms often reached hurricane velocity. The ducks' feathers were invariably blown onto the chickens, and the chickens' feathers were invariably blown onto the ducks. Frequently the wind scooped the cellar from beneath the house but left the house intact, hoisted the well from under the pump but left the pump intact, and carried the whole farm away but left the mortgage intact. An inexperienced dog dared to bark at an approaching "twister." The ensuing entry of air turned the animal inside out.

The grasshoppers that ravaged the big farms were as large as mules. Champing huge mandibles and lashing great antennae, the monster insects deliberately bullied the hogs, cows, and sheep. Nothing escaped their voracious appetites. Wagons and well platforms were favored tidbits. Armed with axe handles, buggywhips, and pitchforks, the gargantuan 'hoppers fought viciously in fence corners for the last ear of corn. After devouring the crops they would insolently pick their teeth on the barbs of the barbed-wire fence.

The belief that "rain follows the plow" was held by many a Kansas farmer in the 1880's and '90's. When a drought was persistent, professional rainmakers were frequently enlisted to coax the reluctant clouds. A popular method of producing rain consisted of killing a snake and "hanging it belly-side up on a fence." In the great drought of the 1890's an all but despairing Bohemian farmer ruefully told a passerby: "I've killed three snakes and hung them on the fence, and each time we got a sprinkle of rain. If I could find enough snakes we'd get plenty rain."

The belief that dead snakes suspended belly-side up on a fence would bring rain is said to have originated before the invention of barbed-wire fences in 1874. When laid on a rail or stone fence, *rigor mortis* would invariably cause the snake to twist over onto its belly and thus prevent the "charm" from being followed to the letter. Barbed-wire fences enabled Kansan farmers to penetrate a dorsal segment and so fix the snake in the prescribed position. Thousands of snakes were properly strung on barbed-wire fences, their white-scaled bellies glistening in the brassy sun-glare. But, strange to relate, Nature seldom reacted favorably to the sacrifice of serpents.

The lore-manufacturers of the cattle trails scorned to imitate the extravagances born of the farmers' hopes and fears about mysterious Nature. The cowboy was a man in full, a rootin' tootin' son-of-a-gun, tougher than the leather of his saddle. Had he met a "big wind," he would have galloped dead against it; had he encountered a giant grasshopper, he would have peppered the insect with his six-shooter. Indeed, the ordinary activities of the cowboy out-fictioned the farmers' folk fiction. The 'puncher rode hard, shot fast, drank copiously, and, as verified by subsequent exhumations, often died with his boots on. In his midst moved "Bat" Masterson, "Wild Bill" Hickok, "Doc" Holliday, "Big Nose Kate," and other incredible persons.

On arriving at Newton, Wichita, Abilene, and other Kansas cow towns the pleasure-starved cowpunchers engaged in mad bouts of drinking, gambling, and dancehall cavorting. Sometimes they "painted the town red" by galloping through the streets and firing their "shooting irons" into the air. At Medicine Lodge the cowboys held horse-races down the main street; at night they built bonfires and took turns riding forward to see whose horse would run nearest the flames. The old saying "There is no Sunday west of Newton and no God west of Pueblo" aptly described the Kansas cow towns.

The cowboy's speech was crisp and pungent. The farmer was a "nester" or "drylander," and an inquisitive person an "eyeballer." Courting was termed "sittin' her," traveling by a circuitous route was known as "antigodlin'," and to make your best effort was "to cut a rusty." The phrase "wild and woolly" is said to have originated in Dodge City, where the stock answer to a query about one's past was: "I came up the Chisholm Trail with the buffalo wild and woolly."

Each cow town had its badmen who, if court records are reliable, were mighty, mighty bad. When badman Jack Coulter was killed at Coronado in 1887, his trigger finger is said to have jerked desperately for a half hour after he died. The badmen had a sadistic sense of humor. Sometimes they made citizens dance by shooting at their feet. Or again, by way of mild diversion, a badman tested his aim by shooting through the hat of a passerby. One such Wiliam Tell in Gray County, whose hand was unsteady from drink, pierced both the hat and head of his target.

The hardboiled, devil-may-care attitude of the cowboy shielded a shy brooding nature. His fatalistic philosophy was often a social pose that he upheld publicly but disavowed in private. That the cowboy was deeply concerned with an untimely end, whether it found him booted or abed, is strongly indicated by his songs and ballads. "Sam Bass," "Mustang Gray," "The Cowboy's Dream," and "The Dying Cowboy" evidence a preoccupation with death, which is at direct odds with the generally accepted picture of a swashbuckling 'puncher with two guns on his hip and an "itching trigger finger." That the cowboy was also concerned about an afterlife is illustrated in the following:

THE DIM NARROW TRAIL

Last night as I lay on the prairie
Looking up at the stars in the sky
I wondered if ever a cowboy
Would go to that sweet by and by.

The trail to that fair mystic region
Is narrow and dim all the way,
While the road that leads to perdition
Is posted and blazed all the way.

They say there will be a grand round-up,
Where cowboys like cattle must stand,
To be cut by the riders of judgment
Who are posted and know every brand.

Perhaps there will be a stray cowboy
Unbranded by anyone nigh
Who'll be cut by the riders of judgment
And shipped to the sweet by and by.

Cowboy sports and customs are frequently revived in Kansas by "Cowboy Rodeo" and "Frontier Day" celebrations. Pioneer times are regularly recalled at various old settlers' gatherings held annually throughout the State. Spelling bees, bean suppers, oyster suppers, box socials, amateur "nigger minstrels," and similar old-fashioned amusements are occasionally revived as novelties by clubs and church societies.

The Kansas reservoir of superstitions is fed by streams from the general pool of American taboos and beliefs. A small percentage of the population believe that a tipped new moon presages frost, that surface crops should be planted in the light of the moon and underground crops in the dark of the moon, that bad luck follows spilt salt or a broken mirror, and that misfortune may be warded off by knocking on wood. Beliefs prevalent among Kansas children include "stamping a white horse," the ubiquitous "bread and butter" incantation used in passing on opposite sides of a post, and the performance of "thumbs" when two persons say the same word simultaneously.

The contemporary Kansas Negro has discarded his heritage of Southern superstitions and acquired in varying degree those of his white neighbor. Many still believe that if the church bell gives an after toll, a member of the congregation will soon die; that bad luck will come if you're struck by a broom; and that a sleeping person will tell his dreams if his hand is placed in cold water. The last is said to be a fundamental—and useful— tenet in the credo of wives.

During the last two decades the imaginations of rural Kansans have been relatively lax in populating empty houses and lonely lanes with "hants" and creatures of the underworld. Several such manifestations are reported periodically, however, in the same regions. Greeley County has its Ghost of White Woman Creek, a white-clad shade who, according to legend, drowned herself in the creek when she found her lover lying dead on its bank. A "giant panther" is said to inhabit the farming district along a draw northwest of Norton. Tales of the beast's fiery eyes and hideous screeching are intermittently revived. Since the 1890's residents of Wallace County have reported seeing a strange light bob across the countryside. Some assert that the light is the ghost of a man murdered in the 1890's, but the more literal minded explain the phenomenon as a phosphorescent glow arising from decaying bones on the prairie.

Education

←←←←←←←←←←←←←←←←←←←←←✿→→→→→→→→→→→→→→→→→→→→→→→

THE schools of Kansas have been locally supported and, for the most part, locally controlled since the earliest days. Until 1937 when the State legislature established a State Aid Fund for the benefit of elementary schools in need of additional support, the State government performed neither of these functions except for the State supported institutions of higher learning and the educational institutions for defectives. Yet Kansans generally have been united by faith in the power of learning to make mankind industrious, virtuous, and wise. With this faith the pioneers built their first humble schoolhouses of logs and sod. And because of this belief 450,000 students attend the universities, colleges, junior colleges, high, and common schools of Kansas today.

The first schools were religious missions among the Indians. Approximately twenty-five were established in eastern and central Kansas between the 1820's, when the Presbyterian Neosho Mission was opened in what is now Neosho County, and the late 1850's. Religion and education went hand in hand at these frontier outposts of civilization. Members of peaceful Indian tribes came from far and near to the mission schools and often attended classes with the white children. They learned reading, writing, farming methods, and simple health measures. Ottawa University is a direct outgrowth of the Ottawa Baptist Mission founded by the Reverend Jotham Meeker in 1837, and Highland College at Highland had its origin in the Kickapoo mission established by the Presbyterian Church in 1856.

The first free schools in Kansas were held in private homes, in village stores, or wherever it was expedient. If the settlement boasted no teacher, a housewife with "learning" was drafted to take charge. School texts were scarce and the children learned their lessons from whatever books their parents happened to have. Sometimes this was the family Bible or a worn volume of Shakespeare, occasionally a copy of an eastern newspaper, and not infrequently an almanac.

In 1855 members of the first Territorial legislature adopted the Missouri statutes for use in the Kansas Territory. These provided for the establishment of public schools "free and open to whites." When the first Free State legislature met at Lawrence in 1858, these laws were revised.

Possessing the deep-rooted Yankee conception of schools as neighborhood affairs, the lawmakers created a system of school districts administered by county superintendents and a Territorial superintendent of schools. To the county superintendent they gave the power of creating and altering the school districts; the individual districts, with their personnel and tax problems, were put under the control of local school boards. For the upkeep of the new school districts, the lawmakers levied a tax upon real and personal property, requiring each district to maintain schools entirely from its tax-derived revenues.

Each succeeding legislature has added to the Kansas school laws until today the system is a patchwork. The State constitution, drawn up in 1859, provided for "equal educational advantages for white and colored," and for "males and females alike." An additional clause provided for a State university at some "eligible and sensible point," and for months after the admittance of the State into the Union the problem of location agitated many ambitious Kansas towns.

The University of Kansas was founded at Lawrence in 1865. According to the original plans, the institution was to have been divided into male and female branches—the latter separate from the college proper and taught by women. But when classes began in 1866, with fifty men and five women enrolled, facilities were so limited that segregation was impracticable, and the university opened as the first co-educational institution of higher learning in Kansas.

Education at college and university level, in name at least, was a matter of great importance to early Kansans. Among the New England pioneers who came West to emancipate "bleeding Kansas" were many ardent young college graduates. Education in their minds ranked next in power to the press and the church, and they envisioned seats of learning comparable to the famous universities of the Eastern Seaboard and of Europe. Eastern churches hastened to strengthen their hold upon the new country by founding colleges, competing with town promoters for choice locations and subsidies. Eighteen universities and ten colleges were chartered by the Kansas legislature between 1858 and 1863. Only Highland College, at Highland, Baker University, at Baldwin, and St. Benedict's College, at Atchison, survive.

The Kansas State College of Agriculture and Applied Science was established at Manhattan as the Kansas State Agricultural College. Under the terms of the Morrill Act, approved by President Lincoln in 1862, Kan-

THE CAMPUS, UNIVERSITY OF KANSAS, LAWRENCE

sas was granted 90,000 acres of land for the founding of an institution "related to agricultural and mechanical arts." The institution opened its doors as a Federal land-grant college in 1863.

The State school for the blind, at Kansas City, the State school for the deaf, at Olathe, and the Emporia State Teachers' College, at Emporia, were established by legislative action in the 1860's. A compulsory education law, for children between the ages of eight and fourteen, was passed in 1874. As part of the prohibition movement, provision was made in 1885 for courses in hygiene, "to be taught with special reference to the effects of alcoholic and narcotic stimulants."

Up to this time Kansas had followed the example of eastern States in school legislation, but in the 1880's the State legislature took an independent step by providing for a State-wide system of county high schools in counties of more than 5,000 population. The first was built at Chapman in 1889. Within a few years legislatures in almost every State in the Union had enacted similar bills.

In the late 1890's Kansas took the initiative by adding manual training courses to the Pittsburg public school curriculum. By the end of the century, courses in sewing, cooking, and woodworking had been introduced into the better-equipped schools in towns throughout the State. The Pittsburg State Teachers' College, established by a legislative act of 1903, pioneered in preparing manual training teachers. In the previous year the legislature also founded Fort Hays State College, which occupies a portion of the land once included in the old Fort Hays Military Reservation.

With the turn of the century, enrollment soared and the construction of school buildings boomed. The new and larger plants contained auditoriums, gymnasiums, theaters, swimming pools, and libraries. Vocational agriculture and home economics appeared in their curricula as a result of the Smith-Hughes Act of 1917, providing Federal support for vocational education. The so-called practical subjects—stenography, bookkeeping, and business correspondence—were stressed. The number of school districts multiplied with the organization of new counties until more than 9,000 of them were spread over the State.

There has been a gradual trend toward centralization of education and consolidation of schools. A State school commission was created in 1913, and in 1916 state educational, charitable, and penal institutions were brought together under a single board of administration. Nine years later (1925) all higher education institutions were put under the control of a board of regents, composed of nine members appointed by the Governor, and serving without remuneration. Consolidation of rural schools, though expedient, has not proceeded rapidly. Failure to consolidate, according to a report of the Kansas State Planning Board (*Rural Schools in Kansas: March 1935*) is due to the fact that "the rural school serves not only educational needs, but acts as a political and social center for the community and has a strong hold on the sentiments of the people." There are approximately 8,600 school districts, spread over the State with little regard for wealth or number of pupils, and each still possesses the individual powers designated by the Third Territorial legislature. More than 3,000 districts have a taxable value of less than $150,000, and in 1,000 districts, schools average less than six pupils.

The study referred to above reported on 8,217 schools out of 8,326 organized and operating in cities of the third class and in rural districts. It found an enrollment of 207,377 (December 1934), though the normal capacity of the schools was 331,194. The 1935 legislature passed a law permitting school districts to share the expenses of maintaining one school for two or more districts, while otherwise retaining their separate identities.

Financial difficulties resulted in a wide disparity in school taxes, and in-

NORTH HIGH SCHOOL, WICHITA

equalities in equipment, teaching standards, and educational opportunities in general. Public schools ranged from the magnificent $2,600,000 Wyandotte High School in Kansas City, to one-room buildings, of which there were 7,000 in 1934.

The only State school aid, up to 1937, was from the proceeds of the dog tax and the interest on the permanent school fund. In this year, after decades of discussion in legislative halls, at political meetings, and on campaign platforms about the "evils of the Kansas school system," the State legislature provided that $2,500,000 be appropriated annually between 1937 and 1939 from a State sales tax for the aid of needy elementary schools. The fund is distributed by the State superintendent of public instruction.

High schools in the small towns are often centers of social activities for young and old alike. Conscientious and hardworking teachers prepare schedules of debates, dramatic and musical productions, and athletic events, which draw large crowds and generally provide for the purchase of school equipment. In the early 1930's high school bands developed, glorious in their bright uniforms, and plumed hats. These groups of boys and girls parade resplendently behind a high-stepping student bandmaster, and enliven county and State fairs, inaugurals, and holiday celebrations. Trips with the band to surrounding towns and the State capital are cherished ambitions of high school music students.

Comparatively new in the Kansas educational system is the municipal junior college. Thirteen are maintained, with an approximate attendance of 4,000, and eight similar institutions are under parochial control.

In addition to the five State colleges financed by biennial legislative appropriations, there are eighteen private institutions of higher learning; but the enrollment of the latter group is equal to only one-third of the total for colleges. Four are Catholic institutions, three Methodist, while the Mennonites, Quakers, Baptists, Presbyterians, and Dunkards each sponsor one or more. These institutions are supported from tuition fees, private contributions, and small endowments.

Wichita Municipal University, formerly Fairmount College, was acquired by the city at a special election in 1926. It is the only municipally owned institution of higher learning in Kansas. Since 1926 its enrollment has grown from 400 to approximately 2,000, including 700 Wichita citizens in its extension department.

Adult education, through public night schools and the extension service offered by the State university and other State-maintained colleges, has developed rapidly in Kansas since the early 1920's. Many of the larger cities offer vocational training and academic courses in public night schools, sponsored by the board of education. The Topeka night school, which opened in 1926 with an enrollment of 634, reached an attendance peak of 2,248 in 1933. In 1936 a total of 4,443 persons were enrolled in vocational education classes throughout the State.

The State-wide educational program, sponsored by the Works Progress Administration, has enabled many districts with inadequate funds to offer adult education. On August 1, 1937, there were 18,709 persons enrolled in eleven types of classes at 567 educational centers. Courses included literacy and naturalization, workers' education, public affairs, parent education, homemaking, vocational education, leisure time activities, correspondence instruction, nursery schools, general adult education, and freshman college subjects.

Religion

THE first churchman of whom there is any authentic record in the region now known as Kansas was a Franciscan friar, Father Juan de Padilla, who accompanied Coronado's expedition to Quivira in 1541. He returned to Mexico with the expedition, but journeyed back to spread Christianity among the Plains Indian tribes. It is said that he was murdered by the Quivirans because of his decision to leave them and preach to another tribe. According to some accounts, however, the martyred friar was murdered by his own men.

Almost three centuries elapsed between the death of Father Padilla and any organized efforts to establish the Christian religion in Kansas. In 1822 the Bishop of New Orleans appointed Father Charles de la Croix as a missionary to the Osage. He is known to have visited the Osages living along the Neosho River, and on May 5, 1822, he performed the first recorded baptism in Kansas—that of Antoine Chouteau, a five-year-old half-breed child. Three missions were built among the Osage by the Presbyterian Church in the early 1820's.

In 1830 the Reverend Thomas Johnson, as representative of the Methodist Church, founded Shawnee Mission *(see Tour 4),* the largest and most influential religious outpost in the State. Soon afterward the Baptists and the Friends established missions a few miles west of Shawnee. In 1836 the Roman Catholic Church successfully established a mission among the Kickapoo, in what is now Leavenworth County.

When the first settlers began to arrive, in the early 1850's, nine missions had established churches, schools, and dwellings in the prairie wilderness. Almost a score of others had come and gone in the quarter-century preceding settlement.

With the passage of the Kansas-Nebraska Bill, which created the Kansas Territory and left to residents the disposition of slavery within its borders, a wave of anti-slavery sentiment swept many New Englanders into Kansas. The church press was scathing in its denunciation of the Kansas-Nebraska Bill. Ministers throughout New England appealed eloquently before their congregations to "take up the torch of freedom for bleeding

Kansas." Northern ministers and churches co-operated with the promoters of the New England Emigrant Aid Company in organizing emigration to the Territory.

Thus the slavery issue was bound up with the development of religious groups. The first great movement of emigrants began in the spring of 1854. Members of the New England Company founded Lawrence, the first Free State town in the Territory. The Reverend S. Y. Lum held church services when the town was nothing more than a cluster of camps on the river bank, and ten weeks after settlement began he organized in a hay house (a tentlike structure of poles thatched with wild grass) the first church for white people in Kansas. This organization survives today as the Plymouth Congregational Church.

In addition to the New England Emigrant Aid Company, a number of individual church groups supported abolitionist colonies in the early 1850's. Most widely known of these was the Beecher Bible and Rifle Colony, sponsored by the Congregational minister, Henry Ward Beecher, and so named because Beecher presented each man with a Bible and a rifle "to defend his faith and his ideas of freedom." The colony founded the Free State town of Wabausnee and the Beecher Bible and Rifle Church *(see Tour 3)*, still in existence.

Another Congregational group was the "Kansas Band," consisting of four ardent young abolitionists—Richard Cordley, Sylvester Storrs, Grosvenor Morse, and Rosewell Parker. Graduates of Andover Theological Seminary, they came to Kansas in 1856 to become leaders in the fight for freedom. As pastor of the Plymouth Congregational Church in Lawrence, Cordley became known throughout the Territory as the "abolition preacher." He escaped death by fleeing across the river when Quantrill and his men sacked and burned the town of Lawrence in 1863.

The Ottawa Baptist Mission in Franklin County also became a stronghold for Free Staters in the late 1850's, and churches in the Free State towns of Topeka, Big Springs, Osawatomie, and Manhattan gave freely of money and supplies to aid the cause.

With the close of the Civil War and the end of the struggle over slavery, the church became the center of community life in Kansas. From humble beginnings in dugouts, hay houses, or the open prairie, it developed with the growth of settlement. In communities where there were no ministers, residents gathered to read the Bible and sing hymns on Sunday; and on isolated claims, women often set the Sabbath day apart in thoughtful observance.

It was during these later decades of the century that Kansas, with its broad acres of unclaimed land, became a mecca for European colonists in search of religious freedom or of homes.

In the early 1870's, approximately 400 families of Mennonites (about 1,900 persons) migrated to Kansas from southern Russia and settled in Reno, Harvey, Marion, and McPherson Counties. With prosperous churches scattered over the region, their sect numbered approximately 11,-000 members, according to the latest U. S. Census figures *(Religious Bodies: 1926)*. German-Russians who came to Kansas from the lower Volga region at about the same time, and settled on the rolling plains country of Rush and Ellis Counties, were chiefly Roman Catholics. They established their own villages and, with much labor and sacrifice, erected large stone churches with colored windows and carved interiors, which rise from the prairie, their spires visible for miles *(see Tour 3)*. The settlers gave their best to the church, even depriving their families of necessities to do so.

Although not drawn to Kansas by a desire for personal or religious freedom, as were the immigrants from Russia, colonies of Swedish Lutherans settled in McPherson and Saline Counties in the 1860's and 1870's. Lindsborg is today the center of Lutheranism in the State.

Negroes, newly emancipated, migrated to Kansas from the South, and were helped in adjusting themselves to their new home by Presbyterian and Congregationalist ministers. In addition to the missions and churches organized by these workers, the Negroes independently established Methodist and Baptist churches.

The temperance issue and the fight for prohibition profoundly affected the Kansas churches from the close of the Civil War to the present day. Church organizations, especially those affiliated with the Methodist, Baptist, and Presbyterian faiths, had joined forces with temperance workers, shortly after the Territory was opened for settlement. At its first meeting, in 1861, the members of the Christian Temperance Union resolved:

"That we look to the churches of our State for earnest co-operation in the work of temperance.

"That we invite and expect all ministers of the gospel to actively support our cause and hope that in every part of the State they will take immediate steps to organize auxiliary societies."

Kansas churches accepted the invitation, and many were active in the campaign for a prohibition amendment to the State constitution. In 1879, when the amendment passed both houses of the legislature, a great mass meeting was held in Topeka at which, according to contemporary accounts, "pastors of the various churches were present and took active part in the discussion of the best means of bringing prohibition to the State." The amendment was ratified in the general election of 1880, with great rejoicing in the churches throughout the State.

Temperance was the opening wedge for a general cleaning up of the boisterous, wide-open "cow towns" of the period. Church members—especially women—were the shock troops that drove out gamblers and other undesirable elements, and intemperance was only one of the evils against which the crusade was waged.

Since then the churches have been the leaders in prohibition activities. When the State legislature submitted a repeal amendment to the voters at the general election of 1934, it was due to church efforts that the dry organizations succeeded in stemming the tide of anti-prohibition sentiment in Kansas.

According to the United States Census *(Religious Bodies: 1926)* there were 4,530 church organizations in Kansas. Of these, 1,242 were urban and 3,288 rural. Church membership totaled 747,078, divided almost equally between urban and rural organizations. The three leading denominations with their membership were Methodist Episcopal, 177,165 (all Methodist bodies, 190,894; Roman Catholic, 171,178; Disciples of Christ, 77,409. Membership in Baptist bodies numbered 70,838, in Presbyterian, 56,667 and in Lutheran, 53,751. Membership in Protestant Episcopal churches numbered 9,623, and in Jewish congregations approximately 5,000. Of the total church membership, 28,292 were Negro communicants, including 15,357 Baptists and 10,069 Methodists, with the remainder divided among a score of other denominations. The Negroes supported 328 churches, of which 213 were urban and 115 rural.

The number of church organizations decreased between 1906 and 1926. This was due, probably, to the abandonment of some rural churches when roads improved and the automobile came into general use, and also to the tendency toward consolidation of churches. During the same twenty year period there was an increase of 272,442 in total church membership.

Sports and Recreation

THE scarcity of natural water areas and the need for water conservation and flood control led indirectly to the development of the State's chief recreational asset—its State parks. A plan to establish a system of parks, in connection with the construction of artificial lakes, was first proposed in 1923 by a group of sportsmen and conservationists. Through their efforts the State forestry, fish and game commission was organized in 1925 and necessary legislation was passed to begin a lake-building program in Neosho County. Sportsmen in that and adjacent Labette County donated 215 acres of land to the commission and a dam was built in 1927, impounding 95 acres of water.

The first lakes were financed entirely by State funds. When the Federal relief agencies launched a water conservation program in 1932, Kansas promptly took advantage of that assistance. The Works Progress Administration and the Civilian Conservation Corps have co-operated in developing lakes and surrounding park areas. There are now (1938) twenty-five State parks, the largest of which is in Kingman County (1,562 acres). Artificial lakes are the nuclei of the majority of these parks and, in addition, hundreds of smaller lakes of twenty acres or less have been completed. The Kansas State lake plan has been adopted in neighboring Missouri and Oklahoma.

The State lakes are stocked with fish from the State hatchery at Pratt *(see Tour 5)*, which propagates bass, drum, crappie, bluegill, bull head, yellow perch, and channel cat. These fish are also indigenous to many Kansas creeks and rivers. Besides fishing, the State lakes and parks have facilities for boating, swimming, and camping.

Pioneer hunters and trappers found vast quantities of game and other wild life in Kansas. Gradually many species became extinct or greatly diminished in number. The program of the forestry, fish and game commission has restored a small fraction of the State's game, and increased the opportunities for good hunting. The commission has established a public shooting ground near Jamestown, Republic County, where the water area, normally 765 acres, lies in salt marshlands. There are 40 blinds, each ac-

JAYHAWKERS IN ACTION, UNIVERSITY OF KANSAS

commodating two hunters. A nominal fee is charged for the use of blinds and decoys. The commission also maintains quail farms near Calista and Pittsburg, and a 3,200 acre tract in Finney County which serves as a buffalo range and a prairie chicken preserve.

The supply of quail and prairie chicken has been steadily enlarged, but these game birds still need the protection of a short season. Found in great numbers, and consequently hunted during longer open seasons, are 'coon, squirrels, and mourning doves. Duck hunting in season is popular at the State lakes and along the larger streams.

The jackrabbit drive is peculiar to western Kansas. Advertised for days in advance by handbills and local newspapers, the drive usually starts on Sunday and is attended by great crowds of spectators. A certain area, covering perhaps thousands of acres, is surrounded by beaters armed with clubs and sticks; guns are banned. Hundreds of people take part. Slowly the lines close in on all sides, flushing the rabbits into a large pen or wire enclosure at a central point, where they are clubbed to death. The daily "kill," which in many instances exceeds 6,500, is reported by the local press. Denounced in other sections as a sadistic display, the drive is de-

fended in the western part of the State as an economic necessity, since the
rabbits feed on green wheat.

Similar to the rabbit drive in plan and purpose is the wolf or coyote
drive. A common event in earlier years, these drives were revived in certain regions of Kansas after 1930, when the suspension of bounties by
economizing county governments resulted in a mounting loss of small livestock. A modern touch was recently added when coyote hunters in Franklin County used a low-flying airplane to spot their quarry.

The most popular drives in Kansas, however, are those made with golf
clubs and tennis rackets. Five State-wide golf tournaments are held each
year. A State tennis meet is held annually at Independence, and an interscholastic tournament is held at Emporia. Invitation tennis meets are scheduled each season at Wichita, Dodge City, McPherson, and other cities.

Football, an intercollegiate sport of Kansas colleges since the early
1890's, is now on the athletic program of 400 Kansas high schools. A
so-called "clinical" game, employing rules that marked the beginning of
the transition from the old "push-and-pull" kind of football to the modern open game, was played at Wichita in 1905. The first forward pass in
American football history was attempted and completed in this trial game.

The Thanksgiving Day Football game between the University of Kansas
and the University of Missouri is a traditional contest that dates from
1891. The game is played at the Missouri field and the Kansas Stadium in
alternate years. The annual game between the Kansas State College and
the University of Kansas, played alternately at Lawrence and Manhattan,
is of State-wide interest.

Basketball is the most popular team sport in Kansas. The game was invented by a Kansan, Dr. James L. Naismith of the Physical Education Department of the University of Kansas, in collaboration with Luther H.
Gulick. Kansas basketball teams have thrice won first place in the national
high school tournament, and the University of Kansas is a perennial leader
in the Big Six conference. The annual national tournament for women's
basketball teams is held in March at Wichita.

Kansas is represented in professional baseball by the Salina Millers and
the Hutchinson Larks of the Western Association. The National Semi-
Professional Baseball Congress is held annually at Wichita. State-wide
amateur leagues include the Ban Johnson League for youths, and the
American Legion Junior League for boys between thirteen and sixteen.
Softball, said to have been invented at Topeka in April 1916 by employees
of the Santa Fe Railway, is very popular in the larger cities.

The University of Kansas Relays, a two-day track and field carnival held

INDIAN BOXING TEAM, HASKELL INSTITUTE, LAWRENCE

in the latter part of April at the university stadium in Lawrence, is an event of national interest. Established in 1924, soon after the completion of the stadium, this meet has become a rendezvous for internationally known athletes. Among those who have competed in the Kansas Relays are Jim Bausch of Wichita, 1932 Olympic decathlon champion; Glenn Cunningham of Elkhart, holder of the world's record for the mile and a member of the Olympic team in 1932 and 1936; and Archie San Romani of Pittsburg, middle-distance runner and a member of the 1936 Olympic team.

Professional boxing bouts are infrequent in Kansas, but professional wrestling matches are held at Topeka, Wichita, Pittsburg, Kansas City and Hutchinson. Amateur boxing is popular at Kansas State College, Kansas University, Haskell Institute, and St. Benedict's College. A wrestling tournament is conducted annually by the Kansas High School Association.

Harness racing, a highly developed and popular sport which declined between 1929 and 1934, has enjoyed a recent revival. Race meetings are held at various county affairs and at the Topeka and Hutchinson State Fairs. Spring and autumn coursing meets are held at Abilene. Dog and horse races are annual features at Dodge City. Lawrin, winner of the Kentucky Derby in 1938, was foaled and trained at the Woolford Farms of Herbert Wolf in Johnson County. Polo, almost unknown in the Middle West until a few years ago, is played at Topeka, Wichita, and other major cities.

Acutely aware that its chief places of recreation were the corner lot and the malarial "swimmin' hole," urban Kansas, beginning with the establishment of a playground system at Topeka in 1912, turned its attention toward acquiring suitable recreational facilities. Today there is scarcely a town with a population of more than 1,500 that lacks a golf course, a swimming pool, tennis courts, and baseball diamonds. A recreational program is now being carried on by the WPA in 121 communities.

Journalism and Journalists

JOTHAM MEEKER, a Baptist missionary connected with the Shawnee Indian Mission near the present site of Kansas City, established the first newspaper published in what is now Kansas. Meeker, a printer as well as a minister of the Gospel, came to Shawnee Mission early in 1833 and (according to his diary) began setting type on the first issue of the *Shawnee Sun* on February 18, 1835. This first issue appeared six days later. The *Sun,* a monthly publication, was printed in the native language of the Shawnee tribe, and was the second newspaper to be published in an Indian language—the first being the *Cherokee Phoenix* (1828), issued in the South. No copies of the *Sun's* early issues are known to be in existence; but a copy of one of the later issues, dated November 1841, was found in Kansas City a few years ago.

On September 15, 1854, shortly after the opening of Kansas Territory to settlement, a second newspaper, the *Kansas Weekly Herald,* made its appearance at Leavenworth. Evidently the press proposed to lead rather than to follow the course of progress, for few signs of civilization were visible on the town site of Leavenworth at that time. This departure from usual journalistic practice was criticized by some as preposterous, but most residents of the Territory saw nothing out of the ordinary in the fact that the printing press should thus precede other activities.

The clash between opposing forces within the Territory on the issue of slavery provided the pioneer Kansas editors with abundant copy. Ardent champions as they were of one side or the other in this conflict, the editors actually helped to make the news they reported. During the years of bitter strife that followed the opening of the Territory, printing offices were wrecked or burned by warring factions and their presses demolished or thrown into nearby streams. Lawrence newspapers suffered this fate when the notorious Sheriff Jones and his men sacked the town on May 21, 1856. Jones's men destroyed the plant of the *Herald of Freedom,* edited by Dr.

THE COUNTRY EDITOR—WILLIAM ALLEN WHITE

George W. Brown, smashing the press and throwing type and other equipment in the Kaw River.

The *Kansas Free State,* established January 5, 1855, by Josiah Miller and R. G. Elliott, suffered a similar fate at the hands of the Lecompton raiders and was never revived. Miller, a native of South Carolina, had left that State because of his opposition to slavery. The "border ruffians" considered him fair game on account of his southern origin and arrested him for treason against the State of South Carolina. Acquitted of the charge, he stumped several of the northern States for Frémont during the Presidential campaign of 1856. Returning to Lawrence in the following year, he was elected probate judge and later State senator from Douglas County. Thus the tradition of the Kansas newspaper man as a political leader was early established. A notable example of this tradition was John J. Ingalls who edited the Atchison *Champion* during the Civil War period (1863–6). An important figure in Territorial and State politics, Ingalls was United States Senator from Kansas from 1873 until his defeat by the Populists in 1890. From that time until his death ten years later he devoted himself chiefly to literature and journalism.

In spite of raids and wreckings, the pioneer press developed steadily, and by 1858 there were 22 newspapers in the Territory. This number had increased at the close of the Civil War to 37—exactly as many as existed in the country as a whole at the time of the Declaration of Independence, a coincidence upon which Kansas newspapers like to dwell. Kansas had been torn and desolated by years of strife, its economic life paralyzed, and its general development apparently hopelessly arrested. Newspapers played a major part in the phenomenal development of the next five years by reviving hope and confidence, encouraging immigration, and promoting industry. The State's population grew from 140,179 in 1865 to 362,307 in 1870, and the number of newspapers increased during the same period from 37 to 80.

Captain Henry King played a prominent part in the post-war period of Kansas journalism. A native of Illinois, he served in the Union Army throughout the Civil War and then returned to Illinois to edit the *Daily Whig* at Quincy. In 1869 he came to Topeka, where he edited successively the *State Record,* the *Commonwealth,* and the *Capital.* He was also the first editor of the *Kansas Magazine.* In 1883 he went to the St. Louis *Globe-Democrat* as contributing editor. Promoted to the managing editorship of the *Globe-Democrat* in 1897, he held that position until his death in 1915. Of Kansas journalists in the 1870's and early 1880's, Captain King has written as follows:

We had our rivalries and antipathies, but for the most part they were transient and subordinate, and did not cause any serious disturbance of the fundamental concord. It was in our politics, however, that we were most apt to disregard the impulses of brotherly love and patience. The Kansas newspapers had early manifested a partiality for aggressive and vociferous campaigns. They were fond of putting candidates under the harrow, as they called it—a process which they have not yet entirely abandoned, I am told. Even a toughened veteran like General Jim Lane had been lacerated to the point of calling for mercy from the Atchison *Champion* when Ingalls was editing it. "About the mildest term it ever applies to me," he said, "is miscreant."

The Topeka *State Record* was first published in 1859 by Edmund G. and W. W. Ross. Edmund Ross, while serving the unexpired term of Senator James H. Lane in the United States Senate, incurred the wrath of his constituents by voting in favor of President Andrew Johnson in the latter's impeachment trial. His political career ruined, Ross returned to his former profession and published the Lawrence *Standard* for a number of years.

Prominent among the earlier journalists of Kansas was Daniel W. Wilder, better known in later years for his *Annals of Kansas*. Wilder had settled in Kansas in Territorial days, becoming editor of the Elwood *Free Press* in 1858. In 1861 he became editor of the Leavenworth *Daily Conservative* and purchased Colonel Dan Anthony's interest in that newspaper when Anthony joined the army. He went to Rochester, New York, in 1865 to edit the *Evening Express,* but returned to the *Conservative* three years later. In 1871 he left Leavenworth for Fort Scott, where he became editor of the *Monitor*. In the following year he was elected State auditor, and won a reputation for reforms instituted in that office.

John A. Martin purchased the Atchison *Squatter Sovereign* in 1858 and changed its name to *Freedom's Champion*. During the war he served as lieutenant colonel and later as colonel of the Eighth Kansas Regiment. After his discharge from the service in 1864, he resumed his editorial position with the *Champion* and continued at that post until his election as Governor in 1885. He died in 1889, not long after his retirement from the governorship.

Noble L. Prentis, like Martin a native of Illinois and a Civil War veteran, was associated with Captain King on the Topeka *Record* and *Commonwealth,* was later editor of the Junction City *Union,* and during Colonel Martin's term as Governor (1885–1889) was proprietor of the *Champion* in Atchison. In 1888 he took charge of the Newton *Republican,* leaving that paper for a position on the staff of the Kansas City *Star* which he held until his death in 1900.

Another soldier-editor was Col. Daniel R. Anthony, who founded a

Kansas newspaper dynasty. As one of the proprietors of the Leavenworth *Conservative*, established in 1861, Anthony "scooped" the State press on the news of Kansas' admittance to the Union in that year. At the outbreak of the war he became lieutenant colonel of the Second Kansas Cavalry. After the war Anthony returned to newspaper work, and the Leavenworth *Times*, following its consolidation with several contemporaries, came under his control in 1872. Upon his death in 1904 his son, the late D. R. Anthony, Jr., Congressman for several terms from the First Kansas District, continued publication of the *Times*. The next of the line, D. R. Anthony, III, is publisher of the paper today (1938).

Also prominent in the early post-war period were Marshall M. Murdock, founder of the Wichita *Eagle* in 1872, Preston B. Plumb of the Emporia *Kansas News*, and Sol Miller of the Troy *Kansas Chief*. But these names are of minor importance in comparison with that of Edgar W. Howe, author of *The Story of a Country Town* and of numerous other books that have won for him a national reputation in addition to his fame as a journalist. Howe's newspaper career began in 1873, when at the age of nineteen he became editor and publisher of a newspaper in Golden, Colorado. Four years later he moved to Atchison and began publication in that city of the *Daily Globe*, which under his editorship and proprietorship was a potent force in Kansas journalism for more than a third of a century. Retiring from active newspaper work in 1911, Howe edited and published for several years a magazine called *E. W. Howe's Monthly*. He died at Atchison late in 1937.

Another Kansas editor and publisher of national reputation is Arthur Capper, who like Ed Howe entered newspaper work at the age of nineteen. Beginning as a typesetter on the Topeka *Daily Capital*, he worked upward on that journal through the successive stages of reporter, city editor, and Washington correspondent, to become its publisher and proprietor. In 1893 he assumed editorship of the North Topeka *Mail*, a weekly newspaper later consolidated with the *Kansas Breeze*, which was founded in 1894 by T. A. McNeal and edited jointly by McNeal and Capper. The latter soon established other publications, including *Capper's Weekly*, *Capper's Farmer*, and the *Household Magazine*.

As publisher of the *Capital*, Capper soon became closely identified with the Republican party in Kansas politics, and as that party's candidate he was elected Governor in 1914—the first native Kansan to hold this office. After serving a second term as Governor, he was elected to the United States Senate in 1918 and subsequently re-elected in 1924, 1930, and 1936.

Capper has been fortunate in his editorial assistants, such as the late Harold T. Chase and T. A. McNeal. Chase was editorial writer for the *Capital* from 1889 until shortly before his death in 1936, and his scholarly and keenly analytical writing received more than State-wide recognition. The association with T. A. McNeal, from whom Capper purchased the *Kansas Breeze* in 1895, has continued since that date. Tom McNeal is now (1938) the dean of Kansas editors. A native of Ohio, he came to Kansas in 1879 and was part owner of the Medicine Lodge *Cresset* for fifteen years. He served a term as mayor of Medicine Lodge, was later a member of the State legislature, and for six years held the office of State printer.

Unlike many of his journalistic contemporaries Frank P. McLennan, Capper's most prominent rival in the Topeka newspaper field, never aspired to public office. He came to Emporia from Ohio in the 1870's; published the Emporia *Daily News* with Jacob Stotler and Alexander Butts for several years, and then purchased the bankrupt Topeka *State Journal* at public auction in 1885. McLennan successfully conducted the *Journal* as an independent newspaper for nearly half a century. He also served for many years as vice president of the board of directors of the Associated Press, once remarking that he regarded that position as preferable to the office of United States Senator. He died in Topeka in 1933.

Capper was succeeded as Governor of Kansas in 1918 by Henry J. Allen, a Wichita publisher whose attempt to regulate labor disputes through the Kansas Industrial Court attracted national attention. Beginning as editor of the *Manhattan Nationalist* in 1894, Allen later acquired and operated several daily papers in smaller cities of Kansas. He published the Wichita *Daily Beacon* from 1907 until 1928, when he sold it to Max and Louis Levand. Shortly after the death of Frank P. McLennan in 1933, Allen became editor of the Topeka *State Journal*.

J. A. Wayland, who founded the *Appeal to Reason* at Girard in 1897, was a political journalist of a type seldom found in Kansas, where editors have been prone to promote themselves for public office and to align themselves with the dominant political group. Wayland was an ardent Socialist, and his *Appeal to Reason,* backed by a fortune acquired in Texas real estate speculation, soon became a national organ of the underprivileged. Wayland later leased the paper to Fred Warren, who continued its publication until 1912. E. Haldeman-Julius then took it over, changing its name to *Haldeman-Julius Weekly* in 1922, and later to the *New Appeal* and to its present title, the *American Freeman*.

For several decades, no name in the annals of Kansas journalism has been better known to the American public than that of William Allen White, "the sage of Emporia." Born in that city in 1868, White was reared in Butler County and learned the printer's trade in the office of the El Dorado *Republican*. In 1891, soon after graduation from the University of Kansas, he joined the editorial staff of the Kansas City *Journal,* and was later employed on the *Star* in the same city. In 1895 he purchased the Emporia *Gazette,* which he has owned and edited ever since.

With the publication in 1896 of his famous *Gazette* editorial, "What's the Matter with Kansas?" White achieved national renown almost overnight. Appearing in the midst of a heated Presidential campaign, it assailed the Populist movement then sweeping the Middle West and was given such widespread prominence by the Republican campaign managers that it played an important part in the election of McKinley.

Like Ed Howe of Atchison, White is no less well known as an author than as a journalist. A dozen books of fiction, biography, social and political commentary have appeared from his pen in the past forty years. He has also played an active part in politics and public affairs as an independent "progressive."

Not a few editors and writers who have risen to prominence elsewhere in the country began their careers in Kansas newspaper offices. Wesley Winans Stout, who in 1937 succeeded George Horace Lorimer as editor of the *Saturday Evening Post,* is a native of Junction City who left college in his freshman year to work on the Wichita *Beacon* and was later on the editorial staff of the Kansas City *Star.* Walt Mason, characterized by William Allen White as "the poet laureate of American democracy," wrote the first of his now widely syndicated "prose poems" as a staff worker on the Emporia *Gazette,* to which he had come after serving an apprenticeship on the Atchison *Globe.* Edwin S. Beck, a son of the pioneer Holton editor Moses M. Beck, has been managing editor of the Chicago *Tribune* since 1910. Will T. Beck, a younger son, has continued publication of the Holton *Recorder,* which his father purchased in 1881.

The Kansas City *Star,* although a Missouri newspaper, has often been a potent factor in molding public opinion in Kansas. The late William Rockhill Nelson, founder of the *Star,* soon learned that Republican Kansas offered a more fruitful field for his political theories than traditionally Democratic Missouri. Nelson's successors have continued his editorial policies, and the *Star* has been identified with the liberal element in Kansas Republicanism.

The indomitable spirit of the pioneer editor still prevails in Kansas journalism. Recent years of unprecedented drought and agricultural depression have not daunted the State's press. And, as has been demonstrated in recent political campaigns, Kansas editors have lost none of their traditional trenchancy. More than 700 newspapers and other periodicals, published in Kansas in 1937, included 61 dailies, 497 weeklies (five of which were published by Negroes), 71 monthlies, and 21 quarterlies.

Realizing that the most accurate and complete history of any community lies in its newspapers, Kansas editors have co-operated with the State Historical Society in preserving their issues for students of Kansas history. The periodical section of the society possesses the most complete files of the State's newspapers in this country. In many instances the society's file of a paper is the only one extant. In January 1937 the State Historical Society had 44,307 bound volumes of Kansas periodicals.

Literature

THE first writing inspired by the region comprised in the present State of Kansas was the journal of Pedro de Castañeda de Najera, who in 1541 accompanied the Spanish explorer Coronado on the latter's march through this region in search of the semi-legendary city or province of Quivira. In the three centuries between Coronado's futile quest and the early settlement of Kansas, the region was traversed by other explorers, some of whom—notably, among the later travelers, Etienne Bourgmont, Lewis and Clark and their aide Patrick Gass, and Zebulon M. Pike—have given us factual records of the region in their published journals.

When Kansas became a territory in 1854, the issue between Free Soil and pro-slavery settlers generated a conflict and a debate that raged for several years with the fierce intensity of a prairie fire. The Free Soil cause found its most eloquent literary expression in the writings and speeches of the great New England abolitionists—William Lloyd Garrison, Wendell Phillips, and the poet Whittier. The latter's stirring song of "The Kansas Emigrants" was a rallying hymn for hundreds of New England emigrants, both on the westward march and in their new home. Noteworthy also were Whittier's bitterly satiric "Letter from a missionary of the Methodist Episcopal Church South, in Kansas, to a distinguished politician," his verses on the burial of Thomas Barber, shot December 6, 1855, near Lawrence, and the poem "For Righteousness' Sake" inscribed "to friends under arrest for treason against the slave power." Within the Territory itself, the only authentic literary note in the struggle was struck by Richard Realf, a gifted young English poet who emigrated to Kansas in 1857 and in the course of about a year's residence there contributed several ardent anti-slavery poems to various Kansas newspapers.

The first novel to be written with Kansas as a setting was Emerson Bennett's *The Border Rover* (1857), a blood-and-thunder narrative of heroic settlers and ferocious Indians. Ten years later appeared Evender C. Kennedy's *Osseo, the Spectre Chieftain*, a poem in eight cantos which has the distinction of being the first literary work produced by a permanent resident of Kansas. This was followed five years later by Annie Nelles' *Ravenia, or The Outcast Redeemed.* These extravagances reflected little of the actual Kansas scene and had small literary merit.

Historical and descriptive narratives were prominent in the output of Kansas writers during the last half of the nineteenth century. One of the earliest books in this field was Sara T. D. Robinson's *Kansas: Its Interior and Exterior Life* (1856). Mary E. Jackson turned to past events with *The Spy of Osawatomie; or, The Mysterious Companions of Old John Brown* (1881); and in his *Gleanings from Western Prairies* (1882), the Reverend W. E. Youngman recalled the experiences of a year spent on a frontier ranch in Kansas. Colonel Henry Inman, who had served at various Kansas army posts in the 1850's and 1860's, drew largely upon personal observation and experience in a long list of books written after he retired from the Army and settled down at Larned. With a biography of Senator James Henry Lane (1899), William E. Connelley began an extensive series of studies in Kansas history, biography, and ethnology, including a five-volume history of the State and its people.

One of the few Kansas writers preoccupied with the common life of his own time in the century's later decades was Edgar Watson Howe, editor and proprietor of the Atchison *Globe* from 1877 to 1911. His *Story of a Country Town,* after rejection by several publishers, was privately printed in 1883, and has since achieved a permanent place in American literature. It is a realistic picture of a small prairie town, with emphasis on the more somber phases of midwestern life in the 1860's and 1870's. Howe retired from active newspaper work in 1911, devoting himself thenceforth to authorship, to travel, and (until 1933) to editing and publishing *E. W. Howe's Monthly.* From his home on "Potato Hill" near Atchison he put forth no fewer than twenty-five books, several of which are collections of travel letters. His frank autobiography, *Plain People,* appeared in 1929; and his last book, *Final Conclusions,* was published shortly before his death in 1937.

Despite the common concern with politics, prohibition, and real estate speculation in Kansas of the 1880's and 1890's, the muses were not wholly silent during this period. With his clever verse in both humorous and serious vein, Eugene F. Ware made the pseudonym of "Ironquill" familiar to an audience that extended far beyond the borders of his own State. Collected in book form, the *Rhymes of Ironquill* appeared in 1885, and an enlarged edition was published in 1899. Another popular purveyor of homespun philosophy in verse, Walt Mason, whose "prose poems" have

long been a familiar syndicated feature in hundreds of American newspapers and have been reprinted in ten or a dozen volumes, began writing
for the Atchison *Globe* in 1885. For many years after 1907, Mr. Mason
was associated with William Allen White on the Emporia *Gazette*. In the
last decade of the century, Charles Moreau Harger, then a youthful newspaper editor in Abilene, frequently turned his pen to poetry; and Florence
L. Snow of Neosho Falls wrote a collection of sonnets published under
the title, *The Lamp of Gold*. The first literary appearance of William
Allen White and Albert Bigelow Paine was made with their *Rhymes by
Two Friends* (1893). But the outstanding poetic achievement of this
period was a single poem by John J. Ingalls, who represented Kansas in
the United States Senate from 1873 to 1891. His "Opportunity," written
in 1891 and since reprinted in many standard anthologies, is considered
by competent critics to be one of the finest sonnets in nineteenth century
American literature.

William Allen White, long editor of the Emporia *Gazette* and best
known of contemporary Kansas writers, came suddenly into national
prominence in 1896 with the publication of a newspaper editorial entitled
"What's the Matter with Kansas?" In the same year he put forth his first
independent book, *The Real Issue and Other Stories*. This was followed
by *The Court of Boyville* (1899), a keen depiction of the adolescent
American male; *Stratagems and Spoils* (1901); and *In Our Town*
(1906), which first displayed his unusual ability for portraying typical
small-town life. His most important full-length novels are *A Certain Rich
Man* (1909) and *In the Heart of a Fool* (1918). In later years, he turned
definitely to the field of public affairs with such books as *Politics: The
Citizen's Business* (1924), *Woodrow Wilson* (1924), *Calvin Coolidge*
(1925), and *Masks in a Pageant* (1928), the last a series of character
studies of political leaders whom the author had known more or less
intimately. Mr. White's neglect, during the last two decades, of the notable creative talent evidenced in his earlier books has been often deplored.
"Had it not been for his uncontrolled urge to be a man of action,"
remarks W. G. Clugston, a Kansas commentator, "he might have been
not only Kansas' first man of letters but also one of America's outstanding
creative artists."

In the same year that William Allen White attained national fame with
a newspaper editorial, the Reverend Charles M. Sheldon of Topeka sprang
into equal prominence with a religious novel entitled *In His Steps*, which
deals with the theme of what Jesus might do if confronted with the

problems of a business man in a small midwestern city. Although this book had world-wide circulation, a defective copyright deprived Doctor Sheldon of royalties. He has subsequently written more than thirty novels, most of which were read serially to his congregation before publication.

Second only to Doctor Sheldon among Kansas novelists with respect to prolific output is Mrs. Margaret Hill McCarter, who has made generous use in her books of material from the State's history. Beginning in 1903 with *The Cottonwood's Story,* the list of her writings comprises more than a dozen titles, perhaps the best known of which are *The Price of the Prairies* (1910), a story of Civil War Kansas, and *A Wall of Men* (1912), a romance of the Free Soil struggle. The lights and shadows of Kansas life in the opening decades of the present century are skilfully limned by Dell H. Munger in *Wind before the Dawn* (1914), a realistic tale of prairie farm life. Of somewhat similar character is *Dust* (1921), by Mr. and Mrs. E. Haldeman-Julius, who are also the authors of a later novel entitled *Violence.*

Two of the State's most distinguished writers seem to have bequeathed much of their literary ability to a second generation. Mateel Howe Farnham, daughter of E. W. Howe, was awarded the first prize of $10,000 in Dodd, Mead & Company's 1927 fiction contest for her novel entitled *Rebellion;* and William L. White, son of "the sage of Emporia," has recently created a sensation in Kansas literary and political circles with his first novel, *What People Said* (1938), the plot of which has to do with a financial scandal that rocked the State in 1933. Mrs. Farnham, by the way, is not the only Kansas author who has won the Dodd, Mead & Company prize; in 1933 it went to Mrs. L. M. Alexander of Baldwin for her novel, *Candy.*

Sunflowers, privately printed by Willard Wattles in 1914, is the earliest among several anthologies of Kansas poetry. It made a brave showing for the prairie muse with such selections as Ingalls' "Opportunity," W. H. Carruth's "Each in His Own Tongue," Eugene F. Ware's "John Brown" and "Three States," Ellen P. Allerton's "Walls of Corn," Harry Kemp's "A Wheat Field Phantasy," Wattles' "Carrie Nation" and "Challenge to Youth," Sol Miller's "Pawpaws Ripe," and Charles L. Edson's "My Sage-Brush Girl" with its fine lines:

> I know who wielded the flaming sword that drove my tribe before me
> Into the dusty desert wide, where all the flowers are dead;
> Know why we met in a rainless land when the dream of dreams came
> o'er me;
> We were the disinherited kin of the lords of meat and bread.

Two later anthologies are *Contemporary Kansas Poetry* (1927), edited by Helen Rhoda Hoopes, and *Kansas Poets* (1935), edited by Henry Harrison. Many of the selections in these volumes originally appeared in *The Harp,* a magazine of verse established at Larned in 1925 by Dr. Israel Newman. Mr. and Mrs. Leslie Wallace assumed its management in 1926, with May Williams Ward as editor, and it continued under these auspices until its demise in 1932. Its editor received the Poetry Society of America award in 1937 for her *Dust Bowl* sequence.

Esther Clark Hill, who assisted Willard Wattles in preparing the first anthology of Kansas poetry, had several volumes of verse to her credit at the time of her death in 1932. In Whitelaw Saunders' *What Laughing God?* published by the Poetry Society of Kansas in 1936, and Kenneth Porter's *The High Plains* (1938), the collected work of two gifted Kansas poets has been given permanent form.

Contemporary Kansas literature, according to Nelson Antrim Crawford, is what might be expected "of a State with the population of Kansas, its geographical position, and its recent history." And he adds: "I for one should be glad if Kansas literature would take off its cap and gown and hood and be frankly drunk with the juice of art." In truth, much of that literature has emanated from writers of pronounced academic background and is invested with a pronounced classroom sobriety. But happily Mr. Crawford's own work is characterized by no spirit of dusty scholarship. After serving for several years as head of the department of journalism at Kansas State College, he has since given most of his time to writing and editing. His "Carrying of the Ghost" won the Kansas poetry award in 1920, and among his novels are *A Man of Learning* (1928) and *Unhappy Wind* (1930)—the former a sharp satire on the American educator.

Neither can any taint of acute academicism be rightfully attributed to the work of William Herbert Carruth, for more than thirty years professor of modern languages and literature at the University of Kansas. In addition to much professional work as writer and editor, Professor Carruth found time to compile a two-volume anthology of *Kansas in Literature* (1900) and to create such books of general interest as *Letters to American Boys* (1907), *Each in His Own Tongue and Other Poems* (1909), and *Verse Writing* (1917). With the single exception of Ingalls' "Opportunity," no poem by a Kansas author has been so widely and frequently quoted as "Each in His Own Tongue," which begins:

A Fire-Mist and a planet,—
    A crystal and a cell,—
A jelly-fish and a saurian,
    And caves where the cave-men dwell;
Then a sense of law and beauty,
    And a face turned from the clod,—
Some call it Evolution,
    And others call it God.

Numerous others besides Professor Carruth have helped to make the university at Lawrence a notable center of activity in scholarly and creative writing, although only a few can be mentioned here. Frank W. Blackmar, dean of the Graduate School for many years after 1896, has a long list of historical and sociological studies to his credit, including *The Story of Human Progress* (1896), *a History of Higher Education in Kansas* (1900), and *Life of Charles Robinson, First Governor of Kansas* (1902); he also edited the *Cyclopedia of History of Kansas*. Frank H. Hodder, chosen head of the department of history and political science in 1908, is author of *The Civil Government of Kansas* (1895) and *Outlines of American History* (1911), and editor of *Audubon's Western Journal* (1905). While occupying a prominent post in the history department from 1902 to 1916, Carl L. Becker published *Political Parties in the Province of New York, 1760–1775* (1908), *Kansas* (1910), and *Beginnings of the American People* (1915). Selden L. Whitcomb, in the department of comparative literature, has published four volumes of original verse, in addition to *The Study of a Novel* (1905), *Autumn Notes in Iowa* (1914), and other prose works. Margaret Lynn, professor of English literature, has to her credit *Stepdaughter of the Prairie* (1914) and *Free Soil* (1920), the latter a compelling narrative of the struggle between abolitionist and pro-slavery forces in territorial Kansas. More recently, Alfred M. Lee, in the department of journalism, has published an account of *The Daily Newspaper in America* (1937); and John Ise, in the department of economics, has produced *Sod and Stubble* (1937), a story of pioneer days in Kansas.

Of past and present faculty members at Kansas State College, Nelson A. Crawford has previously been mentioned in these notes. Charles Elkins Rogers, head of the department of journalism, is the author of *Journalistic Vocations* (1931); and Fred A. Shannon of the history department has written *The Organization and Administration of the Union Army, 1861–1865,* which won a Pulitzer prize for the best piece of American historical research work in 1929, and *An Economic History of the People of the United States* (1935).

Among non-academic writers on subjects of specialized interest, one of the most prominent has been George P. Morehouse, whose published works include *The Kansa, or Kaw, Indians and Their History* (1908), *An Historic Trail* (1909), *Padilla, the Priest of the Plains* (1915), *Prehistoric Man in Kansas* (1917), and *Archaeology of Kansas* (1918). William Y. Murphy, for many years editor and proprietor of the Hutchinson *News,* has written a volume on *The Near East* (1913), in addition to two books of travel sketches. Gustav N. Malm of Lindsborg, artist as well as writer, is the author of *Charley Johnson: A Study of the Swedish Immigrant* (1909), as well as of a play entitled *Härute* (1919). Paul Jones, newspaper publisher of Lyons, in his *Quivira* (1929) and *Coronado and Quivira* (1937), supports the thesis that the ancient city sought by Coronado in 1541 centered about the present town site of Lyons. Dr. Karl Menninger, a well-known psychiatrist of Topeka, has reached a wide popular audience with his books on *The Human Mind* (1930) and *Man against Himself* (1938).

Though work of serious import has taken an increasingly prominent place in the literature of recent years, entertainment for young and old is still the primary purpose of many Kansas authors. Especially prolific in this field have been Thomas C. Hinkle, who specializes in animal stories for children; James William Earp, whose tales of railroad life are familiar to readers of the popular magazines; and Edna Becker, who has published several volumes of stories and verse for younger readers. In the realm of detective fiction, Kirke Mechem's *Frame for Murder* was a 1935 selection of the "Crime Club." Entertainment and edification are happily mingled in Arthur E. Hertzler's *The Horse and Buggy Doctor,* which describes the author's experiences as a country doctor in Kansas.

The list of writers who have been residents of Kansas for a time, but whose literary reputations were gained elsewhere, contains several prominent names. Frank Harris, noted Irish-American journalist and author, attended the University of Kansas in the early 1870's, and later worked on a ranch in the Flint Hills country—an experience described in his book, *My Reminiscences as a Cowboy* (1930). Kate Stephens, from 1879 to 1885 professor of Greek at the University of Kansas, later wrote *Delphic Kansas* (1911), *Life at Laurel Town: In Anglo Saxon Kansas* (1920), and *In a State University of the Middle West,* besides several books of more general appeal. Dorothy Canfield Fisher, novelist and essayist, was born at Lawrence, where her father was a member of the university faculty. Albert Bigelow Paine, friend, biographer, and literary executor of Mark Twain and the author of many books in various fields, lived for a while in Fort Scott and has further association with the State through his collaboration with William Allen White in *Rhymes by Two Friends* (1893). Florence Finch Kelly acquired both bachelor's and master's degrees at the University of Kansas in the early 1880's, and her first book, *With Hoops of Steel* (1900), is a story of the cattle country. The poets Harry Kemp and Claude McKay also studied at the university; Kemp afterward worked as a harvest-hand in the Kansas wheat fields, and a number of his poems have to do with the Kansas scene. Langston Hughes, equally prominent with McKay among present-day Negro poets, spent part of his boyhood in the "Mud Town" quarter of Topeka, and later lived in Lawrence. Still another Negro writer of verse, Frank Marshall Davis, was a student at Kansas State College. Meridel Le Sueur is an expatriate Kansan whose short stories have frequently appeared in prominent American magazines; her *Corn Village,* an unflattering sketch of a small Kansas town, aroused no little discussion upon its appearance in *Scribner's Magazine* a few years ago.

A notable landmark in the State's literary history is the *Kansas Magazine,* which began publication in January 1872. William H. Carruth wrote in 1900: "It would strain the resources of rhetoric to express the mingled feelings of wonder and pride with which this literary meteor was viewed by the people of the State." In its brief career of less than two years, under the successive editorship of Capt. Henry King and James W. Steele, this first *Kansas Magazine* did some excellent pioneer work in cultivating a regional literature. The contributions of Henry King, designated "the first Kansas story-teller" by William Allen White, depicted the real estate "boomers" and young Civil War veterans then entering the State. The short stories that James Steele wrote for the magazine under his own and the pen name of "Deane Monahan" were later collected in a book called *Sons of the Border* (1873). Contributors from outside the State included Walt Whitman, John Hay, and James Redpath.

Steele revived the *Kansas Magazine* in 1886, but again gave it up two years later; and a periodical appeared under the same name from 1909 to 1912. It was once more revived in 1933, and is now issued annually under the editorship of Charles E. Rogers and Helen Hostetter of Kansas State College.

Art

KANSAS art, like Kansas literature, was born amid the strife and chaos of Territorial days. The first large group of settlers were concerned primarily with politics and morality and had little time or aptitude for painting and sculpture. Yet a few were impelled to record, with motives similar to those of a traveler who photographs a scene he wishes to preserve, the novel conditions in which they found themselves. With little or no professional instruction, it is doubtful if they thought of themselves as artists in the accepted sense. They left, however, valuable drawings and paintings portraying important events of the Territorial struggle.

Among such "primitives" in the collection of the State Historical Society are the illustrations in the 12-volume diary of Samuel J. Reader, a Topeka pioneer. Having taken a homestead near North Topeka in 1855, Reader devoted himself, during the following 54 years, to a written and pictorial account of his life in the State—a narrative illustrated with pen and ink drawings, and by oils and water colors. Reader was self-taught; and although his figures are crudely drawn and awkwardly proportioned, his perspective is sound and his handling of color is original and full of variety. In his treatment of detail he strives for literal accuracy.

Some of the most eventful days in Kansas history are described in Reader's diary. He was a soldier in the Free State Guards and fought in the battle of Hickory Point. During the Civil War he saw action at the Big Blue with the Second Regiment, Kansas Militia. Five of his illustrations, enlarged, hang in the museum of the State Historical Society. These include oil paintings of his meeting with John Brown, the Second Regiment in action at the Big Blue, and the battle of Hickory Point. Two incidents of Price's raid are portrayed in water color: a Confederate cavalry charge, and a group of Union prisoners with Confederate troops after the battle.

Other sketches of pioneer scenes preserved at the historical museum are the pen and ink drawings of John F. Ayr, J. E. Rice, and William Breyman. Ayr and Rice, who settled in Lawrence soon after its founding, made

MEMORIAL TO PIONEER WOMEN, TOPEKA

several sketches of the early town. Breyman's drawing of the prison at Lecompton, where he and a score of other Free Staters were confined, gives a graphic impression of the place.

The years immediately following the establishment of peace in Kansas were almost barren in the fine arts. Kansans of the period found the task of wringing an existence from the stubborn soil or developing their mercantile enterprises too exacting for leisure interests. The spirit of the times is symbolized in an amusing way by a canvas in the State Historical Society's collection representing a mammoth watermelon from which a farmer, having climbed upon it with a ladder, has chopped out a plug as large as a wheelbarrow.

Also belonging to this period is a collection of scroll-saw woodwork by the late J. T. Glenn, pioneer resident in Wamego. Glenn used native black walnut to fashion intricate bookcases, writing desks, and picture frames, and miniature churches which served as clock cases. Several items in this unique group, which is on exhibition in the historical society, incorporate fine filigreed effects, while others are somewhat overweighted with ornamental curlicues.

The aboriginal Indians of Kansas produced baskets, bead work, and pottery, and Indian craftsmen at the Potawatomi and Kickapoo reservations in northeast Kansas still practice these arts. Many outstanding examples of Indian artifacts and of arts and crafts have been collected in Kansas museums, notably at the State university and Fort Hays State Teachers' College.

Much of the success of the Kansas agricultural exhibit at the Philadelphia Centennial Exposition of 1876 was due to Henry Worrall, its designer. Worrall's oil painting of the exhibit hangs in the State historical museum.

There were a few attempts to stimulate the arts during the 1880's, notably the organization in 1883 of the State Art Association. The association aimed to establish a permanent art collection in Topeka, hold annual competitive exhibitions for Kansas artists, and maintain an art school. The first loan exhibit was opened in the Topeka Public Library on March 16, 1885, and the first session of the school began the following year. After a short time the school failed to attract students, membership in the association dwindled, and the organization lapsed into inactivity. The art collection, however, supplemented by recent additions, is still on exhibition in the library at Topeka. Among its paintings, a realistic work by Alfred Montgomery depicts a barrel, a scoop shovel, a partly-filled sack, and a dozen ears of corn on a granary floor. Montgomery, whose extreme literalness in rendering commonplace farm subjects aroused facetious comment among his contemporaries and earned him the title of "farmer-painter," introduced art instruction into Topeka high schools in 1887. His painting *Down on the Farm,* exhibited at the Paris Exposition of 1890, was later sold for $10,000. At the same exposition another Kansan, John Douglas Patrick, was awarded a medal for his huge 9 by 12 foot canvas entitled *Brutality.*

John Noble and George M. Stone were the first native-born artists to win more than local recognition. Noble was born in Wichita, then a roaring frontier cow town. Many of his early paintings were nudes which adorned the back bars of local saloons. One of these, *Cleopatra at the Bath* was mutilated by Carry Nation in her famous raid on the Carey Hotel bar. Noble's mature work was done in Paris and New York. Most popular are his marine studies of the Brittany Coast and his paintings of the "magic city"—New York. He was admitted to membership in the National Academy of Design, an honor since bestowed on two other Kansans: Henry Salem Hubbell, who studied in Paris under Whistler, Laurens, and Constant; and Van Dearing Perrine, self-taught "original" of landscape painting.

George M. Stone, who died in 1931, was best known as a portrait painter, although his Kansas landscapes, while somewhat academic, have a good deal of distinction. The State commissioned him to paint many prominent Kansans. Stone also executed several murals and did historical paintings dealing with Kansas' past. Frederic Remington, noted painter, illustrator, and sculptor of Wild West genre, spent some time on a ranch in Butler County. Here he is said to have obtained material for the works that made him famous. Arthur Sinclair Covey lived in El Dorado for a period; his mural, *The Spirit of the Prairies,* painted for the Wichita City Library, brought him wide recognition.

By the 1890's Kansas had grown sufficiently wealthy to replace many of its frame structures with monumental stone buildings. Among the artisans who came to the State were stone-carvers, including Joe Robaldo Frazee, son of John Frazee, noted pioneer among American sculptors. Frazee was employed by Sargent and Company, stone-cutters. The caps on the Corinthian columns of the State capitol were carved by Jim Halderman, who also decorated the Veale Block, Seventh and Quincy Streets. Heads and coiled dragons carved by John Deliew and George Ward on the Shawnee County Courthouse (1896), also in Topeka, indicate a high degree of artistic sensitivity. The ability of these craftsmen to imbue their stonework with warmth and plasticity is further demonstrated in the classic male and female figures above the entrance to the Santa Fe Hospital in the same city.

Kansas woodcarvers plied their craft during the 1880's and 1890's at the Abilene plant of the Parker Amusement Company, one of the few manufacturers of circus and carnival equipment in the country. Artisans employed by the company carved prancing steeds for merry-go-rounds and decorated circus wagons with bold rococco flourishes. The collection of the company, now established at Leavenworth, includes a lion carved in 1880 and a horse carved in 1890, both of white pine. These animals are done with great verve, nostrils widespread, manes flying, legs tensed to leap. The sides of old-time circus wagons, now used to form the walls of sheds at the Parker plant, are encrusted with involved carvings of white pine. Experts have pronounced these designs exceedingly virile and free in execution. Noteworthy among Kansas' artisan-artists are the Lindsborg woodcarvers, whose portrait figurines are excellent in characterization.

It was in the 1890's, too, that Birger Sandzén, Swedish artist and teacher, arrived in Kansas, where he has since painted and lectured at Bethany College, Lindsborg. It was largely through his efforts that Lindsborg has become an art center unique in the Middle West. As a painter, Sandzén is best known for his individual interpretations of the scenery of the Southwest. His technique derives from impressionism, and is marked by a broad simplicity and a vivid utilization of pure color. His visits to the Colorado Rockies and the New Mexico deserts have provided themes for many of his etchings, lithographs, block prints, and water colors. Sandzén is represented in leading American and European galleries, and his Lindsborg studio remains a gathering place for Midwestern artists.

In the present century, Kansas has been the home or birthplace of many talented artists. Outstanding among these are John Steuart Curry and Henry Varnum Poor. Curry was born in 1897 on a farm near Dunavant in Jefferson County. He studied at the Chicago Art Institute for two years, working his way as a bus boy. After several years as an illustrator, he went to Paris and returned in 1927 to devote himself to a dramatic representation of American experiences. With a sensibility steeped in the Midwest and its people he has painted *Baptism in Kansas, Kansas Stockman, Hogs and Rattlesnakes, The Line Storm, Tornado, The Sun Dogs, Spring Shower, The Gospel Train,* and *Return of Private Davis.* The last three are owned by the Metropolitan Museum of Art. A brief tour with Ringling Brothers-Barnum and Bailey Circus provided the artist with material for *Flying Cadonas,* acquired by the Whitney Museum, New York, and other notable drawings and paintings of circus life. In 1933 he painted

JOHN BROWN, DETAIL FROM MURAL IN CAPITOL, TOPEKA

two murals for the new Department of Justice Building, Washington, D. C.

Curry's rural baptisms, whirling tornadoes, and earthy barnyard scenes have an almost savage quality which was not generally admired by Kansans. There were a few, however, who felt that the artist's work deserved public encouragement. When Curry left the State in 1934 to become "artist in residence" at Wisconsin University, William Allen White ruefully declared: "It takes something more than factories, something more than crowded cities and towns, something more than per capita wealth to make a civilization, and Kansas would be able to hold her head a little higher if she could have taken John Curry under her wing." White's statement began a newspaper campaign that rapidly created local interest in Curry's art. In 1937 Curry received a $20,000 commission to paint murals in the Kansas Capitol. This work, according to Curry, will depict "the historical struggle of man with nature," and will require three years for completion.

In contrast with Curry, whose art derives from contemporary life, Henry Varnum Poor finds his inspiration in more traditional sources. Born in Chapman in 1888 Poor has been termed "the artisan in the artist." Though his studies in art did not achieve full scope until he was past thirty, he is a good craftsman and prolific producer in painting, sculpture,

MUNICIPAL ART MUSEUM, WICHITA

and pottery; and his designed urns, houses, furniture, and tile work. Poor is the leading American craftsman in ceramics. His pottery, done in the difficult Persian technique which requires rapid glazing and prompt firing, has been purchased by the Metropolitan Museum of Art. With his daughter Anne, Poor painted murals in the new Department of Justice Building. The Byzantine ceiling of the Union Dime Savings Bank in New York City is one of his notable tile decorations. His *Fisher Boy* hangs in the Metropolitan Museum of Art and others of his paintings are in the foremost American galleries. A resident of New York State for many years, Poor frequently returns to Kansas. He is a close friend of Birger Sandzén.

Bertram Hartman, Albert T. Reid, Kenneth Adams, Ward Lockwood, and Aaron Douglass are artists of Kansas origin. Hartman began his career at Junction City, where he decorated the walls of a local hotel with scenes from *Robin Hood*. His paintings are in the collections of the Whitney Museum and the Brooklyn Museum, and he has done murals for the New York State Tubercular Hospital. Reid, chiefly known as a cartoonist and illustrator, was associated with the Reid-Stone School of Art, opened at Topeka in 1902. His later work includes murals at the Sabetha post office, depicting the development of mail transportation in Kansas from the days of the pony express to the present. Adams and Lockwood are prominent members of the Taos colony, New Mexico. Douglass, a Negro born in Topeka in 1898, is well known as an easel and mural painter. A student of Negro types, he has done murals for Bennett College, Fisk University, the Sherman Hotel in Chicago, and the Hall of Negro Life at the Texas Centennial Exposition.

Albert Bloch of Kansas University is a painter of considerable imagination and sensitivity. He is represented in the Chicago Art Institute, the Columbus Gallery of Fine Arts, and the Phillips Memorial Gallery, Washington, D. C. His colleagues at the university include Karl Mattern, water colorist, Raymond Eastwood, an authority on the technique of oil painting, and Bernard Frazier, who has done distinctive sculptures and dioramas. John Helm Jr., of the department of design at Kansas State College, Manhattan, does etchings and water colors of the Kansan scene.

Merrell Gage, Bruce Moore, and Reginald Wentworth are the foremost Kansan sculptors. Gage, a former pupil of Gutzon Borglum, reflects the influence of his teacher in his *Lincoln* and *Pioneer Women's Memorial* on the State capitol grounds. Also in Topeka are his *Flight,* in the foyer of Memorial Hall, and in Mulvane Art Museum his plaster bust of John Brown, *The Flutist,* and *Mother and Child.* Moore's *Pelican Fountain,* designed for the city of Pratt, won the Speyer Memorial Prize in 1935, a National Academy award. Reginald Wentworth's most recent work is the panel above the entrance to the new high school at Russel, which depicts an Indian raid of 1869.

Among local art institutions the Kansas Federation of Art, formed in 1932, has sponsored, together with other events, a noteworthy show of batiks, jewelry, metalwork, and textile designs by Kansas craftsmen. C. A. Seward (1884–1939), first director of the federation and its president in 1937, did etchings, woodcuts, and lithographs. He helped organize the Prairie Printmakers in 1930. He was also active in the Wichita art group, together with William Dickerson, painter, printmaker, and director of the Wichita Art Association's art school.

The Topeka Art Group, organized in 1924, is fostered by the department of art at Washburn College. Wallace Baldinger, head of the department, and his associate, James A. Gilbert, are painters of local distinction. Carl Bolmar, Topeka artist and critic, works in oils, water colors, and chalk plates. He is employed by the Topeka *State Journal,* the last large daily in Kansas to use chalk plate illustrations.

The formation of the Kansas unit of the Federal Art Project in 1936, revealed a hitherto unsuspected reservoir of talent. Three hundred pictures by project artists have been placed on permanent exhibition; oils, prints, and water colors have been loaned to fifty institutions; murals have been painted for the Topeka High School, the State College, Manhattan, and the University of Kansas, Lawrence. The Index of American Design, a division of the Kansas Art Project, has unearthed, classified, and sketched more than two hundred pieces of Americana.

In sum, Kansas art seems to have entered a period of indigenous growth. A realistic attitude is in evidence among the younger artists, many of whom are inclined to the belief that man's art should in a large measure be concerned with the conditions of his life. In this and in other respects Kansas art participates in the general trend of Midwestern art. Benton of Missouri, Wood of Iowa, and Curry of Kansas have outlined a regional program which is certain to be taken into account by other artists.

Music and the Theater

PIONEERS from New England, traveling westward in the 1850's, fortified their spirits with the stirring and prophetic cadences of Whittier's son of "The Kansas Emigrants," written for the first company of emigrants and "sung when they started, sung as they rode, and sung in the new home."

Temperamental differences in Northern and Southern character were reflected in the pioneer Kansan's songs. New England settlers preferred the old Puritan hymns, and the more popular of their secular ballads, such as "Baby's Gone," "Empty Is the Cradle," and "Willie Has Gone with the Angels," were of a definitely lugubrious nature; while such sprightly sentimental ditties as "The Yellow Rose of Texas Beats the Belle of Tennessee" and "Sweet Violets, Fairer than All the Roses," were introduced by settlers from the South.

The first decade of Kansas State history paralleled the War between the States and the period of Reconstruction. Kansas soldiers entered their first battle singing a contemporary song that breathed the Kansan spirit of that day, when Gen. Nathaniel Lyon's volunteers from the newly created State charged a superior force of Confederates at Wilson's Creek on August 10, 1861, singing "John Brown's Body." Lyon was killed and his little command was driven from the field, but "John Brown's Body" became one of the most potent battle songs of the war.

The thousands of settlers who entered Kansas in the decade following the Civil War brought with them the popular tunes of the time, and to accompany these they wrote ballads, some humorous, some plaintive, describing the tribulations of pioneer life. Especially popular among such ballads were "Frank Baker," sung to the tune of the "Irish Washerwoman," and "Kansas Land," sung to the tune of the old hymn "Beulah Land." A specimen verse with chorus from the latter goes as follows:

We went away awhile last fall
A month or so and that was all;
We earned enough to last us through,
Up to this time we made it do.

146

Chorus:

>Oh, Kansas sun, hot Kansas sun,
>As to the highest bluff we run
>We look away across the plain
>And wonder if it ne'er will rain,
>And as we look upon our corn
>We think but little of our farm.

The first formal musical organization in Kansas was a band of four pieces formed in 1854 by Forest Savage in the then newly founded town of Lawrence. But the first serious approach to the art came in 1869 with the founding of the Topeka Music Union. Mrs. Samuel J. Crawford, wife of the Civil War Governor, was a leader of the organization, serving as pianist at its recitals. The Modoc Club, one of the best known male choruses in the Middle West, was organized at Topeka in 1876, and subsequently toured the country from coast to coast. The club is still active in the capital city. A faculty member of Washburn College returned to Topeka in 1878, after a year at Harvard, and organized what is said to be the first college glee club west of the Mississippi.

"Home on the Range," composed in 1873, was the first widely popular song of genuine Kansas origin. Dr. Brewster Higley, a homesteader on Beaver Creek in Smith County, wrote the words, and Dan Kelly, who lived near Harlan in the same county, composed the music.

Chalkley ("Chalk") M. Beeson, a Dodge City frontiersman and a talented musician, became proprietor of the Long Branch Saloon in Dodge City through a mortgage foreclosure in 1876. Determined to make his establishment a center of culture as well as a rendezvous for thirsty cowpunchers, he instructed his associate, Roy Drake, to provide the customers with high class music. Drake hired Harry Adams, an itinerant musician, and one "Professor" Miller, who had come West to teach music. With these two and Beeson, Drake formed a creditable four-piece orchestra.

"Chalk" Beeson also helped to organize the Dodge City Cowboy Band, which met for its first rehearsal on May 27, 1879. Soon after its formation the band was financed by the local cattlemen's association, and each bandsman displayed on his broad-brimmed hat the cattle brand insignia of an individual sponsor. The Cowboy Band achieved national renown in the following decades, and appeared in most of the larger cities of the United States. Attired in full cowboy regalia, it provided "Wild West" atmosphere and a good quality of instrumental music.

Although music and the flowing bowl are traditionally allied, the prohibition movement added more to the music of Kansas (granted that scraps of doggerel set to simple tunes may be called music) than did the

COWBOY BAND, DODGE CITY(1884)

fermented grape or the distilled corn. The Kansas Women's Christian Temperance Union compiled lists of "battle hymns" which, during the 1880's, were taught to children and included in programs at temperance rallies. Seldom creative musicians, the dry crusaders were principally concerned with inspirational words, and in most instances borrowed the melody from a convenient hymnal. Among the songs dear to militant champions of prohibition were "We'll Turn Our Glasses Down," "Come and Join Our Army," and "We Are a Band of Soldiers."

Kansans who served in the World War sang the ubiquitous "Old Gray Mare" and "There's a Long, Long Trail," but scarcely less popular were the Rabelaisian strains of "Christopher Columbo" and "Glorious, Glorious," traditional favorites of the fraternity house. "The Dying Hobo," "Frankie and Johnny," "I've Been Working on the Railroad," and other ballads introduced by itinerant harvest hands in the pre-combine days, were revived by khaki-clad Kansans whose grandsires in uniform had chanted "John Brown's Body."

The Oratorio Society of Lindsborg, one of the country's famous choral ensembles, was organized at Bethany College in 1882. The original choir of forty voices has since grown to a chorus of five hundred. Annual presentations of *The Messiah* and other great choral works attract thousands of music lovers to this village on the remote Kansas prairie.

Encouraged by the response accorded the Oratorio Society of Lindsborg, other Kansas colleges have developed a variety of music festivals. The College of Emporia, Southwestern College, Bethel College, Baker University, and the State Teachers' Colleges at Hays, Emporia, and Pittsburg have all been active in this field. Music has become an established course in the curriculum of every college in the State.

The departments of music in the high schools of Kansas have been notably developed during recent years. The first accredited course of music study in the secondary schools of any city in the United States was given at Parsons in 1908. Later, Kansas was one of the first States to require four years of college preparation for high school music instructors. Today every high school in the State has one or more musical organizations.

Kansas is especially known throughout the Middle West for its music contests, an Old World custom revived in Kansas through the influence of the Swedes at Lindsborg and the Welsh at Emporia. Annual contests at Hays, Emporia, Lawrence, Winfield, Lindsborg, and Pittsburg are attended by thousands of high school students and others. A recent outgrowth of this activity is the county music festival, in which organizations from county high schools meet in the chief towns or cities for a mass presentation of musical programs, under the direction of conductors supplied by the colleges.

The knowledge and appreciation of music thus being fostered will doubtless result in increased original composition. Though Kansas has not yet gained much attention in this field, outstanding work has already been accomplished. Dean Thurlow Lieurance, of Wichita, has won wide recognition for his interpretations of Indian music; Dr. Charles Skilton, of the University of Kansas, is distinguished for his choral and orchestral works, including several on American Indian themes; and Professor Carl Pryor, also of the University of Kansas, has written many excellent instrumental compositions. Of note in the concert and operatic field are Laura Townsley McCoy of Great Bend, Kathleen Kersting of Wichita, Harold B. Challiss of Atchison, and Marian Talley formerly of Colby.

Karl Krueger, of Atchison, is the best known of Kansan conductors. Formerly conductor of the Seattle Symphony Orchestra, Mr. Krueger returned to the Middle West in 1934 to form the Philharmonic Orchestra of Kansas City, Missouri. Under his direction this latter group has developed into an orchestra of national importance. In the summer of 1937,

Mr. Krueger served with notable success as guest conductor in Vienna, Austria.

Since the advent of the "talkies," the dust on Kansas stage boards has settled heavily. But in the heyday of the "opera house," the State was visited by most of the leading theatrical troupes. Repertoire companies of the 1870's toured from Kansas City on the east to turbulent Dodge City on the frontier. Prominent among these companies was the Louis Lord Troupe, which, to judge from contemporary newspaper notices, was all but worshiped by drama-hungry pioneers.

In Hays, Abilene, Dodge City (the "Cowboy Capital"), and other cattle towns, the entertainers performed in saloons and dance halls. Eddie Foy made his first successful appearance at the Springer (Comique) Music Hall in Dodge City on July 15, 1878. Accompanying him on the same bill were Belle Lamont, Jim Thompson, and Nola and Billie Forrest. Of his engagement in Dodge City, Foy wrote in later years: "I wish I could present to an audience of today an adequate picture of one of those old western amusement halls. Writers and artists have tried to do it, the movies have tried it, but all in vain—the sounds are lacking—the songs and patter at one end, where the show began at eight o'clock and continued until long after midnight; the click and patter of poker chips, cards, dice, wheels and other devices at the other end. . . . All around the room, up above, a sort of mezzanine, ran a row of boxes—and they were boxes, indeed, as plain as a packing case—where one might sit and drink and watch the show."

Topeka, Atchison, Leavenworth, and other major cities in eastern Kansas saw most of the dramatic hits of the 1880's. In the Corinthian Hall at Atchison Thomas W. Keene appeared in *Richard III,* John T. Raymond as Mark Twain's character of "Colonel Mulberry Sellers," and Mrs. Samuel W. Piercy in *Deception.* Troupes that visited Topeka and the chief towns on the Missouri River included McIntyre and Heath's minstrels, and the "Anthony and Ellis Mammoth Ideal Uncle Tom's Cabin Company" with Kate Parkington as Topsy.

Between 1890 and 1925, Topeka, Wichita, and other major cities were on the regular circuit of road shows starring foremost actors or presenting the most popular musical comedians. Topeka audiences saw Joseph Jefferson, Robert Mantell, and Frederick Ward in many of their best known vehicles.

At present, partly because of its proximity to Kansas City, Missouri, Topeka is visited by but one or two road shows a year. Wichita, farther

removed from Kansas City, sees a larger number of legitimate stage productions. The stock company and the tent show, popular twenty-five years
or more ago, have been recently revived. Several companies play profitable
engagements in the larger cities, and during the summer months make a
tent show tour of the smaller towns.

The decline of the commercial theater in Kansas has been happily paralleled by the rise of little theaters in the colleges and larger cities. Little
Theater units are active at Pratt, Liberal, Kinsley, Ulysses, Garden City,
Great Bend, Dodge City, and Hutchinson. A civic theater was organized
at Topeka in 1937. The Peter Pan Players, organized at Wichita in 1931
under the sponsorship of the American Association of University Women,
presents five plays for children each year, with casts restricted to children
in elementary schools.

Dramatic groups are active at Washburn College, Baker University,
Southwestern College, University of Kansas, Kansas State College, St.
Benedict's College, Mount St. Scholastica College, and the State Teachers'
Colleges at Hays, Emporia, and Pittsburg. Outstanding productions have
been presented by the Kansas Players, of the University of Kansas; the
Gilson Players, of Emporia State Teachers' College, directed by Franklin
Gilson; and the Twin College Players, of St. Benedict's College and
Mount St. Scholastica College.

Kansans of note in the contemporary theater include Fred Stone and
Hale Hamilton of Topeka, Howard Thompson of Paola, and Brock Pemberton of Emporia. Pemberton, once a reporter on the Emporia *Gazette*,
has produced among other Broadway successes *Enter Madame, Miss Lulu
Bett, Strictly Dishonorable, Ceiling Zero,* and *Personal Appearance.* Howard Thompson has written several musical comedies, the best known of
which are *Little Jesse James* and *East Is West.* One of the leading characters in *Little Jesse James* is "a girl from Oskaloosa, Kansas," and a song
in the same production is entitled "My Home Town in Kansas." Hale
Hamilton starred in George M. Cohan's *Get-Rich-Quick Wallingford;*
and he has appeared as a supporting player with James K. Hackett, E. H.
Sothern, and John Barrymore.

Fred Stone, comedian of stage and screen, spent his boyhood in North
Topeka. Old residents recall that he acted in amateur theatricals sponsored
by the Kansas Avenue Methodist Church. At the age of nine he stretched
a tight wire across his back yard to train for a career under the "big top."
A few years later he electrified North Side residents by walking across
Kansas Avenue on a wire fastened three stories high. Later he joined a

circus. His first success on the stage was in the role of the scarecrow in *The Wizard of Oz*. With the late David Montgomery he formed the famous team of Montgomery and Stone. In 1935 he appeared with his daughter Paula in Sinclair Lewis's *The Jayhawker*, a play based on the career of a distinguished citizen of Kansas, James H. Lane.

Architecture

THE pioneers who settled along the northeastern border of Kansas in the 1850's found timber and stone with which to build their homes. They set up log cabins or simple one-room houses of stone. Less often they built tent-shaped structures of poles thatched with grass, called "hay houses." These were little more than "straws in the wind" and were abandoned as soon as possible, but they served their purpose as easily and quickly erected buildings. The first church services in Lawrence were held in a hay house.

The settlers who pushed westward to the treeless Plains found no stone, while the only timber was scrubby willow and cottonwood along the shallow streams. Thus they were forced to build with the only material available—the earth itself. The dugout, a sod-covered hole, at one time outnumbered any other kind of dwelling in western Kansas. Sodhouses, or "soddies," were built with heavy slabs of top soil bound together by roots of growing buffalo grass. The "soddy" was box-like, squat, and dingy, its roof pitched at no greater angle than was required to shed rain.

A few sodhouses were in use as late as 1938, but the rare soddy that stands today is preserved largely because of its historical interest. There are Kansans, however, who still remember how to build a soddy. In 1933, when living quarters had to be provided for a Civilian Conservation Camp stationed near Dodge City, soddy experts were found who built satisfactory barracks of earth.

Even after the first decades of settlement, permanent dwellings were not designed in the contemporary Greek Revival style of the eastern sections of the United States. Temple porticos, carved entablatures, and fluted Doric columns were elaborations whose transplanting was precluded by the rigors of the Kansas frontier. Practicality was the order of the times. The four walls were unadorned save by openings to provide light and entrance; the roof was designed to shut out the elements; reasonable comfort was the ultimate aim of the builder.

The grim simplicity of early Kansan houses was not due to a lack of aesthetic sense in their builders, but rather to the fact that there were few

A SOD RANCH HOUSE (1898)

skilled masons or carpenters in the territory. Sawmills and brickyards were scarce, and the construction of the humblest dwelling involved prodigious labors. Buildings of architectural interest were nevertheless erected. Foremost among these scattered few is the old Planter's Hotel in Leavenworth, built in 1856. It is a three-story brick structure ornamented with two oriels, a porte-cochere, and a cornice trimmed with a double band of dentils.

Several frame houses built in the early 1860's in the ghost town of Albany, in Nemaha County, reveal a definite New England influence. A two-story structure beside the dusty road that was Main Street in the one-time village has a hip roof, small window panes, and an inset doorway. A nearby farmhouse of similar design has a low-roofed addition at the rear, with a deep porch under the eave. The design of these structures, however, is not typical of the architecture in the State.

The construction of railroads through Kansas in the 1870's enabled settlers to receive portable houses f.o.b. They consisted of a framework on which wide planks were nailed; the cracks were then sealed with strips and the plank roof was usually covered with tarpaper. Meagerly furnished, portable houses were sufficiently comfortable for bachelors proving homestead claims, and for merchants intent on garnering quick profits in boom towns. Sometimes when the permanency of a prairie settlement became assured, entire blocks of portable houses were set afire and destroyed to make way for substantial buildings.

The German-Russian immigrants who settled in Rush and Ellis counties in 1875 at first made their homes in board "tents," but these makeshifts were soon discarded in favor of the somewhat less crude dugout and sod-house. For a while many German-Russians clung to the European custom of living in compact villages where they kept their stock, driving to and from the fields each day. The German-Russians in time became thoroughly Americanized. Today their villages are like other prairie communities, except for the large churches, so favored by these people. Their homes invariably stand in the shadows of lofty spires that rise from the land like gigantic carpet tacks. Poetically termed "Cathedrals of the Plains," these edifices are adorned with modified Gothic, Romanesque, and Byzantine details.

In the 1880's the more prosperous Kansans replaced their plain houses with ornate structures weighted down with undigested Old World styles. Mansard roofs bristled with wrought iron, towers sprouted from saw-tooth gables, and sharp-eaved dormer windows peeped coyly from beneath gingerbread cornices. Many of these structures, their rampant decorations antithetic to the current trend for simplicity and functionalism, are still standing in Topeka, Lawrence, Leavenworth, and Atchison. An architect, viewing the Victorian mansions of Atchison, once remarked, "It's the result of a Kansas cyclone and nobody ever did anything about it."

Many courthouses built in the eighties and nineties are Richardsonian-Romanesque in design. The Riley County Courthouse at Manhattan and the Harvey County Courthouse at Newton, with almost identical exteriors, are outstanding examples of this style of architecture. Plans for these and many other courthouses of this period were bought by county commissioners from salesmen who went through the State with folders containing a dozen or more courthouse designs, all of which were influenced by Richardson.

The State Capitol at Topeka is of neoclassic design, with a hexastyle portico, a balustrade running the length of the roof, and pilastered pediments along the side walls. E. Townsend Mix prepared the original plan. John G. Haskell, who also designed the Cottonwood Falls Courthouse, superintended the construction of the first or east wing, completed in 1866. The remaining three wings, built at intervals between 1866–1903 and joined cross-wise, follow the general plan of the east wing. The center of the structure is crowned with a lofty copper-covered dome. The capitol, whose design was inspired by that of the National Capitol, has been picturesquely though not entirely accurately described as "the farthest western advance of Graeco-Roman culture."

Since 1915 many of the old county courthouses have been replaced by modern structures. Noteworthy among these is the neoclassic Wyandotte County Courthouse at Kansas City. It is a five-story temple-like building with hexastyle portico, elaborate cornice ornamented with rococo flourishes, and an attic story, decorated with swags. The building was designed by Wight and Wight of Kansas City, Missouri.

Representative of the late 1920's, when communities vied with each other in building monumental public schools, is the Topeka Central High School, designed by T. R. Griest of that city. It is a slender three-story structure of brick, trimmed with stone, its three wings forming a half hexagon. A tall Gothic tower rises above the central wing. Less striking architecturally, but of greater bulk, is the Wyandotte High School in Kansas City, a huge H-shaped building embellished with Lombardic-Romanesque detail. Sculptures by Emil Robert Zettler, based on Indian forms, adorn the façades. The school was designed by Hamilton, Fellows, and Nedved of Chicago, in association with Joseph W. Radotinsky of Kansas City, Kansas.

The five-story Reno County Courthouse, erected in 1930, with its setbacks and angular recesses above the main doorway, is a radical departure from traditional architecture. It was designed by W. E. Hulse of Hutchinson, Kansas. The floor plan is unusual in its high-ceilinged main room, surrounded by a mezzanine similar to that of banking houses.

A wave of school construction, motivated principally by aid from the Federal Government, has swept across the State since 1930. The design of the high school at Russell, completed in 1938, follows the principles of the "form and functionalists," set forth in the late nineteenth century by Louis Sullivan and the Chicago School, and is a notable example of the "prairie" style, with both plan and structural material adapted to the local environment. It is a three-story rectangular building of local limestone, with a low-pitched tile roof. Except for the entrance, flanked by fluted piers and surmounted by a sculptured panel, the structure is bare of adornment. A. R. Mann of Hutchinson was the architect.

The Wichita High School, North, is another excellent example of the prairie style of architecture. Glenn Thomas was the architect. It is a buff brick building with a red tile roof, and lines similar to those of the State Capitol at Lincoln, Nebraska. A square tower 90 feet high is banded with ceramic panels depicting buffaloes and Indians in shades of red, blue, brown, and yellow. The green glazed tower windows are each ornamented with a red arrow; the main entrance is decorated with polychrome and terra cotta figures designed by Bruce Moore.

Polychrome sculptures, depicting Indian arts, crafts, and environments, decorate the buff walls of the Wichita Art Museum, a cast stone structure of modern design. Clarence S. Stein, of New York City, was the architect; the decorations are by Lee Lawrie. The angular mass of the exterior, augmented by juxtaposed rectangular planes, produces a studied play of light and shadow.

Two of the finest business structures in Kansas—the National Bank Building and the Capitol Building and Loan Association Building—face each other across Kansas Avenue in Topeka. The 14-story bank, of modern set-back design, is the tallest business structure in Topeka. It was designed by Thomas W. Williamson & Company, of Topeka. The loan association building is a six-story structure of tan brick with a sharp-gabled roof of red tile. The piers and finials of the south and west façades are decorated with terra cotta sculptures which symbolize in sunflowers, sheaves of wheat, and heroic figures, the pioneering phase of Kansas history. The building was designed by George Grant Elmslie; the decorations are the work of Emil Robert Zettler.

The development of residential architecture in Kansas is not unlike that of any other city in the Middle West. The typical Kansas house is a one- or two-story frame structure with a large front porch that is often screened or trellised. The Kansas climate, however, has begun to exert a noticeable influence on housing construction. Sleeping-porch additions in increasing number give comfort for sultry summer nights. Indeed, one-story towers, open on all sides, have been added to otherwise conventional residences. Unlike the ornate, bracketed, and conical towers of the 1880's these structures are utilitarian in appearance.

Virtually all contemporary house styles are represented in the restricted residential areas of Kansas cities. Dutch-Colonial bungalows, trim English cottages, and adaptations of French and Italian Renaissance villas stand beside wide-porticoed post-Colonial houses. Residences that stress form, function, and material with equal emphasis are comparatively rare. Noteworthy in this connection is the Wichita home of Henry J. Allen, designed by Frank Lloyd Wright. An irregular ell of buff brick with leaded windows and a low tile roof, the structure appears to be a natural outgrowth of the slope on which it stands.

The typical Kansan farmhouse is a one- or two-story frame structure that resembles the urban dwelling in almost every detail except the porch.

HOME OF HENRY J. ALLEN, WICHITA

In summer the front porch of a city house is suitably furnished for out-door living, but the front porch of the average farmhouse is seldom used. It is often sparely constructed and scarcely ever built to the height and width of the façade as are many porches of city dwellings.

Reflecting the chief industries of the region, the most prominent struc-tures on the country skyline are the large wood and stone barns of the cattle-raising sections; flat-sided grain elevators of wood, concrete, or sheet metal in the wheat-growing lands; and concrete silos that look like stubs of gray chalk dotting the dairying areas. The size and shape of these structures are entirely utilitarian—the barns spread wide to receive stores of hay; the tall grain elevators, commonly known as "prairie skyscrapers," supply the gravity required for rapid loading of grain; and the tubular silos permit the compact storage that a structure with corners would not allow, thereby lessening the spoilage caused by exposure to air.

The elevators and grain storage bins at Kansas City and other wheat centers in the State are austere examples of functional design. These buildings form huge upright "L's" on the plain. The vertical arm consists of the elevator, its block-like mass pitted by small square windows. The horizontal arm at the base of the elevator consists of tubular storage bins whose curved sides resemble the folds in a giant cartridge belt.

<<<<<<<<<<<<<<<<<<<<<<<<✿>>>>>>>>>>>>>>>>>>>>>>>>

PART II

Cities and Towns

<<<<<<<<<<<<<<<<<<<<<<<<✿>>>>>>>>>>>>>>>>>>>>>>>>

Arkansas City

Railroad Stations: 5th Ave. and E St. for Atchison, Topeka & Santa Fe Ry.; 6th and Chestnut Sts. for St. Louis & San Francisco R.R.; 2nd and Monroe Sts. for Midland Valley R.R.; Summit and Tyler Sts. for Missouri Pacific R.R.
Bus Stations: SW. corner Summit and Chestnut Sts. for Santa Fe Trail, southern Kansas, and Red Ball Lines.
Taxis: 24-hour service to all parts of city and outlying districts; fare 10¢ per person for 18 blocks.

Accommodations: Three hotels, two tourist camps.

Information Service: Chamber of Commerce, City Building, NE. corner 1st and Central Sts.

Motion Picture Houses: Three.
Golf: 9-hole municipal course in Municipal Park, N. end of Summit St.; greens fee 25¢.
Swimming: Municipal Park.

Annual Events: Arkalalah Hallowe'en festival, sponsored by business men.

ARKANSAS CITY (1,075 alt., 13,946 pop.), pronounced Ar-kan'-sas, three miles north of the Oklahoma border at the confluence of the Walnut and Arkansas Rivers, is a shipping and refining center for oil fields at the north, east, and south. Long lines of tank cars emerge from the city on its four railroads; freight yards are piled high with incoming shipments of oil machinery and pipeline supplies. The local oil refinery has a daily capacity of 20,000 barrels.

The rivers, following almost parallel courses to their junction, flank the city on the east and west. The business district, atop a hill between the two streams, has modern shops with tile façades, and older structures of native limestone. Summit Street, the main thoroughfare, begins in bottomlands along the Arkansas, climbs to the business section, descends through a residential area on the opposite slope, and trails off in farming country at the north. Summit Street shop windows, in addition to the usual displays, also feature various colored trinkets to catch the eye of the Indians. Because the city caters to oil areas in two States, Oklahoma license plates are almost as numerous along Summit Street as those of Kansas.

The founders of Arkansas City arrived at the site on January 1, 1870. The settlement, platted the same year, was named Walnut City. It was soon renamed Adelphi, and subsequently Creswell in honor of the Postmaster General in President Grant's cabinet. The community was incorporated as a city under its present name on June 10, 1872.

Although surrounded by bands of hostile Indians, the settlement was unmolested. This immunity was earned largely through the efforts of Henry Norton, who arrived in 1870. His honesty in dealing with the Indians immediately won their friendship and, eventually, their unreserved confidence. He went to their villages unaccompanied and was permitted to see their religious ceremonies. At his invitation, the Indians visited the settlement frequently, buying supplies, and trading furs and horses. Occasionally they came in their finest regalia and entertained the settlers with tribal songs and dances. In payment the whites gave them colored beads, tasseled handbags, plumed hats, and barbecued meat.

By the end of 1870 the settlement boasted a cluster of stores, a score of houses, two sawmills, and a newspaper, the Arkansas City *Traveler*. Founded by M. G. Mains, this sheet was named for the old fiddle tune, "The Arkansas Traveler," and early issues carried a fiddle below the masthead. The community in these years was a rendezvous for horse thieves who stole stock from settlers in Kansas and drove the animals into Oklahoma. "Buffalo Bill" Cody, then United States Marshal, made the vicinity his headquarters during the early seventies. At times, however, settlers administered the law as indicated in the following item from the *Arkansas Valley Democrat:* "S. P. U.'s take notice: There will be a meeting of the Stock Protection Union this evening at the Bland School House. Every member is requested to be present as business of great importance is to be transacted. Don't fail to come out men. We have work to do."

C. M. Scott of the *Traveler*, soon afterwards hinted poetically at the nature of the work done by the Stock Protective Union with:

> He found a rope and picked it up,
> And walked with it away—
> It chanced that on the other end,
> A horse was hitched, they say;
> They found a tree and tied a rope
> Unto a swinging limb—
> It happened that the other end
> Was somehow hitched to him.

The steamboat *Aunt Sally*, first to ascend the Arkansas River to Arkansas City, arrived on a Sunday morning in June 1878. Services were in progress at the village church, but at the first sound of the steamer whistle the pastor and the congregation rushed out to welcome the boat. Local merchants, intent on developing an inland shipping point, promptly purchased the *Kansas Miller*. On its first trip the vessel grounded on a sandbar. Subsequent journeys were unsuccessful and the *Kansas Miller*, renamed the *Walnut Belle*, was converted into a pleasure boat.

The growth of Arkansas City was stimulated in the 1880's by the discovery of gold in the region. Assays indicated rich deposits and the community seethed with activity. Mining operations revealed but little metal and the boom soon subsided.

When the first of the Cherokee lands in Oklahoma Territory was opened in 1889, hundreds of settlers made the run from Arkansas City. Four years later the Cherokee Strip—that land between the original southern border of Kansas and the corrected southern border *(see HISTORY)*— was opened to settlers. In the late summer of 1893 between 50,000 and

60,000 people swarmed into Arkansas City, which at that time had approximately 5,000 inhabitants. On the day of the rush, September 16, 1893, the streets were deserted by 7 a.m. Those who did not participate gathered at the south end of town to watch the excitement.

Afoot, on horse, in heavy lumber wagons, buggies, covered wagons, and all manner of horse-drawn vehicles, the settlers lined up to await the gunshot which signified that the Strip was open. Impatient settlers inspected wagon wheels, harness, and saddles in a last-minute checkup. At high noon came the signal and the boomers dashed across the line. For an instant the row held unbroken and then, as settlers on fast horses outdistanced the others, it splintered into a tangle of wagons, buggies, and shouting drivers.

By the beginning of the present century Arkansas City had lost its frontier aspect and had become a conventional market town. The discovery of oil nearby in 1914 and in the post-War years altered the economic course of the city. Indians, made rich by wells brought in on their lands in northern Oklahoma, came to Arkansas City to splurge. They came by train, on horseback, or even on foot, and returned to their homes in gleaming new automobiles piled high with gaudy wares. Not a few of the cars were purchased because of a tricky gadget on the dashboard or a chrome figurine on the radiator cap.

Two decades of wealth, however, have scarcely changed the outward appearance of the Indians in the region. Apart from an occasional giant diamond on a rough brown hand, or a massive gold watch-chain dangling from a bright-colored shirtfront, there are no marks to distinguish the rich from the poor. The shabbiest Indian may, as residents put it, "own half of Oklahoma."

Arkansas City has two flour mills, a meat packing plant, foundries, creameries, a sand and gravel plant, overall factories, and an oil field machine shop.

POINTS OF INTEREST

The W. E. COLLINS HOUSE (private), 315 S. B St., a one-story frame structure, is a tribute to W. E. Collins, a fantastic promoter compared by Kansans to the Col. Mulberry Sellers of Mark Twain's Gilded Age. Collins, by means of an artful tongue and a flair for baby-kissing, convinced local citizens in the eighties that he had "wide influence" in the Senate and House of Representatives. When he offered to visit Washington, D. C., and exert his power on behalf of the backward river village, the delighted citizens gave him this house, six lots, and paid his traveling expenses. His subsequent lobbying was unsuccessful, but a glib explanation of his failure enabled him to remain in the good graces of the townspeople when he returned.

HIGH BLUFF, E. end of Madison Ave., on the E. bank of the Walnut River was the CAMPING PLACE OF BUFFALO BILL CODY and a party of approximately half a hundred cavalrymen when they patrolled the border in 1869 and 1870. The bluff and area immediately surrounding was formerly the property of a Cherokee Indian, Two-Boys-Stray-Shadow, or James Hightower, as he was more commonly known. In this wooded region two old Indian pole trails met. The two trails, the Rosebud and the Arrowhead, went out of use shortly after the white men settled in the region but faint pole tracks remain at the top of the bluff today.

NATURAL BRIDGE, at the base of the bluff, is formed by two huge rocks that arch over a spring. On a limestone boulder beneath the arch are the letters "B. B.," Buffalo Bills's initials carved in 1869. A small star separates the two letters.

The KANOTEX REFINERY *(open by permission of superintendent)*, M and Tyler Sts., employs approximately 250 men and has a capacity of between 15,000 and 20,000 barrels of oil daily. The plant manufactures automobile lubricants and gasoline.

Atchison

Railroad Stations: Union Depot, 2nd and Main Sts., for Atchison Topeka & Santa Fe Ry., Chicago Burlington & Quincy R.R., Missouri Pacific R.R., and Chicago Rock Island & Pacific Ry.
Bus Station: 120 N. 5th St. for Missouri Pacific Trailways.
Taxis: Fare 10¢.
Traffic Regulations: Stop signs at principal intersections. Speed limit 25 miles per hour.

Accommodations: Four hotels; boarding houses, tourist camps.

Information Service: Chamber of Commerce, 4th St. entrance, Y.M.C.A. Bldg., N.E. corner 4th and Commercial Sts.

Theaters and Motion Picture Houses: Memorial Hall (Soldiers' and Sailors' Memorial), 819 Commercial St., occasional road shows. Three motion picture houses.
Athletics: Amelia Earhart stadium and athletic field, 14th and Atchison Sts.; Missouri Pacific baseball grounds, 14th and Utah Sts.; St. Benedict's College field for intercollegiate sports.
Swimming: Lions' pool in summer, 12th and Commercial Sts. Y.M.C.A. indoor pool, 321 Commercial St., open for men Mon., Wed., Fri., Sat., Sun.; for women Tues., Thurs.
Tennis: Shelly Park, 16th and Commercial Sts.; Reisner Park, 10th and Kearney Sts.; four courts at 8th and Santa Fe Sts.; one at 5th and R Sts.; one at 8th and Mound Sts.
Golf: Forest Hills Course, 0.25 m. W. on US 73, 9 holes, greens fee 50¢.
Ice Skating: Jackson Park.
Boxing: (Intercollegiate) St. Benedict's College gymnasium; occasional professional boxing, Memorial Hall, 819 Commercial St. ·

Annual Events: Automobile Industrial Show, Memorial Hall, March; High School band concerts, 8th and Santa Fe Sts., every Wed. night during June and July; St. Benedict's College and interscholastic football games, Oct.–Nov.; American Legion Armistice Day celebration, Memorial Hall; Music Week, presented by grade school children during Christmas Week, Memorial Hall.

ATCHISON (795 alt., 13,024 pop.), on the west bank of the Missouri River in a vast amphitheater gouged out during the glacial epoch, is surrounded by low hills. This staid little industrial city is rich in historic interest and proud of the nationally famous personages who have claimed it as their birthplace or former home.

Atchison was laid out with strict attention to symmetry, its streets being straight and evenly platted. In the narrow valley of White Clay Creek, a tributary of the Missouri River, that forms a natural dividing line between the north and south residential districts, are the retail, industrial, and wholesale districts, and the railroad yards. The stream, where it runs through the city, is confined in a large storm sewer. Old elms and broad, well-kept lawns add charm to the residential districts.

While the residential architecture of Atchison clings to the traditional

165

styles of another era, public and commercial architecture follows contemporary trends. In downtown Atchison few of the historic buildings remain. With the exception of two five-story buildings—the Hotel Atchison and a modern office building—the majority of business houses are modest two-story structures, some with modern fronts. Some of the industrial plants and business establishments date back to the 1880's. A bank, organized in 1859 has a slogan "Older than the State of Kansas," and the Blair Flour Mill was established in 1866.

Negro residents, who form nearly 10 per cent of the population, are not segregated, although there is a small district of modest frame dwellings on the edge of a bluff north and east of the business district that is inhabited almost exclusively by Negroes. A considerable number of the more prosperous live in comfortable modern homes scattered throughout the residential sections. Negroes are represented in most of the trades and professions.

From 1875 to 1938 a toll bridge spanning the Missouri River was the only connecting link with the Missouri side of the stream. It was replaced by a free bridge constructed as a PWA project and opened to traffic July 2, 1938.

Recorded history goes back to 1724, when the expedition of M. de Bourgmont, military commander of the French colony of Louisiana, crossed what is now Atchison County to establish friendly trade relations with the Indians of the Platte region. Francois Marie Perrin du Lac, another French explorer, passed through in 1802–1803 and his journal tells of finding stones that he carried away to be analyzed. Although he lost them, the stones are believed to have been iron ore.

Lewis and Clark while encamped on Independence Creek six miles north of Atchison, were the first to celebrate Independence Day on Kansas soil. On July 4, 1804 they fired a salute in observance of the occasion and issued an additional gill of whiskey to the men.

In the winter of 1818, a detachment of soldiers, members of the First Rifle Regiment of Maj. Stephen H. Long's Yellowstone expedition established the first military post in Kansas on a large island in the river six miles south of Atchison. French trappers had previously discovered this island and christened it Isle au Vache (Cow Island). When Major Long joined the detachment in July 1819, he brought the first river steamboats seen in this section. Many members of this expedition were prominent in the development of the West. Maj. John O'Fallon became one of the wealthiest and most influential leaders of St. Louis, Mo., and a private, Bennett Riley, became military Governor of California and was honored by having Fort Riley (see Tour 3) named for him.

A council was called for August 24, 1819 after the Indians fired on the soldiers encamped on Cow Island. At the last moment, several chiefs refused to attend because of their disagreement as to precedence in rank, but peace was declared, according to one account, rather "because of the gunfire, rocket and flare displays, and flag hoisting, than because of Major O'Fallon's eloquence."

By 1850 the California gold rush and the general western trek had

FREE BRIDGE, ATCHISON

brought settlers to this desirable river landing. Most of the homesteaders were anti-slavery but the Missouri settlers determined to use Atchison as a wedge in making Kansas a slave State. They filed claims there for the privilege of voting and kept the community in a constant state of unrest. They even named the city in honor of an ardent slavery advocate, David R. Atchison, United States Senator from Missouri, and, at one time, Acting Vice President of the United States. Although he was not a Kansan, Atchison attended the celebration for the opening of the townsite, and in his speech, exhibited his broad tolerance by admitting that "some Northerners are fairly worthy men who wouldn't steal a nigger themselves."

The city was incorporated August 30, 1855, by a special act of the territorial legislature, and the toss of a coin decided the first mayor. At this time the Southerners raised $400 to start their newspaper, the *Squatter Sovereign*, a vehement champion of slavery, which fought so bitterly with the Free State paper that a duel between the two editors appeared inevitable. Indeed, the editor of the *Sovereign* issued a challenge, but his rival refused to accept it.

The drifting population of the 1850's and 1860's contributed to the lawlessness that characterized the ribald frontier days. The first minister to come to Atchison (1855) lost most of his audience to a chuck-a-luck game across the street. The Reverend Pardee Butler, a Free State minister, attempted to reform the city in the 1850's and, for his efforts, was rewarded with a lone and hazardous voyage on a raft down the "Big Muddy." Ignoring the threats of his attackers, he returned to Atchison a few months later, and narrowly escaped hanging. According to the minister's subsequent report of the proceedings, "after exposing me to every sort of indignity, they stripped me to the waist, covered my body with tar, and then for want of feathers, applied cotton wool. Then they sent me naked upon the prairies."

The Northerners, however, gained in power and by 1857 their arrogance led to violence. Some of them purchased the *Sovereign* and completely reversed its policies. Others began to pilfer from Missourians in the hills across the river.

John Brown, Free State protagonist, also figured in Atchison's history. Hearing that Brown was traveling nearby in 1857, a group of Southern sympathizers went out to capture his party, but were captured instead. Brown ordered one of the prisoners to pray.

"I only know, 'Now I lay me . . .' " the man objected.

"Then say it!" Brown commanded, and the frightened prisoner knelt and recited the child's prayer.

Though they remained but two years, the Mormons, an independent group, established the first large settlement in 1855. Their farm, four miles west of the city on the south side of US 73, was enclosed by ditches, which have been obliterated by cultivation and erosion. This encircling moat was used to prevent cattle from straying.

Lincoln visited Atchison December 2, 1859, and addressed a group here, using the same speech with which he won the Presidency later at Cooper's Hall in New York City. The Atchison *Champion,* published by John A. Martin, did not report the visit because the editor, like most Kansas Republicans, was supporting Seward. Even the man who introduced him had to refer to his notes before naming a "Mr. A. Lincoln." But Lincoln won his audience, although it consisted mostly of hecklers and the curious. It was reported that he admonished his audience with these words: "You cannot secede from the Union! If you do, you will hang as surely as John Brown hanged today."

From Atchison in 1859 the first telegraph message from the West to the East was dispatched and in the same year the city achieved the distinction of being the first west of the Mississippi to have direct connection with St. Louis and the East. At the first city council meeting, it was decided to issue $100,000 in bonds to establish a railroad from St. Joseph, Mo., to Atchison, 15 miles west of any other railroad point. A charter was obtained from the Missouri legislature and in the winter of 1859–1860 the new line was completed and in operation.

With the advantage of a good steamboat landing and the best wagon road leading West, Atchison flourished from the first. Early day trail and river traffic was tremendous. The city directory of 1860 casually remarked that the entire trade carried on by private enterprise with Utah and the forts was from Atchison. In 1862 Ben Holladay bought the equipment of the bankrupt Russell, Waddell & Majors Freighting Company and moved its headquarters from Leavenworth to Atchison. At one time, following its organization in 1856, the company boasted 6,000 teamsters, 50,000 head of oxen, and more than 5,000 wagons. According to the estimate of the original company, they carried 21 million tons of freight through Atchison. Sometimes as many as 1,600 wagons stopped here in a single night. Butterfield's Overland Dispatch, established in Atchison in 1864, was one of the most important freighters, having 55 wagonmasters, 1,500 drivers, 1,200 mules, and 9,600 head of oxen. Holladay acquired Butterfield's Dispatch in 1866.

Carrying the mails from Atchison for the West on the overland stages was a million-dollar business. Mail coaches departing daily took 17 days to make the round trip from Atchison to Denver. Postage was $5 an ounce —and the finest of tissue was fashionable as writing paper.

The Atchison Topeka & Santa Fe Railway was another local enterprise. Ambitious to become the eastern terminus for a great south and west system, the municipality voted a bond issue of $500,000 as a basis for the venture, and in 1859 a company was incorporated by an act of the territorial legislature. Construction was delayed, however, and it was not until 1872 that the road to Topeka and Wichita opened, providing the first unit of a great railway system. Other roads were established and Atchison developed into an important railroad center.

In 1880 the city reached the peak of a steady growth in population and industry. It had three breweries, which were closed by State prohibition in 1881, two flour mills, railroad shops, and packing houses. Since 1900, it has become important as a wholesale and jobbing center. The city ranks fourth in Kansas and tenth in the United States in the production of hard wheat flour, three mills having a combined capacity of 5,600 barrels a day. A foundry established in 1871 is now one of the largest concerns in the United States exclusively engaged in the manufacture of locomotive parts. Atchison's industrial output also includes overalls, leather goods, plumbing fixtures, and processed eggs and poultry. The newest industry, the result of several years of research and experimentation, is the manufacture of industrial alcohol for motor fuel.

The two spaces reserved for Kansas in Statuary Hall in the Capitol at Washington, D. C., are occupied by statues of Atchison men—John J. Ingalls, author and United States Senator, and George Washington Glick, a Kansas Governor and national leader in the Democratic party. Atchison was the birthplace of Amelia Earhart Putnam, the noted aviatrix; Maj. Gen. Harry A. Smith, a World War commander, who received several decorations for bravery, and later was commandant at Fort Leavenworth; and Mateel Howe Farnham, the novelist daughter of Ed Howe, who won a $10,000 prize offered by the *Pictorial Review* Magazine and Dodd, Mead & Company, publishers, with her book, *Rebellion*.

POINTS OF INTEREST

The SITE OF THE OLD MAYFLOWER HOUSE, SE. corner 2nd and Main Sts., is occupied by the Union Depot. The hotel, built in 1857–1858, was an important starting place for stagecoaches traveling into the West.

The SITE OF THE MASSASOIT HOUSE, 201 Main St., where distinguished visitors were entertained in the early days, is occupied by ·a wholesale drug company. Lincoln spent a night in the hotel after making a campaign speech. Fugitive slaves were hidden in the old hostelry during the days of conflict, and it was there that Horace Greeley ate his first dinner in Kansas.

In a tiny PARK, Main St. between 3rd and 4th Sts., adjoining the depot on the west, is a stone marker that commemorates the visit of the Lewis and Clark expedition, July 4, 1804.

The LOCOMOTIVE FINISHED MATERIAL PLANT *(open 8-5, weekdays)*, E. end of Park St., is the only plant of its kind in Kansas and one of the largest in the United States. Established as a foundry in 1871 by John Seaton, the plant has been engaged since 1906 in the manufacture of locomotive parts. Material is sold to nearly every railroad in the United States and to railroad companies in Mexico, Japan, and several European countries. The plant employs an average of 400 men.

An OLD BUILDING *(open 8-5 weekdays)*, NW. corner 4th and Commercial Sts., housed the first telegraph office. It was from this office that the first telegraphic message was sent from the West to the East in 1859. The building, a three-story structure of brick painted yellow, erected in 1858, is occupied by law and real estate offices.

PIONEER HALL *(open 8-5 weekdays)*, NE. corner N. 4th St. and Kansas Ave., a two-story brick building built in 1872, has served a variety of purposes. It housed the first congregation of the Christian Church of Atchison, organized in 1882, and served as a civic hall and headquarters for a volunteer fire department. The building, now used by a Negro club, has not been altered.

The BIRTHPLACE OF AMELIA EARHART PUTMAN *(private)*, SW. corner Santa Fe St. and N. Terrace, a two-story brick and frame house of Victorian design, overlooks the Missouri River from the crest of a bluff. It was in this house, now occupied by another family, that the noted flyer spent most of her childhood with her grandparents. Former playmates recall the aviatrix as a studious child who, in moments of relaxation, liked to play Indian or go on "make-believe" trips in an old-fashioned carriage in a neighbor's barn.

The ATCHISON COUNTY COURTHOUSE, SW. corner N. 5th and Parallel Sts., completed in 1897, is a three-story limestone structure with a clock tower, designed in the Romanesque style by George P. Washburn of Ottawa, Kans.

A marker on the lawn commemorates the address made by Lincoln December 2, 1859, although the speech actually was delivered in a Methodist Church on Parallel Street between 5th and 6th Streets.

The W. P. WAGGENER HOME *(private)*, 819 N. 4th St., is a good example of the pretentious architecture of the 1880's and 1890's. Built in 1885 by the late Balie P. Waggener, father of W. P. Waggener, the three-story brick building has four porches and an arched main entrance. Typical of the architectural furbelows of the period are two copper griffins on the ridge of the roof.

A law library, on the third floor, has approximately 10,000 volumes including the statutes of every State and Territory.

ST. BENEDICT'S COLLEGE *(campus open at all hours)*, NE. corner N. 2nd and Division Sts., is a Catholic institution for young men, with a spacious, well-kept campus skirting the Missouri River and providing a magnificent view of the river valley. Established in 1858 by the Order of St. Benedict, the college confers degrees of Bachelor of Arts and Bachelor of Science and has an enrollment (1938) of 250 students. The present buildings, the first of which were completed in 1885, are designed in the Romanesque and Tudor Gothic styles.

The TUDOR GOTHIC MONASTERY *(admittance only to office and parlors)* is (1938) being erected on the campus. Designed by Brielmaier & Son of Milwaukee and modeled after the Benedictine monasteries of the Middle Ages, the E-shaped edifice of native stone with white trim will cost approximately a million dollars.

The ED HOWE HOME *(private)*, 1117 N. 3rd St., where the journalist and author died October 3, 1937, is a simple two-story brick structure with white stone trim. "The Sage of Potato Hill" was the author of numerous magazine articles and several books, the best known of which is the *Story of a Country Town.*

SOLDIERS' AND SAILORS' MEMORIAL HALL *(open for special events)*, 819 Commercial St., is a two-story brick and limestone building of classic design. It was erected in 1922 as a memorial to the Atchison County men who lost their lives in the World War. The AMERICAN LEGION MUSEUM *(open on application to caretaker)* is on the second floor. In addition to a number of Indian relics, the museum includes a captured German flag, brought from a fort near Coblenz, Germany, by Maj. Gen. Harry A. Smith, former resident of Atchison.

The ATCHISON AGROL PLANT *(open 8-5 weekdays)*, SW. corner S. 13th and Main Sts., manufactures a blend of alcohol and gasoline for use as motor fuel. Established in 1935 as a research unit of the Chemical Foundation of America, the plant began operating on a commercial basis December 2, 1937, and has a capacity of 10,000 gallons daily.

The OLD McINTEER HOUSE, NW. corner N. 13th St. and Kansas Ave., built in 1881, and designed in the manner of an Irish castle, with a profusion of gables and towers, has been converted into an apartment building.

The GLOBE PUBLISHING PLANT *(open 8-5 weekdays)*, 123 S. 5th St., a two-story building of red brick with a stone foundation, is the home of the Atchison *Daily Globe*, founded by Ed Howe in 1877. Walt Mason began writing his rhymes in prose form while working as a reporter for Howe, who objected to the publication of "poetry" in his newspaper.

MOUNT ST. SCHOLASTICA, 801 S. 8th St., a Catholic high school and college for young women, has a 42-acre campus. Founded as a grade school in 1863 by the Benedictine Sisters, the college draws students from remote sections of the United States and from France and Canada.

The large administration building of brick and stone, designed in the Tudor Gothic style by Brielmaier & Son of Milwaukee, was completed in 1924. A new chapel of Roman design, with a façade of stone, and the remainder in mingled shades of buff brick, was designed by the same architects. A lacework of stone at the main entrance is surmounted by a large rose window of carved stone and colored glass.

The school has a total enrollment of 275 and the college awards the degrees of Bachelor of Arts and Bachelor of Science.

MAUR HILL, 1400 S. 10th St., is a Catholic preparatory school for boys. Established in 1920 by the Fathers of St. Benedict's College, Maur Hill is a successor of Midland College, an English Lutheran institution. Five modern buildings, four of which are Tudor Gothic in design, are on the spacious campus. A bronze statue near the campus entrance depicts St. Maur and St. Placid, teachers of youth, seated at the feet of St. Benedict, patron saint of the Benedictine Order.

JACKSON PARK, entrance 1600 S. 6th St., is a rugged 140-acre tract with circuitous one-way drives that skirt precipitous bluffs. From the highest point in the park, Guerrier Hill, there is a good view of the Missouri Valley. Park facilities include a bandstand, small lakes, swings, and other amusements for children, and a small zoo. A World War cannon and a large stone monument were placed in the park in memory of the Atchison men who served in the World War. The drives are lined with beds of iris of different varieties and colors, which bloom in May.

The KANSAS STATE ORPHANS' HOME (open on application), 0.5 m. NE. of city limits on Waggener Rd., consists of nine buildings of modern brick construction on an attractive 240-acre tract of land. The home, which provides broad educational, domestic, and recreational facilities, was established in 1885 as a refuge for orphaned children of soldiers.

POINTS OF INTEREST IN ENVIRONS

Independence Creek, 5.9 m.; Hickory Point, 27 m. (see Tour 12); Atchison County Lake, 22.4 m. (see Tour 12A).

‹‹‹‹‹‹‹‹‹‹‹‹‹‹‹‹‹‹‹☼›››››››››››››››››››››››

Coffeyville

Railroad Stations: 13th St. between Willow and Spruce Sts. for Missouri Pacific
R.R.; E. 7th St. for Missouri-Kansas-Texas R.R.; E. 8th St. for Atchison, Topeka
& Santa Fe Ry.; 8th and Walnut Sts. for Union Electric Ry.
Bus Stations: Bus Terminal, 8th and Walnut Sts., for Southern Kansas Greyhound,
Santa Fe Trailways, and Missouri-Kansas-Oklahoma Bus Lines.
Taxis: 15¢ per person in city; service in rural districts at moderate rate.

Accommodations: Two hotels; municipal camp grounds in Forest Park, at east edge
of city limits; three privately-owned tourist camps.

Information Service: Chamber of Commerce, 721 Walnut St.

Radio Station: KGGF (1010 kc.).
Motion Picture Houses: Three.
Swimming: Pfister Park Pool, NW. edge of town on Buckeye St., adm. 10¢; Nata-
torium, 2826 Walnut St.; Municipal Pool for Negroes, 3rd and Ash Sts.
Golf: Edgewood Golf Course, W. edge of city on US 166, 18 holes, greens fee 25¢,
weekdays, 35¢ Sunday.

Annual Events: Montgomery County Fair, Sept.; Industrial Festival, Oct.

COFFEYVILLE (744 alt., 16,198 pop.), lies immediately north of the
Kansas-Oklahoma line in a sandy basin bounded on the west and south by
a low range of hills, and on the east and north by the Verdigris River.
The city is quartered by Eighth Street, running east and west, and Walnut Street, running north and south. The business section is at the center,
and residences occupy all but the north quarter, the industrial area.

James A. Coffey hauled two loads of lumber from Humboldt, about
sixty miles north, and built a house and trading post near the present intersection of Fifteenth and Walnut Streets in July 1869. The construction
of the Lawrence, Leavenworth & Galveston Railroad through the region
in the following year resulted in the growth of a settlement around Coffey's establishment. The village, named Coffeyville, was south of what is
now Twelfth Street and west of Walnut Street, near the northern border
of the Cherokee Strip *(see HISTORY).* Great cattle lands extended southwest. The Cookson Hills to the east and south were a rendezvous for desperadoes in their grim game of cat-and-mouse with frontier sheriffs.

Coffeyville throve on cattle and railroad trade. Cattlemen and cowboys,
who flocked to the settlement by scores, called it Cow Town. The population numbered several hundred at the end of the first year. Cafes, saloons, dance-halls, and gambling houses multiplied. Cowboy "law" with
its round of riots, brawls, and shootings, prevailed. Twelfth Street, the
main thoroughfare of Cow Town, was known as "Red Hot Street." Old-
timers allow that it was well-named.

Octave Chanute, civil engineer for the railroad, acquired a tract north
of Cow Town in 1871 and platted "a railroad addition to the town of

173

Coffeyville." A subsequent act of the legislature, sponsored by the railroad company, provided for its incorporation as a separate town. When the first election was called in March 1872, citizens of the older Coffeyville realized that their town was in danger of losing its name. Highly indignant, they filed suit in the district court challenging the legislature's act. They won the case and the act was declared unconstitutional.

Parkersburg at the southeast, meanwhile, taking advantage of the quarreling Coffeyvilles, became an increasingly formidable rival for border trade. To protect their interests the two Coffeyvilles joined forces and were incorporated as one town in 1873.

The Dalton family settled near Coffeyville in 1882. Adaline Lee Younger, mother of the tribe, was said to be a relative of the notorious Younger boys who terrorized the Missouri Valley States in post-Civil War days. The bloody Dalton raid, favorite theme of Coffeyville's crackerbox historians and story-tellers, occurred on October 5, 1892. In a running gunfight, following attempted bank robberies, four bandits and four citizens were slain. "The city," said the Coffeyville *Journal,* "sat down in sack cloth and ashes to mourn for the heroic men who had given their lives for the protection of property . . . and the maintenance of law in our midst."

Coffeyville boomed in 1903 with the development of natural gas and oil fields in Kansas and nearby Oklahoma, so that by 1910, with a population of about twenty thousand, it ranked sixth in size among the cities in the State. Its transition from an average market town to an important industrial city, its present status in southeast Kansas, was completed by 1915.

Local factories produce flour, bricks, pigments, tank cars, chemical products, stockfeeds, roofing tile, structural steel, and machinery used in the oil industry. About a thousand inhabitants are employed in refining petroleum and manufacturing gasoline and lubricants. Since 1930 Coffeyville has been a center of organized labor activities in Kansas. Labor leaders participate in all civic enterprises and Labor Day is celebrated annually by the entire population.

POINTS OF INTEREST

The MEMORIAL AUDITORIUM *(open),* 1008 Maple St., is a three-story structure of brick and limestone, built in 1925 in memory of Coffeyville citizens who served in the World War. Six Doric columns above the east entrance are flanked by life-sized figures of stone, symbolizing war and peace. The south façade is similarly columned. The auditorium seats 2,800 and is the scene of the annual Industrial Festival.

The PLAZA, 9th and Walnut Sts., contains a group of buildings at its center, several of which figured in the Dalton raid. The building at the south end of the Plaza block, now occupied by a real estate office, formerly housed the Condon Bank. Its façade is scarred by bullets fired at the Dalton gang.

Shortly after 9:30 a.m., on October 5, 1892, Jack Moore, William Powers, and Bob, Grat, and Emmett Dalton galloped into Coffeyville, hitched their horses in an alley between 8th and 9th Streets, just west of Walnut Street, and strode boldly to the Plaza. Grat, Moore, and Powers entered the Condon Bank. Bob and Emmett swaggered across the street into the First National Bank.

C. M. Ball, cashier of the Condon Bank, when ordered to surrender the funds, stalled for time by telling the bandits that the safe was operated by a time lock that would not open until 9:45 a.m. "That is only three minutes yet, and I will wait," said the outlaw's spokesman. Bob and Emmett, meanwhile, forced the employees of the First National Bank to open the vaults, and stuffed a grain bag with $21,000 in gold and currency.

The bandits had been recognized and the alarm had been given. Two hardware stores, Bowell's and Isham's, threw open their supplies of guns and ammunition to the citizenry, who stationed themselves behind wagons and sent a volley of shots through the windows of the Condon Bank.

When the firing broke out, rheumatic old men who had hobbled with difficulty a moment before, dived into convenient barrels with acrobatic agility. Pedestrians crawled headfirst under culverts and remained there trembling, unmindful of protruding hindquarters. Men of wide girth squeezed behind thin hitching posts or scrambled under porches. Scarcely a box, fence, or doorway on the Plaza was unoccupied.

The bandits who had been tricked into waiting for the time lock to open (the safe had been opened at 8:00 a.m.), burst from the Condon Bank and raced through a withering crossfire toward the alley where their horses were tied. "They were running with heads down," said a witness of the gunfight, "like facing a strong wind."

Bob and Emmett ran from the rear door of the National Bank. Emmett carried the grain bag over his shoulder while Bob, Winchester in hand, covered his retreat. Firing with deadly precision he wounded Thomas G. Ayers, and killed George Cubine, Lucius M. Baldwin, and Charles J. Brown.

Bob and Emmett reached the entry to "Death Alley" where they joined Grat, Moore, and Powers. Converging townsmen fired steadily at the bandits. Bob emptied his gun and then slumped, mortally wounded, at the base of a barn. Summoning his last ounce of strength, Grat shot and killed Marshal Charles T. Connelly. Powers fell headlong, his body riddled. Moore struggled onto his horse and died in the saddle a half mile away. Emmett, shot through the hips, his right arm shattered, but still clutching the bag of money, mounted his horse and returned to where Bob lay dying. As he extended his arm to pull Bob up beside him, he was knocked from the saddle by a slug in the back.

Thus ended the Dalton raid. Less than fifteen minutes had elapsed since the bandits entered Coffeyville. The 16-year-old Emmett was the only survivor. He had been hit twenty-three times. Sentenced to life imprisonment, he was subsequently pardoned after serving fourteen and a half years. He later established himself in California as a contractor and real estate dealer. He died at Los Angeles, aged 66, on July 13, 1937.

FOREST PARK, 8th St. at the east limits of the town, a 40-acre tract, is the site of the Montgomery County Fair held annually in September. In addition to the fair-ground buildings, there are picnic grounds, children's playgrounds, fields for football and baseball, and camp grounds at the north end which are equipped with running water, gas stoves, and screened shelter houses.

The NATATORIUM, 2826 Walnut St., is a health resort built by W. P. Brown in 1909. It contains a dance floor, a gymnasium, mineral springs, medicinal baths, and an outdoor swimming pool of mineral water.

POINTS OF INTEREST IN ENVIRONS

Walter Johnson's Former Home, *0.5 m. (see Tour 7).*

Dodge City

Railroad Stations: Front and Central Sts. for Atchison, Topeka & Santa Fe Ry.; 3rd and Trail Sts. for Chicago, Rock Island & Pacific Ry.
Bus Stations: 613 2nd St. for Southwestern Greyhound Lines, Santa Fe Trailways, Red Ball Bus Lines, Intrastate Bickel Bus Line, and Dodge City to Jetmore Line.
Airport: 3 m. E. on Military Ave. No scheduled service.
Taxis: 10¢ and upward, according to number of passengers and distance.

Accommodations: Six hotels; tourist camps.

Information Service: Chamber of Commerce, Central and Military Aves.

Radio Station: KGNO (1340 kc.).
Motion Picture Houses: Three.
Swimming: Community Pool, Wright Park, 2nd and Water Sts.
Golf: Country Club, N. end of Avenue C, 9 holes, greens fee 25¢ weekdays, 50¢ Sun.; Westlinks Golf Club, 1.5 m. N. from W. Chestnut St. on 14th Ave., then 0.5 m. on Chilton Road, 18 holes, greens fee 25¢ weekdays, 35¢ Sun.
Dog and Horse Racing: Wright Park, 2nd and Water Sts.

Annual Events: Southwest Tractor Show, April; Red Cross First Aid and Water Safety School, May or June; Great Southwest Free Fair, Sept.; Pioneer Picnic, Sept.; Community Christmas program.

DODGE CITY (2,485 alt., 10,059 pop.), on the Arkansas River, is the seat of Ford County and the metropolis of southwest Kansas. The city, with its modern business and public buildings and attractive homes, breaks the monotony of the Kansas short grass country. The newer development of the business section has steadily advanced northward, the heart of the present commercial district lying two blocks north of old Front Street, the early-day business thoroughfare, paralleling the Santa Fe Tracks. The 100th Meridian W. passes through Dodge City and marks the division between central and mountain time.

From the old Front Street area in the lowlands around the Arkansas River the residential district also spreads northward over a series of low hills. As in many western cities, there is a scarcity of large trees, but there is a growing interest in tree planting, and the streets of the newer additions are bordered with young trees, elms predominating.

Situated in one of the greatest wheat-producing areas in the world, Dodge City has been called "the buckle on the Kansas wheat belt." As the point of supply for an agricultural and cattle-raising area, it is naturally the trading and cultural center. Industrial development was followed by a gradual production expansion, with enlarged distribution facilities for agricultural machinery and implements. During the late 1920's and the early 1930's, Dodge City experienced a period of vigorous economic development. Wheat crops in 1929 and 1930 created bank clearings in 1930 of $105,347,955—evidence of the financial security that enabled the city to weather several years of depression without serious consequences.

In 1835 the Army established a small post at the mouth of Mulberry Creek. As late as 1864, however, the only indications of colonization in the Southwest were the settlers' emigrant trains, and the freighters' outfits taking supplies from Fort Hays to the Indian Territory. Indian attacks, led by such noted chiefs as Satanta, Dull Knife, and Wild Hog, were a constant threat to travelers. Raids were especially frequent at the junction of the Santa Fe Trail and the Arkansas River Trail, a favorite campground for the wagon trains and the Government freighters on the Fort Hays-Camp Supply route. To protect this site, the Government, in 1864, established Fort Dodge, naming it for Col. Henry I. Dodge, and placing in charge his nephew, Grenville M. Dodge. It was one of the most important of the frontier forts and several Army Officers of note—among them Miles, Custer, Hancock, and Sheridan—held posts there. The 100th meridian W. was the approximate west boundary of the reservation.

In 1871 a sod house, the first building on the townsite of Dodge City, was erected five miles west of Fort Dodge by H. L. Sitler. The spot was near a lone cottonwood tree—standing near the entrance of Wright Park —that marked a long-used ford across the Arkansas River. Sitler, a Government teamster, with a contract to supply wood for Fort Dodge, invested his earnings in cattle. The "soddy" was built as a cow camp and as a stopping place for freighters and buffalo hunters. It was outside the boundaries of military regulations. For obvious reasons the first Dodge City business houses—tent saloons—were located near Sitler's place.

During the same year, Charles Myer, a veteran buffalo hunter, established a trading post on the Dodge City site, and did business with the hunters of a wide area to the north and south of his station.

In 1872 railroad construction gangs established headquarters near the Sitler camp and soon the clutter of tents and portable shacks became known as Buffalo City. A townsite was laid out later in the year, under the name of Dodge City, by A. A. Robinson, chief engineer of the Santa Fe Railway. In September the first passenger train pulled into the drab little town, bringing the advance influx of immigrants, buffalo hunters, card sharps, gamblers, and adventurers—the heterogeneous, transient population that gave early Dodge City its questionable but picturesque reputation.

Revenue was unbelievably large from the great herds of buffalo on the plains. For many years these great lumbering animals had been killed for sport and food; but with the coming of the railroad, their commercial value became evident. Before a depot could be built, the buffalo hides were hauled in by the thousands and piled up on the ground to await shipment. When this industry was at its height, R. M. Wright, Dodge City historian, estimated that 25 million of these animals were in the Dodge City hunting territory; and added that many persons as well informed as himself put the probable number at 100 million. Hunters could travel for days without losing sight of the vast herds. Tom Nixon, buffalo hunter, once killed 120 in 40 minutes. A good shot, quick-witted and agile, could

CITY HALL, DODGE CITY

earn $100 a day. The era of the buffalo hunter was comparatively brief. Before the end of 1875 the great herds of shaggy animals were practically exterminated. But the railroad was responsible for a greater industry pushing its determined way into Dodge City—the cattle industry.

Milling, bawling, Texas longhorns, driven by hundreds of cowboys and trail bosses, came over the Texas Trail, a shortcut drifting west from the Chisholm Trail to Dodge City, where the herds were shipped east on the Santa Fe Railway, or driven north to the Ellis and Wakeeney railheads on the Union Pacific Railroad. In addition, herds of young steers were rested and watered at Dodge on their way to the great grazing areas in the Northwest. These drives were enormous undertakings. Herds of 17,000 to 40,000 were brought in at one time, driven by cowpunchers scarcely less wild than their bucking, bellowing charges.

So, in 1882, Dodge City took its turn as the cowboy capital of the Southwest and rode high on the wave of prosperity. Outfits of cattlemen jostled freighters, hunters and soldiers in the streets that echoed to the ribald songs and yells of the cowboy, and the wild oaths of the bull-whacker and the muleskinner. The law was 100 miles away at Hays—a town not without high color of its own.

The motley elements that made up the community were far too diverse for harmony. The freighter and the trader had nothing in common, except

a mutual and intense dislike. The same condition existed between the cowboys and the buffalo hunters. And the soldiers, considering themselves
duly authorized fighters, were not averse to taking a hand—a high hand
—whenever and wherever a row started. Results necessitated the establishment of Boot Hill Cemetery.

With the notable exception of Wild Bill Hickock, who centered his
activities at Hays and Abilene and is never definitely known to have visited
Dodge City, most of the gunmen famous in the annals of the Southwest
served terms as marshal or sheriff in the "Cowboy Capital." Jack Bridges,
the first marshal, and several of his successors held no commissions of
authority from the community but were hired by the saloon keepers and
gamblers to preserve some semblance of order among their boisterous
patrons.

Bat Masterson, who came to Dodge City as a boy of eighteen in 1872,
followed a varied career as sub-contractor for the railroad, buffalo hunter
and scout before his election as sheriff in 1877. Defeated for reelection,
he went to Tombstone, Arizona, where he helped Wyatt Earp, also a
former Dodge City peace officer, in his efforts to clean up that notorious
mining town. Bill Tilghman served as one of Masterson's deputies during
his term as sheriff while Ed Masterson, the sheriff's older brother, was
town marshal.

Sheriff Masterson wore clothes of the latest cut, a pearl gray bowler
hat, and a diamond stickpin. He often carried a cane, but in spite of his
foppish attire he was feared as one of the deadliest gunmen on the
frontier.

Other famous marshals included Mysterious Dave Mather, reputed to
be the lineal descendant of Cotton Mather; Prairie Dog Dave Morrow,
so-called because he carried on a profitable business of trapping prairie
dogs and selling the little animals to tourists at $5 a pair; and Luke Short.

Life at Dodge City was not all violent and tragic. Though the racing
cowpony and the detonation of the sixshooter were common sights and
sounds of the town, there were many citizens who carried on their business quietly during the day and took no part in the uproarious night life.
These persons and their preferences were respected.

After the great herds were ruthlessly reduced to a few scattered remnants, hunters and homesteaders were forced to descend to the comparatively dull business of gathering up and selling the bones of the thousands
of slaughtered buffalo. They were piled in huge ricks along the railroad
and shipped East for fertilizer. By 1881 it was estimated that Kansas had
received more than two million dollars for bones alone. During this period
it was a popular saying that in Dodge City buffalo bones were legal
tender.

In 1884, Dodge City held a Fourth of July celebration unique in the
history of the State and Nation. A bull fight, with "distinguished matadors, all in Andalusian costume, . . . and 12 bulls," was given for the first
and, records say, the only time in the United States. The affair was much
talked of and generously advertised, creating wide-spread interest of several sorts. Humane societies protested vigorously. State and Federal author-

MEMORIAL IN BOOT HILL CEMETERY, DODGE CITY

ities wired orders to stop the show; it could not be given in the United States. Mayor A. B. Webster wired tersely in reply, "Dodge City is not in the United States" and went on about his business of completing the elaborate arrangements.

On the morning of July 4th a great crowd was on the streets to see the grand parade. The procession, headed by the mayor, included the Dodge City Cowboy Band and the gaudily dressed matadors. At the fair-grounds more than 2,000 people found seats in the huge amphitheater especially built for the occasion.

The fight was repeated on the next day with an even better selection of fighting bulls, more thrills and excitement. The *Ford County Globe* of July 8, made this boastful comment:

Those present can testify that it was a genuine bull fight on each of the two days, just as we said it would be, and parties who witnessed the performances are free to say that they never beheld one, either in Old Mexico or Spain, that was more in dead earnest than the ones given in this city.

Gradually, as other shipping terminals were established, Dodge City became less important as a center of the cattle industry, and in 1884 the State legislature, alarmed at the increase of the cattle disease known as Texas fever, passed legislation forbidding the importation of Texas cattle between March 1 and December 1, the season of the long drives. This ended the era of the cattle trail.

The city retained a moderate importance as a shipping point for the large herds pastured in Southwest Kansas until the blizzard of 1886 destroyed the herds and the Kansas cattlemen gave up the battle with the homesteaders, which had been raging since the tide of settlement began to sweep over this section of the State in 1885. Many ranchers drove the remnants of their herds into the unorganized territory south of the State line. Others fenced a few thousand acres of grazing land and continued on a smaller scale, but by 1890 large areas near Dodge City had been broken up and sown to wheat and other crops.

From the days of the gambler and the card sharp, down through those of the cowpony race, the bull fight, and the greyhound-jackrabbit coursing, there had been a keen relish for sporting events. Today it finds outlet in dog racing and in the raising and racing of saddle and harness horses, and thoroughbred coursing hounds. The Wild Indian Kennels, just west of Wright Park, are the largest in the Middle West. A familiar sight in the environs of Dodge City is a beautiful thoroughbred jumper, followed on his morning canter by a dozen or more graceful racing dogs.

The city has a modern school system including a junior college, a denominational academy, and a business college. There are two well-equipped modern hospitals and more than a dozen churches, several of which are of architectural interest.

POINTS OF INTEREST

BOOT HILL, 4th Ave. and Spruce St., a promontory of "gyp-rock" (gypsum), and clay rising 100 feet above the Arkansas River Valley, was an early-day lookout.

About 1872 two cowboys, camped on this hillsite, had a gunfight. One was killed and the murderer fled. The dead man, friendless and unknown, was wrapped in his blankets and buried where he fell—with his boots on. So was Boot Hill dedicated.

Deaths in Dodge City during the first five years were frequent—and usually sudden. Often the victims were known only by a first name or an alias. Public concern with the last rites was brief. Some had rude pine coffins; others, wrapped in their blankets were buried as they fell—with boots on, or under their heads for a pillow.

Merritt Beeson, local historian, and son of Chalk Beeson, widely known Dodge City pioneer, says the burial of Alice Chambers, dance hall girl, on May 5, 1878, was the last on Boot Hill.

In 1879, when a schoolhouse was built on the site, the bodies were moved to Prairie Grove Cemetery; and with one exception were buried side by side, in four rows. Alice Chambers lies a short distance away, alone.

In 1927 the city bought Boot Hill as a site for the CITY HALL, built in 1929 and 1930. It is a two-story structure built of yellow brick and concrete, with a tile roof, and houses the offices of city officials, and the fire and police departments. A. R. Mann of Hutchinson was the architect. Near the main entrance is the COWBOY STATUE, a well-proportioned figure modeled in concrete, representing the western cowboy in the act of drawing his gun. To the left of the entrance is the LONGHORN STATUE— the heads and yoke of an ox team molded in concrete on a concrete base. These monuments recalling the Dodge City of the 1870's and 1880's, were modeled by the late Dr. O. H. Simpson, a local dentist.

Near the hall is a clever but rather macabre hoax, also modeled by Dr. Simpson, and "planted" as a bit of atmosphere for a Rotarian convention held in Dodge City in 1930. This is an imitation graveyard with markers at several "graves" bearing the fictitious titles of early-day tough characters—"Shoot-em-up Ike," "One-Eyed Jake," "Toothless Nell." Partially exposed and weathered concrete skulls and boot toes give the expected thrill.

The local Rotarians, infected by the spirit of Dr. Simpson's hoax, "planted" an old cottonwood tree on the hillside and passed it off to visitors as the historic gallows tree from Horse Thief Canyon. It still stands—a rope, dangling suggestively from a high crotch, draped around the dead trunk.

A veteran Dodge City peace officer, attired in cowboy regalia, is stationed in a small tent south of Boot Hill graveyard site. Tourists who visit the Hill are entertained with anecdotes of early day Dodge City and are requested to sign their names in the Boot Hill guest book.

WRIGHT PARK, 2nd Ave. and Water St., N. of the Arkansas River, was named in honor of Robert M. Wright, a pioneer citizen and former mayor. In it are the MEMORIAL FOUNTAINS, honoring World War veterans; the HOOVER PAVILION, a cream-colored stucco building used for entertainments and public meetings named in honor of G. M. Hoover, Dodge City banker who left a bequest of $95,000 for civic improvement; and the Great Southwest Free Fair Buildings. Multi-colored rock—white and black, and varied shades of orange, red, and amber—from the Sawlog, an upland stream near Dodge City, is used in various park constructions.

The OLD LONE TREE, 2nd Ave. and Water St., a cottonwood, near the entrance of Wright Park, marks the site of the ford on the Arkansas River when the town was founded in 1872. The tree is dead, but the trunk has been preserved. A memorial plate shows a prairie schooner and emigrants in bas-relief.

The SITE OF THE FIRST BUILDING, 305 2nd Ave., is marked with a bronze tablet set in the wall of the present building. It is the approximate place where H. L. Sitler built his sod house in 1871.

The SITE OF THE FIRST SCHOOL, NW. corner 1st Ave. and Walnut St., was marked in 1927 by a bronze tablet set in a five-foot sandstone boulder, bearing the inscription, "Here public education had its beginning in the Southwest in 1873."

The SANTA FE MARKER, NW. corner 2nd Ave. and Trail St., is a red granite boulder about three feet high, erected in 1906 by the D. A. R. and the State of Kansas. The inscribed bronze tablet bears the dates when the old Santa Fe Trail was in use, 1822–1872.

The SITE OF OLD FORT DODGE MILITARY RESERVATION, Central and Military Aves., is marked by a tablet set in the pavement in front of the main entrance to the Lora Locke Hotel. Part of the city is built on the old reservation and the hotel is on the western boundary line.

Two SUNDIALS, Front St. and Central Ave., stand side by side, in the Santa Fe station park. They are 44 feet in diameter and separated by a space of 44 feet. Visible from the windows of passing trains, the east dial tells central standard time, the west dial, mountain time. The 100th meridian W. passes between them.

The FIRST PRESBYTERIAN CHURCH, NW. corner Central Ave. and Vine St., is of the English Gothic style of architecture, designed by Harry W. Jones of Minneapolis, Minn. It was completed in 1925 at a cost of $150,000. The structure is of Kansas limestone trimmed with Carthage, Mo., limestone. In the church auditorium is a pipe organ, built in Lawrence and installed at a cost of $12,800.

THE SACRED HEART ROMAN CATHOLIC CHURCH, NW. corner Central Ave. and Cedar St., designed in the Spanish Mission style, is constructed of limestone with red-tile, gable roof and domed belfry. Above the arched entrance is a life-size figure of Christ. The interior of the church is finished in tan stucco and the high ceiling of the nave is supported by rough-hewn beams, stained a dark brown color. Above the altar is an oil painting, "The Crucifixion," by George M. Stone. Designed by Cram and Ferguson of Boston, the Church was completed in 1915 on the site of the first Catholic Church in Dodge City built in 1879. Adjoining the church on the north are a parish house and a parochial grade school, which harmonize with the church in design and construction.

The CITY LIBRARY (open 11-9 weekdays, 2-6 Sun.), NW. corner 2nd and Spruce Sts., an Andrew Carnegie beneficiary, is a one and one-half story brick building of modified Romanesque design, constructed in 1910. Fred Lipps of Dodge City was the architect. The library contains 14,000 volumes.

POINTS OF INTEREST IN ENVIRONS

Beeson Museum, *1.4 m.,* Old Fort Dodge and the State Soldiers' Home, *5 m.;* Willroad Gardens, *5 m. (see Tour 4A).*

Emporia

Railroad Stations: Neosho St. and 3rd Ave. for Atchison, Topeka & Santa Fe Ry.; 6th Ave. and East St. for Missouri-Kansas-Texas R.R.
Bus Station: Mit-way Hotel, 5th Ave. and Commercial St., for Santa Fe Trailways, Emporia-Eureka bus Line.
Taxis: Minimum fare, 10¢.
Buses: Three intra-city lines, fare 8¢.
Traffic Regulations: Traffic lights at intersections in business district. Parking limitations indicated by street signs. Speed limit 25 miles per hour.

Accommodations: Seven hotels; three tourist camps.

Information Service: Chamber of Commerce, 6th Ave. and Merchant St.

Radio Station: KTSW (1310 kc.).
Motion Picture Houses: Three.
Golf: Emporia Country Club, N. end of Rural St., greens fee $1.
Tennis: Peter Pan Park, State Teachers' College campus.
Boating, Fishing, and Ice Skating: Peter Pan Park.

Annual Events: St. David's Day, March 1; County Music Festivals, High School, Grade, and Rural Schools, late in March, early in April; Spring Music Festival, College of Emporia, April; State High School Music Festival, Teachers' College, April; Statewide Scholarship Contest, Teachers' College, May; Santa Fe Brotherhood Picnic, July; Community Play, *Mid-Summer Night's Dream*, Peter Pan Park, July and August.

EMPORIA (1,133 alt., 14,067 pop.), seat of Lyon County, division point of the Santa Fe Railway and trading center of a farming and dairying region, lies on a low ridge between the Neosho and Cottonwood Rivers. Although its streets appear to have been laid through a forest of elms and maples, Emporia was in fact platted on a treeless plain carpeted with bluestem grass and on the surrounding slopes and valleys broad pastures of bluestem still flourish near fields of corn and wheat.

The business district, centered at 6th Avenue and Commercial Street, is composed of two- and three-story brick structures that range architecturally from the beetling-corniced roof of the 1890's to the bland utilitarian façade of the 1930's. Four blocks past the business district Commercial Street runs plump into the Kansas State Teachers' College which, with the College of Emporia, enables local civic leaders to call their town the "Educational Center of the West."

The residential area consists largely of frame houses interspersed with brick bungalows and an occasional Victorian structure. Trees are plentiful; lawns are frequently marked with profuse shrubbery. Berkeley Hills, a restricted neighborhood at the northwest of the city, contains trim modern houses of English and Dutch Colonial architecture. The streets in this section deviate from the usual gridiron pattern and follow curved courses.

The inhabitants are mainly of Welsh and English extraction. St. David's

Day, honoring the Welsh patron saint, is annually observed by a program at the Bethany Congregational Church and the serving of tea with "bara brith," a Welsh shortbread.

Emporia manufactures cheese, candy, mattresses, stock feeds, patent medicines, and flavoring extracts. There are three grain elevators with a combined storage capacity of 75,000 bushels. The Santa Fe Railway maintains stockyards and feeding pens for livestock temporarily quartered here enroute to eastern markets, that can accommodate 12,000 cattle and 60,000 sheep.

Emporia was established in 1857 by the Emporia Town Company, four of whose five members were residents of Lawrence, Kansas. The townsite was bought from the estate of an Indian, A. Hicks, for $1,800. George W. Brown, president of the town company and editor of the Lawrence *Herald of Freedom,* named the proposed town for an ancient city in northern Africa which, according to Rollin's *History of the Carthaginians,* was a place of great wealth and importance.

Set down on the prairie where bluestem grass grew shoulder-high, the settlement consisted of an inn, a store, and a shanty in which Preston B. Plumb, only member of the town company to reside in Emporia, published the *Kanzas News.* The first issue of this sheet, dated June 5, 1857, contained the town charter, a section of which prohibited the use and sale of "spirituous liquor" within the townsite. Thus Emporia was the first "dry town" in the Middle West.

A stageline was established between Emporia and Lawrence in the latter part of 1857. Aided by publicity in the *Kanzas News* and the *Herald of Freedom,* the settlement made comparatively rapid strides. The population of the township numbered 541 by the summer of 1859. Throughout that year and into the next a severe drought withered the countryside and impoverished its settlers. No rain fell for sixteen months. The water supply at Emporia gave out, necessitating laborious journeys to the Cottonwood River.

Heavy rains fell in 1860 and Emporia resumed its progress. At a Fourth of July picnic given in the village that year, Preston B. Plumb mounted a rough platform beneath a brush arbor and delivered a bitter denunciation of slavery. In 1862, practicing what had been implied in his previous preaching, Plumb organized a company of 144 men and served in the remaining years of the Civil War as captain, major, and, finally, lieutenant-colonel of the 11th Kansas Cavalry. On returning to civilian life he was elected to the Kansas legislature. In 1877 he was elected United States Senator from Kansas, an office he held until his death in 1891.

In post-Civil War years the Emporia region attracted cattlemen who, buying gaunt Texas steers for as little as a dollar each, "put taller" on the animals by turning them out to graze the long bluestem grass. About $80,000 worth of cattle were sold in Lyon County during 1866. The "fattening" industry was subsequently blighted by settlers who fenced off the land. The cattlemen objected to the "spoilage" of the range, but their protests were brushed aside by the incoming army of homesteaders.

In 1867 the citizens of Lyon County voted $200,000 to insure the construction of the Missouri-Kansas-Texas Railroad into Emporia. The first train on this route arrived December 22, 1869. A similar sum was appropriated by the county government in 1869 to aid the extension of the Santa Fe Railway. The first Santa Fe train entered Emporia on September 14, 1870. In that year Emporia was incorporated as a city of the second class.

Equipped with railroad transportation and situated amid a fertile farming region, Emporia thereafter prospered as a trading center. Gas for illumination was installed in 1880; streetcars drawn by mules were put in operation the following year; and in 1885 an electric light plant was established. The Santa Fe Railway built a stockyard in 1887, which was enlarged between 1905–1909 at a cost of $90,000. A railroad yard construction and improvement project undertaken by the Santa Fe in 1923 was completed in 1926 at an estimated cost of five million dollars.

Lack of an adequate reserve of water was for many years the Achilles' heel of Emporia. In the drought of 1859 John Hammond, town carpenter, had sunk a well on Mechanic Street and found water at 180 feet, but this supply was not sufficient to satisfy the needs of a growing community. In 1880 a water plant was built by the Cottonwood River, but the quality of the water obtained from this stream proved inferior and, six years later, the plant was moved to the Neosho River.

The level of Neosho River, however, frequently dropped to an extremely low point under the summer sun and Emporia was periodically threatened with a water shortage. In such an emergency during July 1913, Emporians were forbidden to water their lawns and advised to boil all water used for drinking. Dan Dryer, commissioner of public utilities, was mildly ridiculed by the Nation's press in August 1920 because of his quite reasonable demand that the amount of water in Emporia bathtubs not exceed four inches.

In 1926 Emporia, aided by the Federal Government, solved its water problem for all time. The Kahola Valley, 25 miles northwest of the city, was dammed. The 400 acres of water thus impounded assure Emporia of an inexhaustible supply. The project was completed in 1938.

Emporia is the birthplace of William Allen White, eminent journalist and publisher of the Emporia *Gazette.*

POINTS OF INTEREST

The EMPORIA PUBLIC LIBRARY *(open 9-9 weekdays; 2-6 Sun.)*, 6th Ave. and Market St., is a one-story brick structure designed by Felt & Co. of Kansas City, Mo., and built in 1905–1906. It contains 30,000 volumes, complete files of all Emporia newspapers, including the *Kanzas News* (1857–59), and a valuable collection of old clippings, magazines, and secretarial books.

PETER PAN PARK, Randolph and Rural Sts., a 50-acre landscaped tract, has at its northwest corner a lake from which radiate winding paths that open on picnic grounds and a wading pool. A natural amphitheater, equipped with a stage and a loudspeaking system, is used for Sunday evening vespers, amateur theatricals, and various public meetings.

Peter Pan Park was donated to Emporia by Mr. and Mrs. William Allen White in memory of their daughter, Mary, who was fatally injured while horseback riding in 1921. Destined to be Mary White's permanent memorial is the tender editorial that her father wrote upon her death. This prose threnody has been reprinted in a score of anthologies. "Probably if her father has any sort of lasting fame beyond the decade following his death," William Allen White has said, "it will come from this editorial."

SODEN'S MILL *(open on application at office)*, 1017 S. Commercial St., a three-story corbel-stepped structure of cement and rough stone, was built in 1860 by W. T. Soden. For many years before it ceased operating in 1924 this mill supplied most of the flour used in Lyon County. After almost a decade of idleness the building was restored by L. S. Anderson and F. J. Alderson and re-opened as a mill. The walls of the first floor, near the water line, are six feet thick, reinforced by steel bars. Rafters and beams are of black walnut, pinned and braced with pegs. The second floor is similarly constructed of lighter timber. The upper walls are eighteen inches thick. Much of the old machinery, including the rollers, is in use. A new water wheel, propelled by about half the water formerly used, supplies about twice as much power as did the old wheel.

The SODEN HOUSE *(private)*, the west side of Commercial St. near the Soden Mill, is a two-story Victorian mansion, built in the 1870's for W. T. Soden. The brick walls are broken by bay-windows and an irregular out-thrust cornice, which forms a series of hat-like profiles around the structure. The mansard roof, effusively ornamented with wrought iron railings, is capped by a lookout tower.

The WILLIAM ALLEN WHITE RESIDENCE "RED ROCKS" *(private)*, 927 Exchange St., a large two-story house of Colorado sandstone, with Victorian-Gothic gables and dormer windows, was built in the 1880's for Judge Almerin Gillette. Since 1900 "Red Rocks" has been the home of William Allen White *(see LITERATURE, NEWSPAPERS, and HISTORY)*.

White was born in Emporia on February 10, 1868. A part of his youth was spent in El Dorado where he attended high school. Following his graduation he studied at the College of Emporia for two years, working during vacations for the El Dorado *Republican* and the Emporia *News*. In 1886 he enrolled at the University of Kansas, working part-time for the Lawrence *Journal*. He left the university before graduation to follow a career that took him successively to the Kansas City *Journal*, the Topeka *State Journal*, and the Kansas City *Star*.

In 1895 he returned to Emporia, borrowed $3,000, and bought the Emporia *Gazette*, a small daily and weekly. As an editor young White attracted no particular attention until the appearance of his "What's the Matter with Kansas?" editorial in August 1896. His vitriolic answer to the question thus posed was widely circulated by the Republican party in

SODEN'S MILL, EMPORIA

the presidential campaign of that year. Editor White, elevated to Nation-wide prominence overnight, thereafter consolidated his position with a score of books and numerous articles.

Despite attractive offers from metropolitan newspapers, he remained in his home town. Dubbed the "Sage of Emporia" for his interpretations of national affairs, his counsel was sought by the leaders of the Republican party. Not always a deep-dyed party man, he several times bolted the Kansas G.O.P. In 1924 he ran for Governor as an independent candidate to protest against the growing Ku Klux Klan complexion of the Republican party in Kansas. Although defeated he polled votes sufficient to discourage the entry of the Klan into subsequent contests.

White has received honorary degrees from three colleges and four universities. President Wilson appointed him United States delegate to the proposed Russian Conference at Prinkipo in 1919, and in 1931 he served with President Hoover's Organization for Unemployment Relief. He is a trustee of the College of Emporia, the Rockefeller Foundation, the Will Rogers Memorial Association, and, since 1925, a member of the Institute of Pacific Relations.

The EMPORIA GAZETTE BUILDING, 517 Merchant St., is a two-story structure of pressed-brick. Part of the first floor and the entire basement are used to publish the Emporia *Gazette,* White's widely quoted newspaper. Among past employees of the *Gazette,* is Walt Mason, the "rippling rhymer," who began working for White in 1907. His prose-poems, which he began writing while working as a reporter on the Atchison *Daily Globe,* gradually caught the public's fancy, outgrew the *Gazette's* small audience, and, as a syndicated feature, appeared in the largest dailies in the country. Mason lived in Emporia until 1920 when he moved to California, his present home (1938).

The SECOND CHRISTIAN CHURCH (Negro), SE. corner 8th Ave. and Congress St., is a small box-style structure built in 1859 for use by the white congregation of the Christian Church. Shortly afterwards the building was moved to Americus to serve as the courthouse while that town was seat of Lyon County (1858–60). It was subsequently returned to Emporia and again used by the Christian Church until the early 1890's when it was sold to the Negro congregation of the Second Christian Church. Excellently preserved, the structure appears much as it did in pioneer days.

The COLLEGE OF EMPORIA, W. end of 12th Ave., an accredited co-educational institution with an average enrollment of 400 students, was founded in 1882 by the Kansas Synod of the Presbyterian Church. On the 50-acre campus overlooking Emporia are the administration building, Lewis Hall of Science, Thomas Hall (men's dormitory), Mason Gymnasium, and Emporia and Dunlap Halls (women's dormitories). A semicircular drive *(entrance at the southeast corner of the campus)* skirts the main buildings, the most prominent of which is the ADMINISTRATION BUILDING or KENYON HALL, a three-story brick and stone structure of modified Gothic architecture designed by Felt & Co. of Kansas City, Mo., and completed in 1929 at a cost of $275,000. It contains classrooms, administrative offices, a little theater, and society meeting rooms. In the north wing is a WAR MEMORIAL CHAPEL, the walls of which bear plaques commemorating several past presidents of the college and those students who served in the World War.

Another building on the campus is the ANDERSON MEMORIAL LIBRARY *(open: 8-5 Mon.; 7-9 Tues., Wed., Thurs.; 7:30-5 Fri.; 7:30-12:30 Sat.),* a two-story new-classic building of Kansas limestone fronted by a Grecian portico, was designed by Charles Squires of Emporia and dedicated in 1902. On the second floor is MISSIONARY HALL, which contains a library of missionary literature and a collection of curios gathered by alumni of the college employed in foreign missionary work.

The library is named for Col. John B. Anderson, a railroad official who died in 1897. While a division superintendent of a railroad in Pennsylvania, Anderson had invited the employees to use his library. Among those who accepted was Andrew Carnegie, then a telegraph operator. Following Anderson's death in later years, Carnegie, grown wealthy, proposed to commemorate his early friend by financing the construction of a library in Pittsburgh, Pa. Mrs. Anderson of Manhattan, Kans., preferred that the library be established at the College of Emporia, an institution in which her husband had been interested. Carnegie assented. Books from Colonel Anderson's private library supplied the nucleus of the present collection which includes more than 22,000 volumes.

The KANSAS STATE TEACHERS' COLLEGE, 12th Ave. and Commercial St., is a co-educational institution with an average enrollment of 1,500 students. As the Kansas State Normal School, the college was organized in 1865. The opening sessions, held in the upper room of a stone schoolhouse, were attended by 18 students. The first building was erected in 1867 through private gifts and a legislative appropriation. The present name was adopted on February 20, 1923.

The 46-acre campus, enclosed by a low brick wall, is shaded by more than 70 varieties of trees, including Russian olive, Chinese elm, and Irish juniper. The main entrance at the foot of Commercial Street opens on a sunken garden which contains a fountain and a lily pool. The garden is bordered by peach, pecan, catalpa, and mulberry trees.

Directly north of the sunken gardens is PLUMB MEMORIAL HALL, a four-story, T-shaped structure of brick and stone, its main entrance flanked by two massive columns. The building was designed by Charles H. Chandler and completed in 1917. The front wing houses the administrative offices of the college; the rear wing contains Albert Taylor Hall, an auditorium which seats 2,000.

Southeast of Plumb Memorial Hall is the LABORATORY SCHOOL, a three-story building of brick and terra cotta, designed by Charles D. Cuthbert and completed in 1929. The structure incorporates advanced ideas in school planning. It contains kindergarten classrooms equipped with stages and fireplaces, a library, a clinic, a science laboratory, and an auditorium-gymnasium.

South of the Laboratory School is the MUSIC HALL, a three-story building of brick and terra cotta, designed by Charles D. Cuthbert and erected in 1928. It contains 18 studios, 33 practice rooms, several rehearsal halls, and an air-conditioned auditorium where weekly student recitals and monthly public concerts are presented.

Near the drive that extends from Commercial Street is the KELLOGG LIBRARY *(open: 7:45-9 Mon., Tues., Wed., Thurs.; 7:45-8:30 Fri.; 7:45-6 Sat.)*, named for Lyman Beecher Kellogg, first president of the college. The structure was designed by John F. Stanton, and completed in 1903. The library contains more than 70,000 volumes. NORTON SCIENCE HALL, a three-story building of brick and terra cotta, is named for Henry B. Norton, first instructor of natural science at the college. The structure was designed by John F. Stanton and built in 1907. It houses the departments of physics, biology, chemistry, and health education. A MUSEUM *(open 8-5 weekdays)*, in the hallways on each floor, contains fossils, minerals, industrial exhibits, and biological specimens.

Facing Lake Wooster at the north of the campus are the women's dormitories, Abigail Morse Hall and Morse Hall Annex. The remaining buildings on the campus include the gymnasium, the Student Union building, and the power plant.

POINTS OF INTEREST IN ENVIRONS

Lyon County State Lake, *14.2 m.;* Cottonwood Falls, *23 m. (see Tour 4A).*

++++++++++++++++++++++++⌗+++++++++++++++++++++++

Fort Scott

Railroad Stations: 623 E. Wall St. for St. Louis & San Francisco Ry.; 312 National Ave. for Missouri-Kansas-Texas R.R.; 219 N. National Ave. for Missouri Pacific R.R.

Bus Stations: Goodlander Hotel, 2 S. National Ave. for Santa Fe Trailways, Southern Greyhound Lines and Missouri-Ozark Lines.

Accommodations: Eight hotels; five tourist camps; boarding houses.

Information Service: Goodlander Hotel, 2 S. National Ave.; Chamber of Commerce, Marble Bldg.

Motion Picture Theaters: Three.

Swimming: Municipal pool, 7th and Main Sts.; Bridal Veil Park pool (Negro), W. 2nd St.

Picnic and Playgrounds: Gunn Park, W. end of 9th St.

Annual Events: Holy City, sacred cantata, last Sunday in March; Dairy Show, Sept., three days.

FORT SCOTT (800 alt., 10,763 pop.), the outgrowth of a frontier military outpost, lies on the south bank of the Marmaton River, five miles west of the Missouri Line. A city of "jogging" streets and fine old trees, with buildings older than Kansas itself sandwiched in between modern structures, Fort Scott is a blend of pioneer and modern America. At the junction of three railroads, the city is important as a distribution and shipping point and also as a manufacturing center in southeastern Kansas. The Saturday afternoon bustle of farmers and their wives in and out of stores, produce stations, and cafes indicates the place of agriculture in the community's economy.

The business district extends south from Market Square, a triangular plot bounded by Market, Oak, and National Avenues. National Avenue, which bounds Market Square on the west, bisects the town from north to south. Immediately adjacent to the business section on the south and west is Fort Scott's older residential district, center of the social activities of the 1880's and 1890's. Gabled brick and stone structures for the most part, with broad porches and deep windows, the houses are in good repair and in many instances are occupied by descendants of the original owners. Great elm trees form long green arches over the streets in this section, and stone hitching posts still stand in front of many of the houses.

Approximately one mile from the business section on the south and west are the newer residential districts with recently paved streets, straight young trees, and rows of trim frame and stucco houses. Three railroads cut through the north portion of the city near the river and the industrial section.

Fort Scott has one of the first municipally-owned junior colleges in the

State, with an enrollment of approximately 400. Schools, churches, lodges, and clubs are centers for the community's social and cultural life.

Owing, no doubt, to the town's early military history and to the fact that many of the residents are descendants of the first soldiers stationed at old Fort Scott, patriotic organizations have been especially active within the city from its earliest days and residents make even the lesser patriotic days gala occasions. Carroll Plaza, today as in the past, is the scene of these celebrations.

Provisions were made for a camp between Fort Leavenworth and Fort Gibson when the old Military Road between the two was surveyed in 1837, but it was not until 1842 that a fort was founded at a point approximately midway between the two and named in honor of Gen. Winfield Scott. Designated as the "Plaza," a parade ground was laid out and by the summer of 1843 a number of military buildings, including officers' quarters, soldiers' barracks, stables, a hospital, and a guardhouse, were completed, all facing the parade grounds. Surrounding the square and its buildings was a stockade, built of huge timbers 12 feet high. An iron gate in the west side of the stockade was the only opening.

Fort Scott was garrisoned until 1855, when the Government abandoned it, selling the lumber in the stockade and auctioning off fort buildings. After the sale of the buildings Fort Scott carried on as a tiny settlement; travel continued over the Military Road and the town grew in importance through trade with soldiers, settlers, and Indians. Lying only five miles from the Missouri Line, the town, before and during the Civil War, became the rendezvous for both Free Staters and pro-slavery sympathizers, and guerrillas and ruffians along the border plundered and stole from both sides.

One of the old fort's officers' quarters was occupied by the Free State Hotel in the late 1850's, so named because it was a favorite stopping place for such Free Staters as John Brown, Charles Jennison, Capt. James Montgomery, and scores of sympathizers not so well known. The hotel became nationally known through the columns of the New York, Philadelphia, and Baltimore papers as the headquarters of Captain Montgomery, who made widely publicized raids upon pro-slavery sympathizers in the vicinity.

Local tradition in Fort Scott asserts that the term *Jayhawker* originated with the patrons of the Free State Hotel. Pat Devlin, an Irishman and a member of Captain Montgomery's band, so the story goes, returned late one afternoon from plundering pro-slavery farmers along the Missouri-Kansas border. Asked where he had been he replied that he had been "jayhawking." "The jayhawk," he went on to explain, "is a bird in Ireland that catches small birds and bullyrags the life out of them like cats do mice. I'm in the same business myself and I call it jayhawking." Jayhawker was taken up by Captain Montgomery as a nickname for his band and finally stuck as a name for all Kansas.

The Western Hotel, stopping place for pro-slavery men, stood directly across the Plaza from the Free State Hotel in the days preceding the Civil

War, and rivalry between the two hostelries was as bitter as that between the North and the South. Here, it is said, the Marais des Cygnes massacre *(see HISTORY)* was plotted and here two pro-slavery men organized a Blue Lodge by which they hoped to drive Free State men from the Territory by scaring them off their claims. The Free Staters, in turn, organized the Self-Protective Association headed by Captain Montgomery.

Friction between the two factions came to a head in October 1857, when Judge Joseph Williams of the United States District Court, a pro-slavery sympathizer, began to hear the lawsuits between the Free State and the pro-slavery men over homestead claims. Declaring that all decisions were going against the Free State claimants because of partiality shown by the court, the anti-slavery faction set up its own court in a log cabin a few miles from town. This they called the "Squatters' Court" and, as no Bible was handy, witnesses were sworn on an old medical book, *Dr. Gunn's Family Physician.*

Pro-slavery sympathizers arrested a man named Rice, who was charged with the murder of one of their comrades, and held him at the Free State Hotel pending his trial in the district court. Montgomery, with about 70 men, returned to Fort Scott to release the prisoner. A storekeeper named Little, who was also United States marshal, fired into the group outside the hotel from the transom of his shop. Immediately one of Montgomery's men returned fire, shooting Little through the forehead as he looked out. Shots rang out through the Plaza for several minutes. Montgomery and his party surrounded the store, believing it garrisoned with pro-slavery men. Ruffians in the band looted nearby stores. The Free Staters broke into the store and Montgomery stopped the looting. The Free State man was released. By 1860 the border was quiet again.

After the outbreak of the Civil War Fort Scott again assumed importance as a military post, large quantities of supplies being stored there for the use of troops stationed as far south as the Red River. Lt. Col. Lewis R. Lewell, commanding the Sixth Kansas Cavalry, was appointed Post Commander in 1862, and fortifications, consisting of breastworks, stockades, and three blockhouses—Fort Henning, Fort Insley, and Fort Blair—were erected. Gen. James H. Lane, who was appointed Union commander for recruiting in the department of Kansas in July 1862, also established his headquarters at the fort.

Fort Scott, during the 1860's and 1870's, was noted for its gaiety. Even during the tense days before the war the Free State Hotel was as gay a spot as was to be found in southeastern Kansas. Here, according to early newspaper accounts, the "élite of the town" gathered and frequently "danced and joshed each other until seven o'clock in the morning."

The Wilder House, just off the Plaza on Main Street, replaced the Free State Hotel as a rendezvous in the late 1860's. Famed in the vicinity is the reply of the hotel-keeper when new arrivals asked, "Is this the Wilder House?" "You stay here awhile," he would drawl, "and you'll find there ain't a wilder house in the country."

The Tri-Weekly Stage ran between Kansas City and Fort Scott in the 1860's, the name of which, as the town wags explained it, meant "to go out one week and try to get back the next." The fare between the two points was $10 and "carry a rail," the term of the day for walking alongside the stagecoach when the roads were bad. "If the roads were good," an historian writes, "a man passenger only had to carry a rail about a third of the way. But it was worth the price to ride into the Wilder House with a grand flourish."

Cohn's Restaurant and Confectionery on East Wall Street became the social hub of the town in the 1880's. "The Delmonico of the West," one local newspaper called it, "a royal restaurant with dining parlors handsomely painted and papered in the highest style of art, the popular and stylish resort of the city. . . ." Cohn, restaurateur of parts, among other elaborate dishes contributed "Quail à la Marmaton" and "Turkey à la Pawnee" to the art of cuisine.

By the beginning of the twentieth century, however, social life was greatly subdued. The town was developing as a manufacturing and trading center. Then in the early 1900's came a slump in business activity, a gradual let-down after a half century of bustling activity.

For years farmers in the vicinity produced grains and vegetables with only moderate success. In 1910, however, a survey was made and Fort Scott business men offered to promote the establishment of ice cream factories and creameries if the farmers would devote their resources to the raising of dairy cattle. Local banks extended credit to farmers who bought dairy cows and marketed their milk in Fort Scott. Progress was slow in the beginning for money was scarce and a limited market retarded production. In 1918 the Borden Company erected a condensery, furnishing a year-around market which insured the success of the dairying program.

In 1938, thirty milk trucks covered the territory, carrying approximately 150,000 pounds of milk a day into Fort Scott. Farmers receive almost $1,000,000 yearly for the dairy products, the greater portion of which is spent in this vicinity or deposited in local banks. Dairymen and business men promote a Dairy Show annually. In addition to the dairy industry Fort Scott has two railroad shops, an overall factory, a monument factory, foundries, and paving brick plants. A hydraulic cement plant just north of town is among the largest of its kind in the Middle West and deposits of coal, which accompany the cement rock deposits, furnish fuel for the plant's operation. The mining of coal is an industry of steadily increasing importance in the area.

Fort Scott was the home of Eugene Fitch Ware, author and editor (see LITERATURE).

POINTS OF INTEREST

CARROLL PLAZA, east of the business district and bounded by Marmaton, Blair, Fenton, and Lincoln Aves., is a grass-grown square, once the parade ground for soldiers stationed at the old fort. It is the oldest area in the city, having been laid out in 1842. Although the points of the square were undoubtedly intended to be directly north and south, a slight miscalculation was made and its sides lie diagonal to Fort Scott's main streets. On the square and facing it are the remaining fort relics.

Near the SE. entrance is FORT BLAIR *(always open)*, a Civil War blockhouse. Originally built on the corner of 2nd and Scott Streets, it was moved to its site on the Plaza in 1924. The blockhouse is constructed of sawed slabs, thoroughly spiked, covered with shingles and weather-boarded with rough native lumber. Numerous openings in its sides were used as loopholes for rifle fire. A bandstand near the center marks the SITE OF THE OLD FORT POWDER MAGAZINE built in 1842. A stone canopy, near the bandstand, marks the SITE OF THE OLD FORT WELL that was dug immediately after the first soldiers arrived at Fort Scott. The canopy, constructed in the early part of the present century, is a reproduction of the original built in the 1840's.

The SITE OF THE OLD FORT STABLES, NE. corner Fenton and Marmaton Sts., occupied by a storage barn, is designated by a bronze marker. Another bronze marker, midway in the block, marks the SITE OF THE FRONTIER BARRACKS.

The FORT SCOTT MUSEUM *(open 9-5, daily)*, 103 Blair St., occupies one of the three remaining officers' quarters built during the first year of the fort's existence. The museum, the property of the Fort Scott Historical Society, contains souvenirs of the early fort, a collection of Indian relics, and, among other things, pictures of the town as it was in the 1850's and 1860's. These are framed and mounted on walnut pedestals made from pillars of a fourth officers' quarters that stood at the opposite end of the block. The museum building, a two-and-one-half-story house of Georgian Colonial design was operated as the Free State Hotel in the late 1850's. It was remodeled in 1938 as a WPA project.

The GOODLANDER CHILDREN'S HOME *(open with permission of superintendent)*, 107 Blair St., is in another of the officers' quarters. The home, founded January 17, 1903, and named for C. W. Goodlander, who provided funds for its opening, is non-sectarian. It is supported by an annual appropriation of $500 from the State, monthly contributions from Fort Scott business men and residents of Bourbon County, and through the proceeds from "Tag Day" held annually in Fort Scott to raise money for improvements.

The OFFICERS' QUARTERS *(open with permission of manager)*, 111 Blair St., the third of the remaining buildings, has been made into an apartment house although the building has undergone little change.

Immediately behind the three officers' quarters are several small STONE HOUSES used by the troops as store houses. Behind these are the FORT STABLES built with stone walls 14 inches thick. The stables are two stories high with a huge hand-hewn beam between the stories.

The SITE OF THE OLD FORT GUARDHOUSE, corner of Lincoln and Fenton Sts., occupied by the city jail, is designated by a bronze plaque. The guardhouse was built in 1843.

The FORT HOSPITAL, 106 Fenton St., is now used as a storage barn. Occupying its original site the old building has undergone little change except that the porches have been removed.

The NATIONAL CEMETERY, on E. National Ave. 1 m. E. of National Ave., was established by act of Congress in 1862 and dedicated as

a burial place for United States soldiers. The cemetery's 10 acres are enclosed by a stone fence, with entrance through a folding iron gate. Four
mounted cannon guard the rostrum on the knoll near the center of the
grounds. From a tall shaft in the center of the rostrum the American flag
flies over the graves of Civil, Spanish-American, and World War soldiers.
Here, too, is the grave of Eugene F. Ware.

East National Avenue, the approach to the cemetery, is known locally
as "orphan street." Neither the city nor the State claim the thoroughfare,
and it has been allowed to fall into bad condition.

The HOME OF EUGENE WARE *(private)*, SW. corner Eddy
and 2nd Sts., is known as the Drake Home. A two-story white frame
structure, the house has been remodeled throughout since Ware made his
home there in the 1880's and 1890's. Eugene Fitch Ware is best known
for his *Rhymes of Ironquill*, which ran through 13 editions. He came to
Kansas as a young man shortly after the Civil War, was admitted to the
bar, and in the latter part of the century served for a number of years as
editor of the Fort Scott *Monitor*.

POINTS OF INTEREST IN ENVIRONS

Rock Creek Lake, *9 m.;* Elm Creek Lake, *25.1 m. (see Tour 5);* Crawford
County State Park, *27 m. (see Tour 13).*

Hutchinson

Railroad Stations: 3rd Ave. and Walnut St. for Atchison, Topeka & Santa Fe Ry.; C and Main Sts. for Missouri Pacific R.R.; Ave. D and Main St. for Chicago, Rock Island & Pacific Ry. and Arkansas Valley Interurban Ry.
Bus Stations: 18 E. 2nd Ave. for Cardinal and Southern Kansas Stage Lines, and Greyhound and Santa Fe Trailways.
Airport: Municipal airport, E. city limits, N. of US 50S; no scheduled service.
Taxis: 10¢, upward.
Traffic Regulations: Traffic lights; straight ahead or right on green, left turn on amber, stop on red.

Accommodations: Eight hotels, boarding houses, tourist camps.

Information Service: Chamber of Commerce, 203 W. 1st Ave.

Radio Station: KWBG (1420 kc.).
Theaters and Motion Picture Houses: Little Theater, Richardson Hall; five motion picture houses in winter, four in summer.
Swimming: Carey Municipal Park, Park and Main Sts.; Stevens Swimming Pool, 1501 E. 1st Ave.
Golf: Carey Municipal Park, 18 holes; greens fee 25¢ weekdays, 35¢ Sundays and holidays; Country Club, 8 m. NW. on county road, 18 holes; greens fee $1. Prairie Dunes Golf Club, 4 m. E. on county road, 9 holes; greens fee $1, weekdays; $2 Sundays and holidays.
Tennis: Public courts in Carey Municipal Park.
Baseball: Carey Municipal Park.
Wrestling and Boxing: Convention Hall, Ave. A and Walnut St.

Annual Events: Fourth of July Fiesta; Kansas State Fair, Sept.

HUTCHINSON (1,530 alt., 27,085 pop.), fourth largest city in Kansas, lies slightly south and east of the center of the State on the north bank of the Arkansas River. The city spreads out in the level valley land in the form of the letter "T", its base extending eastward and its broad arms reaching north and south. Although typical of the cattle country in its friendliness, its lack of social distinctions, and in the clean way its broad streets meet the open prairie, Hutchinson is a city of mills and factories.

Laid out with a lavish hand by pioneers who had more land than anything else, Hutchinson has long straight streets, broad lawns, and many parks. Unlike most Kansas river towns, it did not begin at the river's edge, but grew from a tiny cluster of houses on Cow Creek which follows a parallel course approximately one-half mile north of the river. Creeping southward until it reached the river and at the same time pushing into the prairie land on the north and east, Hutchinson has practically swallowed up the narrow creek. Busy streets cross the creek bed in the residential sections and it is routed through huge tiles beneath the structures in the heart of the business section.

Main Street, crossing the subterranean channel of Cow Creek at Avenue A, cuts squarely across town from north to south. Through a district of shabby stores and garages near the river it passes into the main business section, emerging finally into the better residential districts as it nears the northern outskirts.

Business houses for the most part are brick structures two and three stories in height with here and there a four-, five-, or eight-story building occupying an important corner. Homes near the business section date back to the 1890's and the early 1900's, built by the first fortunes made in salt and cattle and in prairie real estate. Surrounding these are houses of California bungalow type, flanked by rows of prim new residences of varying architectural designs. The lower-income residential areas of Hutchinson are west and east of the business section, their neat but shabby streets hugging close to the river and the railroad tracks.

The irregular bulk of flour mills and the concrete cylinders of grain elevators dominate the industrial area, which lies approximately a mile east of the retail district. Nearby are salt plants, a refinery, railroad yards, and numerous smaller industrial concerns. Along the railroad tracks on the west side of Hutchinson is a second industrial district, and across the Arkansas River at the south city limits is still another group of mills and elevators, another refinery, and a nationally known salt plant.

The importance of the salt industry to the city of Hutchinson is evident to the casual observer, and "Salt City" is often substituted for Hutchinson in names of business firms. Built above salt deposits, reputedly among the richest in the world, Hutchinson's chief industry is the mining, processing, and shipment of salt. Deposits that underlie the greater part of the metropolitan area and the surrounding country are approximately 600 feet below the surface and range from 300 to 350 feet in thickness. The city's three salt-processing plants ship 3,000,000 barrels of salt annually to markets in all parts of the United States and geologists estimate that the supply is practically inexhaustible. Plants and mines employ approximately 600 men.

Although somewhat less spectacular, Hutchinson's wheat shipping and storage industry attains heights in "wheat years" untouched by the comparatively steady salt industry. As the seat of Reno County, the most important wheat-producing area of Kansas, Hutchinson is a key city for the shipment and milling of grain from the adjacent area and from the great fields of southwestern Kansas. With eight elevators and three flour mills, Hutchinson has storage facilities for more than 10,000,000 bushels of grain. Claiming to be the smallest city in the world with its own grain market dealing in futures, Hutchinson points to a ten-year average of grain receipts at its markets in the period from 1925 to 1935, exceeding 46,-000,000 bushels a year. Thirty grain firms maintain offices in the city.

Surrounded on all sides by oil fields, Hutchinson's petroleum industry has developed gradually, but gives promise of exceeding both salt and wheat in importance. A producing well, flowing at the rate of 3,600 barrels of high gravity oil a day, is only nine miles east of the city and more than 1,500 additional wells are within a radius of 100 miles of the city limits. Adjacent to Hutchinson on the east is Kansas' most productive gas well, yielding 128,600,000 cubic feet a day. Hutchinson has two refineries, numerous distribution and supply companies, and long dark lines of tank cars mingle with those loaded with wheat in its railroad yards.

Named for its founder, C. C. Hutchinson, the city was platted in November 1871, its first streets lying on both sides of Cow Creek near the spot where the new Santa Fe Railway was to cross the Arkansas River. To encourage settlement by sober, industrious persons, Hutchinson included a clause in the deed to each lot specifying that if liquor were sold or given away thereon at any time prior to 1875, the property and all improvements would revert back to the original owner. After 1875 Hutchinson hoped that the moral sentiment of the settlers would be strong enough to control the liquor traffic.

To the builder of the first house on the townsite Hutchinson offered to give one of the choice lots in the settlement. This prize was won by A. F. Horner who moved a black walnut building from the nearby town of Newton. This was not the first prize Horner's portable house had won for its builder. When the town of Brookville was founded on the Kansas Pacific Railroad in the early 1870's its promoters, like Hutchinson's, offered a town lot to the persons who built the first house. Horner quickly built a house 20 by 60 feet which won the prize, but soon moved it to the new town of Florence on the Santa Fe Railway to win another lot.

Horner was settled in the draughty house in Florence when the Santa Fe pushed westward to Newton and promoters of that settlement offered a similar prize. In due time Horner won it with his mobile walnut house. Moving it for the last time to Hutchinson, Horner placed it on a lot at the corner of First and Main Streets where it remained until it was torn down to make room for a more modern structure. The building served as C. C. Hutchinson's real estate office, the town's first post office, and first hotel.

When Hutchinson was incorporated as a third class city in August 1872, Horner's much-traveled building was only one of a number of low buildings along Main Street. The town boasted a newspaper, the Hutchinson *News,* an inn, and a cluster of stores and houses. The promoters plowed a wide furrow around the settlement to protect it from the fires that swept so swiftly across the level grass-covered prairie, and, since stones for street markers were scarce, citizens marked off streets with buffalo bones. The Santa Fe Railway reached the Arkansas River crossing—and Hutchinson—in the summer of 1872, but pushed westward almost immediately.

Having visions of Hutchinson as a prairie metropolis and a seat of culture and learning, the settlers made plans for churches and schools soon after their arrival. The first regular church meetings were held in a building that on weekdays served as a butcher shop. During the second summer of Hutchinson's existence residents voted $15,000 in bonds to build a school building. Literary and musical societies were formed early, and in 1882 the Hutchinson opera house was built by public subscription on the northeast corner of First Avenue and Main Street. The *News* carried long paragraphs on the activities of Hutchinson's cultural societies and the

IN A SALT MINE, HUTCHINSON

town's social leaders sponsored home talent performances at the opera house for special occasions, when "traveling talent" was not available.

By 1885 Hutchinson had attained a certain importance as a shipping and trading center. The production of Turkey Red wheat, a variety particularly adaptable to prairie soil, was increasing yearly, and its increase was accompanied by the growing importance of Hutchinson as a milling center.

A few years later, following the discovery of natural gas, a wave of prosperity swept southwestern Kansas and in 1887 Sam Blanchard of Hutchinson drilled the first well in the vicinity on a farm south of the city. At approximately 300 feet the drill struck salt and although local residents were mildly amazed to learn that salt deposits existed beneath the city they hardly considered prospects of a future industry until New York promoters had a plant in operation almost in the heart of the city. By 1888 almost a dozen salt plants were in operation in and near Hutchinson and the city's salt industry was permanently established less than two years after the mineral was discovered.

Growing slowly and experiencing no booms, Hutchinson had a population of 9,000 in 1900 and by 1910 had grown to more than 16,000. In the 1920's oil wealth began to filter in from the south and west, and the plentiful supply of cheap natural gas fuel attracted many smaller industries.

Hutchinson is the home of Gov. Walter A. Huxman, 27th Governor of the State, and one of the five Democrats elected to the office since Kansas was admitted to statehood in 1861.

POINTS OF INTEREST

The RENO COUNTY COURTHOUSE, NW. corner 1st Ave. and Adams St., completed in 1930, is a fine example of modern architecture. The structure which cost approximately a half-million dollars, is of Indiana Bedford stone, Virginia marble, and yellow brick. In the courtroom, the most highly decorated chamber in the building, is a mural painting by the New York artist Adrenanti, an allegory of mercy, justice, and execution.

The SOLDIERS' MONUMENT, in 1st Ave. Park, 1st Ave. and Walnut St., was erected to the memory of veterans of the Civil War by members of the Joe Hooker Post, G. A. R., of Hutchinson. The monument, dedicated in 1919, is surmounted by the figure of Abraham Lincoln with life-size figures of soldiers and sailors of the Civil War upon each corner.

The SUN DIAL MONUMENT, in Sylvan Park, NE. corner Walnut St. and Ave. B, commemorates President Harding's visit to Hutchinson in 1923 when he spoke at the park's dedication.

The KANSAS STATE INDUSTRIAL REFORMATORY *(open on application)*, S. end of Reformatory Ave., is a penal institution for delinquents between 15 and 25 years of age. It comprises 1,300 acres within the city of Hutchinson and controls 21 farms with a combined acreage of 4,000 acres adjacent to the city. The average wheat yield of the institution is 18,000 bushels, and the sale of surplus swine contributes $8,000 annually toward its upkeep. The automobile tag factory, where Kansas State automobile license tags are manufactured, has an output of 4,000 tags a day. The institution houses approximately 1,000 inmates.

The BARTON SALT PLANT *(open on application; guides)*, Cleveland and Campbell Sts. processes salt by evaporation. Water is forced into the salt wells and the salt brought to the surface in the form of salt brine. In time the moisture evaporates and impurities in the salt are removed.

The CAREY SALT PLANT *(open on application; guides)*, Poplar St. and Avenue B, also processes salt by evaporation.

The CAREY LABORATORY *(open on application; guides)*, on the grounds of the Carey plant is among the largest and most complete laboratories of its kind in the United States. Here salt from the mines is tested and new methods for purifying devised.

The CAREY ROCK SALT MINE *(open mornings only; guides)*, E. end Carey Blvd. at city limits, although owned by the Carey Company operates separately from the plant.

Mine visitors descend 645 feet to the mine bottom by way of an electric elevator in one minute and twenty seconds. Here they are permitted to explore the 200 rooms of the mine and see the maze of subterranean

SALT PLANT, HUTCHINSON

railroad tracks by which salt is transported to the elevators. Rooms are
50 feet in width, 300 feet in length and have ceilings of rock salt from
7 to 10 feet high.

The "skip," or elevator, with a four-ton capacity raises the salt to the
mill on the surface in slightly more than a minute although its speed may
be increased to enable it to carry 1,000 tons of salt from the mine floor
in an eight-hour working day. Cars that convey salt from the mine rooms
to the "skip" carry between 20 and 25 tons of salt each trip and are filled
by motor-driven loaders which complete the task in 15 minutes.

The mine is electrically lighted and electric power is used throughout,
the company claiming that in this mine electricity is more extensively used
than in any other salt mine in the world.

The shaft of the mine was begun in May 1922 and completed in June
1923. Former Governor Jonathan M. Davis touched the button which
brought the first official "skip" of salt to the surface on June 23, 1923.
The mine employs approximately 60 men, and the mill, unlike other plants
in Hutchinson, processes salt by crushing and sifting.

CAREY MUNICIPAL PARK, Main St. between Park Ave. and the Arkansas River, a gift of Emerson Carey to the city of Hutchinson, is entered by a drive that affords a view of the Arkansas River, the park lagoons, sunken gardens, swimming pool, baseball field, golf course, playgrounds, and picnic grounds, and circles back to the entrance past the police rifle range.

The EMERSON CAREY MEMORIAL FOUNTAIN, at the park entrance, is an electrically lighted fountain backed by a decorative stone arch. The spray design of the fountain changes constantly for an hour and a half without repeating the same pattern. Dedicated October 24, 1935, the fountain was built by subscriptions from Hutchinson business men and dedicated to the memory of the late Emerson Carey, former owner of the Carey salt interests and prominent Hutchinson philanthropist.

The MORTON SALT STABILIZED HIGHWAY, connecting Main St. with the Morton plant, was built by accident. At intervals loads of salt were dumped into soft places along the old dirt road that once connected the plant with the city pavement until the thoroughfare was completely surfaced with salt. Through experimentation and constant upkeep by plant workers the road has become a satisfactory thoroughfare for heavy trucks and wagons.

The MORTON SALT PLANT *(open on application; guides),* at the N. end of Morton Salt Stabilized Highway, is one of the seven Morton salt plants in the United States. It refines salt by purifying and evaporating brine from deep wells. The staff of the plant's laboratory does research work for the entire western division of the company's holdings, an area which includes Kansas, Texas, California, and Utah.

POINTS OF INTEREST IN ENVIRONS

Burrton oil fields, *17.2 m. (see Tour 4A).*

Kansas City

Railroad Stations: Union Station, center 7th St. Viaduct, W. side 7th St. Trafficway, for Union Pacific R.R. and Chicago Rock Island & Pacific Ry.; Kansas City Terminal Station, 434 Central Ave., for Missouri Pacific R.R. and Chicago Great Western R.R.; 1900 Olathe Blvd. for Missouri-Kansas-Texas R.R.; 26th St. and Powell Ave. for Atchison Topeka & Santa Fe Ry.; 100 S. 8th St. (Rosedale) for St. Louis-San Francisco Ry. Union Ticket Offices, 914 N. 6th St.

Bus Station: Union Bus Depot, 754 Minnesota Ave. for Missouri Pacific, Union Pacific, Greyhound, Cardinal Stage, and Santa Fe Lines.

Airports: Fairfax Airport, 2.5 m. NE. of business district on Fairfax Rd., U. S. Naval Base, training field and planes for hire; no passenger service. Kansas City Municipal Airport, 102 Richards Rd., Kansas City. Mo. 3 m. E. of Kansas City, Kans., business district, for Braniff, Hanford, and the Transcontinental & Western Air Inc. Lines.

Taxis: Minimum fare 10¢.

Piers: 1st St. and Minnesota Ave.

Streetcars: Fare 10¢, tokens four for 35¢, unlimited weekly pass $1.60. Supplementary bus lines weekly pass $1.25.

Traffic Regulations: Turns may be made in either direction at intersections of all streets except where traffic lights or officers direct otherwise. Stop signs at intersections and school crossings, parking limitations signs on main business streets.

Accommodations: Two hotels, tourist camps.

Information Service: General, Chamber of Commerce, 727 Minnesota Ave.; road information, Kansas Motor Club, 642 State Ave.

Radio Station: KCKN (1310 kc.).

Motion Picture Houses: Three downtown and 11 neighborhood houses; two for Negroes.

Swimming: Clifton Park Pool, 21st St. and Riverview Ave.; Klamm Park Pool, 22nd St. and Cleveland Ave.; Edgerton Park Pool (Negro), 3rd St. and Edgerton Ave.; Shawnee Park bath-house, NW. corner Pyle St. and Osage Ave.; Rosedale Pool, 29th St. and Springfield Ave. Admission 5¢ to 4:30 p.m., 10¢ evenings, holidays, and Sundays. Pools open during July and Aug.

Golf: Victory Hills Golf Club, 18-hole, greens fee, 50¢ weekdays, 75¢ Saturday, $1 Sunday, 5 m. W. on US 40 to Vance Rd.; Quivira Lake Golf course, 9-hole, greens fee, 50 cents weekdays, $1 Saturday, $1.25 Sunday, 9 m. SW Argentine-Holliday Rd., arrange courtesy card of admission at Chamber of Commerce or Quivira Club.

Tennis: Heathwood Park, 10th St. & Stewart Ave., 2 courts; Westheight Manor Park, 20th St. & Wood Ave., 6; Bethany Park, 11th St. & Central Ave., 4; Shawnee Park, 7th St. & Osage Ave., 2; Emerson Park, 29th St. & Strong Ave., 4; City Park, 4122 Rainbow Blvd., 12; Klamm Park, 22nd St. & Cleveland Ave., 6; Quindaro Park, 34th St. & Parkview Ave., 4; Parkwood Park, 9th St. & Quindaro Blvd., 2; Big Eleven Lake, 11th St. & Washington Blvd., 4.

Riding: Royal Riding Academy, Calvin Lake, 3 m. W. on Reidy Rd.; Wonderland Park stables, 44th St. and Muncie Blvd.

Annual Events: Kansas Day celebration, Jan. 29; Military ball on Mon. following Lent; Music Week, first week after Easter; Mexican fiestas, May 5, Sept. 15 and 16; Wyandotte Garden Club Flower Show last week of May; American Royal Live

WYANDOTTE COUNTY COURTHOUSE, KANSAS CITY

Stock and Horse Show, Oct. or first of Nov.; American Legion Posts: Annual ball sponsored by Company G of 137th Infantry, date set by committee.

KANSAS CITY, Kansas (773 alt., 121,857 pop.), at the confluence of the Missouri and Kansas Rivers at the eastern edge of the State, is the largest city in Kansas and the seat of Wyandotte County.

Its position is one of great natural advantages. Situated in the heart of the central plains region, Kansas City, with Kansas City, Missouri, forms the industrial center for this vast region. Kansas City, Missouri, joins it on the east, and so closely are they connected there is no apparent division. On the north, south, and west are undulating farm lands, checkered with fields of wheat and corn. Here, too, are stores of natural resources; small oil and gas wells, rich limestone deposits, and stream beds yielding sand valued at one million dollars annually. Near to the city are dairy farms, truck gardens, and suburban estates. Highways are lined with commercial signs, tourist camps, and wayside markets.

Within the city limits the undulating character of the terrain is intensified. The Kansas River, flowing from the southwest, approximately bisects the urban area, and on either side of the narrow valley is spread a series of hills and precipitous bluffs. Seventh Street Trafficway, traversing the city from north to south, has as many "dips" as a roller-coaster railway, notwithstanding the three viaducts bridging the river and seven railway lines.

Due to the hills and to the manner of its growth, its streets are not regularly patterned—for Kansas City has not grown around a single industrial unit; it is a consolidation of villages. Eight individual towns were merged to form the present corporate limits, resulting in many angling and broken thoroughfares, and in five "main" streets, each centered in its own business and residential district.

Although there is no apparent division between the two cities, Kansas City, Kansas, has jealously retained a definite identity. The city points with pride to the fact that a majority of the great industrial plants in the river bottoms are on the Kansas side of the line, although they are always included in an industrial survey of the Missouri city.

Greater Kansas City, which includes both cities and their suburbs, has spilled over a large area in four counties, two in each State. On the Kansas side it has grown steadily southward until it has crossed the Wyandotte County line into Johnson County, where there are many comfortable suburban homes. Paradoxically, Kansas City, Missouri's, most exclusive residential development, Indian Hills, is also well within the borders of Johnson County, Kansas.

On June 26, 1804, Lewis and Clark passed through the territory on their expedition to the Pacific Coast. They landed on the neck of land between the two rivers that is called "Kaw Point," a part of the present city, and rested for two days, making observations, and overhauling equipment.

Two years later, after crossing the Rocky Mountains to the Pacific, they stopped at this point on their return voyage. On Monday, August 15, 1806, Clark wrote in his diary: "The Kansas is very low at this time. About a mile below it we landed to view the situation of a high hill, which has many advantages for a trading house or fort; while on shore we gathered great quantities of pawpaws, and shot an elk. The low grounds are now delightful, and the whole country exhibits a rich appearance. . . ."

This was the first written description of the territory. Twelve years later it was made a part of the reservation granted to the Delaware Indians. Twenty-five years later—1843—it was purchased from the Delaware by the Wyandot, who laid the foundation for the present city.

The Wyandot, the last of the emigrant tribes, came from Sandusky, Ohio, as a band of 700—not savages, but an educated, and in many instances a cultured people. Intermarried with whites from generations back, they were more white than Indian; their leaders were men of influence and ability. They laid out the town, Wyandot City, in 1843, the first log cabin being completed and occupied on December 10. Within twelve months, despite flood and sickness and the delay of the Federal Government in paying them for their Ohio reservation improvements, they had built a school, the first free school in Kansas; a church, the organization of which they brought from Ohio; a store owned in common by the nation; and a council house in which they were to take far-reaching action.

The Wyandot were farmers, devoted to rural pursuits rather than urban practices; and the little city grew very slowly until 1849, when the California gold rush placed it on the great highway to the Pacific—an alarming situation to Wyandot leaders. From past experiences, they knew that the white men invading their precincts, sooner or later, would covet their lands and that what white men wanted they would obtain. All they could do was increase the value and obtain the best price possible. To accomplish this they must induce white men to settle among them; and to bring white men they must assume a Territorial status.

With this object in view, they met on October 12, 1852, in their council house and elected Abelard Guthrie, a white man married into the tribe, as a delegate to the Thirty-second Congress. Guthrie was not admitted to Congress, but his presence in Washington forced the Territorial question —a fact of which Wyandot leaders were fully cognizant. On July 26, 1853, they met to take the more compelling action of organizing Kansas-Nebraska into a provisional Territory, electing William Walker as Governor, and re-electing Guthrie to the Thirty-third Congress.

Although this action also failed of recognition, it did serve to project the little city of Wyandot into the national limelight. Kansas, by the Missouri Compromise, was neutral territory. If it came into the Union as a Free State, the balance of power would be thrown to the North; and it was known that a majority of the Wyandot were with the North. (In 1848 when their church was divided, 135 of the 200 members had espoused the Northern cause.) Thus, in this little Indian Settlement was staged a preliminary to the national conflict *(see HISTORY)*.

In the meantime, in 1855, the Wyandot petitioned for and received the rights of citizens with their lands in severalty. This enabled them to dispose of their property, which they did promptly; within a short time Wyandot City passed into the hands of white men, and the Wyandot as a nation disappeared from Kansas. Although advanced in civilization, they were not equal to the white man's often unscrupulous shrewdness; and in 1868, having dissipated the proceeds of the sale of their property, they petitioned to be reinstated as wards of the Government. The petition was granted. Those who chose were restored to the nation and given a home with the Cherokee in Oklahoma. The few families who preferred to retain citizenship, remained in the city, where some of their descendants still reside.

The white settlers who succeeded them established a post office in the spring of 1857, opened two banks the same year, and transformed the quiet village into a booming town, which they called "Wyandotte."

Other towns sprang up nearby. Quindaro, on the bank of the Missouri a little to the north and west, was founded in 1856 by Abelard Guthrie, Charles Robinson, and others, and was named for Guthrie's Wyandot wife, Quindaro Brown Guthrie. Intended as a Free State port to compete with the pro-slavery towns of Westport, Missouri, and Leavenworth, it was widely advertised and grew rapidly, for two years rivaling Wyandotte. Ambitious for the trade of the Southwest, Wyandotte built a road to the Kansas River and established a free ferry. Quindaro retaliated with a similar road and ferry. Wyandotte then—after effecting incorporation January 29, 1859, and electing its first mayor, James B. Parr, in February—shifted its business section from Nebraska Avenue to the levee, where a block of business buildings was erected—and Quindaro had no answer. One of

IN THE STOCKYARDS, KANSAS CITY

those buildings was "Constitutional Hall," wherein, July 1859, the constitution of Kansas was written; and by that constitution the county of Wyandotte was erected with Wyandotte as the county seat. Quindaro's prosperity declined and came to an end during the Civil War.

In 1860, James McGrew established a slaughter house in the bottoms now occupied by the stockyards; in 1866 the railroad connecting Wyandotte with Topeka was completed; and in 1868, Edward Patterson and J. W. Slavens began the first packing house with an annual kill of 4,000 animals. However, it was due to Charles F. Adams, descendant of Presidents John and John Quincy Adams, that Kansas City became a meat packing center. Adams acquired several large tracts of land in the Kansas River Valley, now occupied by Armourdale and the central industrial district, and built the first of the stockyards. He then persuaded Plankington and Armour to remove the packing house they had set up in Missouri to Kansas that it might be convenient to his stockyards. This they did in 1871, beginning the present Armour plant and the first of the major packing units. Today Kansas City has eleven packing houses, including those of the "Big Four"—Armour, Swift, Cudahy, and Wilson—requiring the services of seven trunkline railroads.

Around the railroad and packing houses other towns grew up. Old Kansas City, Kansas, on the strip of ground between the Kansas River and the Missouri line, was platted in 1868 and incorporated October 22, 1872; Armstrong, on the hill to the south, was established in 1871. Armourdale, named for the packers, in the low ground south of Armstrong, was founded in 1871 and incorporated in 1882; while Riverview, built on the hill between Armstrong and Wyandotte, came into being in 1879.

These towns, all within a figurative stone's throw and animated with boom times, soon were crowding each other; the need for consolidation became apparent. Agitation was begun in 1876, but it was not until 1880 that Riverview petitioned and became a part of Wyandotte. In 1886 old Kansas City and Armourdale were annexed by legislative enactment, and Armstrong was included as intervening territory. Much discussion arose over the proper name for the consolidated city. Wyandotte held out for its name, but as it was argued that municipal bonds would sell better under the title of Kansas City, Kansas, that was finally adopted.

Still the city was not complete. Across the Kansas River to the south were Rosedale and Argentine. Rosedale took its name from the wild rose covering the bluffs when it was a wayside stop on the Santa Fe Trail. It was platted in 1872 and received impetus from the rolling mill opened in 1875. Argentine grew up around the Santa Fe Railway shops and yards, established in 1880, and the plant of the Consolidated Kansas City Smelting and Refining Company, which drew raw materials from all over the country and sent its smelted gold and silver to the mints of the world. Argentine, so named from the Spanish word for silver, became a part of the city by petition in 1909; Rosedale was forced in by legislative enactment in 1922. Meanwhile, Quindaro, having rescinded its incorporation and reverted to Quindaro Township, was absorbed by natural expansion. And so the present city was formed.

The "Exodusters," freed Negroes from the South, and European peasants—Germans, Russians, Poles, Croats, Czechs, Slovakians—lured by the prospects of freedom in a new land, increased the city's population in the late 1800's.

The coming of the Negroes spread over a period of twenty years following the Civil War, but the peak was reached between 1878 and 1882. In that four-year period twenty thousand are said to have landed on the city's levee. Large numbers were sent on to Atchison, Topeka, and other towns in the State; others were returned to the South. The majority, however, remained in Kansas City and were absorbed by its growing industries. Homes were found along Jersey Creek in a settlement called "Rattlebone Hollow," and in old Quindaro; while literally hundreds squatted on the levee, putting up shanties of scrapwood to form what was known as "Juniper," or "Mississippi Town."

"Mississippi Town" went out of existence in 1924, when it was condemned as an unsightly nuisance, and that part of the levee was transformed into the Woodswether industrial district. "Rattlebone Hollow" is still extant, although the Negroes are not confined to that area. As their economic conditions improved and numbers increased, they have spread over virtually the entire city, forming a substantial civic group. Negro institutions include a university, a hospital, and a high school. There are also two Negro weekly newspapers.

The European immigrants first settled around the packing houses, but have since moved to other parts of the city. "Strawberry Hill," a part of old Riverview, is a Slavic settlement which retains many native customs, although this racial group is fast being assimilated.

Kansas City's industries, except for odors from stockyards and packing houses, are not obtrusive. Yet they are present to an astonishing extent. Hay market and grain storage facilities are the largest in the world. Stockyards and meat-packing houses are second only to Chicago; and not even Chicago has all of the "Big Four," with complete processing plants, as Kansas City has. Serum plants, manufacturing serum for the protection of animal health, rank first in the United States. Soap factories draw raw materials from various parts of the world and distribute their manufactured products throughout North America. Fabricating steel mills are the largest west of the Mississippi; and flour mills, oil refineries, railway shops and yards, and innumerable other activities contribute importantly to its economic stability.

In the early days of Kansas City's industries, the bulk of traffic was carried by steamboats on the Missouri River. Today (1938) this river traffic is being revived. The city owns 90½ acres of levee land and, in conjunction with the Public Works Administration, is engaged in an immense levee development project. Aiding this work, Congress, by an act of July 3, 1930, provided for a survey to determine the possibility of reestablishing barges not only on the Missouri River, but on the Kansas as well. Navigation of the Missouri is now a reality, and barges of 1,000-ton capacity are planned to operate on the Kansas to a distance of 9.5 miles above its mouth.

POINTS OF INTEREST

1. HURON BUILDING, 907-909 N. 7th St., 12 stories in height, is the city's tallest building. Built in 1923 by the Elks Club, with a ballroom and roof garden, it is now devoted to offices.

2. WYANDOTTE COUNTY COURTHOUSE, 7th St. between Ann and Barrett Aves., built in 1927, was designed in the neoclassic style by Wight & Wight of Kansas City, Mo., and constructed of Bedford stone and reenforced concrete. The front is decorated with a frieze of Greek plaques symbolizing the leading industries of Kansas, fluted Doric columns, and carved inscriptions. Interior walls of the first floor are of Italian travertine with floors of terrazzo, bordered with tile and Tennessee mar-

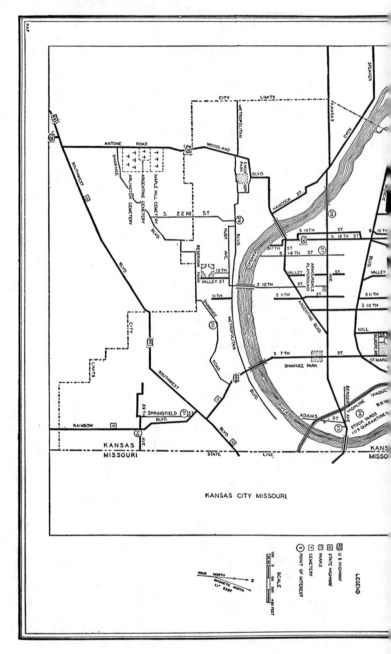

KANSAS CITY MISSOURI

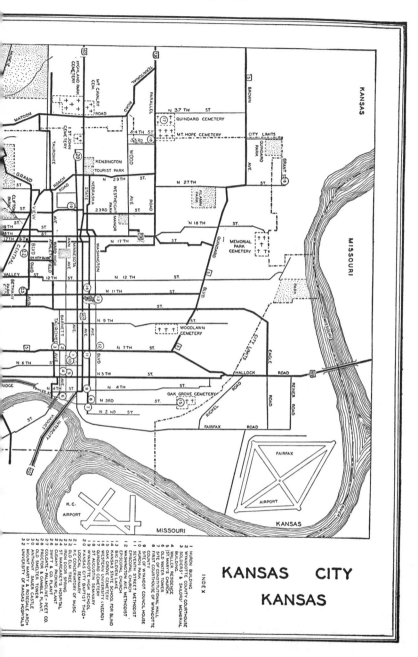

KANSAS CITY

KANSAS

ble. On the third floor, the main hall, with its barrel-vaulted ceiling, forms the beautiful Hall of Courts.

3. SOLDIERS' AND SAILORS' MEMORIAL BUILDING *(open)*, 7th St. between Barnett and Tauromee Aves., of neoclassic design—somewhat freely adapted—was erected in 1924 as a monument to Wyandotte County's World War heroes and is really two buildings, combining a civic auditorium with the Memorial Hall, which contains military trophies, memorial tablets, and photographs. Rose and Peterson of Kansas City were the architects.

4. The WALLER RESIDENCE *(private)*, 524 Ann Ave., a one-story frame structure, was brought by boat from Cincinnati in 1858, and is one of the oldest in the city. Governor Charles Robinson is believed to have once used the front room for his office.

5. ST. MARY'S CHURCH, NW. corner 5th St. and Ann Ave., the city's first Catholic church, was founded by Father Anton Kuhls, who also founded the first hospital. The site of three acres was purchased in 1865 from Mathias Splitlog, a Wyandot, for $800, and the first building was erected on the SE. corner of 6th and Ann Ave. that year. The present building of gray limestone, designed in the English Gothic style, was dedicated in 1903. Three altars of white oak, brought from Louisville, Ky., were temporarily lost in the 1903 flood, but arrived in the city on Saturday morning before the dedication on Sunday. At noon 25 men were set to work, completing the installation at midnight.

6. The OLD WATER TOWER *(not open)*, Fowler St., 100 yards S. of Ann Ave., 40 feet high, suggesting the lookout of a feudal castle, was erected in 1905–1906 as a part of the old Kansas City, Mo., water plant. Prior to the 1903 flood, the connection was a pipeline bridged over the Kansas River. The bridge was washed out in the flood, and a tunnel was then made under the river and the tower erected. During the World War a guard station was maintained in the tower to prevent dynamiting 'or other possible destruction.

The PANORAMIC VIEW, from the end of Missouri Pacific Bridge, Minnesota Ave. and 2nd St., is sweeping and comprehensive. Directly in the foreground is the junction of the Missouri and Kansas Rivers, forming Kaw Point, where Lewis and Clark landed in 1804. To the right is the overhead span of the Inter-city Viaduct and the James St. Bridge. Across the Kansas River SE. is the hill described by Clark as advantageous for a trading house or fort. At the foot of this hill is the strip of ground where the Wyandot camped and 60 died while their leaders negotiated land from the Delaware. Directly ahead, on the left side of the Missouri River, is the Municipal Airport, with planes flying above waters where once chugged slow-moving steamboats; and beyond it are the elevators and towers of North Kansas City. On the left, back across the Missouri, is the Fairfax industrial district, with the cone-topped tanks of the Phillips Petroleum Company, and the floorlike fields of Fairfax Airport, and immediately to the left is the site of the business block of old Wyandot, with the new terminal elevator and dock directly in front.

7. SITE OF CONSTITUTIONAL HALL, 2nd St. and Nebraska Ave.,

is occupied by the Chicago & Great Western Elevator. Constitutional Hall, built in 1858 by Lipman Meyer at a cost of $4,000, was a four-story brick building poorly constructed and never finished, although the constitutional convention assembled there in July 1859, and framed the constitution of Kansas. Undermined by water, it collapsed in May 1861.

8. FIRST COURTHOUSE OF WYANDOTTE COUNTY *(private)*, 328 Nebraska Ave., a weathered, two-story frame building on a high terrace, was purchased from Isaiah Walker, a Wyandot, on July 11, 1860, for $1,800. It then stood on the back of the lot and was used as Wyandotte's first post office. The county commissioners moved it to the front of the lot and erected a log jail at the back. The jail has been demolished, but the old courthouse is occupied as a residence by its present owner.

9. SITE OF WYANDOT COUNCIL HOUSE, 4th St. at alley between Nebraska and State Aves., is designated by a wooden marker with the inscription, "Site of Wyandotte Indian Council House 1843–1861." The one-story, frame building that stood on the site was the first free school in Kansas and the council house of the Wyandot nation.

10. HURON PARK, Minnesota Ave. between 6th and 7th Sts., heart of the downtown district, was "permanently reserved and appropriated" as a burial ground by the Wyandot in the treaty of 1855. In 1859, when the Wyandotte City Town Company plat was filed, it was designated as public grounds under the title of "Huron Place," with 150 square feet on each of its four corners dedicated to church sites. Churches were erected but have since been removed. Within the park are the Carnegie Library, Municipal Rose Garden, and the Indian Cemetery.

The CARNEGIE LIBRARY *(open 9-9 daily)*, an elaborate version of Italian Renaissance architecture, was designed by W. W. Rose of Kansas City and erected in 1920–1924. It contains among other paintings: *The Pioneer Woman* by G. M. Stone of Topeka; *Cherubs*, ascribed by local critics to Rubens; and two large canvases, *Rebecca at the Well* and *Ishmael and Hagar*, by Giobe Montine. The latter two were owned by Elizabeth Patterson of Baltimore, wife of Jerome Bonaparte and hence sister-in-law to the Emperor. They are supposed to have been the gift of the Emperor himself. After the marriage was dissolved by Napoleon, the paintings were placed on the market and purchased by Mrs. Mary E. Craddock, widow of a former mayor, who presented them to the library.

The MUNICIPAL ROSE GARDEN *(open daily and evenings)*, developed in 1935, contains between 8,000 and 9,000 plants.

The INDIAN CEMETERY (Wyandot National Cemetery, locally called Huron Cemetery), a scant two acres joining the library grounds on the west, contains the remains of such Wyandot chiefs as Warpole, Tauromee, George I. Clark, Big Tree, Serrahas, Squeendchtee, and Esquire Grey Eyes, the Wyandot preacher. On the family stones are the names of the Northrups, Zanes, Garrets, and others. The oldest stone is dated 1844. After removal of the Wyandot from Kansas, obliteration threatened the cemetery. In 1906, business men, with an eye to its commercial value, caused a bill to be slipped through Congress, authorizing the sale of the site and removal of the bodies to the second Wyandot cemetery at Quindaro. Wyandot descendants remaining in the city resisted the measure, because in the 1850's, when they sold most of their property, it was stipulated that their burial ground should be preserved. Litigation was carried through all the courts in the country, reaching the United States Supreme Court in 1910. That body upheld the decisions of the lower courts, which had ruled in favor of the bill; but because of aroused public sentiment, Congress, in 1913, repealed the statute and converted the cemetery into a city park, extending sepulchral rights to the Wyandot. Closely associated with the cemetery is the name of Lydia B. Conley, a member of the Zane family, who led the fight to keep it intact. When removal of the bodies was attempted, she padlocked the gates, erected a temporary shelter known as "Fort Conley," and mounted guard with a warning that it would be "peril to trespass." As a qualified lawyer, she pleaded the case before the Supreme Court, being the first woman to appear before the court. In the winter of 1936–1937 Miss Conley obtained a restraining order to prevent a proposed parking lot at the east side of the burial grounds; and on June 7, 1937, she threatened bodily harm to park department employees who were cutting grass and trimming trees in the cemetery proper. For this she was arrested and given a 10-day jail sentence.

11. SEVENTH STREET METHODIST EPISCOPAL CHURCH, SOUTH, NE. corner 7th St. and State Ave., erected in 1888, is a red brick building with a square tower and steeple. The church was founded in 1848, when 65 members of the Wyandot "Church in the Wilderness," espousing the cause of the South, followed the example set by the Georgia conference and seceded from the mother church.

12. WASHINGTON AVENUE METHODIST EPISCOPAL CHURCH, NW. corner 7th St. and Washington Blvd., erected in 1924, is a three-story building, constructed of native stone, and designed in the English Gothic style, with exceptionally beautiful mullioned windows of cherry red and royal blue glass. Charles E. Keyser of Kansas City was the architect. The church organization dates back to 1844, when the Wyandot built "The Church in the Wilderness." Bronze plaques in the vestibule commemorate John Stewart, Negro missionary who first brought the Methodist Church to the Wyandot in Ohio; and Lucy B. Armstrong, daughter of a succeeding missionary and wife of a prominent Wyandot.

13. BIG ELEVEN LAKE, 11th St. from Washington Blvd. to State Ave., was, according to local legend, the haunt by night of sinister characters and the scene of many diabolical murders, the bodies supposedly committed to its muggy waters. In 1934 it was drained, the bottom sanded, and the banks sodded and decorated with a scalloped rock design. After being refilled by the springs that feed it, it was stocked with fish from the State Hatchery. The draining took place before a large and curious audience, but when it was emptied, no human skeletons were found, only a gold watch, an automobile tire, an assortment of tin cans, and some fish.

14. KANSAS STATE SCHOOL FOR THE BLIND *(visitors by appointment)*, State Ave., between 11th and 12th Sts., a unit of the State educational system, is on an oak-studded hillside of 9.6 acres. Curving

drives lead to the 12 red brick buildings, the first of which was erected in 1866 as an asylum for the blind.

15. OAK GROVE CEMETERY, N. end of 3rd St., 12½ acres, overlooking the Missouri River, one of the oldest in the city, was purchased from Sophia Walker Clement, daughter of Gov. William Walker, in 1868. Many pioneer families and notables connected with the city's history are buried here, prominent among whom were Mary Tenney Gray (1833–1904), "Mother of the Women's Club Movement," so called because she initiated the Kansas Federation of Women's Clubs; William Walker (1800–1874), Wyandot chief; and Mary A. Sturges (1809–1892), Union Army nurse.

16. WESTERN UNIVERSITY (Negro), NW. corner 27th and Grant Sts., a coeducational institution, maintained by the African Methodist Episcopal Church with State aid, was begun about 1862 as the Blatchely School by the Reverend Eben Blatchely, a Presbyterian. Later it became the Freedman's University and was converted into a normal school in 1872, when the first State aid was provided. From Blatchely's death in 1877, the school made little progress until 1896, when the Reverend W. T. Vernon took charge. Under his management it has achieved a junior college rating. The six red brick buildings are closely assembled on a hill overlooking the Missouri River. On the campus is a statue of John Brown, sculptured in Italy and unveiled June 9, 1911.

17. QUINDARO CEMETERY, NE. corner Smith and Parallel Rds., second Wyandot cemetery, was founded in 1852. The first interment was that of Eliza S. Whitten, wife of the missionary, whose crumbling headstone is dated January 3, 1852. Beside it is the stone of Lucy B. Armstrong (1818–1892). Nearby was the grave (unmarked) of Katie Sage, alias Sally-Between-the-Logs, who as a child in Virginia, was stolen from her white parents by the Wyandot, brought up as a member of the tribe, and married successively to three Wyandot chiefs.

18. ST. AUGUSTIN SEMINARY *(open by appointment)*, Parallel Rd., between 33rd and 34th Sts., was founded as the Kansas City University in 1895 by Dr. Samuel F. Mather, descendant of Cotton Mather, with the assistance of the Methodist Protestant Church. Dr. Mather, 84 years old, passed away a few hours after the plans were consummated without seeing the realization of a life-long dream. The university attained a standard rating, but was never liberally patronized. On January 10, 1935, it was taken over by the Recollect Augustinian Fathers and converted into a mission seminary for priests. Three widely spaced brick buildings on a shaded hilltop form the seminary group.

19. WYANDOTTE HIGH SCHOOL, SE. corner N. Washington Blvd. and Minnesota Ave. covering three acres, is designed in the Lombardic Romanesque style, with an "H"-shaped plan. Plans were drawn by Hamilton, Nedved & Fellows of Chicago, assisted by the firm of Joseph W. Radotinsky of Kansas City. The construction of this brick and stone building required the largest piece of fabricated steel ever produced by the Kansas City Structural Steel Company—an "I" beam, 100 feet long, weighing more than one ton to the foot.

20. KANSAS CITY BAPTIST THEOLOGICAL SEMINARY, Roach Rd. between Armstrong and Barnett Aves., was opened in October 1902 as a training school for ministers, ministers' wives, women church workers, and home missionaries. A feature of the institution is the Pratt-Journeycake Library, 11,000 volumes of theological and general references and other books. The library was founded by Nannie, daughter of the Delaware chief, Charles Journeycake, who married Lucius Pratt, son of John G. Pratt, Delaware Baptist missionary, as a memorial to her father and father-in-law.

21. KANSAS CITY CONSERVATORY OF MUSIC *(open 8:30 to 5 daily)*, 40 S. 18th St., although a branch of the Kansas City Conservatory of Music, Kansas City, Mo., has its own board of trustees and is independently managed and financed. It is fully accredited with the National Association of Schools of Music and offers a Bachelor of Music degree. In 1937, it had an enrollment of 586 and during the first semester furnished talent for more than 150 outside programs. Josephine Jirak, winner of the Sembrich fellowship and a radio soloist, is one of its alumni. It is housed in a brick and frame building on a terraced corner lot.

22. AN OLD ELM TREE, SW. corner 17th St. and Grandview Blvd., an historic landmark, once shaded the camps of Indians. More than 200 years old, topped and broken, its trunk patched with cement, it has never failed to put out leaves in the spring.

23. IRON DOOR SPRING, SW. corner 11th St. and Ohio Ave., was formerly walled and equipped with an iron door—hence the name—but is now covered with a concrete slab. Situated in a small valley, it was one of the springs about which the Indians camped to receive their annuities.

24. ST. MARGARET'S HOSPITAL, Vermont Ave. between Harrison and 8th Sts., oldest in the city, was founded by Father Anton Kuhls. The first building was erected in 1887 at a cost of $20,000, more than $19,000 of which came from Father Kuhl's own pocket. The present three-story building is closely bordered on three sides by a church and other buildings. Owned and operated by the Sisters of St. Francis, it has accommodations for 300 patients.

25. CUDAHY PACKING PLANT *(open 9-11; 1-2 Tues.-Fri., guides)*, SE. corner Kansas Ave. and Railroad St., is one of the "Big Four" in the meat packing industry.

26. SWIFT & COMPANY PLANT *(open 9-5; Tues.-Sat., guides)*, corner Adams St. and Berger Ave., is also one of the "Big Four."
Both plants slaughter animals at the rate of 600 per hour, only 32 minutes being required from killing pens to refrigerated rooms.

27. COLGATE-PALMOLIVE-PEET COMPANY *(open 10-12; 2-4 weekdays; guides, large parties by appointment)*, 14th to 17th Sts. on Kansas Ave., manufactures soap products. The company imports vegetable oils from China, Ceylon, the Philippine and Fiji Islands, Cuba, southern Europe, and Africa, and perfumes from France, Switzerland, Bulgaria, Italy, and North Africa.

28. PROCTOR & GAMBLE PLANT *(visitors by appointment)*, Kansas

Ave. between 19th St. and Kansas River, manufactures nationally known soap products.

29. The OLD SMELTER TOWER *(not open)*, 22nd St. and Metropolitan Ave., Argentine district, 185 feet high, is a relic of the internationally known Kansas City Consolidated Smelting and Refining Company, around which Argentine was built.

30. ANTHONY SAUER CASTLE *(private)*, 945 Shawnee Rd., is a three-story towered structure of Viennese design, built in 1871, on a 200-acre estate, by Anthony Sauer, native of Vienna, from a fortune amassed in pioneer freighting. All materials, except stone for the foundation, were shipped by water from St. Louis. Marble for mantels was brought from Italy, Vermont, and Kentucky. Stone lions at the front are the work of an Italian sculptor. Crystal chandeliers were brought from Austria, lace curtains from Brussels, and mirrors from Florence. A handsome vase painted by Madame Le Brun, was another prized possession. A solid walnut stair with rosewood rail extends from tower to basement. The estate has dwindled to three acres, but the house (occupied by a daughter of Anthony Sauer) retains much of the original furniture.

31. MOUNT MARTY AND THE ROSEDALE ARCH, Seminary and Springfield Sts., Rosedale district, designed in Ionic style by J. LeRoy Marshall, was erected in 1923. It commemorated the organization on Mount Marty, in 1917, of the 117th Ammunition Train of the famous "Rainbow Division," which served in France under Gen. Henri Gouraud, and also honors Wyandotte County men who served in the War. Ground was broken for the arch on July 30, 1923, General Gouraud taking part in the ceremony.

32. UNIVERSITY OF KANSAS HOSPITALS (Bell Memorial Hospital), SE. corner 39th Ave. and Rainbow Blvd., were founded in 1905 as the Bell Memorial by Dr. Simeon B. Bell, pioneer physician of Rosedale, who donated to the University of Kansas land and money for the initial buildings. These buildings and grounds, now the School of Medicine, are on the NE. corner of Seminary and Broad Sts. The present site of the hospitals proper, 15 acres, was purchased in 1920 with contributions from alumni and friends and appropriations by the city and State. The buildings of brick and limestone, consist of the main hospital and administration building, nurses' home, and various wards. There are also several temporary wooden structures known as "barracks."

POINTS OF INTEREST IN ENVIRONS

Wyandotte County Lake and Park, *12.4 m.;* Delaware Burial Ground, *7.6 m. (see Tour 3);* Shawnee Mission, *1.4 m.;* Home of Frederick Chouteau, *7.6 m.;* Home of Charles Bluejacket, *7.9 m. (see Tour 4).*

Lawrence

Railroad Stations: 7th and New Jersey Sts. for Atchison, Topeka & Santa Fe Ry.; N. 2nd and Locust Sts. for Union Pacific R.R. and Chicago, Rock Island & Pacific Ry.; 2nd and Maple Sts. for Kansas City, Kaw Valley & Western Ry.
Bus Stations: 638 Massachusetts St. for Southwestern Greyhound Lines and Interstate Transit Lines (Union Pacific Stage); 1024 Massachusetts St. for Santa Fe Trails System.
Airport: On US 40, 1.5 m. NE. of town; no scheduled service.
Taxis: Minimum fare 25¢.
Buses: Fare, 8¢.
Traffic Regulations: Usual; all plainly indicated.

Accommodations: Three hotels, five tourist camps.

Information Service: Chamber of Commerce, 746 Vermont St.

Radio Stations: WREN (1220 kc.); KFKU (1220 kc.).
Motion Picture Houses: Four.
Athletics: University of Kansas Stadium, Mississippi St. between 10th and 12th Sts., for school athletic events; Haskell Institute Stadium, 24th and Barker Sts., for Indian school athletic events.
Swimming: Jayhawk Plunge, 6th and Michigan Sts.
Golf: Hill View Golf Course, 2 m. SW. of Lawrence on US 59, 9 holes, sand greens, greens fee 25¢.

Annual Events: Kansas Relays in mid-April; Midwestern Band Festival, part of Music Week in May, Midwestern high school band competition; Commencement Exercises at University of Kansas, early in June; Christmas Vespers at University of Kansas on Sunday before holiday vacation.

LAWRENCE (840 alt., 13,726 pop.), the principal educational center of the State is divided by the Kansas River into two segments—North and South Lawrence. Home of the University of Kansas, Haskell Institute, and Lawrence Business College, the city is also important as a shipping point for potatoes, corn, wheat, and alfalfa grown in the rich valley land around it, and as an industrial center.

South Lawrence or "Lawrence" as distinguished from "North Lawrence" clings to the north, east, and south slopes of a hill that forms the divide between the valleys of the Kansas and Wakarusa Rivers, and spreads down into the level bottomland on the south and east. Massachusetts Street, the city's main thoroughfare, for the most part skirting the foot of the east slope of the hill, bisects the town, and extends from the river southward through the business district to the outskirts.

The older residential districts on the first gentle slopes of the hill west of Massachusetts Street, have an atmosphere of nineteenth century New England with brick paved streets, low retaining walls, broad landscaped lawns, and old mansions of brick and stone designed in the Mid-Victorian style. The newer sections, on the western and southern limits, are as modern as those in the average prosperous Kansas city.

North Lawrence is a semi-suburban community of modest homes and small stores clustered about the Union Pacific Railroad yards and extending along the two highways that enter the city from the north.

Little remains of the old Lawrence that played such an important part in the history of Kansas during its struggle for statehood. The dusty streets that resounded with guerrilla war cries and hoofbeats of the galloping horses of William Quantrill, John Brown, and Charles Robinson are now wide trafficways lined with business houses or comfortable dwellings. "The Hill," overlooking the town and known as Mount Oread, is no longer crowned by Free State fortifications but by the buildings of the University of Kansas.

Modern homes, the property of local chapters of national college fraternities, stand where early settlers built log cabins; and streamlined cars, usually borrowed from indulgent fathers back home, sweep down the brick-paved hillsides. The fine old homes in Lawrence, which have escaped being turned into student rooming houses, stand aloof behind protective screens of shrubbery.

Completing the contrast is Haskell Institute, a Federal Government high school and junior college for Indians, where smartly-clad Indian co-eds and white-collared braves seek to adjust themselves to a new culture, replacing lacrosse and the old war cries with football and "Rah! Rah! Haskell!"

Founded in 1854 by the New England Emigrant Aid Company and named for Amos A. Lawrence of Boston, a prominent member of the company, the town was originally planned as the capital of Kansas. Dr. Charles Robinson was hired by the New England financiers to look after their interests.

As the center of Free State activities the town was a hotbed of warfare throughout the Territorial years. By March 1855 Lawrence was a growing and prosperous town with 369 voters. Late in November of that year, Charles W. Dow, a Free State man, was shot at Hickory Point, ten miles south, by Franklin N. Coleman, a pro-slavery settler, and the enmity between northern and southern settlers of Kansas and Missouri reached the boiling point. This incident precipitated the Wakarusa War (see HISTORY).

Jacob Branson, with whom Dow lived, was rescued by Free State friends after he was arrested by Samuel J. Jones, sheriff of Douglas County. Sheriff Jones, a pro-slavery man, retaliated by tricking Territorial Governor Wilson Shannon into sending out the militia (which then consisted largely of Missourians who had come across their State Line to Kansas at the call of Sheriff Jones) to put down the "rebellion" at Lawrence. This army camped at Franklin about three miles east of Lawrence.

Finally after a week of siege the citizens of Lawrence sent a delegation to the Governor to acquaint him with the true state of affairs. Incredulous, the Governor went to Lawrence to examine the situation and, seeing that he had acted too hastily, called the leaders of both sides together and drew up a peace treaty.

On May 21, 1856, Sheriff Jones returned to Lawrence—this time under the pretense of serving some writs. Before he and his forces left, the town's newspaper offices were dismantled, their presses broken to pieces, and their type thrown in the Kansas River, several stores and residences were robbed, and Dr. Robinson's home was burned. One man, a member of the Jones band, was killed. Citizens of Lawrence declared that an American flag, whipping in the breeze atop the Free State Hotel, knocked off a brick that dropped on his head.

After five years of strife the Free State faction was triumphant. The Wyandotte Constitution, under which the State was admitted to the Union, was adopted October 4, 1859, and two months later an election of provisional State officers was held in which Dr. Charles Robinson was chosen Governor of the new State. Robinson's fellow townsman and political rival, Gen. James H. Lane, was elected to the office of United States Senator by the first State legislature, which convened in February 1861.

At daybreak on August 21, 1863, Lawrence citizens were aroused by the sound of firing and the shouts of guerrilla raiders who swept down on the town from the east, led by the notorious irregular, William Clarke Quantrill. After shooting down the Reverend S. S. Snyder in his barnyard, two miles east of town, Quantrill's command, numbering 450 men, all mounted and heavily armed, galloped toward the city. Opposed to them were only a few unarmed recruits, twenty of whom were mowed down by the raiders.

The guerrilla band moved north on Rhode Island Street and was soon racing down Massachusetts Street, Lawrence's main thoroughfare, toward the Eldridge House. The guests of this inn were spared and allowed to go to the City Hotel while the guerrillas sacked the Eldridge and set fire to the building. The raiders then divided into squads of six or eight men and scattered over town, slaying and burning. After four hours they withdrew, leaving 150 dead and the major portion of the town in ruins. So futile was the resistance offered by the surprised and terror-stricken citizens that the Quantrill band retired with the loss of only one man.

Twice sacked and burned in the first decade of its existence, Lawrence rose from its ashes like the fabled Phoenix, although progress was somewhat halted during the Civil War. The Kansas Pacific, one of Kansas' first railroads, was built through the town in 1864 and with the increasing development of diversified agriculture in the fertile valleys on either side of it, Lawrence became a prosperous trading and shipping point.

Less affected by synthetic booms than many Kansas cities, the growth of the town has been gradual, and its economic structure has been established on a substantial foundation. Among the industries of the city are a large flour mill that utilizes power from the Kansas River, an organ factory, a paper box factory, a cannery, a wholesale seed house, a wholesale grocery, and a poultry packing plant. Lawrence is also the site of one of the largest fraternal insurance companies in the United States.

Paul Starrett, building and structural engineer, who made important contributions to the practical design of skyscrapers in Chicago and New York City during the early twentieth century, was born (1866) in Lawrence. He wrote *Paul Starrett: Changing the Skyline,* in 1938.

GREEN HALL, UNIVERSITY OF KANSAS

THE UNIVERSITY OF KANSAS

The University of Kansas, on the summit of Mount Oread, overlooks the broad Kansas River Valley on the north and the historic valley of the Wakarusa on the south. The 160-acre campus is noted for its purple lilac hedge in the spring and for the scenic panorama of one of the richest sections of the State. University buildings, for the most part, border a drive that follows the crest of the ridge. Below the drive, on the north, is a broad expanse of woodland and bluegrass that stretches down the slope to the stadium and athletic field. Potter's Lake, a placid little pond, which in the morning light reflects the great bulk of the Administration Building, lies in a hollow near the western edge of the campus.

Because of its proximity to Kansas City, Mo., the University draws a considerable portion of its student body from that city. The rhythmic "Rockchalk, Jayhawk, K. U." battle cry of the Kansas "Jayhawks" is outstanding among college yells. The famous yell is a rallying cry for former Kansans the world over. It was heard in the Philippine jungles where former students fought as members of the 20th Kansas Regiment, and on the battlefields of France.

Freshmen and other new students pledge fidelity to K. U. and its ideals in the symbolic torch ceremony which is usually held during the last week in September. The ceremony begins on North College Hill, the site of the first building, where the novitiates are told the story of the University's beginning. Members of the Torch Society kindle a beacon fire and, as the new students march down the hill to the stadium, a runner lights a torch from the fire and carries it to the Rock Chalk Cairn where a second fire is kindled. In the stadium the students gather about an altar of fire which burns before an illuminated seal of the University. Representatives of the freshman class are handed flaming torches by upperclassmen, symbolizing the transference of culture and knowledge. After a brief address by the chancellor, the students pledge allegiance by repeating a modified form of the Athenian oath. In conclusion the chancellor places a freshman cap on the head of a torch bearer, indicating that male members of the class must wear the little caps until the end of the football season.

K. U. points to many illustrious names on its alumni roster, including U. S. Senator William E. Borah of Idaho, Gov. Alf M. Landon, William Allen White, and Gen. Frederick Funston.

On the athletic field K. U. has developed a number of Olympic entrants, including Everett Bradley and Jim Bausch, decathlon contestants and Glenn Cunningham, one of the greatest middle distance runners of all time.

Amos A. Lawrence, who conceived the idea of the University, gave notes and stocks to the amount of $12,000 to be held in trust for the proposed institution. It was first chartered in 1859 as Lawrence University, but this attempt, like several others in the years before Kansas became a State, ended in failure. After Kansas was admitted into the Union plans were revived, and through the efforts of Dr. Charles Robinson, Lawrence was chosen in 1861 as the seat of the State university. An act of the legislature the following year provided for its organization and in September 1866 the first classes were held in Old North College, the University's first building, with an enrollment of 55. In 1938 the University (co-educational) had an enrollment of 5,200. The university has colleges of arts and sciences, law, medicine, pharmacy, education, engineering and architecture, fine arts, business, and a graduate school. The chancellor is its executive head.

◄◄◄◄◄◄◄◄◄◄◄◄◄◄◄◄◄◄◄◄✖►►►►►►►►►►►►►►►►►►►►

Campus Tour—*1.6m.*

S. from 12th St. on Oread Ave.

The MEMORIAL UNION BUILDING *(open 7:30 a.m.-10 p.m. weekdays)*, SW. corner 13th St. and Oread Ave. is of modern design constructed of brick and limestone. Pond and Pond of Chicago were the architects. Dedicated in 1927 to former students who lost their lives in the World War, the building, in which are a cafeteria and lounge, is for the use of campus visitors and extra-curricular activities of students. Murals in the lounge are the work of WPA artists of the Federal Art Project.

The DYCHE MUSEUM *(closed for repairs 1938)*, NW. corner 14th St. and Oread Ave., was built in the early 1900's to house the extensive natural history collection of the late Prof. L. L. Dyche. Constructed of native limestone with white limestone trim and ornamentations of white limestone and brick, the structure is of modified Romanesque style and is adorned with naturalistic carvings of birds and beasts, the work of an Italian stone cutter. Its arched portal, approached by a broad flight of steps, is modeled after that of St. Trophime in Arles in southern France. The building was designed by Root & Seimans of Kansas City, Mo.

The THAYER MUSEUM OF ART *(open 10-5 weekdays; 2-5 Sun. and holidays)*, NE. corner 14th St. and Oread Ave., served as the university library from 1894 to 1924. After the completion of the new Watson Library it was remodeled to house the $150,000 art collection, donated to the University by Mrs. Sally C. Thayer of Kansas City, Mo., as a memorial to her husband, the late W. D. Thayer, Kansas City merchant. Constructed of red sandstone, the three floors of the building are utilized to exhibit the collection. In the basement is a display of Indian blankets, baskets, and pottery. The first floor contains a collection of rare volumes, histories of art, reference books on arts and crafts, and a collection of 500 pieces of English porcelain and eighteenth century English glassware. Another collection includes a large exhibit of textiles from many nations, a collection of coins, Japanese lacquer and silverware, and Chinese tapestries. In the central gallery of the second floor is a collection of Japanese prints and Chinese paintings, and in a smaller room is an exhibit of American handicraft including old furniture, coverlets, hooked rugs, and samplers.

At 14th St., Oread Ave. becomes Campus Drive; R. on Campus Drive.

GREEN HALL (R) houses the School of Law. It is a buff colored brick structure with huge stone columns that form a wide front portico approached by a broad flight of stone steps.

In front of the building is a STATUE OF "UNCLE JIMMY" GREEN, dean of the School of Law from 1879 to 1919. The work of the late Daniel Chester French of Stockbridge, Mass., the bronze statue is set on a granite base and represents the dean standing with one of his students.

FRASER HALL (L), the oldest building on the campus, is a gaunt four-story structure of native limestone completed in 1872. Its great bulk is topped with twin towers that have almost flat tops and are encircled by iron railings.

On the second floor is the WILCOX MUSEUM *(open 8-5 weekdays)*, named for Prof. A. M. Wilcox, its founder, who was a professor of Greek for 43 years. It contains facsimile reproductions of various objects of antiquity, a collection of Greek and Roman coins, vases, lamps, articles of dress, specimens of Roman glass, and full-sized plaster casts of the works of noted Greek sculptors.

The PIONEER STATUE, E. of the entrance of Fraser Hall, is a bronze figure of a pioneer with spade in hand, the work of Frederick C. Hibbard of Kansas City, and a gift of Dr. Simeon D. Bell. A marker commemorates the site of the barracks and trenches of 1864, dug in preparation for Price's raid *(see HISTORY)*.

The WATSON LIBRARY *(open 7:30 a.m.-10 p.m. weekdays)*, Campus Drive, (L) west of Fraser Hall, is a three-story Bedford limestone structure, Collegiate Gothic in style and designed by Ray M. Gamble, State architect. Completed in 1924, it contains about 291,900 volumes. It was named for Carrie M. Watson, librarian from 1887 until 1921.

HAWORTH HALL *(open 8-5 weekdays)*, Campus Drive (L), is a two-story native stone structure with shops for students of mining in the rear. It contains the PALEONTOLOGY MUSEUM with a large collection of fossils, most of which came from chalk beds along the Smoky Hill River. There is also a GEOLOGICAL MUSEUM including specimens of igneous and sedimentary rocks, crystals, ores, and building stone.

The ADMINISTRATION BUILDING, (R) across the Drive from Haworth Hall, is of Italian Renaissance design and constructed of brick faced with yellow terra cotta. It is the largest building on the campus, and contains the BRYNWOOD COLLECTION of paintings *(open 8-5 weekdays)*, loaned to the University by Chester Woodward, Topeka alumnus.

SNOW HALL, Campus Drive (R) just west of the Administration

Building, is Collegiate Gothic in design with walls of Bedford lime-stone. It was completed in 1929 and houses the natural science depart-ments, some departments of the School of Medicine, and the FRANCIS HUNTINGTON SNOW ENTOMOLOGICAL MUSEUM *(open 8-5 weekdays)*, considered one of the finest insect collections in the United States.

Campus Drive swings N. at the W. end of campus becoming West Cam-pus Rd.; R. on 11th St.

MEMORIAL STADIUM *(open for athletic events only)*, main en-trance at 11th and Alabama Sts., a concrete horseshoe, is the scene of the University of Kansas football games, the Kansas Relays, and the com-mencement exercises. Completed in 1927, it has a seating capacity of 38,000.

The ROCK CHALK CAIRN, approximately 100 yards south of the stadium on the slope of a hill, is a pile of historic stones including remnants of North College and of old Snow Hall.

NORTH COLLEGE HILL, 11th St., N. end of Mount Oread, is a plateau-like elevation bounded by 10th, Ohio, and Indiana Sts. Here Old North College, the first building, was erected in 1865. It was torn down in 1923 and replaced by CORBIN HALL, a three-story building of brick and stucco, housing a women's dormitory.

The hill is the scene of noisy pre-game football rallies climaxed by the pre-Thanksgiving game ceremony. On the night before the annual Thanks-giving game with the University of Missouri, loyal followers of the Kansas Jayhawks gather around a crackling bonfire and join in the ceremony of burning the Missouri Tiger in effigy.

OTHER POINTS OF INTEREST

The POWER DAM, just east of the bridge that spans the river at Massachusetts St., furnishes power for many of Lawrence's industries. It is the only dam on the Kansas River.

In ROBINSON PARK, overlooking the river at 6th and Massa-chusetts Sts. is the OLD SETTLERS' MONUMENT, a giant boulder brought to Lawrence by the Santa Fe Railway Co. from the mouth of Shunganunga Creek near Tecumseh. On it is a bronze plaque bearing the names of the first settlers who arrived in 1854.

The SITE OF THE FIRST METHODIST CHURCH, 724 Vermont St., is indicated by a stone marker bearing the inscription: "Site of First Methodist Church in Lawrence. Bought July 6, 1855. Building erected 1857. Used as a morgue, August 21, 1863." The last date is that of Quantrill's raid.

The CARNEGIE LIBRARY *(open 10-8:30 weekdays; July and Aug. 10-12 a.m., 6-8:30 p.m.)*, NW. corner 9th and Vermont Sts., was originally a one-story building constructed of tan brick, completed in 1904. A $35,000 addition was added in 1937 as a PWA project. The library contains 27,000 volumes.

The PLYMOUTH CONGREGATIONAL CHURCH, 923 Vermont St., a red brick structure with a modern community house on the south, houses the oldest church organization in Kansas. On October 1, 1854, the Reverend S. Y. Lum delivered the first sermon in Lawrence. The congregation was organized two weeks later with seven members. Meetings were held in the Pioneer Hotel.

"A few rough boards were brought for seats," wrote Mrs. Sara Robinson, "and with singing by several good voices among the pioneers the usual church services were held. The people then, as on many succeeding Sabbaths, were gathered together by the ringing of a large dinner bell."

SOUTH PARK, between 11th and 13th Sts., and divided by Massachusetts St., has an area of 12.8 acres. The eastern section of the park is attractively landscaped and contains a bandstand where public concerts are given. Franklin D. Roosevelt, as a candidate for Vice President, spoke from this bandstand in September 1920.

The SITE OF THE MASSACRE OF RECRUITS, near the sidewalk at 935 New Hampshire St., is indicated by a stone marker. It was near this spot that Quantrill's guerrillas shot down twenty unarmed boys during the raid of August 21, 1863.

The SITE OF THE ROBINSON HOME, 1115 Louisiana St., is commemorated by a granite marker. Dr. Charles Robinson built a home here soon after his arrival in 1854. It was burned by Sheriff Jones' raiders May 21, 1856.

The JOHN SPEER HOME, 1024 Maryland St., used as an implement shed and in a state of dilapidation, was built by one of the town's first settlers. In front of this house Larkin M. Skaggs, the only member of Quantrill's band who lost his life during the raid, was killed by White Turkey, a Delaware Indian.

HASKELL INSTITUTE *(campus open at all hours; to visit classes apply superintendent)*, 23rd St. and Barker Ave., is the largest Indian school in the United States. Haskell was opened in 1884 as one of three non-reservation boarding schools provided by an Act of Congress in 1882. The purpose of the institution, according to its founders, was "to provide an opportunity for the American Indian to acquire an education which would fit him for useful citizenship." Land for the original campus of 280 acres was donated by the city of Lawrence. The school was known as the Indian Training School of Lawrence until 1890 when it was named for Congressman Dudley C. Haskell of Kansas who was influential in locating it in the State.

This initial attempt to educate the Indian in the ways of the white man was regarded as a radical innovation, especially by the considerable group of people in the western States who still adhered to the belief, fostered by years of bloody warfare, that "the only good Indian was a dead Indian."

Classes opened with twenty-two students and a faculty of three members. While enrollment was unrestricted as to age, tribe, or residence, the first enrollees were younger children from the reservations whose parents felt compelled to send their boys and girls to Lawrence to "learn the white man's ways." Consequently the first academic courses were elementary and many of the children had to be taught to speak English as well as to read and write.

The first superintendent was Dr. James Marvin, who had lately retired as chancellor of the University of Kansas. Doctor Marvin held office for one year and was replaced by Col. Arthur Grabouski, a retired Army officer who instituted a rule of strict military discipline. Colonel Grabouski was succeeded by former Gov. Charles Robinson.

Enrollment increased rapidly and at the end of the second year had reached 200, representing 31 tribes. As older students began to enroll courses in home economics for the girls and handicraft and agriculture for the boys were developed. By 1895 new academic courses had given the school a rating equal to that of a standard elementary school and junior high school.

As the older Indian boys came in increasing numbers Haskell began a program of organized athletics. In competitive sports, especially football, the Indians displayed a remarkable skill. As the fame of Haskell elevens spread, the Braves were invited to compete with some of the larger colleges and universities in the Missouri Valley area. In later years they played in every section of the country.

Although Haskell has never produced an athlete who equalled Carlisle's Jim Thorpe, many of its gridiron heroes have received national or sectional recognition. The list includes Bill Bain, the Hauser brothers, Chauncey Archiquette, John Levi, Buster Charles, and Louis "Little Rabbit" Weller. Pete Hauser, who played on a Haskell team that defeated the Universities of Kansas, Nebraska, and Missouri, was one of Walter Camp's All-American selections in the early 1900's. John Levi, a giant Arapahoe, starred in the early 1920's and was recognized as one of the finest fullbacks of his generation. The Little Rabbit, an eel-like Caddo halfback, thrilled Kansas football crowds from 1928 to 1931 with his sensational runs.

In 1931 Haskell's enrollment reached its peak of 1,240. Two years later the Reverend Henry Roe Cloud, a full-blood Winnebago, was appointed superintendent, the only Indian who ever held the office. He was succeeded in 1935 by Russell M. Kelley, the present (1938) institutional head.

In 1934 a new Indian educational policy resulted in the elimination of the agricultural courses and the curtailment of enrollment. The new plans originally provided for the abandonment of non-reservation schools, but because of a storm of protest Haskell was permitted to continue. Haskell now offers a four-year high school course and a two-year postgraduate commercial course. Enrollment is limited to students from Kansas, Iowa, Montana (except the Flathead Reservation), North Dakota, South Dakota, North Carolina, Michigan, Oklahoma, Nebraska, Minnesota, and Wyoming. In 1938 there were approximately 600 students. Applicants who are of less than one-fourth Indian blood are not accepted.

Except for their racial characteristics Haskell students look very much like their neighbors at the University. Indian co-eds keep pace with the current styles in campus wear, and boys dress in the casual garb affected by college men throughout the country.

A tour of the campus may be made by following a circular tree-lined drive from the Barker Street entrance. The drive passes the Administration Building, a one-story frame building of bungalow-type; Pocahontas Hall and Winona Hall, girls' dormitories; Sacajawia Hall, Home Economics Building. Keokuk Hall and Osceola Hall, now used as boys' dormitories, are the oldest buildings on the campus. Both were built in 1884 and are of local limestone construction, four stories high and of the institutional-type of architecture. Other buildings in the following order are: Sequoia Hall, the Academic Building; Tecumseh Hall, the boys' gymnasium; Hiawatha Hall, the girls' gymnasium; the Auditorium; Pontiac Hall, the vocational building; and Powhatan Hall, which contains apartments for teachers. The buildings are predominantly of the institutional-type, ranging from two to four stories in height and are of brick and local limestone construction. Left from the entrance is the STADIUM, with a seating capacity of 17,000, donated to the Institute by Indians in appreciation of the work done for Indian youth. It was dedicated November 11, 1926.

The REUTER ORGAN FACTORY (*open 8-5 weekdays*), 6th and New Hampshire Sts., manufactures custom-built pipe organs and is the only factory of its kind between the Mississippi River and the Pacific Coast. The company was organized at Trenton, Ill., in 1917 and moved to Lawrence three years later. The plant is housed in a four-story, factory-type building of brick. Normal production varies from 50 to 60 organs a year and the company employs approximately 45 persons.

The KAW VALLEY CANNING PLANT (*open 8-5 weekdays*), E. 10th and Maryland Sts., is a three-story, factory-type building of brick. The factory was established in 1885 by the late Jabez Watkins. In 1930 it was leased to the Columbus Foods Corp. and has since operated under their control. Providing a cash market for truck farmers in the Kaw Valley areas near Lawrence, the cannery operates continuously from April, when the spinach crop is harvested, until late November, when the last of the pumpkin crop is ready for canning. Large quantities of peas, sweet corn, tomatoes, and green beans also are canned. An average of 75 persons are employed during the season. Since 1930 the average annual output has been 75 carloads.

The ELDRIDGE HOTEL, SW. corner 7th and Massachusetts Sts., a five-story brick structure of modern design erected in 1925 is the fourth hotel on this site. The Free State Hotel, the first on the townsite, was burned by Sheriff Jones' raiders, May 21, 1856. In 1863 Col. S. W. Eldridge built another hotel on the corner, but this building was burned by Quantrill's men a few months after its completion. Before the end of the year, Colonel Eldridge began the construction of a third building that occupied the site until it was razed in 1924 to be replaced by the new Eldridge.

TRINITY EPISCOPAL CHURCH, 1009 Vermont St., now used as a parish house, is the oldest church building in Kansas. It is English Gothic in design, constructed of native limestone, and was erected in 1858. The present church, just north of the old building, is also of native stone and of similar design. It was completed in 1871 and has been remodeled in recent years.

The SITE OF THE OLD SNYDER HOME, approximately 400 yards south of the intersection of 19th and Haskell Sts., where the Reverend S. S. Snyder of the United Brethren Church was killed by Quantrill's band as they entered Lawrence, is marked by a WELL.

POINTS OF INTEREST IN ENVIRONS

Lecompton, *12.2 m. (see Tour 3);* Oak Hill Cemetery, *1.1 m.;* Franklin Cemetery, *2.4 m.;* Pioneer Cemetery, *3.4 m.;* Hole in the Rock, *16.9 m. (see Tour 12).*

Leavenworth

Railroad Stations: Main and Delaware Sts. for Missouri Pacific R.R., Union Pacific R.R., and Chicago, Rock Island & Pacific Ry.; 8th and Shawnee Sts. for Atchison, Topeka & Santa Fe Ry.; 5th and Choctaw Sts. for Chicago, Burlington & Quincy R.R.; Choctaw St. and the Missouri River for Chicago Great Western R.R.
Bus Stations: 303 Delaware St. for Missouri Pacific Trailways; 230 Delaware St. for interurban to Kansas City; National Hotel, NE. corner 4th and Cherokee Sts. for Leavenworth-Kansas City Bus Line.
Airport: Fort Leavenworth Airport, 3.9 m. N. of business section on US 73, emergency service for private planes.
Taxis: Minimum fare, 10¢.
City Buses: Fare 8¢ to all parts of city and to Federal Penitentiary and Fort Leavenworth.
Traffic Regulations: Two-hour parking in business section from 8 to 6.

Accommodations: Three hotels; cottages for tourists.

Information Service: Chamber of Commerce, 516 Delaware St.

Theaters and Motion Picture Houses: Abdallah Shrine Temple, 511 Shawnee St., Shrine circuses, concerts, occasional road shows. Three motion picture houses.
Swimming: City park pool, 13th and Shawnee Sts., and pool for Negroes, 2nd and Kiowa Sts., adults 25¢, children 10¢.
Golf: Shrine Park, two blocks S. of city limits on Maple Ave. 9 holes, greens fee 25¢; Greenwood Country Club, 4 m. SW. on State 92, 9 holes, greens fee 25¢.
Riding: Fort Leavenworth, 2.5 m. N. on State 92, open only to members of fort riding class, class fee $10 monthly.

Annual Events: Competitive R.O.T.C. drill April or May; horse show May and Oct.; steeplechases, polo games, and air shows at irregular intervals.

LEAVENWORTH (760 alt., 17,466 pop.), on the west bank of the Missouri River, spreads out over high bluffs and rolling hills, overlooking the Big Muddy, its green "bottoms," and adjacent farm lands. The business district is on fairly level ground in the narrow valley of Three Mile Creek, a shallow stream which flows between steep banks and makes a natural line of demarcation between downtown Leavenworth and the south residential district.

Bounded by the river on the east and by the military reservation of Fort Leavenworth on the north, the city's growth from the retail and industrial district has been largely to the south and west. There are a number of modern homes among the old Victorian mansions that line its well-shaded streets, but the architecture of the city is predominantly that of the eighties and nineties.

Fort Leavenworth, known as "the mother-in-law of the Army" because of the more than 200 Leavenworth girls who have married army officers, is just beyond the city limits two and a half miles northwest of the busi-

COMMAND AND GENERAL STAFF SCHOOL, FORT LEAVENWORTH

ness district. It consists of an 8,000-acre reservation with appropriate residences and administrative buildings, and it also contains the Federal Penitentiary and the United States Prison Annex, formerly the Army disciplinary barracks.

The Penitentiary, locally called the "Pen," a towering city of gray stone and red brick, has its entrance at Thirteenth and Metropolitan Streets, 1.9 miles from the business section. Escapes from its impregnable walls are rare, but there have been some notable exceptions. On November 7, 1901, before the institution was completed, 26 inmates marched away in a fusillade of bullets. On April 20, 1910, six convicts forced an engineer to crash a locomotive through the heavy prison gates; and on December 11, 1931, seven men, armed with revolvers smuggled to them in a barrel of shoe polish and using Warden Thomas B. White, his secretary, and a guard as shields, made a break for freedom. In each case, however, liberty was of short duration.

Catholic and Protestant churches are well supported and constitute a potent civic force. Residents at the fort have their own cliques and social circles, although women in riding habit and men in Army khaki are familiar figures in the city, particularly during the summer encampments. Prison guards make their homes in Leavenworth and occasionally the families of convicts establish temporary residence.

Although the manufacture of furniture predominates, there are various other industries whose production includes structural steel, cotton gloves, flour, stoves and ranges, mine and mill machinery, meat packing products, and coal. Diversified farming, truck gardening, and livestock raising are practiced in the vicinity, and a luscious variety of strawberry—the Aroma —developed by local fruitgrowers, has acquired a wide market.

The earliest known inhabitants of Leavenworth County were the Kansa Indians, a migratory tribe, followed by the Delaware and the Kickapoo. Lewis and Clark passed the townsite July 2, 1804, camped to the north, and left a description of the country in their journals. Seventeen years later trade with Santa Fe was initiated, and in 1827 Col. Henry H. Leavenworth erected Cantonment Leavenworth—now Fort Leavenworth—to protect traffic on the Santa Fe Trail. The first white settlers in the county and State were the farmers at the cantonment and missionaries employed among the immigrant tribes a few years later.

Leavenworth, the town, had its origin at a meeting of pro-slavers in Weston, Mo., a few days after the passage of the Kansas-Nebraska bill (May 30, 1854). Ambitious men in Missouri coveted the rich lands in Kansas, and David R. Atchison, proponent of slavery, advised his friends in Weston to go over and help themselves—which they did even before the Territory was established. Although the townsite was on the Delaware Trust Lands and provisions of the treaty precluded their settlement until they were surveyed and sold to the highest bidder, Missourians surged across the border and preempted the choice locations. Some brought families and built crude huts in order to present the appearance of bona fide settlers. Most of the claims were speculative, but by the end of June 1854 there was scarcely an acre not claimed in this fashion.

The town company, the first in Kansas Territory, was organized June 13, 1854; the 320 acres embraced in the joint claim were surveyed, platted and divided into shares; and "New Town," as it was at first locally known, was created. The name, Douglas, in honor of Stephen A. Douglas of Illinois, was suggested and generally favored; but H. Miles Moore, a townsite proprietor, argued that the sale of lots would be stimulated by leading outsiders to confuse the city with the military post, which was in an exceedingly desirable situation, and "Leavenworth" was adopted.

The city was progressing smoothly when the Delaware Indians, incited by settlers from the rival town of Atchison, sent a formal complaint to Washington, protesting against the invasion of their lands, and an order to drive off all squatters was issued. It was realized then that the dash into Kansas was illegal, but by agreeing to pay a price fixed by the Government, the squatters contrived to appease the Indians and were allowed to remain, although the final sale of the land was not consummated until February, 1857.

Meanwhile, plans went ahead for the town's advancement. On September 15, 1854, the *Kansas Herald*, first English newspaper in the Territory, was published under a tree on the town's levee. On October 9 the first sale of town lots was held, and the following summer—by an act of the legislature convened July 20, 1855—Leavenworth became the first incorporated town in Kansas Territory.

Early elections of the community were notoriously corrupt. Residents of Weston and other points in Missouri floated down the Missouri on steamboats to stuff ballot boxes with fraudulent votes. The pro-slavery and Free State parties nominated candidates for the Territorial council and assembly, and a canvass made before the first election (March 30, 1855) revealed the district as capable of polling 305 votes. But the election inspectors accepted 964 "legitimate" votes and allowed the pro-slavery candidates an overwhelming majority.

Nor was it wise to protest the frauds. William Phillips, a young Free State lawyer, tried it and was advised to leave the Territory. When he refused, he was stripped to the waist, tarred and feathered, and escorted to Weston, Mo., where he was ridden on a rail to the accompaniment of clanging bells and pans, and eventually placed on a slave block and auctioned off for one cent by an old Negro.

But despite political violence, Leavenworth grew. Its proximity to the fort gave it military protection and made it the commercial terminus for the roads radiating from the fort into the Territory. Business firms were attracted. In the fall of 1854 Murphy and Scruggs established a sawmill. By the following February the Leavenworth Hotel had been erected; a tailor, shoemaker, and barber had hung out their signs; and two blacksmith and three carpenter shops were established. In the spring of 1856 J. L. Abernathy, with the slender capital of $600 began the Abernathy Furniture Company; the following fall Majors Russell and Waddell *(see TRANSPORTATION)* made it headquarters for their vast transportation system.

Employing thousands of men and oxen and hundreds of wagons, this firm did more for the development of the town than several decades of average increase. The first year it expended more than $15,000 for stores, and for blacksmith, wagon and repair shops, thereby attracting other traders. Outfitters, formerly located at Independence, Westport, Weston, and St. Joseph, Missouri, now moved to Leavenworth as the new base of supply for the West and Southwest. And to all this exchange was added the $600,000 annually spent by the fort in salaries and for supplies.

On March 25, 1858, after two previous attempts—at Lecompton and Topeka—a constitutional convention assembled in Melodeon Hall at Leavenworth and framed the Leavenworth Constitution. This document was patterned after the Topeka Constitution and was sent to Congress while that body was debating the Lecompton Constitution. One of its provisions recognized the Negro and gave him the right to the ballot; another provided that the question of universal suffrage be submitted to a vote. Congress never took action on this constitution but its purpose was accomplished by the eventual defeat of the Lecompton Constitution.

Four years after its founding, July 15, 1858, Leavenworth suffered a fire in which 32 stores and $200,000 worth of property were destroyed. Yet, by 1861, with a population of nearly 8,000, it was the largest city in the newly formed State and a money center equal in importance to cities of five times its size. It boasted eight banks and five newspapers, shops, stores, and manufacturing plants. It had telegraphic connections with the East and was looking forward to railroads. It had an organized board of education and a school system.

Meanwhile the political sentiments of the community had shifted strongly to the North and throughout the struggle of the Civil War Leavenworth was loyal, furnishing eighteen companies for defense of the Union. On April 18, 1861, when a river steamer flying a Confederate flag docked at the levee, a crowd assembled with "Old Kickapoo," a battle-scarred cannon, and ordered the flag lowered. Then the mob went aboard and forced the skipper to raise the American standard.

Leavenworth's importance was recognized in the development of railroads, and one of the first charters granted by the Territorial legislature was to the Leavenworth, Pawnee and Western (afterwards the Eastern Division of the Union Pacific) in 1855. As the starting point for western travel, Leavenworth was selected for the eastern terminus. But after surveying, grading, and assembling supplies, difficulties arose; and the terminus was moved to Wyandotte in the summer of 1863. This was a serious setback, duplicated in 1879 when a branch line of the Hannibal and St. Joseph from Cameron, Mo., resisted all Leavenworth's efforts and selected Kansas City, Mo., as its point of connection. These losses to Leavenworth gave Kansas City the advantage which resulted in its ultimate ascendancy; although until 1880 Leavenworth, with more than 20,000 people, was still the largest city in Kansas, humming with trade and manufacture. Since 1900, however, it has fallen to sixth place.

The city has many manufacturing interests, wholesale and retail establishments, and is serviced by one main and five branch line railroads.

POINTS OF INTEREST

PLANTERS' HOUSE *(private)*, NE. corner Shawnee and Main Sts., now operated as an apartment house, is a four-story building of red brick, once a popular hostelry of the West. It was opened in 1856 by indignant pro-slavery men who heartily disapproved of the Free State policies of the old Leavenworth Hotel, then on the northwest corner of Main and Delaware Streets.

Although it catered to guests of pro-slavery sentiment, one tolerant person proposed that Free Soilers who paid their bills and deported themselves as gentlemen should be suffered admittance. The barroom was patronized by enemy politicians, so the management kept one pro-slavery and one abolitionist bartender on duty at all times.

The hotel was host to many famous guests, including Abraham Lincoln, who delivered a campaign speech December 3, 1859, from the steps of Stockton Hall; Stephen A. Douglas, who spoke from the balcony of the Planters'; and Horace Greeley. It was the temporary abode of Gen. William T. Sherman, who, during a brief period of law practice in Leavenworth, is said to have lost the only case he tried.

A kidnapping occurred January 13, 1859, at the Planters'. Temporarily thwarted in an attempt to arrest Charley Fisher, a Negro employee, on the charge that he was a fugitive slave, a deputy United States marshal obtained a ladder, stuck his head in a window and threatened to blow out the landlord's brains. This persuaded the landlord. Assisted by two other men, the marshal handcuffed Fisher and took him across the river into Missouri. But while his captors enjoyed a brief siesta, the Negro escaped and filed off his shackles. His abductors were arrested, tried, and found guilty of kidnapping a slave. However, no existing law provided punishment for such an offense and they were released.

The SITE OF STOCKTON HALL, 401 Delaware St., now occupied by the Leavenworth National Bank, was the scene of Lincoln's campaign speech December 3, 1859, in which he attacked the Stephen A. Douglas theory of State sovereignty. Stockton Hall was a privately-owned auditorium arranged for theatrical presentations and public gatherings. One of the most significant meetings in State history was held here in the summer of 1858 for the organization of the Democratic party in Kansas. It was destroyed by fire January 25, 1864.

The NATIONAL HOTEL, NE. corner 4th and Cherokee Sts., was visited by Carry Nation during her bar-wrecking campaign of the 1900's, but the pleasant smile of Jesus Mella, the affable host, dissuaded her from the intention. During her visit curious citizens pressed their noses against windows and crowded through the doors to view the famous hatchet-wielder. Many retired to the bar for drinks and, it is reported, provided the saloon a record for one day's business that remained unchallenged.

The LEAVENWORTH COUNTY COURTHOUSE *(open 8-5, weekdays)*, Walnut St., between 3rd and 4th Sts., a stone building, was erected upon the ruins of its predecessor, which was almost completely destroyed by fire in 1911. The well-kept grounds, with flower beds and venerable trees, provide an attractive setting, particularly in the spring and summer.

The FORMER HOME OF THOMAS CARNEY *(private)*, 411 Walnut St., now used as the Presbyterian manse, is a two-story, ten-room house of stucco-covered brick, with a wide porch on two sides. Started in 1855 by Jeremiah Clark, the property and building were later purchased by Governor Carney, second Governor of Kansas, who completed the house and built a wall around the entire block. Part of this wall remains.

The PUBLIC LIBRARY *(open 9-9 daily; closed Sun. during summer)*, SE. corner 5th and Walnut Sts., a building of red brick with arched windows, was occupied in 1902 and financed by an endowment from Andrew Carnegie. It has approximately 39,500 volumes, but contains no special collections.

The J. C. LYSLE MILLING PLANT *(open 10-12 and 1:30-4, Mon.-Fri.)*, 512 Choctaw St., houses one of the oldest flour mills in Kansas, the company being founded in the early 1870's. During the late 1880's the company introduced Kansas hard wheat flour to Europe and, for a number of years, was the largest exporter of Kansas flour to markets of the United Kingdom.

By a series of automatic processes, in which the wheat travels more than a mile to the packing room, the grain is separated from foreign matter by screening, scoured to remove residual dirt, dampened, and ground into flour and feed.

The Y.W.C.A., 529 Delaware St., contains a relic of Lincoln's visit. In a bookcase on the second floor is a Wedgwood pitcher with a yellowed paper pasted to its bottom. A faded inscription reads:

"From this pitcher Mr. A. Lincoln drank a glass of beer, when a guest of my father, Mark W. Delahay, in 1859, at Leavenworth, Kansas, Kiowa St., near 3rd St.—M.E.D."

A THREE-WHEELED MOTOR CAR is on display at the Bayer Brothers Carriage & Motor Works *(open by appointment)*, 725 Shawnee St. Made in 1905, this was one of four motor cars designed and manufactured by Henry Bayer and Charles Doyle, an expert though bibulous mechanic of Cleveland, Ohio. The three-wheeled vehicle, propelled by a two-cylinder motor, has a gasoline tank under the seat, and a long iron rod on the right side, which serves as a steering device. Three pedals operate the clutch, brake, and emergency brake.

This car is in running condition and, according to the Bayer family, an offer from Henry Ford of $1,000 and a new Ford sedan has been refused.

The ABERNATHY FURNITURE PLANT *(open by appointment)*, 205 Miami St., covers 2,500 square feet of space. The company was established in 1856 and is one of the oldest enterprises in Leavenworth. Founded by J. L. Abernathy it is now the largest industry in the city occupying two plants, and employing some 400 men the year round in the manufacture of a general line of household, school, and office furniture, as well as mattresses and other household supplies—most of which are distributed in the western part of the United States.

MELLA'S CASTLE, NE. corner 6th and Shawnee Sts., the most incongruous building in Leavenworth, was constructed in the 1880's, designed in the manner of an Italian villa, and named Terrace des Italiens. The vine-covered stone building was erected by the widow of Dr. J. W. Brock, who had served in the Union army. It has been transformed into a restaurant and night club.

The ABDALLAH SHRINE TEMPLE *(open by permission)*, 509-511 Shawnee St., the "Mother Temple" of Kansas, was chartered March 28, 1887. The original building, which has a stucco front and two sphinxes between the doorways, has been augmented by another structure of brick, trimmed in white stone. The temple's auditorium, with a seating capacity of 1,500, is the largest in Leavenworth.

The CATHEDRAL OF THE IMMACULATE CONCEPTION, 711-715 N. 5th St., once one of the largest and most imposing churches west of the Mississippi, was started in 1864 and dedicated December 8, 1868.

Designed in the Romanesque style, the building served the first organized parish in the Territory and is still the cathedral of the Leavenworth Diocese. The paintings by Leon Pomrade on the ceiling and walls remain remarkably clear.

Bishop Meige was appointed in 1850 by Pope Pius IX as vicar apostolic of the Indian Territory, but it was not until May 15, 1855, that he visited Leavenworth, celebrated Mass, and decided upon the town as his permanent residence.

The PARKER AMUSEMENT PLANT *(open by appointment)*, 1000 S. 4th St., has manufactured and shipped merry-go-rounds, ferris wheels, and other carnival amusement devices to remote parts of the world, but now engages principally in repair work on the merry-go-rounds it has leased or sold.

Moved from Abilene, Kans., in 1910 by C. W. Parker, one of the founders, the factory soon won the appellation, the "Wooden Horse Ranch." According to Paul Parker, a son, the Sultan of Java came here in 1916 and ordered a merry-go-round complete with 48 horses. The Sultan, it developed, had 48 wives, and his subtlety was employed to prevent a jealous uprising in his harem. He paid $16,000 for the merry-go-round and during its construction stayed at the Parker home. After his return to Java he sent Mrs. C. W. Parker a large mirror framed with ivory, still in the family's possession.

At EVERGREEN SANITARIUM *(private)*, first block S. of the city limits on Maple Ave., a rambling two-story stucco building with a flat roof, Carry Nation spent her last days. She died there June 2, 1911. The Evergreen Sanitarium has been discontinued and the building is now used as a private institution known as the Stoddard Sanitarium.

PILOT KNOB, a long wooded ridge in SW. Leavenworth, provides a commanding view of the surrounding country. The highest point in Leavenworth, Pilot Knob possessed early-day significance as a trail marker. A large pile of stone on the southern point was one of several between Leavenworth and a ford over the Kansas River at Lawrence, serving as guides for the Sac and the Fox, the Miami, and other Kansas tribes on their excursions to Fort Leavenworth and Weston, Mo.

An ancient cemetery on the hill has been almost obliterated. Isaac Cody, father of William F. (Buffalo Bill) Cody, who died October 12, 1857, was one of the first buried there. Buffalo Bill's mother died six years later and was interred beside her husband. Many unidentified skeletons, however, have been removed to other cemeteries.

The HOME RIVERSIDE COAL MINE *(open by appointment, usually at night)*, SE. corner 2nd and Maple Sts. produces bituminous coal and is tunneled under the Missouri River. The shaft is 750 feet deep. Before the mine was equipped with electricity, burros pulled the coal cars. With the coming of electricity the donkeys were removed, but it was necessary to expose them to the light gradually in order to prevent blindness.

FORT LEAVENWORTH *(grounds open, buildings by permission)*, Metropolitan and Grant Aves., was an outpost of civilization 30 years before Kansas Statehood. It served as the first executive headquarters of the first Territorial Governor. As a training ground for army officers, it is accorded an eminent position among military posts. Grant Avenue, the main thoroughfare, connects with other paved highways and narrow, tree-shaded drives. A studious atmosphere pervades the fort, particularly in the vicinity of the Command and General Staff School. Traffic is required to move slowly here.

"Cantonment Leavenworth" was established by Col. Henry H. Leavenworth in 1827 and four companies of the Third Regiment under Colonel Leavenworth's command were immediately set to work building the cantonment. Tents pitched on the west bank of the Missouri River soon were replaced with huts of logs and bark, occupying the approximate site of the present Main Parade, north of Kearney Avenue, between McClellan Avenue and Sumner Place. As a protection against Indians, a stone wall was built on higher ground on the south.

Soon malarial fever depleted the little garrison. The sickness recurred in 1828 and 1829. Cholera, too, was taking a heavy toll from the frontier army and nearly wiped out some of the Indian villages in the vicinity of Fort Leavenworth. The situation became so critical that on April 28, 1832, Gen. Winfield Scott issued the following order:

Every soldier or ranger who shall be found drunk or insensibly intoxicated after the publication of this order will be compelled, as soon as his strength will permit, to dig his grave at a suitable burying place large enough for his own reception, as such grave cannot fail to be wanted for the drunken man himself or for some drunken companion.

The first post office in this region was established here May 29, 1828. It was an outfitting point for troops in the Mexican War and later for California gold seekers. Many famous names are associated with the history of the fort; among them Kit Carson, Wild Bill Hickok, and Buffalo Bill Cody, the last of whom spent his boyhood in the vicinity. In 1834 the First Dragoons, organized in 1833 as the first cavalry regiment in the Army, was ordered here and showed to a great advantage over the slow-moving infantry in the pursuit of well-mounted Indians.

Congress designated Fort Leavenworth as temporary capital of the Territory. But the first Governor, Reeder, arriving October 7, 1854, found inadequate quarters, and soon sought more commodious housing at Shawnee Mission (see Tour 4), in Johnson County. During the Civil War thousands of volunteers were mustered in and trained here and important ordnance stores were guarded. But the expected southern attack never came.

From this fort went officers to serve in the Spanish-American War; and it became an active training center during the World War. Gen. John J. Pershing and Marshall Ferdinand Foch visited the fort after the war and tendered their praise.

At the south end of Scott Avenue is the COMMAND AND GENERAL STAFF SCHOOL, a combination of four buildings—Sheridan, Grant, Sherman, and Wagner Halls—which ranks second only to the Army War College in Washington, D. C., as a training school for officers. Of yellow brick, with broad entrances, the long consolidation of buildings is surmounted with a tower with illuminated clock dials on its four sides.

Established in 1881 by order of Gen. William T. Sherman, who before the Civil War was a lawyer in Leavenworth, the school has constantly improved in its broad objective of training officers for command and for general staff duty. Names of the Nation's greatest military leaders have been associated with its growth and progress. A school library includes virtually every military book in existence. About 250 officers graduate yearly.

The RESIDENCE OF THE COMMANDANT, No. 1 Scott Avenue, was built about 1861 to house the officer in charge. It has undergone considerable reconstruction and is now one of the most attractive residence buildings at the fort. It is occupied (1938) by Brigadier General Leslie J. McNair.

At 611 Scott Avenue is the site of the FORMER HOME OF HIRAM RICH, the post sutler, where Andrew H. Reeder took his meals during his brief stay at Leavenworth. It has been completely rebuilt into a modern two-story English Colonial house and has been occupied variously by post sutlers, department and post commanders. It was constructed of logs about 1841.

A MONUMENT TO GEN. ULYSSES S. GRANT stands in a tiny triangular park at the confluence of Scott and Grant Avenues. This bronze statue was designed by Lorado Taft and erected in 1889.

North of this monument is the HISTORIC STONE WALL erected by Colonel Leavenworth's men in 1827.

A bronze marker was placed through the efforts of the Capt. Jesse Leavenworth Chapter, Daughters of the American Revolution.

A BRANCH OF THE SANTA FE AND OREGON TRAILS started approximately 100 yards south of the present Missouri Pacific Railroad station at the foot of what is now Riverside Avenue. The ruts where pioneers landed their wagons and teams from river steamboats and pulled up a steep grade can still be traced between the trees. The wagons moved along the present route of Kearney Avenue on west to make connections with the well-trodden Santa Fe and Oregon Trails.

At 12-14 Sumner Place is the FORMER HOME OF GOVERNOR REEDER, representing in part the oldest building at the fort. It is a two-story structure with a porch or gallery extending along the entire breadth of its upper story. Built of native stone in 1834, a brick extension was added in 1879 and later the entire building was stuccoed. It is just north of the site of the old Dragoon barracks.

On the southwest corner of Scott and McPherson Avenues is POPE HALL, occupying the site of an old assembly hall, school building, and post chapel, erected about 1850, which served as the first executive headquarters of the Territory. Governor Reeder maintained his offices here from October 7 to November 24, 1854.

A COLONIAL STYLE BRICK HOUSE, at No. 17 Sumner Place, is one of the oldest and most interesting at the fort. It was built about 1840 and became the home of the post commanders, who were hosts to numerous distinguished guests here until 1890. Since then it has served as officers' quarters.

On the northwest corner of McPherson and Riverside Avenues is the U. S. PRISON ANNEX, formerly the U. S. Military Prison and Disciplinary Barracks, which was started in 1875. Previous to that time military prisoners were sent to penitentiaries with civilian convicts. The walls and buildings are of gray stone quarried on the Reservation.

Three times have prisoners engaged in strikes here. In 1919 the prison was crowded beyond capacity with "conscientious objectors," radicals, and I.W.W.'s, who overflowed into a stockade. Many were men of good character who had received excessive sentences amid the war hysteria for trivial offenses. Bitter resentment against such injustice flared into violence

January 25, 1919. A Negro struck his white opponent after a card game, and during the ensuing racial conflict many Negroes were taken to the prison hospital suffering from severe beatings. The white men who beat them were sent to "the hole," a place of isolation. A prison labor gang went on a "folded arms strike" January 29, and refused to work. One of the conscientious objectors said their chief grievance was the needless prolongation of their war-time sentences. When a strikers' committee conferred with prison officials later in the day, they were told that this matter of holding the war prisoners after peace had been taken up with Washington only a week before. Col. Sedgwick Rice, the Fort Commandant, ordered the release of men from "the hole," and left for Washington to present the case to the War Department. The "fold-arms" prisoners returned to work.

But neither pardons nor commutations resulted, and another strike was called in May 1919 with a demand for recognition of a prisoners' committee. This revolutionary demand was granted. A board of officers sent by Washington arrived July 7 to review the cases, but before action was taken the prisoners were on strike for a third time. The warden practically acquiesced in the demands of the prisoners' committee, and a veritable government by soviet was established. The situation became so tense that extra prison guards and additional troops were stationed inside and outside the prison walls. Machine guns were placed at strategic points, cells were searched for weapons, and the men were put on a diet of "bread, water and toothpicks." By July 26 the cowed prisoners asked to be returned to work, and to their regular meals, but Colonel Rice chose to extend the punishment until July 29, when they were returned to work at full rations. On August 3, 1919, 128 of the mutineers were taken under heavy guard to Alcatraz Island.

The old prison now serves as an annex to the Federal Penitentiary, principally for the confinement of narcotic addicts.

The FORT LEAVENWORTH MUSEUM *(open weekdays 1-5; Sun. and holidays 2-5)*, is in a small brick building just west of the 17th Infantry barracks on McPherson Avenue. The first floor contains a collection of vehicles including the carriage in which Abraham Lincoln rode from Troy to Leavenworth, Kansas, December 1859; an old prairie schooner; and several stagecoaches, Army transport wagons and hansom cabs. On the second floor is a collection of Indian artifacts found within a radius of a few miles of the fort and dioramas depicting Kansas history, the work of the Kansas WPA Museum Project.

The NATIONAL CEMETERY *(open 9-4)*, opposite entrance to the golf course on Biddle Boulevard, is surrounded by a stone wall and contains hundreds of neatly aligned small stone markers over the graves of soldiers who fought in the War of 1812, the Indian campaigns and the Mexican, Civil, Spanish, Philippine, and World Wars. Gen. Henry H. Leavenworth, the fort's founder, is buried here. He died July 21, 1834, while leading an expedition against the Pawnee four days before orders were issued promoting him to the rank of brigadier general. He was buried at Delhi, N. Y. In 1901 his body was returned to Fort Leavenworth.

FEDERAL PRISON, LEAVENWORTH

A massive granite shaft unveiled on Memorial Day, May 30, 1902, bears an inscription to his memory. This tract was set aside for a cemetery in 1860 and bodies from two older burial grounds at the fort were rein- terred here, some without identification. They included soldiers and civil- ians who had died in the vicinity of the fort and others brought in from the plains along the Santa Fe Trail. Among the known dead are five offi- cers of the Seventh Cavalry, including Capt. T. W. Custer, a brother of Gen. George A. Custer, who died in the battle of the Little Big Horn; Prvt. John Urquhart, one of the "hot heads" of Charleston, S. C., who fired the volley on Fort Sumter; and six Confederate soldiers mortally wounded in the battle of Westport. A monument marking the grave of Col. Edward Hatch lists 54 battles in which he was engaged.

South of the National Cemetery is the SUMMER TRAINING CAMP, where R.O.T.C. students from colleges and C.M.T.C. cadets are given military training for six week and four week periods, respectively. Rows of plain, one-story frame buildings provide "mess," bath, and ex- ecutive quarters during the sessions, when the camp is a mass of neatly aligned army tents.

POINTS OF INTEREST IN ENVIRONS

Leavenworth County State Park, *29.6 m. (see Tour 3);* U. S. Veteran's Adminis- tration Facility, *3.9 m.;* St. Mary's College, *4 m.;* Home Site of Buffalo Bill, *6 m. (see Tour 12A).*

Lindsborg

Railroad Stations: E. Lincoln St. for Union Pacific R.R.; 1st and E. Grant Sts. for Missouri Pacific R.R.

Bus Stations: Olson Cafe, 134 N. Main St. for Missouri Pacific, Southwestern Greyhound, Cardinal, and Santa Fe Bus Lines; passengers also picked up at Carlton Hotel, corner Main and Lincoln Sts.

Traffic Regulations: No U-turns in the business district. Speed limit 15 m. No parking limits.

Accommodations: Two hotels; rooms in private homes.

Information Service: Carlton Hotel, and Western Union Service.

Motion Picture House: One, not open Sundays.

Annual Events: Art Exhibit at the Swedish Pavilion during Easter Week. *The Messiah* presented every Palm Sunday and Easter at Bethany College; Community Fair held at Ling Gymnasium, Oct.

LINDSBORG (1,332 alt., 2,016 pop.), in the valley of the Smoky Hill River within the central Kansas wheat belt, is the center of an Old World culture unusual in this section of the country. Settled by a Swedish society, Lindsborg took its name from the first syllable of the surname of three society members—S. P. Lindgren, S. A. Lindell, A. P. Linde—and *borg* (Sw., *castle*). The population is composed almost entirely of persons of Swedish birth or descent.

Outwardly, Lindsborg is like a score of other agricultural communities. Sturdy brick and limestone buildings line its main street. Most of the homes in the residential districts are neat frame structures with closely cut lawns. Only in an occasional glimpse of a tiny garden, an arched window, or the slender, grey spire of Bethany Church does the town reflect its character to the casual observer.

Every year on Palm Sunday, music lovers from all sections of the Middle West crowd into Presser Hall to hear a presentation of Handel's oratorio, *The Messiah,* sung by a chorus of 500 voices. The Oratorio Society is the center about which the Annual Messiah Festival has grown. The festival continues through Holy Week with concerts, contests, and recitals until Good Friday, when a rendition of Bach's *Passion According to St. Matthew* is given, concluding on Easter Sunday with a second performance of *The Messiah.*

Lindsborg was organized in 1868 by the Chicago Swedish Company and its first building was the company's house, where religious services were held and business was transacted. The following year the first dwelling house was erected by the Swedish Merchants' Association and the first store and post office was opened, with J. H. Johnson, the storekeeper, as postmaster.

McPherson County was organized in 1870 with the village of Sweadal, two miles from Lindsborg, as a temporary county seat, but in September 1870 it was moved to Lindsborg. A petition asking for relocation of the county seat was presented to the board of commissioners in April 1873, signed by the citizens of McPherson, King City, and Gotland. An election was called, and these three towns competed with Lindsborg.

The McPherson town company offered land as a site for the courthouse and rooms for the county offices for a period of ten years or until a courthouse could be completed. When the votes were counted McPherson had 605 out of the total vote of 934 and the county offices were moved to that town. There were rumors of illegal voting, due to the fact that the vote cast exceeded the county's population by nearly 200, but charges were never pressed.

The story of the Messiah Festival, however, is the story of Lindsborg. In the late 1800's, while on a European tour, Dr. Olaf Olsson of Augustana College, Rock Island, Ill., heard a rendition of the Handel oratorio in Exeter Hall, London. Returning home, he attempted to develop a similar chorus in Rock Island, but was unsuccessful, although some recitals were given. In 1878, Dr. Carl Swensson, recently graduated from Augustana, was appointed to the pastorate of Bethany Church. Having heard the recitals in Rock Island, he became imbued with the idea of founding a Messiah chorus in Lindsborg, and, with the assistance of his bride, Alma, he began the undertaking in 1881.

From the village and the adjacent farms the young couple gathered a group of fifty singers. The Swedish pioneers, with their natural love of music, were enthusiastic pupils, but rehearsing was difficult, for only a few of them had ever seen a music score before. Bad roads and primitive means of transportation delayed rehearsals. In many instances the trip to Bethany Church for the Sunday afternoon practice sessions took three or four hours.

Despite these obstacles the work continued and on Easter Sunday 1882 the chorus gave its first recital. An orchestra was imported from Rock Island, Dr. Olsson acted as director and organist, and the chorus was conducted by Joseph Osborn. Concerts were held in neighboring towns that year and receipts were given to Bethany College, founded in 1881, of which Dr. Swensson was the first president. So encouraged were the founders by the interest in the chorus that *The Messiah* was repeated the following year, and since 1889 has been presented annually on Palm Sunday and Easter Sunday.

During its half century of existence the choir has appeared outside Lindsborg on only four occasions. The most notable performance was given at Convention Hall, Kansas City, Mo., in 1930. It was in that year that the new Presser Hall, a magnificent music temple, was completed on the college campus. Mrs. Swensson, who is 78 years of age (1938), still sings a soprano role in the chorus she helped establish and has missed but one performance since the first recital in 1882.

No person in the chorus receives pay. As early as 1892, however, Dr. Swensson began engaging artists and singers of national reputation to

ART MUSEUM, BETHANY COLLEGE, LINDSBORG

give special concerts during the festival week. In that year, Remenyi, one of the foremost violinists of the time, appeared in a recital. Since then many noted musicians have taken part in the activities of festival week, among them Nordica, Schumann-Heink, Gadski, Galli Curci, Giannini, Matzenauer, Ysaye, Marion Talley, Sigrid Onegin, Frances Alda, Claire Dux, Erika Morini, Richard Crooks, Elsa Alsen, and Helen Marshall.

The director of the choir (1938), Dr. Hagbard Brase, has held this position since 1914. Dr. Brase is a native of Sweden and a graduate of the Royal Conservatory of Music at Stockholm. He is a member of the American Guild of Organists and has achieved success as a composer and conductor.

Lindsborg is also well-known as the home of Prof. Sven Birger Sandzen, a painter of international reputation. Professor Sandzen, the dean of Kansas artists, has been a member of the faculty of Bethany College since 1894 and is now (1938) professor of Art History and director of the Art School of the Lindsborg institution.

Wood carving is another Old World art that is practiced in Lindsborg, and many outstanding character interpretations have been produced by Lindsborg artisans. The figures are usually carved from basswood and seldom exceed ten inches in height. Some are faithful representations of American characters, others portray Old Country costumes and activities.

Probably the most notable of Lindsborg's wood carvers are Anton Pearson and John A. Altenborg.

POINTS OF INTEREST

BETHANY COLLEGE, Swensson and 2nd Sts., was founded in 1881, largely through the efforts of Dr. Carl A. Swensson, who served as its first president. Classes opened on October 15, 1881, in a building completed during the previous summer. The following year the college was placed under the directorship of the Swedish Lutheran Church, and was incorporated. Its students come, for the most part, from Swedish Lutheran families in the Kansas Conference district of the church. The college, which is co-educational, has an average annual enrollment of about 400. Departments include preparatory, normal, commercial and college training, art, and music.

Dr. Ernst F. Pihlblad, dean of Kansas college presidents, has been president of the college since 1904.

Among the nine buildings on the compact, elm-shaded campus is PRESSER HALL *(open 8-5, school days),* scene of the annual music festivals since 1931. It was named in honor of Theodore Presser, music publisher of Philadelphia, in recognition of his gift of $75,000 to the institution. The building was designed by Henry C. Eckland & Co. of Kansas City, Missouri, and ground for the three-story brick and concrete structure was broken by the Crown Prince of Sweden on his visit to Lindsborg, March 17, 1927. In November 1928 the first wing, including the auditorium, which has a seating capacity of 2,750, was completed. The studio wing, with studios, classrooms, rehearsal halls, and practice rooms, was completed in 1930.

Benefit concerts contributed materially to the building fund and the structure was completed without indebtedness. Mme. Schumann-Heink, who said, "America has no other Lindsborg, I want to have a hand in this one," gave a benefit recital on May 16, 1926, and on November 2, 1928, Marion Talley, formerly of the Metropolitan Opera, as her contribution, dedicated the auditorium at a recital. The pipe organ is the gift of Francis J. Plyn of Niles, Michigan.

The MAIN BUILDING, a five-story structure of brick and limestone, was completed in 1886. It contains a dining hall, classrooms, chapel, men students' living apartments, science laboratories, and the museum. BETHANY COLLEGE MUSEUM *(open 8-5, weekdays),* on the first floor, contains a collection of natural history and ethnology exhibits. It has a valuable numismatic collection containing more than 3,000 specimens of rare gold, silver, copper, and bronze coins.

BETHANY CHURCH is a gray stone structure of classic design with a steeple rising 150 feet and topped with a cross. Here Dr. Swensson held the first *Messiah* concert. Two wings have been added to the original building which served for a time as a part of Bethany College. Above the altar is a painting by G. N. Malm of Lindsborg, *Christ at Bethany,* in which the Christ is represented with Lazarus, Martha, and Mary. Left of the altar is *The Ascension,* and on the right *The Resurrection of Lazarus,* both by Birger Sandzen.

The church was organized in 1868, and on August 18, 1869, Dr. Olaf

Olsson arrived to assume the pastorate, which he occupied until he was called to the presidency of Augustana College.

In 1878, when Dr. Swensson succeeded to the pastorate, the church had 323 communicants. At his first annual meeting it was decided to sell a part of the land granted the church by the Missouri Pacific Railroad and to use half of the proceeds in building an addition to the church, laying the other half aside to be used as a fund for Bethany College.

The SWEDISH PAVILION *(open 2-5, school days),* home of the Bethany College Art Department, was presented to the college by the Swedish Government through W. W. Thomas, former U. S. Minister to Sweden and Norway. It was part of Sweden's exhibit at the St. Louis World's Fair in 1904 and was reconstructed on the Bethany College campus shortly after the close of the exposition. Built of wood with a red tile roof, the design is based on the old style of Swedish manor house with a main hall and two smaller buildings connected by porticos. All material used in its construction was brought from Sweden. In the pavilion are paintings by Kansas artists.

BIRGER SANDZEN'S STUDIO *(open on application),* 421 N. 2nd St., a one-story building of frame and stucco, contains a collection of prints, bronzes, wood carvings, and oils. Among the paintings by contemporary artists are *The Brown Bottle,* and *Portrait of a Child* by Henry Varnum Poor, former Kansan. Just outside Dr. Sandzen's studio window is *The Little Triton,* a bronze statue by Carl Milles, which was presented to a group of Milles' Lindsborg friends with the stipulation that it stand in Dr. Sandzen's garden. It was on display at the Texas Centennial Exposition at Dallas in 1936.

POINTS OF INTEREST IN ENVIRONS

Coronado Heights, Soldier Cap Mound, *3.7 m.;* Sharp's Creek, *6 m.;* Shelter Belt Nursery, *12.6 m.;* Salemsborg, *22.6 m. (see Tour 9).*

Manhattan

Railroad Stations: 4th and El Paso Sts. for Chicago, Rock Island & Pacific Ry.; 1st and Yuma Sts. for Union Pacific R.R.
Bus Stations: Wareham Hotel, 418 Poyntz Ave. for Greyhound Lines; 5th and Poyntz Ave. in rear of Scheu's Cafe, for Sante Fe Trailways, Interstate Transit Lines.
Buses: Intra-city, fare 5¢.
Taxis: Minimum fare, 10¢.
Traffic Regulations: Traffic lights on Poyntz Ave. in downtown business section. No U turns in business district.

Accommodations: Three hotels; seven tourist camps.

Information Service: Chamber of Commerce, 4th and Humboldt Sts.

Radio Station: KSAC (580 kc.).
Motion Picture Houses: Four.
Athletics: Memorial Stadium, Kansas State College campus, for college athletic events.
Swimming: Free swimming pool in City Park, 11th and Leavenworth Sts.
Tennis: City Park, 11th and Leavenworth Sts.
Golf: Manhattan Country Club on Bluemont Hill, 18 holes, greens fee 50¢, weekdays, 75¢ Sun. and holidays; Stagg Hill, 2.5 m. W. on US 40, 18 holes, greens fee 50¢.

Annual Events: Farm and Home Week, Jan.; Annual Engineers' Open House, given by the students of the Engineering Division, Kansas State College, March; Kansas State College Homecoming, Oct.; State High School Band Contest, Nov.

MANHATTAN (1,012 alt., 10,136 pop.), seat of Riley County, lies in a natural bowl carved out of a limestone formation during the glacial age. The Big Blue River flowing from the north through the upland pastures meets the Kaw River one mile east of the city limits. Before the great flood of 1903 the Big Blue ran past the city at the foot of Poyntz Avenue, the main street, but the flood formed a new channel one mile east of the old river bed, washing away hundreds of acres of rich farm land.

Encircled by low hills, Manhattan is an oasis of green during the late summer months when the bluestem grasses that cover the hills are turned to an autumnal brown by the sun. With streets well-shaded by spreading elms, the city, seen from the adjoining countryside gives the appearance of a great park. Here and there the outline of one of the taller buildings is visible above the mass of green.

The city extends a little more than a mile west from the old river channel, spreading to the north and south from Poyntz Avenue, a wide thoroughfare that ends abruptly as it encounters the first slopes of the limestone hills. The State College campus adjoins the city on the northwest and most of the new residential development is in this area. South of Poyntz Avenue an older section of modest homes extends to the Rock

Island tracks. Along the railroad is a small area inhabited by Negroes and Mexicans.

Many of Manhattan's business houses and residences and all of its public buildings, including those of Kansas State College, are built of native limestone.

Kansas' second largest educational institution, the State College, is the center of activity in Manhattan. Stores depend upon the patronage of the farm territory and the 4,500 students. The city supports four newspapers. These include a morning and an evening daily and two weeklies of city and rural circulation. Five periodicals are published by educational groups.

The city has two business districts, one downtown and another adjoining the college campus. The uptown district has been known as "Aggieville" since the days when the college was known as the Kansas State Agricultural College and its students as the "Aggies."

Successive settlements of Germans, Swedes, and Irish have placed descendants of the New England and Ohio founders in a minority in contemporary Manhattan but the spirit of the crusading pioneers prevails. The city supports eighteen churches and these religious groups exert a strong influence in its social life.

Manhattan was one of the last towns in the State to lift the ban on Sunday theaters. This compromise with the champions of strict Sabbath observance was the result of a heated controversy between church leaders and business men. State College students flocked to Junction City, Wamego, and other neighboring towns to attend Sunday night movies and proprietors of cafes and soft drink emporiums in the college town complained that they were losing trade because of this weekly exodus. In 1934 the question was submitted to a vote and proponents of Sunday amusement won by a small majority. Since then Manhattan has been more successful in keeping students' dollars at home.

Years before the first white settlers came, a large Kaw Indian village stood near the mouth of the Big Blue. The exact site of this village is undetermined, but it is believed to have been in the area between the old river bed and the new channel. Early explorers reported the existence of the village, which disappeared before the first settler arrived.

Two towns were established on the present site of Manhattan late in 1854. Col. George S. Park of Parkville, Missouri, platted a townsite and called it Poleska. Soon afterward a second settlement, called Canton, was established near the mouth of the Big Blue by a committee from the New England Emigrant Aid Company. This settlement was soon consolidated with Poleska under the name of Boston. On April 27, 1855, a party of colonists left Cincinnati on the steamboat *Hartford*, destined for the new Boston. They navigated the Ohio River to its junction with the Mississippi and then to St. Louis where they were delayed for several days by authorities who suspected them of being abolitionists. Resuming their journey toward Kansas City by way of the Missouri River the Ohioans arrived at the mouth of the Kaw late in May. There they were delayed because of low water.

Tardy spring rains finally raised the river to what was believed to be a navigable level, but near St. Mary's Mission the boat, carrying, in addition to the colonists, a load of freight that included ten portable houses, stuck on a sandbar. The passengers were unloaded and proceeded to their destination by land, but within a few days, after another rise in the stream, the boat arrived.

The Ohioans at first selected a site for their colony near the present Junction City, and named it Manhattan. The leaders of the party, John Pipher, Andrew J. Meade, and H. Palmer finally, however, closed a deal with the Boston Association whereby they were given half of the Boston townsite, and by mutual agreement Boston was renamed Manhattan.

Manhattan's pioneers were Free State men, and before the arrival of the party from Cincinnati, the New England group had voted to install one of their number, Samuel D. Houston, as Free State representatives to the First Territorial legislature. Houston was the only Free State man elected to this body.

With the development of agriculture in the fertile river valleys, Manhattan became important as a trading center. Two railroads, the Rock Island and the Union Pacific, extended their main lines through the town in the seventies and eighties and it became a shipping point for farm produce and for cattle from the upland grazing areas.

In 1859, Bluemont College, the forerunner of Kansas State College, opened its doors. As the college grew, the city prospered. In 1910 the city endeavored to expand its trade territory by voting $20,000 in bonds for the construction of an electric railway between Manhattan and Fort Riley. This line brought a proportion of the soldier trade from Camp Funston to Manhattan during the World War, but with the advent of the paved highway it went into decline and was finally abandoned.

Although Manhattan's economic structure is largely based on agriculture and livestock raising, the city has a number of small industries including two hatcheries, a creamery that manufactures butter, cheese and ice cream, a monument works, a flour mill, two packing companies that process eggs and poultry, and a serum plant. Two planing mills turn out cabinets, door frames and boxes, and a third manufactures egg cases and shipping crates.

POINTS OF INTEREST

The CARNEGIE LIBRARY *(open 10-5 weekdays)*, NW. corner Poyntz Ave. and 5th St., erected in 1904, is a two-story brick and limestone building of neo-classic design. Operated as a municipal library, it contains 30,000 volumes.

The FIRST METHODIST EPISCOPAL CHURCH, NW. corner Poyntz Ave. and 6th St., erected in 1925, is of English Gothic design, constructed of native limestone. In the church is the old bell of the steamer *Hartford* that brought the settlers from Cincinnati in 1855. The original congregation was organized in 1858.

ST. PAUL'S EPISCOPAL CHURCH, SW. corner Poyntz Ave. and 6th St., built in 1865 of native limestone, was designed by Richard Upjohn. It is an excellent example of the Gothic Revival style of architecture.

CITY PARK, 11th St., between Poyntz Ave. and Fremont St., is a 45-acre tract equipped with playgrounds, a swimming pool, and tennis courts. It is attractively landscaped, containing approximately 1,000 trees. Near the Leavenworth Street entrance is a band pavilion with a seating capacity of 1,000, erected under the sponsorship of the Manhattan Ministerial Alliance, where band concerts and open-air church services are held during the summer. Rose gardens, sponsored by the Manhattan Kiwanis Club and a rock garden sponsored by the Rotary Club attract visitors from all parts of the country.

Near the center of the park is the TATARRAX MONUMENT, a shaft of grey marble, ten feet high, resting on a truncated base of limestone four feet high. The monument was designed by J. V. Brower, one of the founders of the Quivira Historical Society.

An OLD STAGECOACH, formerly used in Yellowstone Park, stands just west of the monument. It was donated to the city by the Union Pacific Railroad. Near the stagecoach is the LOG CABIN MUSEUM *(open Sun. afternoons during the summer months);* containing a number of pioneer relics.

The KANSAS STATE COLLEGE, 14th and Anderson Sts., has an attractively landscaped 155-acre campus on which there are twenty buildings of native limestone construction and modified Gothic design.

In 1857 an association was formed to build a college in or near Manhattan. Under the direction of the Reverend Joseph Denison, Isaac Goodnow, and Washington Marlatt funds were raised for the purchase of a farm one mile west of the present State College campus. A three-story building was erected in 1859 and the college, opened under the direction of the Methodist Episcopal Church, was given the name of Bluemont College. The Reverend Joseph Denison was chosen president. The college did not prosper and in 1862 it was offered to the State as an agricultural and mechanical college under the provisions of the Morrill Land Grant Act. A resolution of the State legislature, approved by Gov. Thomas Carney, February 3, 1863, created the Kansas State Agricultural College, a co-educational institution. Kansas State has graduated engineers, journalists, and scientists in addition to its trained agronomists.

In 1931 the State legislature changed the name of the college from Kansas State Agricultural College to Kansas State College of Agriculture and Applied Science. It took Kansas sports writers quite a while to forget the habit of referring to Kansas State athletic team as "The Aggies" but the new appellation "wildcats" finally superseded the traditional nickname.

In the early fall of 1934 Kansas State became the center of a controversy on compulsory military training. The Morrill Act, under which the college was established, reads as follows:

. . . where the leading object shall be, without excluding other scientific and classical studies, and including military tactics, to teach such branches of learning as are related to agriculture and the mechanical arts.

The school year of 1934 opened with a military training strike by three freshmen who refused to drill and gave their abhorrence of war as a jus-

AIRVIEW, KANSAS STATE COLLEGE, MANHATTAN

tification. College authorities were insistent. Patriotic organizations took up the fight for compulsion. Pacifist groups offered legal and moral support to the striking students. Eventually the question was referred to the State legislature at the session of 1935. Proponents of the forced drill prepared legislation making it compulsory. Backed by the American Legion and the college authorities the bill was passed. Students who object to drill must seek their education at other colleges.

Prof. Fred A. Shannon of the department of history won a Pulitzer award for historical research in 1929. In 1933 the *Kansas Magazine* was revived by Russell Thackery of the department of industrial journalism *(see LITERATURE)*. Prof. John Helm, Jr., of the department of architecture, is now (1938) director of the Kansas State Federation of Art.

Kansas State had an enrollment of 4,457 in 1938.

In ANDERSON HALL, the college administration building, is a MUSEUM *(open 8-5 daily during the school year)*, that contains a collection of antique furniture, a pottery collection, and other articles of interest.

In THE COLLEGE LIBRARY *(open 8-5 daily during the school year)*, is an art collection, including portraits, oils, and water colors. Some of the paintings and murals, by WPA artists, were presented to the college by the Federal Art Project of Kansas. On the fourth floor of the library is an arch of stone letters forming the words, Bluemont College, 1859. This arch was set above the entrance to old Bluemont College. It was taken from an old barn a number of years ago and placed in the library.

FAIRCHILD HALL contains a large MUSEUM OF NATURAL HISTORY *(open 8-5 during school year)*. There are many specimens of mounted animals and reptiles as well as a collection of live snakes, lizards, and alligators. Other exhibits include a large collection of mounted birds, Indian artifacts, and a geological collection.

Kansas State College owns 1,428 acres of land, much of which is used for agricultural experiments. At the extreme southwest corner of the campus is a MEMORIAL STADIUM where the Kansas State athletic teams compete with the other members of the Big Six conference. The stadium was completed in 1922.

SUNSET CEMETERY, Sunset and Evergreen Aves. (R), on the crest of a hill overlooking the city, contains the SOLDIERS MONUMENT, erected in 1898 by the Lew Gove Post, Grand Army of the Republic. It is an oblong shaft surmounted by an old cannon. A singing tower has been erected in a new section of the cemetery.

DENISON CIRCLE, in the center of a winding drive at the intersection of Evergreen and Sunset Aves., a sodded plot of ground 100 feet in diameter has in its center THE REVEREND JOSEPH DENISON MONUMENT, a memorial of red glacial boulders to the first president of Kansas State College.

MEMORIAL ARCH, Evergreen and Poyntz Aves., was erected in memory of Amanda Arnold, one of Manhattan's first school teachers. The arch was taken from the old Central School building.

POINTS OF INTEREST IN ENVIRONS

Fort Riley, *14.6 m. (see Tour 3)*; Beecher Bible and Rifle Church, *22.1 m. (see Tour 3)*.

Medicine Lodge

Railroad Station: W. Kansas St. for Atchison, Topeka & Santa Fe Ry.
Bus Station: Hart Hotel, 1st and Main Sts., for Anthony Stage Lines.

Accommodations: Two hotels and two tourist camps.

Motion Picture House: One.
Golf: Municipal Golf Course, Peace Treaty Park, E. limits of city, 9 holes, greens fee 25¢.
Tennis: High school grounds, 1st and Main St.

Annual Event: Peace Treaty Pageant, October of years with numerals ending in 2 and 7.

MEDICINE LODGE (1,500 alt., 1,655 pop.), seat of Barber County, is a trim little town, spreading out comfortably on a hillside overlooking the Medicine River and its timbered valley. Low brick buildings line the broad main street and spreading trees shade modest frame houses in the residential section.

Expanding gradually from Main Street, the thoroughfare upon which the town's first log houses were built in the early 1870's, Medicine Lodge has grown with the surrounding country, adding new blocks and new streets as more space was needed with little thought of a definite city plan. Its streets jog and turn and oftentimes end blindly, and those on the outskirts meet the open farmland suddenly.

Medicine Lodge, a country town with a rural serenity about it and a trading center for farmers in the river valley, has a certain importance as a shipping point for the vast wheat and cattle country to the south and west. Its one industrial touch is the gypsum mill where gypsum rock, mined in the hills that extend north and south on the west side of the townsite, is made into cement and a fine grade of plaster used for making molds and wall decorations. The mill furnished much of the plaster used in Federal buildings in Washington, D. C.

Once each five years, Medicine Lodge presents a Peace Treaty Pageant commemorating the Medicine Lodge Peace Treaty negotiated by U. S. Government representatives and the chiefs of five plains tribes in October 1867. The first pageant was held in 1927 on the sixtieth anniversary of the signing of the Treaty and others have been held at five-year intervals since that date.

The pageant, sponsored by the Medicine Lodge Peace Treaty Association, reenacts the signing of the treaty and hundreds of Medicine Lodge residents and Indians from Oklahoma reservations participate. It is held in a natural amphitheatre in Memorial Peace Park, on the eastern limits of Medicine Lodge. Widely advertised, it is attended by thousands of persons from Kansas and neighboring States.

For years before the settlers arrived Indians in the region believed the spot to be under the protection of the Great Spirit. Prairie fires, which periodically destroyed tree growth along the western rivers, had passed around the region making it seem that the waters of the Medicine River possessed a magic power to protect the green woodland clinging to its margin.

Representatives of all tribes in the Southwest met in peace at a little medicine lodge which is said to have stood on the river bank near the present townsite. Here they fasted and prayed and bathed in the curative waters of the sacred river so that their bodily ills might be healed.

When settlement of the Territory was brought almost to a standstill by constant Indian wars in the 1860's, representatives of the Federal Government made plans for a great peace council between the Indians and the white men. Scouts, soldiers, settlers, and gold-seekers were enlisted to carry word to tribes that Government representatives desired to meet them and negotiate a treaty of peace at a place of their own choosing.

After months of tribal councils and powwows the tribes chose the site of their medicine lodge on the banks of the wooded river. Two factors influenced their choice. They believed that near their ancient sanctuary the Great Spirit would watch over all that took place. The spot, too, was miles from the white man's civilization and here, in their own country, they believed there was less danger of treachery on the part of the white men. Plans were completed for the meeting in the early fall of 1867 and in October of that year at the present site of Medicine Lodge 15,000 Indians met with 600 Government representatives in what is said to be the largest gathering of Indians and whites in the history of the United States.

The commissioners, whose duty it was to negotiate the treaty with the chiefs of the five plains tribes (Kiowa, Comanche, Arapaho, Apache, and Cheyenne), were all men of prominence in war and Government affairs. N. G. Taylor, orator and scholar, was president of the commission. Gen. W. T. Sherman, Civil War hero, and S. J. Crawford, Governor of Kansas, were there as advisors. Others who played important parts were Col. A. G. Boone, grandson of Daniel Boone, Col. Edward W. Wynkoop, agent of the Arapaho and the Cheyenne, respected by the whites and possessing the trust and confidence of the Indians, Col. James H. Leavenworth, agent of the Kiowa and the Comanche, Kit Carson and William Mathewson, Indian fighters and scouts, and Jesse Chisholm, for whom the Chisholm Cattle Trail was named. Henry M. Stanley, later known for his explorations in Africa and his search for David Livingstone, covered the event for the New York *Tribune*.

Towering above all the Indians in native intellect, and bearing a remarkable resemblance to Andrew Jackson, was Little Raven, orator and chief of the Arapaho. A. A. Taylor, later Governor of Tennessee, attended the council as a secretary. In an account of the event published in the early 1900's he said: "Little Raven's speech before the commission on the question of damages . . . his reference to the ill treatment the Indians had received from the whites was scathing, and his plea for protection and better treatment in the future was the most touching piece of impassioned oratory to which I have listened before or since."

Of no less importance to the gathering were Satanta, chief of the Kiowa; Young Bear, Iron Mountain, and Painted Lips of the Comanche; Wolf Sleeve, Iron Shirt, and Crow of the Apache; and Black Kettle, Bull Bear, and Slim Face of the Cheyenne.

Council meetings were held in a large tent near the river bank. Commissioners and Indian chiefs sat on camp stools in a circle and secretaries wrote on large packing boxes. Thus after three years of constant warfare, Indians and whites met peaceably, exchanging words instead of blows and concluding arguments with mutual concessions. Each chief spoke before the council and the grievances and claims of each tribe were settled individually. At the end of the two weeks' negotiations the treaty was signed. It fixed the southern boundary of Kansas and stipulated that south of that line should be Indian Territory "as long as grass grows and waters run." It ended a war of three years' duration, thus clearing the way for white settlement of the entire southwest. As a result of the treaty the populations of Colorado, North Dakota, South Dakota, New Mexico, and Arizona were augmented, making it indirectly responsible for the entrance of those States into the Union.

White men are known to have settled in the region shortly after the signing of the treaty, but it was not until 1873 that John Hutchinson and a party of men laid out the town of Medicine Lodge on a 400-acre site on the river bank. The town's first public buildings were a hotel and a store, surrounded by a cluster of log houses. In 1874, known as the "grasshopper year," swarms of insects destroyed the corn and vegetables that would have sustained the new settlers during the next winter. Experiencing its share of business failures and hardships brought about by droughts, floods, and blizzards, the town continued to grow slowly and, without the stimulus of a boom period, overcame the effects of each disaster.

In 1884 Medicine Lodge was a straggling country town without a railroad, and the cattle business was its chief source of income. The community boasted only one outstanding institution, the Medicine Valley Bank of which E. Wylie Payne was president and George Geppert was cashier. On May 1, 1884 four men rode into town and attempted to hold up the bank. They killed Geppert, mortally wounded Payne, and fled south, with a posse of townsmen hastily organized by Barney O'Connor, a prominent cattleman, in pursuit.

Aided by a group of cowboys the posse surrounded the bandits in a narrow canyon in the Gypsum Hills southwest of town. Trails leading out of the canyon were barred by riflemen, who covered an unarmed member of the posse sent into the canyon to demand their surrender. Realizing that they were trapped, the four men walked out with upraised hands and were placed in a small frame house which served as a jail.

Payne died shortly after nightfall. When word of his death passed through the crowd, the rumbling of voices in the streets was punctuated with cries of "Lynch them! Lynch them!"

The leader of the gang, killed in an attempt to escape from the jail, was John Henry Brown, city marshal of Caldwell, "reformed" bad man and former companion of the robber and killer, "Billy the Kid." Brown had a record of excellent work in Caldwell and had been presented with a gold-mounted Winchester rifle by residents of the town. With Brown were Ben Wheeler, assistant marshal of Caldwell, and Billy Smith and John Wesley, cowboys from Texas. Wheeler, Wesley, and Smith came to their death, according to the report of the coroner's jury, "by hanging at the hands of a mob, composed of persons unknown."

The town's first newspaper was the *Barber County Mail,* founded in 1878 by M. C. Cochran. In 1879 the paper was purchased by J. W. Mc-Neal and E. W. Iliff, who changed its name to the Medicine Lodge *Cresset.* At this time T. A. (Tom) McNeal became associated with the paper. Tom McNeal served a term as mayor of Medicine Lodge, was State printer for six years and is now (1938) one of the editors of the Topeka *Capital* and the dean of Kansas newspapermen.

It was in Medicine Lodge in the summer of 1890 that "Sockless Jerry" Simpson, Populist leader, began the career that gained him Nation-wide publicity. Simpson, a resident of Medicine Lodge, acquired the name "Sockless Jerry" in his campaign for Congress against James R. Hollowell, a Republican. Appearing upon the same platform with his opponent one day Simpson attempted to brand Hollowell as an advocate of luxury with the statement, "My opponent wears silk stockings." Hollowell, stooping to pull up Simpson's trouser leg to display a few inches of bare ankle retorted, "My opponent wears no socks at all."

Simpson was victorious in the election held the following fall and as "Sockless Jerry" Simpson of Kansas held an important place in State and national politics for a decade.

Carry Nation, militant reformer and prohibitionist, moved to Medicine Lodge in the late 1880's; she and her husband, David Nation, rented a tiny stone house just west of Main Street. It was not until the last year of the century, however, that she began her crusade against liquor which later took her to all parts of the United States and to England.

In the 1890's dissension ran high in Medicine Lodge and in the surrounding country between cattlemen who wanted an open range and settlers who wanted to make homes, build fences, and till the soil. By 1900, however, the feud subsided and today cattlemen own great ranches to the south and west of town and farmers raise their chickens and hogs, plant their gardens and till the soil in the fertile valley along the river. The two industries—cattle raising and farming—contribute about equally to the economic life of Medicine Lodge.

POINTS OF INTEREST

The PEACE TREATY MONUMENT N. end of Main St. was erected by the United States Government and the Medicine Lodge Peace Treaty Association in 1929. It is a marble statue of a frontiersman and an Indian clasping hands.

CARRY NATION

MEMORIAL PEACE PARK, E. limits of city on US 160 is a wooded area containing a natural amphitheatre, recreational facilities, and a network of foot trails. The park is the scene of the Peace Treaty Pageant produced every five years to commemorate the Medicine Lodge Peace Council.

The HOME OF CARRY NATION *(private)*, NE. corner Fowler Ave. and Oak St., is a one-story gray stone structure marked by a bronze plaque presented by the W.C.T.U.

Mrs. Nation's first public demonstration occurred in Medicine Lodge on a Saturday afternoon in the summer of 1899 when she and a few of her associates held a prayer meeting in front of one of the town's seven saloons, singing to the accompaniment of a small hand organ. By that time Medicine Lodge had become a thriving trading center and the streets were jammed with farmers, cattlemen, and townspeople. A large crowd soon collected about the little group of women and Mrs. Nation, encouraged by the audience, launched into a tirade on the evils of liquor. Each time she paused for breath and inspiration her companions waved their arms and sang:

> They who tarry at the wine cup,
> They who tarry at the wine cup,
> They who tarry at the wine cup—
> They have sorrow, they have woe.

Then suddenly, clutching a big, black umbrella by the stem, Mrs. Nation stormed the door of the saloon. The proprietor, however, watching the activities from inside the window, had anticipated the move and Mrs. Nation found the door locked and bolted. Pounding on it she shouted to him: "You are a child of Satan. You will go to Hell!" And then, waving her umbrella and singing "John Brown's Body Lies A-mouldering in the Grave" she led the group down Main Street to her home. According to her autobiography, written about five years later, it was then that she experienced "the birth pangs of a new obsession and realized that she was to become the 'John Brown of Prohibition.'" Mrs. Nation retained her residence in Medicine Lodge for several years after the turn of the century, but she directed her militant attentions elsewhere. Early in 1900 she used stones and bricks to smash a saloon in Kiowa, also in Barber County, but it was not until she reached Wichita during the latter part of that year that she first used the hatchet for which she became nationally known.

The GYPSUM MILL (open 8-5 weekdays), Harvey St. at the W. limits of town, prepares raw gypsum for use in plaster by the calcine process. The plant has a capacity of 50,000 tons per year and gives employment to approximately 100 men.

POINTS OF INTEREST IN ENVIRONS

Gypsum Hills, 4 m.; Twin Peaks, 6 m. (see Tour 6).

Newton

Railroad Stations: A. T. & S. F. Ry. depot, SE. corner 5th and Main Sts., for Atchison Topeka & Santa Fe Ry.; 6th St. and Kansas Ave. for Missouri Pacific Electric Ry.; 123 W. 5th St. for Arkansas Valley Interurban Ry., service between Wichita, Hutchinson, and Newton.
Bus Station: A. T. & S. F. Ry. depot for Santa Fe Trailways System.
Taxis: Minimum fare 10¢.

Accommodations: Nine hotels, three tourist camps.

Information Service: Chamber of Commerce, 500½ Main St.

Motion Picture Houses: Three.
Swimming: Newton Swimming Pool, Athletic Park, west end of 1st St.
Golf: Newton Golf Club, 0.6 m. S. of city limits on US 81, 18 holes, greens fee 50¢.
Tennis: Municipal courts, Athletic Park, west end 1st St.; Themian Park, west edge of city between 7th and 8th Sts.

Annual Events: Newton Trade Show, March; Mennonite Music Festival, May; Institute of International Relations, June; Labor Day celebration, Sept.

NEWTON (1,439 alt., 11,034 pop.), seat of Harvey County, is a trading center for the surrounding wheat country, and a main division point of the Santa Fe Railway. The city lies amid gently rolling hills. Main Street is bisected by tracks down which rattle endless freight trains carrying oil and grain to the east, merchandise and farm machinery to the west. About twenty-five passenger trains, including sleek streamliners, halt daily at the Main Street Depot.

Local economy is governed to a large extent by the activities of agriculture and the Santa Fe Ry., particularly the latter. Almost a thousand inhabitants are employed in the shops, offices, and rail mill of the Santa Fe. Railroad news often crowds politics and information of world import onto the second page of the local papers. Labor Day is an important annual festival celebrated with parades, oratory, fireworks, and brass bands.

Five per cent of the population is Mennonite. Some of them have renounced their traditional vocation of farming to enter business; there is a Mennonite Mutual Fire Insurance Company and Bethel College is Mennonite. Of the 23 churches in the community, the largest congregations are the Methodists and the Mennonites.

A house built by A. F. Horner in Brookville, Kan., in the early 1870's was the first dwelling in Newton. Horner built it in order to win a town lot offered by the promoters of Brookville for the first house erected there. Within a few months Horner moved his 20-by-60-feet dwelling from Brookville to Florence, to Newton, to Hutchinson, winning in turn the lots offered by each town's promoters for the first dwelling. In July 1871 the Santa Fe Railway extended its line to the settlement which thereby succeeded Abilene as the terminus of the Chisholm Trail. The cattle trade turned Newton into a "cow town" overnight. Saloons, dancehalls, and gambling houses for pleasure-starved cowboys sprouted from the plain. Although this phase of Newton's growth only lasted until January 1873, when the railroad was extended to Wichita, fifty persons are estimated to have met sudden death in its saloons and dancehalls.

Most fearless of the gunmen in the booming settlement was Art Delaney, better known as Mike McCluskie, a railroad agent hired as marshal by local saloonkeepers and gambling house proprietors. McCluskie shot and killed William Bailey, a Texas gambler. Hugh Anderson, a friend of Bailey's who had driven a herd of longhorns to Newton from his father's ranch in Texas, swore to kill McCluskie on sight. He was backed by Jim Wilkerson, a sure-shot Kentuckian, and two fellow Texans, Will Garret and Henry Kearnes.

On the night of August 9, 1871, McCluskie sauntered into the gaming room of the Tuttle Dance Hall, accompanied by Riley, a thin tubercular youth of eighteen, who worshipped the gunman and followed him around like a faithful dog. Although warned that Anderson and his friends had chosen this night to avenge Bailey's death, McCluskie lingered at the gaming tables. Riley lounged near the door.

The door burst open and Hugh Anderson, Garret, Kearnes, Wilkerson, and several cowpunchers strode into the room. The click of poker chips stilled and the roulette wheels slowed to a stop. McCluskie leaped to his feet and reached for his gun. Anderson fired. McCluskie spun around and dropped, mortally wounded.

The frail Riley went berserk. Snatching a pair of pistols from his ragged clothing, he began pumping lead. When he ceased firing, Anderson and five of his henchmen lay bleeding on the floor. Jim Wilkerson was fatally shot, two of the cowboys were dead, Garret, Kearnes, and Anderson were wounded.

Riley ran from the room. Tom Carson, the new marshal, organized a posse to search for the youth, but he was never seen again.

The Tuttle Dance Hall Massacre aroused the "better element" to reform Newton. As an initial attempt the Reverend H. M. Haun, a fearless Methodist missionary, stalked into the Gold Room Saloon and announced that he intended to conduct a religious meeting. "Go ahead, parson," the loungers assented, "a little of the Word of God won't hurt us none." Thus prompted, Haun held services behind an untapped keg of beer. As he intoned the final Amen, two cowboys swept off their Stetsons and, with six-shooters in hand, took a collection. Gold coins clinked into the hats. Presenting the money with a flourish, the volunteer deacons bowed the parson out graciously with a request that he return sometime for another meeting.

Bernard Warkentin, a descendant of the group of German Mennonites who migrated to Russia during the reign of Catherine the Great, was one of the first of his faith to reach Kansas. In 1872 he settled at Halstead, 12 miles west of Newton, and established a small flour mill operated by water from the Little Arkansas River. He later helped immigration agents of the Santa Fe Railway by encouraging his kinsmen to leave the Russian steppes for the Kansas prairies. Many of these devout, industrious people settled near Newton, introducing an Old World culture to the region and greatly furthering its agricultural development. With them they brought precious Turkey Red wheat (see AGRICULTURE). In 1885 Warkentin organized the Newton Milling and Elevator Company, which subsequently became one of the largest in central Kansas.

Newton was designated a division point of the Santa Fe Railway in 1873. The water supply proved to be inadequate, however, and in 1879 the division offices were removed to Nickerson. In 1886 the Santa Fe built the Hutchinson cut-off, which circumvented Nickerson and weakened its position as a division point. The townspeople of Newton, seeing a chance to regain the division point, began to negotiate with railroad officials. An agreement was reached in 1894 whereby the Santa Fe promised to re-establish a division point at Newton if an abundant supply of good water could be provided there.

Learning that Professor Erasmus Haworth of Lawrence had completed a geological survey of Kansas, which showed that the old bed of the Smoky Hill River extended through Harvey County, the citizens of Newton enlisted his aid. Professor Haworth unhesitatingly selected a point in the bed nearest the city, which when drilled, produced a vast supply of subterranean water. For this valuable service the Professor charged Newton $13.50.

Re-designated a division point and possessed of an inexhaustible water supply, Newton forged ahead steadily, and by 1910 the population numbered 7,862. Besides its railroad industries, Newton has a creamery, four bakeries, one of which supplies a state-wide market, and four mills that annually produce 700,000 barrels of flour.

POINTS OF INTEREST

The SITE OF THE FIRST WATER WELL, 5th and Main Sts., dug by Capt. David Payne in 1872, is marked by a bronze plate. Captain Payne was a typical frontiersman, soldier, and Indian scout. He commanded a company of the 19th Kansas Volunteer Cavalry in the Indian Wars of 1867. After contributing to the development of Harvey County, where for many years he lived as a homesteader, he entered the movement to settle Oklahoma (then Indian Territory) with whites. In Kansas history he is known as the "Daddy of the Cherokee Strip."

The FROG AND SWITCH SHOP (open by permission of the superintendent), between the main line Santa Fe tracks W. of 1st St., (also known as the Santa Fe Rail Mill), supplies track fastenings for the entire Santa Fe system. It was established in 1897 and until 1927, when new facilities were installed, its operations were confined to sawing off battered rail ends. With the advent of oxyacetylene welding this work was gradually dropped.

The CARNEGIE LIBRARY (open 9-5 weekdays), 203 Main St.,

is a two-story building of classic design, with two Ionic columns of cut stone supporting the portico. Construction is of brick and limestone. The building was completed in 1903 and contains approximately 15,000 volumes.

The HARVEY COUNTY HISTORICAL SOCIETY MUSEUM *(open by arrangement with custodian)*, 713½ Main St., contains a collection of historical articles including the goose quill pen with which Gov. John P. St. John signed the Prohibition Amendment to the Kansas Constitution in 1880. The original draft of the amendment, written by J. W. Ady, Newton attorney and member of the State legislature, is also preserved.

ATHLETIC PARK, west end of 1st St., a 20-acre tract on Sand Creek, contains a deer park, an outdoor stage, an artificial lake, a stadium for night football and baseball, and a municipal swimming pool with submarine lighting.

BETHEL COLLEGE, 0.5 m. N. of the city limits on State 15, is the oldest and largest Mennonite educational institution in America. It was chartered on May 23, 1887, following an agreement between the Kansas conference of the Mennonite Church and the municipal government of Newton, whereby the latter offered financial aid to establish a college at Newton.

The cornerstone of the Administration Building was laid atop a small hill north of the city in October 1888, but building operations were stopped after a few months when Newton, owing to a depression, was unable to supply funds for continuance of the work. Construction was resumed in 1893, when the Administration Building was completed at a cost of $35,000. The college was opened in September 1893, with 60 students enrolled.

Bethel was maintained as a preparatory school and junior college until 1908 when the curriculum was enlarged to that of a four-year standard college. The first Bachelor of Arts degrees awarded by a Mennonite college west of the Mississippi were received at Bethel in 1912 by a graduating class of six men, two of whom are now (1938) members of the faculty. The present curricula include courses in music, commerce, elocution, fine arts, and liberal arts. The German department is outstanding.

The landscaped campus is shaded by elm and maple trees. Grouped around the Administration Building are the Alumni, Music, Dining, and Science Halls. These structures are of brick and native stone. In front of Science Hall are two deeply notched cylindrical THRESHING STONES brought from Russia by pioneer Mennonites. The stones were drawn by oxen over wheat strewn thick on the ground, thus removing the grain from the stalk. The threshing stone is the symbol of Bethel College.

Since 1937 the college has been a sponsor of the Kansas Institute of International Relations, held here in June at the end of the school year. Other sponsoring and contributing organizations are the American Friends Service Committee, the Congregational Christian Council, the Kansas Yearly Meeting of Friends, the Board of Christian Education of the United

Brethren Church, and the Peace Committee of the General Conference of Mennonites.

The annual Mennonite Music Festival is held at Bethel College in the latter part of May. Mennonites come to this event from all parts of Kansas. Handel's *Messiah* is sung in English and German by more than 500 voices.

POINTS OF INTEREST IN ENVIRONS

Halstead, Riverside Park, Kit Carson Tree, Halstead Hospital, *8.9 m. (see Tour 4A)*.

Ottawa

Railroad Stations: 135 W. Tecumseh St. for Atchison, Topeka & Santa Fe Ry.; 307 E. 1st St. for Missouri Pacific R.R.
Bus Stations: North American Hotel, 3rd and Main Sts., for Greyhound Bus Lines, Santa Fe Trailways, and Missouri Pacific Bus Line.
Taxis: 10¢ per person within the city limits.

Accommodations: Two hotels; three tourist camps.

Motion Picture Houses: Three.
Swimming: Forest Park, W. end of Tecumseh St.
Golf: Ottawa Country Club, 0.5 m. E. of N. Main St. on Logan St., 9 holes, greens fee 50¢.

Annual Events: Eastern Kansas Baptist Assembly, first week in Aug.; Franklin County Fair, Sept.; Christmas Festival.

OTTAWA (891 alt., 9,563 pop.), seat of Franklin County, is named for the Ottawa Indians whose reservation once occupied the surrounding area. Designated a "city of religion and education" by its townsmen—a claim bolstered by 6 public schools, a university, and 23 churches—Ottawa is also the trade center of a prosperous farming and stock-raising region.

The city lies in a saucer-like valley around the Marais des Cygnes River (pronounced *merry deseen* locally). Its residential section is composed largely of frame houses, set behind broad lawns, and shaded by mature elms. Main Street binds the community together physically, by spanning the river, and economically, by reason of the shops packed tightly along its south extent.

Ottawa manufactures flour, ice cream, farm machinery, and electric refrigerators. There are several hatcheries, two mail order printing houses, a stone-crushing plant, and a foundry and woodwork factory. Car shops and a division headquarters are maintained by the Santa Fe Railway. Water and light facilities are municipally owned.

Ottawa had its origin in 1832 when the Ottawa Indians ceded their Ohio lands to the United States in return for 34,000 acres of what is now Franklin County. The Government appointed John Tecumseh Jones to assist the tribe in establishing itself on the new reservation. Jones was a half-breed Potawatomi who had been graduated by the Baptist Education Society, from which grew Colgate University, N. Y.

Arriving in Kansas the Ottawa found abundant game, grass, and water, but the hot dry air—the antithesis of the humid climate at their Ohio reservation—caused many to sicken and die. The Reverend Jotham Meeker of the Shawnee Mission, 60 miles to the northeast, traveled frequently to the ailing Indians, doctoring them as best he could. Finally, in the summer of 1837 he and his wife moved to the Ottawa reservation and established the Ottawa Indian Baptist Mission. As described by Meeker, they made their home in "a rough small cabin, intended for a stable and without a chimney, floor, or window." Among the missionary's meager possessions was an old Seth Adams press with which, at Shawnee Mission in 1835, he had printed the Shawnee *Sun* in the Shawnee language *(see NEWSPAPERS)*.

The Ottawa were a peaceful, intelligent people. Meeker taught them simple agricultural methods while his wife nursed the sick; together they instructed the tribe in spelling, reading, and the gospel. On his press Meeker printed the *Laws Governing the Ottawa Indians,* which many of the younger members of the tribe were soon able to read. Word of Meeker's work reached neighboring Indians and aroused their curiosity. Sac and Fox braves, clad in their finest regalia, would creep close to the mission, listen to the music or the voice of the preacher, and then silently depart.

John Tecumseh Jones, or, as he was better known, Tauy Jones, was of great help to the Meekers, and in time he became associated with them in their missionary work. In 1845 he married Jane Kelly, a white missionary. He was subsequently adopted into the Ottawa tribe, largely, it is said, because of the affection the Indians held for his wife.

When border warfare broke out the Ottawa Indian Baptist Mission became a headquarters for Free State adherents. Tauy Jones and the Reverend Meeker were staunch abolitionists. A two-story hotel that Jones built near the mission in the 1850's was burned by pro-slave sympathizers in 1856. John Brown, warm friend of Jones, told the Massachusetts Legislature of this event in 1857: "I saw it while it was still standing, and afterwards saw the ruins of the most valuable house and property of a highly civilized, intelligent, and exemplary Indian, which was burned to the ground by the ruffians. . . ."

Incoming settlers found the site of Ottawa highly desirable because of a natural ford at that point across the Marais des Cygnes River. The land belonged to the Indians, however, and a settlement was not at once established. In the spring of 1864 I. S. Kalloch, a Baptist preacher, C. C. Hutchinson, Ottawa Indian Agent, James Wing, Ottawa Chieftain, and Tauy Jones obtained the desired tract through their positions as members of the recently formed Ottawa University board of trustees. A town company was promptly organized and the site was surveyed in March 1864. Five months later the nascent town was designated the seat of Franklin County. A toll bridge was built above the ford, which, with a sawmill, Tauy Jones' store, and a hostelry known as the Ottawa House, supplied the economic nucleus of the settlement.

Shortly after its establishment Ottawa was damaged by a cyclone. Describing it, an early settler, A. F. Richmond stated, "I could see the cyclone coming. It looked like a ball of fire and it roared like thunder. It would go up in the sky and come down again. Whenever it hit the ground it made explosions like a cannon. There was a long tail on that cyclone that revolved. It came down and hit the front of our house; took off all the doors and windows in the front, and destroyed all the furniture in the front room and filled the room with old pieces of bottles, old tin cans, old worn out shoes and boots, bric-a-brac, pieces of iron, dead cats and dogs."

A treaty to move the Ottawas to Indian Territory in Oklahoma was signed on February 23, 1867. As the Indians vacated the region white settlers flocked in and Ottawa consequently prospered. In 1871 the community voted $60,000 and donated a site valued at $70,000 to assure the establishment of the machine shops of the Leavenworth, Lawrence & Galveston Railroad. The shops, built in 1872, employ 200 workers.

Electricity was generated in Ottawa in 1888, less than four years after New York City's Pearl Street Station—first plant in the country to produce electricity for public use—had been put in operation. Following a year of experimentation, the Ottawa plant began supplying power for public use in 1889. A field of natural gas was discovered near the city in the opening decade of the present century and harnessed for commercial use. Several industries were thereafter established; false frame fronts on Main Street were replaced by brick structures; and by 1910 the population stood at 7,500.

POINTS OF INTEREST

OTTAWA UNIVERSITY, 9th and Cedar Sts., a co-educational Baptist institution, offers four-year courses in art, music, and science. The university has 17 instructors and an average enrollment of 400 students. There are four buildings on the 30-acre campus, all built of Kansas limestone. Owing to a tradition whereby graduating classes donate a tree, a shrub, or an ivy plant, the buildings are encrusted with vines and the campus is heavily wooded. A choir composed of students in the Music Department presents Handel's *Messiah* annually in December at the First Baptist Church, 4th and Hickory Sts.

At the first Baptist Convention in Kansas, held at Atchison in 1860, plans for a college were adopted and the proposed institution, named in honor of Roger Williams, was chartered by the Territorial Legislature on February 20, 1860. Tauy Jones subsequently urged that the Ottawas be admitted to the school. Representatives of the Baptist Church and the Ottawa tribe accordingly met on December 5, 1860, and worked out a plan whereby the Ottawas agreed to donate 20,000 acres to Roger Williams University; the trustees agreed to finance the construction of buildings, to educate fifty Indian children between the ages of 4 and 14 each year for 30 years, and to thereafter establish ten perpetual scholarships for Indians. These provisions were incorporated in a treaty on June 24, 1862, but as the Ottawas were removed to the Oklahoma reservation in 1867, the provisions of the treaty were never carried out.

Throughout the Civil War no attempts were made to construct the school. On April 21, 1865, the institution was incorporated and renamed Ottawa University. Classes were held during 1866 in a temporary building. In the following year the school was closed to await the completion of its own structure, the present Tauy Jones Hall, which was finished in 1869. Instructions were resumed in May of that year, with only three

Indians in the class of 83 students. The Ottawas held rights in the university until 1873 when by Act of Congress the remainder of the original grant of 20,000 acres (about 11,000 acres) were put in Government trust along with $16,000 obtained through land sales.

TAUY JONES HALL *(open during school hours)*, the oldest building on the campus, is a three-story limestone structure, erected in 1869. It was gutted by fire on January 5, 1876, but the walls remained firm. In the succeeding months the Reverend Robert Atkinson, president of the college, hewed walnut logs to rebuild the interior. Aided by the townspeople of Ottawa, he reroofed the structure and classes were resumed in 1876. The hall was damaged by a second fire in 1921. Two years later it was extensively remodeled in keeping with the original design. Six dormer windows were replaced and the interior was outfitted with hardwood floors, beamed ceilings, and walnut doors. The building now houses the music department and a MUSEUM which contains fossils, minerals, Indian artifacts, and Kansas memorabilia.

FOREST PARK, W. end of Tecumseh St., an 80-acre wooded area, contains playgrounds, tennis courts, horseshoe courts, picnic grounds, and a swimming pool. Throughout the summer weekly concerts are presented by the Ottawa Band. The annual Franklin County Fair is held here.

The MEMORIAL GATEWAY at the main entrance to the park was dedicated on November 3, 1899, in memory of Franklin County citizens who served in the Spanish-American War with Company K of the 20th Kansas Regiment. The ornamental iron gates are supported by octagonal limestone pillars, 13 feet high. The central pillar is surmounted by a bronze eagle. The money to build the gateway ($1,600) was provided by popular subscription.

The MAIN STREET BRIDGE, Main St. at the Marais des Cygnes River, a steel and concrete structure built in 1925, is arched above the ford that was used during the 1850's and 1860's by soldiers, settlers, traders, and freighters following the Osage Trail. While crossing the river at this point in 1856, Cyrus Curran, Indian trader, turned to the members of his party and said: "I've been across this ford a good many times and I never cross but that I think that some day there'll be a town built here."

The FRANKLIN COUNTY COURTHOUSE, SE. corner 4th and Main Sts., is a three-story structure of red brick and Kansas limestone. The blue slate roof has turrets at the corners, with intermediate gables and a cupola at each end of the apex. The west cupola above the Main Street entrance contains an illuminated clock with four dials. The east cupola contains a bell which strikes the hours. At the apex of the west gable is a statue symbolizing Justice. The courthouse was designed by George P. Washburn & Son, and completed in 1893 at a cost of $46,535. Washburn, one of the most prolific and talented of Kansan architects in the 1890's, also designed the courthouse at Atchison.

POINTS OF INTEREST IN ENVIRONS

Indian Burial Ground, *3 m.;* Site of Old Baptist Mission, *3 m.;* Tauy Jones' House, *2.5 m.;* Chippewa Burial Ground, *6 m. (see Tour 12).*

Salina

Railroad Stations: Union Station, 400 N. 13th St., for Union Pacific R.R., Missouri Pacific R.R., Atchison, Topeka & Santa Fe Ry., and Chicago, Rock Island & Pacific Ry.
Bus Stations: Santa Fe Ave. and Ash St. for Cardinal and Santa Fe; 230 N. Santa Fe Ave. for Southwestern Greyhound, and Interstate Transit Lines.
Buses: (Street System) From intersection on Santa Fe and Iron Aves. to N., S., E., and SW. city limits. Fare, 5¢ with one transfer privilege.
Airport: Municipal, 2.5 m. SE. on E. Crawford St. No scheduled service.
Taxis: Minimum fare, 10¢.
Traffic Regulations: Traffic lights in business zone; stop signs at intersections with boulevards; no one-way streets.

Accommodations: Ten hotels; five tourist camps.

Information Service: Chamber of Commerce, SW. corner Ash and 5th Sts., Kansas Motor Club, Lamer Hotel, Santa Fe Ave. and Ash St.

Radio Stations: KSAL (1500 kc.); KFBI (1050 kc.).
Theaters and Motion Picture Houses: Memorial Hall, 9th and Ash Sts., for concerts. Five moving picture houses.
Swimming: Municipal pool in Oakdale Park, E. end Mulberry St.
Golf: Northview Country Club, 2 m. E. on Iron Ave., thence 2 m. S. on a country road, 18 holes, greens fee 50¢; Municipal Golf Course, 6 m. N. on US 81, 9 holes, greens fee 25¢.

Annual Events: Salina Racing Association, pacing, trotting, and running races, Kenwood Park, E. end of Prescott Ave., Aug.; 4-H Club Fair, Agricultural Hall, Kenwood Park, 1st week in Sept.

SALINA (1,220 alt., 20,155 pop.), seat of Saline County, lies in a basin four miles southwest of the confluence of the Saline and Smoky Hill Rivers. The main part of the city, extending across tablelands to the north and south, is shaped like a huge block "I." The Smoky Hill River loops through the east side of the "I," intersecting an arm of the city which reaches to the crest of low hills on the east.

The inner framework of the "I" consists of Santa Fe Avenue, an exceptionally broad thoroughfare that terminates north at St. Johns' Military School, and south at the Kansas Wesleyan University. The south segment of this avenue is lined with rambling mansions built in the 1890's. Many of the structures are occupied by their first owners. The central segment of the avenue is walled with business structures which range from two to ten stories in height. A short distance north of the business district Santa Fe Avenue is crossed by the main line tracks of three railroads. Grain elevators and flour mills tower east of the avenue, bordering the tracks.

Salina's streets intersect at regular right angles except in the Highland Court section at the southwest corner of the city, and the fashionable residential area on the hills at the east. Curved drives and "Y"-mouthed

SANTA FE AVENUE, SALINA

boulevards in these neighborhoods are flanked by close-cropped lawns on which stand trim houses of contemporary design. In the body of the city the main east-west streets are continued over the river on concrete bridges. At other points the streets follow the contour of the stream.

Salina is the virtual metropolis of central Kansas. In the heart of the hard wheat country, the city is a trading and recreational center for thousands of farmers. On Saturday nights the business sections on Iron and Santa Fe Avenues are ablaze with neon signs. Rows of dusty motor cars are nosed in at the curbs and groups of rural shoppers crowd the sidewalks.

Wheat is the alpha and omega of the region. Remarks about the weather are not mere tokens of conversation for drought or prolonged rain may be the difference between a lean and fat purse. In June wheat becomes "The Wheat" of anxious inquiry. Under the brassy sun the yellowish stalks droop and turn golden. Blue-overalled men go into the fields and a burnished stream of grain pours into Salina. Often the storage bins are filled to overflowing so that the grain is piled on the ground like sand.

Salina ranks third as a flour milling center in Kansas and fifth among the cities of the United States (1937). The five local mills have a daily capacity of 10,000 barrels of flour. The granaries and elevators can hold seven million bushels of wheat, enough—so townsmen boast—to supply a loaf of bread to each person in the United States. Salina also manufactures flour mill machinery, furnaces, gravity pumps, cement products, bricks and tile, playground equipment, and agricultural implements. Two large oil fields are within forty miles of the city.

Salina is the home town of Guy T. Helvering, present U. S. Commissioner of Internal Revenue (1938), and a former mayor of the city.

William A. Phillips, a Scotchman who had come to Kansas in 1855 as a special correspondent for the New York *Tribune,* journeyed through the unsettled section of the territory in 1857, searching for an attractive townsite. Of the places he saw he was best pleased with the site at the point where the Smoky Hill River twists sharply from its southern course and flows to the east. In 1858 Phillips returned to the region, accompanied by two fellow Scotchmen, James Muir and A. M. Campbell, and staked out a townsite.

Saline County was organized in February 1859. In the following month the Territorial legislature chartered a town company composed of Phillips, Muir, Campbell, and two newcomers, D. L. Phillips and A. C. Spilman. A. W. Phillips established a store and A. M. Campbell began operating a free ferry across the river. The settlement was at first dependent on trade with occasional Indian hunting parties, but, as the westernmost post on the Smoky Hill trail, it throve in 1860 as a "jumping off" place for gold-hunters traveling to Pike's Peak.

The Civil War stopped both the westbound traffic and the growth of Salina. W. A. Phillips promptly enlisted with the Union Army. In 1862 he was made colonel of a regiment composed of Cherokee Indians. Later he served as attorney for that tribe. In 1873 he was elected to the U. S. House of Representatives.

In the course of the war Salina was twice jolted from its lethargy. In early 1862 word was received that hostile Indians were preparing to massacre the twelve families at the settlement. A stockade was hastily built. The Indians, presumably deterred by this defense, did not attack. But in the autumn of the same year Salina was caught unawares by twenty bushwhackers who robbed the settlers of their food, horses, munitions, and tobacco.

At the close of the war W. A. Phillips returned to Salina and laid plans to stimulate its growth. Through his efforts the Union Pacific Railroad was extended to the settlement in 1867. J. G. McCoy alert livestock dealer, visited Salina and proposed that it become the terminus of the cattle drives. Fearing that the "Texers" and their droves of "mossy horns" would disorganize their community, the citizens rejected his offer. McCoy thereupon departed in a pique to Abilene, a dreary cluster of huts which he subsequently transformed into one of the great western "cow towns." In commenting on Salina McCoy declared that it was "a very small dead place, consisting of about one dozen log huts, low small, rude affairs, four-fifths of which were covered with dirt for roofing. . . . The business of the burg was conducted in two small rooms, mere log huts."

The development of Salina was thereafter greatly accelerated by the railroad. Josiah Copley, correspondent for the *Gazette* of Pittsburgh, Pa., visited the settlement several months after McCoy and reported that the population had increased to almost two thousand. Large groups of settlers began to enter Saline County. A colony of 60 Swedes from Galesburg, Illinois, arrived in 1868; 200 homesteaders from Ohio came in 1869; and 75 ex-residents of Henry County, Illinois, arrived in 1870.

Despite the inhabitants' previous rejection of the cattle trade, Salina became a minor center of that industry in 1872. Gun-play and carousing were sternly suppressed, however, and the community remained comparatively placid. In 1874 the cattle trade gravitated farther west and Salina's "cow town" era ended. The resultant economic gap was more than filled by agriculture. Great crops of wheat began to pour into Salina during the 1870's. A $75,000 steam-powered flour mill was built at the town in 1878.

In the early part of 1874 Dr. E. R. Switzer of Salina obtained alfalfa seed from California for 50 cents a pound and planted it on his farm. Green shoots came up, only to be destroyed by drought and grasshoppers. Dr. Switzer considered the experiment ended. But rain fell in September and the alfalfa grew again. "I concluded," Dr. Switzer later said, "that a grass that would go through drought and grasshopper plague was the thing for Kansas." The doctor thereafter pioneered in introducing alfalfa to Kansas farmers. From Saline County the legume spread outward to become in 1935 the State's fourth largest crop.

By 1880 Salina was assured of a place among the principal cities of Kansas. Its population exceeded 3,500 and its industries included 3 flour mills, 6 grain elevators, a carriage and wagon factory, and an agricultural implement works. Between 1885–90 three railroads were built through the community.

Four-fifths of Salina was inundated by the Smoky Hill River in 1903. The inhabitants had ample time to retreat to the heights east of the city without loss of life. In June 1938 heavy rains again sent the Smoky beyond its banks and a small section of the city was flooded. Property damage was negligible and no lives were lost.

POINTS OF INTEREST

OAKDALE PARK, entered at the N. by Oakdale Drive and at the W. by the E. end of Mulberry St., a 50-acre tract shaded by elm and walnut trees, contains a swimming pool, tennis court, picnic grounds, and CLAFLIN HALL, an open air auditorium. At the North entrance is the SPANISH WAR AND G. A. R. MEMORIAL GATE, erected by Saline County at a cost of $13,000. It was designed by George H. Honig and completed in 1918. On the marble columns beside the gate are heroic bronze figures of a Civil War soldier and a Spanish-American War soldier.

KENWOOD PARK, entered by the foot bridge at the E. end of Oakwood Drive or by the E. end of Prescott Ave., a 90-acre tract within a bend of the Smoky Hill River, is the site of the annual meet of the Saline Racing Association, and the 4-H Club Fair *(see ANNUAL*

EVENTS). The 4-H Club Fair is held in AGRICULTURAL HALL, a large brick pavilion built by Saline County at a cost of $65,000.

ST. JOHN MILITARY SCHOOL, Santa Fe and Otis Aves., an Episcopal school with an average enrollment of 100 cadets, offers elementary and college preparatory courses for boys. The school was established in 1887 at which time VAIL HALL a four-story brick and stone structure of modified Gothic-Romanesque design was built. An octagonal tower is attached at the west wing and a square with pyramidal roof tower rises three-stories above the east wing.

KANSAS WESLEYAN UNIVERSITY, Claflin St. and Santa Fe Ave., is a Methodist Episcopal institution with an average enrollment of 400 students. The university, established in 1886, is housed in five modern structures on a 40-acre campus. At the center of the group is the HALL OF PIONEERS, which houses the administrative offices, classrooms, and Sams Memorial Chapel. A two-story brick and stone structure with Gothic detail, designed by Zerbe and Wilmarth, it was dedicated to the pioneers of Kansas in 1926. Carnegie Science Hall, built in 1908, houses the university library and museum. The LIBRARY *(open 7:45-12, 1:25-5:30, 7-10 weekdays during the school year)* has 20,000 volumes. The MUSEUM *(open same hours as the library)* contains botanical, zoological, and geological specimens.

MARYMOUNT COLLEGE, E. end of Iron Ave., a Catholic institution for girls with an average enrollment of 200, offers four year accredited courses in art, music, science, and home economics. The college was established in 1922 by the Sisters of St. Joseph. The main building occupying a knoll overlooking Salina, is a three-story E-shaped structure of stone, castellated and buttressed in the Gothic style. The central wing houses the Immaculate Conception Chapel. The two flanking wings contain the college offices, classrooms, and dormitories. On the walls of the GREEN ROOM, the main reception room, are paintings of *The Holy Family* and *John and Jesus* by Elizabeth Sirani, seventeenth century Florentine artist.

MEMORIAL HALL, 9th and Ash Sts., a municipal auditorium, is a three-story brick structure trimmed with concrete. It was designed by C. W. Shaver and dedicated in 1922 as a "Memorial to our Veterans of all Wars." The auditorium seats 4,000.

The SALINA PUBLIC LIBRARY *(open 10-9 weekdays, 3-5 Sun. during winter; 9-1, 6-9:30 weekdays during summer),* SW. corner 8th St. and Iron Ave., is a two-story brick and stone structure with neo-classic detail. The original building, completed in 1903, was designed by Fred Gum of Salina. An addition built in 1928 was designed by Ben Byrnes of Salina. The library contains 38,000 volumes, five paintings by Birger Sandzen *(see ART),* and a valuable collection of old magazines and books, among them a complete set of McGuffey's readers. On the second floor is an HISTORICAL MUSEUM *(open 2-5 and 7-9 Mon.-Fri.; 2-5 1st and 3rd Sun. of month),* which contains pioneer memorabilia and a reference library of more than 500 volumes.

CHRIST CATHEDRAL (Episcopal), 134 S. 8th St., cathedral of the

Diocese of Salina, is a native limestone structure of English Gothic design. The altar is of Carthage marble, with reredos of Silverdale limestone. The central tower contains 11 bell chimes, donated by Mrs. A. L. Claflin in memory of her husband, a pioneer resident. The interior woodwork of black oak was carved by members of the Lang family of Oberammergau, Bavaria. The cathedral was designed by Henry Macomb and Charles M. Burns of Philadelphia, and dedicated in 1907 as a memorial to Hermon Griswold Batterson, a missionary of the Episcopal Church. Funds for the building were donated by Mrs. Hermon Griswold Batterson, of New York City.

POINTS OF INTEREST IN ENVIRONS

Indian Burial Pit, *4.5 m. (see Tour 3)*, Salemsborg, *16.2 m.*, Coronado Heights, *19.1 m. (see Tour 9)*.

Topeka

Railroad Stations: 5th and Holliday Sts. for Atchison, Topeka & Santa Fe Ry.; 701 N. Kansas Ave. for Union Pacific R.R. and Chicago, Rock Island & Pacific Ry.; 501 Adams St. for Missouri Pacific R.R.
Bus Stations: Union Bus Depot, 123 W. 6th St. for Missouri Pacific and Santa Fe Trailways, Capitol Highway Stages; Union Bus Terminal, 120 W. 6th St. for Greyhound and Union Pacific Bus Lines.
Airport: Municipal Airport, 3600 Sardou, 3 m. NE. of capitol N. of US 40, no scheduled service.
Taxis: 25¢ for first two miles, 10¢ each additional ⅔ mile.
Buses: Fare 8¢, tokens 2 for 15¢.
Traffic Regulations: Lights at principal intersections in business section. Stop signs on arterial streets. Speed limit, 35 miles per hour on W. 6th Ave. (US 40) and W. 10th Ave., 30 miles per hour on Topeka Blvd. Bridge, 25 miles per hour on all other streets. Parking meters, 5¢ for one hour, on Kansas Ave., parking restrictions on other streets in business district plainly indicated by signs. No one way streets.

Accommodations: Twenty-two hotels, 2 for Negroes; 10 tourist camps.

Information Service: Kansas Motor Club, Elks Bldg., 7th and Jackson Sts.

Radio Station: WIBW (580 kc.)
Theaters and Motion Picture Houses: Grand Theater, 615 Jackson St., occasional road shows; eleven motion picture houses, one for Negroes.
Swimming: Municipal pools, Gage, Ripley, and Garfield Parks.
Golf: White Lakes Club, 1 m. S. on US 75, 18-hole, greens fee 25¢. Washburn Golf Club, 17th St. and Jewel Ave., 9-hole, sand greens, greens fee 25¢. Topeka Country Club, 26th and Lincoln Sts., 18-hole, greens fee $1.
Tennis: Municipal courts in Gage, Garfield, Ripley, Edgewood, Westlawn, Euclid, and Chesney Parks.
Boxing and Wrestling: American Legion Stadium, 6th St. and Gage Blvd.
Football: Moore Bowl, Washburn College, 17th St. and College Ave.

Annual Events: Kansas Day Club, Jan. 29 (Republican); Washington Day Club banquet, Feb. 22 (Democratic); State High School Basketball Tournament, March; Mexican Fiesta, July; Community 4th of July celebration, Gage Park; Kansas Free Fair, Sept.; State Horseshoe Pitching Contest, Sept.; State Chess Tournament, Sept.; Civic Concert Series, Oct. to May; Community Forum Lecture Series, Nov. to March; Community Christmas Tree.

TOPEKA (886 alt., 64,120 pop.), capital of Kansas, seat of Shawnee County, and third city in population, is bisected by the Kansas, or Kaw River, as it is more familiarly known. On the north side of the stream the city extends across the fertile Kaw Valley to the slope of a low range of hills. On the south it spreads over a ridge that divides the watersheds of the Kaw River and Shunganunga Creek, extending across the creek bottoms, and up the gradual slope of another range of low glacial hills.

Kansas Avenue, the main street, extends from the northern to the southern limits of the city, lined for almost half its length with business houses.

In the territory adjacent to the river, extending across a level expanse of bottom, is the principal industrial and wholesale district. Here are four meat-packing plants, wholesale houses, flour mills, and small factories. This section, the oldest part of the town, was laid out parallel to the river banks, northeast, southwest, while the streets of the newer addition follow the cardinal points of the compass.

South from Third Street to Fifth Street, Kansas Avenue ascends the slope of the divide, bordered by small shops, hotels, motion picture theatres, and second-hand stores. Concentrated between Fifth and Tenth Streets is the modern retail business and professional district. Quincy and Jackson Streets, flanking the Avenue on either side, show increasing business and commercial development. The Avenue's architecture varies from the ornate, heavy-corniced structures built in the 80's and 90's to the modern 14-story National Bank of Topeka Building. Construction is predominantly of brick. At Tenth Street the commercial aspect of Kansas Avenue begins to change. At Eleventh Street it enters a residential section built in the 1890's.

Topeka Boulevard, once Topeka's "Park Avenue," is lined with pretentious mansions built between 1880 and 1915, but the motor age has caused the exclusive residential district to move west until it is nearly three miles from the business section.

Most of the newer homes are built in the additions on the south and west. Many of the pretentious Victorian mansions are now comfortable rooming and boarding houses, within walking distance of the business district. Tall shade trees, forming cool green archways above Topeka's wide streets, give the city its chief claim to civic beauty. The town founders, finding that land was cheap and shade was scarce, platted the thoroughfares lavishly and lined them with elm, hackberry, walnut, and maple trees. Each succeeding generation of home-builders has carefully preserved this tradition.

Westboro, a restricted residential district in the southwest, is the only section of the city that does not follow the formal street plan having been laid out in lanes, courts, drives, and terraces. Its homes follow many styles of architecture, the Dutch and Georgian Colonial predominating.

Descendants of the Negro "Exodusters" who came to Topeka in 1879–1880 now number approximately 8,000 (1938). The oldest and most compact Negro community is "Tennessee Town" established by five hundred Exodusters in 1880. This district extends west from Buchanan Street to Washburn Avenue and south from Tenth to Huntoon Streets, and it is inhabited by more than two thousand Negroes. When "Tennessee Town" was settled it was west of the city limits but the town has grown around it until it is now almost in the center of Topeka's West Side. Today, its streets are paved and its homes are neat one-story frame structures. There are other Negro residential districts in North Topeka and in areas along the railroad tracks. The city has three Negro elementary schools; Negroes are represented in most of the trades and professions.

While the white residents are largely of Anglo-Saxon stock, there are scattered groups of Russo-Germans, Swedes, and Mexicans. The Russo-

Germans work in the Santa Fe shop, and live in a little settlement in North Topeka known as "Little Russia." Mexicans are concentrated near the railroad yards and are employed in the Santa Fe shops or as section laborers.

Topeka's excellent transportation facilities and its position in a prosperous agricultural area have made it an important distribution and trade center. Streets in the retail districts are thronged with shoppers from the surrounding countryside. Before the motor age, when farmers drove into town, they were provided with hitching posts along broad Kansas Avenue; and wagon and feed yards catered to their convenience. Today their automobiles, dusty and serviceable, and usually carrying produce, are parked alongside the shining city cars on "the Avenue" while their owners shop or transact business at the courthouse. Parking meters, insuring the motorist an hour's parking privilege for five cents, have replaced the old hitching posts and the feed yards have given way to modern "one-stop" motor service stations.

In 1842, two French-Canadians, Joseph and Louis Pappan, the latter a progenitor of the late Charles Curtis, married Kaw Indian half-breeds and settled on Kaw lands in what is now Shawnee County. They established a ferry across the Kaw River at the site of Topeka which they operated until the stream was bridged in 1857. The Pappans were probably the first white settlers in the region.

Topeka, however, owes its existence to Col. Cyrus K. Holliday, a young Pennsylvanian who came to Kansas Territory in 1854 with $20,000 and an urge to build a railroad. He interested a group of former New England capitalists in his proposition, and accompanied by a few of the pioneers walked into Lawrence one day in 1854 to explain his plan to Dr. Charles Robinson, agent of the New England Emigrant Aid Company. The future rail magnates had made the 45-mile journey from Kansas City on foot.

Robinson was interested and, failing to convince his visitors that Lawrence was an ideal site for the railroad center, suggested that they take a trip up the Kaw to pick out a spot. Holliday agreed and the group set out. Twenty-one miles west along the river was the thriving village of Tecumseh, the initial stop. Tecumseh business men, however, appeared to have heard of Holliday's $20,000 and they asked an enormous price for the site. This display of avarice cost Tecumseh dearly. The frugal Yankees proceeded up the river five miles to the site of Topeka where they formed a town company, after closing a deal for a tract of land with Enoch Chase, a local land owner who had purchased large tracts from the Kaw Indians.

Holliday was elected president of the company and the Lawrence delegation took stock, as did Chase. The company met in a log cabin December 5, 1854, to complete organization. Holliday proposed to call the town Webster after Daniel Webster, but the others wanted to give it something with a local flavor. After much discussion the Reverend S. Y. Lum suggested Topeka, an Omaha Indian word meaning a good place to dig "potatoes" (the Indians designated all edible roots as potatoes).

The following year, due to the efforts of Dr. Robinson, a large contingent of New Englanders arrived and Topeka grew into a sizable settlement. Before another year passed Colonel Holliday and his associates had completed plans for the construction of the railroad that became the Santa Fe. Topeka thrived and became a rival of Tecumseh for the seat of Shawnee County. The rivalry was that of a Free State and a pro-slavery community, since Tecumseh was settled by Missouri slave owners.

The first Kansas constitution was framed by a convention of Free State men who met in Topeka in 1855. With only Free State men voting, the document was quickly approved, provisional officials and a legislature were chosen. Members of the legislature, however, were arrested by United States troops when they convened at Topeka, July 4, and the "Topeka Government" was speedily overthrown.

In 1857, the year the city was incorporated, the first bridge across the Kaw was completed. High water carried it away the following summer and Tecumseh residents chortled as the wreckage floated by on its way downstream. It was Topeka's turn to laugh a few months later when it won over Tecumseh in a county seat election, October 4, 1858.

Dr. Robinson returned to Lawrence after the details for the founding of Topeka had been completed. The Kansas Constitution, adopted at Wyandotte, under which the Territory was admitted to the Union, provided for an election to select the capital city. Topeka and Lawrence were aspirants, and Robinson, a candidate for Governor, was believed by the people of Lawrence to favor the selection of their town. Consequently, they supported the doctor. Robinson and Gen. Jim Lane, however, threw their influence behind the Topeka movement. The result was that Robinson was elected and Topeka chosen as the capital of the new State.

Meanwhile, Holliday unfolded his plan. He presented to the State a tract of the townsite to be used as a capital park. He promoted the Atchison, Topeka & Santa Fe Railway which in 1869 started building westward from Topeka, and had the general offices and machine shops of that system established in Topeka in 1878. Holliday's name, appropriately, is preserved in Holliday Street on which stands the Santa Fe depot, and in the Cyrus K. Holliday Junior High School on Topeka's east side, which is attended by sons and daughters of Santa Fe shop employees.

Although the growth of Topeka and the State was retarded by the drought of 1860 and the ensuing period of the Civil War, Topeka kept pace with the phenomenal revival and period of growth that Kansas enjoyed from the close of the war in 1865 until 1870. A town of 700 inhabitants in 1862, it had grown to more than 5,000 in 1870.

In October 1864, Topekans erected a stockade of cottonwood logs for protection against Price's raid. The flimsy roofless structure was derisively called "Fort Folly" by citizens who pointed out that it would be scant protection against artillery. The Second Regiment of the Kansas State Militia, however, engaged in a bloody skirmish with Price's forces at the Big Blue River near Kansas City, Missouri. The regiment, composed of men from Topeka and Shawnee County under the command of Col. George Veale, met a vastly superior enemy force on October 22. Although forced to retreat, the regiment inflicted severe losses and helped to check Price's advance. The Topeka battery, attached to the regiment as Company K, took up a position in a lane near the crossing of the river where they repulsed

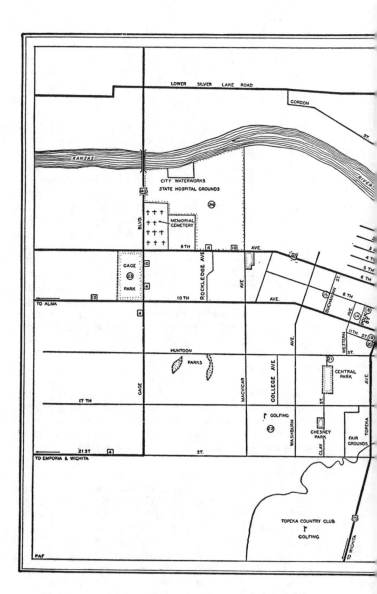

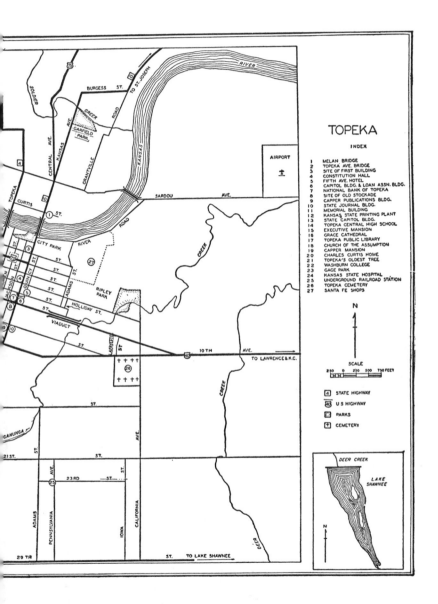

TOPEKA

INDEX

1 MELAN BRIDGE
2 TOPEKA AVE. BRIDGE
3 SITE OF FIRST BUILDING
4 CONSTITUTION HALL
5 FIFTH AVE. HOTEL
6 CAPITOL BLDG. & LOAN ASSN. BLDG.
7 NATIONAL BANK OF TOPEKA
8 SITE OF OLD STOCKADE
9 CAPPER PUBLICATIONS BLDG.
10 STATE JOURNAL BLDG.
11 MEMORIAL BUILDING
12 KANSAS STATE PRINTING PLANT
13 STATE CAPITOL BLDG.
14 TOPEKA CENTRAL HIGH SCHOOL
15 EXECUTIVE MANSION
16 GRACE CATHEDRAL
17 TOPEKA PUBLIC LIBRARY
18 CHURCH OF THE ASSUMPTION
19 CAPPER MANSION
20 CHARLES CURTIS HOME
21 TOPEKA'S OLDEST TREE
22 WASHBURN COLLEGE
23 GAGE PARK
24 KANSAS STATE HOSPITAL
25 UNDERGROUND RAILROAD STATION
26 TOPEKA CEMETERY
27 SANTA FE SHOPS

N

SCALE
250   0   250   500   750 FEET

▣ STATE HIGHWAY
▣ U S HIGHWAY
▣ PARKS
✚ CEMETERY

DEER CREEK

LAKE
SHAWNEE

N

two spirited cavalry charges but succumbed to a third. Eight men were killed, four wounded, and ten, including Captain Ross Burns, were taken prisoner. Burns stood by his piece until he was clubbed into insensibility and dragged from the field.

During the late 1880's Topeka passed through a boom period that ended in disaster. There was a vast speculation on town lots. One promoter advertised in foreign newspapers that his lots were 12 miles from the post office, but his description of Topeka was that of a city on the scale of Chicago. Subdivisions were platted at points several miles west of the present city limits. In 1889 the bubble burst and many investors were ruined. Topeka, however, doubled in population during the period and was able to weather the depressions of the 90's.

In the spring of 1903 a flood of the Kaw River inundated North Topeka, which lies in the valley. Weeks of continuous rain throughout the watershed transformed the Kaw into an angry torrent five miles across.

Breaking through its low banks the Kaw cut a new channel through North Topeka and on the south side the water rose as far as Second Street. Hundreds were marooned in their homes and 29 persons were drowned. Property damage amounted to $2,288,000. North Topeka was an industrial section with a number of large flour mills and lumber yards. Indians had warned the early settlers not to build a city on the banks of the river, recalling a great flood of 1844.

High water in 1908, 1923, and 1935, created uneasiness among residents of North Topeka, but the dikes constructed a few years after the 1903 flood prevented a repetition of the disaster.

Having survived the depressions of the 1890's, and the flood period, Topeka welcomed with enthusiasm the new motor age. The Topeka *State Journal* on April 3, 1911, reported: "Work is progressing rapidly in tearing down the old Culp livery barn at 508 Quincy Street, preparatory to the erection of an undertaking establishment. Automobile license No. 627 was issued today." By 1920 the motor had replaced the horse in city transport and the city fire department was motorized. During the next 15 years motor buses gradually replaced the old trolley cars on Topeka's streets, two new hotels were opened, and the city definitely had entered the modern era.

Today, the city is an insurance center with home offices of seven life insurance companies, two fire insurance companies, and one crop insurance company. Also of importance in its economic background is the printing industry, with four large independent plants in addition to the one maintained by the State. Topeka's largest single industry, however, is the Santa Fe Railway, which maintains repair shops and general offices and furnishes employment to 5,000 Topekans.

POINTS OF INTEREST

1. MELAN BRIDGE, Kansas Ave. at Kansas River, between Crane and Curtis Streets, is a concrete arch bridge, reenforced with steel, constructed in 1895. It consists of six spans and is 900 feet in length. Two railroad bridges and the streetcar bridge were washed out in the 1903 flood, but

the Melan Bridge withstood the high waters, although both approaches were destroyed. Prior to 1938 it was the only connecting link between North Topeka and the south side.

2. The TOPEKA BOULEVARD BRIDGE, Topeka Ave. at Kansas River, between W. 2nd and W. Gordon Sts., was dedicated August 27, 1938. This 4,400-foot steel and concrete structure, designed by Robert J. Justice, of the State Highway Department, is the longest bridge in the State highway system and was built at a cost of $1,500,000 with the State, the city, and the Federal Government sharing the expense. A PWA grant matched State funds for construction of the central span and WPA shared the cost of the two approaches, which eliminate railroad grade crossings. The bridge contains the largest continuous girder plate ever built in the United States, a span 893 feet long, resting on piers and without an expansion joint. The bridge has eliminated the bottle neck that was created by the necessity of routing all north-south traffic across the old Kansas Avenue bridge.

3. The SITE OF FIRST BUILDING, NW. corner Kansas Ave. and 1st St., is commemorated by a bronze marker on the front of the Poehler Mercantile Building. It was a log cabin built by four of the town founders, December 3, 1854.

4. CONSTITUTION HALL, 429 Kansas Ave., with the principal façade remodeled, is, as indicated by a marker on the sidewalk, the original two-story stone building erected in 1855 in which the "Topeka Constitution" for the State of Kansas was written. Today it is occupied by offices and a jewelry store and differs little in appearance from the other square brick front buildings in the block.

5. The FIFTH AVENUE HOTEL, SW. corner 5th and Quincy Sts., a four-story brick structure with Mansard roof, designed in the manner of the French Second Empire, was for many years Topeka's leading hotel. It was built in 1870. On January 22, 1872, Grand Duke Alexis of Russia, returning from a buffalo hunt in the western part of the State, was guest of honor at a banquet given here by Gov. James M. Harvey and the Kansas legislature. The Grand Duke's party included officers of the Russian Imperial Navy. American visitors of note were Generals Phillip H. Sheridan and George A. Custer.

6. The CAPITOL BUILDING AND LOAN ASSOCIATION BUILDING (1924), NE. corner 6th St. and Kansas Ave., designed by George Grant Elmslie of Chicago, is not based upon any traditional style of architecture. The building is constructed of tan brick, polished granite, terra cotta, and reenforced concrete. The decorative sculptural terra cotta is the work of Emil Zettler of Chicago. In the panel over the main entrance is symbolized the American home, and the agricultural and industrial activities that support the homes of Kansas. Figures on the south side of the building symbolize Kansas and its progress.

7. The NATIONAL BANK OF TOPEKA, NW. corner 6th St. and Kansas Ave., a 14-story structure, is Topeka's tallest office building. It was designed by Thomas W. Williamson & Company of Topeka, in the neoclassic style of architecture and completed in 1932. Materials used in

the construction are white Indiana limestone, polished granite, and steel. The entrance to the bank is finished in antique travertine trimmed with bronze.

8. The SITE OF OLD STOCKADE, NW. corner 6th St. and Kansas Ave., is marked by a plate on the sidewalk in front of the National Bank Building. Called "Fort Folly" by doubting citizens, the roofless, log structure was erected in 1864 as protection against Confederate raiders under Price.

9. The CAPPER PUBLICATIONS BUILDING *(open 8-5 weekdays)*, SE. corner 8th and Jackson Sts., owned and operated by Arthur Capper, senior United States Senator from Kansas, is the home office and publishing plant of several farm publications of national circulation, and of the Topeka *Daily Capital,* a morning newspaper. Completed in 1909, the three-story graystone building adorned with Corinthian columns, is of French Renaissance style. Holland and Squires of Topeka were the architects. The *Capital* achieved attention in 1900 when its editor, Maj. J. K. Hudson, placed the editorial policy of the paper under the direction of Dr. Charles M. Sheldon, prominent Topeka minister, for one week. Dr. Sheldon, in his first editorial said: "The editor of the Capital asked me to assume entire charge of the paper for one week and edit it as a Christian newspaper."

Dr. Sheldon, during his short tenure in the editorial sanctum of the *Capital,* eliminated all news of crime, prize fights, and scandal, and published columns in support of the prohibition movement. After noting the response to Sheldon's "Christian" newspaper, publishers generally were in agreement that there was no demand for this type of publication.

10. The STATE JOURNAL BUILDING *(open 8-5 weekdays)*, SE. corner Kansas Ave. and 8th St., a classic two-story edifice of white stone and terra cotta, was designed by James E. Holland of Topeka. The late Frank P. McLennan, publisher of the *State Journal* from 1885 until his death in 1933 directed the designer of the building to make it as nearly as possible a replica of the Herald Tribune Building in New York, N. Y. Henry J. Allen, former Governor and United States Senator, is its present editor (1938).

11. MEMORIAL BUILDING *(open 8-5 weekdays)*, NE. corner 10th and Jackson Sts., is a four-story structure of white marble designed by the late Charles H. Chandler, State architect. It is of the French Renaissance style. The cornerstone was laid September 27, 1911 by President Taft and the building was dedicated May 27, 1914, to the soldiers and sailors of Kansas. It contains the offices of the State Historical Society and of the Kansas Department of the American Legion, the Spanish War Veterans, and the Grand Army of the Republic.

The NEWSPAPER SECTION *(open)*, on the first floor, contains more than 42,000 bound volumes of Kansas newspapers dating from 1854. A total of 725 Kansas newspapers and periodicals are received for filing (1937).

In the ART COLLECTION *(open)* on the first floor is the Philip Billard Memorial, *Flight,* a 4-ft. statue by Merrell Gage, formerly of Topeka. It was presented to the Historical Society by the Topeka Rotary Club in memory of Lieut. Philip Billard of Topeka, who was killed in line of duty near Issoudon, France, July 24, 1918. Billard was the first Topekan to own and operate an airplane.

The STATE HISTORICAL LIBRARY *(open)*, on the second floor, contains a collection of newspaper clippings, atlases, and historical reference books.

The MUSEUM *(open 8-12; 1-5 weekdays)*, third and fourth floors, contains the Bower Archeological Collection; the Perkins Mineral Collection; the F. L. Sexton collection of sea shells, and the Goss Collection of birds. In the historical section are numerous articles of interest including a sword found in western Kansas on the handle of which is inscribed the name of Captain Juan Gallego, one of Coronado's band; a drop of the blood of Abraham Lincoln, which fell on a Ford's Theater program; two original sod plows invented in Kansas; and the doors of the house of representatives that were smashed during the Populist uprising in 1893. A recent acquisition is the airplane in which Phil Billard made some of his early flights over the city in 1915 and 1916.

12. KANSAS STATE PRINTING PLANT *(open 8:30-5 weekdays)*, SW. corner 10th and Jackson Sts., housed in a three-story building of brick and stone on State-owned property was erected in 1906.

The plant is equipped with one perforating press, two high-speed automatic presses, six cylinder presses, two open feed presses, and two high-speed envelope machines. Approximately 200 men are regularly employed and the plant has a normal daily output of 85,000 pieces of printed matter. During the biennial sessions of the State legislature the force is increased to 300 to meet the increased volume of work and the plant is operated 24 hours a day, production increasing to 250,000 pieces of printed matter daily. The plant also publishes text books used in the public schools of Kansas.

13. The KANSAS STATE CAPITOL *(open 8:30-5 weekdays)*, is in the center of a ten-acre landscaped park covering a square extending from 8th St. to 10th St. and W. from Jackson St. to Harrison St. The only motor drive entering the ground is an extension of W. 9th St. Long curving asphalt walks lead up to the north and south entrances from Van Buren St. The west driveway, with its entrance at 9th and Harrison Sts., is used only by pedestrians.

The design of the Kansas Capitol is based upon that of the Capitol at Washington, D. C. The plan is composed of four wings, extended in the form of a Greek cross with a large rotunda at the center. These elements are somewhat lacking in proportion and uniformity of design owing to the fact that they were constructed at different times and designed by different architects. Construction of the east wing was begun October 17, 1866, from plans submitted by John G. Haskell and E. Townsend Mix of Lawrence. It was occupied in December 1869. Its classic hexastyle portico, supported by fluted Corinthian columns, has a long flight of granite steps leading up to the main entrance at the second floor. The limestone walls of the central wing on either side of the portico are adorned with pilasters of the same order. Stone used in the construction of this wing was quarried near Junction City *(see Tour 3);* the rotunda and the other wings are of Silverdale limestone *(see Tour 10).* The west wing was constructed in 1880 and is a replica of the east wing.

Work on the north and south wings and the rotunda began in 1883, but it was not until twenty years later that the completed building was officially accepted by the State. Like the older sections, the north and south wings are approached by flights of granite steps and have the main entrance at the second floor beneath a Corinthian portico. The pediment on each portico was blocked out in preparation for the carving of symbolic figures, but, although a sculptor prepared models for this work, he could not reach an agreement with the State, and the pediments remained unadorned. The best stone carving of the exterior is on the north wing where the delicate Corinthian detail was skillfully executed under the direction of James Halderman.

The rotunda with its lofty dome rising to a height of 304 feet, on an octagonal drum, was designed by John F. Stanton, State architect. The great central dome is more slender in proportion than that of the National Capitol, and is octagonal in shape. The weathered cap of the dome is òf copper which the elements have turned to a bluish green color. It is topped with a lantern cupola, also copper covered, with a balustraded platform at its base from which there is an impressive panoramic view of the city and its environs. This platform is reached from the interior by means of a circular iron stairway extending from the fifth floor. The outer drum of the dome, designed in two stages, is adorned with a superimposed ordinance of Doric and Corinthian columns, at the first and second levels, respectively. Light is admitted to the interior through large arched windows in the drum as well as through a row of medallion windows in the lower portion of the dome. The interior of the rotunda is decorated with murals by Abner Crossman of Chicago. These paintings are around the base of the drum. One group of figures depicts Religion, Knowledge and Temperance; the second, Plenty; the third, Peace; and the fourth, Power.

The Florentine decorations in the SENATE CHAMBER, which occupies the third floor of the east wing, were added during the 1880's, at a cost of $300,000. The twenty-eight columns and pilasters encircling the room are decorated with hand-hammered copper in a design of ivy, morning glories, and roses. Seats are arranged in a semicircle about the rostrum and there are visitors' balconies at the front and rear of the room. Tennessee marble frames the doors and the walls are paneled in Mexican onyx.

REPRESENTATIVE HALL, on the third floor of the west wing, is less elaborate than the Senate Chamber but of similar plan. Wainscoting on the walls is of imported marble, trimmed with Italian Carrara.

Sgt. Boston Corbett, alleged slayer of John Wilkes Booth, was doorkeeper for the house of representatives for a short time during the legislative session of 1887. Corbett, a religious fanatic who shot Booth in defiance of orders to take the assassin alive, justified his act by saying that God had told him to avenge the death of President Lincoln. While he was

THE CAPITOL, TOPEKA

acting as doorkeeper he became violently insane, threatened the lives of fellow employees and was arrested and committed to the State Hospital for the Insane. He later stole a visitor's pony from a hitching post at the hospital and escaped to Mexico.

During the session of 1893 several Populists contested the seats of Republican members and each party claimed the right to organize the house. For several days the two bodies held sessions on opposite sides of the hall. Finally, on February 14, the elections committee of the Republican house summoned L. C. Gunn, a Populist, to testify as a witness in one of the election contest hearings. Gunn refused to obey the summons and was arrested by a Republican sergeant-at-arms. He immediately instituted habeas corpus proceedings and the legality of the Republican house was brought before the supreme court. The Republicans next arrested Ben Rich, chief clerk of the Populist body. Enraged Populists stormed the hall, rescued Rich and barricaded the door after clearing out the Republican faction.

The following morning, after battering down the doors with a sledge hammer, Republicans surged into the hall and ejected their rivals. On February 17 an agreement was reached whereby the Populists held their sessions in another room and the Republicans retained the hall. Eight days later the supreme court recognized the Republican body as "the legal and constitutional house of representatives of the State of Kansas," bringing the Legislative War to an end.

The STATE LIBRARY *(open 8:30-5 weekdays)*, occupying the third floor of the north wing is divided into three departments: the REFERENCE DEPARTMENT, the LAW DEPARTMENT, and the STORMONT MEDICAL LIBRARY. There are approximately 112,000 volumes in the reference and law departments, exclusive of pamphlets and unbound periodicals. These departments are supported by State appropriations.

The Stormont Medical Library, established in 1889 by a gift of $5,000 from Mrs. Jane C. Stormont, is supported by the income from this dona-tion. Books are selected by a committee appointed by the State Medical Association. This section contains more than 2,000 volumes.

LINCOLN STATUE, by Merrell Gage, southeast corner of the capital park, is of cast iron and depicts the Civil War President seated in an arm chair in a meditative pose. Unveiled February 12, 1918, this was the first statue in Kansas to be executed by a Kansas sculptor.

The OLD COTTONWOOD TREE, 9th St. entrance (L), is a giant tree as old as the capitol itself. According to legend, it sprouted from a stake that was used to secure a guy rope during construction of the first wing of the building. Under its rustling leaves three Presidents have spoken—Harrison, McKinley, and Taft. The late Charles Curtis stood beneath its spreading branches and received notification of his nomination for the Vice Presidency. Here, too, in 1936, Gov. Alf M. Landon was formally notified of his nomination as Republican candidate for the Presidency.

FOUNTAIN TREE, just west of the north entrance to the capitol, is a living hydrant. From the faucet in the trunk of this elm, city water is drawn. Years past, an open water main protruded several inches above the ground and became filled with dirt in which an elm seed lodged and the tree sprouted. The tree put out roots above the rim of the pipe and extended them into the earth confining the pipe in the hollow of the trunk. Observing this phenomenon, a custodian bored a hole into the trunk and inserted a small pipe to which he attached a faucet.

The PIONEER STATUE, also by Merrell Gage, stands in the southwest corner of the grounds. The statue portrays a mother guarding her two children. She is holding a baby in one arm and a boy kneels at her side. A long rifle lies across her knee. The statue rests on a granite base.

14. The TOPEKA CENTRAL HIGH SCHOOL *(open 8-5 weekdays)*, 10th and Taylor Sts., was completed in 1930 at a cost of $2,000,000. Designed by T. R. Griest of Topeka, the building is of Collegiate Gothic architecture, constructed of pressed brick and native stone. The auditorium has a seating capacity of 2,500. In the Gothic tower is a carillon, donated by the late David W. Mulvane as a memorial to his wife. A foreyard of the old United States frigate *Constitution* is used as a flagpole at the Polk Street entrance. It was presented to the school in 1930 by the United States Navy through the efforts of the late Charles Curtis.

15. The EXECUTIVE MANSION, SW. corner 8th and Buchanan Sts., was purchased by the State in 1901. It was built as a private residence in 1889 by Erastus Bennett, a Topekan who had acquired a fortune by buying European horses and breeding them for Kansas farms. The three-

EXECUTIVE MANSION, TOPEKA

story, 32-room mansion of brick and terra cotta is of the ornate late Victorian style, surmounted with a cupola.

16. GRACE CATHEDRAL, SW. corner 8th and Polk Sts., the Cathedral of the Kansas Diocese of the Protestant Episcopal Church, is a twin-towered limestone structure designed by George M. Seyman of Kansas City, Mo. Its exterior is patterned after the medieval cathedrals of England and Normandy. The interior walls are of masonry, the ceiling of plaster and wooden beams, copied in detail from Westminster Hall, London. The flat, three centered arches under the clerestory wall are designed in the English Perpendicular Gothic style.

An altar piece by the late George M. Stone, Topeka artist, was presented to the church in 1919. It is an interpretation of "The Transfiguration" and depicts Christ with Moses and Elijah on the mountain top before the apostles, Peter, James, and John. The canvas is ten feet by twelve feet and the figures in the foreground are life size.

The pulpit is adorned with eleven figures by Alois Lang, Bavarian woodcarver, representing the Saviour, the Four Evangelists, St. Paul and the Five Angels of Adoration. The rose window is composed of glass left over from a rose window of Westminster Abbey, London, several boxes of which had been stored in the abbey since 1760. The framework was made in Topeka and shipped to London where the glass was fitted. A cherished relic is THE BAPTISMAL SPOON *(for permission to view, apply at rectory west of cathedral)*, one of five made by King Olaf of Norway in 1571, which was presented to the church by Mrs. Julius Severin Greu.

The cathedral has a seating capacity of 1,100.

17. The TOPEKA PUBLIC LIBRARY *(open 10-8 weekdays)*, SW. corner 8th and Jackson Sts., is a two-story building of brick and limestone, erected in 1882 with funds provided by two railroad companies, the donors stipulating that it should be erected on the capitol square. It is of modified Romanesque design. The library contains 30,000 volumes.

18. CHURCH OF THE ASSUMPTION, NW. corner 8th and Jackson Sts., is a buff-colored brick Roman Catholic church designed by Carroll & Defoe of Kansas City, in the Romanesque style. It was built in 1924 on the site of the first Catholic church in Topeka, erected in 1862.

19. The CAPPER MANSION *(open 8-5 daily)*, NW. corner Topeka Blvd. and 11th St., is headquarters for radio station WIBW, owned and operated by Capper Publications. The house, a two-story limestone and concrete structure of the Italian villa type, was designed by Root & Seimans of Kansas City and completed in 1912. It was the residence of Kansas' senior Senator during his two terms as Governor of the State (1915–1919). Capper's successor, Gov. Henry J. Allen, also occupied the Capper mansion during his tenure of office. For several years, Kansas' two United States Senators lived on opposite corners of Topeka Boulevard and 11th Street, but Senator Charles Curtis' resignation to accept the nomination for Vice President ended Topeka's senatorial monopoly.

20. CHARLES CURTIS HOME *(private)*, SW. corner Topeka Blvd. and 11th St., is a three-story late Victorian structure built of red brick and limestone. Curtis, grandson of a Kaw Indian chief, spent his boyhood on the reservation. Admitted to the bar in 1881 he launched upon a long and successful political career. Kansas had just adopted prohibition. Elected to the office of county attorney or prosecutor of Shawnee County, Curtis began his career as the scourge of the "jointists," as the illegal saloonkeepers were termed, thus establishing the Kansas tradition, that the successful young office seeker must be an avowed prohibitionist. While the young prosecutor was hammering the liquor trade, his law partner was a recalcitrant old gentleman who was said to be one of the jointists' regular customers. A citizen asked him, "How does it happen that you drink so much liquor when Charley is a strict prohibitionist?" To which came the alleged reply, "Well Charley's closing 'em up and I'm just drinking up the supply on hand." Shawnee County and the Congressional District of which it was a part rewarded Charley Curtis by electing him Representative in 1892, which position he held until 1907 when he was elected to fill an unexpired term in the United States Senate. He represented Kansas in that office until he resigned in 1928 to accept the nomination for Vice President on the ticket with Herbert Hoover. He died in Washington in 1936.

21. TOPEKA'S OLDEST TREE, SE. corner Huntoon and Clay Sts., is marked with a plate placed at its base by pupils of nearby Central

Park School. It is a giant locust, with widespreading branches and a trunk three feet in diameter, and is said to have been a full grown tree when the town was founded in 1854.

22. WASHBURN COLLEGE, 17th St. and College Ave., established in 1865 as a denominational college under the direction of the Congregational Church, represents the New England culture long dominant in Topeka. The 160-acre elm-shaded campus, which stretches away to the Shunganunga Valley on the south, was donated in 1858 by John Ritchie, Topeka pioneer. When the college was incorporated, this site was considered too remote from the settlement (it was more than a mile west of the city limits) and classes opened in a stone building known as Lincoln College at 10th and Jackson Streets, the present site of the Memorial Building. As donations began to swell the endowment fund trustees decided to use the Ritchie tract. The first building on the campus was erected in 1870 and the college was renamed for Ichabod Washburn of Worcester, Mass., one of the donors. Washburn's athletic teams are known today as the "Sons of Ichabod" or "The Ichabods."

There are nearly a score of buildings including Rice Hall, Carnegie Library, MacVicar Chapel, Whiting Field House, Thomas Gymnasium, Boswell Hall, the Observatory, Holbrook Hall, Benton Hall, a women's dormitory; and Mulvane Art Museum. Four sororities and two fraternities have erected chapter houses on the campus since the Kansas Supreme Court ruled in 1933 that fraternity houses are not tax exempt unless they are on school property. Buildings are constructed of Kansas limestone and of varying Romanesque, classic, and modern design.

Washburn is a co-educational nationally accredited college with a liberal atmosphere, offering courses in liberal arts, fine arts, journalism, and law. Its law school has a high rating and many law students from the State University complete their preparation for an LL. B. degree here after receiving their A. B. at the Lawrence institution.

The college has an annual enrollment of 700 to 800 students. Since 1910 it has been conducted as a non-sectarian institution.

MULVANE ART MUSEUM (open 8 a.m.-5 p.m.; 7 p.m.-9:30 p.m. weekdays; 2 p.m.-5 p.m. Sun.), a two-story limestone building, is in a small grove near the northwest edge of the campus. It is Italian Renaissance in style and was constructed in 1923. It houses the college department of art and contains a collection of painting and sculpture. In the Hall of Sculpture on the first floor are three pieces by Merrell Gage, former instructor in the college department of art: *John Brown, Mother and Child,* and the *Flutist.* In the collection of oils on the second floor are Henry Salem Hubbell's the *Orange Robe;* the *Frosty Morning* by John F. Carlson, and Bierstadt's *Rocky Mountain Landscape.* An oil portrait of the late Joab Mulvane, Topeka art patron, whose $50,000 bequest made the museum possible, is the work of George M. Stone.

RICE HALL, a three-story limestone building with red tile roof, constructed in 1870, is the oldest building on the campus. It contains a small MUSEUM OF NATURAL HISTORY (open 2-5 weekdays during school year), which includes mounted specimens of birds and animals and a collection of insects. Near Rice Hall is the OLD COLLEGE BELL, which hung in the Rice Hall belfry before the fire that partially destroyed the building in 1907. It was used to call students to classes and to ring out the glad tidings of a football victory. The bell was salvaged after the fire, but was never restored to its old place in the belfry.

23. GAGE PARK, 6th Ave. and Gage Blvd., 146 acres, Topeka's largest recreational center, contains a swimming pool, tennis courts, baseball diamonds, picnic grounds, a rock garden, and a small zoo.

The REINISCH ROSE GARDEN, in the southwest section of the park, a memorial to the late E. F. Reinisch, former park superintendent, has been termed the perfect rose garden by national experts. It has received prize awards in several contests.

The OLD SETTLERS' MEMORIAL CABIN *(open 9 a.m.-10 p.m. daily)*, north and east of the Reinisch Rose Garden, was originally on the farm of Adam Bauer, near Topeka. It was removed to Gage Park in the early 1930's. The cabin is of walnut logs and its dooryard enclosed by a rail fence. It contains numerous pioneer relics including two sewing machines, a spinning wheel, rifles, pistols, and cooking utensils. In the dooryard are several old wagon wheels, two feed troughs hewn out of logs, and many other household and farm implements used in pioneer days.

24. KANSAS STATE HOSPITAL *(grounds open at all hours)*, 6th St. and Randolph Ave., its 22 buildings half-hidden by a heavily-wooded park, is reached by a drive that is an extension of Randolph Avenue. The institution grounds cover an area of 320 acres. The main drive leads to the administration building, a yellow brick structure with a turreted roof. At this point it turns right and follows a circuitous route past a row of brick buildings in which the 1,800 patients are housed. An area of approximately 80 acres is attractively landscaped. Left of the main buildings are poultry houses, cattle barns, a green house, and implement sheds. Nearly 240 acres are under cultivation and the institution maintains a dairy farm. Farm produce and dairy products are consumed in the hospital dining rooms and the income from surplus products is applied to the annual maintenance fund. The hospital, established in 1878, is one of three State supported institutions for treatment of the insane. All types of mental cases are treated here.

25. UNDERGROUND RAILROAD STATION *(open by arrangement with owner)*, in the rear of a private home at the SW. corner 23rd St. and Pennsylvania Ave., is a small, one-story building constructed of walnut slabs. The station was established in 1855 by Daniel Sheridan, an associate of John Brown, as a connecting link in the Underground Railway system that enabled escaped slaves from Missouri to make their way through Kansas and Nebraska to a haven of safety at Tabor, Iowa. From the cellar beneath the building a tunnel connected with an opening in a pasture 100 yards east. Most of the tunnel has caved in and all traces of the exterior opening have been obliterated but the passageway is still visible from the basement.

26. TOPEKA CEMETERY, 10th and Lafayette Sts., contains a monument to the Kansas soldiers who died in the Battle of the Blue. It is a

LOG CABIN (1870), GAGE PARK, TOPEKA

white granite shaft 75 feet high, dedicated May 30, 1895, by Col. George Veale, who commanded the 2nd Kansas Militia in the battle.

27. The SANTA FE SHOPS *(open 8-5 weekdays on application to the superintendent)*, 3rd and Holliday Sts., consisting of a dozen factory-type buildings of brick and stone and a network of track, cover an area of 225 acres, part of the old Cyrus K. Holliday farm. An average of 2,000 men are employed here in repairing locomotives and other rolling stock.

POINTS OF INTEREST IN ENVIRONS

Old Stagecoach Station, *2.9 m.;* Alf M. Landon Mansion, *3.5 m.;* Kansas Vocation School, *3.9 m.;* State Industrial School, *4.1 m.;* Old Baptist Mission, *6.5 m.;* Burnett's Mound, *6.7 m.;* Chief Burnett's Grave, *8.3 m. (see Tour 3);* Lyons Castle, *11 m. (see Tour 11).*

Wichita

Railroad Stations: Union Station, E. Douglas Ave. at Santa Fe St., for Atchison, Topeka & Santa Fe Ry., Chicago, Rock Island & Pacific Ry., and St. Louis & San Francisco Ry.; 302 W. Douglas Ave. for Missouri Pacific R.R.
Bus Stations: Union Bus Station, NE. corner Broadway and William St., for Southern Kansas Stage Lines, Southern Kansas Greyhound Lines, Cardinal Stage Lines, Santa Fe Trailways of Illinois, and Santa Fe Trails Stages.
Buses: (Street System) From Douglas Ave. to all parts of the city; fare 7¢, or tokens 5 for 25¢.
Taxis: Minimum fare, 10¢, governed by zones.
Airports: Municipal Airport, 4 m. SE. on State 15, Braniff Airways and Transcontinental and Western Air.
Traffic Regulations: All plainly indicated; no one-way streets.

Accommodations: Nineteen hotels.

Information Service: Kansas Highway Patrol, 1721 N. Broadway; Kansas Motor Club, Hotel Lassen, 153 N. Market St.

Radio Stations: KFH (1300 kc.), KANS (1210 kc.).
Theater and Motion Picture Houses: Arcadia Theater, Water and William Sts.; the Municipal Forum, Water and English Sts., for concerts and road shows; thirteen motion picture houses.
Swimming: Municipal, South Riverside Park (R), off Central Ave. at Arkansas River.
Boating: Israel (Riverside) Boathouse, E. end of Murdock Bridge, for canoes and rowboats; motor launch ride to Little River Dam, 10¢.
Golf: Municipal, in Sim Park, W. end of 11th St., greens fee 25¢; Meadowlark, 4 m. SE. on State 15, greens fee 25¢; Westlink, 6 m. W. on US 54, greens fee 25¢; Canyons, 1 m. W. Municipal (State 15) Airport, greens fee 25¢; Crestview Country Club, 21st and Oliver Sts., greens fee 25¢.
Riding: Bridle and Saddle Club, 3.75 m. E. on Central Ave.; Gill Riding Stable, from downtown E. 1 m. to Hydraulic Ave. and S. 3 m.

Annual Events: Farm Power Equipment Show and Southwest Road School at Forum, Feb.; State choir and orchestra joint concert, Mar.; Girls' National Basketball Tournament, Forum, Mar.; spring concerts of Minisa Chorus and Orchestra of Wichita Municipal University, May; spring concerts by the Singing Quakers of Friends University, April; National Semi-pro Baseball Tournament, Stadium, Aug.; annual pageants (historical), and stock show, Nov.

WICHITA (1,283 alt., 111,110 pop.), seat of Sedgwick County, lies on tablelands at the confluence of the Arkansas and Little Arkansas Rivers. A fifth of the city is built west of the Arkansas River; a smaller fraction lies on the tongue of land between the junction of the rivers. The rest of Wichita sprawls east of the rivers, its north-south bulk bisected by a drainage canal. The city is closely knit by concrete bridges, six of which span the Arkansas, eight the Little Arkansas, and twenty-four the drainage canal.

The area west of the Arkansas River, commonly called West Wichita, is composed of residential districts. Houses for the most part are large structures of brick and stone with an occasional frame dwelling extravagantly decorated in the gingerbread style of the 1880's. The repeated pattern of lawns, houses, and neighborhood shopping districts is broken by the campus of Friends University, Mount Carmel Academy, and the Masonic Home.

The attractive residential section on the peninsula between the rivers is called Riverside. The trim bungalows that occupy this area are ranged beside avenues that terminate north at the banks of the rivers, and south at the lawns and wooded groves of Sim Park and Central Riverside Park. The latter contains one of the rare stands of virgin timber that remain in this section of Kansas.

Wichita east of the rivers consists of business, residential, and industrial blocks. The business district—more metropolitan than those of other Kansas cities—is centered around the junction of Main Street and Douglas Avenue. Two-and-three-story shops heavily corniced in the style of the 1890's cluster at the base of tall office structures and department store buildings whose ten-to-seventeen-story heights are the nearest approach to skyscrapers in Kansas. On Wichita Street, between English and Lewis Streets, is Tractor Row, an area two blocks long so-named because it is wholly occupied by dealers in tractors and farm power equipment.

The avenues north and south of the business district are lined with elm and cottonwood trees which shade the lawns of comfortable residences. This neighborhood is bounded on the east by the tracks of the Santa Fe Railway. East of the tracks to the drainage canal is a low-income section of small cottages and box-style houses. Beyond the drainage canal the streets rise gradually to the slope that flanks the eastern section of the city. On the crest of the slope are the neat brick and frame houses of the residential area known as College Hill. Along the north-south extent of this section are six cemeteries, and Fairmount Park, College Hill Park, St. Mary's Academy (Roman Catholic), and the Wichita Municipal University.

At the east fringe of the College Hill district are various restricted residential areas, most unusual of which is Eastborough at the extremity of Douglas Avenue. Eastborough was developed as an expensive residential addition, but in July 1930 oil gushed forth from a pool that underlies the region. Today stately Georgian houses share the Eastborough horizon with the steel girders of oil derricks.

The buffer section that lies between the Santa Fe Railway and the drainage canal trails off at the north in a vast industrial area. Ranged along the tracks of the four railroads that thread this section are a stockyard, railroad shops, grain elevators, and oil stills and tanks. Wichita ranks fourth as a national milling center and sixth as an interior market for grain. Six local mills have a combined daily capacity of about 12,000 barrels of flour. Four oil refineries can produce about 11,000 barrels per day. Five meat packing plants make Wichita the center of that industry in the Southwest. Other industries include the manufacture of textiles, leather goods, building materials, food products, farm machinery, airplanes, tools, and dies, and drilling and oil field equipment.

Wichita was named for the Wichita Indians who, having been driven into Texas by the Osage's invasion of Kansas, returned to their native region in 1863 and built a village of grass lodges near the mouth of the Little Arkansas River. James R. Mead, aided by Jesse Chisholm, a half-breed Cherokee, established a trading post near the Wichita village in 1864. In the following year, at the close of the Civil War, Mead sent Chisholm into the Southwest with a wagonload of goods to exchange for buffalo hides. While returning Chisholm encountered a severe storm but pressed on toward Wichita, his heavily laden wagon cutting deep tracks in the prairie soil. Thus was blazed the Chisholm Trail, the broad highway through the wilderness over which in subsequent years traveled scouts, traders, Indians, ranchers, and cowboys.

Following the removal of the Wichita tribe to Oklahoma Territory after 1865, Mead's trading post became the nucleus of a settlement. A herd of 2,400 Texas longhorns was driven up the Chisholm Trail in 1867, past the cottonwood pole hut and several dugouts at the site of Wichita, and on to the Union Pacific Railroad at Abilene. Throughout 1868 the Chisholm Trail was beaten hard by the hooves of Texas cattle. The settlers at Wichita began to provide accommodations for the herd-driving cowboys. E. S. Munger built the Munger House and a second settler built the "first and last chance saloon," where thirsty cowpunchers could get their first drink coming up the trail and their last before returning to Texas.

Thousands of steers passed over the Chisholm Trail in 1870. In that year Wichita was platted. In 1871 the Santa Fe Railway was built midway between Wichita and Abilene to Newton, which town superseded Abilene as the "cow capital," but when the railway was extended to Wichita in 1872 Newton was relegated to the "cow capital" limbo and Wichita boomed. Before the end of the year about 350,000 cattle were driven to the new "cow capital"; a Government land office was established; and Col. Marshall M. Murdock began publishing the Wichita *Eagle*. Shops, cafes, saloons, and dance halls were hastily built. Scouts, Indians, gamblers, cowboys, Mexican ranchers, and homesteaders milled in the streets, crowded into dance halls and barrooms, and frolicked to the music of a brass band that was especially imported by the proprietors of a gambling house. Costumes ranged from the checkered suits worn by "sports from back east in Kansas City" to the chaps and sombrero of the cowboy, the buckskin breeches and jackets of the scouts and plainsmen, and the brightly colored blankets worn toga-like by Indians. Signs posted at the outskirts of the town declared: "Anything goes in Wichita. Leave your revolvers at police headquarters and get a check. Carrying concealed weapons is strictly forbidden."

The Reverend Luther Hart Platt, widely known as the "fiddlin' preacher," made desperate efforts to improve the moral tone of the ebullient cow town. Occasionally he would stalk into a saloon, clear his throat and intone a popular ballad, accompanying himself on the fiddle. When

TERMINAL ELEVATOR, WICHITA

the crowd gathered round he would play several hymns and then lay aside his fiddle to preach. At the conclusion of the sermon he would invite his listeners to attend the coming Sunday services in the dugout schoolhouse, and then depart, fiddle under arm.

Within this decade scores of settlers arrived at Wichita. Land speculation became rife and property values soared. The Chisholm Trail was criss-crossed with barbed-wire barriers and by 1880 virtually oversown with wheat. The cattle trail was consequently shifted farther west to Dodge City and Wichita entered a period of decline. Gamblers, saloon-keepers, and merchants vacated the city to cash in on the prosperity of the new "cow capital." Land values collapsed at Wichita in 1886, bankrupting many a townsman.

The settlers who had fenced off the prairie and thereby contributed to the fall of "cow capital" Wichita, more than atoned for their fault throughout the 1880's and 90's. Grain from their farms soon equalled the wealth formerly brought by cattle, and Wichita took a new lease on life as a trade and milling center. During the harvest rush wheat-laden wagons often stood on the streets for thirty-six hours before they could be weighed and emptied at the mills. It was not uncommon to see carts and wagons lined along Douglas Avenue in files ten blocks long.

Where cattle had built dance halls and gambling houses, wheat built churches and schools. All Hallows Academy (now Mount Carmel Academy) was founded in 1888; Fairmount College (now Wichita Municipal University) was established in 1892; and Garfield University (now Friends University) was established in 1898. An interest in art, music, and literature was contemporaneously kindled among the townspeople.

By 1900 the population exceeded 24,000. Wichita thereafter all but doubled its population each decade, reaching 86,000 in 1920. Shortly after the World War oil was discovered in the "door-step pool," so-called because of its proximity to the city. Wealth derived from this source was used to build large business structures in the downtown section and palatial residences in restricted subdivisions. Local economy was further stimulated by post-war interest in airplane manufacturing, which industry had been previously established in the city. Wichita business men, eager to bolster Wichita's claim as "Air Capital of America," built factory after factory, until by the middle 1920's fifteen had been erected. These firms built 1,500 planes in 1928, or one-fourth of the total commercial output of the country. About 2,500 planes were produced the following year.

The depression of 1929 sent Wichita's airplane industry into a disastrous tailspin, but four companies withstood the crash. Their plants and equipment are today valued at $2,500,000; their total annual production is estimated at $1,500,000. The industry employs an average of 550 workmen.

Noted former residents of Wichita are the late John Noble *(see ART)*; Bruce Moore, sculptor; Kathleen Kersting, operatic star; Earl R. Browder, Presidential candidate of the Communist party in 1936; and Charles B. Driscoll, author and columnist. Wichita is the home town of United States Senator George H. McGill.

POINTS OF INTEREST

FIRST PRESBYTERIAN CHURCH, SW. corner of Broadway and Elm St., a modified Gothic limestone structure with an octagonal tower, was designed by Badgley and Nicklas of Cleveland, Ohio. Huge stained glass windows, designed by A. A. Leyendecker, rise from the wainscoting to the peak of the arched ceiling. The church was built in 1910. The SARA BLAIR CASE MEMORIAL EDUCATION BUILDING, adjoining the church, is a three-story limestone structure, built in 1936. It was designed by Glenn Thomas of Wichita.

The CATHEDRAL OF THE IMMACULATE CONCEPTION (Roman Catholic), SE. corner of Broadway and Central Ave., popularly known as St. Mary's Cathedral, occupies the northwest corner of the onetime homestead of James R. Meade, a founder of Wichita. The cathedral was dedicated in 1912. Of modified Romanesque and Italian Renaissance architecture the façade of the structure is adorned with four massive columns of Vermont gray granite. The design of the copper dome is based upon that of the domes over the twin churches of Piazza del Populo in Rome. E. L. Masquery of St. Paul, Minn., who designed several of the exposition buildings at the St. Louis World's Fair (1904) was the architect.

The SEDGWICK COUNTY COURTHOUSE, NW. corner of Central Ave. and Market St., is a six-story limestone structure, built in 1890. From the town clock in the tower swings a pendulum that weighs nearly a half-ton. The building was designed by W. H. Sternberg of Wichita.

The HISTORICAL MUSEUM OF THE SEDGWICK COUNTY PIONEER SOCIETY *(open 8-5 weekdays),* in the main corridor on the second floor of the courthouse, contains pictures of the early day local scene; Indian weapons and utensils (principally Arapahoe and Cheyenne); and examples of pioneer women's sewing, weaving, and knitting.

The SOLDIER'S AND SAILOR'S MONUMENT, on the south lawn of the courthouse, was designed by E. M. Viquesney and erected in 1912 in memory of the Union force that served in the Civil War. It consists of a bronze figure of Liberty, flanked by four life-sized figures of Union soldiers and sailors.

The UNITED STATES POST OFFICE AND COURTHOUSE, NW. corner of Market and 3rd Sts., a four-story, white stone structure of neoclassic design, was planned by architects of the U. S. Treasury Department and completed in 1932. The interior is lavishly finished with marble, walnut, and gold leaf. The wall panels in the recess behind the bench in the district courtrooms are of marble quarried in Germany; the panels on the ceiling of the circuit courtroom are decorated with 23-carat gold leaf.

The WICHITA PUBLIC LIBRARY *(open 9-9 weekdays),* 220 S. Main St., is a two-story stone structure with a green tile roof. It was designed by Anthony Allaire Crowell and built in 1915. On the Mezzanine floor are three mural paintings by Arthur Sinclair Covey—*Promise, Fruition,* and *Afterglow*—which depict the progress of civilization on the prairies. The library contains 127,000 volumes.

The MUNICIPAL FORUM, NW. corner of Water and English Sts., is a three-story structure of extra-sized brick, owned and maintained by the city of Wichita. Its auditorium seats 4,800. The structure is used for conventions, expositions, political rallies, and large-cast road shows. Adjoining the forum are an exhibition arcade and a two-story brick Exposition Building. The latter structure, at the SW. corner of Water and William Sts., contains the ARCADIA THEATRE where concerts and road shows are presented. The total floor space of the Forum, the exhibition arcade, and the Exposition Building is 211,340 square feet. The Forum was built in 1910 and the Exposition Building in 1918.

The WICHITA ART MUSEUM *(open 11-5 daily except Mon.; showings changed monthly; free except for special exhibitions; motor bus service Sun. only)* is at the south entrance of Sim Park, 619 Stackman Drive. It is a cast stone structure with severely modern lines, designed by Clarence S. Stein of New York City, and completed in 1935. Polychrome sculptures by Lee Lawrie, depicting Indian arts and crafts, adorn the entrance. The construction of the museum was financed by a grant of the Public Works Administration, and a $70,000 bequest from Mrs. Louise Caldwell Murdock.

In the permanent collection are a frieze by Walter Ufer, a black panther in lacquered bronze by Bruce Moore, and paintings by Dewey Albinson, E. L. Blumenschein, Max Bohm, Maurice Braun, Ed L. Davison, William Dickerson, B. J. L. Hordfeldt, E. Kopietz, John Noble, Birger Sandzen, Elizabeth Sprague, and Walter Ufer.

8. RIVERSIDE PARK ZOO *(open 9-5 daily)*, River Blvd. and Nims Ave., contains an aviary, an animal house, fish ponds, an alligator pond, and a bear den. The main building, half a block north of Woodman Bridge on Nims Avenue, houses monkeys, lions, and other jungle beasts.

9. THE HIKER, SW. corner of Nims and Murdock Ave., an heroic bronze figure of a soldier, was designed by Newman Allen. It was erected in 1926 by members of Lawton Camp No. 18 of the United Spanish War Veterans, in honor of the Spanish-American War veterans of Wichita and Sedgwick County.

10. The OLD MUNGER HOUSE *(private)* 920 Back Bay Blvd., built of wide upright boards painted white, is generally believed to be the first house in what is now Wichita. It was constructed in 1868. Buffalo hair was used to reenforce the plaster of the interior walls. Its original owner, D. S. Munger, was at times justice of the peace, postmaster, and innkeeper of the settlement. He made the first plat of Wichita. His house—then situated one hundred yards east of its present site—was at the very center of the village. Cowboys wounded on the trails or in drunken brawls customarily came to Munger for hospitalization of sorts in the present structure. The purveying of food and shelter was, however, Munger's principal pursuit, in which connection the Wichita *Eagle* of April 12, 1872, said: "The Munger House in the original town is a bower now and a paradise for homelike, quiet-stopping people. Mr. Munger is alive to the interest of his guests, and sets a good table and keeps clean beds. What more does a traveling public demand? No pause for reply."

11. WICHITA HIGH SCHOOL, NORTH, NW. corner of 13th St., and Rochester Ave., the newer of the two high schools in Wichita, was opened in the autumn of 1929. Constructed of buff brick with a red tile roof, it is architecturally noteworthy as an example of the "prairie" style. The walls are trimmed with cream-colored Silverdale (Kansas) stone, and decorated with sculptured figures in polychrome and terra cotta. Near the top of the 90-foot tower that surmounts the school are four panels of colored terra cotta which depict Indian and buffalo scenes. The structure was designed by Glenn Thomas of Wichita; the ornamentation and decorative panels are the work of Bruce Moore, Wichita. *Two Indians*, a painting by Walter Ufer, hangs in the first floor corridor of the school.

12. MINISA BRIDGE, 13th St. and Little Arkansas River, was planned to harmonize with the Wichita High School, North. It is ornamented with Indian and buffalo heads designed by Bruce Moore. The structure was dedicated in 1932 and named Minisa (Ind. *red waters*) by high school students who chose the word from the title of a composition by Thurlow Lieurance, authority on Indian music.

On MEAD ISLAND *(no bridge or convenient method of transportation)*, So. of Minisa Bridge, is a GRASS HOUSE of the type in which the

AIRVIEW, RIVERSIDE PARK, WICHITA

Wichita Indians formerly dwelled. The structure was built in 1927 by descendants of the tribe, now living in Oklahoma. It consists of a pole and willow rod framework, thatched with grass. Coronado noted grass lodges at the village of Quivira in 1541 *(see ARCHITECTURE)*.

13. SIM MEMORIAL PARK, entrance at the W. end of Beal Ave., consists of 183 acres beside the Arkansas River. The site was given to Wichita in 1917 by Mr. and Mrs. Colar B. Sim in memory of their son, Arthur. It contains a municipal golf course, archery grounds, and picnic groves equipped with roasting ovens and concrete tables. A drive parallels the river through the park and emerges at the south near the intersection of Pine Street and River Boulevard.

14. The WICHITA HORSE AND MULE MARKET *(open 8-6 weekdays)*, 521 E. 21st St., is a branch of the Wichita Union Stockyards Co., managed by the Wichita Horse and Mule Commission Co. The Wednesday auction sales are attended by buyers from foreign countries and

many parts of the United States. A carload of trail mules are annually purchased at this market for use in Grand Canyon National Park.

15. The WICHITA UNION STOCKYARDS EXCHANGE BUILDING *(open 8-5 weekdays)*, NE. corner of 21st St. and Meade Ave., was built in 1909. It houses the Union Stockyards National Bank, the offices of the Union Stockyards Co., numerous commission firms and stockfeed companies, the U. S. Market News Service, and the remote control studio of radio station KFH. The yards (110 acres) north of the Exchange Building have a capacity of 5,000 sheep, 15,000 hogs, and 21,000 cattle. The area is paved with brick, electrically lighted, and drained by a special system of sewers.

16. The DERBY OIL REFINERY *(open by permission)*, 1100 E. 21st St., is representative of the oil industry in Wichita. Crude oil is pumped to the refinery from the Eastborough Pool, which lies between Douglas and Central Avenues, a mile east of Oliver Street.

17. The MUNICIPAL UNIVERSITY OF WICHITA, 21st and Hillside Ave., an outgrowth of Fairmount College founded in 1892, is a co-educational institution created in 1926 by a referendum vote in Wichita. The curriculum is composed of courses in education, science, business administration, and the fine and liberal arts. The university has an average enrollment of 1,500 students. Its president (1938) Dr. William M. Jardine, was formerly U. S. Secretary of Agriculture (1925–29), and Minister to Egypt (1930–33). The College of Fine Arts is directed (1938) by Thurlow Lieurance, D. M., known for his research among Indians, and for his Indian musical compositions, "Minisa," and "By the Waters of Minnetonka."

The university has offered courses in police science since 1935. Through a cooperative arrangement between university officials and the Wichita Police Department, young men, invested with full police authority, are employed as cadets while studying a two-year course in criminal law and police science. They attend classes in the morning and perform a half tour of police duty each day.

The university occupies an 80-acre campus overlooking Wichita. There are six brick buildings and several frame structures, the latter remaining from Fairmount College. The main buildings are Fiske Hall and the Administration Building.

MORRISON LIBRARY *(open 8:30-10 weekdays)*, facing Fairmount Ave. at the south of the campus, is a yellow brick structure of neoclassic design trimmed with stone. It was designed by Robert R. Ross, dedicated in 1910, and named for Nathan F. Morrison, former president of Fairmount College. The library contains 60,000 volumes, many thousand pamphlets and periodicals. It is a depository of the Federal Government. The CARTER MEMORIAL ROOM contains 2,000 volumes of the complete works of classical English and American authors, many of which are first editions.

The NATURAL HISTORY MUSEUM *(open during class hours)*, in the Science Hall north of Morrison Library, contains marine fossils, geological specimens, Indian artifacts, a large collection of bird and small mammal specimens, World War memorabilia, and Palestinian field, shop, and household utensils. The latter were procured through Selah Merrill, former U. S. Consul to Syria.

18. The OLD MISSION CEMETERY, main entrance 21st St. and Hillside Ave., has a CARILLON that attracts large audiences to summer evening concerts.

19. The CARRY A. NATION MEMORIAL FOUNTAIN, Douglas Ave. just E. of Santa Fe St. on Union Station Plaza, was dedicated in 1918 by members of the Women's Christian Temperance Union. It consists of a granite slab with a dedicatory plaque and a drinking fountain. The memorial is a block east of the OLD CAREY HOTEL (now Eaton Hotel), the barroom of which was raided in December 1900 by Mrs. Nation. As related in her autobiography, Mrs. Nation "walked into the Carey barroom and threw two rocks at the picture; then turned and smashed the mirror that covered almost the entire side of the large room. Some men drinking at the bar ran out . . . I took the cane and broke up the sideboard, which had on it all kinds of intoxicating drinks. Then I ran out across the street to destroy another one (saloon)." The picture at which Mrs. Nation "threw two rocks" was John Noble's *(see ART)* painting of *Cleopatra at the Bath,* a work described by Mrs. Nation as "the life-sized picture of a naked woman."

20. The McKNIGHT MEMORIAL, SW. corner of Grove St. and Douglas Ave., was designed by Alexander Proctor and erected in 1931 in honor of J. Hudson McKnight who donated the 70-acre tract on which the nearby Wichita High School, East, is built. The memorial consists of a life-sized bronze figure of a trapper leaning on his rifle beside the seated figure of an Indian with bow and arrow in hand.

21. The HENRY J. ALLEN HOUSE *(private),* SW. corner of Roosevelt Ave. and Second St., designed by Frank Lloyd Wright, is a two-story structure of buff brick, built in the form of an irregular ell. Rising from a slope, which is protected on the Second Street side by a retaining wall, the house appears to be underslung in comparison with its setting, an effect accentuated by the low-pitched tile roof. When built in 1920 this residence was considered a radical departure in residential architecture.

Henry J. Allen, publisher of the Wichita *Beacon* (1907–28), and now editor of the Topeka *State Journal* (1938), was elected to the Governorship of Kansas in 1918 while serving with the American Red Cross in France. He was reelected in 1920. Nine years later he was appointed to fill the unexpired term of United States Senator Charles Curtis, who had been elected to the Vice Presidency.

22. The UNITED STATES VETERANS' FACILITY *(open by permission),* NE. corner of Bleckley Drive and Kellogg St., was opened in November 1935 as a general observation hospital for war veterans. The fourteen buildings and their equipment are valued at $1,250,000. The main building is a four-story Georgian Colonial structure with dormer windows, stone quoins, and a white cupola. Bleckley Drive, which leads

to the main entrance, is named for Lieut. Erwin Bleckley, a native of Wichita who was shot down in his plane while attempting to deliver rations to the "Lost Battalion" in the World War.

23. The FIREMEN'S AND POLICEMEN'S MEMORIAL, on McLean Blvd. between Douglas Ave. and Second St., consists of a stone and concrete wall with plaques that bear the names of Wichita firemen and policemen killed in the line of duty. It was designed by Ed Forsblom and built in 1934.

24. LAWRENCE STADIUM, NE. corner of Maple and Sycamore Sts., was built in 1934 and named for Robert Lawrence, Wichita pioneer. The construction cost ($125,000) was shared by Wichita and the Federal Government. The stadium has seats for 6,000 and standing room for 2,000. State and national semi-professional baseball tournaments are held here annually.

25. FRIENDS UNIVERSITY *(QUAKER)*, University and Hiram Aves., founded in 1898 by the Society of Friends, is a co-educational institution open to students of all denominations. The university has an average enrollment of 400. The curriculum consists of courses in Music and the Liberal Arts.

UNIVERSITY HALL, a five-story structure of red brick and native stone, surmounted by a clock tower, is the main building on the 17-acre campus. On its fourth floor is a Museum *(open 8-5 weekdays; Sun. by appointment)*, which houses mound builder and Indian artifacts, Chinese lacquer work and royal pewter, mineral and fossil specimen, and Aztec and Inca pottery.

26. The WICHITA MUNICIPAL AIRPORT, 3.3 *m.* southeast of Wichita on State 15, a mile square tract with concrete landing strips 4,800 feet long, is at the junction of two of the most important lighted airways in the country.

The AIRPORT ADMINISTRATION BUILDING, a two-story structure of buff brick, contains a passenger station, airport and airline offices, and a radio station of the U. S. Weather Bureau which is operated in conjunction with the Department of Commerce. An airplane motif figures in the interior and exterior decorations of the structure. A passenger plane in flight is depicted in a frieze above the main entrance. The building was constructed in 1935 at a cost of $150,000.

27. The STEARMAN AIRCRAFT FACTORY *(open by appointment)*, opposite the Municipal Airport, is housed in a one-story structure of buff brick. The factory produces training planes for the U. S. Army and Navy.

POINTS OF INTEREST IN ENVIRONS

Santa Fe Lake, *19.6 m. (see Tour 5)*; Indian Peace Treaty Monument, *9.4 m.*; G. A. Stearns Stock-breeding Farm, *13.3 m.*; Camp Bide-A-Wee, *17.3 m. (see Tour 9)*.

PART III
Highways and Byways

TWO-YEAR-OLD TIMBER BELT PLANTING

Tour 1

(St. Joseph, Mo.)—Marysville—Belleville—Norton—St. Francis—(Denver, Colo.); US 36.
Missouri Line to Colorado Line, 420 m.

St. Joseph & Grand Island R.R. parallels route between Elwood and Hiawatha; Chicago, Rock Island & Pacific Ry. between Elwood and Troy; St. Joseph & Grand Island R.R. between Hiawatha and Hanover; Chicago, Burlington & Quincy R.R. between Hanover and Haddam; Chicago, Rock Island & Pacific Ry. between Belleville and Norton; Chicago, Burlington & Quincy R.R. between Norton and Oberlin, Atwood and St. Francis.
Hard-surfaced roadbed over half the route, remainder graveled. Open all year except during severe snowstorms.
Usual accommodations.

Section a. MISSOURI LINE *to* BELLEVILLE, *166.5 m.,* US 36

This route traverses a region of apple orchards, and the wheat, alfalfa, and corn fields of the fertile Glacial Uplands, the Blue Hills Uplands, and the southern part of the great midwestern corn belt.

US 36 crosses the Missouri Line, 0 *m.,* 1 mile west of St. Joseph, Mo. *(see MO. Tour 1),* on a high bridge over the tawny, clay-banked Missouri River.

ELWOOD, 0.5 *m.* (816 alt., 849 pop.), is a poplar-lined suburb, most of its inhabitants working in St. Joseph, which was once smaller than Elwood and a rival of the town.

In a country first explored by French traders in 1719, Elwood was founded by a promoter named Rose who in 1856 invested $10,000 in the townsite and named it Roseport. By painting a glowing verbal picture of the great inland port his town would be some day, Rose induced other investors to join him in forming a town company.

Roseport was growing rapidly when the company directors discovered that Rose was an ex-convict. They drove him away and placed a man named John B. Elwood in charge of the government, renaming the town in his honor. Elwood grew in size and importance until it became the largest city in Kansas Territory. In this flourishing river port the Great Western Hotel, three stories high and 100 feet square, the first hostelry in this region, was built. Abraham Lincoln, campaigning for the Presidential nomination in 1859, chose Elwood as his first stop in Kansas.

In the spring of 1860 the shifting currents of the Missouri River cut away a large portion of the Elwood townsite. The Great Western Hotel was demolished, homes floated downstream, and large numbers of the town's population moved away. Many went to St. Joseph, then recently founded on the other side of the river.

On April 3, 1860 William H. Russell of Leavenworth instituted the Pony Express (US 36 in general follows the route of the Pony Express as far west as Marysville), with St. Joseph as the eastern terminus, and Elwood as a wayside station. The Pony Express, first postal system to connect the eastern part of the United States and the Pacific Coast with any degree of speed, had 190 relay stations along its 2,000-mile route. Some of these, called home stations, had taverns for housing employees; others, called way stations, were merely stables. Riders were paid from $50 to $150 a month, according to their ability and the risk and responsibility of their assignment. Mail to California had heretofore been carried by sea either around the Horn, or to the Isthmus of Panama and thence by ship to San Francisco. Russell established the Pony Express to prove that mail could be carried rapidly overland. He charged $5 for each half-ounce of mail carried.

Until supplanted by the Overland Stages from Leavenworth and a transcontinental telegraph line established in 1861, the Pony Express made two trips a week between St. Joseph and Sacramento. The first riders started simultaneously at each end of the route. The fastest relay trip in Pony Express history was made in seven days and seven hours.

After the Civil War Elwood again grew in population, but was damaged by repeated floods of the Missouri River. St. Joseph always stood high and dry, as if waiting to receive the refugees from the rival town. At one time the population of Elwood dropped as low as 100.

WATHENA, 6 m. (818 alt., 854 pop.), now the market for a large horticultural area, was named for a Kickapoo Indian chief who proudly allowed the settlers to hold church services in his wigwam. The town's first settlers, who came in 1840, were "Squaw" Pete Cadue, a French trader, and his Indian wife.

The townsite is dominated by the imposing ST. JOSEPH'S CHURCH (Roman Catholic). This structure, designed in the Gothic style, has a large tower topped with a cross set with electric lights. When the present church was built in 1935, the 800 members were assisted by Protestants and other residents in meeting the cost of $35,000.

The improved highway between Wathena and Atchison was once the roadbed of Kansas' first railroad. Built in the 1860's, it entered the State at Elwood, ran west from Wathena, then turned southwest to Atchison. It was abandoned as unprofitable after a few years of use.

A roadhouse, 7.8 m., built in the form of a red apple, was erected to advertise the Kansas orchard region.

TROY, 13.1 m. (1,093 alt., 1,042 pop.), the seat of Doniphan County, in the rolling fertile hills of the Missouri River valley, is important as a shipping point for local fruit-growers.

It is estimated that there are 10,000 acres of apple orchards in the vicinity of Troy. Almost everyone in Troy and the surrounding country participates in the annual Apple Blossom Festival (late April) and the Apple Harvest Festival (early Sept.). There are agricultural exhibits, parades, and carnival attractions.

APPLES FROM THE COOPERATIVE PACKING PLANT, TROY

Founded in 1855 as a Territorial county seat, Troy was incorporated in 1860.

The *Kansas Chief,* Troy's first newspaper, was owned and edited by Sol Miller, author of the satirical poem "Paw Paws Ripe," which tells of a "man of five-and-forty years with beard of grizzled brown," and his family:

> Nine boys and girls with rheumy eyes,
> Stowed in with beds and tins,
> Were all so nearly of a size,
> They well might have been twins.
> The mother as a penance sore,
> For loss of youth and hope,
> Seemed to have vowed, long years before,
> To fast from comb and soap.
>
> * * * *
>
> Don't tell me of your corn and wheat—
> What do I care for sich?
> Don't say your schools is hard to beat,
> And Kansas soil is rich.
> Stranger, a year's been lost to me,
> Searchin' your Kansas siles,
> And not a pawpaw did I see,
> For miles, and miles, and miles!

The pawpaw, often called the Missouri banana, is a fruit shaped like a fat cucumber, containing a number of large brown seeds imbedded in a sweet pulp that tastes like a well-ripened banana. It is native to Missouri but rare in Kansas except along the Missouri Line. Because Missourians were fond of the fruit while New Englanders considered it nauseating, the pawpaw, in the days before the Civil War, was a symbol of the Kansas antislavery settlers' scorn for proslavery Missourians.

When Abraham Lincoln, campaigning for the Presidential nomination in 1859, made a speech in Troy the event received only brief mention in the local papers, which were all opposed to him.

Around Troy are tobacco plantations, rare in Kansas, and on the south edge of the town is a TOBACCO STOREHOUSE, a large barn-like frame structure.

SPARKS, 22 m. (910 alt., 75 pop.), is a small roadside community, once a railroad station near the parent town of Highland. Called Highland Station, it was promoted during the winter of 1869–1870 by a company of railroad owners and investors from Highland. When the railroad was discontinued, Highland Station declined. The remaining citizens of the town in 1933 took a new name in honor of John Sparks, pioneer leader.

Right from Sparks on State 7 is EAGLE SPRINGS (*medicinal waters, swimming pool*), 4.5 m., a health and pleasure resort locally noted for the beauty of nearby bluffs.

IOWA POINT, 6.3 m. (795 alt., 75 pop.), on the western edge of the broad valley, was once the largest Kansas town on the Missouri River. It was founded in 1855 on land given to the Reverend S. W. Irvin by the Iowa Indians. Within a year it had an estimated population of 3,000, but the intense partisan strife between Free State and proslavery settlers soon disrupted the town's commercial life. In 1857 it began an abrupt decline. Iowa Point was a station on a branch of the Burlington R.R. between Sparks and Rulo, Nebr., until the line was abandoned in 1933. State 7 follows the old roadbed along the west bank of the Missouri River. The town now consists of but a few houses and stores and the abandoned railroad station.

WHITE CLOUD, 11.3 m. (1,037 alt., 476 pop.), an old river town facing the wide sweep of the curving Missouri River, has a background of tall wooded bluffs. This village, named for a chief of the Iowa tribe of Indians, was developed by booster chicanery and ballyhoo typical of many boom towns in Kansas. In 1856 John Utt and Enoch Spaulding, two of a group of promoters from Oregon, Mo., expecting that all the Indian lands would be available for purchase that year, selected the present site of White Cloud for a town and pre-empted it, although it was still owned by the Indians. The company had $45,000 in paid-up capital stock and started to erect a town; but one of the members, R. J. Gatling (who later invented the Gatling gun), pointed out that if they built their city on the Indians' land, the Indians could legally sell it to rival investors. So they delayed extensive improvements until the time when they could buy the land. The settlement had a ferry landing, a store, a frame house, and several log shacks when in June 1857, the promoters purchased the site from the United States Government. They announced a great auction sale of town lots for July 4; advertised a barbecue, plenty of liquor, band music, dancing, and patriotic oratory, and arranged steamboat excursions from other Missouri River towns. Actors, bartenders, barbers, and circus "spielers" were hired to impersonate investors. The "sooners" who had come to the townsite and recklessly put up buildings without acquiring title to the lots, lost their property in the auction. When a desirable lot was put up for sale, the town owners' employees outbid the building's owners, so that the promoters, by buying from themselves and paying the money to themselves, acquired all the sooners' buildings free, retained the most desirable lots, and permitted the outsiders to buy the adjoining property. The *bona fide* sales amounted to $23,798; sales of food, whiskey, and steamboat tickets to 6,000 visitors amounted to a similar sum. Thus the promoters netted a profit of $30,000 or $40,000, still had their $45,000 of capital, and owned the best lots in town.

After the decline of Iowa Point, White Cloud succeeded its downstream neighbor as the river metropolis of Doniphan County, but suffered a slump when railroad development ruined the steamboat traffic on the Missouri. Sol Miller founded the White Cloud *Chief* here in 1857. An old BRICK BUILDING (L), at the western end of the business district, was built by Miller in the late 1860's and occupied by the *Chief* until the paper was moved to the county seat in 1872. It is now occupied by a grocery store. On the side of a hill overlooking the business district one block (R) from Main St. is the POULET HOUSE *(private)*, a pretentious three-story structure of red brick, built in 1880 by Alexis Poulet, White Cloud banker. It is a garish blend of Victorian and French architecture, with a gabled cupola rising above the roof and balconies of iron grillwork in the rear at the second and third floors. Poulet, a Frenchman from New Orleans, settled at Iowa Point and conducted a profitable mercantile business; he came to White Cloud in 1858. His son, Acton Poulet, who was born and reared here, served as representative of an American oil company in the Orient from 1909 until 1922 when he was appointed United States Consul at Saignon, French Indo-China. The building is used as a rooming house by its present owner.

Right from Main St., 0.4 *m.* on a winding drive up a steep incline to the CREST OF A BLUFF that affords a view of three States—Kansas, Missouri, and Nebraska—and of the Missouri River, which flows 200 feet below. The White Cloud area contains many Indian burial mounds and ruins of villages built by the Pawnee and the Kansa (Kaw).

HIGHLAND, 26.2 *m.* (856 alt., 788 pop.), a quiet, old-fashioned town amid green hills, is the seat of the Presbyterian Church in Kansas and the home of the oldest institution of higher learning in the State.

In 1837 Highland was part of an Indian reservation for the Iowa, Sac, and Fox tribes. Two miles northeast of the present townsite was a Presbyterian mission that had been founded for the Indians by "Father Irvin" (the Reverend S. M. Irvin), a Presbyterian missionary. There were many white settlers in the region by 1854 when two promoters—Gen. John Bayless and J. P. Johnson—chose this site for a town and named it Highland.

A log school, built in the settlement in 1856, was placed shortly afterward under the control of the Highland Presbytery and named the Highland Presbyterian Academy. In response to a petition of the trustees, the Kansas Territorial Legislature in 1857 granted the school a charter under the name of HIGHLAND UNIVERSITY.

In addition to the president's residence, the plant includes a dormitory with 17 rooms; the main building, a two-story red brick structure erected in 1858, and now enlarged and modernized to house the library and conservatory; and the new college building, a two-story structure of pressed brick, which contains the president's office, auditorium, laboratories, and recitation rooms. Highland is a co-educational junior college with an annual enrollment of about 150.

Near the center of town is the HIGHLAND PRESBYTERIAN CHURCH, a plain, substantial structure, built in 1914 to replace a frame building erected in the late 1880's and destroyed by fire in October 1913. The church traces its origin to the old Presbyterian mission where it was organized in 1843 with a membership of six persons. The Reverend S. M. Irvin was its first minister.

HIAWATHA, 40.8 m. (1,095 alt., 3,302 pop.), seat of Brown County, set among fruit trees and flower gardens, is one of the most beautiful towns on the Kansas prairies.

Its sky line is dominated by an attractive courthouse designed in the Greek Revival style. Hiawatha is one of the few Territorial boom towns that survived and prospered after Kansas had become a State. Founded in 1857, it became the seat of Brown County in 1859 and has grown steadily since.

The annual Hiawatha Hallowe'en Frolic was organized by Mrs. John Kerbs, an early resident, to stop the Hallowe'en pranks played on her by youngsters. The feature of the event is a parade, usually two or three miles long, which includes comedians hired by the chamber of commerce, competitive flower floats, and exhibitions by local boys and girls. After the parade a dance is held in the city auditorium.

Hiawatha's Fall Festival, usually held in September, includes agricultural exhibits, a street carnival, and dances. An annual flower show, also originated by Mrs. Kerbs and sponsored by the Hiawatha Chamber of Commerce, is held later in the fall.

In the HIAWATHA MORRILL FREE LIBRARY is a small HISTORICAL MUSEUM (open 2-5; 7-9; except Sun. and holidays).

In MOUNT HOPE CEMETERY at the southeast edge of Hiawatha, is the DAVIS MEMORIAL, an unusual monument with a vault, pavilion and eleven life-size portrait statues, carved in Italian marble. It was erected, after his wife's death, by John M. Davis, a retired farmer. Davis, who is still living (1938), expects to be buried beside his wife.

The first pair of statues shows the Davis couple newly wedded. The next four sets show them at later stages in their married life. The last set of portraits—before the death of Mrs. Davis—reveals the couple as aged and weary, but sitting very erect on over-stuffed parlor armchairs of marble. Mrs. Davis' hair, still abundant and wavy, is combed back and fastened in a Psyche knot. Her husband of 50 years has heavy hair and a flowing beard.

The final statue, of granite instead of marble, shows Mr. Davis sitting alone in his great armchair beside which stands another bearing the legend The Vacant Chair. Here the old lover, apparently past 80, has shaggy eyebrows, a longer beard than before, and looks like the portraits of George Bernard Shaw. The ten marble statues were carved in Rome by Italian artists who were sent photographs of Mr. and Mrs. Davis. The final granite image of the husband was done by a Vermont sculptor. This couple, whose married life is so enduringly recorded, had no children.

Hiawatha is at the junction with US 73 (see Tour 12A).

FAIRVIEW, 52.1 m. (1,240 alt., 367 pop.), is a comparatively modern and thriving agricultural trade center with a small hotel in the center of town and a TOURIST CAMP on US 36 just outside the city limits.

At Fairview is the southern junction with US 75 *(see Tour 11).* Between Fairview and Sabetha, US 36 and US 75 are one route.

SABETHA, 59.2 *m.* (1,300 alt., 2,332 pop.), an agricultural trading point, has well-kept homes and a neat business district. According to legend, the town was named by a pious Biblical student who reached this point in the 1850's on his way to California. One of his oxen died here on a day which he calculated to be the Hebrew Sabbath—so he named his camp Sabetha.

The genesis of Sabetha, however, was a settlement called Albany Hill, established in 1857 by pioneers from Castle Creek, N. Y., who named it for the capital of their native State. Albany Hill was two miles north of Camp Sabetha, but when a railroad was built through the county in 1871 and a station erected at the old camp site, Albany Hill's inhabitants moved to the more advantageous place.

In the SABETHA POST OFFICE is a mural by Albert T. Reid, former resident of Concordia, Kans., which depicts a stagecoach and a Pony Express rider.

Right from Sabetha on an improved road is ALBANY, 2.2 *m.,* remnant of a Free State town. The two-story frame house with a hip roof (L) was an important station on the Underground Railroad. John Brown, the violent abolitionist, is said to have spent his last night (February 1, 1859) in the Territory of Kansas at Albany.

Left from Sabetha on an improved road is the SITE OF LOG CHAIN TAVERN, 15 *m.,* on what is now Log Chain Farm, beside the route of the old Fort Leavenworth military road. The tavern was named for a nearby road so boggy that a log chain was frequently used to pull out vehicles caught in the mire. In 1858 Mark Twain and Horace Greeley were guests at the tavern, which was noted throughout the West for its hospitality. Just before the Civil War it was used by John Brown and Jim Lane as a station on the Underground Railroad. Local legend has it that Abraham Lincoln and William H. Seward spent a night at the tavern in the late autumn of 1859. Most historians discredit this, however, and insist that Lincoln was never this far west.

LAKE SABETHA *(fishing, free picnic and campground),* 65.5 *m.* (R), covering 115 acres, was built in 1936 with the help of Federal funds as a town water supply. It is surrounded by natural forest land.

ONEIDA, 68.5 *m.* (1,217 alt., 224 pop.), was founded in 1873 by Col. Cyrus Shinn of Virginia on a plot of 400 acres purchased for the promotion of a great city. Sixty-four years after its founding it had increased its first recorded population by only ten or twelve inhabitants.

Colonel Shinn gave a free lot to everyone who would settle here, but forbade the sale of liquor, thus creating one of the first prohibition towns in Kansas. Its original name of Shinntown was changed to Oneida as soon as the colonel died.

SENECA, 75.3 *m.* (1,150 alt., 1,864 pop.), seat of Nemaha County, on the banks of the sluggish Nemaha River, is very similar in appearance to Sabetha; its sky line is dominated by church spires.

Seneca was founded in 1857 to rival Richmond, a town three miles away on a feeder of the Oregon Trail, also called the California Trail. Seneca boosters planted oats in a section of the trail and detoured it through their town. When the oats came up with the first spring grasses, the old trail had the appearance of having been abandoned. Thus immigrant traffic was brought to Seneca. A few years later, when a Pony Express station was established here, and later when this became an Overland stage depot, Richmond people moved to Seneca.

In 1921–1922 Seneca was the home of Jean Harlow, the platinum blonde motion-picture actress. Miss Harlow (then Harlean Carpenter) attended the elementary school.

The old SMITH HOTEL, at the corner of S. Main and 4th Sts., is a two-story building, now a rooming house. This structure, moved from the corner of N. Main and 7th Sts., was an inn serving both Pony Express riders and passengers on the Overland stages.

Three feeders of the Oregon-California Trail either met or crossed in the vicinity of Seneca. One from St. Joseph crossed Baker's Ford, a few miles north of town; another ran directly west through Seneca to Marysville; and the Fort Leavenworth Military Road came in just west of town.

Left from Seneca on State 63, graveled, to the junction with a dirt road, 1 *m.*; L. here to MAXWELL SPRINGS, 1.2 *m.*, once a watering place on the old Overland Trail, now the Seneca city water supply. Nearby are ruts left by early day covered wagons.

On State 63 at 5.5 *m.* is the NEMAHA COUNTY STATE PARK, including 582 acres of natural woodland and a 356-acre lake *(fishing)*.

BAILEYVILLE, 80.1 *m.* (1,293 alt., 636 pop.), a little prairie town founded in 1880 and settled largely by Germans, was formerly known as Haytown because it was a shipping place for prairie hay.

At 94.6 *m.* is the junction with an improved road, State 99.

Right on State 99 is BEATTIE, 1 *m.* (1,292 alt., 434 pop.), one of the first towns in Kansas to have a city government composed entirely of women (1899). Home of the late Linden Kirlin, inventor of farm implements, it is interesting for its huge limestone quarry.

An old PONY EXPRESS BARN, 4 *m.*, is a sturdy structure built of local granite.

MARYSVILLE, 106.8 *m.* (1,154 alt., 4,013 pop.) *(see Tour 10)*, is at the junction with US 77 *(see Tour 10)*.

At 110.1 *m.* is the junction with an improved road.

Right on this road is BREMEN, 4 *m.* (1,327 alt., 82 pop.), a tiny community of decaying old buildings of German architectural influence.

Left from Bremen on a dirt road to the PONY EXPRESS STATION, 7.5 *m.*, now a farmhouse. The house, a frame structure, is weathered and dilapidated, its unpainted siding warped and sagging, its windows askew. Beside it is a stable of stone with a wooden loft whose hewn timbers reveal the marks of a broad axe, although they are now blackened with age and honeycombed with dry rot. From this mow, hay has been forked down to horses for more than 75 years.

West of Marysville a short series of hills borders the highway. On one of these hills is a large boulder, visible for a long distance. It is said to have served as a trail marker for Indians.

At 117.8 *m.* is the junction with State 15E, improved.

Right on State 15E is HANOVER, 3 *m.* (1,232 alt., 880 pop.), a village of scattered houses and stores resembling the outskirts of a large city. Hanover, most of whose settlers came from Germany, was founded in 1869 and incorporated as a third-class city in 1872. It was named for the former home of its first settler, G. H. Hollenburg, who was for years its leading citizen. The Days of Forty-Nine celebration, most important event of the year locally, is sponsored by the Hanover Business Men's Club and lasts for three days. To advertise it, local men allow their whiskers to grow and the women wear old-fashioned sunbonnets.

Hanover was, for a time, the home of Prof. Don Carlos Taft, father of Lorado Taft (1860–1936), the sculptor, who frequently visited his parents here. Hamlin Garland, the author, was married to the sculptor's sister, Zuline Taft, in Hanover in 1899.

In the city park is the usual PONY EXPRESS MONUMENT, a block of granite four feet tall bearing a Pony Express marker. In the Hanover Cemetery is a MONUMENT TO G. H. HOLLENBURG, a bluish-gray shaft capped with a large granite ball. Hollenburg was appointed to the Emigrant Counsel in 1874. He died and was buried at sea en route to Germany in July of that year.

The NEUGEBAUER ROCK GARDEN (open) is 60 feet wide and 100 feet long. Relics in this garden include Indian rubbing stones, skin scrapers, and a totem pole; also specimens of petrified wood from thirteen States. In the center of the garden is a 3,000-pound rock castle modeled by the owner from a picture of a medieval European fortress.

In the HANOVER HERALD PLANT is a collection of relics from the former Hanover House, a stagecoach tavern built in 1870 and operated until 1880 when State prohibition drove many of its patrons to Nebraska. Noted for its good food the Hanover House sheltered hundreds of wealthy Germans seeking land in the new country. In the eleven volumes of its register, included in the *Herald* collection, are the names of many who played leading parts in the development of Kansas and Nebraska. Two dinner bells from the Hanover House have holes worn in the side by their "Dongers" or clappers.

The old RANCH HOUSE OF C. H. HOLLENBURG, 5.4 *m.*, was built in late 1850's. This long narrow structure, first known as Cottonwood Ranch, was a stagecoach depot visited by Mormons in their trek westward to Utah. Around the house, where the prairie has never been plowed, are ruts left by wagons on the overland trail.

The Nebraska Line is at 12 *m.;* L. here on a dirt road to a granite OREGON TRAIL MARKER, 15 *m.*, at the place where Washington County, Kans., adjoins Gage and Jefferson Counties, Nebr. Triangularly shaped, each of its sides faces one of the counties.

WASHINGTON, 129 *m.* (1335 alt., 1,370 pop.), is built around the strikingly attractive WASHINGTON COUNTY COURTHOUSE, one of the few civic buildings in Kansas designed in the modern style. It was built in 1933 at a cost of $87,500 after the old courthouse and sections of the business and residence districts had been destroyed by a cyclone, July 4, 1932. Because most of the population had gathered in the city park for a celebration when the storm struck, the property destruction was not accompanied by a heavy loss of life. After the storm Washington enjoyed a building boom at the expense of insurance companies.

Largely an agricultural shipping and trading center, Washington's main industry is the manufacture of butter and cheese. These products are shipped to cities in Kansas and Nebraska.

Washington was founded in the 1860's by a company of townsite promoters who named the town in honor of the first President of the United States. The country around Washington was first explored by the S. H. Long expedition in 1820.

The COUNTY HOME for the dependent aged, S. 2nd St., two blocks west of the First National Bank, a two-story white frame house, is the boyhood home of Paul Swan, chief mechanical engineer of the Byrd expedition to the South Pole.

A county stock show is held at Washington annually in September.

Left from Washington on State 15W, a graveled road, is ASH CREEK, 2.5 *m.* Near the bridge is MORMON SPRING, one of the many small springs in the bed of the creek. Mormon Spring is identified by a large sandstone rock, on which is carved a wagon wheel and the names of numerous Latter Day Saints who stopped here for water in the middle 1850's while on their way to Utah.

MORROWVILLE, 139.4 *m.* (1,335 alt., 246 pop.), founded in 1884, was named for its founder, Cal Morrow, State Senator (1876–1890). Until 1896 the town was called Morrow, but its name was changed to Morrowville after the railroad company had complained that its ticket agents were confused when travelers asked for "a ticket to Morrow (tomorrow)."

At 160 *m.* is the junction with an improved road.

Left on this road is CUBA, 2 *m.* (1,577 alt., 403 pop.), often called the Bohemian capital of Kansas because it is the center of the largest Bohemian colony in the State. Its main street, modernized only by filling stations and SOKOL HALL, has nearly all the buildings that were put up when the town was founded in 1884. Saturday night in Cuba is reminiscent of one in an Old World village. Hundreds of farm folk sit in parked cars to drink beer and eat sausage, laughing, and talking in English and Bohemian. Some of them smoke their long, curved-stemmed Bohemian pipes, while orchestral strains float out from the dance floor in Sokol Hall.

Cuba was founded by Bohemians and Swedes in 1873 approximately 2 miles south and west of the present townsite, but residents moved their store buildings and homes in order to be on the railroad when the Burlington and Missouri River built through here in the middle 1880's. In Cuba the various racial stocks and sectional cultures include Bohemians, Swedes, Scotch, Irish, Spanish, French Canadians, and Yankees from Massachusetts and Vermont.

Every winter, series of plays are presented by the third and fourth generations of the Bohemian residents. The players take particular pride in being letter perfect in the Bohemian language.

BELLEVILLE, 166.5 *m.* (1,514 alt., 2,383 pop.) *(see Tour 9),* is at the junction with US 81 *(see Tour 9).*

Section b. BELLEVILLE *to* COLORADO LINE, *253.5 m.,* US 36

The country between Belleville, 0 *m.,* and Phillipsburg is a continuation of the high, rolling Blue Hills Uplands. West of Phillipsburg, in the High Plains region, the landscape becomes smooth and monotonous; marks of erosion are less frequent, and watercourses are rare. This is still in the corn belt, though much wheat is also raised in spite of periodic droughts.

Between Oberlin and Atwood the rugged country is the result of erosion; green cactus and Spanish bayonet pierce the whiteness of rimrock arroyos and magnesium limestone hills. Cut through hillsides and bridged over canyons, the highway resembles a Roman aqueduct in a region of foothills.

West of Atwood the terrain levels out into a high, flat plain.

SCANDIA, 10 *m.* (1,530 alt., 608 pop.), an agrarian market town with a poultry hatchery as its principal industrial plant, was founded in the late 1860's by a Swedish immigrant company from Chicago, Ill., and settled by a colony of Scandinavians. Most of the Swedes have moved elsewhere and Scandia is now inhabited by descendants of native-born Americans.

In the P. T. STROM HOME *(open)* is a small but interesting COLLEC-
TION OF INDIAN RELICS, old guns, and miscellaneous pieces.

The Fort Riley to Fort Kearny (Nebr.) military road, used by Federal
troops sent out to fight Indians, once crossed what is now Scandia.

On a hill just east of Scandia are the marked GRAVES OF NINETEEN
IMMIGRANT MORMONS, killed here in an Indian battle.

COURTLAND, 17.1 *m.* (1,501 alt., 430 pop.), a small, neat village,
like Scandia, was settled largely by Swedes. Its name was originally
spelled "Cortland." It was incorporated as a third-class city in 1892, and
is now important only as a railroad shipping point.

1. Right from Courtland on a dirt road to the junction with another dirt road,
7.5 *m.;* L. here to the SWIHART EXPERIMENTAL FARM *(visitors welcome)*, 14 *m.*
As many as 1,500 different crops have been raised here in a single year; specimens
of these crops are frequently displayed at exhibitions throughout Kansas.

2. Left from Courtland on a dirt road to the junction with another dirt road,
6 *m.;* R. on this road to REPUBLIC COUNTY STATE PARK *(hunting, fishing,
picnicking)*, 6.5 *m.* Its lake, comprising 700 acres, is maintained by the State Fish
and Game Commission but unlike most Kansas State- and county-controlled lakes,
shooting is allowed on part of the reserve.

FORMOSO, 23.2 *m.* (1,515 alt., 381 pop.), is a typical western Kansas
railroad town, partly shielded from the constant prairie winds by a low
range of hills to the northwest. It was founded in the late 1870's and
named Omio, the lament used by Indians who were forced by settlers to
abandon their tribal camping ground on this site. When a railroad came
in 1884 the town was given its present name.

MANKATO, 34.4 *m.* (1,787 alt., 1,404 pop.), seat of Jewell County,
in an attractive setting of evergreen, ash, and elm trees, is the market center for a highly productive grain and livestock area.

The JEWELL COUNTY COURTHOUSE, three stories high, of modern design and constructed of local limestone, is the work of Joseph W. Radotinsky of Kansas City, former State architect. It was completed in 1938 as a
WPA project, costing $125,000.

The original name, Jewell Center, was changed to Mankato shortly
after the town's founding, to avoid confusion between this and Jewell
City, an older town in the same county.

US 36 enters the LIMESTONE VALLEY SOIL EROSION PROJECT
at 41.5 *m.* where demonstrations of several methods of erosion control are
being conducted in a district 22 miles long and 15 miles wide. Five hundred drought-stricken farmers have been given work here, and more than
$500,000 in Federal funds have been expended.

SMITH CENTER, 65.3 *m.* (1,804 alt., 1,736 pop.), seat of Smith
County, varies the usual courthouse-square pattern of western county-seat
towns by scattering pioneer business buildings and residences along a
mile-long street. The old red brick structure housing the weekly *Pioneer*
exposes blank walls along a side street in the same block with the modern
tapestry-brick Community Hall and City Library.

L. T. Reese, a founder of the town and an organizer of the county,
still lives (1938) in Smith Center, and takes great pleasure in telling with

utmost frankness his version of the town's history: "I was advised by older heads to take a homestead in the exact center of the county with the aim of making it the county seat. I came here with a partner and we filed on 320 acres at a time when the only settlements in the county were along the Solomon River in the southwestern part of the county. The little town of Cedarville on that river expected to be the county seat."

To create a county the legislature had to designate the county area and give it a name. Then a minimum of 600 *bona fide* settlers, who had established residences, "organized" the county—that is, appointed temporary county officers and set up a temporary county seat. Bonds were next issued to pay salaries and build roads, bridges, and a courthouse.

"A dozen of us settlers went to Topeka to see the Governor and organize the county," continues Reese, "but when we were admitted to his presence we were informed that a dozen settlers were not enough; it required hundreds. We left the Governor's office very dejected, but were accosted by a man who said: 'Why don't you put the names of all your friends in the East on the list as *bona fide* settlers, then organize Smith County and go home and wait for these settlers to come?' We had a terrible task in thinking up 600 names, but finally we got it done. Then we appointed our county officers and went back to have the Governor confirm them . . . but we found that our three county commissioners all lived in one district. We had to have one from each of three districts, and we didn't have any men in the other two districts. We were disheartened again and were ready to go home beaten until someone promised that if we would pay a certain cash honorarium to him we could falsify the residences of two of our members to conform to law, and he would guarantee that the Governor would not notice the irregularity. . . . We had the money, so we paid, and went home with the county organization; my farm was the county seat."

In the SMITH CENTER LIBRARY is a small HISTORICAL MUSEUM *(open 9-5 weekdays)*, containing a chair made of cottonwood by the town's first settler, and a drawing of a "clog and chunk" fence invented by a Smith County pioneer, Phil Breon, and used on his farm in lieu of barbwire. The "clog and chunk" fence consisted of a single strand of wire suspended between two posts. A cord about ten feet long, attached to the wire with a slip knot, would, when fastened to the right forefeet of horses or cattle, allow the animals to graze the length of the wire. An ox yoke and other implements that belonged to the "clog and chunk" fence inventor are also in the museum.

The words of "Home on the Range," voted a "hit" tune in 1934 and once described in a press conference by President Franklin D. Roosevelt as his favorite ballad, were written in 1873 by Dr. Brewster Higley who homesteaded a claim on Beaver Creek in Smith County. Dan Kelly who lived near the town of Harlan in the same county composed the music. "Home on the Range" became locally popular; it was played by dance orchestras and sung around cowboy campfires. So far as is known, both words and music were first published in 1910 in *Songs of the Cattle Trail and Cow Camp,* compiled by John A. Lomax. In 1934 William Goodwin and his wife, of Tempe, Arizona, filed suit in the United States District Court of New York against radio networks and motion-picture producers. The Goodwins asked damages amounting to $500,000, claiming that they had written and copyrighted "Home on the Range" in 1905 under the title "My Arizona Home." The defendants instructed their attorney, Samuel Moanfeldt, to find out who really wrote it. Moanfeldt discovered that Lomax had learned the song from the lips of cowboys, so he went to Dodge City, Kans., and interviewed old-timers who made affidavit that they had sung the song in 1880, more than 25 years before Goodwin claimed he had written it. Still seeking the real author Moanfeldt traveled through Arizona, New Mexico, California, Nevada, Utah, Idaho, and Oregon before, on the advice of a Kansas woman, he came in 1936 to Smith Center and was directed to the home of Clarence (Cal) Harlan, then 87 years old. Mrs. Harlan is a sister-in-law of Dan Kelly; Harlan, at the age of 24, was the first to sing the song in public.

"Pa," said Mrs. Harlan, "get down your guitar and let's see if we can't sing it for the gentleman." Accompanying themselves on guitar and banjo the old couple sang the song as they had first sung it 63 years before. While they sang, the lawyer turned to their neighbors and said: "This proves the point. I've got that lawsuit beaten."

He photographed the old couple and made a phonographic recording of their singing. This record, together with the testimony of forty of their neighbors, proved that the song had belonged to Smith County before it belonged to the Nation at large.

At 66.1 *m.* is the junction with a private dirt road *(visitors may enter).*

Right on this road is PLASTER'S CASTLE *(unoccupied),* and the SITE OF SITTING BULL'S FORT, 1.5 *m.* Generations before white men came to Kansas, this point was a center of trade between Indian tribes. Flint knives and arrowheads were fashioned here and the Indians made a lodge of a soapstone mound by hollowing it out with flint tools. In 1867, when Sitting Bull leagued many Midwestern Indian tribes for a last stand against the whites, this stone lodge was converted into a fort and used as a hiding place for steel arrowheads, scalping knives, and guns that had been illegally sold to the Indians by manufacturers' agents. A deadline extending southwest to the desert and northeast to Canada ran through the fort. Sitting Bull warned white settlers not to cross that line. There are some old-timers in Smith Center who remember Sitting Bull's ultimatum.

After the Indians had been subdued and put on reservations, this tract was homesteaded in 1872 by William A. Plaster, who dreamed of building a castle. Making his home in the old soapstone dugout, Plaster began working on his quixotic project. When it was only one-story high his funds failed, so he abandoned his dream of turreted towers and roofed the building over. Rectangular in shape with a flat roof, Plaster's Castle, once the largest building in Smith County, relieves the monotony of a desolate hillside.

At 69.3 *m.* is the junction with a dirt road.

Right on this road is REAMSVILLE, 11 *m.* (1,812 alt., 27 pop.), a decadent prairie hamlet with an old DUTCH MILL that dominates the landscape for miles around. Built of hand-hewn beams, this mill was started in 1882 by Charles G. Schwartz. It had cogwheels of wood and fans with a spread of 72 feet. When operating, it ground corn meal and graham flour on a toll basis for local farmers.

PHILLIPSBURG, 95.3 *m.* (1,939 alt., 1,543 pop.), seat of Phillips County, has a courthouse square with an oasis-like park irrigated by the streams and springs that furnish the town's water supply.

Phillipsburg was named for Col. William A. Phillips, early day writer, politician, and colonel of the Cherokee regiment of the Civil War. Designated as the county seat by the Kansas Legislature, Phillipsburg was platted in 1872 and incorporated as a third-class city in 1880.

This region averages only 18 inches of rain annually, but the rich black topsoil in Phillips County is underlain with a deep porous clay which stores water like a sponge. Consequently, there are green fields of corn around Phillipsburg when the corn in other parts of Kansas has been seared by the sun.

Two blocks south of the Bissel Hotel is the WINSHOP ROCK GARDEN AND LOG CABIN *(open)*, built by an 83-year-old man to resemble the foothills of the Rocky Mountains in miniature. The landscape contains figures of antelope, deer, elk, coyotes, and bears; toy swans and frogs float on the ponds; in the lakes are live fish. At night the rock garden is illuminated by colored electric lights.

Two blocks east of Main St. on the highway (R) is still another ROCK GARDEN *(open)*, unusual for its massive rocks rather than its plants. It was built by a local railroadman.

A SWIMMING POOL *(free)*, at the west edge of Phillipsburg, is filled with natural salt water—the remnant of a prehistoric sea left bottled up in a clay bed.

The annual rodeo *(1st week in Aug.)*, attracts about 14,000 people who camp near the town in order to admire the roping, riding, or bull-dogging of longhorn steers, or be amused by the lassoing of jackrabbits. Contestants come from Wyoming and Montana to display their skill.

At 97.3 *m.* US 36 crosses a TIME ZONE BOUNDARY. West of this point Mountain Standard Time is used; watches of west-bound tourists should be set back one hour.

FORT BISSEL (R), 100.8 *m.*, a rough rock structure, was hurriedly erected in the spring of 1873 when the commander of Fort Hays sent a military scout to warn settlers that warring Apache might be expected any hour. The Apache, however, did not attack.

At 122.4 *m.* is the junction with US 83 *(see Tour 8)*. Between this place and a point at 135.2 *m.* US 36 and US 83 are one route.

At 123.9 *m.* is the junction with an improved road which traverses a spacious lawn of buffalo grass lined with trees and flowers.

Right on this road is the STATE TUBERCULOSIS SANITARIUM *(permission to visit is granted in the administration building, first building from the road)*, 0.3 *m.*, opened in 1913, as a sixteen-bed hospital. It was built by the State on land purchased by citizens of Norton. It now includes an administration building, a 268-bed hospital, a power plant, a greenhouse, several barns, and other farm buildings.

NORTON, 129 *m.* (2,275 alt., 2,767 pop.), seat of Norton County, is the center of a large agricultural and dairying region. Its buildings are modern and its business district consists of several streets.

Norton had its beginning in Billingsville, a town founded by and named for N. H. Billings. In the same year that Billingsville was platted (1872), it was designated as a temporary county seat by means of a fraudulent petition. Settlers later organized the Norton Town Company and laid out Norton about 500 yards northeast of Billingsville. The town company's plat was erroneously recorded. W. B. Rogers, who owned an adjoining tract, attempted to file it as the town of Norton. In the long court fight that followed, many irregularities in the town company's records were found. At the conclusion of the case Billingsville was forced to reorganize and file its plat as an addition to the town of Norton.

The NORTON MANUFACTURING COMPANY IRON FOUNDRY *(open on application)*, casting farm-machinery parts, has an international market.

ELMWOOD PARK *(scenic drives, wading pools, picnic grounds)*, one block east and two blocks south of the post office, is bounded on the south by Prairie Dog Creek. Comprising forty-five acres, this park was built by Federal relief labor at a cost of more than $30,000. The Norton County Fair, which attracts large crowds from all parts of northwestern Kansas, is held here annually the first week in September.

At the southern edge of Norton is a SWIMMING POOL *(open daily in summer)*, a roller-skating rink, and a dance pavilion *(dances 1 to 4 nights weekly)*.

At the northern edge of town, beside the Norton Cemetery, is the junction with a dirt road.

Left on this road is ROBINSON DRAW, 1 *m.*, which extends northwest and southeast along the creek at this point. It was here that W. W. Robinson settled with his family in 1873. While building the large, stone ROBINSON HOUSE (R) near the road, the family lived in a nearby dugout. Southwest of the house, on top of a bluff is a NATURAL ROCK WELL *(permission to visit granted at stone house)*, discovered by W. W. Robinson while he was quarrying stone. This narrow crevice, walled by rock, always contains from 8 to 10 feet of water and is believed to have its source in an underground watercourse.

NORCATUR, 147.3 *m.* (2,631 alt., 524 pop.), a wind-swept village of the High Plains, is dominated by a large red brick building (L), the Norcatur Rural High School.

First named Rockwell City, the village was founded a short distance northeast of its present site by a shrewd pioneer woman, Mrs. William Rockwell. When the Lincoln Land Company purchased a townsite southeast of her unsuccessful Rockwell City, Mrs. Rockwell, learning that the company was allied with the railroads and purchased townsites only where the railroads planned to have stations, abandoned Rockwell City and was among the first to buy lots in the new townsite, called Norcatur because of its proximity to the Norton-Decatur County line.

In 1878, just after a band of Cheyenne under Chief Dull Knife had gone on the warpath, a young man riding a sweating horse dashed into Norcatur, waving a bloody hand.

"The Indians! The Indians!" he shouted, as he spurred his horse.

The settlers converted the sod house of Isaac Whitaker into Fort Whitaker; a log cabin belonging to Sidney Case, hastily equipped with one gun and several pitchforks, became Fort Case. The women and children were crowded into these two "forts." Captains Case and Whitaker began drilling the men for action. Told to extinguish the lights when they heard any loud noise, the women mistook Captain Whitaker's authoritative commands to his men for the shouts of attacking savages.

"The yelling of those women would have put a pack of coyotes to shame," one old-timer averred. "We had to go shut 'em up 'fore we could go on with our drills."

After three tense days it was learned that the young man who gave the alarm had accidentally wounded himself with his gun while drunk. The Indians were a product of his imagination. Somewhat sheepishly, the citizens resumed their daily routine.

Norcatur is the home of Eldon Auker, American League pitcher and a former Kansas State College athlete.

In the OBERLIN CEMETERY (L), 164.1 *m.,* a granite monument commemorates the settlers killed in the LAST INDIAN MASSACRE IN KANSAS. In September 1878, Cheyenne led by Chief Dull Knife murdered more than a score of persons, including six members of the Laing family, whose rude tombstones of native rock are near the monument.

OBERLIN, 165.5 *m.* (2,561 alt., 1,629 pop.), seat of Decatur County, is an up-to-date, prosperous hillside village of substantial buildings. Its residents possess the friendliness and cordiality typical of the West.

SMICK MEMORIAL PARK *(athletic field, picnic grounds and playgrounds),* at the southeastern edge of town, three blocks east of the courthouse, is named in honor of E. B. (Cal) Smick, an educator in the community. Landscaped and planted with shrubs, flowers, and trees, the 10-acre park is in pleasing contrast wtih its semiarid surroundings.

The annual Armistice Day celebration here includes track events and baseball or football games. A pavement dance in the evening completes the activities.

Right from Oberlin on US 183 is the 481-acre DECATUR COUNTY STATE PARK NO. 2 *(fishing),* 1.5 *m.,* with a 160-acre stocked lake.

Many sheep and cattle graze on the hilly pastureland that surrounds Oberlin. The most prolific form of vegetation is the Russian thistle, a blessing in time of drought when no other green succulent herb will flourish. During such periods the young plants are eaten by cattle, made into ensilage, and cut for hay. The mature thistles are too woody and thorny to be grazed or cut for hay. They assume a rounded bushy shape, break from their roots in the fall, and, impelled by the wind, go rolling and bouncing over the plains, dropping seeds from their pods. Sometimes this briery bush is as tall as a man and 3 feet thick. Where the highway is sunken the thistles will drift into the cut, cling together like a barbwire entanglement, and make the road impassable till they are burned.

In February 1909, residents report that a severe windstorm piled thistles high on the streets of Oberlin and buried one house to a depth of 20 feet. Only the chimneys were visible above the stack of tinder-dry thistles. Members of the family were afraid to light their breakfast fire, lest the sparks fly from the chimney and ignite the pile. After the storm had

LAMBS FATTENED FOR THE STATE FAIR

abated, neighbors with spades and corn knives chopped a tunnel through the thistles and rescued the marooned family.

Throughout the countryside the barbwire fences catch masses of weeds. These present such resistance to a strong wind that posts are sometimes snapped off in a gale.

ATWOOD, 193.9 m. (2,843 alt., 1,166 pop.), seat of Rawlins County, was founded in 1878, a mile and a half northeast of its present site, and named for Atwood Matheny, son of the town's founder. It was moved in 1880. In 1885 it was plunged into the inevitable county-seat fight, ultimately defeating the rival village of Blakeman.

The township made 100-acre LAKE ATWOOD *(boating, fishing)*, by building a dam across South Beaver Creek.

A Tourist Camp (R), 203.6 m., exhibits the works of a former cowboy and old settler of Atwood who paints landscapes in ready-mixed house paint. The tourist camp also has specimens of local "bastard" granite, so-called because geologists cannot account for its presence in sedimentary formations.

McDONALD, 214.2 m. (3,369 alt., 442 pop.), a quiet village of colorless frame houses, was established as a railroad boom town in 1887 by R. L. McDonald, the ranchman who owned the land. The Rawlins County Fair is held annually just south of McDonald. In years when the rainfall is sufficient to produce crops, this fair has good livestock and agricultural exhibitions.

Right from McDonald, on an improved road, is BONE HILL, 12 *m.*, a steep bluff, so-named for a pile of buffalo bones at its base. According to tradition, these are the bones of an entire herd of buffalo stampeded over the bluff by Indian hunters.

At 223.4 *m.* is the junction with a dirt road.

Left on this road is BIRD CITY, 0.5 *m.* (3,452 alt., 740 pop.), a village of weather-worn frame shops and houses brightened by a block of neat bungalows landscaped with shrubbery, shade trees, and well-kept lawns. A modern community hall of local stone is in the city park. The town was named for John Bird, its founder. Dr. Frank E. Townsend, author of the old age pension plan, once homesteaded here.

The FORMER HOME OF BANTY ROGERS *(private)*, SE. corner Ketchem Ave. and 5th St., a one-story frame structure, was occupied for many years by the man who taught Col. Charles A. Lindbergh aeronautics. After his trans-Atlantic flight Lindbergh flew over Bird City in his plane, the *Spirit of St. Louis,* and dropped a note of tribute to his old teacher. Rogers left Bird City in 1930, but still owns the house.

ST. FRANCIS, 238.3 *m.* (3,291 alt., 944 pop.), a rural trading and shipping point and seat of Cheyenne County, is a one-street western town. One side of this wide thoroughfare is solid with pioneer business buildings; the other has a few stores, scattered between vacant lots.

The town was founded in 1885 a few miles from its present site and called Wano. When the coming of a railroad caused the townsite to be moved it was renamed Emerson for Capt. A. L. Emerson, one of its founders. To avoid confusion with another Kansas town of the same name, this village was called St. Francis in honor of Captain Emerson's wife.

Aside from a few filling stations, a landscaped park, and an 800-seat concrete stadium, St. Francis has changed but little since 1888 when it was selected as the county seat. Most of the inhabitants are descended from the Protestant Germans, the Russo-Germans (Mennonites), and the Bohemians who settled the town in the middle 1880's.

The climax of the wars with the Plains Indians in Kansas came in 1868, in the Battle of Beecher Island on the Arikaree, just across the Colorado Line from Cheyenne County. Gen. William T. Sherman, hearing that Indians were entering northwestern Kansas, ordered Col. George A. Forsyth, with fifty men, to turn them back.

After pursuing the Indians for five days, the party camped on the north bank of the Arikaree River, opposite small, sandy Beecher Island. Early the next morning, about a thousand Cheyenne attacked the camp. The men hastily retreated to the island, abandoning their food and equipment. In the thickest of the fighting, an arrow was driven so deeply into Scout Harrington's skull that his comrades were unable to remove it. Later a bullet fired from an Indian's gun struck the shaft and knocked it from Harrington's head.

Ringed in by the enemy, there seemed no way of escape. Colonel Forsyth twice sent scouts to summon aid from Fort Wallace, about 90 miles south. Meanwhile the besieged, their water supply depleted, cared as best they could for festering wounds and subsisted on horseflesh, much of which was putrid. The relief party arrived on the ninth day. Forty-six of Forsyth's command—half of whom were wounded—were rescued. It was estimated that the Indians lost between 700 and 800 men, among whom was the chief, Roman Nose.

A large volume of underground water flows eastward from the Rocky Mountains through the sand and gravel underlying Cheyenne County. In the ravines and river bottoms, wells 4 to 12 feet deep tap this flow, from which more than 200 miles of irrigation ditches are supplied locally.

In the vicinity of St. Francis pieces of petrified wood and fossils have been found. Many of these specimens, washed out by a flood in 1935, are on exhibit in the Kansas State Teachers' College at Hays *(see Tour 3)*.

The 13-acre lake *(fishing, boating, camping)* at 244.3 *m.* is used for irrigation as well as recreation. Despite adverse soil and climatic conditions, trees have been planted and attempts made to landscape the adjoining land.

At 253.5 *m.* US 36 crosses the Colorado Line, 171 miles east of Denver, Colo.

‹‹‹‹‹‹‹‹‹‹‹‹‹‹‹‹‹‹‹☼›››››››››››››››››››››

Tour 2

Manhattan—Clay Center—Stockton—Goodland—(Colorado Springs, Colo.); US 24.
Manhattan to Colorado Line, 335.2 m.

Union Pacific R.R. parallels route between Clay Center and Miltonvale, between Glasco and Beloit, and between Bogue and Colby; Missouri Pacific R.R. between Beloit and Stockton; Chicago, Rock Island & Pacific Ry. between Manhattan and Clay Center, and between Colby and Kanorado.
Roadbed is bituminous surfaced most of distance, paved, or oiled the remainder; open all year, except during infrequent blizzards.
Good accommodations in all county-seat towns.

Northwest of Manhattan, US 24 twists through rugged limestone hills, timber-clad and sparkling with small streams. Most of the route crosses slightly undulating pasture and wheat land. West of Hoxie are miles of level plains that seem to stretch endlessly to the level horizon, but just east of the Colorado Line the route traverses a rough hilly area.

MANHATTAN, 0 *m.* (1,012 alt., 10,136 pop.) *(see MANHAT-TAN)*.

Points of Interest: Kansas State College of Agriculture and Applied Science, experimental farms, City Park with log museum and monument to Chief Tatarrax, Amanda Arnold Arch.

Manhattan is at the junction with US 24-40 *(see Tour 3)*.

RILEY, 18.9 *m.* (1,108 alt., 431 pop.), is at the junction with US 77 *(see Tour 10)*. Between Riley and a point at 22.9 *m.* US 24 and US 77 are one route.

LEONARDVILLE, 24 *m.* (1,375 alt., 392 pop.), a quiet village on a prairie upland, is a trading center of an agricultural area. It was settled largely by Germans and Swedes in the 1860's.

CLAY CENTER, 39.7 *m.* (1,200 alt., 4,386 pop.), seat of Clay County, was named for Henry Clay. The business district is built around the courthouse square. The town has a broom factory and a toy factory that supply national markets, but its chief importance is as a shipping center for wheat, corn, hay, dairy, and poultry products.

Founded in 1862, Clay Center became the county seat in November, 1866, and in 1868 the first courthouse was built at a cost of $1,600. The Junction City and Fort Kearney R.R. reached Clay Center in 1873 and by 1880 the town had a population of almost 2,500. Disastrous floods of the Republican River, which flows south and west of the townsite, damaged Clay Center in 1903, 1915, and 1925.

DEXTER PARK *(picnic grounds, concerts every Wed. evening)*, on Grant Ave. between 6th and 7th Sts., has a MONUMENT TO THE DEXTER BROTHERS, early settlers. CITY PARK, on South 4th St., near the municipal light plant, contains a rock garden.

At the southeastern edge of Clay Center are fairgrounds where the Clay County Fair is held every year *(usually in Sept.)*.

In the courthouse square is a monument to soldiers of the Civil War, a slender slab of stone erected in 1911.

At 46.8 *m.* is the junction with a dirt road.

Left on this road is IDANA, 1 *m.* (1,253 alt., 170 pop.), dominated by two churches and a mill.

At 3 *m.* is the junction with another dirt road; L. here to FLAT TOP HILL, 4.5 *m.*, often called Table Mound. The hill was a landmark for Indians and early settlers. In the center of its butte-like peak is a spring, now used as a watering place for cattle.

MILTONVALE, 58.1 *m.* (1,378 alt., 814 pop.), was named for Milton Tootle, who founded the town in 1879. The MILTONVALE WESLEYAN COLLEGE, housed in a two-story limestone building on a knoll near the west edge of town, offers a four-year theological course, a junior college course, and complete courses in music. In 1938 this college had an enrollment of approximately 150.

At 70.5 *m.* is the junction with US 81 *(see Tour 9)*. Between this place and a point at 72.5 *m.* US 24 and US 81 are one route.

GLASCO, 80.7 *m.* (1,318 alt., 707 pop.), was founded in 1870 as Del Ray. It has a packing house, a hatchery, a creamery, and a flour mill. The Glasco Stock Show, held annually in September since 1903, and one of the most widely attended events in Cloud County, includes agricultural and household exhibits and a carnival.

Left from Glasco on an improved road, within a ROMAN CATHOLIC CEMETERY, 0.3 *m.*, is a plot reminiscent of Flanders Field, its 16 crosses aligned beneath a flagpole. The gateway to this cemetery, a MEMORIAL TO WORLD WAR SOLDIERS, has two white stone columns with inscribed brass plates.

SIMPSON, 86.1 *m.* (1,383 alt., 273 pop.), backed by the hilly terrain of the Solomon River Valley, was built in 1870 on the site of an old Pawnee village. It has survived a series of Indian raids and crop failures. The first white men to attempt settlement were driven away by the Pawnee; later, when the Pawnee were finally subdued, the Cheyenne attempted to seize this territory which was exceptionally fine for buffalo hunting. It was early in the 1880's before settlers could feel comparatively safe from Indian attacks. Then came grasshopper plagues and crop failures that caused food shortages; these disasters were followed by prices so low that the poverty-ridden pioneers burned corn for winter fuel.

Simpson is now a shipping center for a large farming and stock-raising region.

ASHERVILLE, 90.2 *m.* (1,343 alt., 200 pop.), founded in 1867 on the site of a stockade built for protection against Indians, is one of the oldest settlements in Mitchell County. The only modern note is a school building (L), in the northern part of town. An emergency first-aid station is maintained here.

BELOIT, 100.2 *m.* (1,378 alt., 3,502 pop.), is the seat of Mitchell County. Its long main street is lined with old buildings of local limestone interspersed with an occasional modern structure.

The first house on the townsite was a log cabin erected in 1868 by A. A. Bell, on the north bank of the Solomon River. The name of the settlement was changed in the early 1870's from Willow Springs to Beloit, for Beloit, Wis., the former home of T. F. Hersey, a town promoter. On March 26, 1872, Beloit was surveyed and the plat recorded; in August of the same year it was organized as a third-class city, with Hersey as mayor.

Beloit is surrounded by a rich agricultural district, and has several small industries; flour milling, the chief among them, utilizes the water power of the Solomon River.

On the northern edge of Beloit on State 9 (R) is the STATE INDUSTRIAL SCHOOL FOR GIRLS *(open, visitors apply to superintendent)*. Its brick and stone buildings include five cottages for girls, two cottages for officials, a school, a laundry, and several farm buildings. The institution houses approximately 150 girls ranging in age from 8 to 18 years. Vocational training is stressed. Girls leave the school when they are 21 years old, but the merit system provides for paroles at an earlier age.

GLEN ELDER, 110.8 *m.* (1,425 alt., 617 pop.), bounded on the south by Solomon River and on the east and northeast by Limestone Creek, is built along an elm-shaded street. First platted two and a half miles northeast of its present site and named West Hampton, Glen Elder was moved when a flour mill was built on the present site in 1871.

At 116.8 *m.* is the junction with a dirt road.

Left on this road is WACONDA SPRINGS *(hotel accommodations, hospital)*, 1 *m.* (1,428 alt., 25 pop.), a small health resort. Behind the hospital are three springs. GREAT SPIRIT SPRING, the largest and best known, rises to the top of a mound in the bottom lands of the Solomon River. The mound, about 42 feet high, is level on top. At its center is the spring, a smooth body of water about 50 feet in diameter. Always filled to the brim, it appears about to overflow; instead, the water seeps through the porous rock sides of the mound.

It is said that the Indians, believing these waters sacred, named the springs Waconda, for the chief deity of the Kaws. Another explanation of the name is that a powerful Indian chief opposed the son of a rival chief as a suitor for his daughter, Waconda. In a battle between the two tribes Waconda's lover was wounded, and weak from loss of blood, fell into the stream. When Waconda accused her father of killing the young brave he became angry, shot an arrow through his daughter's head and threw her body into the spring where the spirits of the lovers still dwell.

The waters from Waconda Springs received an award at the Chicago World's Fair in 1934. They contain 1,120 grains of sodium chloride, sodium sulphate magnesium, and epsom salts to a gallon.

CAWKER CITY, 117.8 *m.* (1,473 alt., 739 pop.), was so-named in the early 1870's as the result of a poker game played by its founders. E. H. Cawker won. It is the site of a small manufacturing company but is largely dependent on farm trade.

The RICHARDSON MANUFACTURING COMPANY *(open 8-5 weekdays)*, one block south of US 24 on First Ave., manufactures miscellaneous agricultural implements and a patented machine for stripping beans.

The OLD ALDRICH HOME *(private)*, N. edge of the city on Pennsylvania Ave., a two-story, red brick structure of Victorian design, was built in the 1880's by Levi L. Aldrich (1849–1917), a newspaper publisher who founded the Cawker City *Free Press* in 1878, and later became publisher of the *Public Record*. Mrs. Emma B. Aldrich (1845–1925), wife of the pioneer editor, was the first woman in Mitchell County to hold a higher grade teacher's certificate. She later served as county superintendent of schools. In 1883 she was one of forty women who met at Denver, Colo., and organized the Woman's Relief Corps. Her husband, a Union veteran, was active in Grand Army of the Republic circles and edited the *Camp Fire,* a publication of the veterans' organization.

DOWNS, 124 *m.* (1,483 alt., 1,383 pop.), in the bottom lands of the South Fork, Solomon River, is a railroad center in an agricultural region producing oats, rye, rape, alfalfa, sorghum, sugar beets, broom corn and rice corn. The town was named for Major Downs, a local railroad superintendent at the time of its founding. Downs has the usual main street lined with business establishments.

OSBORNE, 136.5 *m.* (1,557 alt., 1,881 pop.), seat of Osborne County, was named for Vincent B. Osborne, early Kansas cavalry sergeant, and settled largely by Pennsylvania Dutch. A clean and modern town in the heart of the fertile Solomon Valley, it is a shipping point for the surrounding cattle, wheat, corn and sorghum area.

Just east of the Osborne post office is an attractive sunken garden.

At 137.7 *m.* is the junction with an improved road.

ALTON, 151.2 *m.* (1,651 alt., 383 pop.), a rural trading center, was originally called Bull City for Gen. H. C. Bull, one of its founders who flipped a nickel to win the honor from Lyman T. Earl, another founder. The name was changed to Alton in 1885 for Alton, Ill., from where many of the settlers had emigrated.

In 1879 an exciting event occurred in this little locust-shaded village, when a pet elk killed General Bull and three men who tried to save him. The horns of the elk hang in a little shop (locally called a museum) on Alton's main street.

STOCKTON, 170.1 m. (1,775 alt., 1,291 pop.), is a spacious western cow town on tableland overlooking a basin formed by the South Fork and the Solomon River valley. Stockton was so-named by early day cattlemen because of the livestock raised in the surrounding country.

The annual Western Kansas-Nebraska Fair *(latter part of Aug.)* is held in Stockton, with carnival attractions, school and home exhibits, and a stock show.

At Stockton is the junction with State 1, improved.

Left on State 1 to the junction with another improved road, 2 m.; R. on this road is the ROOKS COUNTY STATE LAKE (under construction, 1938), 4.5 m. When completed the lake will cover an area of approximately 60 acres and will be stocked with fish by the State Forestry, Fish and Game Commission. Water will be impounded by damming Boxelder Creek, a tributary of the Solomon River. Begun in 1934 as an FERA project, the work was continued under the WPA program and is expected to be completed in 1939.

West of a TIME ZONE BOUNDARY, 173 m., Mountain Standard Time is used and watches of west-bound travelers should be set back one hour.

At 187.1 m. is the junction with a dirt road.

Left on this road is the junction with another dirt road, 3 m.; R. on this road past a few farmhouses and much poor pasture land characterized by low bluffs and dunes to NICODEMUS, 5 m. (2,200 alt., 67 pop.), an unincorporated town and the only all-Negro community in Kansas.

Nicodemus, sole survivor of Kansas' three colonies settled by the "Exodusters" *(see HISTORY)*, is not affluent. Children play in the dusty street before wooden or stone huts that contain only bare necessities—often wooden chairs and a table, a stove and an iron bed. A tavern is the sole business place. Only the churches have electric lights and the nearest telephones are at Bogue, 6 miles away. The residents, employed by Negro farmers of Graham County, go to Stockton or Hill City for supplies or for conferences with their Negro lawyers or their white bankers. From their meager share of the harvest,' which they hoard for winter use, a tithe is set aside for the annual Emancipation Celebration.

The "Exodusters" were organized in 1873 by Benjamin (Pap) Singleton *(see HISTORY)*. In establishing Nicodemus he was aided by Topeka Negro leaders and W. R. Hill, a white man from Indiana, who was speculating in land in Western Kansas at that time and was attracted by the large fees that homesteaders paid for assistance in obtaining land and file papers. The first group reached this townsite in the autumn of 1877, too late to plant crops. Their savings had been spent for railroad fares and the payment of fees. Unable to purchase lumber or other building materials, they lived in crude dugouts or burrows. For fuel, they burned buffalo chips, sunflower stalks, and faggots cut from clumps of dwarf willows and cottonwoods. During the first year no houses of any kind were built above the ground. They received little aid from the white settlers of the county, who resented them so bitterly that Hill, blamed for bringing them in, was forced to flee. (When he returned to this section later, however, he was held in high esteem and Hill City was named for him.)

NEGRO FARMER

This community was named Nicodemus not for the Biblical character but for the legendary Nicodemus who came to America on a slave ship and later purchased his liberty. Of him the plantation Negroes of the South sang:

> Nicodemus was a slave of African birth,
> And was bought for a bag of gold,
> He was recokoned as a part of the salt of the earth,
> And he died years ago, very old.
>
> Nicodemus was a prophet, at heart he was wise,
> For he told of the battles to come;
> Now he trembled with fear when he rolled up his eyes
> And he heeded the shake of his thumb.

Members of the Nicodemus colony added the following hopeful chorus:

> Good time coming, good time coming,
> Long, long time on the way;
> Go tell Elijah to hurry up pomp,
> To meet us under the cottonwood tree
> In the great South Solomon Valley to build up
> The city of Nicodemus at the break of day.

Crop failures followed in monotonous succession. Even in 1883, a good crop year elsewhere in western Kansas, Nicodemus was seared by southwest winds. Many colonists, discouraged, abandoned their claims. Others found seasonal work with white farmers in the county. From a population of 500 in 1880 the town had declined to less than 200 by 1910.

One of Nicodemus' most able leaders, the Reverend Roundtree—who wore a brand on one cheek as punishment for having received educational instruction from his master's son—taught the new citizens to read and write. At a State Fair in Michigan his pleas for the colony of Nicodemus brought several carloads of food and a sum of money. Assisted by Zach Fletcher, another resident, he was successful in having Baptist and Methodist churches erected. These buildings are still used by the community. Although most of the colonists have had to begin work at an early age, some have been graduated from college and a few have held county offices. Probably the most notable of these was E. P. McCabe, State auditor (1885–1889), who later became a Territorial official in Oklahoma.

The stone PRISCILLA ART CLUB BUILDING *(open)*, W. end of Main St. (R), built in the boom days of the 1880's by one of the town's important early day social and cultural groups, was never occupied because of faulty construction.

The NICODEMUS SCHOOLHOUSE *(open)*, near the southwest edge of town, a one-room frame structure painted white, was built in 1882 and is still in use.

Left 0.8 *m.* from Nicodemus on an unimproved road to the junction with another unimproved road; R. 1.3 *m.* on this road to 12-acre SCRUGGS GROVE *(dance pavilion, picnic tables)*, where the annual Emancipation Celebration is held. Kansas Negroes observe August 4 as Emancipation Day because, according to legend, that was the day on which Nicodemus' master laid aside his whip. Negroes from all parts of the State as well as visitors from Oklahoma and Missouri join in a barbecue and watermelon feast under the cottonwoods. Square dances for the older residents are varied with modern steps for the younger Negroes.

At 195 *m.* is the junction with a graded road.

Left on this road is BOGUE, 2 *m.* (1,203 alt., 135 pop.), a rural trading center, founded in 1888 and named for a locomotive engineer. It was not incorporated until 1935.

At 7.8 *m.* on this road is the BUSS TAXIDERMY *(open)*, a two-story stucco building used as a dwelling by Mr. and Mrs. Charles Buss and as a museum for their collection of stuffed birds, reptiles, and other animals. Most of the specimens are of wild life found in Graham County. Included are badgers, coyotes, skunks, raccoons, prairie dogs, owls, eagles, blue birds, red-winged blackbirds, pelicans, herons, prairie chickens, horned toads, lizards, and turtles. Another collection includes a mammoth tusk found in the county in 1934 and other geological and paleontological specimens.

At 203 *m.* is the junction with a graded road.

Right on this road to a pasture gate (R), 2.5 *m.* Through the pasture gate 3.2 *m.* to TINDALL HILL, a sandstone promontory rising 150 feet above the plain. The slopes are overgrown with gooseberry bushes, sumac, wild grape vines, and buffalo grass. At the base of the hill is Coon Creek, a clear winding stream. Tindall Hill is a popular picnic spot for residents of Graham County. The sandstone deposits have been quarried extensively and used for surfacing highways.

Although HILL CITY, 204.2 *m.* (2,134 alt., 1,027 pop.), seat of Graham County, is on a hill bordered by two creeks, it was named for one of its founders and early settlers, W. R. Hill.

John Stanley, the first resident of the townsite, arrived in 1877. Hill City was surveyed in 1880; two years later it was incorporated with Hill as mayor.

"Hill City, like Kansas," admitted a local writer, "has come through cyclones, hot winds, prairie fires, county seat fights, and droughts until today (1936) she is the largest . . . city in Graham County. Not only in their ability to survive disasters but also in their fondness for civic organizations are the residents of this town typical of their State. In addition to having membership in church guilds and literary and social clubs, Hill Citians are active in such groups as the American Legion, Rotary, the

FARM WOMEN'S LITERARY MEETING

Y.M.C.A., the Masons, Oddfellows, Woodmen, and their various women's auxiliaries. Even though all the local members of the G.A.R. are now dead, its women's division still holds meetings. Almost everyone belongs to some group and almost every group, from the elementary school to the veterans, has a band that, clad in striking costume, drills for prizes on every gala occasion."

Right from Hill City on State 21, an improved road, to the only SOD HOUSE *(open)* in Graham County, 1.5 *m.* This reproduction, a fine example of the prairie pioneer's architecture, was built in 1925. It has two rooms with dirt floors, plastered walls, two windows, and a door. When the pioneers passed beyond the forested lands—which ended approximately at Kansas City, Mo.—and pushed out on the treeless plains where neither wood nor stone was available for building, they cut the hard prairie turf into bricks to form walls that would support the weight of a roof and give protection from the weather. These sod walls were no deterrent to snakes or rodents, however, and, since the houses were often half dug-outs, with one side of their roofs projecting from a hillside, grazing buffalo would sometimes crash through the roof and join the occupants below.

At 2 *m.* is the junction with a dirt road; R. here to KNOUF GROVE *(rustic benches and tables, nominal fees),* 7 *m.,* a shady cottonwood grove with a spring, a pleasant place for picnics.

At 216.4 *m.* on US 24 is the junction with an improved road.

Left on this road is MORLAND, 1 *m.* (2,302 alt., 385 pop.), a rural trading and shipping point, in the sandy valley of the Solomon River. The town was organized in 1886 and named Fremont in honor of General Fremont, but when the railroad came 3 years later it was renamed for a railroad official.

Morland held a treasure hunt in the spring of 1936 that attracted widespread interest. A local merchant, who had hired drillers to sink a water well on his property, announced that the drill had struck a hard metallic substance and was covered with shiny particles that looked like gold. Within a few hours the town was buzzing with news of the discovery of a box or chest filled with Spanish doubloons or gold bars. The well was being sunk in a former channel of the river, and imaginative citizens concluded that Spaniards or "forty-niners," when attacked by Indians, had thrown their treasure into the stream. Soundings indicated that the object was approximately 2 feet wide and 4 feet long.

Efforts to bring the treasure to the surface were made extremely difficult by the loose sand. There were frequent cave-ins and the work was hazardous. Eventually it became too expensive for one man to finance and a company was organized with a capital of $200. For weeks the "box" resisted all efforts to dislodge it. In the meantime Morland enjoyed a boom. The curious came from miles around and local restaurant proprietors and soft-drink vendors realized unusual profits. Finally it was announced that the "box" would be raised on a Saturday afternoon and a large crowd, including representatives of several metropolitan newspapers, poured into Morland to see the treasure. A block and tackle were made fast. The pulley creaked and the "box" rose slowly to the edge of the pit. It was a large chunk of limestone.

At 217.9 m. is the junction with an improved road.

Right on this road is 86-acre ANTELOPE LAKE, 1.5 m. (hunting, boating, fishing), constructed in 1934–35 as an Emergency Relief project. The dam is constructed with floodgates which can be opened during periods of heavy rainfall to divert water into ditches with which adjacent wheat fields are irrigated.

STUDLEY, 221.2 m. (2,381 alt., 100 pop.), on an uneven plateau just north of the South Fork of the Solomon River, was settled by former residents of Yorkshire and named for Studley, England. The surrounding area contains attractive English-type homes and cattle and sheep ranches. Irrigation has enabled residents to reproduce the gardens of old Yorkshire.

Left from the highway is the J. FENTON PRATT HOUSE (private), a stone structure of Victorian architecture, surrounded by a garden and trees. The main portion of the residence was constructed by Pratt for his English bride in the 1880's.

West of Studley the land gradually rises; numerous low hills and draws are covered with yucca and soapweed. The roots of the latter plant make rich suds when powdered and mixed with water; they were used for soap by trappers, settlers, and Indians. When blooming in June, the yucca plant has tall cream-colored spikes of blossoms that stand like ghostly sentinels along the draws.

At 239.7 m. (R) on the south bank of Sand Creek is the SITE OF OLD PORT BYRON, a pioneer cattle town. Here in early days was a camp and bedding ground for herders and cowboys on the trail over which cattle were driven from Texas to Kansas and the Northwest. The town began in 1879 as a dugout saloon. The story is that a cowboy named Richards with a friend, Billy Hudson, started the dugout saloon so that they might watch the cattle trails for another cowboy named Fisher, who had severely wounded Richards a year before. Fisher never came.

Indians often camped near the dugout saloon, but with the exception of the Cheyenne they were all friendly. According to old accounts, local settlers feared drunken cowboys more than the Cheyenne.

HOXIE, 240.1 *m.* (2,654 alt., 800 pop.), seat of Sheridan County, is a modern trading and shipping village. Hoxie had its beginning in a village named Kenneth that was situated 3 miles north of the present site. In 1886 when the Missouri Pacific R.R. made plans to come through the county, the settlement was moved and renamed for a vice president of the railroad company. Though the railroad failed to arrive till some time after Hoxie had been founded, the village prospered.

West of Hoxie US 24 traverses the High Plains, which stretch unbroken for many monotonous miles. Early summer in crop years *(see AGRICULTURE)* finds this area covered with waving yellow fields of wheat interspersed with green corn.

At 243.2 *m.* is the junction with a private dirt road.

Left on this road is an OLD SODDY, 1 *m. (occupied, visitors welcome),* built about 1896, and somewhat modern compared with the first soddies erected on these plains.

HALFORD, 265.3 *m.* (3,086 alt., 18 pop.), is at the junction with US 83 *(see Tour 8).* Between this place and a point at 267.3 *m.* US 24 and US 83 are one route.

Along the highway west of Halford barren spots of earth, resembling ant hills, extend outward from the edge of the road. These are places where the crop-devastating bindweed has been destroyed by salting the earth. The bindweed is a white morning-glory that strangles wheat or corn by enmeshing the crops' roots and absorbing all the nutriment from the soil. The most effective way to kill it is with salt; but salt makes plains country soil unfit to grow vegetation for a quarter of a century.

The sales pavilion (L), 273 *m.,* is a livestock market where traders can buy and sell stock grades of hogs and cattle. Formerly the railroad stockyards in Colby handled this business, but now only finished hogs and cattle are handled in Colby.

COLBY, 274.4 *m.* (3,138 alt., 2,153 pop.), seat of Thomas County, an attractive town with green trees and lawns, is built along a main street broad enough to permit parking in the center.

On this site, before the town was built, there had been a post office, the earliest in Thomas County. The town, named for J. R. Colby, an early settler, was incorporated as a third-class city in 1886. It now serves a large agricultural area as a wholesale, shipping, and trading center. Since 1910 Colby has had a municipal light and water plant that supports all other civic expenses and keeps the town tax-free. Rates compare favorably with those of privately owned utilities.

The Thomas County Fair is held here annually *(3rd week in Aug.).*

West of Colby is the KANSAS AGRICULTURAL EXPERIMENT STATION *(open),* in a group of white-painted buildings surrounded by shrubbery, and well-kept grounds. This station cost approximately $30,000, covers 266 acres, and operates under the direction of the U. S. Department of Agriculture and the Kansas State College.

At 276 *m.* is the junction with a township dirt road.

Right on this road is 5-acre HEMSTROM PARK *(nominal rates, swimming pool, baseball, dancing, picnicking, boating)*, 4 *m.*

EDSON, 300.4 *m.* (2,573 alt., 80 pop.), was named for an early settler, Ed Harris, and his son.

Right from Edson on a dirt road is the KUHRT FARM *(open)*, 12 *m.*, known for its shorthorn cattle which have won many prizes in stock shows throughout the United States.

GOODLAND, 313 *m.* (3,687 alt., 3,626 pop.), is a modern western county seat, with a few attractive office buildings, a railroad division office quarters, and a modern courthouse, ranged along a wide main street.

The population of Goodland varies noticeably from year to year. Prior to the motor age 50 percent of local employment was furnished by the railroad; now, owing to the decline in rail traffic, only 15 or 20 percent depend upon this industry. The permanence of Goodland, however, seems assured by its water supply. Thirty feet beneath the surface, a layer of sand extending westward to the Rockies is replenished by a constant underground flow from the melting snows of those mountains.

Locust, elm, poplar, and evergreen trees shade the one-and-one-half acre GOODLAND CITY PARK, which has a fountain and wading pool in its center. The Northwest District Free Fair *(last week in Aug.)* is held at the fairgrounds on the northern edge of town.

During the drought of the early 1890's, officials of the District Fair, then only a county organization, advertised in railroad depots for hundreds of miles in Kansas and Nebraska that Melbourne, called the "Australian Rain Maker," had been hired to display his magic on the fairgrounds and would be paid $1,500 if he could bring forth one inch of rain in 24 hours.

"It was the opening day in September," wrote Fred Stewart, authority for the story of Goodland rain making, "windy, dusty, and parching dry. No rain fell here after the rain maker's experiment. But during the twenty-four hours of Melbourne's time limit, we received telegrams from towns along the railroad northeastward into Nebraska saying: 'Shut off the rain maker; we are drowning.' Floods washed out bridges and did immense damage."

Melbourne's method consisted of pouring sulphuric acid on zinc to release hydrogen, which was supposed to rise and unite with oxygen in the air to form water.

After experiments of two local men, O. P. Smith, a chemist, and E. F. Murphy, a railroad agent, had been followed by a shower, they incorporated and sold all their shares at par. The corporation was hired by Californians to make rain in several farming valleys, and the Mexican Government, harassed by a great drought, also sought the Goodland Rain Makers, but before the company could perform, the Mexican drought ended.

A later rain-making company, organized by a Goodland druggist, Dr. L. Morse, operated for 15 or 20 years. A transcontinental railroad, running through the town, put on three laboratory cars for its own rain makers and toured all their roads in Kansas. "In 1892," continues Fred Stewart, "our finest prospect for wheat began burning up in July. The postmaster, Billy Walker, gave $50 to Dr. Morse to buy chemicals to make it rain. I helped him carry the chemicals to a barn, including a 10-gallon carboy of sulphuric acid so heavy I had to drag it. He started his experiment at 10 o'clock in the morning. At two in the afternoon, the town sidewalks were afloat and kids were riding on them for rafts." O. P. Smith, the chemist who organized the first rain-making company, still lives in Goodland (1938).

Goodland introduced several innovations in the usual county-seat fight. In 1886 Eustis was appointed by the Governor as temporary county seat pending a popular election. Its rivals were Voltaire, Sherman Center, and Itaska, "the Queen City of Kansas." In the November election all the officials of the Eustis faction, except one, were returned to office. When the votes were to be counted, all factions sent representatives heavily armed with pistols, clubs, and bowie knives.

Another county seat election was held in 1887 after Goodland had been organized. Goodland was supported by settlers from Sherman Center and Itaska, who wished to wrench the prize from Eustis. Voltaire was also asked to join the new town, but refused and spent seven years dying. The Homesteaders' United Association, a local organization to protect settlers against claim jumpers, sided with Goodland and ordered twelve repeating rifles from Pennsylvania. Goodland won the county seat without firing a shot.

The members of this militant force built a courthouse in Goodland, but Eustis refused to surrender the county books, and influential residents secured an injunction forbidding their removal to Goodland. Goodland promoters then secretly posted 300 armed men in their empty courthouse and sent the new sheriff, John Nevert, to arrest, individually, every able-bodied man in Eustis on false charges. The male population of Eustis was thus charged with cattle stealing, wife beating, polygamy, murder, escape from the penitentiary, arson, larceny, mayhem, and harboring an unlicensed dog. Each man, knowing himself to be innocent of the charge, submitted to arrest, eager to clear himself before a judge. When all these men had been brought into the courtroom, the judge started a mock trial that the victims took seriously. Meanwhile the army of 300 slipped out of the courthouse and dashed for Eustis to seize the records. "I saw them go," Col. George Bradley, old-time resident, reported, "so I rushed in and reported it to the prisoners at the bar. This broke up the trial."

"I had a horse and buggy," Bradley continued, "and I raced over the prairie on the north flank of the Goodland army. Their leader cried 'halt,' but I ignored him and they opened fire—their bullets kicking up dust all around me. I reached Eustis and saw the horde seize the records. 'Negro Bob,' a big colored doorman at the Eustis Hotel, in an attempt to be pleasant and noncommittal, spoke to Mr. Fletcher, one of the H. U. A. members saying: 'Are you white men out hunting?'"

"'Yes,' growled Fletcher, 'hunting coons.' And he hit the Negro with his Winchester, raising a bump on his head. This was the only casualty of the entire campaign. Goodland secured all the records except the precinct election returns of 1887, these, George Benson, county clerk, had hidden in a trunk in his own house." The Goodland Town Company offered Benson two town lots and several hundred dollars in cash for the return of the election records, according to Bradley who concludes:

"I raced back to Eustis, entered Benson's store basement, broke open the trunk, and took away the election returns. When Benson arrived he sounded the alarm that he had been robbed. It was really comical. Meanwhile the Kansas Supreme Court had been appealed to and made a judicial examination of witnesses in every precinct. M. B. Tomlin, about to open a bank in Goodland and eager to make sure of its legality as the county seat, offered to hire me as a detective and to pay $1,500 for the missing election returns. Before I could go get them, the report of the Supreme Court's confirmation of Goodland became known and the stolen returns were not needed. I kept them several years and then threw them in the fire."

A truckload of live jackrabbits was shipped from Goodland in 1935 to stock the game preserves of Illinois. But these large rabbits of the semi-arid plains could not adapt themselves to damp wooded areas, and died.

Sherman County was the scene of a corn-breeding experiment in the early 1900's. G. W. Sherrod produced a flinty hard corn named Sherrod's White Dent that matured in 100 days, often producing three large ears to the stalk. White Dent was later replaced by a yellow corn which yielded a soft inferior grain but required a shorter growing season.

The soil around Goodland is derived from the sediment of a chalk sea, estimated to have existed 200 million years ago. Petrified sea turtles and marine coral are found along Sappa Creek. Fossil remains of a 40-feet marine reptile, called Mosasaurus, are also found in this region.

KANORADO, 333.2 m. (3,906 alt., 359 pop.), so named for its position near the Kansas-Colorado Line, is a small railroad shipping point with two grain elevators, one hotel, two tourist camps, a number of small business establishments, a consolidated school, and a nine-hole golf course.

At 335.2 m. US 24 crosses the Colorado Line, 150 miles east of Colorado Springs, Colo. (see COLO., Tour 5).

<<<<<<<<<<<<<<<<<<<<✿>>>>>>>>>>>>>>>>>>>>

Tour 3

(Kansas City, Mo.)—Kansas City—Topeka—Manhattan—Salina—Hays —(Denver, Colo.); US 24-40, US 40.
Missouri Line to Colorado Line, 451.1 m.

Union Pacific R.R. parallels entire route.
Concrete paved roadbed between Kansas City and Wilson, remainder of the route
is either bituminous mat or oil surfaced. Heaviest east-west traffic arcoss Kansas.
Open all year except immediately following occasional blizzards.
Good accommodations in all county seat towns.

This route, connecting several of the State's most important towns, borders the Kansas River between Kansas City and Junction City; between
Junction City and a point just east of the Colorado Line, it roughly
bisects the area between the Smoky Hill River and the Saline River.

Section a. MISSOURI LINE *to* MANHATTAN, *128.9 m.,* US 24-40,
US 40

West of Kansas City US 24-40 crosses a pleasant, rolling country from
whose high points are sweeping views of farm lands and wooded hills. It
skirts Lawrence, where the university buildings are visible on the summit
of Mount Oread, and winds with ever-changing views of woods and
waters, through the Kansas River bottoms, flanked on both sides by rugged
hills. Between Manhattan and Junction City the route climbs these white-
ribbed limestone hills.

On the intercity viaduct over the Kansas River, US 24-40 crosses the
Missouri Line, 0 *m.,* west of Kansas City, Mo. *(see MO., Tours 2 and 3).*

KANSAS CITY, KANS., 1.2 *m.* (771 alt., 121,857 pop.) *(see KAN-
SAS CITY).*

Points of Interest: University of Kansas Hospital, Baptist 'Theological Seminary,
Horner Institute of Fine Arts, Western University (Negro), Old Huron Indian
Cemetery, and others.

At 3.7 *m.* is the junction with oil-surfaced Louisa Smith Rd.

Right on this road is the OLD QUINDARO CEMETERY, 4 *m.* Near the cemetery
is the SITE OF AN OLD LOG CHURCH built by Wyandotte Indians in 1849 when
their original church was divided over the slavery question.

The VICTORY HILLS GOLF CLUB *(open, nominal rates),* 7 *m.,* has (L)
an 18-hole course, bent grass greens, and a modern clubhouse.

WHITE CHURCH, 8.8 *m.* (1,038 alt., 116 pop.), a village built
around a post office and a general store, is the site of a Delaware Methodist mission erected in 1832. Approximately a thousand Delaware Indians living in the vicinity attended the mission, which had five buildings
and large stables. Missionary annals of the 1850's describe the Delaware
as "intelligent and industrious and eager to accept the teachings of the
Methodist Church." They had been in contact with English civilization
since the founding of Virginia. When the question of slavery arose and
the Methodist Church split, the Delaware at White Church took their
stand with the new southern branch of the church, which favored slavery.

Right one block on Betton Road is the MEMORIAL WHITE CHURCH, a
one-story structure of Romanesque design, constructed of local limestone.
The original log structure, destroyed by fire in 1844, was replaced by a
white frame building which the Indians called White Church; for this the
town was named. After the frame building had been destroyed by a

cyclone in 1886 it was replaced by the present stone building. In 1932, after a century of Methodism, it became a community church.

Directly behind the church, on a hillside shaded by oak trees, in the BURIAL GROUND OF THE DELAWARE is the GRAVE OF CHIEF KETCHUM, leader of the tribe for 26 years and one of the signers of a treaty in 1868, by which his tribe agreed to move to Indian Territory. For many years after the removal of the Delaware from Kansas, members of the tribe returned annually to pay homage to their dead—pilgrimages that account in large measure for the preservation of the cemetery.

Near the center of the cemetery is the SITE OF AN OLD LOG CHURCH built by Wyandotte Indians in 1849 when their original church was divided over the slavery question. The spot is marked by a linden tree bearing a long scar on its trunk. According to local legend the scar was caused by the fire which destroyed the church on the night of April 8, 1856.

At 11.1 *m.* is the junction with Corum Road, paved.

Right on Corum Road to WYANDOTTE RECREATIONAL PARK *(swimming, boating, picnic grounds, fishing, shelter houses, concession stand)*, 2.5 *m.*, covering 1,500 acres enclosed by a rail fence. A lake is encircled by 12 miles of trails and footpaths; a 20-mile drive follows the shore line.

The MAYWOOD PRESBYTERIAN CHURCH (L), 11.6 *m.*, founded in 1885, is, with a white-painted frame building and an old cemetery, all that remains of the town of Maywood.

VICTORY JUNCTION, 15.2 *m.* (950 alt., 50 pop.), is at the junction with US 73 *(see Tour 12A)*. In a triangular plot (R) at the junction of the two highways is a bronze statue of an American soldier. US 24-40 was dedicated in 1920 to Kansans who lost their lives in the World War and markers were erected along its course at intervals; between Victory Junction and Fort Riley it is still known locally as the Victory Highway, although the route officially became US 40 in 1927.

Fruit growing and dairying supplement grain and truck farming to some extent around Victory Junction. Grapes are grown extensively and one of the largest commercial varieties of strawberries was developed here.

A brief stretch of high, treeless farm lands separates the wooded section near Kansas City from the valley. West of Victory Junction the rolling hills descend slowly to lowlands indicated in the distance by a line of trees.

The WREN BROADCASTING STATION *(visitors welcome)*, is (L) at 25.8 *m.*

At 27.8 *m.* is the junction with State 16, a paved road.

Right on State 16 is TONGANOXIE, 0.2 *m.* (875 alt., 1,109 pop.), a trading center for the farming area midway between Kansas City and Lawrence. Climbing a slope from the railroad track on the east, Tonganoxie's main street is lined with cream stations, hardware shops, drug and dry goods stores, and the usual business concerns of the small farming community, all housed in stiff little brick and limestone buildings, remnants of the 1880's and 1890's, with which its elm-shaded residential district forms a pleasing contrast. In an attempt to recover part of the trade lost when the highway that formerly followed Tonganoxie's main street was

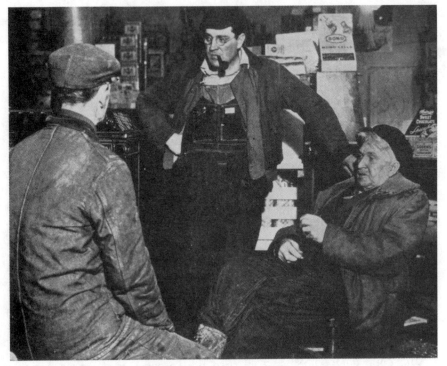

IN A COUNTRY STORE

rerouted to by-pass the town, its residents placed many signs along the highway asking travelers to "Stop at Tonganoxie."

At 3 *m.* is the 506-acre LEAVENWORTH COUNTY STATE PARK *(boating, swimming, fishing, camping, hunting, hiking)*. Its 175-acre lake is stocked with bass, crappie, and catfish.

South and west of Tonganoxie US 24-40 dips into the widening Kaw River valley where fields of oats, corn, and potatoes extend in checkerboard pattern from both sides of the road. Approximately 2 million bushels of potatoes are grown annually in this valley. The long symmetrical rows of potato plants seem to realign themselves, first into diamonds and then into squares.

A Victory Highway Marker (R), 37.4 *m.,* honoring Douglas County citizens who died in the World War, consists of a massive stone base upon which a bronze eagle hovers above a nest of its young.

A tourist camp and roadhouse, 39.8 *m.,* built to resemble an Indian village of tepees, is at the southern junction with US 59 *(see Tour 12)* which unites with US 24 for 10.2 miles west of this point.

Right here on US 24-59, an alternate route to US 40 through the Kansas River valley, which avoids the Lawrence and Topeka traffic and the hills and curves on US 40.

PERRY, 14.5 *m.* (845 alt., 418 pop.), an attractive village founded as a railroad boom town in 1865, serves as an agrarian shipping and trading center. BUM'S PARK (L), at the intersection of the business district and the highway, was so-named because it is a favorite lounging place for loafers.

West of Perry the highway passes a series of low bluffs overlooking the Kansas River which makes a great bend between this point and the Topeka city limits.

US 24 traverses the northern outskirts of North Topeka at 26.4 *m.,* an area of suburban homes and small truck farms.

At 31 *m.* is the junction with US 75 *(see Tour 11).*

The STATE INDUSTRIAL SCHOOL FOR BOYS (R), 32.2 *m. (grounds open to visitors; buildings on application),* with 27 buildings in a grove of elm trees, covers 500 acres. In this correctional institution boys between the ages of 6 and 16 are instructed in regular school work, music, mechanics, barbering, painting, engineering, woodworking, and shoe repairing; military training is also given.

At 33.1 *m.* is the junction with US 40.

LAWRENCE, 42 *m.* (840 alt., 13,726 pop.) *(see LAWRENCE).*

Points of Interest: University of Kansas, Haskell Indian Institute, Spooner-Thayer Museum, Plymouth Church, and others.

Lawrence is at the southern junction with US 59 *(see Tour 12).*

From US 40 at 45 *m.* the red-roofed limestone buildings of the University of Kansas are visible (L) on the crest of a hill known locally as Mount Oread.

Between Lawrence and Topeka, US 40 follows a winding route through a range of hills. The Kansas River valley (R) and the Wakarusa River valley (L) dip from the highway, their multicolored fields of corn, wheat, alfalfa, and pasture land separated by green hedgerows. From the higher points the tree-covered bluffs of the Kansas River are visible far to the north.

The marked SITE OF THE COON POINT CAMPING GROUND (R) of early overland travelers, 50.8 *m.,* is at a junction with a graveled road.

Right on this road is the junction with a dirt road 0.1 *m.;* L. here, 0.3 *m.,* to the unmarked SITE OF FORT TITUS, on a farm *(visitors welcome),* belonging to F. H. Nace. The fort was built by Col. H. T. Titus, who brought a battalion of Southerners to Kansas in 1856, to fight the Free Staters of Lawrence and Topeka *(see LAWRENCE).* He participated in the sacking of Lawrence, May 21, 1856, when the type of the *Herald of Freedom* was strewn through the dusty main street. According to some accounts, the Free Staters gathered the type in grain baskets, winnowed it out in the breeze, and melted it into Minie balls. Samuel Walker, leading 600 Free Staters, attacked Fort Titus in August 1856. The Free Staters' cannon, called Old Sacramento, was loaded with Minie balls. After the first shot one of the attackers shouted: "Now give them another edition of the *Herald of Freedom!"* The fort was destroyed and Colonel Titus, seriously wounded, was captured with his men, but soon released through an exchange of prisoners.

At 3 *m.* on the graveled road is LECOMPTON (846 alt., 288 pop.), a quiet village on the sides of the rolling hills above the south bank of the Kansas River. It was founded in 1854 and named for Samuel D. Lecompte, the first chief justice of the Kansas Territory.

When the first Territorial legislature, in session at Shawnee Mission, voted to remove the permanent seat of government to Lecompton in August 1855, a 13-acre tract on the east side of the settlement was set aside by the legislature, and Congress was induced to make appropriations for the construction of a large stone capitol here. Between 1855 and 1858 Lecompton was the center of the political struggle in which, President Pierce charged, Territorial officials and influential persons were more interested in filling their pockets with realty profits than in the great issue dividing the Nation.

In 1858 the Territorial legislature passed a resolution to adjourn to Lawrence because of "a general lack of accommodations" at Lecompton. That same year the Lecompton constitution was submitted to President Buchanan and the voters in the Territory. The President urged its adoption and the admission of Kansas as a slave State. The electorate of the Territory, however, repudiated the document with an overwhelming vote. The legislature, meanwhile, continued to convene at Lecompton and immediately adjourn to Lawrence, a formality that was practiced until the admission of Kansas as a State in 1861.

LANE UNIVERSITY, adjacent to the Lecompton Rural High School (one block E. of the business section), was established in 1865 by the United Brethren Church and built on the foundations of the unfinished Territorial capitol. It was named for James H. Lane, ardent abolitionist, and stressed religious education. In 1903 Lane University was merged with Campbell University at Holton *(see Tour 11)*. Subsequently, it was moved to Kansas City, Kans., where it became known as Kansas City University. Still later it was moved to Nebraska.

The ROWENA HOTEL, at the south end of Main St., a plain building of crumbling stone, was one of the five hotels that did a flourishing business when Lecompton was the territorial capital. It provided the first quarters for Lane University till a college building was erected on the site of the unfinished capitol; then the Rowena was converted into dormitories.

In CONSTITUTION HALL, on the west side of Main St., a two-story frame house of modest proportions, the Lecompton constitution was written.

Just north of Lecompton and east of the bridge spanning the Kansas River is the SITE OF SIMMONS' FERRY LANDING, which played an important part in the commercial life of Lecompton in the 1850's. The ferry was a dugout skiff made of a large sycamore log. William K. Simmons, its owner, and the first white settler in the vicinity, was one of the organizers of the Lecompton townsite. An early-day traveler related that he approached this crude boat with some misgiving, but Simmons said reassuringly: "Don't feel skeery, mister, for she's as dry as a Missourian's throat and as safe as the American flag."

Right 2 *m.* from Lecompton on an improved road to the junction with another improved road; R., 2.5 *m.*, on this road to the STANTON HOME *(private)*, a two-and-one-half-story structure with a hip roof, built of local limestone, on a thickly wooded height. This house was erected by Frederick P. Stanton, Territorial Governor in 1857. Weary of the petty strife, he built the structure for seclusion and during 5 years of residence here invited no guests.

BIG SPRINGS, 56 *m.* (949 alt., 40 pop.), is a roadside settlement on the slope of a hill. The springs (now dry) for which the town was named once flowed a short distance to the north of the townsite. In the 1850's this was the only watering place between Lawrence and Deer Creek, just east of Topeka. The Free State Party held its first convention here in 1855.

Directly across from the yellow brick Community Church, crumbling stone walls mark the SITE OF THE FIRST UNITED BRETHREN CHURCH in Kansas, built in the 1850's.

The parallel depressions on the side of a grassy hill (R), at the east limits of Big Springs, are the wagon tracks of the Lecompton Trail used in the 1850's.

The Victory Highway Monument (L), 56.3 *m.*, honors the World War veterans of Shawnee County.

TECUMSEH, 63.9 *m.* (860 alt., 350 pop.), once a county seat town ambitious to become the State capital, is now but a cluster of houses sheltered by huge elms and maples. The town was founded in 1852 by a party of proslavery men. Two years later the population numbered almost 2,000.

Plans were made for the erection of a courthouse, and the future of the busy settlement seemed assured.

Late in 1854 Cyrus K. Holliday, a young lawyer from Carlisle, Pa., offered to buy a portion of Tecumseh, but its founders asked too high a price. Holliday obtained land 5 miles up the river and founded Topeka in December of that year. By 1856 the two towns, one proslavery and one Free State, were bitter rivals for designation both as the county seat and the State capital.

In the first county election, held early in 1858, Tecumseh won the contest for the county seat but the citizens of Topeka asserted that Tecumseh's victory was effected by fraudulent means. In an election held later that year, Topeka won and Tecumseh began to decline.

The KANSAS VOCATIONAL SCHOOL (L), 67.4 m., housed in two- and three-story buildings of local limestone on a 110-acre campus, is a State maintained institution. It was founded in 1895 on the plan of the Tuskegee Institute at Tuskegee, Ala., where Negro boys and girls between the ages of about 10 and 20 years are taught trades. Out-of-town students live in dormitories on the campus. Enrollment in 1937 was 118.

Beside a spring shaded by a large oak tree at 68.4 m. (R) is a stagecoach station built in the 1850's; it is now a barn. In the 1850's and 1860's the spring was a watering and camping place for immigrants, gold seekers, and freighters with their wagon trains. The stone residence in front of the barn was built later.

At 68.9 m. on the outskirts of Topeka is the junction with California Ave., a paved street.

Left on California Ave. to the junction with 29th St., graveled, 1.5 m.; L. on 29th St. to 400-acre LAKE SHAWNEE (swimming, boating, fishing), 3 m., in a 1,017-acre wooded park. Foot and bridle trails and a 10-mile drive follow the shore line.

TOPEKA, 71.3 m. (886 alt., 64,120 pop.) (see TOPEKA).

Points of Interest: Statehouse, Washburn College and Mulvane Art Museum, Kansas State Historical Society with Library and Museum, Gage Park and Reinisch Rose Garden, State Hospital, Santa Fe Shops.

Topeka is at the junction with US 75 (see Tour 11).

At 74.3 m. is the junction with W. 6th St. (US 40 and Gage Blvd.). At Gage Blvd. US 40 turns R.

1. Left (straight ahead) on W. 6th St. to the HOME OF ALFRED M. LANDON (private), 0.5 m. (R), Governor of Kansas (1933–37) and Republican candidate for the Presidency in 1936. Built of brick, painted white, this Georgian Colonial mansion overlooking the Kansas River valley was designed by W. E. Glover of Topeka and completed late in 1937.

2. Left on Gage Blvd. to the junction with State 10 (10th St.), 0.5 m.; R. 2.8 m. on State 10 the junction with a dirt road; R. 0.2 m. on the dirt road to the OLD BAPTIST MISSION (open), a three-story stone structure built in 1848, now used as a barn. The mission was discontinued in 1859. The Indians asked to have it reopened in 1869 but the Baptist church did not have enough funds to do so.

At 3 m. on Gage Blvd. is the junction with a graveled road; R. 0.7 m. on this road to BURNETT'S MOUND (L), named for Abram Burnett, a Potawatomi chief who lived at the base of the mound on the south bank of Shunganunga Creek. Burnett weighed 450 pounds, and was known in eastern Kansas for his intelligence and shrewdness. He was born in Michigan about 1811 and came to Kansas in 1848, where he lived until his death in 1870. His name appears on many of the treaties made between the Potawatomi and the United States Government.

At 2 *m.* on the graveled road is the junction with an oil-surfaced road; L. 0.3 *m.* on this road to a farmyard gate (R); R. 0.8 *m.* on the trail through a farmyard and pasture to BURNETT'S GRAVE marked by a 12-foot marble shaft.

US 40 crosses the Kansas River at 75.1 *m.* on a narrow bridge.

SOLDIER CREEK, at 78.5 *m.* (R), was the scene of a liquor raid while Kansas was still Indian territory. Because Congress had passed a law forbidding the sale of liquor to Indians, Federal soldiers, overtaking a whiskey trader as he camped on the banks of the stream, dumped his liquor into the water. The disappointed Indians named the stream Soldier Creek.

SILVER LAKE, 85.6 *m.* (913 alt., 336 pop.), on the site of a Potawatomi village, was named for a lake that once extended south from the townsite.

To the east of this point is the PROPOSED SITE OF KIRO DAM, a flood-control project advocated by the U. S. Army Engineer Corps, which would submerge this valley, necessitating the removal of Wamego and several other towns, and the abandonment of thousands of acres of rich farm land. Topeka businessmen favored the project, believing that the proposed 50-mile-long lake and the wages paid thousands of workers during the 3 years of construction work would enrich the capital city. Residents of Wamego have led the fight against the building of the dam, protesting the proposed abandonment of their townsite, and maintaining that the value of the valley as a food-producing area far exceeds its potential value as a flood-control project.

Across the railroad tracks from Silver Lake (R) in the Silver Lake Cemetery, a tall slender shaft on the western slope of a hill is a MONU-MENT TO LA FROMBOISE, chief of the Potawatomi. Several of the chief's descendants reside nearby.

ROSSVILLE, 91.2 *m.* (928 alt., 701 pop.), a rural trading center in the fertile valley of the Kansas River, was founded in 1871 on land that was formerly part of the Potawatomi Reservation. Many of the early settlers in the Rossville area were of French and Belgian descent. The present townsite of 100 acres was purchased from a pioneer, Anthony Navarre. First called Edna, the town was renamed for W. W. Ross, the Potawatomi agent.

During the early years of its existence Rossville was a trading center for the Potawatomi Prairie Band, whose diminished reservation was a few miles north of the town. Residents of the frontier village were friendly with the Indians but they were alarmed June 4, 1876, when nearly 100 armed warriors rode into town at daybreak, awakening the citizens with war whoops. A contemporary newspaper correspondent wrote: "The occasional discharge of a shot and the glimpses one had of brave men darting hither and thither in their night clothes, armed with everything from a scythe to a Belgian rifle, led me, with very little stretch of imagination, to believe and realize that all the horrors of a regular Indian massacre were being enacted."

The Indians, however, were in pursuit of four horse thieves who had camped on the city square with a number of ponies stolen from the tribe. The thieves fired on their pursuers, fatally wounding Chief Lah-Kah-wah, before they were captured. Rossville men urged the Indians to place the captives in their custody but the warriors, infuriated by the loss of their leader, dragged the horse thieves to Cross Creek, west of town, where their bodies were found a few days later.

ST. MARYS, 98.8 *m.* (957 alt., 1,304 pop.), a Roman Catholic community, is composed of neat houses set in compact rows flush with the highway. It had its beginning in a Potawatomi Indian mission founded by Jesuit missionaries in 1848. In 1878, when the name of the town was changed from St. Mary's Mission to St. Mary, the U. S. Post Office Department acquiesced to the citizens' request to retain the final "s", but the railroad still lists the town as "St. Mary."

At the east edge of the town (R) is ST. MARYS COLLEGE *(open)* on the site of the old mission of which it is an outgrowth. Many of the priests in Kansas are ordained here. St. Marys College formerly offered courses for youths of high school and college age, but, since the early 1930's, the curriculum has been restricted to clerics. The average enrollment is 200.

The brick and limestone college buildings, largely classical in style, are on a wooded hillside. The college maintains a dairy farm stocked with purebred Holstein cattle.

Above the entrance to the 2,000-acre campus is a MEMORIAL ARCH dedicated to Lt. William T. Fitzsimmons, one of the first three American soldiers killed in the World War, and to other alumni who died in the war.

Just west of the college on US 40 (L) is the CHURCH OF THE IMMACULATE CONCEPTION *(open),* a limestone structure of modified Gothic design. Within hangs the IMMACULATE CONCEPTION *(best viewed in morning light),* an original by Benito, Italian court painter of the early 16th century. The picture was given to the Potawatomi by Pope Pius IX and brought to Kansas in 1854 by Bishop Meige. Also prized by local churchmen is a Latin record of Potawatomi activities, written in 1837 by Jesuits among whom were Father De Smet (1801–1872), explorer and Indian missionary, and Father Galliland, founder of St. Mary's Mission.

At 107.6 *m.* the route crosses the Vermilion River, so-named by the Indians, according to legend, because the blood of the braves of two warring tribes temporarily turned its water red.

WAMEGO (pronounced Wah-me'-go), 112.9 *m.* (989 alt., 1,647 pop.), is a well-kept old town, between the shallow-banked Kansas River on the south and low rolling hills on the north. Landscaped hillsides on the outskirts of town add to its attractiveness. In spring boxes of pansies, the official town flower, brighten the business section.

Wamego does not levy local taxes. The income from municipally owned utilities defrays the town's expenses, including the maintenance of a 25-bed municipal hospital. Except for a snowplow factory, the town is dependent on farming.

The WAMEGO CITY PARK (R), on the east limits of Wamego, was developed by the volunteer labor of Wamego businessmen, who transplanted trees from the woods near the river, and built the shelter house, fireplaces, benches, and fountains with rocks gathered from the hills. The DUTCH MILL, on the highway (R), was brought stone by stone from a Pottawatomie County farm—where it had been built by a Hollander in 1875—and reassembled here in 1923.

At Wamego is the junction with State 99, graveled.

State 99 branches south and crosses the Kansas River at 0.1 *m.* This route leads through the area settled by the Beecher Bible and Rifle Colony, which was organized in New Haven, Conn., in 1856 by ardent abolitionists *(see HISTORY).* During a meeting held at North Church prior to the colonists' departure, Capt. C. B. Lines, president of the company, reminded the audience that no provision had been made for weapons. Henry Ward Beecher, who had just delivered an invective against slavery, agreed to furnish money for twenty-five rifles if the New Haven citizens would buy the other twenty-five needed. With his check for $625 Beecher sent a Bible for each member of the company and a farewell letter prophesying: "You will not need to use arms where it is known you have them. It is the essence of slavery to be arrogant before the weak and cowardly before the strong."

FOUR CORNERS, 3 *m.,* is the junction with a graveled road and State 29, a dirt road.

1. Right **3** *m.* on State 29 is WABAUNSEE (1,180 alt., 90 pop.), a crossroads town with a store, a garage, and a cluster of houses flanking a dusty country road. Most of its first settlers are dead and their descendants have moved away; few of its original walnut-beamed stone houses remain; and many of the newer residents are not aware of the town's history.

The Beecher Bible and Rifle Colony—which had bought supplies in St. Louis with a common fund, before steaming up the Missouri to Kansas City in the *Clara* —arrived here April 28, 1856, and immediately founded the town. They had the land surveyed into sections and had a committee appraise the various claims. Some were valued as high as $120, others as low as $5. A large number of the sites were valued at par, the average for the whole. Then the land was auctioned to the highest bidders. All the money received for the sites in excess of their appraised values was prorated among those whose land was valued below par—an early-day version of the "share the wealth" program.

Settlers with land along the river were given the largest bonuses by the committee in the belief that bottom land would breed malaria. Today these bottom land farms are among the most productive in the State.

A few months after its founding Wabaunsee became a station on the Underground Railroad, and the rifles of the colonists were used effectively to prevent slave owners from capturing fugitives whom they had traced to this point.

The BEECHER BIBLE AND RIFLE CHURCH *(open),* on the southern outskirts of the town, is a rectangular stone building. On its sides are three long, narrow windows which have their original shutters. Above the front entrance is a tiny rose window. Atop the church is a squat tower whose bell, once used to call the settlers to worship, has been silent for years.

The interior is plain. A choir loft, from which an attic leads to the bell tower, extends across the back wall. The narrow pews—hard, square, and uncomfortable— remain in their original places, divided by a center aisle that separates the men's side from the women's.

When the congregation was organized in 1857 and affiliated with the Congregational Church, it first met in a tent and then in a temporary building until this structure was finished in 1862. The Reverend Harvey Jones, first pastor, served for nearly three years. Robert Banks, a resident of the region since 1855 and later a member of the colony, was the stonemason. Mrs. Banks mixed the mortar.

Throughout his life Beecher retained an interest in the Bible and Rifle Colony,

DUTCH WINDMILL, WAMEGO

and especially in this church in which the colonists met annually to reread the letter that had accompanied his gifts.

Shortly after the fiftieth anniversary of its organization (June 1907), the congregation of the Beecher Bible and Rifle Church began to dwindle. Improved methods of transportation permitted younger members to attend services in the more modern Congregational churches of Wamego or Manhattan. In 1920 regular services were discontinued.

In the WABAUNSEE CEMETERY are the graves of the Goulds, the Cottrells, and the Mitchells, all members of the original colony.

2. Left 3.2 m. from Four Corners on the gravel road to the HOMESTEAD OF CAPT. WILLIAM MITCHELL (private), a member of the Beecher Bible and Rifle Colony. The log cabin built by Captain Mitchell in 1857 is the dining room of the present two-story frame structure. The cabin loft in which fugitive slaves were frequently hidden in the late 1850's is used as a studio by Miss Maude Mitchell, artist-daughter of Captain Mitchell. Relics in the house include the pulpit Bible of the Beecher Bible and Rifle Church, a hammer, a rifle, and a broadaxe used by the colonists, and a Dutch oven taken in a jayhawking raid.

On State 99 at 12 m., in the Mill Creek valley, is ALMA (1,053 alt., 811 pop.), founded in 1857 and named for the city in Germany whence many of the settlers came. In addition to their descendants, who form the larger part of the town's population, Alma has a Negro group, the remnant of a colony of "Exodusters" (see HISTORY).

The WABAUNSEE COUNTY COURTHOUSE, built in 1931, is a two-story structure of Carthage stone, designed in the modern style by W. E. Glover, Topeka architect. Within are a colorful mosaic map of the county and a MUSEUM (open) maintained by the Wabaunsee County Historical Society. The museum contains a portrait of

Chief Wabaunsee of the Potawatomi, for whom the county was named, and a number of Indian artifacts and pioneer relics.

West of Wamego the road ascends to the crest of the first rim of hills on the north side of the valley. Scrub oaks line the highway and the slow-moving Kansas River (L), bordered with elms and cottonwoods, is a silver line through the expanse of green.

ST. GEORGE, 120.1 m. (993 alt., 216 pop.), which lies in the Black Jack Hills, is one of the earliest settlements in Pottawatomie County and the first seat of county government. The contest that resulted in the removal of the county seat to Westmoreland inflamed the towns in the county. It was claimed that in Wamego all the employees of the Union Pacific voted, regardless of their legal place of residence, and that St. Marys registered names from the tombstones in the old cemetery.

At a filling station 120.3 m. (L), water from Black Jack Springs, thought by the Potawatomi to have medicinal properties, is dispensed free.

The Big Blue River (as distinguished from the Little Blue, one of its tributaries) at 125.5 m. empties into the Kansas River. The Kansa had a good-sized village at this river junction, which, as near as can be identified from the French chronicles, was visited by de Bourgmont, explorer-trader, in 1724. It was still in existence as late as 1830 when the United States Army was policing this part of the Louisiana Purchase (see HISTORY).

On an unmarked site on the bank of the Big Blue River, believed to be approximately 1½ miles above the point where US 40 crosses the stream, occurred the only bellicose activities of the Potawatomi in Kansas. The serene and civilized Potawatomi, enraged by repeated Pawnee raids, went on the war path in 1851 and virtually annihilated the warriors of that tribe.

Many Indian relics have been found in this region.

The Flint Hills, known in this section as the Bluestem Hills, crowd closer to the river east of Manhattan, their blue tops visible in the distance.

MANHATTAN, 128.9 m. (1,012 alt., 10,136 pop.) (see MANHATTAN).

Points of Interest: Kansas State College of Agriculture and Applied Science with experimental farms, City Park with log museum and monument to Chief Tatarrax, Amanda Arnold Arch.

Manhattan is at the junction with US 24 (see Tour 2). US 40 branches southwest (L).

Section b. MANHATTAN to COLORADO LINE, 322.2 m., US 40

This route is through the Kansas wheat belt, the valleys of the Smoky Hill and Saline Rivers, and the High Plains alternately banded with wheat and grasslands. The wheat belt, most productive around Abilene, extends west of Salina. Excellent grazing country with sparsely timbered rocky hills extends between Brookville and Ellsworth. West of Russell the highway traverses vast oil fields, and wheat prairies that ascend gradually toward the Rocky Mountains.

West of Manhattan, 0 *m.,* US 40 climbs the long, steep grade of STAGG HILL, the summit of which affords a sweeping view of the river, the valley, and wooded hills in the distance. The group of institution-like buildings (R) in the valley is the REBEKAH INDEPENDENT ORDER OF ODD FELLOWS HOME for the aged *(open by permission).*

Traffic is heavier between Manhattan and Junction City than on any other stretch of US 40, except in the immediate vicinity of Kansas City.

OGDEN, 9.9 *m.* (1,050 alt., 418 pop.), called the "last place on the map" in the 1860's, is a one-street market town whose limestone buildings reflect the stolid German influence of Theodore Weichselbaum, pioneer merchant. A stone structure on the western edge of town (R), later used as a barn, was an old brewery in the 1870's. Beer was cooled in a hillside cave behind the buildings.

(Because of the heavy traffic, sharp curves, and dense timber, cars are forbidden to pass each other between Fort Riley and Junction City.)

US 40 crosses the boundary of the FORT RILEY MILITARY RESERVATION at 10.9 *m.,* which covers 24,000 acres of virgin prairie marked by steep, stony hills (R) and rich bottom land (L). In the growing season this is a good place to observe the various wild grasses, dwarf shrubs, and flowering plants that originally carpeted the Kansas prairies. Farming operations have extirpated much native Kansas flora, and even in the unplowed sod of the Fort Riley reservation many varieties of plant life have become extinct because of the gradual impoverishment of the soil.

The SITE OF CAMP FUNSTON (L), 11.7 *m.,* named for Gen. Frederick Funston *(see Tour 12),* was one of the largest U. S. military training camps in use during the World War. A stone MONUMENT TO GEN. LEONARD A. WOOD (1860–1927) stands in a grove of young cottonwoods. During the first few months of the camp's existence no rifles or guns were available so General Wood had his division drill with wooden rifles, wooden field guns, and even wooden horses. This method proved so successful that when the animals and ordnance finally arrived the men quickly acquired complete proficiency. The dim outlines of a network of roads visible behind the monument are all that remain of the camp of 4,000 buildings which housed 80,000 men.

A chimney silhouetted against the bluff (R), a REMNANT OF GENERAL WOOD'S WARTIME HEADQUARTERS, has become a World War shrine and steps have been built to it.

Four men were brutally slain and a fifth disfigured for life in a robbery of the Camp Funston Bank, January 12, 1918. The murdered men were James Hill, John Oehlsen, Charles F. Winters, founder of the bank, and John W. Jewell, editor of *Trench and Camp,* the camp newspaper. After knocking Winters unconscious with a blow from the butt of his pistol, the murderer forced Kearney Wornall, a bank employee, to bind and gag Hill, Jewell and Oehlsen. As the four men lay helpless on the floor, he killed them with a hand axe and then attacked Wornall.

Customers who entered the little frame building a few minutes later found it a shambles. The safe and cash drawers had been ransacked. Recovering consciousness later in the day, Wornall said that he believed he could identify his assailant. As this news spread through the camp it reached Capt. Lewis R. Whisler, Company E, 345th Infantry. "Is it true that Wornall will recover?" he asked excitedly of a corporal whom he heard discussing the affair with another soldier. Assured that it was, the captain turned away remarking, "Then they will catch the murderer," walked into his quarters and ended his life by firing two bullets into his head. Most of the stolen money, approximately $62,000 in bloodstained currency, was found hidden in the wall of Captain Whisler's quarters. Officers of the camp said that the captain had been acting strangely for some time and expressed the opinion that he had become mentally deranged from overwork. He was a former resident of Salina.

PAWNEE FLATS (R), 13.7 m., is an old rifle range opposite the SITE OF PAWNEE (L), which was Kansas' first "permanent" Territorial capital and the Free State town that Andrew Reeder, first Governor of Kansas Territory, was accused of having promoted for his own profit.

The OLD CAPITOL, a two-story limestone building, was restored by the Union Pacific R.R. and is maintained as a public MUSEUM (open), furnished as it was in the 1850's. The building was used as the State capitol for 4 days, before the proslavery majority unseated the Free Staters and adjourned to Shawnee Mission. The proslavery administration at Washington included the site of Pawnee in the military reservation and thus disposed of Reeder's Free State boom town.

CAMP WHITESIDE (R), 14.2 m. (permission to enter buildings or quarters, obtainable from officer in charge), has long rows of gray barracks backed by green hills ribbed with rimrock. According to local legend, this is the terrain reproduced on the Kansas State seal. These hills are the locale of Tawny and Silver and other animal stories by Dr. Thomas C. Hinkle. Camp Whiteside is used in summer by the Kansas and the Missouri National Guards, and other reserve military units.

FORT RILEY, 14.6 m. (1,064 alt., 3,500 pop.), is the only cavalry school maintained by the United States Army.

The Cavalry School Horseshow (adm. free), and Race Meet (nominal admission fee), held during the last week in May, are annual events that draw visitors from many parts of the country. Polo games at intervals throughout the spring and summer months also attract large crowds.

The permanent garrison consists of three cavalry regiments (one Negro); a field artillery battalion; a company of mounted engineers; an air corps squadron; the cavalry school detachment; the school for bakers and cooks; the detachments for quartermaster; medical, veterinary, and signal corps; ordnance department; and chemical warfare service. School for Reserve and National Guard officers and non-commissioned officers of the mounted service are also maintained.

In 1852 the movement of caravans on the Santa Fe Trail and the encroachment of trappers, so aroused the Indians that it became necessary to protect travelers. In October of that year, Maj. E. A. Ogden, Quartermaster at Fort Leavenworth, then the westernmost point, was ordered to

TERRITORIAL CAPITOL, FORT RILEY

select a suitable site for a station near the confluence of the Smoky Hill and Republican Rivers. Maj. R. H. Chilton and Troop B of the dragoons were the escort for the party, who named the site Camp Center. Construction was begun in 1853 and it was renamed in honor of Maj. Gen. Bennett Riley of Buffalo, N. Y.

In 1855 Congress appropriated funds to transform Fort Riley into a cavalry post and laborers were brought in from Missouri. More than a hundred persons, mostly civilians, died of cholera at the fort that summer. The main body of troops, away on an Indian campaign, escaped the epidemic.

After the Civil War the construction of the Kansas Pacific R.R. caused serious Indian uprisings. Troops were needed to protect settlers and railroad workmen; thus in 1866 the 7th Cavalry was organized at the post. The Indian campaigns of 1867 and 1868 took the 7th northward and westward, ending Fort Riley's brief importance as the center of operations. Col. A. J. Smith was in charge of the post, with George A. Custer second in command. The exceedingly small garrison was not increased until 1869, when a school of light artillery was established and maintained for two years.

In 1887 Congress passed a bill which provided for the School of Application for Cavalry and Light Artillery at Fort Riley. The school was organized in 1891 under Col. James W. Forsyth of the 7th Cavalry, Custer's old command, but an adequate curriculum was not offered until

1904. In 1908 the name was changed to Mounted Service School. In 1917 the instruction personnel was ordered away, and from then until after the World War the post became a training center for reserve officers.

At Fort Riley is the junction with the camp's main drive, paved, which encircles the grounds.

Left on the main drive in the order named are the officers' swimming pool, the stadium, apartments, enlisted men's swimming pool, cavalry headquarters, a sub-post exchange and post office, the post baker, and the motor transportation garage and shops. Right around the post bakery, then L. at an intersection across the Kansas River on a ONE-WAY BRIDGE brought from France after the World War *(watch clock at either end to make sure no vehicle is coming from other direction)* to Marshal Field, Fort Riley's airdrome. Return across the bridge, turn west on Custer Ave. to the East Riding Hall, Cavalry Headquarters, the Post Headquarters Library and Telephone Exchange, the book department salesroom and the printing plant, the post Theater, the post exchange and the bowling alleys, the post guard-house, and the swimming pool. Right on Pleasanton Ave. to Sheridan Ave.; L. on Sheridan Ave. to Waters Hall and the Wounded Knee Monument, a memorial to the 7th Cavalry, which was led against the Sioux in South Dakota by Col. James W. Forsyth. Maj. Gen. Nelson A. Miles's report of the "disaster" includes: "the unfortunate affair at Wounded Knee Creek December 29, 1890 in which 30 officers and soldiers and 200 Indians (men, women, and children) were killed or mortally wounded, prolonged the disturbance. . . ." "For his (Forsyth's) conduct on that day and the previous day Col. Forsyth was relieved from command." A few yards north of the Wounded Knee Monument is US 40.

The OGDEN MONUMENT (L), 14.8 *m.*, on a hillside overlooking Fort Riley, is built on the site described by early surveyors as the geographical center of the continental United States. This monument, in memory of Maj. E. A. Ogden, who died at Fort Riley in 1855 during an epidemic of cholera, was erected in the 1880's.

Behind Ogden Monument (L) is a NATIONAL CEMETERY established in 1855 during the cholera epidemic. Here is the GRAVE OF BVT. MAJ. FREDERIK A. A. ROSENCRANTZ (1825–1879), who, trained as an officer of the Royal Guard of Sweden, offered his sword in defense of the Union and served in the Army of the Potomac.

JUNCTION CITY, 18.9 *m.* (1,077 alt., 7,407 pop.), seat of Geary County, has developed as a trading point for soldiers from the Fort Riley Reservation. Its old stone houses show the influence of Swedish stone-masons. Junction City is the boyhood home of Bertram Hartman, New York artist, and Dr. Thomas C. Hinkle, author of animal stories.

Founded in 1858 and so-named because it is at the junction of the Republican and Smoky Hill Rivers, Junction City became the seat of Davis County, organized in 1855 and named for Jefferson Davis, then Secretary of War. In 1889 the county was renamed in honor of John W. Geary, third Territorial Governor of Kansas.

In the early days Junction City was near the Kansa reservation and tribesmen frequently visited the city. Once in 1867 a Kansa war party arrived, much to the alarm of the pioneer residents. The Kansa had just met the fierce Cheyenne in a bitter encounter, and had taken 25 enemy scalps. They offered the scalps for sale on the streets of the town. Some were purchased by the townspeople at prices ranging as low as 10 cents each.

On the dining room walls of the BARTEL HOUSE, a three-story, red brick hotel of Victorian design at the northwest corner of 6th and Washington Sts., are murals of scenes from the life of Robin Hood, painted by Bertram Hartman (see ART). The hotel was built in the 1890's. On its south wall is a bronze tablet marking the site of an old stone house in which settlers took refuge from Indians in 1861. Across the street at the entrance to the City Park is a monument in memory of Civil War heroes. At the end of W. 6th St. is a children's playground (flower gardens, swimming pools, tennis courts, fireplaces, tables).

The MUNICIPAL AUDITORIUM, on Jefferson St. between 8th and 9th Sts., was built as a PWA project, the city and the Federal Government sharing the cost of $213,600. It is a two-story structure of brick and limestone, designed in the modern style by Charles Shaver of Salina. The auditorium, which has a seating capacity of 1,800, is used for conventions, athletic events, theatrical performances, and community social gatherings. The building was dedicated by Gov. Walter A. Huxman, March 6, 1937, at the climax of a three-day "munifesta." Visitors from all over the State attended and hundreds of couples danced in the auditorium to music provided by an orchestra imported for the occasion. The building also contains the offices of city officials and the police and fire departments.

Some of the best building material in Kansas is the magnesium limestone quarried from the bluffs around Junction City.

Junction City is at the junction with US 77 (see Tour 10). Between this place and 20.9 m. US 77 and US 40 are one route (see Tour 10).

In CHAPMAN, 30.3 m. (1,113 alt., 819 pop.), trading center for a stock-raising area, is the FIRST COUNTY HIGH SCHOOL in the United States. This three-story structure of local limestone, built in 1889 and still in use, stands on US 40 (R) on the west edge of town. The brick wing is a later addition. The idea of establishing a State-wide system of county high schools was conceived in the early 1880's by Prof. J. H. Canfield of the University of Kansas, father of Dorothy Canfield Fisher, novelist. Through his efforts the legislature enacted a bill in 1887, providing for the establishment of high schools in all Kansas counties with populations exceeding 5,000. Within a few years the legislatures of almost every State in the Union had enacted similar bills.

THE MULBERRIES (private), on US 40 (R) at the extreme west edge of town, was the home of Henry Varnum Poor, the artist and potter (see ART), born in Chapman in 1888. This two-story frame structure, named for nearby mulberry trees, is occupied by the painter's sister and brother-in-law, Mr. and Mrs. Herbert Stone.

Two of Poor's paintings are in the CHAPMAN BANK (open 9-4 weekdays). The first, above the cashier's desk at the right of the entrance, is a marine study of the California coast. The other, on the rear wall of the room, is a scene in the Garden of the Gods near Manitou, Colo.

Aberdeen Angus cattle, from the herd which Sir George Grant brought to Victoria in the 1870's, are raised extensively in this area. Better Live Stock Day, attended by several thousand persons from many parts of the

United States and occasionally from foreign countries, is held every spring on a farm near town. West of Chapman (R) is an old INDIAN BURIAL GROUND.

At 35.8 *m.* is the junction with State 43.

Left on State 43 is ENTERPRISE, 1.5 *m.* (1,150 alt., 764 pop.), a milling town, to which Carry Nation came, uninvited, in the 1900's and, in the absence of the saloonkeeper, demolished his property with an axe. The women of Enterprise, regarding this act as unladylike, pelted Carry with rotten eggs and ran her out of town.

Just east of Abilene the valley widens, the soil becomes sandier, and the hills along the valley's rim are softened with a blue haze. Wheat fields increase in size and number, their broad expanse broken at intervals by fields of emerald green alfalfa.

This region was settled in the 1870's and 1880's by Germans from Wisconsin who lived in ox-drawn wagons until they built their homes. In later years the settlers declared that they came to Kansas because they had heard that here they might pull and eat turnips in the fields on Christmas. During the hardships that followed their moving, the pioneers often wondered why they had left comfortable homes for the occasional privilege of pulling turnips in December.

ABILENE (Syr., *grassy plain*), 41.5 *m.* (1,161 alt., 5,658 pop.), at the confluence of Turkey Creek and the Smoky Hill River, is a prosperous-looking town, its streets lined with well-kept lawns and the rambling comfortable houses of retired farmers.

Abilene, seat of Dickinson County, one of the most productive wheat-raising counties in the State, is an important shipping point for farm produce. Its hotel facilities, unusually good for a town of its size, make it a popular convention center. Since 1934 the National Coursing Association has held a spring and a fall meeting in Abilene. Greyhounds from many parts of the United States are entered in the events and although the association does not make official awards it recognizes the winning animals as national champions. Large kennels are maintained in and near the city.

The annual Central Kansas Free Fair is held here in September.

Abilene in the 1860's was one of the roughest towns in the Middle West and perhaps the most widely known of all the Kansas cow towns. On the post office lawn, at the north edge of the business section, is a boulder marking the TERMINUS OF THE CHISHOLM CATTLE TRAIL over which more than 3 million head of cattle were driven in the 1860's and 1870's.

When Abilene was made the terminus of the Union Pacific R.R., the Chisholm Trail was extended northward to the railhead. Joseph G. McCoy, an Illinois cattleman, saw the possibilities of creating a huge market for Texas cattle here and built stockyards covering several acres of the east edge of town to accommodate 3,000 cattle. Throughout Texas he advertised Abilene as an excellent place to market. The next spring thousands of Texas longhorns were herded northward on the Chisholm Trail.

The origin of the lunch wagon, a night-life feature of western towns before the automobile age, is attributed to cow town days in Abilene.

When the Texas cattle trade was at its height in 1871, as many as 5,000 cowboys were often paid off simultaneously here. Hotels and restaurants were not available for an army like this, so the cowboys slept on the prairie and ate at their chuck wagons. The only accommodations they wanted were saloons, gambling houses, and brothels that blared all night. The chuck wagons of the various outfits were rolled into town to feed their carousing members. From this grew the custom that prevailed from Kansas City to New Mexico, of hauling lunch wagons downtown at night and parking them in front of saloons.

"Texas Abilene" was on the south side of the railroad tracks where the longhorns were driven into stock pens to await shipment while the Texas cowpunchers camped nearby. Facing the tracks today in that section of Abilene is the OLD GULF HOUSE, now called the National Hotel, a flat-roofed, two-story limestone structure opened in 1871.

In the early days the "tough district," a mile and a half north of town, consisted of 25 or 30 one-story frame houses each with 10 to 20 rooms. Later this district was known as "McCoy's addition" and "Devil's Half-Acre." The Abilene *Chronicle* stated in 1871 that there were more cut-throats and desperadoes in Abilene than in any other town its size on the continent.

When Abilene was incorporated in 1869, an attempt was made to "clean up." After many marshals had been either killed or driven out, Tom Smith, of Kit Carson, Colo., applied. Polite, soft-voiced, deferential, yet courageous, he enforced a deadly-weapon ordinance and the licensing of saloons.

Wild Bill (James Butler) Hickok, the best-known gunman in the old West, succeeded Tom Smith as marshal of Abilene. Wild Bill's feats with revolvers were almost fabulous. He could dent a tossed coin with a bullet before it hit the ground. With a gun in each hand, he could keep a tomato can dancing in the dust. He could perforate a hat brim while it spun in the air. While serving as marshal in Abilene, he killed two murderers—fleeing in opposite directions—so rapidly that a boy witness swore on oath that only one shot had been fired.

Referring to Hickok's shotgun patrol of Abilene, Mayor McCoy later said, "Talk about a rule of iron! We had it! But we had to kill a few roughs." Wild Bill's flair for picturesque dress approached dandyism. At the height of his career he gave up the fringed and beaded buckskins of his scouting days, and affected a Prince Albert coat, checked trousers, and an embroidered waistcoat. Sometimes a silk-lined cape completed the outfit. He carried silver-mounted pearl-handled revolvers when dressed up; for everyday wear he favored a pair of heavy double-action army pistols. Hickok was credited with 43 killings before he came to Abilene where, according to some biographers, he increased his total to 100. "There is no use in trying to override Wild Bill, the marshal," warned the *Chronicle,* "his arrangements for policing the city are complete and attempts to kill police officers or in any way create disturbance, must result in loss of life on the part of violators of the law."

Philosophizing on his record in manslaughter, Wild Bill once remarked,

"Killing a bad man shouldn't trouble one anymore than killing a rat, or a mad dog."

Eastern writers made a hero of Wild Bill and a theatrical producer had a play written about him in which Hickok "killed" a number of "Indians" by firing blanks at them. The troupe toured the country east of the Mississippi and played in New York; by the time they reached St. Louis, Hickok, bored with stage life, wished to end his contract, but the other actors protested. In the next performance Hickok stood over the "dead Indians," blistering their bare thighs with hot wads from his gun until they jumped over the footlights and ran shrieking up the aisle to the street. Wild Bill chased them to the river, into which they plunged and swam away. When they returned all agreed to the cancellation of the contract.

In 1876 Wild Bill joined the gold rush to the Black Hills. While in a friendly poker game in Deadwood, S. Dak., he was killed by Jack McCall, a drunken, cross-eyed gambler. Lurching into the saloon, McCall shot Wild Bill in the back of the head. Hickok slumped over the table, with his outspread fingers holding the "dead man's hand"—aces and eights!

SOLOMON, 51.8 *m.* (1,171 alt., 1,032 pop.), surrounded by wheat fields, is a shipping center, and a junction point on the Union Pacific R.R.

At 54.8 *m.* US 40 crosses the Solomon River, a shallow stream flowing between banks fringed with cottonwoods. Early day scouts saw this stream drunk dry by an immense herd of buffalo.

NEW CAMBRIA (Lat., *Wales*), 59.7 *m.* (1,200 alt., 130 pop.), a shipping point, arouses to activity only during the wheat harvesting season. Formerly New Cambria was called Donmyer for an early settler. Woodward's Ferry, once operated northeast of town on the Saline River, was marked on the map of the first governmental survey of Kansas Territory.

At 62.5 *m.* is the junction with a graveled road.

Left on this road is an INDIAN OSSUARY *(adm. 25¢),* 1 *m.,* protected by a small frame structure on the farm of George E. Kohr. Here, preserved just as they were when unearthed in October 1936, are 109 whole skeletons and other bones. Dr. Waldo R. Wedel, assistant curator of archeology of the U. S. National Museum, Smithsonian Institution, and A. T. Hill, Director of the Nebraska Historical Society Museum, Lincoln, Nebr., who visited the site consider this one of the most remarkable archeological finds in the Middle West. Archeologists believe that the pit was a communal burial place for members of one of the Plains tribes. Four layers of skeletons have been unearthed in the pit, the majority of which lie on their right sides in a flexed position, facing the rising sun. Necklaces of clam-shell beads, pottery, and other artifacts found here are on display. Because no glass beads or metal objects have been uncovered, it is thought that these Indians were buried before white men reached this part of Kansas. The first skeleton in the pit was found by Howard Kohr, whose interest in archeological work had been aroused by the discovery (July 1936) and excavation of the site of an Indian lodge on his farm near the present burial pit. G. L. Whiteford, Salina police sergeant and amateur archeologist, discovered the lodge; because of the extremely delicate work required in the excavation of the burial pit, Whiteford supervised this work also.

Looming against the sky a few miles east of Salina are the great hulks of gray-white grain elevators.

SALINA, 65.5 *m.* (1,220 alt., 20,155 pop.) *(see SALINA).*

Points of Interest: St. John's Military College, Wesleyan University, Marymount College, and others.

AT THE AUCTION, HORTON

Salina is at the junction with US 81 *(see Tour 9)*.

The bluffs and hills west of Salina are rich in paleontological remains. Fossils of marine shells, sea reptiles, and fishes, bones and teeth of prehistoric animals, and petrified wood and leaves have been found here.

BROOKVILLE, 81 *m.* (1,353 alt., 237 pop.), is a refreshing oasis in treeless farming country. Many years ago the Union Pacific sponsored the planting of maples in the small city park here, and today some of their trunks measure more than 14 feet in circumference.

Surrounding the town are picturesque hills, used by Jesse James (1847–82) and his gang as a hide-out. The town was a popular camp site for gold seekers and pioneers bound westward in covered wagons. A landmark in the little town is the OLD CENTRAL HOTEL, a two-story building of local limestone, noted for its cuisine since the 1870's. It is now operated (1938) by a daughter of the first proprietor.

Shortly after it was founded in 1871 Brookville was the scene of an Indian raid. Warned of the Indians' approach by the crew of a train from the west, the settlers took refuge in the roundhouse to await the attack. The Indians had surrounded the building and were piling railroad ties against the wooden doors to burn the settlers out, when an engine under steam crashed out through the doors, rolled across the turntable, and, whistle shrieking and bell ringing, started to Salina for help. The Indians fled.

In the JOHNSON ROCK GARDEN *(open to visitors)*, on the north edge of Brookville, is an unusual collection of native stones.

West of Brookville US 40 crosses hilly pasture country, broken by clumps of cottonwoods. Dull green rocks, red soil, red water in the ponds, white ranch houses, cattle, and occasional trees against a background of grotesque hills form the landscape. Kafir corn is grown in the valleys. This country is part of the High Plains, a semiarid region.

At 97.1 *m.* is the junction with a graveled road.

Left on this road is KANOPOLIS, 2.4 *m.* (1,576 alt., 860 pop.), one of the most extensive "paper" towns ever conceived. It was founded in 1886 and for a time the promoters kept presses busy day and night printing advertisements of what they dreamed was to be a big city by 1900. The site was laid out to accommodate 150,000 inhabitants and lots sold for as much as $1,000 apiece. Four blocks were reserved for the statehouse which, in 1893, the Populist Party tried to move here from Topeka.

Kanopolis was built on the SITE OF OLD FORT HARKER, a military post established in 1864. As an operating and distributing point, Fort Harker was one of the most important posts west of the Mississippi. It was abandoned in 1873. West of the post office on Ohio Street, Kanopolis' main business thoroughfare, is the OLD GENERAL HEADQUARTERS *(private)*, a two-story building, now used as an apartment house. The lower half of the building is constructed of local brown sandstone, the upper half of frame. The OFFICERS' QUARTERS *(private)*, across the street from the General's Headquarters, two sandstone cottages of Georgian Colonial design, are used as dwellings. Two blocks west on Ohio Street (R) is the OLD GUARDHOUSE *(private)*, a square two-story structure, of local sandstone. The interior has been converted into apartments.

Today a majority of the people of Kanopolis, of which a large part are Mexicans, are employed in the salt mines.

Salt mining is an important industry in this region. The salt stratum, at a depth of 650 feet is 185 feet in thickness. SALT MINES *(permission to enter obtainable from superintendent)*, are visible from the highway at intervals.

At ELLSWORTH, 101.4 *m.* (1,534 alt., 2,072 pop.), seat of Ellsworth County, called the forest city because of its variety of trees, the wheat belt overlaps the grazing country. Founded in 1869, the settlement was named for Lt. Allen Ellsworth, Company H, 7th Iowa Cavalry. As the rails pushed westward Ellsworth had its day as a "wild and woolly" cow town, but it is now a progressive agricultural community with law-abiding citizens, good schools, many churches, and comfortable homes. As a cattle-shipping center in the 1870's, it was characterized by rowdyism, gambling, and crime. Not all the bad men who left their bones in Ellsworth died with their boots on, however, for cholera broke out in the middle 1880's and scores of bodies were hastily buried in unmarked graves about the settlement.

The Grand Central Hotel, built in 1872, is now known as the WHITE HOUSE and stands on N. Main St. On the old registers are the names of Buffalo Bill Cody and Wild Bill Hickok.

At the southern edge of Ellsworth is the MOTHER BICKERDYKE HOME *(open by permission)*, named for Mary Bickerdyke, Civil War nurse. The institution was founded in the late 1890's as a home for Civil War nurses and the mothers, widows, and daughters of Civil War veterans. It is maintained by the State and houses approximately 50 women. There are a number of cottages, a hospital, and a cluster of low frame and stone buildings in a 160-acre park. Future plans for the home include the admission of World War nurses and near female relatives of World War soldiers.

Right from Ellsworth on State 14, improved, to LINCOLN, 25 m. (1,374 alt., 1,732 pop.), called Lincoln Center by its founder, who planned to make it the seat of Lincoln County. The town was platted May 9, 1871. It and the county were named for Abraham Lincoln. In a referendum held February 19, 1872, Lincoln Center received 232 votes, Abram, its rival, 176. Soon after the election most of the buildings in Abram were placed upon wheels and moved across the prairie to this place.

In 1879 Lincoln was incorporated as a city of the third class. A railroad connecting the city with Salina makes it a shipping point for wheat and livestock. Quartzite and limestone are quarried locally, an industry that provides considerable employment.

The McDONALD BLACKSMITH SHOP, 134 N. 4th St., a one-story frame structure formerly a dwelling, is the only remaining building of the onetime town of Abram.

Right from Lincoln 1.8 m. on State 18 to the junction with an improved road; R. here 2.1 m. to the ABRAM MONUMENT (L), a triangular sandstone boulder on the site of the first town in Lincoln County. The shallow depression near the monument is the cellar of the first courthouse, built in 1871.

Abram was organized on a bitterly cold day in January 1871, and immediately designated a temporary county seat. When Lincoln was founded the following spring an intense rivalry developed between the two towns. Late in the summer Ezra Hubbard and John Healey of Abram had an argument about the ownership of a piece of timber Hubbard was using in the construction of a mill. Healey accused the miller of stealing his timber; Hubbard, enraged, seized his carbine and killed Healey. The slayer was arrested and placed in jail.

Soon a drunken mob of 40 or 50 men gathered, clamoring for vengeance. The authorities, it was related, made no serious efforts to protect their prisoner and the mob burst into the building, seized Hubbard and beat him insensible. Later one of the mob leaders returned and crushed Hubbard's skull with a mallet.

Citizens of Lincoln made much of this lawless episode in their arguments for moving the county seat. A man named Buzick was tried for Hubbard's murder and acquitted. Abram jealously tightened its hold on the county government, but the voters sealed its doom in the following year.

At 2.6 m. on this road is the junction with a dirt road; L. here to the MOFFATT MONUMENT, 0.8 m., a quartzite boulder in a pasture 100 feet (L) from the road, which commemorates four buffalo hunters killed by the Cheyenne. During the desperate attempts of the Indians in 1864 to repel the white invaders who were destroying the buffalo, their food supply, two brothers named Moffatt, and their companions, Houston and Tyler, were surprised and slain near here by a band of 100 Cheyenne.

Indian raids were frequent at the time. War parties of Kiowa, Pawnee, and Cheyenne roamed the region until the early 1870's and the settlers were in constant fear of attack. Most dreaded of all the roving bands were the Dog Indians, or Dog soldiers (Kiowa and Cheyenne), whose sworn purpose was the extermination of the white invaders. They were a blood brotherhood and chose their own leaders, whose authority they recognized as superior to that of hereditary tribal chiefs. Often, when the tribes were pledged to peace with the white men, the Dog soldiers ignored the truce and continued to raid the settlements.

WILSON, 117.2 m. (1,684 alt., 1,038 pop.), is a farm market and milling town. Its promoters, prophesying that it would be the wildest, biggest, and boomingest cow town in the West, called it Bosland (Lat., bos, *ox* or *bull*), a name that survives only on the town plats and recorded deeds.

At 124.7 *m.* is the junction with an improved road.

Right on this road in LUCAS, 19 *m.* (1,493 alt., 630 pop.), is the GARDEN OF EDEN *(open),* once the home of S. P. Dinsmoor. The house, built of concrete logs to resemble early log cabins, was completed in 1907. It is surrounded by scores of concrete figures—all made by Dinsmoor from more than 113 tons of cement.

In front of the house the figures of Adam and Eve with out-stretched arms form an entrance arch. A concrete serpent coils in a treetop above them; a concrete devil leers from a nearby roof.

Dinsmoor died in 1932 at the age of 89. His embalmed body lies in a concrete coffin of his own fashioning, covered with a glass top. This coffin, which was displayed by him before his death, is in a niche in the wall of the mausoleum and below it lies the body of his first wife in a steel vault entirely encased in concrete. Poised on the roof of the mausoleum is a concrete angel. Over all is poised a red, white, and blue concrete flag.

West of Wilson oil derricks appear as grey skeletons against the sky.

RUSSELL, 140.3 *m.* (1,828 alt., 2,352 pop.), in the center of the oil district, was established in the 1870's by a colony of 70 settlers from Ripon, Wis. They were "good, sober, industrious people," according to old accounts, who allowed neither gambling nor saloons. The town's population today is made up largely of people of German-Russian descent, also rated good, sober, and industrious although they were never prohibitionists.

WALKER, 152.3 *m.* (2,000 alt., 110 pop.), is a tiny German-Russian settlement built about QUEEN ANNE'S CHURCH (Roman Catholic), a limestone structure of modified Gothic design, which serves as the center of spiritual and social life for the frugal and industrious farmers of the surrounding wheat area.

Left from Walker on a dirt road to the junction with another dirt road, 5 *m.;* R. on this, at the confluence of Victoria and Big Creek, is the REMNANT OF OLD FORT FLETCHER, 5.5 *m.,* established in 1865 to protect scattered settlers and workers in railroad construction camps from the Indians. The crumbling ruins of one stone building, the old rifle pits, and the roasting pits used by settlers and construction men remain.

In 1931 W. D. Phillip and sons, ranchers in the vicinity, erected on the site of the fort a MONUMENT TO ELIZABETH A. CUSTER, wife of General Custer. Mrs. Custer narrowly escaped death here in 1867 when a flood damaged the fort.

VICTORIA, 156.5 *m.* (1,919 alt., 637 pop.), is a German-Russian community built to resemble a native Russian village. Houses with sharply peaked roofs are flush with the street. Heavy, solid-wood shutters cover the windows and many of the structures have only a back door, which opens onto a rectangular court. In Russia peasants working on their distant farms came into their village homes only for weekends to trade and attend church; this type of building protected their homes from raids of the wild, roving Kirghis tribes. The persistence of this architecture in Kansas is attributed to a similar fear of Indians.

Victoria is the center of German-Russian settlements totaling approximately 50,000 persons in Russell, Ellis, Trego, and Rush Counties. Although their neighbors refer to these people as Russians, or "Rooshans," they are of pure German blood, their ancestors having migrated to Russia

WATER BOY

as did the Mennonites upon the invitation of Catherine the Great in the 1760's. Slightly more than a century later, their descendants came to America when a successor of Catherine revoked the privileges they had enjoyed under her rule.

Roman Catholic in faith, the settlers have retained many of their original customs, especially those associated with the church. They are thrifty and industrious, and for the most part have remained close to the soil.

Many attend several or all of the masses on Sundays as well as the afternoon services, vespers, and benediction. Feast and holy days are celebrated with special services. On the feast of Corpus Christi every man, woman, and child takes part in a procession that, weather permitting, winds about the countryside, making a circuit of nearby villages. The marchers recite the rosary and litanies while members of the choir sing Latin and German hymns.

During divine services the conduct of even the younger children is very devout. Occasionally worshippers pray with outstretched arms symbolizing the crucified Saviour. Special prayers, often attended by members of the entire community, are offered for the repose of the souls of the dead; and children are usually baptized immediately after birth.

Rising magnificently from the low houses around it are the two spires of the St. Fidelis Church, called by William Jennings Bryan the Cathedral of the Prairies. Designed by John R. Comes of Pittsburgh, Pa., and Joseph Marshall of Topeka, the structure is 221 feet long and 73 feet wide with a transept 107 feet in width. Built of local limestone and Romanesque in style, its two towers are 141 feet high. The church seats 1,700 persons, almost three times the population of the town.

Victoria was originally two colonies. German-Russians settled to the north of the present townsite in 1875 and English colonists settled directly south of it in 1871. The two were not united under the name of Victoria until 1913.

Sir George Grant, of London, conceived the idea of founding an English colony in America and in 1871 bought a large tract of land from the Union Pacific R.R. and platted a townsite which he named Victoria in honor of Queen Victoria. During the next year he advertised in England and in 1873 returned to America with a shipload of young Englishmen—sons of wealthy families—who had regular remittances from home. With the colonists, also came a shipment of fine horses, Aberdeen Angus cattle, and Southdown sheep.

The young English colonists, uninterested in cattle raising, spent the greater part of their time riding over the prairie in pursuit of jack rabbits and coyotes. Freed from parental restrictions, they frequented saloons and dance halls and lived with joyous abandon. Several longed for their native lakes, so they dammed Big Creek and impounded enough water to make navigation possible for a distance of 8 or 9 miles. A steamboat, brought across the prairie by floating it in the streams and rivers whenever possible and pulling it in large oxcarts at other times, was launched in Big Creek.

One historian says, "Kansas has witnessed many incongruous spectacles. There have been gold mining enterprises, street cars traversing little else than raw prairies, red-coated Britons galloping over the buffalo grass and other such paradoxes but never before or since was there such a mirage-like sight as a steamboat chugging along in the midst of the prairie filled with a cargo of young British merrymakers."

Finally the colonists' indifference and a series of droughts reduced the income from the Victoria Colony to the vanishing point. At the end of 5 years the project collapsed and the colonists moved to other parts of the United States or returned to England.

The German-Russians, who in the meantime had founded the colony of Herzog to the north, were prepared by heritage and training for life on the prairies. Skilled in agriculture, they prospered from the first and their enthusiastic reports of the fine conditions in America brought new members; eventually they absorbed the deserted site of the English colony, which became the seat of the settlement.

On US 40 is a stone marking the Grave of Sir George Grant (R), who lived long enough to see the lands he had obtained for his countrymen owned by others.

1. Right from Victoria on an improved road to the junction with a dirt road, 6 m.; L. on this road is CATHERINE, 10 m. (2,000 alt., 625 pop.), a German-Russian agricultural village founded in 1876 by the first emigrants to leave the

lower Volga region in Russia for settlement in Kansas. Their ancestors had been invited into Russia by Empress Catherine the Great to set up colonies, which she hoped would form models for her backward peasants. Dominating the village is ST. CATHERINE'S CHURCH (Roman Catholic), an imposing Gothic-type structure of local stone. Its classically proportioned twin spires dominate miles of level countryside. In the church is a revered relic of the earliest days of the colony—a rude WOODEN CROSS. For several years, until they were able to build a church, the settlers held their services in the open air at the foot of this cross.

2. Left from Victoria on an improved road is PFEIFER, 10 *m.* (2,000 alt., 200 pop.), home of German-Russian immigrants from a town of that name in Russia. At Pfeifer is the HOLY CROSS CHURCH (Roman Catholic) with three steeples on the west facade. The center one with a bell loft is 150 feet high. Over the main entrance a mosaic by Brachi, a Venetian artist, shows the return of Christ as judge of mankind. Upon the tile floor at the entrance is the inscription: Mein Haus ist ein Bethaus (Ger., *My house is a house of prayer*).

On the large LANG FARM *(open)*, 160.6 *m.* (R), once known as the Behan Ranch, is a barn with an immense clock installed in 1880. Its face is 6 feet in diameter, its pendulum weighs 50 pounds, and the minute hand is 3.7 feet long. Huge stones on long ropes, used as weights, are held by ratchets and drawn up by a hand crank. When the clock strikes the hours it can be heard for miles.

HAYS, 166.5 *m.* (2,000 alt., 4,618 pop.), is a neat town, with a long main street lined with two- and three-story brick and limestone buildings. A trading point for a large wheat-raising area, Hays' business activity slumped noticeably with the years of drought and crop failures in the early 1930's, but climbed to new heights in 1936 when oil fields were developed in the vicinity. The once quiet streets and hotel lobbies are crowded with oil-field workers and oil speculators, and each new well brings a period of feverish activity and excitement.

In 1933 and 1934 Hays was the center of a movement to repeal prohibition in Kansas. The Kansas Anti-Prohibition Society was started here in 1933 together with the Kansas *Repealist,* published monthly until the defeat of repeal at the general election of 1934.

The parents of Marion Talley, the singer, and those of Walt Disney, the movie cartoonist, formerly resided near Hays.

ST. JOSEPH'S CHURCH (Roman Catholic), NW. cor. 13th and Ash Sts., constructed of local limestone, is a composite of Gothic and Romanesque styles, designed by Joseph Marshall of Topeka. The present church, dedicated in 1904, replaced an older church built in 1886. A large stained-glass window portrays Joseph, patron saint of the church, and the Virgin Mary.

ST. ANTHONY'S HOSPITAL *(open)*, 307 W. 13th St. adjacent to St. Joseph's Church, is operated by the Sisters of Saint Agnes, and represents an investment of $600,000. Three stories high, the structure is built of local limestone, and brick with terra-cotta trim. It has accommodations for 110 adult patients.

Hays City, founded in 1867 as an outgrowth of Fort Hays, frontier military post, was a gathering place for scouts, cattlemen, soldiers, and desperadoes during the early years of its existence. The town grew rapidly, and by 1877 the population numbered almost 6,000.

Fort Hays, directly south of the city, was abandoned in 1889 since the Indian wars had ended. The 7,000 acres owned by the Federal Government became an idle military reservation. In 1900 the tract was given to the State of Kansas for educational and scientific purposes. On 7th St., adjacent to the south limits of the city, is the FORT HAYS STATE COLLEGE (co-educational), in eight buildings on an 80-acre campus. This is one of three State teachers' colleges in Kansas and has an annual enrollment of 500 students.

In the FRONTIER HISTORICAL PARK *(open)*, immediately south of the college campus, are the remnants of Fort Hays. The northeast corner of the park is leased to the Hays Country Club Association for a golf course *(private)*. On what was once the fort's parade ground wagon tracks, made by the heavy freighter wagons traveling from Fort Hays to Fort Wallace, are still visible. The OLD BLOCKHOUSE *(private)*, with its cemented but plainly marked loopholes, is now a clubhouse.

Directly across the road from Frontier Park is the 3,600-acre FORT HAYS AGRICULTURAL EXPERIMENT STATION *(open)*, controlled by the U. S. Department of Agriculture and Kansas State College. Here experiments in dry-land farming, soil-erosion prevention, livestock breeding, and forestry are conducted; the findings, published periodically as bulletins of the U. S. Department of Agriculture or of the experiment station, are issued to farmers. Branch stations—performing experimentation supplementary to that undertaken at Hays—are at Colby *(see Tour 2)*, Tribune, and Garden City *(see Tour 4)*.

In the residential district, at 18th and Fort Sts., is the SITE OF BOOT HILL, early burial place. Estimates place the number of persons interred at 75, most of whom died "with their boots on." When basements were dug for houses in this district, many skeletons were unearthed—some in coffins, some in rude boxes, and some with no encasement.

In the 1860's Buffalo Bill Cody is said to have killed 4,280 buffalo near Fort Hays within 18 months. The meat was sold to railroad workers' camps and the commissary of the fort.

Left from Hays on US 183, bituminous-surfaced, is LA CROSSE, 25 *m.* (2,061 alt., 1,355 pop.), seat of Rush County, a modern little city amidst oil and natural-gas fields. La Crosse was founded by David and Denman Stubbs, pioneers from Missouri, who, upon learning 'that the borders of Rush County had been changed by a legislative act, saw that Rush Center would lose its designation as a county seat since it was no longer at the center of the county. In 1876 the Stubbs brothers surveyed two roads across the county, bisecting it from north to south and from east to west. At the junction of these roads they platted La Crosse (Fr., *the crossing)* and made a bid for the county seat. After a prolonged dispute with Rush Center, La Crosse became the permanent seat in 1888. A two-story frame building on the west side of Main St., now occupied by a pharmacy, was the first courthouse in Rush County. In the course of the county seat quarrel this structure was shunted back and forth between the rival towns four or five times.

ST. JOSEPH'S COLLEGE AND MILITARY ACADEMY (Roman Catholic), 168.8 *m.,* offers military training and courses comparable with those of accredited high schools and junior colleges. The institution was opened in 1931; enrollment in 1938 was 256. The main building, a four-story brick structure trimmed with white Carthage limestone, is of Collegiate Gothic design. C. A. Smith of Salina was the architect. North of the main building is a small frame structure which houses the agricultural department. South of the main building, in a landscaped garden, is the SHRINE OF THE LADY OF OUR LORD, built by students in 1937. The shrine, approximately 30 feet high, is surmounted with a statue of the Virgin.

US 40 enters grassy, rolling hill country west of Hays. A line of trees (R) marks the course of a creek.

ELLIS, 180.4 *m.* (2,119 alt., 1,957 pop.), established in 1867 on Big Creek as a railroad tank and pumping station, was named for George Ellis of the 12th Kansas Infantry. Ellis is a division point on the Union Pacific R.R. which maintains repair shops here. A cow town in the days of the Texas cattle trade, Ellis was also a disembarkation point for many colonists coming to western Kansas by railroad. Walter P. Chrysler, motorcar magnate, received his public school education and learned the machinist trade here.

In the yard of the municipal power plant is a lighted fountain with rainbow-colored spray.

At 181.4 *m.* US 40 crosses a time zone boundary. West of this point Mountain Standard Time is used; westbound travelers should set their watches back one hour.

WAKEENEY, 199.7 *m.* (2,456 alt., 1,408 pop.), seat of Trego County, was named for Ward and Keene, a Chicago business firm that bought land here for speculative purposes. The town was established in 1878. In 1879 the General Land Office was moved here from Hays, bringing hundreds of people to file homestead claims. For years after its founding fire guards were regularly plowed around Wakeeney to check the prairie fires that ravaged the region. Thousands of buffalo, killed for their hides, had been left on the prairies and in the 1880's their skeletons proved a welcome source of livelihood to the new settlers. Fertilizer plants paid $9.50 a ton for bones and often as many as one hundred tons were piled near the Wakeeney railroad station awaiting shipment.

Wakeeney is a market center and a distribution point for produce and farm machinery. The annual Trego County Free Fair is held here *(last week in Aug.)*.

West of Wakeeney great pastures and fields of wheat mark the beginning of the High Plains region of Kansas.

Beneath this level country lie rich deposits that have contributed geologic specimens, including fossilized birds, lizards, sharks, and bones of prehistoric animals, to many collections throughout the United States. A formation known as moss agate, an opaque stone sold in Colorado as "Colorado agate," also underlies this region.

COLLYER, 212.3 *m.* (2,578 alt., 243 pop.), a small trading point, was founded in 1878 by a soldier and sailor colony from Chicago. It was named for the president of the organization, the Reverend Robert Collyer. A. B. Baker (1858–1930), for several years assistant director of the National Zoological Park of the Smithsonian Institution, formerly resided here.

At Collyer is the junction with a graveled road.

Left on this road is the junction with a dirt road, 10 *m.;* R. on this to the junction with another dirt road, 12 *m.;* L. on this to a pasture gate, 13 *m.;* R. through the gate are CASTLE ROCKS, 13.5 *m.,* chalk remnants that have been eroded by rain, wind, and shifting soil into pillars and domes. These unusual formations, in the Smoky Hill Valley near the Butterfield or Smoky Hill trail, were formerly used by Indians as a lookout point and hiding place.

QUINTER, 219.7 *m.* (2,664 alt., 570 pop.), is the social and trading center of thrifty Dunkards. Agriculture, stock raising and oil production contribute equally to the prosperity of the town. A community *chorus,* assisted by guest artists, presents a sacred oratorio each year at Christmas.

Right from Quinter on a graded road to the 124-acre SHERIDAN COUNTY STATE LAKE, 7.3 *m. (fishing, boating),* formed by constructing a dam across the Saline River. The park surrounding the lake covers more than 400 acres.

SHELTER BUILDINGS, being used (1939) temporarily by the CCC for barracks, messhall, hospital, and recreation hall, are built of adobe brick, with roof, floors and partitions of lumber and plaster. Adobe bricks can be made from any soil that is not too sandy. After the earth has been revolved in a cement mixer until it is a thick mud, rye or oats straw is added. This mixture is then placed in box-like molds of wood, 16 inches long, 8 inches wide, and 4 inches deep. When partly dried the bricks shrink and are removed by turning the mold upside down. In extremely hot weather a little water is sprinkled on the bricks at this stage; otherwise they are left to season slowly for two or three weeks.

GRINNELL, 241.5 *m.* (2,939 alt., 303 pop.), named for a U. S. Army officer stationed at Fort Hays, and settled by frugal German farmers, is a shipping point for livestock and wheat. In 1872, according to a railroad guide published at the time, Grinnell was "a section house, railway tank, six dugouts, and two large turf houses for the purpose of drying buffalo meat." The air is so dry in this region that meat stripped off in layers can be dried and preserved indefinitely. Early settlers, who used this method to preserve meat, called the product "jerked" meat because of the manner of tearing it from the carcass.

Because OAKLEY, 253.3 *m.* (3,029 alt., 1,159 pop.), a market center and shipping point, is the largest town in Logan County and has modern accommodations (municipal swimming pool and golf course), and adequate transportation facilities provided by the transcontinental highway and the Union Pacific R.R., civic leaders made an effort in 1937 to have it made the county seat instead of the more isolated Russell Springs. Oakley offered voters of Logan County a new courthouse if they would agree to the move, so an election was ordered. The village of Winona was the third aspirant. The final tabulation, however, gave Oakley a plurality of one vote, considerably less than the majority required by law.

Oakley is at the junction with US 83 *(see Tour 8).*

McALLASTER, 284.2 *m.* (3,156 alt., 25 pop.), is a trading and shipping point, with a general store and a filling station.

In 1870 an expedition from Yale University collected vertebrate fossils along the north bank of the Smoky Hill River, west of this point. Among the specimens found were the foot and other bones of a gigantic flying reptile.

WALLACE, 296.9 *m.* (3,310 alt., 100 pop.), is the skeleton of a town of 1,500 that throve here in the 1870's. It wasted to its present proportions upon the cessation of frontier activities. Many of the plain frame and stone buildings in the town are remnants of that period.

The Union Pacific R. R. established a station at Wallace in 1870, choosing the site because it was the most accessible point on the railroad from Fort Wallace, a frontier military post established a mile and a half southwest of the townsite in the middle 1860's. The railroad built a roundhouse, a stone office building, and a row of houses for its workers. A cluster of homes and shops soon arose about the railroad center.

Until 1878—when the Santa Fe Ry. and the Burlington R.R. were built—the Union Pacific line was the only route between the Platte River in Nebraska and the Gulf of Mexico, a distance of 2,000 miles. Thus, Wallace, a shipping point for this vast area, became one of the most important towns in the Southwest.

The town's permanent population in the 1870's and early 1880's was made up of railroad workers and merchants for the most part; its floating population consisted chiefly of cattlemen, quick-shooting cowboys, buffalo hunters, and gamblers. Fred Harvey established a railroad-eating house here in the 1870's, the first of what was to become a cross country chain of restaurants.

Frank Madigan, son of Thomas Madigan, pioneer Wallace merchant, wrote: "The buffalo hunters, bone pickers, and cowboys who made up a considerable part of the population of Wallace were a care-free, fun-loving bunch of fellows with little respect for human life. Killings were common and practically all went unpunished, as the friends of the killers would testify that it was in self defense."

After several unsuccessful attempts to organize the county, Wallace became the temporary seat of Wallace County in 1887, but in 1889 Sharon Springs became the permanent county seat. Fort Wallace had been abandoned in 1881 and by the late 1880's the Union Pacific R. R. had extended its line into Colorado and abandoned its roundhouse and shops at Wallace. Settlers left the region in long caravans during the years of drought in the early 1890's. Wallace enjoyed a momentary revival in 1907 upon the installation of a municipal water system, but it has declined steadily for the last two decades.

Right one-half block from the center of town is the stone FOUNDATION OF ROBIDOUX'S STORE established in 1870 by Peter Robidoux, a French Canadian. This is said to have been at one time the largest department store between Kansas City and Denver. Robidoux made a fortune during the years when Wallace was prosperous.

As business declined in the late 1880's, Robidoux vowed that if ever the day came when he failed to sell a single item in his establishment he would lock its doors forever. That day came in 1895 and on the following morning the doors of Peter Robidoux's store remained shut. They were not opened again until after his death in October 1927. When the store was closed its stock, valued at $20,000, included buggies, cowboy outfits, harness, expensive cutlery, nails, bags of beans, flour, sugar, and many varieties of canned foodstuffs.

In the COUNTY VAULT, a small stone building on US 40 (R) in the heart of town, the county records were kept while Wallace was the county seat.

Left from Wallace on a dirt road to the Union Pacific R.R. tracks, 1 *m.;* R. at the tracks to the junction with another dirt road, 1.7 *m.;* L. on the second dirt road to the SITE OF FORT WALLACE (R), 2.7 *m.,* marked by a lone hackberry tree.

This last frontier post in Kansas was established in 1865 as Camp Pond Creek to protect settlers and cattlemen from the Indians, and to advance Army occupation of the West. In 1866 Camp Pond Creek was renamed Fort Wallace in honor of Gen. W. H. L. Wallace, a Mexican War veteran who also served in the Indian wars in Kansas. Fort Wallace was built as a four-company post, and could accommodate only 500 men. Between 1866 and 1869 the troops stationed here were detailed to escort stagecoaches, express wagon trains, Government officials, quartermaster trains, and railroad surveyors and laborers so that the regular garrison was numerically small. Nevertheless social formalities were observed. Musicales and skits were presented by residents of the post; on Sunday evenings the band gave concerts; and officers and their wives had evenings "at home." The canteen bar and nightly poker games provided further entertainment.

From Fort Wallace, in September 1868, went a company to the rescue of a little band of soldiers, who, in the Battle of Beecher Island on the Arikaree, had held out for 9 days against 1,000 Indians *(see ST. FRANCIS, Tour 1).* General Grant visited Fort Wallace in 1868 and Generals Sheridan, Custer, and Bankhead were stationed here at various times. The most important battle near the fort occurred in 1867, while General Custer was in command. About 125 Indians and 22 soldiers were killed.

FORT WALLACE CEMETERY (L) is enclosed by a wall of local limestone. A MONUMENT TO THE SOLDIERS, also of limestone, was erected here in 1867. Restoration of the monument and the wall was made possible by State appropriation in 1930. Ornamentation and inscription on the monument are in good condition. Many of the soldier dead have been removed to other military cemeteries; but about 60 remain—mostly cholera victims.

SHARON SPRINGS, 305.7 *m.* (3,400 alt., 792 pop.), seat of Wallace County, a well-shaded market town in treeless plains country, is on both sides of the Smoky Hill River. Sharon Springs, founded in 1886, has a wide trade territory. The surrounding region was ideal cattle country until the era of mechanized wheat farming.

The BROCK HISTORICAL COLLECTION *(open),* on exhibition at the Sharon Springs bank, includes portraits of the Peter Robidoux family, a ledger from Robidoux's store with the accounts of many noted people who traded there, and a good picture of Fort Wallace in its prime.

1. Right from Sharon Springs on State 27, improved, to the junction with a dirt road, 4 *m.;* L. on this to the junction with another dirt road, 6 *m.;* R. to the top of a hill and the OLD MAID'S POOL, 8.5 *m.,* a sunken area 125 yards in diameter, apparently with neither inlet nor outlet. Its unfailing freshwater supply is believed to be from the underflow of the Smoky Hill River. The water content of the pool rises and falls, depending somewhat on the season's precipitation. An Indian legend attributes the sinking of the earth here to the Great Spirit, who disliked the outcome of a battle on this site. Two tribes had fought all day and at night the seemingly victorious group had camped on the hill. During the night the hilltop camp site disappeared leaving only the present depression, filled with water. It is a place of mystery, and, according to local historians, Indians will not visit it.

2. Left on State 27 is TRIBUNE, 30 *m.* (3,543 alt., 436 pop.), a High Plains wheat center. Greeley County, organized in 1888, was named for Horace Greeley; and Tribune, which became its county seat, was given the name of Greeley's newspaper, the New York *Tribune.*
Tribune was settled in 1885 at which time it was called Cappaqua. In the fol-

lowing year a number of neighboring towns sprang up, each hoping to be the county seat. The leading aspirants were Horace, Hector, Greeley Center, and Tribune. Hector and Tribune promoters merged their towns, abandoning the old Hector townsite 4 miles northwest of Tribune, and thus won the county seat election.

A Wallace County newspaper in 1886 reported the organization of Tribune in the following news items: "Down at the little town of Tribune, erstwhile called by the poetical name of Cappaqua, where the lady settlers are largely in the preponderance, they have a serenading club, organized for the purpose of welcoming visitors and those who come to stay. Every stranger who enters the town to stay overnight is entertained with beautiful songs by the club. The singing and the presence of a bevy of young ladies are said to be attracting large numbers of young men in that direction so the society will probably be 'evened up' in Tribune before long."

Right from Tribune 1 *m.* on State 96, improved, is a STATE EXPERIMENT STATION *(open)*, established on a small tract in 1912 by the Kansas State College of Agriculture and Applied Science. In 1934 the tract was enlarged by the gift of 130 acres from the Missouri Pacific R. R. Experiments are conducted largely for the purpose of determining the types of crops adaptable to this section of the State, and seed is produced for distribution to farmers. The institution also maintains herds of beef and dairy cattle and studies diseases of livestock.

WESKAN, 318.1 *m.* (3,841 alt., 205 pop.), a wind-swept village with a name composed of the first three letters of the words, "Western Kansas," is a trading center for wheat farmers on both sides of the State Line.

At 322.2 *m.* US 40 crosses the Colorado Line 196 miles east of Denver, Colo. *(see COLO. Tour 7)*.

⫷⫷⫷⫷⫷⫷⫷⫷⫷⫷⫷⫷⫷⫷⫷⫷⫷⫷⫷☿⫸⫸⫸⫸⫸⫸⫸⫸⫸⫸⫸⫸⫸⫸⫸⫸⫸⫸⫸⫸

Tour 4

(Kansas City, Mo.)—Baldwin City—Council Grove—Great Bend—Garden City—(La Junta, Colo.); US 50, US 50N.
Missouri Line to Colorado Line, 485.6 m.

Atchison, Topeka & Santa Fe Ry. roughly parallels route between Kansas City and the Colorado Line; Missouri Pacific R.R. between Admire and Herington; Chicago, Rock Island & Pacific Ry. between Herington and Marion.
Paved roadbed for most of distance, a few short stretches of improved road. Open all year, except immediately after an occasional heavy snowstorm.
Usual accommodations.

This route parallels, and at times is identical with, the eastern part of the old Santa Fe Trail over which wagon trains journeyed from Westport Landing (now Kansas City, Mo.), to Santa Fe, New Mexico. Its course is through farm country of eastern Kansas, the bluestem pastures of the Flint

Hills west of Osage City, the great wheat fields of central Kansas near McPherson, the newly developed oil fields near Lyons, and the plains regions of the western part of the State.

Section a. MISSOURI LINE to JUNCTION WITH US 50N AND US 50S, 49.5 m., US 50

Southwest on Ward Parkway from its junction with Mill Creek Parkway in Kansas City, Mo., US 50 crosses the Missouri Line (see MO. TOUR 4), 0 m., 0.5 miles west of the Country Club Plaza, and traverses fairly level country, once an open prairie along which, in early days, wagons started on their long trip to Santa Fe.

SHAWNEE CEMETERY, 0.8 m. (L), enclosed by an iron fence, is one of the oldest white burial grounds in Kansas. It contains the marked GRAVE OF THE REVEREND THOMAS JOHNSON, founder of Shawnee Methodist Mission, and that of his wife.

At 1.1 m. is the junction with Mission Road, improved.

Right on this road is SHAWNEE METHODIST MISSION, 0.3 m., twice the territorial capital of Kansas, which consists today of three aging brick structures standing in the form of a triangle. Since their recent acquisition by the State, the buildings have been partially restored and the 12-acre grounds landscaped under the direction of the Kansas State Historical Society. Midway between the two southern buildings is a clear spring, which, used for centuries by the Indians, still flows even in years of severest drought.

In 1838 the Missouri Conference of the Methodist Episcopal Church directed the Reverend Thomas Johnson, a young Virginian who had been for eight years a missionary among the Shawnee, to build a manual training school for the children of the tribes among whom the conference labored. Selecting a 2,240-acre site three miles west of old Westport, Mo., Johnson soon had two large buildings under way and had planted 176 acres of corn and a 12-acre apple orchard, the first in Kansas. The mission school opened in October 1839, with 4 teachers instructing 72 children from 10 tribes. Attendance soon exceeded 100, which included a number of children of the Negro slaves owned by Johnson. Boys were instructed in farming and trades; girls were taught to spin, weave, cook, sew, and keep house. When the slavery question split the Methodist Church in 1845, Shawnee and all other Kansas missions joined the Methodist Church, South.

The SCHOOLHOUSE proper, a large barrack-like structure erected in 1839 and standing at the east angle of the present triangle of buildings, contained class and study rooms, a chapel, teachers' living quarters, and a boys' dormitory. The chapel has been converted into a MUSEUM (free), which contains the pulpit and Bible used by Johnson, a green upholstered walnut chair presented to the missionary by President Buchanan, the original land grant for the mission, and many documents in Johnson's hand.

The walls of the schoolhouse show few signs of age. The original black walnut doors are in place, but much of the building has been modernized and furnished with little regard for the preservation of its original appearance, except in two rooms on the second floor and in the long low room on the third floor that served as a dormitory for Indian boys. These retain their rough-hewn floors and crude fireplaces. Where the heavy plaster has fallen from the ceiling, hand-hewn lathing appears. Large wooden pegs were used to fasten beams and rafters.

The HOME OF THE SUPERINTENDENT, in the south angle of the triangle, was used as a girls' dormitory and boarding house, having a spacious dining hall seating more than 200 persons. Built in 1839, it has been kept in adequate repair for living quarters.

To the north stands the former DORMITORY AND BOARDING SCHOOL, a two-story structure erected in 1845, now empty, although it was long used as a barn. To this building on November 24, 1854, Andrew H. Reeder, first Territorial Governor, moved his executive offices from Fort Leavenworth, where he had been inaugurated on October 7 of that year. Later he selected Pawnee *(see Tour 3)* as the permanent capital and convened the first Territorial legislature there early in 1855. Charging Reeder with speculating in Pawnee real estate, the pro-slavery party unseated all but two of the Free Staters and hurriedly passed a law transferring the seat of government back to Shawnee Mission.

The legislature took complete possession of the large schoolhouse building. The House of Representatives sat in the chapel, the council in a room on the second floor. Here the statutes of Missouri were adopted virtually in their entirety and slavery was legalized in the Territory of Kansas by the "bogus statutes of 1855," as they were stigmatized by Free Staters, who refused to recognize them. On August 8, 1855, the legislature established the capital at Lecompton, and several months later the executive offices were moved there.

The mission declined rapidly after this time. The Indians sold their lands and moved away. Border troubles increased the school's difficulties. At the outbreak of the Civil War, Thomas Johnson, although himself a slave owner, pledged his allegiance to the Union cause, and his son, Alexander, became a soldier in the Union Army. The Johnsons abandoned the mission in 1864 and moved to their farm near Westport, Mo., where Johnson was killed by a band of Quantrill's guerrillas on the night of January 2, 1865.

The SHAWNEE MISSION RURAL HIGH SCHOOL, 3.6 *m.,* a modern brick building, stands on the approximate SITE OF A QUAKER MISSION founded for the Shawnee in 1834. A red granite boulder marks the site of the three-story mission buildings. Nothing now remains of the school but a CHAIN-AND-BUCKET WELL under a wooden canopy.

At 4.5 *m.* is the junction with US 69 *(see Tour 13),* which unites with US 50 for a few blocks.

SHAWNEE, 7 *m.* (1,000 alt., 553 pop.), a suburban market center, was once an Indian village, and became a bustling town on the Kansas frontier during the early days of the Santa Fe Trail. Known as Gum Springs, it was for a time the largest town in Kansas Territory, being the seat of Johnson County from 1855 to 1858 when Olathe supplanted it.

Right from Shawnee on State 10, paved, to the junction with an improved road, 0.5 *m.;* L. here, 0.6 *m., to the* HOME OF FREDERICK CHOUTEAU *(private).*
Chouteau, a member of the family of French fur traders that founded St. Louis, Mo., built the house for his Shawnee wife in 1830, shortly after the first settlement of the Territory. The front portion of the house is the original frame structure built by Chouteau; the stone addition in the rear is of a later date.
At 0.9 *m.* on State 10 is (L) the HOME OF CHARLES BLUEJACKET *(private),* Shawnee chief and Methodist minister. Built in the early 1830's, the house, a shabby two-story frame structure, was occupied by Bluejacket until 1871 when he migrated with his tribe to Indian Territory, where he died in 1897.

OLATHE, 19.7 *m.* (1,023 alt., 3,656 pop.), the seat of Johnson County, is a prosperous market town of pleasing residences and stately elms. It was founded in 1857 on a green prairie knoll carpeted with blue and scarlet verbena, the white lacy blooms of wild parsnip, pink-petaled wild roses, and scores of other flowers. When Dr. John T. Barton, one of the founders, decided to call the town by an Indian name meaning *beautiful,* he had difficulty in explaining to the Indians what he wanted. As he pointed to the flowering meadow a Shawnee exclaimed, "O-la-the!" and it was so named. (The Shawnee word for beautiful is *wes-see.*)

William Clarke Quantrill, notorious guerrilla leader, raided Olathe in

1862. Riding in at midnight, he captured revelers in the town's three saloons and routed sleepy citizens from their beds. A clergyman who did not answer when called was killed. Men were lined up in the town square, and a score of Union Army volunteers were taken prisoner. After loading plunder on wagons and wrecking the newspaper office, the Quantrill band marched the prisoners toward Missouri. They were finally released after taking an oath that they would never bear arms against the Confederacy.

Olathe was the home of John P. St.John (1833–1916). It was during ex-Governor St.John's first administration (1879–1881) that Kansas adopted a prohibition amendment, largely through his efforts. He was the Presidential candidate of the National Prohibition Party in 1884 but was defeated by Grover Cleveland. Republicans blamed him for the defeat of their candidate, James G. Blaine, by splitting the Republican vote, and St.John became the center of a storm of abuse. So bitter was the feeling against him that he was frequently hanged in effigy. In later years St.John said, "No man living in America today has been the object of more bitter attack and burning hatred than myself."

In the town square is the JOHNSON COUNTY COURTHOUSE, a brick and granite structure with bracketed cornice, two-story gable porch, hip roof, and towering cupola. So popular is the courthouse with couples eloping from Missouri and eastern Kansas that the town has become a local Gretna Green. Judge Bert Rogers, father of Charles (Buddy) Rogers, orchestra leader and motion picture actor, presides (1938) in its "Cupid's Parlor," which is decorated with more sentiment than restraint. Love birds adorn the fringed lamp in the parlor and many photographs of Buddy embellish the walls.

On the southeastern corner of town square is a Santa Fe Trail marker.

On US 50 near the northern edge of town (L), is the KANSAS SCHOOL FOR THE DEAF *(open on application)*, established in 1866 for the education of deaf children of elementary and high school age. Some 250 boys and girls live and attend classes in its modern brick buildings set in a shady landscaped park. The school stresses vocational training, teaching trades, agriculture, and domestic science.

The HYER BOOT FACTORY *(open on application)*, N. Chestnut St., a remodeled three-story stone hotel built before the Civil War, had its humble beginning in the 1870's when Charles A. Hyer, a German shoemaker teaching his craft at the Kansas School for the Deaf, opened a small shop of his own. His first customer was a cowboy, for whom he designed a handsome pair of soft leather boots. Many ranchers and cowboys came to admire and buy his fine handiwork, as did cavalry officers and other fastidious horsemen. The factory now employs sixty men in fashioning fine riding boots, including many that are elaborately ornamented to meet the exacting demands of Hollywood cowboys.

OLATHE PARK, in the center of town, has a large municipal swimming pool.

Left from Olathe on a graveled road to LAKE OLATHE, 2.5 *m. (open)*, which covers 57 acres and is well stocked with fish. Cabins around the lake are privately owned.

Just east of the concrete bridge on which US 50 crosses Cedar Creek, is a Santa Fe and Oregon Trail marker, 22.5 *m.,* one of a series of 98 boulders and monuments that have been placed throughout Kansas on these historic routes. On the west bank of the creek is an old stone building that housed the workers who built the first railroad through this region in 1871.

Before GARDNER, 28.2 *m.* (1,065 alt., 493 pop.), a rural trading center, developed there was a sign post here reading, "Road to Oregon" (R) and "Road to Santa Fe" (L). Ruts made by wagons traveling the Oregon Trail are visible a short distance north of town. Founded in 1857 by Free Staters and named for Governor O. B. Gardner of Massachusetts, the town cast only three of its 103 votes for the pro-slavery Lecompton constitution. One of the first Free State conventions in Kansas was held here in 1858.

Right from Gardner on a graveled road to the 340-acre JOHNSON COUNTY STATE PARK, 3 *m. (fishing),* well landscaped with numerous trees and containing a fine lake.

EDGERTON, 33.6 *m.* (966 alt., 278 pop.), a tidy hamlet, succeeds two vanished towns, McCamish and Lanesfield. The former was laid out about three miles to the northeast in 1857; Lanesfield, named for James H. Lane, fiery orator and leader of the Kansas antislavery Democrats, was later founded about a half mile west of McCamish. When the Santa Fe Ry. skipped both towns, in building through the region in 1870, the inhabitants of the two settlements moved nearer the railroad and called their new town Edgerton, for the chief engineer of the railroad. Only a country schoolhouse now marks the site of Lanesfield; McCamish has vanished completely.

BALDWIN CITY, 44.6 *m.* (849 alt., 1,127 pop.), a quiet college town, is dominated by the yellow limestone buildings of BAKER UNIVERSITY, a co-educational Methodist school with an enrollment of 350. Opened in 1858, it is the oldest four-year college in Kansas. One of its earliest recorded donations is a $100 check received from President Abraham Lincoln in February 1864. While the record does not indicate the circumstances, Thomas A. Evans, alumni secretary of the university, says that it was given to the Baker financial agent who visited the President at Washington.

OLD CASTLE HALL, in which the college's first classes were held, is preserved on the campus as a monument. In the vault of the university LIBRARY *(open during school hours),* is the noteworthy QUAYLE COLLECTION OF BIBLES, assembled by Bishop William Quayle, once president of the institution. The collection contains Bibles that belonged to Robert Southey, Robert Browning, and Robert Louis Stevenson; synagogue rolls; early English versions of the Scriptures and rare Arabic translations on vellum.

In 1874 Dr. Andrew Taylor Still, a country doctor who had studied and practiced medicine for many years, laid before the officials of Baker University a new system of treating human ailments without drugs, which he called osteopathy. His ideas met with such a cold reception that Doctor Still left Kansas and took up practice in Missouri, where he established the first school of osteopathy at Kirksville in 1892.

In Territorial days Baldwin was the scene of a bitter fight between pro-slavery Missourians and Free State Kansans. The Missourians attacked under the leadership of a Congressional Representative; the Free Staters were concentrated at Baldwin under various leaders. The fight came to a halt when Governor Shannon ordered United States troops under Colonel Sumner to send the belligerents home and release all prisoners. On their way back to Missouri pro-slavery men plundered Osawatomie *(see Tour 12B)*.

At 49.5 *m.* is the junction with US 59 *(see Tour 12)*, and with US 50S *(see Tour 4A)*.

Section *b*. JUNCTION WITH US 50, US 50S, AND US 59 *to* GARDEN CITY, *364.3 m.*, US 50N

West of the junction with US 59, 0 *m.*, US 50N traverses a fine upland farming country, the soft-coal mining region near Scranton, the grassy Flint Hills dotted with red cattle, the grimy oil fields about Lyons, and the highly developed area of irrigated farm lands near Larned and Garden City.

OVERBROOK, 16 *m.* (1,070 alt., 460 pop.), is the center of a district once important for the mining of bituminous coal, but now devoted to diversified farming and cattle raising.

At 23.1 *m.* is the junction with US 75 *(see Tour 11)*.

West of the junction coal mines are visible on both sides of the highway. Most of the mines are small and owned by individuals who truck their coal to Topeka to be sold by the load.

SCRANTON, 26.5 *m.* (1,100 alt., 538 pop.), established in the early 1870's as a coal-mining camp, is now a farmers' market town.

BURLINGAME, 33.4 *m.* (1,045 alt., 1,127 pop.), the oldest settlement in Osage County, is a rambling town with broad shady streets and fairly comfortable homes. Old limestone buildings with long deep windows and strong straight walls, erected in the 1870's and 1880's, line its main street, once part of the Santa Fe Trail. Founded in 1855 as Council City, Burlingame was the county seat and largest town of Osage County, which then included much of Shawnee, Wabaunsee, Lyon, and Coffey Counties, until the dwindling of traffic along the trail brought a decline and the transfer of the county seat to Lyndon. Today it is a rural trade center and shipping point.

At 40.2 *m.* is a junction with State 31.

Left on this road is OSAGE CITY, 0.2 *m.* (1,084 alt., 2,402 pop.), market center of a coal-mining and farming area, has three small community parks, well shaded and well watered *(camping allowed)*.

A mining disaster occurred here in the winter of 1874. Fire broke out in a shaft in which twelve men were working. Their only means of escape was through the mouth of the tunnel, which was filled with clouds of smoke and sheets of flame. The State had not yet passed laws obligating mine owners to provide escape shafts

BUILDING TEMPORARY SILO OF SNOW FENCE AND TAR PAPER

for their workers. William Marks, a fearless miner, carried out the unconscious men one at a time, but only four survived.

BUSHONG, 64.1 *m.* (1,337 alt., 193 pop.), is a quiet hamlet surrounded by large cattle ranches.

The boyhood HOME OF GEN. J. G. HARBORD *(private)*, 67.5 *m.* (L), chief of staff of the expeditionary forces under General Pershing during the World War, was moved here early in 1937 from its original site northwest of Bushong. The one-and-one-half story structure has been remodeled considerably since it was occupied by the Harbord family.

COUNCIL GROVE, 77.2 *m.* (1,234 alt., 2,998 pop.), incorporated by a special act of the Territorial legislature in 1858, lies on the edge of the Flint Hills in the fertile Neosho River valley, which is devoted to cattle raising and diversified farming. The town has long been noted for the size and beauty of its oaks, elms, and maples, many of which were damaged during the drought of the early 1930's.

Council Grove grew up about an old campground in the great oak grove that once stood near a shallow ford across the Neosho River. Long known to the Indians, the ford was also used, so legend has it, by Coronado and his Spaniards in 1541 when they were searching for Quivira *(see HISTORY)*. Almost three centuries later, on August 10, 1825, three federal commissioners from Washington met here with chiefs of the Kansa, and of the Great and Little Osage, who received $500 for signing a treaty allowing the whites to survey and mark a trail from the Missouri River to Santa Fe.

In 1826 Josiah Gregg of Independence, Mo., led the first large caravan across the ford at Council Grove. A year later, it is said, Kit Carson stopped to rest in the grove and carved his name on one of the elms. Travel along the Santa Fe Trail increased rapidly, and by the early 1840's the campground was a busy place. Traders bound for Santa Fe, emigrants, and gold hunters met here and Council Grove soon became the most important station in the 700-mile stretch between Westport and Santa Fe. After the outbreak of war with Mexico in 1846 Col. Alexander W. Doniphan and his Missouri volunteers camped in the grove for several days.

Traffic on the Santa Fe Trail gradually declined and practically ceased in 1866 with the building of the Kansas Pacific 50 miles to the north. In 1871 the town became the permanent seat of Morris County, and, realizing that its roseate commercial dreams were over, settled down to slow but steady growth as an agricultural center.

The Kansa, who had been placed on a diminished reservation near the townsite in 1847, were moved to Indian Territory in 1873, severing the last link with the exciting frontier days. When the railroad came in 1883, Council Grove became a shipping point for livestock. In 1903 the Neosho River went on a rampage and the town was completely inundated. Property damage was estimated at $200,000 and many sections of the town had to be rebuilt.

The MADONNA OF THE TRAIL MONUMENT, NE. corner Union and Main Sts., dedicated to the pioneer women of the plains, was awarded to

Council Grove as having the most interesting history of any town in the State. The monument represents a pioneer woman holding an old-fashioned musket in one arm and a baby in the other, as a small boy clings to her skirts.

Under COUNCIL OAK, 210 E. Main St., the treaty of August 10, 1825, was signed. At the suggestion of George H. Sibley, one of the Federal commissioners, "Big John" Walker, a scout, carved the name Council Grove on the wide-spreading oak under which the council was held. This old but well-preserved tree measures more than ten feet in circumference. On August 10, 1907, the State and the D. A. R. erected a monument opposite the old tree and in the cement foundation sealed a metal box containing old and contemporary historical documents.

The HAYS TAVERN, 112 N. Main St., was built in 1847 by Seth M. Hays, Council Grove's first white settler, who established a trading post near the confluence of Elm Creek and the Neosho River in 1847, a few months after the Kansa had been placed on their reservation here. Although somewhat modernized, this frame structure—which served successively as a home, saloon, supply house, courthouse, and hotel—retains the exterior appearance of its early days when it was the scene of the settlement's most important social activities.

The KAW (KANSA) MISSION (private), SE. corner Huffaker and Mission Sts., a two-story local-stone building of Colonial design, was opened in 1849 by Thomas S. Huffaker. He was sent by the Methodist Episcopal Church to teach the Indians, who, however, were so unresponsive that the mission was shortly closed and remained so till 1854, when it was reopened as the first school for white children in Kansas. In spite of his inability to educate the Indians, Huffaker gained their confidence and respect and did much to maintain friendly relations between the Kansa and the increasing number of settlers, who were in constant fear of an attack by the reservation braves and the roving bands of Cheyenne. They frightened housewives by stalking into their kitchens and demanding food, and annoyed stockmen with their constant depredations on their herds.

In the summer of 1859, Chief Ah-Le-Goh-Wah-Ho enraged by Seth Hays' demand for the return of some horses stolen from a Mexican trader, rode into town one morning with a Kansa war party of 100 braves. When Charles Gilke and a man named Parks had been wounded, one by a bullet, the other by an arrow, Huffaker ran out into the street and commanded the Indians to leave. After a brief parley the war party turned about and rode out of town, but halted on a hill about a mile away, where they were re-enforced by 400 warriors. Responding to the pleas of the terrified townspeople, Huffaker again approached the Indians, demanding that they return to their reservation.

The chief was persuaded to call off the attack and to surrender the two braves who had shot Gilke and Parks. One of the offenders tried to stir up a mutiny but was seized and bound by the Indians. Both prisoners were taken to Council Grove where they were summarily tried and hanged. The bodies were returned to the tribe in a wagon driven by a man named Rocheford. After receiving their dead in stoical silence, the Kansa began their funeral chant, which so frightened Rocheford's oxen that they ran away.

Charles Curtis, Vice President of the United States (1929–33), was a member of the tribe, lived on the Kansa reservation as a boy, and is said to have attended the mission school.

The LAST CHANCE STORE, NE. corner of Main and Chautauqua Sts., a one-story local-stone building erected in 1857, was for several years a post office, then became a Government trading post, and is now occupied by the Morris County National Farm Loan Association. It was so named because it was the last place where supplies could be obtained on the trail between Council Grove and Santa Fe.

HERMIT'S CAVE, on Belfry St. between Columbia and Hays Sts., became the refuge of a mysterious and destitute stranger who arrived in 1862. To improve his shelter, he built up a wall of rocks to meet the overhanging ledge at the top of the cliff, and here, high on the eastern face of the great bluff overlooking the town, he lived with only his dog for company. His name was Matteo Boccalini, he said, and he was a native of Capri. He told of having gone to Rome at the age of eighteen to be ordained for the priesthood, of having become secretary to the Pope, but of later being unfrocked because of a love affair with a young girl. Having incurred the enmity of the Jesuits, he wandered for years, migrated to America, and finally reached the Kansa reservation, from whence he was expelled as "bad medicine."

He lived in fear of being followed, and one day hurried away with a wagon train bound for the Southwest, after having seen a man whom he thought he recognized among some travelers. Two years later Council Grove learned that a priest had been found dead, with a dagger through his heart, in a cave house in the mountains of New Mexico. On the walls of the cave he had carved his name, a cross, and the words "Jesu Maria" and "Capri," exactly as they appeared on the walls of Hermit's Cave here.

In the BELFRY TOWER, corner of Columbia and Belfry Sts., near Hermit's Cave, is a bell originally purchased by the Plymouth Congregational Church at Lawrence in 1863. After the Lawrence church had rejected it because it was cracked, Council Grove, needing a church and school bell as well as an alarm to warn settlers of Indian raids or prairie fires, bought it for $9 and hauled it overland by ox team. After serving almost 40 years it finally fell from its tower and was placed in this monument, which was erected with contributions from school children and was dedicated on September 19, 1901, to President William McKinley, who was buried on that day.

The POST OFFICE OAK, on E. Main St. between Union and Liberty Sts., was an unofficial post office during the days of heavy travel on the Santa Fe Trail. For a time this was the only place for mail exchange between Junction City and Santa Fe. A stone cache held the messages of passing caravans.

CUSTER'S ELM, six blocks south of Main St. on Neosho St., a giant tree 100 feet in height and 16 feet in circumference, is said to have shelteıed the camp of Lieutenant Colonel Custer in 1867. Custer was leading an expedition against hostile Indians in western Kansas when he passed through Council Grove.

At 90.2 m. is the junction with a dirt road.

Left on this road to the SITE OF DIAMOND SPRINGS, 4 m., once a green oasis and a favorite stopover for travelers on the long dusty Santa Fe Trail. Frontiersmen enclosed the land about the springs, which are now dry, with a corral of local stone to protect themselves and their stock from the Indians. Stops were made here either at night or during the heat of the day, for wagon trains traveled only in the cool of early morning or late afternoon.

HERINGTON, 102.6 m. (1,324 alt., 4,519 pop.) (see Tour 10), is at the junction with US 77 (see Tour 10). Between this point and MARION, 128 m. (1,310 alt., 1,959 pop.) (see Tour 10), US 77 and US 50N are one route (see Tour 10).

HILLSBORO, 139.2 m. (1,426 alt., 1,458 pop.), at the junction of the north and south branches of the Cottonwood River, is the center of a large Mennonite community that extends into neighboring counties.

TABOR COLLEGE, a co-educational Mennonite institution founded in 1908, is on a landscaped square near the eastern edge of the town. The two college buildings, an administration building and a dormitory, are of modern design and are constructed of brick and terra cotta. Tabor offers a two-year course in liberal arts, science, and religion and has an enrollment (1938) of approximately 100.

The ancestors of these Mennonites were largely Swiss and Germans who had migrated to Russia in the eighteenth century when Catherine the Great promised them religious freedom, exemption from military service, and freedom from taxation for a period of thirty years. Catherine's successors revoked these privileges, however, and members of the sect migrated to America in the early 1870's. Those who settled in central Kansas have made it one of the most prosperous farming regions in the State. Its great golden wheat fields had their origin in the tiny patches planted by the first Mennonite settlers who had grown Turkey Red wheat successfully on the steppes of southern Russia and who brought bags of seed with them. Kansas farmers had previously grown only soft spring wheat, but by the early 1880's they were buying large quantities of Turkey Red wheat from their Mennonite neighbors and importing hundreds of bushels of seed from Russia. By the late 1890's this rust-resistant hard winter wheat had supplanted soft spring wheat almost completely (see AGRICULTURE).

Until recent years the Mennonites clung tenaciously to their religion and Old World customs, characterized by great simplicity in their home life, dress, entertainment, and religious services. Many lived for years in America without becoming naturalized citizens because their religion did not sanction the taking of oaths. Even today members often refuse to vote, except in school elections, or take part in governmental affairs.

Hillsboro has a Mennonite publishing plant that prints religious books and weekly newspapers in German, which many people here speak as fluently as they do English.

West of Hillsboro US 50N is bordered by fields of alfalfa, wheat, and corn.

LEHIGH, 145.4 *m.* (1,522 alt., 315 pop.), is a cluster of small buildings and derricks near the center of a large oil field.

McPHERSON, 165.5 *m.* (1,480 alt., 6,147 pop.), seat of McPherson County, was named for Maj. Gen. James B. McPherson, Commander of the Army of the Tennessee, whose equestrian statue stands in the courthouse park. A shipping and refining point for the central Kansas oil fields, McPherson has expanded rapidly in recent years, having been relatively untouched by the depression.

McPherson and the surrounding farm lands were settled by Swedes who were followed by Germans, Bohemians, and French Canadians. The thrifty descendants of these pioneers own their own farms for the most part and many draw royalties from the oil produced on their lands.

McPherson has two Carnegie libraries; one was donated to the city, the other to McPHERSON COLLEGE (Dunkard), whose eight brick and limestone buildings stand on a landscaped campus at the eastern edge of town. A co-educational institution, it has an enrollment of 400. The Dunkards, frequently called Dunkers or Tunkers, are members of the Church of the Brethren, a sect of Baptists that in 1708 grew out of the Pietist movement in Germany. Although most of the out-of-town students belong to the sect, the college no longer stresses the Dunkards' opposition to oaths, alcohol, tobacco, and warfare.

Dr. J. Willard Hershey, a professor of chemistry at McPherson College, has produced the largest synthetic diamonds manufactured in the United States. Sir Hubert Wilkins used Hershey's mixture of helium and oxygen gases on his submarine North Pole expedition in 1931.

CENTRAL COLLEGE AND ACADEMY (Free Methodist), at the southern edge, of the town, is a secondary school and junior college with an enrollment of approximately 100. Founded in 1914, the institution has a 15-acre campus with three modern, well-equipped buildings, in addition to four residences for faculty members and students nearby. Students must conform to Free Methodist practices, which forbid smoking, dancing, college fraternities, attendance at motion picture theaters, and the wearing of jewelry. Visiting between the sexes is limited to supervised social interviews.

The gymnasium of the new McPHERSON CITY AUDITORIUM was used by the local Globe Refinery basketball team, which won the national amateur championship in 1936 and participated in the Olympic games in Germany.

McPherson is at the junction with US 81 *(see Tour 9)*.

West of McPherson sunflowers grow rank from June until frost. Although designated the official State flower in 1903, the sunflower, curiously enough, is not native to Kansas. Its seeds came from the Southwest, in mud and dirt clinging to the broad wheels of freight wagons plying the Santa Fe Trail in early days. The small variety that grows wild along the roadside and in uncultivated fields is regarded as a pest, but varieties producing large seeds are cultivated for chicken feed.

At 192.1 *m.* is the junction with an improved road.

Right on this road to LITTLE RIVER, 1 *m.* (1,504 alt., 618 pop.), the trade center of a rich wheat-raising area, named for the Little Arkansas River which flows a short distance north of the town.

LYONS, 199.2 *m.* (1,696 alt., 2,939 pop.), a small city of substantial houses and shady lawns grouped about the Rice County Courthouse, is dependent on salt and wheat, the principal crop of the surrounding countryside.

In the middle 1870's, when the towns of Atlanta and Peace (Sterling) were rivals for the county seat designation, it was decided at a hotly contested election to place the seat in the exact center of the county, more than a mile north and east of Atlanta. A new town was laid out there in 1876 and named for Truman J. Lyons, on whose property it was founded. Four years later Lyons was incorporated as a second-class city.

In 1890 the shaft of the first salt mine was sunk in the vicinity. The mines of the two salt companies operating here have 16 miles of air-conditioned tunnels. The highly crystalline salt is mined without the use of timbering. Columns of salt support the roofs of the mines which resemble mammoth vaulted caverns. A small electric railway hauls the blocks of salt to an elevator, which lifts them to the surface. Salt is also extracted from wells drilled in the vicinity. After fresh water has been forced into them, the brine is pumped out and evaporated in vats, leaving salt crystals.

Lyons experienced a boom in the middle 1920's with the development of new oil fields nearby. In 1936 Rice County led Kansas in oil production, having an output of 11,427,072 barrels, almost 20 per cent of the State's total.

In the COURTHOUSE a large collection of relics, believed to be of the Quivira expedition of Francisco Vasquez de Coronado, includes Spanish lances, fragments of chain mail, and a Toledo sword blade, all plowed up on a farm near the old Cow Creek crossing on the Santa Fe Trail.

A local historian believes that Coronado's search for the fabulous Seven Cities of Cibola ended here *(see HISTORY)*.

Left from Lyons on State 14, paved, to STERLING, 10 *m.* (1,657 alt., 1,868 pop.), a town with a wide main street and modern schools, churches, and business houses. Founded in 1872 as Peace, it was incorporated under its present name in 1876.

At the north end of Main Street is (R) STERLING COLLEGE (200 enrollment), a United Presbyterian institution established in 1886 as Cooper College. The original building, Cooper Hall, is a gaunt limestone structure near the north campus limits. Three newer buildings of brick and limestone serve as girls' dormitory, gymnasium, and school of music. Sterling is co-educational and offers degrees in liberal arts, fine arts, and science.

On the banks of Cow Creek, 207.5 *m.*, are (L) ruts made by wagons on the Santa Fe Trail. Nearby is a Santa Fe Trail marker on one of the Plains Indians' favorite spots for ambushing freighters.

ELLINWOOD, 221.2 *m.* (1,782 alt., 1,115 pop.), a clean and symmetrical town surrounded by a forest of oil derricks, was founded as a post office in 1871, just before the last of the Plains Indians were put on reservations. A railroad, built through the town the following year, attracted new settlers and Ellinwood became a shipping and trading point.

Since 1930, when development began in Barton and Rice Counties, Ellinwood has been the center of one of the State's largest and most productive oil fields. On the outskirts of the town scores of newly painted cottages have been erected by the oil companies for their workers, who have their own schools and community organizations. Although rather monotonous in appearance, these mushroom settlements are an improvement on the rows of unpainted shacks and dingy tents that characterized the booming oil towns of the past generation.

Right from Ellinwood on a graveled road to the ROBL BIRD-BANDING STATION *(open on application)*, 2.5 *m.*, a private refuge conducted by Frank Robl, district game warden and a deputy Federal game protector. No hunting is permitted on the 500 acres surrounding the 16-acre refuge. Here migratory birds are marked with leg bands so that their flights back and forth across the country can be studied. More than 15,000 birds have been banded by Robl since he began his work here in 1928. Some 400 geese, 1,000 ducks, and several flocks of sandhill cranes regularly stop here on their flights south, usually in October; they return north in March. Although there is no winter shelter, mallard ducks and Canadian geese sometimes stay all year. They nest about the reedy pond in summer and become so tame that Robl and his assistants can handle them. During the severe winters the birds consume as much as 300 bushels of wheat and oats, in addition to what they themselves can obtain.

Bordering a horseshoe bend in Walnut Creek, 226.5 *m.*, is (R) the FORT ZARAH STATE PARK *(outdoor stoves, excellent campground)*, a three-acre tract marked with a Civil War cannon. In early days OLD WALNUT CROSSING (L), just off the highway, was a favorite stopping place for traders, explorers, and plainsmen.

Fort Zarah, a link in the chain of frontier forts that guarded the Santa Fe Trail, was established by Gen. Samuel R. Curtis, September 6, 1864, and named for the general's son, Maj. H. Zarah Curtis, who was killed in the Baxter Springs Massacre *(see Tour 7)*. It had one building, two stories high, constructed of sandstone from a nearby bluff.

The 3,700-acre Fort Zarah Military Reservation was established by order of President Andrew Johnson, September 30, 1868. The lessening of Indian depredations and the decline of traffic along the trail soon removed the necessity for a post at this point, so the fort was dismantled in December 1869. An act passed by Congress in 1871 provided for the resurvey and sale of the reservation lands.

According to one historian, the abandoned fort became "a general rendezvous for bats and marauders," until piece by piece, the stone walls of the building were carried away by settlers to be used in the construction of dwellings. The last trace of the old fort disappeared before the end of the century.

GREAT BEND, 231.4 *m.* (1,843 alt., 5,548 pop.), named from its position on the sweeping curve made by the Arkansas River as it loops through central Kansas, is a shipping, wheat, and oil center. Settled in 1871, two years after the abandonment of old Fort Zarah, the town grew rapidly after the railroad reached it in 1872. The first building on the townsite, the Southern Hotel, was erected by the town company. Tom Stone, the landlord, was a burly man with huge "handle-bar" mustaches. He loved to wear vermilion-colored shirts and an old military sash from which protruded the handles of two big revolvers. In spite of his terrifying appearance Stone was a pleasant fellow and a popular host.

In 1874–75 Great Bend was a railhead on the Chisholm Cattle Trail and its crowded, boisterous saloons and dance halls gave it a reputation as a "hot spot" among cowmen and freighters. With the cattle trade came the usual entourage of gamblers, gunmen, and other undesirable characters. Although Great Bend merchants enjoyed a brisk business during the cow-town era, many of the townspeople lived in terror of the rough element and welcomed the passage of a State law in 1876 which established a deadline for Texas cattle thirty miles west of the town.

One of Great Bend's first city marshals, H. B. "Ham" Bell, now (1938) a resident of Dodge City, came to Great Bend from Maryland in 1875. The Kansas Pacific brought him to Ellsworth but there was no railroad or stageline operating between that town and Great Bend; so he asked a local liveryman what he would charge to drive him to his destination. "It'll cost you a dollar a mile and it's forty-five miles," replied the driver. When Bell protested, the man pointed to a large lake along the western horizon and explained that the route was extremely hazardous because it passed through the shallow waters of this lake. The driver demanded payment in advance and Bell reluctantly produced the $45. "The lake, however, proved to be a mirage," Bell relates, "and I learned too late that I was figuratively as well as literally being 'taken for a ride.' My driver refused to make a settlement and seemed to regard the chicanery as a legitimate trick to play on an unsuspecting tenderfoot."

For many years the town's chief industry was flour milling, but its streets and hotel lobbies are crowded now (1938) with men in khaki shirts, boots, and stained riding breeches, all talking the jargon of the oil fields. With oil wells to the north, south, and east, a boom spirit has gripped the town. Great stacks of heavy timbers for rigging, of fabricated steel for derricks, of tubing, casing, and pipe are piled high in supply yards. During 1937 many new business establishments were opened and hundreds of new houses were built here. In spite of all this bustle and feverish growth the town has retained a neat and orderly appearance.

BARTON COUNTY COURTHOUSE, a four-story structure of Bedford limestone, stands in the center of the city in a landscaped square, which also contains the MOSES MEMORIAL BAND SHELL, donated in 1926 by descendants of Clayton L. Moses, Great Bend pioneer, and a bronze statue of a Union soldier, erected as a G. A. R. memorial in 1915.

Right from Great Bend on State 8, a paved road, to 40-acre LAKE BARTON (*gas, water, ovens for picnickers; fishing, no hunting*), 7 *m.*, which supplies the railroad shops at Hoisington with water. The Barton County Club has leased 120 acres adjoining the lake (*dance pavilion, shelter house, boathouse; $1 a day fee charged to non-members*).

DUNDEE, 235.3 *m.* (1,899 alt., 32 pop.), was settled in the 1870's by Mennonites who patterned the settlement after their villages in Europe. Colonists lived together in the village and pooled the surrounding land in one big farm. The large number of acres necessary to support a family in this region made the scheme impracticable, however, and the settlers soon took up individual farms. Their descendants still attend the old Mennonite church in Dundee.

PAWNEE ROCK, 245.6 *m.* (1,941 alt., 399 pop.), is at the junction with an improved road.

Right from Pawnee Rock on this road to PAWNEE ROCK STATE PARK, **0.5** *m. (shelter house, picnic grounds)*, formerly a rendezvous for Plains Indians and the scene of many savage battles in the early days. The Santa Fe Trail passed near its base and some historians believe that Coronado's expedition (1541) came to this place with Indian guides who used the hill as a landmark. The rock's name, according to most historians, refers to the fact that the Pawnee often met here in council. But in his book *The Old Santa Fe Trail* Henry Inman declares that it was so named because of a battle fought here between the Pawnee and the whites, in which Kit Karson participated.

From the rock is a sweeping view of the Arkansas, Ash, and Walnut Rivers, and of the city of Larned to the southwest. A mass of Dakota sandstone, the rock originally stood almost 100 feet high, but some 18 feet of stone was stripped from the top by early settlers, who used it to build houses, and by the Santa Fe Railway in laying its roadbed along the route of the old trail in the valley.

The State acquired the five acres comprising the present park in 1908, and in 1912 erected the PAWNEE ROCK MONUMENT, a 30-foot shaft of Barre granite, designed by Silverstro Caro, an Italian sculptor of Topeka.

LARNED, 254.1 *m.* (2,023 alt., 3,532 pop.), a trading center and seat of Pawnee County, lies at the confluence of Pawnee Creek and the Arkansas River. The business section has a modern aspect with store fronts of brick, stucco, stone, and tile.

The settlement's first building was a frame structure moved from Fort Larned, floated across Pawnee Creek, and rented as a saloon by Henry Booth, an Englishman. Upon the arrival of the railroad later that year, a one-story wooden hotel was erected near the depot. Although it had unplastered rough-sawed walls, canvas ceilings, and canvas partitions between the rooms, it was regarded in its day as spacious and luxurious. In 1874 the first public school was set up in a recently vacated building across whose two front windows ran the nine-inch red and yellow letters S-A-L-O-O-N. Pupils sat on beer kegs before the bar which served the teacher as a desk.

In a shady landscaped park north of the business district stands the PAWNEE COUNTY COURTHOUSE, a modern brick building with Ionic pillars and a long double flight of stone stairs rising to the portico floor. A collection of early relics is on exhibit in the lower corridor. In the Junior High School is the HEIMSOTH PALEONTOLOGY COLLECTION, which includes the 15-foot tail of a mosasaurid, a giant mail-clad prehistoric lizard; the bones of the tail are complete, numbering 110.

At the south end of Main Street, between Pawnee Creek and the Arkansas River, on a site formerly known as Island Park, is an old INDIAN BATTLEGROUND, where a bloody conflict between the Pawnee and invading Cheyenne under Chief Black Kettle was witnessed by Colonel Henry Inman in 1860 while on his way to Fort Larned. According to Inman, the

Pawnee chief had him tell the enemy that the Pawnee were waiting for them on the willow-covered island between the two streams. As the last of the Pawnee reached the island and disappeared behind the willows, 200 Cheyenne warriors led by Yellow Buffalo advanced, chanting their war song, and plunged into the stream with a shout of defiance, holding their rifles and powder bags above their heads. The Pawnee allowed the Cheyenne to approach within 10 feet before half of them blazed away with their first volley in the very face of the foe. As soon as they saw how many men had been hit the other half followed with the second volley. Then each Pawnee, who, in addition to rifle and bow and arrows, carried two pistols, kept up a steady fire.

Leaving many dead and wounded, the Cheyenne withdrew, only to renew the attack in greater force under Black Kettle, but again they were repulsed with great slaughter, losing fifty men. The Pawnee reported one dead and two wounded, and at sunset remained masters of the field. "But while a victory for the Pawnee, the battle settled nothing," wrote Inman, "for Black Kettle remained and his Cheyennes continued to hunt on the Pawnee grounds."

Left from Larned on State 45, improved, to the junction with an improved road, 0.2 m.; R. here to the HOSPITAL FOR THE INSANE, 3.4 m. (open on application), consisting of brick cottages and residences, modern farm buildings, towering silos, and a large dairy barn, situated on 1,440 acres of farm land in green Pawnee Creek valley.

JENKINS HILL, west of the cottages, figured prominently in the early history of the region as a lookout for both Indians and whites. Army officers considered building Fort Larned on its summit, but because of the hazards of obtaining water in case of siege the plans were abandoned. Stone for the buildings at Fort Larned was quarried from this hill and workmen were under military guard to protect them from Indian attacks. Three white men and six Indians, killed in skirmishes at the hill, are said to have been buried on the western slope.

Left from the base of Jenkins Hill on the bank of Pawnee Creek is a red granite boulder marking the site of the old "dry route" crossing of the Santa Fe Trail, also known as Boyd's Crossing for a saloon established here by A. H. Boyd in 1867.

At 259.1 m. is the junction with a dirt road.

Left 0.5 m. on this road to the SITE OF FORT LARNED (visitors welcome), now part of the 2,500-acre Fort Larned Ranch, owned by E. E. Frizell and devoted to stock-raising and the cultivation of alfalfa and sugar beets. The Camp on Pawnee Fork, as Fort Larned was first known, was established in 1859 to protect travelers on the Santa Fe Trail from Indian attacks. There were two routes from this point to Fort Dodge; one closely followed the Arkansas River and touched Big Coon Creek near Garfield; the other route, shorter but less safe, proceeded 10 or 12 miles up the south bank of Pawnee River and then cut across dry upland to rejoin the other route just east of Fort Dodge.

The name of the post was changed to Camp Alert in 1860, and later in the same year was renamed Fort Larned in honor of the paymaster general of the Army. The first structures, built by the soldiers, were of adobe with sod roofs; these were replaced between 1864 and 1868 by the present stone buildings. The sandstone was quarried at Lookout Mountain, now Jenkins Hill, and the lumber was brought from Michigan by shipping it down the Missouri River and then hauling it overland by ox teams. Although soldiers guarded the quarrymen and teamsters during building operations, the Indians killed several workmen, burned a bridge over the Pawnee, and drove away much stock.

The buildings face a parade ground 400 feet square. In the center is a small mound built as a base for the flagpole. The COMMISSARY QUARTERS have walls two feet thick; wedge-shaped holes along the south side afford wide views of the plains. The OFFICERS' QUARTERS, three buildings with large front porches, were the most impressive; the northernmost was in the exact center of the 11,000-acre military reservation. In one of the old STABLES is a BLACKSMITH FORGE, formerly used at the fort, now part of the ranch equipment. A barn 50 feet wide and 372 feet long is one of the largest in Kansas and was built from the former barracks. A stone marker at the southwest corner of the quadrangle commemorates the establishment of the fort and gives its history. On the northwest corner is an old CANNON, mounted on a limestone base and inscribed, "No. 16, B. H., U. S. 1812."

Fort Larned was the supply base and agency for the Arapahoe and Cheyenne from 1860 to 1868. When Indian stores ran low, the warriors would besiege the post, and at such times the situation occasionally became so tense that United States troops were summoned to prevent serious trouble. In 1861 a sixteen-year-old sentinel, annoyed by the importunities of some 20,000 Indians camped just outside the fort, shot and killed the son of a chief. Colonel Leavenworth called in the chiefs for a parley, but no explanation would satisfy the angry Indians; they demanded that the young man be delivered to them for punishment. Although the post was inadequately garrisoned, and there was no time to summon re-enforcements, the officers threatened to exterminate the tribes by cannon fire if they harmed the boy. "Huh!" the chiefs retorted, "cannon no good." The soldiers quickly wheeled the cannon about, trained it on a horse, and blew the animal to bits. The Indians immediately departed.

In spite of Indian scares there were many social activities at the fort. Full-dress dinner parties were given for officers on inspection trips. Numerous quiltings, taffy pullings, and cock fights were held, and at the occasional dances everyone joined in the quadrille, polka, or schottische to the accompaniment of guitar and cornet.

By 1878 the troops stationed at Fort Larned had pacified the Wichita and the Osage, who had rebelled when the railroads invaded their best hunting grounds. The Indians had been moved to other reservations, and the necessity for the frontier posts was considerably decreased. All the troops at Fort Larned were moved to Fort Dodge, and in 1882 Congress approved a bill to authorize the sale of the reservation. The section of the reservation on which the buildings stand was auctioned to the Pawnee Valley Breeders' Association in 1884, and the remainder was made subject to preemption in tracts of 160 acres.

BURDETT, 278.1 *m.* (2,113 alt., 320 pop.), a shipping and trading center surrounded by broad wheat fields and cattle pastures, was the boyhood home of Clyde Tombaugh (1906–   ), the astronomer who discovered the ninth planet, Pluto, in February 1930, while working at the Lowell Observatory in Arizona. He was honored by the Royal Astronomical Society of London with a bronze medal and the Jackson-Gwilt gift. Tombaugh first began studying the stars with a homemade telescope when he was a boy on his father's farm here.

JETMORE, 305.3 *m.* (2,261 alt., 914 pop.), seat of Hodgeman County, was founded in 1879 as Buckner, but changed its name to honor the railroad lawyer who helped it become the county seat. In the courthouse is a collection of Indian and Pioneer relics, the property of the Hodgeman County Historical Society.

Right from Jetmore on US 283 to NESS CITY, 26 *m.* (2,258 alt., 1,509 pop.), the seat of Ness County, surrounded by great wheat fields. It was founded in 1878 by James and Ross Calhoun, brothers from Iowa, who took a homestead near the present townsite. In recent years oil, developed near the town, has caused a mild boom.

George Washington Carver (1864–   ), noted Negro scientist and educator, lived on a homestead 15 miles west of Ness City from 1888 until 1891, when he sold his 160-acre farm and left the State. Carver engaged in geological research in the vicinity and predicted that oil would be found under the county's rock strata. He frequently visited Ness City and is well remembered by its older residents, many of whom helped to pay for the bronze bust of Professor Carver recently unveiled at Tuskegee, Ala.

At 308.3 *m.* is the junction with an improved road.

Left on this road is 153-acre HODGEMAN COUNTY STATE PARK, 1 *m.* with a large lake *(fishing, boating)*.

At 325 *m.* the route enters the MOUNTAIN TIME ZONE; watches of west-bound travelers should be set back one hour.

KALVESTA, 328.5 *m.* (2,950 alt., 49 pop.), settled in 1874, was a thriving settlement during the early decades of its existence, but is now important only as a rural trading center.

Right from Kalvesta on a dirt road to FINNEY COUNTY STATE PARK, 9 *m.,* *(boating, fishing, cabins, camp accommodations)*. The dam across the 320-acre lake in this park is one of the largest in Kansas.

At 336.2 *m.* is the junction with a dirt road.

Right on this road to the SITE OF RAVANNA, 6 *m.,* contestant for the seat of Garfield County (now abolished).

In 1880 John Bull, a Canadian, preempted a claim which included the townsite and had the proposed name of Bull Town moderated to Cowland. Surrounded by large cattle ranches, Cowland prospered and was rechristened Ravenna for a town of that name in Ohio. A mistake was made on the official papers, however, and the name became Ravanna.

At the organization of Garfield County Ravanna and Eminence became rivals for the county seat designation. Ravanna won in the election of 1887. But Eminence charged fraud, and was designated county seat by a decision of the supreme court. Chagrined, Ravanna claimed that Garfield County had insufficient area to be a county; the supreme court upheld the claim, dissolved Garfield County, and incorporated it with Finney County. A few ruined buildings and a portion of the old courthouse, hastily constructed while Ravanna was the county seat, remain on the townsite.

In 1882 Rabbi Isaac M. Wise of Cincinnati promoted the establishment of a Jewish agricultural colony—one of the few ever attempted in America—called Beersheba, just east of Ravanna. Under the leadership of Rabbi Adelhartz, twenty-four families arrived in the neighborhood that year, took up claims along Pawnee Creek, and built a number of dugout shelters and a sod synagogue. Although helped by Jewish societies in the East, the agricultural venture was not a success. Most of the colonists managed to live on their claims until the late 1880's when they mortgaged or sold them, using the money to return East or to establish themselves in business in western Kansas.

GARDEN CITY, 364.3 *m.* (2,830 alt., 6,121 pop.), seat of Finney County, lies on the Arkansas River in an extensive irrigated belt producing sugar beets as the chief crop. The metropolis of western Kansas, Garden City is green and shining except when "black blizzards" from the High Plains sweep across the valley to bury everything under a thick blanket of dust. A majority of farmers in the region have adopted such measures as strip listing and planting of cover crops to combat wind erosion.

Garden City was founded by several brothers named Fulton in 1878, to the intense indignation and disgust of all cattlemen in the region. In June

1879, the first and last rain of the year fell. "It started the grass," wrote a local historian, "but the crops perished, and many discouraged people moved away." The cattlemen enjoyed a temporary triumph, pointing out that the occasional rains were just sufficient to make the grass grow and that during succeeding dry spells it was "cured on the stalk" and made excellent hay. But farmers persisted in plowing up the buffalo grass.

In the late 1880's, there was wild speculation in land throughout the Southwest, and the town boomed, achieving a population of 6,000. In spite of the warnings of cattlemen, farmers took up lands all the way to the Colorado Line, plowed under the sod, and planted corn. In 1886 they obtained a great crop, "the first and also the last corn crop ever raised in this region," according to a local historian. A period of drought followed and many farmers left the area. During the World War a new tide of settlers flowed in to raise wheat, then in such great demand, on large mechanized farms. Upon the collapse of farm prices after the war the production of wheat declined in the region, which turned increasingly to the growing of sugar beets in irrigated fields along the Arkansas.

In the vicinity of Garden City some 28,000 acres are irrigated with water pumped from an apparently inexhaustible subterranean supply lying from 11 to 40 feet under the surface. Some wells supply water at the rate of 8,000 gallons a minute. This water, according to geologists of the State Water Resources Board, fell in the Rocky Mountains 2,000 years ago and seeped underground until it was impounded here. The irrigated fields about the city have an annual yield of 800,000 tons of beets, which the local factory converts into 22,000,000 pounds of sugar. During the refining season the plant provides 350 men with full-time employment. More than 1,000 hands are employed in the field during the growing season, when beets have to be hoed and weeded on hands and knees with a small hooked knife known as a beet hook. Beet tops are stored in silos and used as feed for livestock.

Less than a decade after the town had been founded, residents voted bonds for the purpose of planting the now substantial trees that shade both business and residential districts. When plans were made to stretch telephone wires along Main Street in 1900, residents objected so strenuously to having their trees mutilated by the erection of poles and wires that the telephone line had to run down the middle of the street.

In the southwest corner of the city on the Arkansas River is 110-acre FREDERICK FINNUP MEMORIAL PARK *(zoo, picnic, and playgrounds)*, given to the city in 1918 by Frederick Finnup, pioneer resident. In the park is the GARDEN CITY SWIMMING POOL *(free)*, all concrete and covering an area 337 feet long by 218 feet wide.

Garden City is at the junction with US 83 *(see Tour 8)*, and with US 50S *(see Tour 4A)*.

Section c. GARDEN CITY *to* COLORADO LINE, *71.8 m.,* US 50

West of Garden City, 0 *m.,* US 50 traverses an irrigated beet-growing section along the tree-studded valley of the Arkansas River. West of

Lakin it cuts through barren eroded upland country until it again enters the Arkansas Valley near Kendall, following the north bank of the stream to the Colorado Line.

HOLCOMB, 6.8 *m.* (2,836 alt., 215 pop.), a hamlet at the head of the Garden City irrigation ditch, is a receiving station for sugar beets. It has a large consolidated school attended by 500 students brought daily in eleven buses from a surrounding area of 125 square miles; a teachers' dormitory adjoins the school building.

This region was once concerned with a lawsuit over riparian rights on the Arkansas River. Kansas filed suit to enjoin the citizens of Colorado from diverting water for the irrigation of beet fields around Lamar because Kansans wanted to irrigate their own beet fields. The Federal court ruled that Colorado residents had a right to use all the water they wanted, adding that it made no difference to the United States whether the sugar beets were raised in Colorado or Kansas. The decision pointed out that if Colorado could not use the water because Kansas wanted it, then Kansas could not use the water if Oklahoma wanted it, and Oklahoma could not use the water if Arkansas wanted it—thus, the water would all go where it was not wanted, into the Mississippi River to break dikes and flood Louisiana.

DEERFIELD, 17.8 *m.* (2,943 alt., 325 pop.), a one-crop town, ships beets to Garden City. Most of its inhabitants work in the beet fields from spring to fall.

At 22.9 *m.* is the junction with a dirt road.

Right on this road to LAKE McKINNEY, 2.8 *m. (open),* an irrigation reservoir storing water for use on lands controlled by sugar companies. It is the largest body of water in Kansas and is well-stocked with fish; in fall and winter months its shores abound with ducks, rabbits, and prairie chickens.

LAKIN, 25.9 *m.* (2,998 alt., 739 pop.), seat of Kearny County, is dominated by a large consolidated high school. It was at one time a rather important shipping point for beef cattle fattened on the buffalo grass that once covered western Kansas. The old pump in front of the courthouse, the only public source of water in the town, is a gathering place for old and young, who congregate here at almost all hours of the day, buckets in hand, to visit or discuss important matters.

KENDALL, 41.6 *m.* (3,380 alt., 150 pop.), a dusty hamlet, was formerly a watering station on the Santa Fe Trail. At that time it was named Aubrey for Francis X. Aubrey, French Canadian scout and guide, the first man to take a loaded wagon train from the Missouri River to Santa Fe in the winter season. On one occasion he rode from Santa Fe to Independence, Mo., a distance of 775 miles, in 5 days and 13 hours to win a bet of $5,000, procuring relays of horses from wagon trains passed along the way. In 1852 Aubrey discovered a new route to Santa Fe. Instead of leaving the Arkansas River at Cimarron Crossing *(see Tour 4A),* he proceeded upstream to the mouth of the Big Sandy, not far from Bent's famous fort at Big Timbers, in what is now Colorado, and there struck southwestward along a high ridge between Raton Pass and Cimarron

River. Aubrey was killed in 1856 by R. C. Weightman, later an artillery major in the Confederate Army, in a quarrel in a Santa Fe saloon.

The crumbling REMAINS OF FORT AUBREY, 49.4 m. (L), a frontier army post, was built by two companies of Wisconsin infantry in 1866 to put down Indian uprisings. It was abandoned early the following year. Near Fort Aubrey are the barely distinguishable outlines of old INDIAN GRAVES, most of which have been rifled.

SYRACUSE, 53.6 m. (3,228 alt., 1,383 pop.), seat of Hamilton County, one of the most favored towns on the High Plains, is a green cool oasis. Inhabitants of distant towns motor here to relax and enjoy the beauty of its tall graceful poplars, weeping willows, and other trees.

Syracuse became the seat of Hamilton County in 1888 after a long fight with Kendall, whose loyal and spirited citizens barricaded their courthouse with barrels of salt, sacks of flour, and bales of hay, to keep the county records after Syracuse had won an election by the expedient of casting 1,178 votes for 614 qualified voters. Kendall petitioned the State Supreme Court to have the election declared fraudulent. Each town had its own county officers for three years; then Syracuse won another election. Once more Kendall charged fraud, but this time Syracuse won the legal battle. "Died: Kendall, 10 miles east," ran the obituary in the Syracuse newspaper.

At 71.8 m. US 50 crosses the Colorado Line, 87 miles east of La Junta, Colo. (see COLO. Tour 9).

←←←←←←←←←←←←←←←←←←☼→→→→→→→→→→→→→→→→→→→

Tour 4A

Junction of US 50-50N and US 59—Emporia—Newton—Hutchinson —Dodge City—Garden City; US 50S.
Junction of US 50-50N and US 59 to Garden City, 356.6 m.

Atchison, Topeka & Santa Fe Ry. parallels route between Ottawa and Garden City. Paved roadbed.
Usual accommodations.

West of Ottawa US 50S follows the valley of the Marais des Cygnes River, once an important trade route for the Osage Indians. Traversing long stretches of undulating prairie sown to wheat and corn, the highway enters the bluestem grazing region in the Flint Hills, rimmed with curiously formed borders of caprock, and emerges in the Great Bend wheat belt, once a paradise for grazing herds. Crossing the Arkansas River at

Hutchinson, the salt-mining center, and again at Kinsley, the route runs along the southern spur of the Smoky Hills Uplands, and then descends into the irrigated bottom lands along the Arkansas River, where trees, shrubs, truck gardens, and fields of beets and alfalfa offer a welcome relief from the general monotony of the high arid plains.

US 50S branches southwest from its junction with US 50 and 50N, 0 *m.* *(see Tour 4).* Between this point and Ottawa, US 50S and US 59 are one route *(see Tour 12).*

OTTAWA, 13 *m.* (891 alt., 9,563 pop.) *(see OTTAWA).*

Points of Interest: Ottawa University, Marais des Cygnes River crossing, Tauy Jones Hall, and others.

Ottawa is at the junction with US 59 *(see Tour 12).*

RANSOMVILLE, 23.2 *m.* (1,138 alt., 5 pop.), now only a cluster of houses, was once an important coal center in Kansas. The first shaft was sunk in 1880 by J. H. Ransom, who enlarged his holdings in 1881 and built thirty cottages for his workers. Increased freight rates in 1882 led to a decline.

Mines are on both sides of the highway. Veins are shallow and are mined by the drift method, consisting of driving tunnels into the hillsides.

At 27.5 *m.* is the junction with an improved road.

1. Right on this road to the junction with another improved road, 4 *m.;* R. on this road to the junction with a third improved road, 5 *m.;* L. on this road to the junction with a dirt road, 7 *m.;* R. on this winding road to a farmyard gate (L), 8.7 *m.*

Through the gate are the RUINS OF THE SAC AND FOX INDIAN AGENCY BUILDING, 9.2 *m.,* completed in 1846, and occupied until 1867, when the tribe was moved to Indian Territory. All that remain are three stone foundations. On a knoll behind are three Indian graves, believed to be those of Sac and Fox chiefs. Chief Keokuk, a friend and helper of the first white settlers, was buried here in 1848. His remains were exhumed and removed to Keokuk, Iowa, in 1883.

2. Left on this road to the junction with a dirt road, 8 *m.;* L. here to the JESSE JAMES CAVE (R), 8.3 *m.,* a hiding place of the outlaw and his gang.

The SITE OF SILKVILLE (L), 29 *m.* (1,010 alt., 8 pop.), is today a handful of whitewashed limestone buildings in a small grove of mulberry trees planted in the 1870's by a colony financed and led by Ernest Boissiere, a French engineer of noble family, who brought manufacturing experts and cocoons from France. The fine silk produced by his workers here won first prize at the Centennial Exposition in Philadelphia in 1876, but the enterprise was soon abandoned. Boissiere then bought dairy herds and operated a cheese factory here, but that also proved unprofitable and he returned to France.

At 42.2 *m.* is the junction with US 75 *(see Tour 11).* Between this place and a point at 45.2 *m.* US 50 S and US 75 are one route.

EMPORIA, 69.7 *m.* (1,133 alt., 14,067 pop.) *(see EMPORIA).*

Points of Interest: Home of William Allen White, College of Emporia, Kansas State Teachers' College, Soden's Mill, and others.

Right from Emporia on State 99, paved, to the junction with an improved road, 13.2 *m.;* R. here to the 138-acre LYON COUNTY STATE LAKE, 14.4 *m.* (boating, fishing), in a 600-acre park.

PLYMOUTH, 77.8 *m.* (1,132 alt., 113 pop.), a roadside community founded in the late 1850's, flourished for a time as a railroad shipping center, but is today a small marketing town frequented by neighboring farmers.

Near the highway is (R) a squat frame structure, PLYMOUTH'S FIRST HOUSE *(private)*, built shortly after the town had been founded. A literary society met in the basement and in the parlor above the Friends held religious services and organized their first Sunday school. Stage drivers stopped for meals or to quench their thirst at the deep well in the yard. The large barn nearby, built in 1864, was PLYMOUTH'S FIRST SCHOOL BUILDING, although the first classes were held in the old house across the street from the first house.

STRONG CITY, 89.9 *m.* (1,174 alt., 805 pop.), is a moderately prosperous rural shipping and trading center; many of its shops and houses are built of limestone from nearby quarries.

In this vicinity a coyote hunt is held every year during the winter. Hundreds of men and boys form a square or circle covering a large area, and gradually close in on their prey. To prevent accidents, clubs are generally used instead of guns.

Left from Strong City on State 13, an improved road, to COTTONWOOD FALLS, 2 *m.* (1,491 alt., 963 pop.), seat of Chase County, an agricultural and live-stock trading and shipping point, named for nearby falls in the Cottonwood River. To this place on the edge of the Flint Hills with their vast expanse of upland pastures, thousands of Texas cattle are shipped every spring to graze on the rich bluestem grasses. The Chase County Fair is held at Cottonwood Falls annually in October and the town sponsors a Fourth of July rodeo.

Founded in 1858 by a group of Free State settlers, prominent among whom was Col. Samuel N. Wood, who had been actively engaged in the factional struggles near Lawrence, Cottonwood Falls became the county seat of Chase County in 1859. "In the long ago younger sons of the British aristocracy were as thick around Cottonwood Falls as bass in South Fork," wrote Jay E. House. "The county actually boasted two or three British titles. George Hughes, radical-minded, soft-hearted son of Sir Thomas Hughes, progenitor of 'Tom Brown,' ranched it there for years. A little farther to the westward in the same Flint Hills, Frederick Remington, the artist, served an apprenticeship as a cowhand. He was one of the Plum Creek outfit, and when they came to town business picked up for everybody. The British invasion had a distinct influence on the speech, intonation, and nomenclature of the country." Jay E. House, later a Topeka and Philadelphia newspaper columnist, worked on a ranch near Cottonwood Falls in the 1890's. Mrs. Willard Greene, whose *Peggy of the Flint Hills* is a popular feature in several Kansas newspapers, began writing her column in the *Chase County Leader,* the town's weekly newspaper.

The CHASE COUNTY COURTHOUSE, in a landscaped square, is one of the most interesting of the old Kansas courthouses. Constructed in 1873 of limestone from quarries in the Flint Hills, the old three-story building is French Renaissance in style, with mansard roof and dormer windows. A cupola topped with a flagpole completely dominates the town's sky line. The building was designed by John G. Haskell of Lawrence, who drew the original plans for the State capitol at Topeka.

At 18 *m.* on this road is the junction with a private road through a pasture *(permission to enter is granted at farm house)*; L. 1 *m.* on this road through three gates *(close after passing so cattle will not get out)* to the KNUTE ROCKNE MEMORIAL, a marble shaft upon a limestone base, commemorating the well-known football coach and seven others who died here in an airplane crash, March 30, 1931.

A few days after the crash Jay E. House, then a Philadelphia newspaper columnist, wrote the following description of the scene: "A grizzled country of narrow, fertile lowlands and wide, depressing uplands, which smiles a few days in the spring and relapses into sullenness during the remainder of the year; a country with cattle on a thousand low-flung and menacing hills and the green and purple of alfalfa in the threads between. That's where Knute Rockne died."

At 96.8 *m.* is ELMDALE (1,206 alt., 246 pop.), a small shipping and trading point.

Left from Elmdale on a dirt road to CAMP WOOD *(open at nominal rates when not in use by the Y.M.C.A.; fishing, boating),* 1.5 *m.,* the State Y.M.C.A. summer camp, consisting of sixteen cabins grouped around a lodge on the shores of a 10-acre lake.

FLORENCE, 113.3 *m.* (1,262 alt., 1,493 pop.) *(see Tour 10)* is at the junction with US 77 *(see Tour 10).* Between this place and a point at 116.5 *m.* US 50S and US 77 are one route.

PEABODY, 129.5 *m.* (1,351 alt., 1,491 pop.), a low and spacious town of the plains, with yellow limestone and red brick buildings shaded by cottonwood and box elder trees, was once a prosperous commercial center, but motor transport has diverted much of its trade to nearby Newton and metropolitan Wichita.

Peabody lies in the Mid-Continent oil fields. Oil once played a prominent part in the town's life, but today most of the local wells are nearly dry.

At 131.4 *m.* is the junction with a graded road.

Right on this road to INDIAN GUIDE, 4 *m.,* a hill used by Indians as a lookout point and landmark. Over this hill went the Kaw trail to the buffalo feeding grounds north of the great bend in the Arkansas River. The Indians often stopped here to tan buffalo robes or to dry buffalo meat; when the buffalo hunting was good, they sometimes wintered here. A granite shaft now stands on the summit of the hill, which was once piled with buffalo bones.

NEWTON, 148.1 *m.* (1,439 alt., 11,032 pop.) *(see NEWTON).*

Points of Interest: Railroad shops, flour mills, Bethel College and others.

Newton is at the junction with US 81 *(see Tour 9).*

At 156.2 *m.* is the junction with a paved road.

Left on this road to HALSTEAD, 1.5 *m.* (1,388 alt., 1,373 pop.), a prosperous and modern town founded in 1873, one of the few villages in the vicinity of Newton and Wichita that have not suffered a severe loss of trade and population during the motor age. Surrounded by fine wheat and cattle country, its principal occupations are milling, shipping, and trading.

At the north edge of Halstead is RIVERSIDE PARK *(picnicking, boating, fishing),* a pleasant stretch of timberland on the banks of the Little Arkansas River. Early in August every year a two-day picnic for the old settlers of Harvey County is held here. According to tradition, the old KIT CARSON TREE back of the bandstand marks the spot where a wagon train led by Kit Carson was ambushed by Indians.

The HALSTEAD HOSPITAL *(open on application),* 328 Poplar St., a three-story stucco building of modern design, was built by Dr. Arthur E. Hertzler, Halstead's first physician and surgeon, whose autobiography *Horse and Buggy Doctor* (1938) attracted Nation-wide attention. The original hospital was a two-and-one-half story frame building completed in 1902. By remodeling and adding new equipment as rapidly as funds would permit, Doctor Hertzler gradually built up this well-equipped fireproof hospital to a capacity of 200 beds. It was his aim to provide facilities at a nominal cost and in the beginning he charged a maximum of $4 a day for hospitalization and a maximum fee of $150 for operations, though patients unable to pay for surgical treatment were never refused admittance. Finding the tax burden too great, Doctor Hertzler sold the hospital to the Sisters of St. Joseph in 1933 for a consideration of one dollar, but has retained his connection with the staff.

BURRTON, 166.3 *m.* (1,451 alt., 649 pop.), an alert prairie community, lies just north of a line of sand hills where in 1937 "wildcatters" opened up a new oil region that turned out to be one of the State's most productive fields.

HUTCHINSON, 181.7 *m.* (1,530 alt., 27,085 pop.) *(see HUTCHIN-SON).*

Points of Interest: Salt Mines, Kansas State Fair, State Industrial Reformatory and others.

Left from Hutchinson on State 17, improved, to the junction with a dirt road, 6.5 *m.;* L. here to YODER, 9.5 *m.* (1,535 alt., 75 pop.), an agricultural trading center populated largely by Amish Mennonites and the hub of a large Mennonite community. These people are often confused with the Russo-German Mennonites *(see Tour 4)* who came directly from Russia to Kansas in the 1870's. Members of the Amish branch are descendants of Pennsylvania Dutch farmers who migrated to Reno County in 1883–84. Yoder was named for Eli Yoder, one of the original settlers, who established a store here in 1889 and became the town's first postmaster. Unlike the Russo-German Mennonites, who are gradually adopting worldly ways, the Amish cling to their hereditary customs and traditional mode of dress. The women wear tiny bonnets and long-sleeved, high-necked dresses of somber-colored material. Hooks and eyes are substituted for buttons on clothing. The men wear long chin whiskers, but shave their upper lips. Automobiles are banned; the Amish men and their families drive to town in old-fashioned buggies drawn by well-groomed horses. A number of Amish families from this community moved to Fairbanks, Iowa, in 1937 because oil developments were encroaching upon their seclusion.

STAFFORD, 226.1 *m.* (1,858 alt., 1,614 pop.), settled in the late 1870's, was known for several years as Sodtown because of old Vickers' Sod Hotel which stood on the site of the present Masonic Hall. When a county was organized in 1879 and named Stafford, in honor of Capt. Lewis Stafford, Company E, First Kansas Infantry, Sodtown immediately changed its name to Stafford, hoping that it would be designated the county seat. Postmaster Charles Johnson hastened to Topeka and returned with assurances that Stafford would be made temporary county seat. But Johnson evidently had not seen "the right people," for Governor John P. St.John bestowed the plum on the town that has since borne his name. St.John became the permanent county seat after a series of elections during one of which a tornado ripped through Stafford, destroying the ballot boxes and nullifying the election.

After more than 50 years of quiet, Stafford suddenly became an oil boom town in 1938 when a wildcat well nearby came in with the roar of a gusher.

ST. JOHN, 235 *m.* (1,908 alt., 1,552 pop.), seat of Stafford County, was founded in 1879 and originally known as Zion Valley, a Mormon town. The first building on its site was a church of the Latter-Day Saints. On its completion in 1875 the Mormons blessed the town to protect it from cyclones. In recent years "twisters" have come within 10 miles of the town, but none has ever struck it.

HARVESTING WITH BINDER

St. John today is a trading and shipping center for a large region producing corn, wheat, barley, oats, and alfalfa. The utilities are municipally owned, thus eliminating city taxes.

MACKSVILLE, 247.8 *m.* (2,025 alt., 868 pop.), is a quiet farming town that used to bustle with activity during the wheat harvest when hundreds of migratory hands poured in to help with the work. Today most of the harvesting is done by motorized machinery.

Much of the country around Macksville is underlain with water that comes from the Rocky Mountains by underground channels and is pumped from wells made by driving specially built pointed pipes through the sandy soil to the underflow.

LEWIS, 263.5 *m.* (2,142 alt., 512 pop.), founded in 1882 by a family of that name from Virginia, is a village that lost one-third of its population when wheat farming was motorized. At the same time Lewis acquired a group of five modern grain elevators overlooking two sprawling rows of store buildings that line a wide main street.

At 267.6 *m.* an elevator and railroad siding (R) mark the SITE OF OHIO CITY. In 1894 two men from Ohio purchased a square mile of land here, divided it into town lots, and recorded the plat at the county seat under the name of Ohio City. Then they returned to Cleveland with a map of the town showing many imaginary buildings and began giving away about 2,500 "choice town lots" to credulous city folk who where asked to pay a notary and recording fee amounting to $8 or $10. These fees constituted the profits of the schemers. Eventually the lots were sold by the sheriff for taxes, and the "city" was legislated out of existence. The site remained good grazing land until sown to wheat 30 years later.

The highway crosses Coon Creek, 274.8 m. at a point where a detachment of U. S. Army recruits escorting their paymaster from Fort Leavenworth to Fort Mann (now Dodge City) were attacked by Comanche and Apache Indians on June 17, 1848.

"Lieutenant, you should double your guard tonight," said an experienced plainsman, "we haven't seen a buffalo in the last two days and that means there are Indians around."

The next morning wolves were heard howling. "Look out, boys," the plainsman warned again, "the wolf packs that are doing that howling are Indians." Soon an immense herd of buffalo approached the camp and the soldiers seized their carbines, breech-loading rifles then new to the plains. When the buffalo shied at the army tents and swerved to the right, 800 Comanches and Apaches came into sight, armed with lances and shields made of the tough hide of a buffalo hull's neck. Holding their shields before them they rode forward to draw the fire of the soldiers, planning to rush in before the recruits' guns could be reloaded. When the Indians saw the soldiers rapidly reloading at the breech after the first volley, they hesitated and then charged.

Several Indians fell, and the war party withdrew about a mile, but a squaw rallied them for a second charge. "Shoot their horses," shouted the lieutenant. When a score of front line mounts went down and others fell over them, the charge was halted 30 yards short of its goal. Pursued by the soldiers, the Indians retreated again and then began a flanking movement. The soldiers had taken up a position on a hill and, as the fighting continued at long range, an Apache chief was killed as he attempted to mount a fresh horse. Suddenly a young Indian boy rode back from the retreating Indian ranks, slipped a lasso around the chief's body and dragged it from the field. The boy was the chief's son, Geronimo, and the soldiers' admiring his courage, held their fire. Geronimo grew up to be the most able Apache warrior who ever opposed the United States forces.

KINSLEY, 275.8 m. (2,050 alt., 2,270 pop.), seat of Edwards County, enjoys a comfortable living from wheat, corn, alfalfa, and poultry products. Many of its houses show the Southwestern influence. Recent public buildings, surrounded by green lawns and shrubs, are of modified Spanish Mission style.

Kinsley was founded in 1873 by a group from Massachusetts who found to their disappointment that the windy, treeless prairies were quite unlike the green wooded hills of their home State. Although the first decade was marred by crop failure and pestilence, in 1884 the local paper called Kinsley "the boomingest boom town in the Southwest." Eastern capital was being poured into the State. "Townsites broke out all over the face of Kansas like the measles," one historian put it. The weekly Kinsley

Mercury became a daily and printed a European edition of 25,000 copies to advertise the town. "KINSLEY! THE CYNOSURE OF ALL EYES, THE COMING GREAT METROPOLIS."

Kinsley citizens envisioned their city as a greater railroad and commercial center than St. Louis or Chicago. Bonds were voted for railroads to connect it with Denver, Memphis, and Atlanta. To the protest that "Kansas is railroad crazy," the *Mercury* replied with a rhymed headline:

"Oh, hear the boom, the rumbling boom!
A shower of golden wheels to dissipate the gloom!"

Town lots to the "value" of $330,000 were sold within a week. Suburban additions were laid out for 6 miles in every direction from town. Street railways and irrigation ditches were projected, a board of trade was organized. In 1888 the bubble burst. "The boom is over," confessed the *Mercury*, printing nine columns of delinquent tax notices. "The young Chicago of the prairies" settled down to more productive pursuits.

Jouett Shouse, organizer of the American Liberty League, calls Kinsley his home, having represented its district in Congress for a time.

OFFERLE, 285.2 *m.* (2,050 alt., 298 pop.), is dominated by the white Romanesque limestone tower of ST. JOSEPH'S CHURCH (Roman Catholic) and several towering grain elevators. Milling is the principal industry of the village.

Old residents tell a strange tale of a band of "forty-niners" who, returning from California in the 1850's, camped on the present townsite for the night, burying buckskin bags containing $50,000 worth of gold dust in a creek bank for safety. An Indian attack at dawn left only one survivor, an eight-year-old girl. In the 1890's she returned to look for the gold dust, but after a day's search gave up the quest and returned East.

DODGE CITY, 312.9 *m.* (2,420 alt., 10,059 pop.) *(see DODGE CITY).*

Points of Interest: Boot Hill, City Parks, Lone Tree, and others.

At Dodge City is the junction with State 45 *(see Tour 4B).*

1. Left from Dodge City on US 283, paved, to the Beeson Rd., 1 *m.;* R. on this road to the BEESON MUSEUM *(adm. 25¢),* 1.4 *m.,* which exhibits some 4,000 items, including cowboy saddles, arrowheads, peace pipes, buffalo robes, and Indian baskets, forming one of the largest collections of Indian and pioneer relics in Kansas. It was assembled and is in charge of Merritt Beeson, son of Chalk Beeson, noted scout and cowboy band leader. Because of his unsurpassed knowledge of the country, Chalk Beeson was official guide of the "Royal Buffalo Hunt" organized by Gen. George Custer to entertain Grand Duke Alexis of Russia on his tour of America in 1871–72.

2. Left from Dodge City on US 154, paved, to the FORT DODGE SOLDIERS' HOME, 5 *m.,* originally a frontier fort, now a home for war veterans. Two of the ADOBE BARRACKS built here in 1864 still stand; both have been veneered with native stone. One is the old fort headquarters, which at various times housed Generals Custer, Sheridan, and Miles. CUSTER'S CHERRYWOOD LIQUOR CABINET is still part of this building's furniture.

3. Left from Dodge City on a dirt road to WILLROAD GARDENS, 4 *m.,* a low-priced housing project built in 1934–36 by a syndicate of Dodge City businessmen. The 69 bungalows, containing from three to six rooms, were sold on small

monthly payments to clerks, businessmen, and industrial workers. Behind the houses are hayfields, vegetable gardens, and community pastures. All the land here is irrigated by means of a network of ditches connected with the Arkansas River. The community center is a three-room frame schoolhouse where two teachers instruct the 60 pupils. The schoolhouse can be turned into a church or hall seating 250 by opening the folding doors between the rooms.

At 325 *m.* the route enters the MOUNTAIN TIME ZONE; watches of westbound travelers should be set back one hour.

Between Dodge City and Ingalls is the EMBANKMENT OF THE ABANDONED EUREKA IRRIGATION DITCH, an ambitious enterprise started in the 1880's. During the boom in those years many such irrigation canals were projected; although by 1890 more than 30 companies had been incorporated for the purpose of building them, this ditch is the only monument to the numerous paper enterprises.

CIMARRON, 332.3 *m.* (2,625 alt., 1,035 pop.), an exceptionally attractive town in rainy years, when its residents can cultivate their lawns and set out trees and flowers, became the seat of Gray County in the early 1880's after a bitter fight with Ingalls.

INGALLS, 338.5 *m.* (2,672 alt., 272 pop.), a small wheat center, once dreamed of itself as the seat of Gray County and the capital of a great irrigated empire.

The dream took shape in the minds of two brothers named Gilbert, who persuaded an eastern manufacturer, Asa T. Soule, to finance the Eureka Irrigation Company. A $400,000 canal, 90 miles long, was planned to divert water from the Arkansas River and irrigate 640,000 acres. "There are now employed 225 men and 360 horses and mules," reported the *Kansas Cowboy* of Dodge City in 1884, "the monthly payroll will be $15,000." Soule astonished frontier folk by bringing five great machines from Chicago to dig the ditch. The gigantic canal, the newspaper exulted, would make the valley "bloom as the rose"; productive harvests could never fail.

Soule supplied the capital (millions, some historians say), the Gilberts supplied ideas and the ditch was dug. Soule erected a hotel, a church, and a store or two at the intake of the ditch, and named the settlement Ingalls —for John J. Ingalls, political leader and writer of the day. Intent on making Ingalls the county seat, Soule built a "gift" railroad to Montezuma, 35 miles away, to win Montezuman votes in an impending election.

Through Soule's largesse Ingalls won; but Cimarron, already the temporary county seat, refused to surrender the county records, even though a court ruling commanded it. Ingalls descended upon Cimarron in a body, and a riot followed in which an innocent bystander was killed. When the smoke cleared away, Ingalls was the county seat in fact as well as in law.

Soule later sold his ditch to other speculators for $1,000,000. In time the ditch went dry, largely through neglect, and Ingalls was left to dwindle to a population of less than 100. In an election in 1896, which Ingalls did not contest, Cimarron became the county seat.

An epilogue to this story was written in 1912 when one of the Gilberts, backed by Denver capitalists, attempted to revive his dream project. Once again water came through the ditches, but drought finally dried up the flow.

Ingalls is at the SITE OF THE OLD CIMARRON CROSSING, where a short cut of the Santa Fe Trail branched southwest toward Raton Pass (New Mexico). Although it saved almost 100 miles, the route was dangerous because some of its water holes were 80 miles apart.

Captain William Becknell of Missouri, who had opened the Santa Fe Trail in 1821, was the first man to make the hazardous journey over this route. On a second trip in 1832, he was racing a party of pack-mule traders to Santa Fe. Handicapped by heavy wagons, Becknell fell behind, and, seeking a short-cut, took the Cimarron cut-off. On the second day the party's water gave out. In desperation the men cut off the ears of mules, drank the warm blood, and stumbled on. On the fourth day Becknell, with tongue black and swollen, led his party across the dry bed of the Cimarron River. Half his men were delirious from thirst. An old buffalo bull, stomach distended as if filled with water, was sighted in the underbrush. Becknell and his men shot the animal, split his belly open, and drank the tepid water. Then those who could still walk followed the spoor through the underbrush to a spot in the dry sand bed of the Cimarron where the bull had pawed out a water hole. The men staggered back with water and saved the party.

For years the exact site of the crossing has been disputed by historians and residents of the region, but D. W. (Doc) Barton, a pioneer Ingalls cattleman, who came here in 1872, says that the town lies in the crotch of the fork, where the short-cut branched south. According to Barton, the trail left the Arkansas River bottom near the present site of Cimarron, extended west along the prairie for about 4 miles, then returned to the river and followed its course to the site of Ingalls. Here the "water scrape route" began, crossing the river and extending southwest through Haskell, Grant, and Morton Counties (see Tour 6).

The ruins of an old Spanish fort stood at the fork of the trail when Barton came to Gray County. Crumbling adobe walls, caved-in dugouts, and traces of corrals were plainly visible in the 1870's, he says, but have long since disappeared.

PIERCEVILLE, 351.2 m. (2,758 alt., 150 pop.), a scattered village centered about a general store, was headquarters in 1872 for the Barton brothers, ranchers with a large herd of cattle. They arranged with the railroad to have the tracks pass their ranch house and laid out a townsite, which they named Pierceville for Charles and Carlos Pierce, members of the townsite company. The railroad quartered 500 workmen in bunk cars parked at Pierceville and hired hunters to supply buffalo and antelope meat. A store, a post office, and several dugouts were built by settlers in the two years that followed.

On July 3, 1874, a local historian recounts, buffalo hunters raced into town with the news that a band of Indians on the warpath had been defeated in an attack on Adobe Walls, Texas, a few days previously, and were headed for Pierceville. The townspeople scattered and hid in the prairie draws. The Indians left Pierceville a mass of smoldering ruins.

The Barton brothers later rebuilt their ranch house, but the townsite became a camping ground for Indians, cowboys, and immigrants until 1878 when the Government reestablished the post office and the town began to rebuild.

GARDEN CITY, 365.6 *m.* (2,830 alt., 6,121 pop.) *(see Tour 4)*, is at the junction with US 50–50N *(see Tour 4)*, and with US 83 *(see Tour 8)*.

◀◀◀◀◀◀◀‿◀◀◀◀◀◀◀◀◀◀◀ ✿ ▶▶▶▶▶▶▶▶▶▶▶▶▶▶▶▶▶▶

Tour 4B

Dodge City—Sublette—Hugoton—Elkhart—Oklahoma Line; State 45. Dodge City to Oklahoma Line, 121.8 m.

Atchison, Topeka & Santa Fe Ry. parallels route.
Hard-surfaced roadbed most of the distance, gravel the remainder. Open except during infrequent blizzards and dust storms.
Accommodations limited; modern hotels in county seat towns; tourist camps.

State 45, the direct route to the Kansas gas fields and to the center of a former dust bowl, passes through a section that has been exploited by two generations of land speculators. The first wave of immigration swept over southwestern Kansas in the 1880's when promoters sought to build great cities on these arid plains. When the boom burst in 1889, thousands of investors were ruined, and a score of towns were left to decay as a majority of settlers abandoned their claims, some returning to their former homes, others joining the rush into the Cherokee Strip. Those who remained used the vast expanse of buffalo grass as pasture for their cattle, making little attempt at cultivation.

Southwestern Kansas became the pawn of empire builders a second time when, in 1912, a Dodge City group persuaded the Santa Fe Railway to build a line into the region. To provide a reason for the railroad's existence, the promoters encouraged settlement and wheat farming. Townsites were platted and lots sold to eager investors. As new towns arose, older towns were deserted. New county-seat wars flared. Thousands of acres of grasslands were plowed and sown to wheat; huge elevators were built to store the expected grain. But climatic conditions were not stable, and, in the two decades that followed, one good yield in three plantings came to be accepted as the norm of prosperity. The one-crop-in-three-plantings series was disrupted by drought in 1931. Crop failures ensued. The denuded soil, pulverized by successive plowings, was scooped up by

DUST STORM APPROACHING WESTERN KANSAS TOWN

the winds and carried along in "black blizzards." In time the entire prairie between Dodge City and the Oklahoma Panhandle seemed on the verge of becoming the desolate rim of the more desolate dust bowl. But rain fell in 1938. The wheat sprouted, the land turned green, and a fair crop was harvested.

State 45 branches southwest from its junction with US 50S *(see Tour 4A)* in DODGE CITY, 0 *m.* (2,420 alt., 10,059 pop.) *(see DODGE CITY)*.

ENSIGN, 14.7 *m.* (2,625 alt., 244 pop.), a cluster of small frame buildings in the shadow of a grain elevator, was established at the height of the first boom in 1887 and named for its founder, G. L. Ensign. The town enjoyed a brief period of prosperity after Asa T. Soule, eastern capitalist, had built a railroad spur from Dodge City through Ensign to Montezuma in order to gain Montezuma's support in a county seat election *(see Tour 4A, INGALLS)*. After Cimarron had become the county seat, the railroad was abandoned and Ensign lapsed into dormancy until 1912 when the Santa Fe built its new line through the town.

MONTEZUMA, 26.5 *m.* (2,625 alt., 424 pop.), another reminder of two railroad booms, was founded in 1887 by speculators who abandoned it after the failure of Asa Soule's enterprise. Twenty-five years later it was aroused from its torpor by railroad promoters. A new generation of speculators arrived, and the town was rejuvenated. In 1913 a prairie fire sweeping in from the south threatened it with destruction; panic-stricken residents loaded their household goods in trucks and wagons and prepared to abandon their homes. Men, women, and children fought the flames with wet gunny sacks and blankets, and, aided by a shift in the wind, succeeded in preventing a disaster. Montezuma throve for a decade as a shipping point, and now (1938), after waiting patiently by the roadside during 7 years of ruined crops, is enjoying an abundant wheat harvest.

COPELAND, 38.9 *m.* (2,630 alt., 423 pop.), founded in 1912, was named for an official of the Santa Fe Railway. Rising high above the little railroad station is a great concrete grain elevator, built by a co-operative grain-marketing company in 1929 at a cost of $125,000. Its capacity of 517,000 bushels was filled to overflowing in 1930 and 1931 when southwestern Kansas harvested record wheat crops. It was again nearly filled in 1938 but during most of the intervening years, the great tube has stood almost empty.

Between Copeland and Sublette the road enters a vast level plain; during drought years the mirage is a common phenomenon here and travelers are often deceived by atmospheric tricks. Large lakes appear along the horizon, only to vanish as they are approached. Before this country was plowed, it was a lush meadow, richly carpeted with buffalo grass.

SUBLETTE, 50.4 *m.* (2,950 alt., 673 pop.), named for William Sublette, the fur trader, is the youngest county seat town in Kansas. It came into existence in 1912 when the new railroad circumvented Santa Fe, the old county seat 7 miles away. Businessmen in Santa Fe soon abandoned their townsite and moved their buildings to Sublette, although Santa Fe remained the nominal county seat until 1920. A courthouse was completed here 2 years later. Decrepit frame structures brought from Santa Fe strike an incongruous note in this otherwise modern town.

At 52.4 *m.* is the junction with US 83-160 *(see Tours 8 and 6).*

SATANTA, 58.8 *m.* (2,911 alt., 508 pop.), was named for Satanta, or White Bear, a Kiowa chief. Many in Satanta are "suitcase farmers," who lease large tracts of land on a share-crop basis and hire men with motorized machinery to plant wheat, gambling the cost of seed and cultivation against the chance that they may "hit a crop" and make their fortunes. One suitcase farmer received $92,000 for his wheat in 1929. His success prompted other suitcase men to sow a vast acreage in the fall of 1930, which contributed substantially to Kansas' record wheat harvest of 240 million bushels in 1931. During the next 7 years, however, the farmers in this vicinity seldom raised enough wheat to replace their seed.

Southwest of Satanta thousands of acres were plowed in the hopeful 1920's and produced a few crops. During the drought this was a wasteland of shifting sand and silt, broken only by an occasional deserted farmhouse with its cluster of half-buried outbuildings. In the fall of 1938 the land was again green and farmers were being paid $1.25 a head a month for pasturing cattle on the growing wheat—a practice that improves the spring crop by preventing the growing grain from becoming too rank in the autumn.

The road crosses the Cimarron River, 64.8 *m.,* which winds through hills covered with yucca, sagebrush, and Russian thistle. The stream is dry at this point almost all year, but on rare occasions it becomes a raging yellow torrent and floods the valley.

MOSCOW, 75.3 *m.* (3,100 alt., 249 pop.), known as New Moscow to its older residents, is the successor of another Moscow, established 8 miles to the south in 1887 and moved here in 1913 to be on the railroad. The town has a modern brick high school that serves nine school districts.

HUGOTON, 88.8 *m.* (3,100 alt., 1,368 pop.), seat of Stevens County, is a neat town with tile, terra cotta, and yellow brick shops lining its main street. Although the community lies deep in the Kansas dust bowl, it has preserved a measure of economic stability by virtue of the surrounding gas field, one of the largest reserves in the United States. Three different formations in the Hugoton field contain gas, and geologists believe that gas underlies all of Stevens County.

Pipe-lines carry Hugoton gas to Denver and other Colorado cities; northeastern lines extend as far as Minneapolis and Detroit. The first well (1927) produced 7 million cubic feet of natural gas. The vast pocket has since been tapped by about 200 local wells. Royalties from land leased to development companies have saved many farmers and ranchers from bankruptcy.

When Hugoton was established in 1885, a literary-minded founder named it Hugo in honor of the French novelist. But, as that name had already been adopted by another town in Kansas, the settlement was renamed. Early efforts to make Hugoton the county seat were stoutly opposed by Col. Samuel N. Wood who founded a rival town, Woodsdale, in 1887. Colonel Wood, a typical pioneer promoter, settled near Lawrence, Kansas, in 1854, and became a leader of the Free State Party. In 1859 he moved to the Flint Hills country and helped organize Chase County, which he represented in the first State legislature. Two years later he established first newspapers in Council Grove and Cottonwood Falls. Following meritorious service in the Civil War, he returned to Kansas.

Resenting Wood's interference with their plans, Hugoton citizens caused his arrest on a libel charge and had him taken from Kansas into what is now Oklahoma. Friends rescued Wood. In an election marked by palpable irregularities, Hugoton was voted the county seat. Woodsdale sulked and Hugoton prospered. That Colonel Woods was not yet defeated became evident in 1888 when the county ordered a referendum on the question of issuing bonds to subsidize the construction of a railroad. When Hugoton residents learned that the proposed road was to circumvent their town and pass through Woodsdale, they marshaled forces and defeated the measure. Charges and countercharges of fraud were exchanged. Overt warfare broke out and the militia was sent to disarm the belligerents.

In this conflict Sam Robinson, Hugoton marshal, had struck Jim Gerrond of Woodsdale over the head with the butt of his revolver in a meeting at a town called Vorhees. A warrant was issued for Robinson and given to Ed Short, Woodsdale marshal, who came to Hugoton to make the arrest. The two marshals exchanged shots on the street, and Short retreated. A month later he learned that Robinson had gone hunting in the neutral strip known as No Man's Land south of the State Line. Assembling a party, Short rode into the strip and surrounded Robinson and his friends in a dugout. But Robinson escaped on a race horse and rode back to Hugoton for re-enforcements.

To prevent a rescue, Short had also sent for re-enforcements, and Sheriff John Cross, a Woodsdale man, organized a posse and started for the strip. On the night of July 25, 1888, Cross, three deputy sheriffs, and a youthful tenderfoot named Tonney were encamped in a hay meadow on the shores of Wild Horse Lake. The Hugoton forces surprised them there and killed the sheriff and his three deputies. Tonney, seriously wounded, made his way back to Vorhees, swearing that the Woodsdale party had been attacked while it slept, although the Hugoton men reported that the sheriff and his posse had met death in a running fight. Again troops were sent in to preserve order, but no arrests were made because the killing occurred beyond the State's jurisdiction.

Two years later, through the efforts of Colonel Wood, twelve Hugoton men were indicted for their part in the "massacre" and brought to trial before a Federal court at Paris, Texas. Five were convicted of murder in the first degree, but the United States Supreme Court ordered a new trial which was never held. In June 1891, as he was leaving the Hugoton court, then held in the local Methodist church, Wood was shot from behind and killed by Jim Brennan, deputy sheriff of a neighboring county, who had been a witness for the defense in the murder trial. Brennan surrendered to the authorities and was taken to Liberal, but was never tried because all of the few hundred men eligible for jury service in Stevens County had been so actively identified with one or the other faction in the long-standing dispute that it was impossible to select an unprejudiced jury.

After the colonel's death Woodsdale declined rapidly, although the post office was not closed until 1910. The townsite was finally abandoned and sold for taxes. The last reminder of the town disappeared in 1934 when the remains of Sheriff Cross and those killed with him at the Hay Meadow Massacre were removed to Moscow and other towns.

The NEGRO BAPTIST CHURCH, on N. Main St., a frame building formerly used by the white Methodist congregation, served as a county court-room in early days. Here Colonel Wood, shot by Jim Brennan, expired in his wife's arms.

Left from Hugoton on US 270–State 51 to the NORTHERN NATURAL GAS COM-PANY ABSORPTION PLANT *(open on application)*, 3.7 m., constructed in 1933 to produce high quality casing-head gasoline, which, when mixed with kerosene, can be used as fuel for automobiles. A 165-mile pipe-line conveys natural gas from 90 wells to this plant. Forced into five cylindrical tanks, the gas is sprayed with min-eral seal oil, which absorbs gasoline vapors. The plant, with a daily capacity of 15,000 gallons, ships 300 to 500 tank cars of gasoline annually. Gases not converted into usable products by the absorption process are carried through an outlet pipe 30 feet high and burned; at night the flame is visible for 20 miles.

The area between Hugoton and Elkhart changed miraculously in the fall of 1938. That year Stevens County raised 328,000 bushels of wheat in the area where the "black blizzards" had almost denuded many fields of their topsoil and had covered others with a deposit of fine silt. In 1934 the Government bought starving drought-cattle here; in 1938 the farmers —with feed enough for 100,000 cattle—were seeking livestock to con-sume their grain.

ROLLA, 104.8 m. (3,648 alt., 437 pop.), the first town platted on the new railroad and settled shortly after the surveyors left in 1912, was originally named Reil for one of the founders. Through an error of the Post Office Department the name became Rolla. The town lies on the edge of the Hugoton gas field; the first well drilled had a production of 14 million cubic feet in 1930. Rolla has a rural high school, an electric lighting and water system, and a score of modern business houses.

Right from Rolla on State 51 to RICHFIELD, 17.7 *m.* (3,648 alt., 106 pop.), a cluster of dugouts and buildings dominated by the Morton County Courthouse, a remnant of the boom in the 1880's when Richfield was a thriving trade center. As platted in 1885 by optimistic speculators, Richfield's townsite covered 640 acres—more than enough to accommodate the entire present population of Morton County. By 1886 the town had a general store, 2 banks, a hotel, a bakery, a drugstore, a lumberyard, and a population of 1,500.

For a short time Richfield prospered; then came the drought of 1889. Banks failed; settlers abandoned their claims; and merchants moved away leaving part of their stock on the shelves. When the Cherokee Strip was opened in 1893 hundreds more left to seek their fortune in Oklahoma. By the end of the year fewer than 500 persons remained in the county. Buildings from deserted towns were moved to ranches and converted into houses, cattle sheds, and corrals. Each autumn the ranchers, with four-horse teams, made the 50-mile trip to Syracuse, the nearest railroad point, for the winter's supplies.

In 1905 a new boom got under way. Land speculators bought 400 quarter sections at $1 an acre. Land values rose; new settlers poured into the country. But Richfield received a crushing blow when the new railroad built in 1913 avoided it.

The MORTON COUNTY COURTHOUSE, a two-story building constructed of local limestone, was completed in 1889.

WILBURTON, 113.8 *m.* (3,648 alt., 150 pop.), another of the boom towns of 1913, consists of frame dwellings clustered about a lumberyard, an elevator, and a railway station. During the dust storms these houses were almost covered by silt. In 1938 they emerged like butterflies from their dusty cocoons—bright with new paint.

ELKHART, 121.3 *m.* (3,648 alt., 1,435 pop.), metropolis of Morton County, was settled in 1913 and enjoyed a brief prosperity as a shipping point for broomcorn. Upon completion of the railroad, freight and produce for shipment were brought here from towns 100 miles distant in Colorado, New Mexico, Texas, and Oklahoma. The World War stimulated a boom reminiscent of that in the 1880's. Elkhart paved its streets, built an electric power plant, and installed an electric pump to replace the windmill at the city well. A decline began in 1926 with the extension of the railroad through Elkhart into Oklahoma.

GLENN CUNNINGHAM PARK, N. end of Main St., equipped with an athletic field and tennis courts, was named for Glenn Cunningham, renowned middle-di *it* ince runner and one of Kansas' greatest athletes. Representing the loc..l high school, Cunningham first attracted attention in 1929 when he established a new State high school record for the mile. Later, while attending the University of Kansas, he flashed along the cinder paths to establish new records and qualified for the United States Olympic team in 1932. In the 1936 Olympics at Berlin he broke the record for the 1,500-meter race, but finished second to the British runner, Jack Lovelock. On receiving his doctor's degree in physical education at New York University (1938), Cunningham announced that he was retiring from competition. Cunningham first took up running to develop

STONE FENCE POST ON TREELESS PLAIN

the muscles of his legs after they had been severely burned when the country schoolhouse he attended was destroyed by a fire in which his brother was fatally burned.

Right from Elkhart on State 27 to the junction with a dirt road, 7.5 *m.*; L. on this road to POINT ROCKS, 1 *m.*, a landmark on the old Santa Fe Trail. Point Rocks, a tall sandstone bluff rising from the northern bank of the Cimarron River, was used as a campground by early travelers because it afforded a commanding view of the surrounding country. Many Indian artifacts and parts of wagon trains, including ox yokes and fragments of wheels, have been found on this site.

A soil conservation project here illustrates several methods of reclamation; one unbroken contour furrow extends for nearly 10 miles. The work of the reclamation agencies—including the restoration of buffalo grass on many formerly bald hills—has been so successful in this area that there are rumors (1938) of another land rush. Agricultural experts warn, however, that a potentially dangerous situation still exists in some sections in spite of favorable rainfall, and that full co-operation of farmers and Government agencies is necessary if the region's agriculture is to be placed on a sound basis.

At 121.8 *m.* State 45 crosses the Oklahoma Line.

◄◄◄◄◄◄◄◄◄◄◄◄◄◄◄◄◄◄◄◄◄✿►►►►►►►►►►►►►►►►►►►►►

Tour 5

(Jefferson City, Mo.)—Fort Scott—Wichita—Pratt—Liberal—(Hooker, Okla.); US 54.
Missouri Line to Oklahoma Line, 396.6 m.

Missouri Pacific R.R. parallels route between Fort Scott and Wichita; Atchison, Topeka & Santa Fe Ry. between Wichita and Pratt; Chicago, Rock Island & Pacific Ry. between Pratt and Liberal.
Concrete paved roadbed except for short stretch of improved road near Oklahoma Line. Open all year, except immediately following snowstorms.
Fair accommodations in all county seat towns; good accommodations in cities.

Except for oil fields around El Dorado and Wichita, US 54 is bordered by farming country—fertile valleys, pastures and broad rolling wheat fields that combine to make Kansas one of the foremost agricultural States.

Near the eastern border the route crosses an area of gently undulating hills and valleys broken at intervals by narrow wooded ravines. Hedgerows separate the farms and occasionally mark off the fields into squares striped with long green rows. Dairying is the principal industry in this region. Large herds of cows are visible from the highway and almost every farmhouse is flanked by a huge cattle barn and a towering silo.

Between Bucklin and Liberal the route traverses an area where wheat is planted. Its rainfall ranges from 8 to 25 inches a year.

Section a. MISSOURI LINE *to* WICHITA; *176.5 m.,* US 54

US 54 crosses the Missouri Line, 0 *m.,* 180 miles southwest of Jefferson City, Mo. *(see Mo. Tour 15).*

FORT SCOTT, 5.1 *m.* (800 alt., 10,763 pop.) *(see FORT SCOTT).*

Points of Interest: Old Military Barracks, Historical Museum, Fort Blair, Carroll Plaza, Market Square, Memorial Building, Home of Eugene Ware, and others.

Fort Scott is at the junction with US 69 *(see Tour 13).*

Just west of Fort Scott was the townsite of the short-lived Vegetarian Kansas Emigration Company, which had its headquarters in New York City. In 1855 the company hired Henry S. Clubb to expound his dietary principle and attract settlers. When several hundred with capital varying from $50 to $10,000 had responded, four square miles of prairie were purchased from the Government and trimmed into the shape of a large octagon with a small octagon in the center on which was to be erected an octagonal building to house a store, a school, a church, a post office, and a town hall. The rest of the geometric figure was divided into 16 farms each facing the central octagon.

Colonists had to arrive in units of 16 or multiples thereof; the plan was to erect four octagonal villages into an octagonal city of 16 square miles, and so on endlessly. Believing that the original village would become the center of a great city, the promoters had worked out a detailed plan which divided each of the vegetarian farms into eight city blocks containing twenty town lots each. All their advertisements stressed the increased value of real estate resulting from this form of settlement. When the supply of vegetarian purchasers of these octagon lots ran out, the promoters organized a sister company for non-vegetarians called the Octagon Settlement Company. Purchasers were to be anti-slavery, anti-liquor, have a good moral character, and be ready to vote for "purifying" laws when Kansas should become a State.

In 1856 nearly one hundred vegetarian blacksmiths, carpenters, and farmers arrived with twenty oxen, five or six horses, and a gristmill, creating a transitory boom. Immigrants were arriving from all directions in April, May, and June, and lots bought in May were sold a few days later at a profit of $150; but the New York promoters failed to supply the promised farm implements and seed grain. There was only one plow in the vegetarian settlement. Mosquitoes, fever, and ague attacked the settlers, many of whom were unfitted for frontier life. The "inexhaustible" springs dried up; what crops were planted were raided by the Indians. There was heavy mortality among children and old folk and, when winter neared, all who were able to travel departed. One woman wrote in her diary: "My husband went to see Mr. Clubb . . . to refund our money . . . no law to regain our money . . . he let us have some corn starch, farina and a little pearled barley." The only reminder of the enterprise is a nearby stream, still called Vegetarian Creek.

ROCK CREEK LAKE *(boating, fishing, camp stoves, picnic grounds, children's playgrounds),* at 10.2 *m.* (L), covers about 70 acres, in a 320-

acre natural park. The lake was built by Fort Scott to supplement its water supply from the Marmaton River.

At 19 *m.* is the junction with a graveled road.

Left on this road to the junction with another graveled road, 7 *m.;* R. here to ELM CREEK LAKE *(swimming, boating, fishing)*, in BOURBON COUNTY STATE PARK *(picnic grounds, footpaths, hunting in season)*, 9 *m.*

In BRONSON, 29.2 *m.* (1,074 alt., 455 pop.), a small market town patronized by neighboring farmers, is the home of Jonathan M. Davis *(see HISTORY)*, Governor of Kansas *(1923–1925)*.

West of Bronson are clusters of gas wells and a few abandoned weed-grown gas fields from which parts of the equipment have been removed. When gas was first discovered in this section, geologists estimated that the supply was inexhaustible and producers worked only high pressure wells; they capped old wells when the pressure went down, and drilled new ones. Today most of the wells are idle.

A GOVERNMENT EMERGENCY LANDING FIELD AND RADIO RANGE (R), 39.1 *m.*, has an oral-type radio beam for the use of mail planes flying between Kansas City, Mo. and Fort Worth, Tex.

In the ELM CREEK SOIL CONSERVATION AREA, 39.6 *m.*, farmers, co-operating with the Federal Government, are experimenting with the control of sheet erosion common on these long slopes. This demonstration area, approximately 14 miles long and five and one-half miles wide, contains 35,000 acres. Examples of terracing, contour farming, and pond building are visible from the highway.

LA HARPE, 41.7 m. (1,036 alt., 756 pop.), once a busy industrial town but now dependent on farm trade, was founded in 1881 by a group of Civil War veterans. It grew slowly until 1898 when the discovery of natural gas in the vicinity brought industrialists to develop the gas fields and to establish factories using the fuel. Workers seeking jobs flocked to La Harpe. Soon a zinc smelter, brick and tile plants, and several smaller manufacturing concerns were thriving. In 1910 the gas supply began to fail, and by 1915 the industries dependent upon it had shut down and their workers had gone to the oil fields farther west.

IOLA, 47.6 *m.* (957 alt., 7,160 pop.), built around a spacious courthouse square, has broad streets lined with spreading elms. Its industrial plants include foundries, a brickyard, a dress and overall factory, a big cement factory, and a milk condensery. Between 1924 and 1937 the milk condensery paid 5 million dollars to farmers of this vicinity. During drought years these checks have often been the farmers' chief source of income. The condensery's policy of importing pure-bred dairy cows to be sold at cost to the farmers on long-time payments has improved the grade of cows in the community and increased their average milk production.

Following the discovery of natural gas near Iola in the late 1890's a zinc smelter, an acid plant, and several smaller concerns were built and operated here until the early 1920's, when the diminishing gas supply forced them to shut down. During the peak of gas production Iola attained a population of approximately 12,000.

Congressman "Farmer" Funston, nicknamed by Republicans "Fog Horn" Funston—whose son, Fred Funston *(see Tour 12)*, was a hero of the Philippine campaign—often came to Iola from his nearby farm and made temperance speeches on the street. It was before the days of amplifiers and radio, but citizens claimed that they could hear Funston's voice from a distance of one mile.

In 1906 a prohibition fanatic stole thirty sticks of dynamite from the cement factory and planted them at night in seven buildings around the square that housed "joints" (illegal saloons). The next morning he lit the fuses. The resultant series of explosions wrecked five buildings but fortunately the other two charges did not go off. Newspapers speculated on the possibility of this man's becoming "the John Brown of Prohibition," but he was committed to an insane asylum.

In RIVERSIDE PARK *(swimming, free camping, picnic and playgrounds)*, five blocks south and five blocks west of the courthouse square, the Allen County Fair and Southeastern Kansas Exposition is held annually *(last 2 or 3 days of Aug.)*, featuring horse and automobile races and agricultural and livestock exhibits.

The KANSAS ROOM of the IOLA PUBLIC LIBRARY contains a collection of historical clippings and pictures and 700 volumes that are either written by Kansas authors or deal with the history of the State.

Iola is at the junction with US 59 *(see Tour 12)*.

From a bridge over the Neosho River, 48.5 *m.* the IOLA DAM (L) and the IOLA WATER WORKS (R) are visible.

West of the Neosho River bridge the highway follows a 10-foot fill built across the swampy lowlands and topped with concrete. Trees and shrubs have been planted on its sloping sides and tall grass grows in the ditches along its base. The surrounding country, subject to floods of the Neosho River, has many ponds bordered with swamp grass and cattails.

From the summit of PIQUA HILL, 53.9 *m.*, is a broad view of the countryside. A line of trees to the east indicates the course of the Neosho River through the green valley; beyond is the tip of the Iola courthouse tower extending above the treetops. On both sides of the highway from this point hills close in about the valley.

PIQUA, 54.9 *m.* (1,034 alt., 259 pop.), a tiny rural village within the semicircle formed by two low ranges of hills, is the birthplace of Buster Keaton, motion picture comedian. While his father and Harry Houdini were operating an Indian medicine show here in the 1890's, a terrific storm blew their tent down, and Mrs. Keaton was taken to a nearby church, where her son was born. She remained in Piqua for two weeks at the home of Jacob Haen.

West of Piqua are large hayfields, the country is more rolling, and the hilltops are covered with tall coarse grass. During the summer, hay balers are at work in the fields on both sides of the highway and large trucks loaded with baled hay, most of them piled to what seems the toppling-over point, travel the highway.

YATES CENTER, 68.7 *m.* (1,099 alt., 2,013 pop.), seat of Woodson County, an important hay-shipping point, stands on the crest of the divide

YATES CENTER

between the Neosho and Verdigris Rivers. Laid out in 1875, the town is built around a landscaped courthouse square. Its old limestone business houses are interspersed with more modern structures whose fronts are of stucco and tile.

Yates Center is at the junction with US 75 *(see Tour 11)*.

West of Yates Center US 54 makes a series of curves through high plateau pasture land, now and then descending into rocky wooded canyons. The route follows the northern edge of the region locally called the Kansas Ozarks.

BATESVILLE, 79.1 *m.* (1,059 alt., 22 pop.), was known as one of the largest hay-shipping stations in the country until a few years ago, when trucking became a popular means of transportation. Though the town was never more than a cluster of houses, hundreds of thousands of tons of hay were shipped annually on the Missouri Pacific R.R. from this point.

When settlers first arrived in the region, grass grew as high as a man's head on the slopes and to a greater height in low sandy places; but years of harvesting have depleted the soil and now the grass seldom reaches a height of more than two feet.

Old-timers describe prairie fires in this region that traveled as fast as a horse could run. Flames leaped high in the air and great clouds of smoke, visible for miles, darkened the sky. Crackling loudly, the tongues of fire devoured everything in their path—stock, homes, crops, and occasionally human lives—leaving behind only charred desolation. Wild animals and birds fled screaming before the wall of fire. Coyotes and rabbits often ran ahead of the blaze for miles and then, crazed, turned suddenly and plunged into the flames to die.

In the more thickly populated regions, settlers fought fire with fire by burning out sections of land, and thus halting the terrible sheet of flame. Lone families, however, were usually forced to flee. Their abandoned homes soon became smoking ruins.

At 80.2 *m.* is the junction with an improved road.

Right on this road to WOODSON COUNTY STATE PARK *(picnic grounds, playgrounds, scenic drives)*, 5 *m.*, comprising approximately 500 acres in the Kansas Ozarks. LAKE FEGAN, a feature of the park, covers 200 acres. During the drought in the summer of 1935, water from Lake Fegan was released for the use of live-stock raisers. Although this water was sufficient to fill all the pools in the bed of Big Sandy Creek for a distance of 20 miles, the supply in the lake was not seriously depleted.

TORONTO, 85.3 *m.* (933 alt., 706 pop.), on the east bank of the Verdigris River, has often been called the Green City because trees, shrubs, and grasses grow abundantly all about it.

Old-timers here claim that in the early days the north wind had a clean sweep from the north pole to the settlement. So strong was the wind, they recall, that no building with a weak foundation could survive its buffeting. After the first schoolhouse had been retrieved from the creek a number of times and trundled back up the hillside, the people tied the building down on its foundation with wire cables fastened to deep-set posts. "Occasionally it waved in the breeze like a flag from a mast," an early settler said, "but it always settled back on its foundation again when the wind died down."

Right from Toronto on a graveled road to DRY CREEK CAVE, 12 *m.* At the mouth of this cave, which is approximately 50 feet wide and 10 feet high, lies a stone about nine feet long that is carved with faces, human figures, animals, birds, letters of the alphabet, and numerous lines and designs. At the time of its discovery by Robert Daly in 1858 this rock was partly covered with dirt and overgrown with moss, indicating that the figures had been cut out many years before.

West of Toronto is the eastern edge of the bluestem region or the Flint Hills whose broad grassy slopes extend from central Kansas into northern Oklahoma. Bluestem grass grows quickly during rainy seasons and generally remains green throughout the long hot summer. Its fattening qualities are excellent and thousands of head of cattle are shipped to this pasture land each spring from Texas, Arizona, and Oklahoma, to remain until the fall marketing season. Herds mill and stamp near the roadside or appear as splashes of red and white on the distant hillsides. Except for a few fences and crossroads the pastures here have changed little in the past half century. The blue haze mentioned so often in early descriptions of the country hovers over the tops of distant hills. Only an occasional oil well strikes a modern note in the panorama of slopes, summits, cattle, and sky.

The Verdigris River is crossed at 96 *m.*

EUREKA (Gr., *I have found it*), 107.8 *m.* (1,075 alt., 3,698 pop.), on the east bank of the Fall River, was founded shortly after the Civil

War and so-named by a classically minded settler who discovered a spring here. This little settlement was an important stopping point on the early cattle trails and later, with the coming of the railroads, became a shipping point for cattle.

When it was still a cattle town Eureka was the home of Eugene Lowery, said to have been the only Negro cowboy in Kansas, if not in the Southwest. Lowery, a fence rider and cowhand, worked for many of the leading cattlemen in the bluestem country and was considered an expert on cattle brands.

After 1915 the oil resources of this region were exploited and Eureka became a busy oil distribution point.

Right from Eureka on a graded road to 274-acre EUREKA LAKE *(swimming, boating, picnic and playgrounds)*, 6 *m.*, developed as a city water supply within a 400-acre park.

Shoestring oil sands, found at depths of about 2,000 feet, occur in northern Greenwood, southeastern Butler, and adjacent counties. The sands appear in lens-shaped deposits ranging from 50 to 100 feet in thickness, from 1 to 1½ miles in width, and from 1 to 7 miles in length. These unusual deposits are so-named because on a surface map they appear to be strung out like elongated beads. The usual stratification of sand or rock may be compared to the layers in a layer cake while the shoestring deposits are more like the irregular mottlings in a marble cake. The resemblance between maps of sand reefs off the Atlantic and Gulf coasts and maps of the shoestring oil sands suggests the origin of the latter. "The conclusion, after careful comparative study," said N. Wood Bass of the U. S. Geological Survey, 'is that these sand bodies are offshore bars that accumulated around the rim of a broad bay on the western shore of the prehistoric Cherokee Sea."

On the highway near the BUTLER COUNTY POOR FARM, 134.2 *m.*, are two statues carved by A. Burris, an inmate of the farm. The larger figure, *American Jurisprudence,* is that of a woman holding aloft a bottle in one hand and the scales of Justice in the other. The second statue, *Crime Against Civilization,* also the figure of a woman, is a protest against the tendency of courts to give the custody of children to women who are unfit to care for them.

A TANK FARM, 138.1 *m.*, consisting of ten 55,000-barrel tanks, is a storage place for oil. When prices are too low to satisfy the producer, these farms are used as reservoirs and become important price-determining factors. Occasionally lightning strikes a tank, setting the oil on fire. The terrific heat of such a fire melts the emptying tank above it. Circular depressions around each tank are to prevent leaking oil from spreading over the field.

ELDORADO (Sp., *the gilded*), 139.3 *m.* (1,285 alt., 10,311 pop.), in the Walnut River valley surrounded by a veritable forest of oil derricks, is in the center of the largest and most productive oil field in Kansas. Its business district is a mixture of sturdy plain limestone buildings of pioneer days and ornate structures built since the oil boom. The town was founded in the 1860's on a site about a mile south of this point, and so-named because of a gorgeous sunset that impressed its founders the evening they arrived. The settlement was moved a short time later in order to be nearer a sawmill on the banks of the Walnut River; it developed as a trading point and cattle town.

After numerous tests, begun in 1903, oil was discovered just west of Eldorado in 1915; since then the town has become a refining and marketing center for petroleum, increasing in size and importance with the development of each new field. Two large and many small refineries *(open by permission of superintendent)* operate here.

Eldorado is at the northern junction with US 77 *(see Tour 10)*. Between Eldorado and Augusta US 54 and US 77 are one route.

Right from Eldorado on State 13, improved, to (R) ELDORADO LAKE *(picnic ovens, boating; small fee for fishing)*, 5 *m.*, covering 315 acres. It was created by the city and is the source of its water supply.

A farmyard gate (L) is at 144.3 *m.* on US 54.

Left through this gate on a country lane to RUTHERFORD CAVES *(secure permission from Rutherford homestead near the gate)*, 0.1 *m.* The caves, a series of rock-walled rooms of varying sizes, have only one known entrance, a dark cavernous passage approximately 10 feet high and 8 feet wide. The source of a salt-water stream which flows from the interior of the passage, and maintains a temperature of 50° winter and summer, has never been determined.

Several attempts have been made to explore the cave to its full depth. In 1906 an expedition from an eastern university attempted to ascertain whether the stream that flows through the cave is a branch of the subterranean river believed to flow beneath the Flint Hills of central Kansas. According to reports of farmers in the vicinity, members of the party traversed six miles of narow caverns before black-damp, a poisonous gas, forced them back. Since that time several geology classes of midwestern universities have explored the cave but none has succeeded in penetrating more than the 6,000 measured feet reached by a group of University of Kansas students in 1934. Harold V. Lyle, a Wichita newspaper photographer, and James Fullerton, reporter, made explorations in 1936 but were forced to turn back when confronted with a low narrow channel that would not admit passage of their photographic equipment. Passage from the main tunnel, which leads from the entrance chamber, is difficult because a huge boulder hangs within a foot of the water at this point and extends back for a distance of 75 feet. Within the cave are many stalactitic formations. The only specimens of animal life found in the cave are a few crawfish in the stream and some mule-eared bats.

AUGUSTA, 156.6 *m.* (1,214 alt., 4,033 pop.), lies on tableland near the confluence of the Walnut and Whitewater Rivers. According to a local legend, this plateau was the scene and point of contention of many Indian battles including one in which several thousand warriors perished.

Surrounded by rich farm lands and productive oil fields, Augusta is a trading center, has one large refinery, and is a distribution point for an oil company. An increasingly important industry is the manufacture of automobile trailers.

Augusta is at the southern junction with US 77 *(see Tour 10)*.

1. Right from Augusta on Ohio St. *(graveled)* are the ATHLETIC KENNELS *(open)*, 2 *m.*, comprising 80 acres, one of the largest greyhound farms in the United States. Dogs raised here are raced on tracks throughout the country.

2. Left from Augusta on State St. *(graveled)* 180-acre LAKE AUGUSTA *(fishing, picnic grounds, tennis courts)*, 1 *m.*, lies in a wooded park.

REFINERY, ELDORADO

For many years, the subject of one of Robert Ripley's *Believe It or Not* sketches—a man with a white beard and long white hair—was a familiar sight along the highway between Augusta and Wichita. Usually seen leaning on a long staff and holding his hat over his breast, he was known locally by many names—including "Walking William," "Man of God," and "The Saint." When asked his name, he replied: "I am William, the Watcher of God."

Although the old man never asked for a ride, he always accepted one when it was offered. But, after riding a short distance, he would exclaim: "Stop the car! The Lord has told me to get out and go back." Beside the road he would resume his prophet's pose until offered a return ride. He denounced all forms of public worship and believed that ministers and priests "will spend eternity in Hades." He died on February 4, 1938, at the age of 89, without revealing his real name.

West of Augusta US 54 traverses rolling plains country in which oil wells give way again to barns, silos, and fields of grain.

At 158.6 *m.* is the junction with an improved road.

Right on this road is 250-acre SANTA FE LAKE *(swimming, boating, fishing; cabins, picnic facilities),* 1.5 *m.* The Wichita Boy Scout Council maintains a summer camp here. Santa Fe Lake is the only body of water in Kansas where sailing regattas are held annually, usually in June.

WICHITA, 176.5 *m.* (1,360 alt., 111,110 pop.) *(see WICHITA).*

Points of Interest: Wichita Art Museum, Sim Memorial Park, Municipal University, Friends University, United States Veterans Facility, and others.

Wichita is at the junction with US 81 *(see Tour 9).*

Section b. WICHITA *to* OKLAHOMA LINE, *220.1 m.,* US 54

The underground water table tapped by wells has been steadily lowered in the section west of Wichita, 0 *m.,* because of the destruction of the grass by plowing. The turf used to hold the rainfall and then allow it to seep into the subsoil; but now the rainfall makes a quick runoff. Flood control experts warn that this region is steadily drying up and will become unhabitable unless vigorous steps are taken to restore the water level.

Steep RED BLUFFS at 40.1 *m.* jut from the level monotony of the plains. Their red sides are mottled with green trees and grasses and cut by tiny streams which have etched crooked little gullies in the soft rock. In the distance zigzagging roads climb the less precipitous sides to the hilltops. Most of these roads have been made by picnicking collegians who want to see if their cars can climb the incline.

KINGMAN, 45.1 *m.* (1,500 alt., 2,752 pop.), on the banks of the Ninnescah River in good farming country, was founded in 1872 on the north side of the river. In 1878 another town company established a second Kingman on the south side. For two years the rival towns of the same name each maintained stores, hotels, and respective newspapers. But in the 1880's, when the surrounding territory was being organized as Kingman County, residents of the two settlements realized that they must unite if they were to obtain the county seat. The north-siders offered free land to the south-siders who accepted the offer, floated their buildings across to the north bank of the Ninnescah, and set them up. Kingman became the county seat.

RIVERSIDE PARK *(cabins, picnic grounds, swimming pool, tennis courts, playgrounds; fishing, boating),* is on the southern edge of Kingman.

At 53.1 *m.* is the junction with an improved road.

Right on this road to NINNESCAH LAKE *(fishing, boating),* 0.3 *m.,* in 1,200-acre KINGMAN COUNTY STATE PARK *(playgrounds, picnic grounds, shelter houses).*

At 56.1 *m.* is the junction with an improved road.

Left on this road to a STATE QUAIL FARM *(open)*, 0.5 *m.*, occupying a 60-acre tract, maintained by the State fish and game commission. Here quail, prairie chickens, and pheasants are raised to replenish wild flocks in Kansas.

One of the requirements for settling the land west of this point was the planting of trees. Dense groves of giant cottonwoods along the highway testify to the industry of the pioneers. These cottonwoods serve as windbreaks and shade from the summer sun, and are valuable as a source of fuel.

Around CUNNINGHAM, 62.3 *m.* (1,537 alt., 412 pop.), which is built in the form of a cross, are vast unfenced fields of wheat that shoulder their way to the town limits. Often during the summer harvest, tractor-drawn gang plows follow directly behind the combines, plowing the ground so that it will lie fallow until planting time in the fall. When the weather is unusually hot, this plowing is done at night; large spotlights on the tractors illuminate the ground.

At 76.3 *m.* is the junction with a graveled road.

Left on this road to the STATE FISH HATCHERY *(open)*, 1 *m.* In the brood ponds some 800,000 fish are hatched each year to be shipped to lakes in all parts of the State. Grasses that attract innumerable insects upon which the fish feed are planted on the banks of the ponds. In the aquarium, a circular structure in the Administration Building, specimens of the hatchery fish are on display.

Also in operation here is the STATE PHEASANT FARM *(open)*, with 15 pens and other structures necessary to care for the birds, which produce about 7,000 eggs annually. These are distributed to sportsmen and farmers in Kansas who hatch and subsequently liberate the birds. Additional pens display rare varieties of pheasants that are seldom seen in a wild state, among which are the Reeves, the silver, the Lady Amherst, and the melanistic mutant.

A MUSEUM *(open)* in the Administration Building contains mounted beavers, raccoons, ducks, swans, cranes, peacocks, quail, prairie chickens and other species of birds and fur-bearing animals.

PRATT, 78.8 *m.* (1,887 alt., 6,322 pop.), a farmers' town, has the smart shops and hotels of a modern city, though overalls are the usual street costume. The Rock Island Ry. shops employ approximately 400 men here. In the midst of a vast wheat country, with good rail connections, Pratt is important as a shipping point.

Founded in 1884, it was named for Caleb Pratt, a Civil War veteran. Two miles east of Pratt at that time was Saratoga, "within shooting distance," as an early country newspaper expressed it. Between 1884 and 1886 the two settlements became bitter rivals for selection as the county seat. After a series of elections in which one and then the other won the designation by alleged bribery, fraud and force, the case was carried to the Kansas Supreme Court. When the time for the hearing arrived, politicians and influential citizens shifted their headquarters to Topeka, but citizens of Pratt County were not idle as they awaited a decision. Boosters of both towns kept their pistols in plain view, while armed scouts patrolled the two-mile stretch of no man's land between the townsites. Once during this period a pitched battle was fought on the outskirts of Saratoga, and on another occasion three Pratt men were wounded by Saratoga citizens.

Late in 1884, when news spread over the countryside that Indians on the warpath were headed in this direction, many settlers, especially those in Saratoga, forgot about the county seat fight in their hurry to gather up a few belongings and flee. By the time the supreme court decreed the last election illegal, and ordered another contest held, there were few people left in the county. Nevertheless, citizens of Pratt quickly called another election and were easily victorious.

Saratoga citizens returned to their homes a few weeks later to find the county seat legally established at Pratt, and the country calm and peaceful. No Indians had arrived. The county seat was not contested again, but for years afterward Saratoga citizens claimed that the Indian scare had been started by residents of Pratt.

A GIRL SCOUT CABIN (L) in a landscaped park is near the west edge of Pratt.

The undulating country traversed by US 54 west of Pratt was once a hunting ground of the Kiowa. Seen occasionally on either side of the highway are the sand hills in which the Kiowa camped and held their powwows. Often they swooped down from these hide-aways and raided defenseless wagon trains. When chased by troops they retreated into the hills, and it was dangerous for the soldiers to follow them because of possible ambush.

William Mathewson, an early scout, tells of seeing 40,000 buffalo in this region at one time. The last of these was killed in 1879.

This district is almost equally divided between large wheat fields and cattle ranches, but near Liberal the wheat gives way to pasture.

In HAVILAND, 100.6 m. (2,240 alt., 641 pop.), a Quaker settlement, the buildings are plain and unadorned and activities center about its tiny meeting house. The town, settled in 1884 by a group of Quakers from Indiana, has had a quiet unruffled existence.

The FRIENDS BIBLE COLLEGE, formerly Haviland Academy, organized in 1892, includes two buildings and grounds comprising one square block near the center of town.

GREENSBURG, 111.1 m. (2,244 alt., 1,338 pop.), with its tall water tank and grain elevator, serves residents of the wheat and cattle lands that surround it. The town was named for D. R. "Cannonball" Green, stagecoach driver along the route now followed by US 54, which is still known locally as the Cannonball Highway.

When the railroad was built through Greensburg, Cannonball—so-called for the speed and dependability with which he drove—was invited by officials of the railroad to be a passenger on the first train between Wichita and Dodge City, traveling a route he had covered many times in his stagecoach. Although resenting the intrusion of trains, he was nevertheless impressed by the complete lunch, even to iced beer, that was served him on the train.

Thanking his hosts, Cannonball invited them to accompany him on his last stagecoach trip between the two towns. They accepted and were traveling with him across the hot prairie when he stopped about noon at a grassy bend in the road. Alighting, he served his guests a delicious meal —identical with the one he had received on the train, including the iced beer.

Carry Nation (1846–1911) rode with Cannonball many times during the first days of her temperance crusade. Once, when Mrs. Nation was a passenger, Cannonball lighted a huge cigar; the reformer reached from the coach window, snatched the cigar from his mouth, and threw it into the dust along the roadside. Immediately Cannonball stopped the coach, picked up Mrs. Nation, and without a word lifted her down to the dusty road. Then he drove off—leaving her surprised, indignant and miles from town.

In Greensburg is a firm that ships live jackrabbits to all parts of the United States. The animals are caught at night by blinding them with a bright light. Jackrabbits have replaced foxes in hunts in some parts of the country.

In Greensburg's MINK FARM *(open)* approximately 200 minks are kept in wire cages. The attendants wear thick gloves as minks are savage and will try to bite anyone within reach.

In the GREENSBURG CEMETERY, imbedded in the MONUMENT TO DUDLEY MITCHELL, a Civil War veteran, is a hardtack biscuit, sent by Mitchell to his home in Illinois while he was serving with Sherman's forces in the South. The family later moved to Kansas, and when Mitchell died had the biscuit mortised into the face of his tombstone.

The older residents of Greensburg are fond of recalling a blizzard in January 1886 that did much to settle the controversy in this region between the cattlemen who wanted to maintain the open range and the farmers who wanted to fence and plow the land. After a week of mild winter weather, the storm broke suddenly, killing many cowboys and thousands of range cattle. For days the temperature remained at 10° and 20° below zero while snow drifted 15 feet deep in places. Several of the ranchers each lost 4,000 head of cattle and all of their sheep and hogs. When the snow melted in the spring, the range was covered with dead "critters" and the impoverished cattlemen were powerless to prevent settlers from taking possession of the land.

In a COMPRESSOR STATION *(open)*, 120.2 *m.,* of the Northern Natural Gas Company newly produced gas is washed and compressed before it goes into the pipe line for delivery to consumers. The station buildings have upper walls made of glass and when lighted at night are visible for miles.

KINGSDOWN, 138.5 *m.* (2,418 alt., 150 pop.), in 1887 consisted of a few shacks along the railroad right-of-way. One evening, during a card game, the players decided to turn their railroad camp into a town and agreed to name it for the first card drawn from the deck—it was a king.

West of MINNEOLA, 153.5 *m.* (2,554 alt., 617 pop.), a prairie town built in the center of a level area called the Flats, is a region of large ranches on slightly undulating prairies of buffalo grass. Most of the ranch houses are small and far apart, but well painted and protected by a

planted grove of trees.The few spacious houses with big porches were
built during the years of high cattle prices.

In FOWLER, 164.5 *m.* (2,481 alt., 724 pop.), a shopping center for
the surrounding farming and stock-raising area and a shipping point for
silica, is St. Anthony's Church (Roman Catholic). This brick structure of Romanesque design by H. W. Brinkman of Emporia is considered
one of the finest churches in southwestern Kansas.

Left from Fowler on a graveled road to the junction with another graveled road,
5.5 *m.;* R. on this road to the Cudahy Silica Mine *(open),* 7 *m.,* one of the largest of its kind. An unlimited quantity of volcanic ash is believed to be available
here. The silica is crushed and dried at the mine, a process which lowers its weight
and thus cuts shipping costs. Silica is an important ingredient in many brands of
cleansing powders, tooth pastes, and soap.

Southwest of Fowler are many small ponds and lakes, most of them
fed by artesian wells. In 1887 B. F. Cox, pioneer settler in the region,
struck an artesian vein while drilling for water on his farm northwest of
Fowler. Gushing several feet above the ground the flowing well drew
crowds of sightseers from many parts of western Kansas. Artesian well
water is held between two impervious layers of rock or clay and is forced
upward through a fissure by hydro-static pressure. The Artesian Valley extends for nearly 40 miles southwest of Minneola, and is from 5 to 15
miles wide. In this area of approximately 500 square miles are more than
300 artesian wells, ranging in depth from 70 to 200 feet.

MEADE, 175 *m.* (2,503 alt., 1,552 pop.), seat of Meade County,
spreads out pleasantly on the prairie. It differs from most western Kansas
towns in that it has many trees, shrubs, and green lawns made possible by
an abundant supply of artesian water, which also fills the swimming pool
in the shady city park. The county courthouse is not in the central square
which was reserved for it by the townsite promoters; these gentlemen
promised to build a courthouse but never did. Meade's main street is 130
feet wide. An annual county fair is held here.

Meade is at the junction with US 160 *(see Tour 6).* Between Meade
and a point at 187.8 *m.* US 54 and US 160 are one route.

1. Left from Meade on State 23, paved, to the junction with State 98, paved,
4 *m.;* R. on State 98 to the MEADE COUNTY STATE PARK, 12 *m.,* 1,240
wooded acres surrounding LAKE LARABEE *(picnic grounds, playgrounds, shelter
houses; swimming, boating, fishing).* Three hundred and twenty acres of the park
have been set aside as a game preserve.

2. Right from Meade on State 23 to the junction with a dirt road, 5 *m.;* R. on
the dirt road to Lone Tree, 6 *m.,* a gnarled cottonwood on a creek bank. Standing
40 feet high and measuring 12 feet in circumference, this tree is estimated to be
100 years old, and for years was the only tree near the old wagon trail from Dodge
City to the Southwest. Set in the side of the tree is a bronze plaque dedicated to
O. E. Short and his party, who were massacred by Indians near this place when they
surveyed Meade County in 1874.

South and west of Meade US 54 traverses eroded country and passes
many large ranches. Occasionally a gas well is seen; now and then a
stream zigzags across the prairie, its bank thinly fringed with cottonwoods.

At 190.1 *m.* is the junction with an improved road.

CEMENT SILOS IN SORGHUM FIELD

Right on this road is (L) the BOOSTER PLANT *(open to visitors when accompanied by an employee)*, of the Panhandle Eastern Pipeline Company, 0.6 *m.* Ten gigantic engines at the plant force natural gas, produced in the vicinity, through huge pipe lines serving a wide territory. A STRIPPING PLANT here draws the casing head gasoline from the natural gas by a process similar to the absoption process *(see Tour 4B)*. The plant operates 15 hours a day, employing 50 men who work in two shifts. They live in a hotel especially constructed for them and in residences near the plant.

At 190.6 *m.* the route crosses the Cimarron River which, aptly described as a mountain torrent that blundered out on the plains, usually contains only a few shallow pools at this point. But a sudden spring thaw or a cloudburst near its source in the mountains of New Mexico occasionally sends floodwaters roaring down the channel like a tidal wave. On August 18, 1938, one of these unpredictable floods demolished the Rock Island bridge three miles west of this place, hurling a freight train into the angry waters. Two transient laborers, riding in a boxcar, were drowned. Eugene Simpson, another itinerant harvest hand, rescued fireman Carl M. Powell by diving to the submerged engine cab and dragging him from the wreckage.

A NEW BRIDGE (R)—600 feet long and 110 feet high—under construction (1938), will shorten the line four miles. When the railroad was building through this section in 1888, Springfield and Liberal were engaged in a county seat contest. Because it was near the center of the county, Springfield had been designated as a county seat and lay directly in the path of the proposed line. The railroad promoters agreed to bridge the river at Springfield if the town would vote bonds to aid in construction. But the Springfield men refused financial aid so the railroad builders resurveyed the right-of-way, avoided Springfield, and built the bridge several miles downstream. Four years later Springfield lost the county seat to Liberal, and soon ceased to exist.

LIBERAL, 215.6 m. (2,839 alt., 5,294 pop.), seat of Seward County center of the southwestern Kansas gas field, has well-paved streets and modern schools and houses. Founded in 1886, Liberal was the terminus of the Rock Island Ry. for many years and became the largest town in Seward County. According to local historians, when this region was settled in the 1880's water was scarce and well owners locked their well houses to prevent wayfarers from watering animals and exhausting the supply. Water sold for 5 and 10 cents a bucketful. One mile west of the present site of Liberal, L. E. Keefer, a pioneer storekeeper and postmaster, lived in a two-story adobe building. Everyone was welcome to drink from his well free of charge. The story that Keefer was liberal with his water spread far and wide and identified the neighborhood as an advantageous stopping place. A few years later, when a small settlement sprang up here, the settlers named it Liberal.

After the railroad had reached Liberal, ranchers from Texas, Oklahoma, New Mexico, and southwestern Colorado came to the town for supplies which were transported in wagon trains by professional freighters. Sometimes ten or twelve spans of mules or fifteen or sixteen yoke of oxen drew the enormous wagons, behind which were attached from one to five trailer wagons.

As many as fifty cowboys with their herds often came to Liberal at one time. They sometimes spent an entire year's wages in a week end of carousing. The making of fancy boots and saddles for their trade developed into an industry that still exists on a small scale. The town was on the border of what was known in the early days as No Man's Land, or the neutral strip, an unclaimed area which knew little or no law and was notorious as a rendezvous for cattle rustlers and bandits. Probate Judge L. A. Etzold, who had settled here before the town was founded and was serving in the courthouse in 1936, relates:

"Cowboys would spend the night gambling, and those that won were good customers in the stores next morning. There was something doing every minute when they were around. If one boasted of how quick he could rope and tie a steer, bets were laid and he had to prove his prowess.

"One day two half-drunken cowboys got on one bronco to make him pitch. One rider was bucked off and the other tried to dismount, but his spur caught in the stirrup and the horse dashed away dragging him, the man's head bumping on the ground at each jump of the galloping horse. Other riders headed the horse and finally ran him into the side of a wagon and the crash disentangled the cowboy's spur. I supposed the man had been dragged to death, but he absorbed the punishment and rode out with his gang the next morning. That's the kind of tough human hickory the cowboys were made of."

Liberal has a gasoline-extracting plant, a flour mill, factories manufacturing farm implements and accessories, a city park with a swimming pool, and a 160-acre municipal landing field.

Liberal is at the junction with US 83 *(see Tour 8)*.

At 220.1 *m.* US 54 crosses the Oklahoma Line, 15 miles northeast of Hooker, Okla. *(see OKLA. Tour 17)*.

Tour 6

(Springfield, Mo.)—Pittsburg—Parsons—Winfield—Medicine Lodge—Ulysses—(Trinidad, Colo.); US 160.
Missouri Line to Colorado Line, 508.1 m.

Missouri Pacific R.R. parallels route between Fort Scott and Wichita; Atchison, Topeka & Santa Fe Ry. between Wichita and Pratt; Chicago, Rock Island & Pacific Ry. between Pratt and Meade.
Roadbed alternately hard-surfaced bituminous mat, oiled, gravel, and dirt.
Good accommodations in all larger towns.

Following an irregular course through southern Kansas, this route crosses coal fields, oil fields, fertile black valleys, forest country, hilly grazing country, and a section of a former dust bowl.

Section a. MISSOURI LINE *to* WELLINGTON, *192.4 m.,* US 160

US 160 crosses the Missouri Line, 0 *m.,* 115 miles west of Springfield, Mo.

In this area, known as the southeast Kansas or Pittsburg district, geologists estimate that there were 295,622,000 tons of coal, half of which has been removed (1938). These beds produced approximately 2 million tons or about 60 percent of the State's output in 1936. The coal occurs in a deep layer about two and one-half feet thick and approximately 100 feet underground, and in a parallel upper layer from 12 to 18 inches thick. As strip mining was not practiced when the field was open, and the upper layer was not thick enough to permit men to work in the galleries that would have been formed by removing the coal, the deeper layer reached by shafts was mined first. Main tunnels were dug and posts or beams put in to support the roof. Next, side rooms were scooped out of the coal strata; first dynamite was used and then miners pried out the residue with picks. Extraction, at present, is by means of steam and electric shovels that strip away the earth from above the coal deposits and pile the clay, rock, and shale into miniature mountain ranges, which are visible in all directions from the highway and are reached on byroads. Operating here is one of the world's largest shovels *(miners will direct visitors to it)*, four times the size of those used in digging the Panama Canal. The huge scoop lifts 20 cubic yards of earth and rock more than 100 feet in the air, and drops the load on a dump pile.

The groups of irregular green mounds are abandoned dumps, now covered with trees and wild blackberries. The pits have filled with water, creating chains of lakes with rocky banks. Many of them have been stocked with crappie, bluegill, channel cat, ring perch, and bass, and some have been cleared of brush *(improved lakes 25¢ for fishermen, which includes rental of boat.)*

FRONTENAC (pronounced Fron-tee-nack), 4 *m.* (934 alt., 2,085 pop.), a pioneer coal-mining town in the Kansas section of the Tri-State coal field, began as a mining camp. In 1887 it was laid out as a town and named for a French general. The Santa Fe Ry. built its switches here and all the coal shipped over that road from the Pittsburg district is forwarded at Frontenac. Its two rows of one- and two-story business houses are flanked by the squat homes of the miners. This town is often called the melting pot of Kansas because its inhabitants are from twenty-one nations—45 percent are Italians; 13 percent are old-stock Americans; 8 percent are French; 8 percent are Germans; and the remaining 26 percent represent seventeen other nationalities.

The replacing of coal as a fuel by oil, gas, and electricity in homes, factories, trains, and steamships; the tendency to ship by truck rather than train; and the change from deep-shaft mining to strip mining, which requires fewer laborers, are the factors largely responsible for Frontenac's decrease in population and income.

From a population of 3,396 in 1910 it shrank to 2,051 in 1930 and, unable to pay its expenses, filed a petition in bankruptcy in 1935 in the United States District Court, praying for a readjustment of its municipal debt (suit still pending 1938). At that time it had the highest tax rate of any town of its size in Kansas.

Immediately adjacent to the Santa Fe depot are the rock and shale dumps of old SANTA FE MINE NO. 2, opened in 1887. Here the greatest explosion in the history of Kansas mining occurred in November 1888, when a defective shot of dynamite caused the loss of almost fifty lives.

At 6 m. is the junction with US 69 (see Tour 13). Between this point and PITTSBURG, 9.5 m. (932 alt., 18,145 pop.) (see Tour 13), US 160 and US 69 are one route.

Along the banks of the NEOSHO RIVER, 34.3 m., the Osage lived from 1808, when they sold their lands in Missouri, until 1865, when they sold this land and moved to the Osage Diminished Reserve on the banks of the Verdigris and Elk Rivers. Artifacts of this tribe have been found in almost every draw and creek bed in the Neosho Valley. Specimens of petrified wood, estimated to be 40 million years old, have been unearthed along the Neosho River. These specimens, found in outcroppings of limestone near the creek banks, are covered with a coral formation believed to have been deposited by the huge inland sea that once covered Kansas.

PARSONS, 44.1 m. (896 alt., 14,903 pop.), on a plateau slightly above Labette Creek, developed as a division point of the Missouri-Kansas-Texas R.R. which maintains offices, shops, and a roundhouse here. It is a shipping and distribution point for grain and dairy products, has stockyards that buy more than $3,000,000 worth of stock annually, and boasts a livestock exchange housed in a $15,000 building.

During the World War the town had a population of approximately 18,000, but as the result of strikes in the shops the railroad moved much of its repair work to other points on the line, and Parsons experienced a noticeable decline. Parsons is the home of U. S. Senator Clyde M. Reed and Governor Payne Ratner.

The KANSAS STATE HOSPITAL FOR EPILEPTICS (open on application), 16th and Gabriel Aves., is surrounded by 630 acres and houses almost 1,000 patients. The institution, founded in 1903, includes thirteen ward buildings, a laundry, a power house and plant, a large dairy barn, several small cattle barns, a poultry unit, two greenhouses, a commissary, a carpenter shop, an employees' quarters, a superintendent's residence, a farm cottage, and an engineer's cottage.

Parsons is at the Junction with US 59 (see Tour 12).

Visible from the highway at 56.1 m. are the BENDER MOUNDS, low hills rising abruptly from a level plain. They were named for the Bender family. William, his wife, their son, John, and daughter, Kate, had moved in 1870 to a hill farm on the old trail from Independence to Osage Mission. (The trail was slightly north of the route followed by US 160.) They lived in a two-room frame building, using the back room as living quarters, and the front room as a store for the sale of tobacco, crackers, powder, shot, and provisions. William Bender and his son were quiet men, highly respected by their neighbors. Kate, a red-haired buxom lass, traveled about the country lecturing on spiritualism. Her beauty is said to have caused many persons to stop at their little trading post.

Between 1870 and 1873 several travelers who disappeared between Independence and Osage Mission were traced to within a few miles of the Bender Mounds. So many stories of mystery, murder, and the supernatural were associated with the area that cautious persons would go long distances to avoid it.

In March 1873, settlers in the neighborhood held a meeting to discuss these strange and alarming disappearances. William Bender and his son attended. A short time later a searching party of fifty men stopped at the Bender house and asked Kate to use her clairvoyant powers in an effort to solve the mystery. This she agreed to do.

A few days later, passers-by noticed stock wandering about the Bender farm and on investigation found that the place had been hastily deserted. In the combined orchard and garden back of the house they discovered a number of bodies, including that of Dr. William York, the last person to disappear. His head had been smashed in, and his throat cut from ear to ear. It had been the Benders' custom to seat guests at the dinner table with their backs to a cloth partition which screened the bedroom. It is believed that from behind this cloth the Benders killed their victims with an axe in order to rob them. In spite of many clues neither Kate, whose plump hands may have committed the murders, nor any of her family were ever found.

At 59.1 *m.* is the northern junction with US 169. Between here and 69.1 *m.* US 160 and US 169 are one route.

CHERRYVALE, 65.1 *m.* (837 alt., 4,251 pop.), in the valley of Cherry Creek, was founded by the Kansas City, Leavenworth, and Southern Kansas R.R. in 1871, and was its terminus for a number of years. In 1889 residents voted a $5,000 bond issue to prospect for coal in the vicinity. At a depth of 600 feet natural gas was discovered. This well, the first of any consequence in Kansas, attracted a zinc smelter, a brick plant, and numerous smaller industrial units to Cherryvale.

By 1912, however, the supply of natural gas had diminished and many of these businesses went elsewhere. A plant in the northwest part of town extracts zinc from the ashes left by the old zinc smelter.

LOGAN PARK *(shelter house, natural-gas stoves, swimming pool, playground, free campground),* is near the center of Cherryvale.

At 69.1 *m.* is the southern junction with US 169, paved.

Left on US 169 is LIBERTY, 5 *m.* (800 alt., 246 pop.). Left from Liberty on an improved road to the junction with another improved road at 7 *m.;* R. on this road to a country lane, which leads through a field to TREATY ROCK, 7.7 *m.* In its southernmost ledge are etchings of elk, cows, horses, buffalo, deer tracks, an Indian profile, and other figures. All point to a basin in one of the larger rocks nearby, and are said by the Osage to have been here when their fathers entered this territory. Though their meaning is unknown, some believe they describe the Seven Cities of Cibola which Coronado sought 400 years ago. Others think the mound is a burial plot or that the signs served to call the Indians' attention to the basin, once a water hole.

INDEPENDENCE, 74.3 *m.* (795 alt., 12,782 pop.) *(see Tour 11),* is at the junction with US 75 *(see Tour 11).* Between this place and a point at 77.3 *m.,* US 75 and US 160 are one route.

TABLE MOUND (R), 77.5 *m.,* a 700-acre elevation with a flat rocky top, appears to be an oval but actually is shaped like a gigantic letter M. This is the legendary home of a lost Indian tribe. Ogeola, chief of the Osage, married Prairie Lily, daughter of Lawara, chief of the mound dwellers. Later Lawara killed Ogeola in a fit of jealousy. Early the next morning a band of 2,000 Osage seeking vengeance attacked the mound dwellers and by sundown had wiped them out. Many arrowheads have been found on the slopes of the mound and in the low country surrounding it.

At 81.5 *m.* US 160 leaves the low country and gradually climbs to a timbered ridge called the Backbone; the highway crosses the Elk River four times in the next 25 miles.

LONGTON, 101.3 *m.* (914 alt., 744 pop.), when founded in 1869 was called Elk Rapids but, to avoid confusion with the neighboring town of Elk Falls, was renamed for a village in England. Today the town is a market center and shipping point for agricultural and dairy products. Blackjack oak trees cover the round hilltops, which are strikingly beautiful with their vivid autumn foliage after the first light frost (about Oct. 15).

ELK FALLS, 110.5 *m.* (930 alt., 288 pop.), named for the falls of the Elk River, was settled in 1870 and became the temporary seat of Howard County. When Boston, a town about 12 miles southwest, was organized in 1871 it immediately became Elk Falls' rival for the county seat designation. The first election, which had been held in 1872 with Elk Falls, Boston, Peru, Longton, and Howard City as contestants, was declared illegal after evidence of fraud had been produced.

A second election was held November 11, 1873. No official figures have been preserved and there are conflicting accounts of the result. A former resident of the town relates that Boston received a majority of 235 votes but other authorities say that Elk Falls had a majority of 232. In either event, Boston claimed to have won the election and called upon Elk Falls to turn over the records. When the demand was refused 150 armed Bostonians marched to Elk Falls, loaded the records in a wagon amid the "consternation, threats and tears of the inhabitants," and hauled them to Boston.

When the sheriff of Howard County demanded the return of the records and the arrest of the mob leaders, Boston, according to its historian, answered the summons by posting armed guards around the town. The records were later removed to Cowley County where they were hidden for several weeks.

Disgusted with the controversy, farmers and residents of other towns launched a movement to divide Howard County, which had an area of 1,300 square miles and was the second largest county in the State. Boston and Elk Falls, united by a common interest, bitterly opposed the division and the county was soon aligned into division and antidivision factions. The former won and the county was so divided (1875) that Boston and Elk Falls were in the southwestern corner of the new county of Elk. Because of the prevailing notion that a county seat should be in the center of the county, they were no longer considered as contestants. Boston soon passed out of existence; Elk Falls has continued as a market center for a limited area in the hill country.

MOLINE, 115.6 *m.* (1,047 alt., 897 pop.), is divided into segments by a small creek that runs through the center of the town. It was founded in 1879 and named for Moline, Ill., the former home of its founder. Surrounded by farming and grazing regions the town is a shipping point for livestock and farm produce. It is also a distribution point for oil field materials. Industrial plants include a small cheese factory, a hatchery, and a plant that manufactures a processed material for surfacing highways. An annual kafircorn carnival is held the last week in September.

Left from Moline on State 99 (improved) to the SITE OF OLD BOSTON, 4.2 *m.*, now an expanse of upland pasture. Boston was founded in August 1871, by seven bachelors from Osage Mission, most of whom were of Irish descent. Other Irish Catholics came to the new town and its roster soon included such names as Nulty, Brogan, Riley, Callahan, Sheehan, Doolahan, and Conners. After entering their town as a candidate for the county seat designation, the ambitious Celts purchased a site and obtained building materials to erect a Roman Catholic church. But Pat Nulty had observed that the county's population was predominantly Protestant and questioned the political wisdom of flaunting their religion before the Methodist, Baptist, and Campbellite settlers. Construction was postponed "until after Boston had secured the county seat." The church was never built. "Pat Nulty had a monopoly on the saloon business," wrote Thomas E. Thompson (1860–1933), Howard newspaper editor. "Once a quiet little old chap essayed to open an opposition saloon, and laid in a little stock of booze, a keg of beer and a jug of blackberry wine, fixed up a pine board bar and stood ready to wait on thirsty customers. Pat locked his saloon, gathered up all the boys, went over and bought drinks for everybody at the new saloon. The pleasure of standing treat was passed around while the new proprietor fairly beamed his hospitality. As the evening advanced and the regular trade discovered Pat's place shut up, they all went over to the new place, and proceeded to put on a regular jubilee. They drank up all the little stock of liquors, largely on credit, and then threw the bar fixtures out of doors and hinted to the new proprietor that Boston wasn't big enough for two saloons, and he never opened up again."

Timber on the hilltops diminishes at GRENOLA, 128.8 *m.* (1,109 alt., 522 pop.). A few miles west of this hamlet the route enters the bluestem pasture region, a section of the Flint Hills, whose broad slopes extend from central Kansas into northern Oklahoma.

At 154 *m.* is the junction with State 15, improved.

Left on State 15 is DEXTER, 7 *m.* (904 alt., 484 pop.), a one-street village that has a HELIUM BEARING GAS FIELD *(inaccessible)* and a HELIUM PLANT *(open by permission of superintendent)*, built in 1927, near its southern limits. The wells in the helium field are hard to distinguish from nearby oil wells, and the plant itself, except for an identifying sign, looks much like an ordinary gasoline refinery.
In 1903 drillers seeking oil on a farm just north of Dexter struck a flow of gas at 350 feet so heavy that its roar could be heard for several miles. Jubilant, the citizens of Dexter planned a gigantic celebration with band music, patriotic speeches, and games, to be climaxed with the lighting of the gas from the well. Circulars announced that "a great pillar of flame from the burning well will light the entire countryside for a day and a night."
A crowd of several thousand gathered. Women sat in groups on the grass near the picnic baskets while children played games, ate bananas, and drank lemonade from the flag-bedecked refreshment stand. Men in their "good clothes" played horseshoes or stood about in little groups, occasionally taking nips from a jug in the back of somebody's buggy.
When the time came for lighting the gas well, excitement ran high. The master of ceremonies finished his address, held his lighted torch impressively high, and touched the uncapped flow of gas. The torch went out. He tried again. Again it was blown out. Three times, as the expectant crowd drew nearer to the well, he attempted to ignite the escaping gas. Each time it failed to burn.
When a sample of the gas was analyzed at the University of Kansas, Prof. H. P.

HELIUM PLANT, DEXTER

Cady explained that it contained less than 15 percent of combustible matter. In 1905, after further analysis, Professor Cady announced that the gas was 1.84 percent helium. This marked the first time that helium had been found in natural gas. Until 1895, when it was detected in the mineral, cleveite, scientists believed that it existed only on the sun. Helium is non-inflammable and less than one-seventh as heavy as air, which makes it superior to other gases for use in dirigibles and balloons. Helium is breathed by deep sea divers and others working under pressure to reduce the danger of the pressure illness known as "the bends," and is also beneficial in the treatment of asthma and similar ailments. Since helium liquefies at a lower temperature than other gases, it is extracted from natural gas at the Dexter plant by a low temperature process.

The Government has contracted (1938) to buy this plant; helium produced here has been used to inflate lighter-than-air craft and in medical treatments. Before the Government erected a helium-extracting unit at Fort Worth, Texas, during the World War, a cubic foot of this gas sold for $2,500. It is now produced for about 1 cent.

The gas from several smaller wells in the United States has a helium content as high as 7 or 8 percent, but their flow is not sufficient to make extraction plants profitable. Although discoveries have been rumored in Russia and elsewhere, helium is not now known (1938) to exist in commercial quantities outside of the United States.

The explosion of the *Hindenburg* in May 1937 reopened the question of allowing foreign countries to purchase helium. Before any can be shipped abroad now (1938) the State Department must approve its exportation and the Department of the Interior must consent to its sale.

WINFIELD, 168.5 *m.* (1,114 alt., 9,398 pop.) *(see Tour 10)*, is at the junction with US 77 *(see Tour 10)*.

US 160 crosses the Arkansas River (pronounced Ar-Kan-zas in Kansas), 175 *m.*, a shallow slow-moving stream fed by Rocky Mountain springs and bordered with cottonwoods, willows, and maples. Spring and fall rains fill its banks but it dries up quickly during periods of drought. An easterner looking up and down the wind-swept sand of the Arkansas in mid-August declared, "That would be a pretty good river if somebody would irrigate it."

In early days the Arkansas was treacherous to ford, being full of deep holes and quicksand. Occasionally its sands would shift within the course of a few hours, and a crossing that was safe one day would become a hazardous hole the next.

WELLINGTON, 194.2 m. (1,189 alt., 7,405 pop.) (see Tour 9), is at the junction with US 81, (see Tour 9).

Section b. WELLINGTON to JUNCTION WITH US 83–160, 225.4 m., US 160

West of Wellington 0 m., the route passes through a country devoted entirely to grazing and the cultivation of wheat. Distances between towns became greater. As the route nears Meade it passes through several large cattle ranches. The terrain is alternately flat and rolling; frequently huge eroded gullies appear along the highway and reddish buttes rear their rugged outlines against the horizon.

Between Wellington and Medicine Lodge, towns are little more than small clusters of buildings hemmed in by vast wheat fields. Many of them boomed in the early 1880's, but were all but deserted with the opening of the Cherokee Strip (see HISTORY) in 1893. Thousands left their homes in southern Kansas to take up claims on the free lands opened by the Government in Oklahoma.

ARGONIA, 21.9 m. (1,242 alt., 546 pop.), claims to have had the first woman mayor in the United States—Mrs. Susanna Salter. A bronze plaque in front of the township hall was erected to her memory. Argonia was incorporated in 1885, four years after Kansas had adopted prohibition. Susanna Salter's husband was the first city clerk, while his young bride was a leader in the Argonia chapter of the Women's Christian Temperance Union. In an election in 1887 some of the "Wets" facetiously put forward Mrs. Salter for mayor and planned to give her twenty votes. Much to their embarrassment Susanna received a two-to-one majority. She gave the town a successful administration, working in harmony with the five masculine members of the city council. When she was speaker at the Kansas Women's Equal Suffrage Association convention at Newton, in the fall of 1887, Susan B. Anthony slapped her on the back, it is said, and cried, "Why, you look just like any other woman."

A short distance from US 160 (R) is the SITE OF OLD RUNNYMEDE, 5 m., a town consisting of a few stores, an inn, and an Episcopal church established in 1889 by the younger sons of English noble families. It was named for Runnymede, England, where John, brother of Richard the Lion-hearted, signed the Magna Charta in 1215.

The young Englishmen came with fine horses, red hunting coats, and polished boots, planning to conduct their colony much on the order of the hunt clubs in England. Lacking foxes, they rode over the prairie hunting rabbits, wolves, and coyotes, and spent their evenings about the campfire telling stories and singing. After a few months their food supply ran low and their scarlet jackets became ragged. The hungry founders of Runnymede, riding lean horses, set out for "civilization" and home.

HARPER, 37.5 *m.* (1,340 alt., 1,485 pop.), a wheat town, bustles with activity during the harvest season early in July, but lapses again into unruffled calm as the last loads of grain leave for market.

Before the combine and tractor replaced transient labor in the 1920's, the harvest hand was king in Harper during the early summer months. Hundreds of these bronzed men in overalls poured into town from all parts of the country for a few weeks' work in the wheat fields. Some came in rattle-trap Fords, others hitch-hiked or arrived in boxcars. They were a vigorous hearty crew, shouting and waving to motorists, welcoming days of hard work in the hot sun, and reveling in great plates of fried chicken prepared by the farm women. When harvest hands were scarce, wheat growers gathered in Harper to meet incoming trains or to stop men on the highways, as a shortage of hands sometimes meant the loss of thousands of dollars, so disastrous was a few days delay in the harvest.

At Harper is the junction with State 14 (improved).

Right on this road to the junction with an improved road, 1.5 *m.;* L. on this road to the ANTHONY MUNICIPAL LAKE *(boating, fishing, picnic and playground facilities),* 2.9 *m.,* in an improved park of 410 acres. This 152-acre body of water was created by a Federal project in 1935.

West of Harper fields of wheat, from 500 to 4,000 acres in extent, flank the highway. In the smaller fields binders cut and bind the wheat. The bundles are fed to a huge threshing machine which pours the grain into sacks while the straw is blown out like smoke. In the larger fields combines cut and thresh the grain in a single operation.

In the ATTICA CEMETERY (L), 52.7 *m.,* a weather-beaten white marble shaft close to the road marks the GRAVE OF N. GRIGSBY, a Civil War veteran from Indiana who died April 16, 1890, at the age of 78. The inscription on the shaft hurls a curse at Grigsby's political foes: "Through this inscription I wish to enter my dying protest against what is called the Democratic Party. I have watched it closely since the days of Jackson, and know that all the misfortunes of our Nation have come to it through the so-called party—therefore beware of this party of treason."

MEDICINE LODGE, 72.1 *m.* (1,468 alt., 1,655 pop.) *(see MEDICINE LODGE).*

Points of Interest: Memorial Peace Park, Peace Treaty Monument, Home of Carry Nation, Gypsum Mill, and others.

Left from Medicine Lodge on a graveled road over the backbone of a ridge, 4 *m.,* are the GYPSUM HILLS. Deep canyons on either side of the road and hills carved by erosion into towering mesas and buttes present a scene of wild beauty. The red shale of the mesas is capped with white gypsum.

TWIN PEAKS, 5 *m.,* two sharp-pointed hills, stand out boldly on the western horizon.

SUN CITY, 91.9 *m.* (1,490 alt., 404 pop.), is a cluster of gray frame buildings.

Left from Sun City on a graveled road to a fork, 1 *m.*

1. Left 5 *m.* from the fork to the junction with a dirt road; L. on the dirt road 0.5 *m.* to a NATURAL BRIDGE of gypsum rock. The under side of its arch is 12 feet above the water level, and its span is approximately 35 feet. A footpath crosses the bridge and, unless the water is high, a path going under the span can be followed.

A tunnel-like cave, cutting through the gypsum rock on the west bank of the stream, has one entrance upstream (south) from the bridge and another immediately downstream. This cave is 260 feet long and so narrow that visitors must walk in single file *(flashlight necessary for exploring).*

2. Right 3 *m.* from the fork, on the dirt Sun City-Wilmore Cutoff, to a GYPSUM MINE *(open).* The mouth of the mine lies at the bottom of a narrow gulch reached by a byroad (R) from the cutoff. From this level a railroad track leads half a mile back into the mine. The main tunnel branches in all directions a short distance from the entrance. The entire hill is honeycombed with tunnels, ranging from 8 to 15 feet in height and from 25 to 30 feet in width, cut through solid gypsum rock. The gypsum is shipped to Medicine Lodge, where it is made into a fine plaster or cement.

At 10 *m.* on the Sun City-Wilmore Cutoff is (R) a schoolhouse and the junction with a narrow rocky pasture road; R. through several gates to HELL'S HALF ACRE, 13 *m.* Here rocks of many colors have been eroded into grotesque and bizarre forms. To the north, a small canyon with a number of trees growing along its narrow floor cuts through the sandstone and exposes the underlying red beds. The white sandstone with its brown and yellow bands and the green foliage contrast vividly with the orange and reds of the canyon. The colored rock is soft and was once used by the Indians to paint their faces and bodies.

Northwest of Sun City is high rolling pasture country, broken frequently by shallow rocky canyons. Cattle graze on the slopes alongside the highway or gather around the occasional water holes. Ranches in this region range from 1,000 to 5,000 acres. An occasional ranch house with its brood of small outbuildings is visible from the highway, usually standing far back from the road on a knoll or the side of a hill overlooking vast stretches of unplowed grazing country. This region was homesteaded in the 1880's by cattlemen who managed to evade the Federal act limiting homesteads to 160 acres, by bringing in employees who lived on a claim for the required length of time and then deeded title to their employer.

BELVIDERE (Ital., *beautiful view*), 105.3 *m.* (1,840 alt., 80 pop.), a roadside community with a grade and high school, a church, and a post office (housed in a private residence), is on the site of the former Osage and Otoe reservations. The GREAVER CABIN, built by one of the county's pioneer cattlemen, stands in an elm grove a short distance east of the present townsite and is believed to have served as a hide-out for the Jesse James and the Younger Brothers gangs of outlaws. The arrival of the railroad in the 1870's brought an influx of homesteaders. Greaver, like all cattlemen, opposed the fencing and plowing of the range. Those who homesteaded near him were either bought out or run off at the point of a gun. At one time the cattlemen banded together, dressed their cowhands and themselves as Indians, and pretending to be a war party, camped at the Medicine River nearby until all settlers had fled.

Right from Belvidere on an improved road to the OSAGE ROCKS, 0.5 *m.,* the scene of a battle in the 1860's between the Osage and the Kiowa in which the Osage chief was killed by Satanta, chief of the Kiowa. Many Indian artifacts have been found in the vicinity.

On the ROBBINS TURKEY RANCH *(open)*, 107.9 *m.*, from 8,000 to 10,000 turkeys are grown each year on its 5,000-acre range. The birds roam at will and large numbers of them are visible from the highway. In November and December they are herded by men on horseback who drive them into pens where they are examined, sorted, and prepared for shipment to many parts of the United States.

COLDWATER, 124.8 *m.* (2,080 alt., 1,296 pop.), seat of Comanche County, and named for a town in Michigan, is a wheat farmers' market and a shipping center. Two blocks west of Main St. is the MUNICIPAL SWIMMING POOL *(free)*.

In the COMANCHE COUNTY COURTHOUSE is a sheaf of fraudulent bonds with a face value of $72,000 on which the taxpayers of this farming community have been paying interest for 44 years (1938). In 1873 a half-dozen promoters came from Topeka into what is now Comanche County. At that time there was only one *bona fide* resident in the area, a buffalo hunter. The schemers asked him to become a county official. Taking up residence in the two small log shacks that constituted the entire town of Smallwood, they filled in ballot tally sheets with 240 names from an old city directory of St. Joseph, Mo. and forwarded them to Topeka. The copying of these names constituted the "special election" at which was "voted" a $72,000 bond issue. When the buffalo hunter asked who would buy such worthless bonds, he was told that there was a ready market for them in Topeka, although they brought only half as much as genuine ones.

These bonds were actually legalized by the majority opinion of a three-man committee of legislators. The two men who upheld the fraud justified their venality by arguing that if such bonds were not recognized, foreign capital would be frightened away from Kansas. This majority report maintained that all but 40 of the original 600 or 700 residents had been driven out "by the Indians." The minority report of Attorney General A. L. Williams declared:

First, Comanche County has no inhabitants and never had. Second, it was by everyone conceded that no one lived there at the time of my investigation. I visited the county myself and I declare that there are no *bona fide* settlers in the county and never were . . . In Smallwood are two log cabins, both deserted of course, without windows or doors. And these constitute the homes of the "householders" of the county. Its sole inhabitants are the Cheyenne and the coyote, the wolf and the wild Indian. Comanche County was organized solely for plunder. To issue these bonds required wholesale perjury and forgery. The county should be disorganized, both by act of the legislature and by decree of the supreme court, and its territory should be attached for judicial purposes to some decent county where law is administered.

In answer the legislature declared that a *de facto* government had legally issued the bonds. But Comanche County remained a virgin prairie used by ranchers for their great herds of cattle. The cattlemen banded together to keep out settlers and succeeded until 1885, when the railroad, reaching this area, brought in thousands of homesteaders and Comanche County was legally organized, with Coldwater as its seat. As soon as the county had been legally established, purchasers of the spurious bonds sued for payment. They were represented by A. L. Williams, who as attorney general had declared the bond issue illegal. A Federal judge declared the obligation binding, and Coldwater found itself so heavily in debt that it was unable to float legitimate bond issues to finance the construction of roads, county buildings, and schools.

At 138.5 *m.* is the junction with a graveled road.

Left on the graveled road to the junction with an improved road, 12 *m.;* L. here to the BRIGGS RANCH *(open),* 12.5 *m.,* entered through a huge cement gateway.

In August 1925, the owners purchased 10 buffaloes, costing from $100 to $400 each, part of the celebrated herd on the Charles Goodnight Ranch in Oklahoma. The buffaloes, kept in a spacious pasture enclosed by a specially constructed fence, had increased to 25 by 1937. *(Animals are untamed and visitors are warned not to approach the fence.)*

ASHLAND, 153.7 *m.* (1,950 alt., 1,232 pop.), seat of Clark County, with its broad paved main street lined with two-story business places, its tree-shaded courthouse square, its modest frame houses, and its city park *(shelters, stoves, free tourist camp),* bears little resemblance to the "wild and woolly" cattle town it was in 1884.

Two great cattle trails of the Southwest, one from Texas to Fort Dodge, the other from Santa Fe to Sun City, crossed at Ashland. Laid out by a group of Kentuckians in 1884, the town became a revictualing center for immigrants, traders, and cowboys following their herds along the trail. It was named for Ashland, Kentucky.

Among the Kentuckians who came to Ashland was Sam Robinson, a tall swarthy gunman, who acquired a reputation as a frontier badman. Robinson left Clark County after numerous escapades had convinced its law-enforcement agents that he was an undesirable citizen. At Hugoton *(see Tour 4B)* he found employment suitable to his talents, and as marshal of that embroiled boom town was one of the leaders in the Hay Meadow Massacre. Forced to flee after the killings, Robinson went to Colorado. There he held up a train, was apprehended and committed to prison.

Chalk Beeson, organizer of Dodge City's famous Cowboy Band, was frequently seen in Ashland during the early years. Beeson owned a ranch in the western part of the county and shipped or bought cattle here on numerous occasions. Many of Dodge City's less respected citizens also paid periodic visits to the town during the cattle-trail days and added to the general disorder which prevailed after the annual roundup.

Ashland became an oil center in 1935 and 1936, when several productive wells were drilled near the town.

Right from Ashland on graveled State Lake Highway to HORSESHOE BEND, 12 *m.* A footpath leads directly to the bend, whose precipitous rock walls in the form of a horseshoe enclose a low grassy meadow of eight acres. Hackberry Creek flows through Horse Thief Canyon and leaves the enclosure at the northwest corner, emptying into Bluff Creek a few feet downstream. In the 1870's this canyon was

SAINT JACOB'S WELL, CLARK COUNTY

the home of "Dutch" Henry, who used it as a place to hide stolen horses and cattle. The "Dutchman" was a frontier Robin Hood who robbed prosperous settlers and frequently shared his plunder with impoverished "nesters." He was a lone rider who trusted no accomplices.

Near the entrance of the canyon Henry fashioned a dugout, roofed it with cottonwood logs, and plastered it with mud. He lived snugly in this crude shelter for more than a year but was finally captured by Mike Sughrue, sheriff of Ford County, and committed to the State penitentiary. One day, while working with a prison road gang, the Dutchman disappeared. He was arrested several months later at Trinidad, Colorado. "I didn't run away," the fugitive protested, "they sent me after a shovel and I just haven't found one yet."

West of Ashland is a pasture-land of huge ranches, with scattered ranch houses and barns. Jackrabbits are so numerous in this section that residents organize jackrabbit drives; hunters comb the territory and drive the rabbits into enclosures where they are killed with clubs.

US 160 passes through BIG BASIN, 173.3 *m.,* a depression covering 2,000 acres, rimmed by high gypsum hills. As it has no outlet, stagnant pools remain here, even during very dry seasons. The basin is said to be a sink in the earth's crust caused by underground stream erosion. Many believe that this area is honeycombed with tunnels, into which a square mile or two of territory may fall at any time; old-timers insist that there is gold in the hills around Big Basin, but none has ever been found.

At 173.8 *m.* on the south rim of Big Basin is the junction with a dirt road.

Right on the dirt road to LITTLE BASIN, 0.5 *m.*, a depression similar to Big Basin and probably of the same origin, although it measures only a half mile across. The bottom is covered with scattered rocks, grass, and a few shrubs. Near its north wall, in a nook sheltered by a high ledge, is a pool of water known as SAINT JACOB'S WELL. Even during long periods of drought, Saint Jacob's well has never gone dry; residents of the country-side describe it as bottomless.

North and west of Big Basin US 160 crosses a flat treeless tableland, so level that the telephone poles along the highway appear to converge in the distance.

MEADE, 194 *m.* (2,503 alt., 1,552 pop.) *(see Tour 5)*, is at the junction with US 54 *(see Tour 5)*. Between Meade and 206.8 *m.* US 160 and US 54 are one route *(see Tour 5)*.

At 225.4 *m.* is the southern junction with US 83 *(see Tour 8)*, which unites with US 160 for a few miles.

Section c. JUNCTION WITH US 83 *to* COLORADO LINE, *90.3 m.,*
US 160

After the junction with US 83, 0 *m.*, US 160 traverses the southern part of the High Plains wheat land, which was settled in the 1880's but was without railroad service until the Santa Fe built a branch from Satanta early in the 1920's, precipitating the last of the Kansas railroad booms. The railroad development company encouraged settlers to plant wheat, and this, united with high prices and the comparative ease of cultivation, led to the plowing of large areas. Wheat replaced the buffalo grass that grew during the rainy seasons and held the soil in place with its intertwined roots, in addition to supplying fodder for buffalo, antelope, and range cattle.

Warnings of danger were unheeded. Prof L. E. Call, director of the Kansas Agricultural Experiment Station, told a meeting at Satanta in 1926, ". . . the excellent crops that are often produced the first years on sod are encouraging the breaking up of a larger proportion of the grass land on many farms than should be brought under cultivation at this time, for grass land, once destroyed, is difficult to replace in western Kansas."

In 1931 southwestern Kansas entered a drought cycle of unprecedented severity. The 1931–1937 period was the driest 7-year stretch in the records of the Dodge City weather bureau (established in 1875). "Black blizzards" raged with mounting intensity throughout 1934. Finally, in 1935, an erosional program was financed by the FERA. Strip listing, contour listing, cultivating with specially designed machinery, and planting of drought-resistant cover crops—chiefly the small varieties of grain sorghums—were used to prevent the wind from carrying the soil away. The program was financed by the U. S. Department of Agriculture during 1936 and 1937, at the end of which time the area subject to wind erosion had been reduced by more than half.

The Kansas Legislature passed a soil blowing act in 1937 *(see SOIL CONSERVATION)* which required that wind erosion be controlled within affected counties. The first reports filed in accordance with this act, revealed that all of Grant County was liable to soil drifting in 1937, but that the area actually blowing had been reduced. Haskell County reported that 75 percent of its farm land began blowing in February 1937, but that most of the blowing had been stopped by June 1 with the aid of the emergency program. Grant, Haskell, and Stanton Counties produced 850,000 bushels of wheat in 1938 which, though far short of a normal crop, represented the first sizeable yield in five years. Rains in the autumn of 1938 put the soil in prime condition for growing wheat.

Yucca, Russian thistles, and sunflowers grow wild in this area. When the thistle dies, it forms huge ball-like tumbleweeds that are wind-driven across the prairie and piled high against fences and buildings (see Tour 1).

To reduce wind resistance, houses in this region are built low, many being half-buried like storm cellars, with roofs only slightly protruding above the ground; the barns are made of metal in a semicylindrical form.

At 15.5 m. on US 160-83 is the junction with State 45 (see Tour 4B).

A gasoline station (R), 20.5 m., at the northern junction with US 83 (see Tour 8), marks the SITE OF SANTA FE, which once had a population of nearly 1,000 and was the seat of Haskell County from 1887 to 1920. Although it was named for the Santa Fe Ry., no line came through here until 1912. Even then it missed Santa Fe and established its own town, Sublette, which immediately circulated petitions for a county seat election. In 1912 the State had granted complete suffrage to women and this election, held February 24, 1913, was the first county election in which Kansas women voted. Santa Fe successfully resisted all efforts to move the county seat until 1920, but ceased to exist soon after it lost the eight-year battle.

The OLD PATRICK RANCH HOUSE (private), 21.3 m., was (R) one of the largest and most modern in the area during the cattle-grazing days. When the first boom hit this buffalo-grass country, "Cattle King" Patrick turned his big hacienda into a hotel and real estate office, and part of his range became the town of Santa Fe.

The TRIMPA RANCH HOUSE (R), 24.1 m., is lighted and heated by the small low-pressure natural gas well, that stands near it.

The farmhouse and a small filling station, 32 m., are in a district owned largely by Mennonites, who have been wheat farmers here since the late 1870's.

In a CARBON BLACK PLANT (open on application), 43.1 m., carbon black, used in the manufacture of paint, is produced by the incomplete combustion of natural gas. Since the extension of the Hugoton gas field (see Tour 4B, HUGOTON) into Grant County in 1936, many new wells have been drilled in this vicinity.

One thousand cattle and 5,000 sheep were grazing on growing wheat in Grant County in the autumn of 1938, and livestock was being shipped in from other points. The single-strand wire fences used in this area to confine stock are charged with enough electricity to shock but not to injure the animals. They soon learn to avoid the wires.

ULYSSES, 50.3 m. (3,045 alt., 1,140 pop.), the seat and only post office in Grant County, was founded in 1885 three miles east of its present site and named for Gen. Ulysses S. Grant.

When Grant County was organized in 1888 Ulysses and Appomattox, a neighboring town, became rivals for the designation as county seat. Leaders in the two towns met several days before the election and agreed in writing that there was to be no bribery or intimidation and that the victorious town was to reimburse the defeated town for the money spent in financing the contest. When the terms of the secret contract leaked out, Appomattox citizens believed themselves betrayed by their leaders, particularly because Ulysses received a large majority of the votes. Enraged Appomattox partisans seized their leaders and threatented to hang them for their supposed duplicity. The prisoners were released after promising that their captors would be repaid the money they had spent in the campaign.

Impoverished by its payment to the Appomattox promoters, by loss of settlers following the drought of 1889, and by the opening of the Cherokee Strip in 1893, Ulysses struggled along by issuing bonds until 1909, when it was threatened with foreclosure. Its citizens, now reduced in number from 2,000 to less than 100, put wheels under their houses, hitched up the horses, and moved three miles across the prairie, leaving the bondholders 40 acres of bare ground on which to foreclose.

Since the natural-gas development began here in 1936 Ulysses has experienced a small boom.

West of Ulysses fields of broom corn begin to appear.

Left from Ulysses on US 270-State 25 to the JEDEDIAH SMITH MONUMENT (L), 12 m. The name is misspelled "Jediah" on the monument. One of the most renowned of the early plainsmen, ranking with Jim Bridger and Kit Carson, Jed Smith is credited with being the first to cross the Sierra Nevada into California, the first white man to lead an expedition overland from California to Oregon, and the first to lead a party over the famous South Pass in the Rockies. Well-educated and devout, Smith prayed regularly and always carried a Bible with him, a habit that was a constant source of wonder to his profane and free-and-easy colleagues.

Taking the Cimarron Crossing Cutoff on the Santa Fe Trail in 1831, Smith lost his way and wandered for days, suffering the terrible agonies of thirst. Finally he reached the Cimarron River here, only to find it dry. He dug frantically in the sand, at length got down to water, and drank ravenously. At that moment a band of Indians fell upon him. Smith killed several of them in a fearful struggle before he was himself killed and scalped. For years thereafter Cimarron Cutoff was known as the "water scrape route."

The monument was erected in 1937 by the 4-H clubs of Grant County with money awarded them as a prize at the Southwestern Kansas Free Fair for their pageant representing the fatal trip of Jed Smith and his party along the Santa Fe Trail.

The HOME OF CHARLES E. VAN METER (L), 70.1 m., is a two-story-and-basement English type house with a central chimney. It is approached by a U-shaped drive bordered with red cedars and Chinese arbor vitae. Van Meter (1853–   ), who came here in 1887 as assistant pastor of a Methodist circuit, was also an editor, farmer, merchant, weather observer, political organizer, county officer, insurance agent, reforestation expert, crop experimenter, and livestock breeder. In 45 years of farming his most successful crop was broom corn. Although at one time he had a herd of 100 shorthorn cattle, he realized that the land then cultivated would not raise enough feed to support the animals.

JOHNSON, 72.4 *m.* (3,330 alt., 514 pop.), seat of Stanton County, was founded by Civil War veterans in 1885, about seven miles to the northwest and named Veteran. The next year the town was moved to its present site and the name changed to Johnson in honor of Col. A. S. Johnson, one of the veterans.

At 84.5 *m.* is the junction with an improved road.

Left on this road to the STANTON COUNTY STATE PARK, 4 *m.*, being constructed (1938) by the WPA. The park will contain 400 acres, 300 of which will be a lake formed by a proposed dam across Bear Creek.

West of the TIME ZONE BOUNDARY, 88.7 *m.,* Mountain Standard Time is used; watches of west-bound travelers should be set back one hour.

At 90.3 *m.* US 160 crosses the COLORADO LINE, 180 miles east of Trinidad, Colo. *(see COLO., Tour 11).*

‹‹‹‹‹‹‹‹‹‹‹‹‹‹‹‹‹‹‹‹✲›››››››››››››››››››››››

Tour 7

(Joplin, Mo.)—Baxter Springs—Coffeyville—Arkansas City—South Haven; US 66 and US 166.
Missouri Line to South Haven, 169.9 m.

Missouri Pacific R.R. parallels route between Chetopa and Cedarvale; Atchison, Topeka & Santa Fe Ry. between Arkansas City and South Haven.
Paved roadbed except for a short stretch between Baxter Springs and Chetopa. The Neosho River sometimes floods this route; highway patrolmen warn travelers when there is danger.
Usual accommodations in larger towns.

This route passes through the lead- and zinc-mining region of southeastern Kansas, the Mid-Continent oil fields near Coffeyville, and a slight portion of the Flint Hills grazing region.

US 66 crosses the Missouri Line, 0 *m.,* at a point 6 miles west of Joplin, Mo. *(see MO., Tour 5),* entering the heart of the State's lead- and zinc-mining, a portion of the productive tri-state region of Missouri, Kansas, and Oklahoma. The trees of this formerly heavily timbered area were cut in early days for mine timbering and log houses. Today, where mining operations have not encroached, a second growth is almost impenetrable. Lying in all directions from the highway are man-made white mountains of chert, residue from the mines, topped occasionally with gaunt black mills and separated by dusty roads, railroad tracks, and patches of rock and cinder-covered wasteland. The chert, or "chat," as it is more commonly known, is used in this region as railroad ballast, for road surfacing, and in concrete aggregate.

The GALENA SMELTER *(open on application),* 0.5 *m.,* a great gray hulk surrounded by a maze of chat-covered roads and railroad tracks, is said to be one of the largest of its kind in the world; 200 tons of lead concentrates (ore as it comes from the mine) are smelted daily into 150 tons of pig lead (molded blocks of metal small enough to be handled and shipped to the manufacturer). Operating 24 hours a day, the smelter employs 250 men. Its buildings and yards cover 20 acres.

GALENA (Lat., *lead ore),* 1 *m.* (874 alt., 4,736 pop.), pioneer lead- and zinc-mining town, is surrounded by smelters, mills, and chat piles that have destroyed the original beauty of the country. The portion of town north of Short Creek has been undermined to such an extent that cave-ins are common and residents must constantly repair streets, damaged homes, and business houses.

This section was once Empire City, bitter rival of Galena in the early mining days. When lead was discovered in the vicinity in 1877, investors and workers flocked to this site. Galena, south of Short Creek, and Empire City, north of the creek, sprang up almost simultaneously. Each town took on the aspect of a frontier mining camp. Red Hot Street, the first business street of Galena which led down toward Short Creek, was soon lined with saloons and gambling houses. Most of the early mines were north of Short Creek and residents of Empire City built a timber stockade ten feet high and approximately half a mile long between the two settlements to prevent a direct route from Galena to the diggings. This was burned by residents of Galena soon after it had been completed.

As mining operations spread to the south and east, Empire City began to decline and was annexed to Galena in 1911.

Left from Galena on an improved road is SCHIMMERHORN PARK *(swimming, boating, fishing, picnicking),* 2 *m.,* comprising 160 acres of wooded land along Shoal Creek. Rock ledges and caves along this creek once sheltered Quantrill, the Daltons, and other notorious badmen.

US 66 at 3 *m.* enters Spring River valley. The large trees, deep grass, and wild flowers that cover its slopes contrast as sharply with the barren ugliness of the mining area as Spring River, a broad limpid stream that flows over a clean rocky bottom, differs from Kansas' usual brown muddy waterways. Many descendants of the Quakers who settled this valley still live on farms west and north of Riverton.

In RIVERTON, 4 *m.* (910 alt., 383 pop.), on the west bank of Spring River, is the EMPIRE DISTRICT HYDROELECTRIC PLANT *(open on application),* furnishing power to 80 communities in Missouri, Kansas, and Oklahoma. Its brilliant lights are visible at night from the concrete bridge on which US 66 crosses the river.

Left from Riverton on an improved road, 0.6 *m.,* the POWER DAM of the Empire District Electric Co. above the mouth of Shoal Creek causes the water to back up into both streams and forms 400-acre LAKE LOWELL. Public and private re-

UNION MEMBERS, GALENA

sorts line the river banks *(boating, swimming, fishing; cabins at moderate rates);* the region is the home of thousands of waterfowl.

BAXTER SPRINGS, 9 *m.* (842 alt., 4,541 pop.), surrounded by lead and zinc mines, has more homes beautified by interior decorators and more attractively landscaped lawns and gardens than most small Kansas towns. Several mine operators live in its shady residential district. It was named for A. Baxter, its first settler, who arrived in 1850 and built a shack and a sawmill beside the springs near the present town's northern limits. As stories of the water's curative properties spread, Baxter built a tavern to accommodate visitors and soon a few stores and a bank were added to the settlement.

In the 1860's Texas cattlemen drove thousands of longhorns to the fine pasture land around Baxter Springs. Especially large drives in 1867 and

1868 boomed the town. When the railroad was built in 1870 Baxter Springs became a wide-open cow town and shipping point so crowded with be-pistoled cowboys and cattlemen that it was called "the toughest town on earth."

By 1888 the railhead had advanced westward and Baxter Springs, having lost the cattle trade, concentrated on the expansion of her industrial, agricultural, and resort possibilities.

The old military trail from Fort Leavenworth to Fort Gibson passed down the town's only thoroughfare—the present Military Avenue.

The SITE OF THE BAXTER SPRINGS MASSACRE is at the end of E. 7th St. On the morning of October 6, 1863, the Federal garrison of a small post here, consisting of one company of cavalry and 65 or 70 colored infantrymen, was attacked by Quantrill's men *(see LAWRENCE)*, while part of the garrison was away on a foraging expedition. After 20 minutes of disorganized fighting, the invaders withdrew. They had lost two men and killed nine Federals.

Maj. Gen. James G. Blunt, accompanied by his staff, a regimental band, and a detachment of troops, approaching Baxter Springs on his way from Fort Scott to his new command at Fort Gibson in Indian Territory, mistook the departing raiders for a welcoming escort, and was quickly surrounded by Quantrill's men who captured almost his entire detachment.

Although reports of witnesses state that Quantrill had already shot all his captives including the wounded, he sent a messenger with a flag of truce to the garrison to suggest an exchange of prisoners. This, according to Quantrill's own report, was to "see if we had any wounded there."

Blunt, who escaped with only seven or eight men, reported: "I soon discovered that every man who had fallen, except three, who escaped by feigning death, had been murdered, all shot through the head. The brigade band, teamsters, and all headquarter's clerks who were first captured were murdered the same way." Eighty-seven of Blunt's men were killed.

In LIBRARY PARK, corner of 10th and Park Aves., is an OLD CONFEDERATE CANNON made in Macon, Ga., and captured at Pea Ridge, Ark., in 1862.

On HANGMAN'S ELM, between Park and Military Aves., two blocks south of the park, 19 men are said to have been hanged in the early days of the town.

In Baxter Springs is the junction with US 166 on which the tour continues westward; US 66 turns south from here and crosses the Oklahoma Line.

In the BAXTER SPRINGS NATIONAL CEMETERY (R), 11.2 *m.*, is a granite monument that commemorates the victims of the Baxter Springs Massacre, most of whom are interred here.

At 15.5 *m.* is the junction with US 69 *(see Tour 13)*.

The farming country in this region is broken at intervals by patches of timber. Small ravines cut through the pastures occasionally, their low sides trampled into a rough No Man's Land of miniature "shell craters" by the hoofs of cattle and baked hard in the sun. This undulating farm and pasture land slopes gently westward.

US 166 crosses the Neosho River, 29.3 *m.*, a slow-moving muddy stream fringed with elms and maples, the former home of the Osage.

CHETOPA, 30.3 *m.* (826 alt., 1,344 pop.) *(see Tour 12)*, is at the junction with US 59 *(see Tour 12).*

Many descendants of the hundreds of pioneers from Ohio, Illinois, Missouri, and Iowa who settled this part of the Neosho Valley in the 1880's are still living on the land homesteaded by their fathers or grandfathers.

The FORMER HOME OF WALTER PERRY JOHNSON *(private)*, 57.4 *m.*, built in 1920, is a frame two-story structure of English design, faced and roofed with brown shingles. A long poplar-bordered lane leads from the highway to the house.

Johnson, born on a farm near Humboldt, November 6, 1887, and considered by many the greatest pitcher ever to "toe the rubber," began his baseball career on the sand lots in California, where his parents moved when he was a boy.

In 1906 "Big Train" Johnson, pitching his second year for the Washington Senators, created a sensation when he shut out the New York Yankees three times in four days, allowing only thirteen hits for all three. After the third game, which was the first of a double header, he was warming up to pitch the fourth when Joe Cantillion, manager of the Washington team, "chased him to the showers." He pitched for the Senators for 20 years, a record unequalled by any other ballplayer.

For years Johnson passed the autumn and winter months on a farm near Coffeyville where he raised Holstein cattle and Orpington chickens, and went 'coon hunting in the heavily wooded areas along the Verdigris River. He built this home at the edge of the city in 1920, but after the death of Mrs. Johnson in 1930, moved from Kansas to Maryland.

COFFEYVILLE, 57.9 *m.* (744 alt., 16,198 pop.) *(see COFFEY-VILLE).*

Points of Interest: Roosevelt Drive, Shadow Pool, subsurface-lighted swimming pool, Forest Drive.

Though derricks are not visible from the highway, the region around Coffeyville is a part of the great Mid-Continent oil field, centering in Oklahoma. The abandoned "stripper" fields are brought back into productivity here by pumping water at high pressure into four wells sunk in the producing sand around a central well. This forces the oil residue in the sands toward the central well from which oil is taken until it begins "watering," an indication that the sands have been washed clean.

Although the installation of the machinery is expensive, abandoned stripper wells can be purchased for such small sums that they usually yield good profits.

An oil TANK FARM *(open by permission of superintendent)* and pumping station are at 75.8 *m. (see Tour 5).*

CANEY, 77.8 *m.* (737 alt., 2,794 pop.) *(see Tour 11)*, is at the junction with US 75 *(see Tour 11).* Between Caney and a point at 81 *m.* US 166 and US 75 are one route.

In the hill country northwest of Caney, villages are far apart.

The hills, a section of the Osage range of northern Oklahoma, are low, round-topped, and forested with maple, hackberry, elm, and blackjack oak, which turns a flaming red in the autumn. Occasional layers of moss-covered rocks jutting out along the ravines form shady retreats in summer.

SEDAN, 99.8 *m.* (841 alt., 1,776 pop.), surrounded by tree-covered hills, has two legends to explain its name. Some claim that it was named for the French city where Napoleon III and his army surrendered to the Prussians September 1, 1870. This group states that when the town was being built late in 1870 Thomas Scurr of Coffeyville, riding into town on a load of lumber, was struck by the resemblance between the heavily timbered hills surrounding the townsite and a picture of Sedan which he had seen in a magazine.

Others explain that before the town was built a sawmill was operated here by a man named Dan. The mill became a popular loafing place for settlers living down the creek. After the chores were done the men would take their pipes and tobacco and tell their women folks, "I'm going up to see Dan." Eventually, anyone bound in this direction was said to be going to "see Dan," and when the town was founded in 1875 the name clung.

At 100.6 *m.* is the junction with State 99, a graveled road.

Right on State 99 is 80-acre DEER CREEK LAKE *(swimming, boating, fishing),* 3.5 *m.,* in a park of 110 acres *(baseball and football field, children's playgrounds, picnic grounds, camp stoves, shelter houses).*

West of this junction the route dips into narrow canyons and climbs the broad summits from which miles of hills and valleys, with their tree-tops and streams, are visible.

CEDARVALE, 116.7 *m.* (914 alt., 1,000 pop.), on a hillside, was laid out in 1870 when a great number of cedar trees were growing in the valley. From the foot of Main Street the Caney Valley stretches to the southwest, flanked in the distance by hills. An irregular line of trees at the base of the slope marks the course of the Caney River.

The citizens, planning an elaborate celebration for the town's first Fourth of July, discovered on July 2, that they had no flag. A modern Paul Revere volunteered to make a wild night-and-day ride to Eureka, about 50 miles north, for material. When he returned late in the evening of July 3, he was met by half a dozen women with scissors, needles, and thread, who spent the rest of the night cutting and sewing pieces of red, white, and blue in order that the Stars and Stripes might banish any doubt as to Cedarvale's patriotism.

West of Cedarvale timber on the hilltops diminishes and US 166 enters a section of the Flint Hills.

ARKANSAS CITY, 149.3 *m.* (1,075 alt., 13,946 pop.) *(see AR-KANSAS CITY).*

Points of Interest: Natural bridge, old Indian trails, Buffalo Bill Cody's campground, Arkansas City Fair.

Arkansas City is at the junction with US 77 *(see Tour 10).*

The route crosses the ARKANSAS RIVER, 151.5 *m.,* and dips into its low sandy valley. Here cottonwood trees, ranging in size from slender sprouts only a few feet high to great gnarled giants with widespread limbs, grow in abundance.

SOUTH HAVEN, 169.9 *m.* (1,218 alt., 442 pop.) *(see Tour 9)*, is at the junction with US 81 *(see Tour 9)*.

<<<<<<<<<<<<<<<<<<<<<<☼>>>>>>>>>>>>>>>>>>>>>>

Tour 8

(Kearney, Nebr.)—Norton—Oakley—Scott City—Garden City—Liberal —(Turpin, Okla.); US 83.
Nebraska Line to Oklahoma Line, 267.4 m.

Chicago Burlington & Quincy R.R. parallels route between Nebraska Line and Norton; Chicago Rock Island & Pacific Ry. between Almena and Gem; Union Pacific R.R. between Colby and Oakley; Atchison, Topeka & Santa Fe Ry. between Scott City and Garden City.
Roadbed improved and paved; open all year except following infrequent snowstorms.
Fair accommodations available in county-seat towns.

US 83 follows in general a north-south course through the rolling prairie land of western Kansas. Traversing the High Plains in the north, the highway passes wheat fields, pasture land, and a small area of irrigated farm land midway along its route, and enters the wind-swept plains near the Oklahoma Line. Along the way it crosses the valleys of the six principal rivers of western Kansas—the North and South Forks of the Solomon, the Saline, the Smoky Hill, the broad Arkansas, and the Cimarron—each a narrow ribbon of green in an otherwise monotonous prairie.

US 83 crosses the Nebraska Line, 0 *m.*, 67 miles south of Kearney, Nebr. *(see NEBR., Tour 5)*.

LONG ISLAND, 10.2 *m.* (2,074 alt., 242 pop.), a trading and shipping point for farmers and cattlemen, was settled in 1871 by a group of Holland Dutch, and was so-named because of its position between two creeks that run parallel for many miles. The Dutch strain is still predominant locally.

Many farms in the vicinity are supplied with running water from nearby streams, and have electric lighting systems and other conveniences more generally associated with the suburban estates of gentlemen farmers.

Five miles west of Long Island was the home of Amos Cole, one of the pioneers of the region who came here in the 1860's. Cole was an easterner who decided that buffalo hunting was not only an exciting sport but also would provide an easy living, not realizing that the Indians lived on the buffalo and regarded white hunters as poachers for whom the proper punishment was death. To survive in his precarious life as a buffalo hunter, Cole had to re-educate himself quickly. He learned the Sioux language, dressed himself in the hunting costume of the Indians, and trained himself to imitate their posture and gait in walking or running. But his disguise was penetrated on several occasions by the Indians, and he managed to escape only after spirited running fights, in one of which he received a bullet in his head. With the disappearance of the buffalo and the Indians, Cole took up a homestead near the county line, where he spent his remaining years.

Southwest of Long Island the rolling prairie rises here and there into low hills, broken by the broad fertile valleys of the larger streams, which are fed by the tributary creeks that come down from the high prairie through winding, canyon-like valleys.

The rugged barrenness of the surrounding upland strikingly sets off the green beauty of Prairie Dog Valley. Its watercourses are lined with thick growth of trees, wild grapes, wild plums, currants, and choke-cherries. In the valley are violets and buttercups and in protected places, wild columbine. The higher prairie land is bright with blue and white daisies, the purple blossoms of the wild onion, the pink of the wild rose, the yucca with its white waxlike flowers, the upland poppy, the prickly pear, the prairie violet, sunflowers, and goldenrod. From May until August appear bluish-purple patches of the flowering locoweed, which is poisonous; it often causes cattle and horses to go temporarily crazy. Many cowponies in early years got the loco habit, it is said, and went on spree after spree.

At 21.7 *m.* is the junction with a dirt road.

Left on this road to 11-acre DOLE'S LAKE, 1 *m. (fishing, boating, swimming, picnicking).*

ALMENA, 24.5 *m.* (2,155 alt., 703 pop.), was named for her home town in Michigan by Mrs. James Hall, wife of an early settler. The town originally was built on the south bank of Prairie Dog Creek, and consisted of a blacksmith shop, a mill, a few shanties and dugouts. Indian tepees once occupied the site where the town now stands. The surrounding land was used by the Indians as a dumping ground and a place for curing buffalo hides. Almena was moved to the north bank of the creek in 1885 when a railroad was built along it.

1. Right from Almena on a dirt road to the junction with another dirt road, 0.5 *m.;* R. on this road to Prairie Dog Creek and a STATE GAME PRESERVE for ducks and geese, 6.3 *m.* Along the nearby creek are beaver dams.

2. Left from Almena on a dirt road to the junction with another dirt road, 6 *m.;* L. on this road to a stone quarry, 2 *m.,* where several incomplete skeletons of horses and rhinoceroses that inhabited Kansas during the Miocene Age millions of years ago have been unearthed. At 0.1 *m.* on the main dirt road is (L) the SITE OF A BATTLE fought in October 1868 between three companies of cavalry and Whistler's band of Ogallala Sioux. The soldiers and Indians slain were buried nearby on the banks of Skull Creek.

At 25.2 *m.* is the junction with State 60, improved.

Left on State 60 to EAGLE'S POINT, 1 *m.* *(crest can be reached only on foot),* so-named by Amos Cole because bald eagles frequently soared over it. The prairie rises in a gentle slope to the top, about 150 feet above the plain, affording a view that on clear days extends 40 miles east and west, and more than 13 miles north and south. Buffalo hunters used this height in early days to sight distant herds.

Immediately southwest of Almena is the South Fork of Prairie Dog Creek. Buffalo Bill Cody reported that in 1869 he had seen a band of Indians kill thirteen Government surveyors at the point where the South Fork enters Prairie Dog Creek. According to his story he was pursued by the Indians but was able to reach Fort Hays in safety.

Much of the land along the highway to the west is cultivated by power machinery. Erosion is cutting ever deeper and larger ravines in the prairie.

At 28.7 *m.* is the junction with a dirt road.

Left on this road to PILOT KNOB, 0.3 *m.,* topped with a ridge of soft limestone 20 feet high and 100 feet long. From the summit is an excellent view of the valley where many Indian battles were fought in the 1860's.

CALVERT, 29.7 *m.* (2,197 alt., 40 pop.), known as Neighborville until the railroad was built through the town, lies in the center of extensive deposits of volcanic ash, or powdered lava, used in the manufacture of glass, scouring powders, and in glazing china and porcelain. Calvert ships 500 carloads of pulverized silica annually. Steam shovels scoop up the pure white siliceous material occurring in layers some 18 feet thick just under the surface of the hills that rise rather abruptly south of the village.

Left from Calvert on a dirt road to a SILICA MINE, 0.3 *m.* *(open with permission of superintendent).*

The creeks in the vicinity are skirted with timber, and their valleys are green with grass, providing good pasturage.

At 31.2 *m.* is the eastern junction with US 36 *(see Tour 1).* Between this place and a point at 44 *m.,* US 83 and US 36 are one route *(see Tour 1).*

At 35.7 *m.* is NORTON (2,275 alt., 2,767 pop.) *(see Tour 1).*

South of the junction with US 36 coyotes are common. In autumn the men and boys form hunting parties and methodically kill these animals to protect their livestock. The hunters spread out in a wide circle and then close in on their quarry. The coyotes killed are sometimes auctioned off for the benefit of various local charitable organizations; their only value is the bounty on their pelts.

Along the streams beaver, now protected by law, have become quite common. Mink and squirrels also live along the creeks, and badgers inhabit the prairie land. Of the nocturnal animals raccoons are most numerous, though there are opossums, skunks, and civet cats. Introduced about 20 years ago, pheasants have propagated rapidly; prairie chickens are now scarce, and quail almost extinct.

West of JENNINGS, 67.2 *m.* (2,541 alt., 344 pop.)—called "Slab City" in the early 1870's because the first shacks were built of rough-sawed native lumber—the soil of the gently rolling countryside is black clay or sandy loam, largely sown to wheat and corn, although much is used as pasture. Some of the grasslands descend in a series of shelves or steps from high plateaus to creek bottoms.

At 69.3 *m.* is the junction with a dirt road.

Right on this road is the JENNINGS STATE PARK, 0.5 *m.* *(swimming, boating, duck hunting, fishing, skating)*, with a 40-acre lake formed by a dam across Prairie Dog Creek.

DRESDEN, 75.8 *m.* (2,731 alt., 231 pop.), named by German settlers for their home in Saxony, is the shipping point for a prosperous livestock area.

In the 1870's Dresden was the center of a buffalo hide boom. Fashion had decreed buffalo robes for carriages and sleighs, and prices for hides soared so high that hundreds of settlers from eastern Kansas and neighboring States came to the plains to shoot buffalo.

At 79.2 *m.* is the junction with a dirt road.

Left on this road to LEOVILLE, 0.5 *m.* (2,541 alt., 90 pop.), a German Catholic community founded by three young men who came from Iowa in 1885, settled on claims nearby, and built a sod church, naming their settlement for Pope Leo. The hamlet looks down on the surrounding countryside from a plateau which is exposed to all the Kansas winds.
The original sod church has been replaced by an imposing edifice of brick and native rock (the largest in northwestern Kansas), having a seating capacity of 740. Its fine workmanship and interior decorations annually attract hundreds of visitors. The church is the center of an agricultural community consisting of a dozen houses and a modern grade and grammar school.

SELDEN, 84.7 *m.* (2,837 alt., 399 pop.), on a large expanse of high level prairie, serves an important wheat-growing area.

Right from Selden on a well-marked dirt road *(sharp turn)* to BROOKWOOD PARK, 4.5 *m.* *(boating, swimming, fishing; picnic grounds, golf course, baseball diamond)*, a pleasant recreation spot with a lake and a grove of native trees.

REXFORD, 96.3 *m.* (2,955 alt., 375 pop.), a substantial village with several large brick buildings along its main street, has in its northern section a grove of shade trees, a rarity in this region. When Rexford was founded, in the early 1880's, the vast flat prairie here was a mat of buffalo grass so thickly strewn with bleaching buffalo bones that it seemed a field of white lilies stretching to the horizon. Many early settlers eked out a livelihood by gathering these bones and hauling them to market, whence they were shipped to fertilizer factories. They composed a pathetic ballad, "The Bone Hunters," and sang it at their dreary task.

After the coming of settlers the immense herds of buffalo quickly disappeared. But wild horses and antelope remained plentiful for some time, and the hunting of these animals proved profitable. A herd of wild horses would be kept running day and night by a group of settlers, who changed men and mounts every morning and evening until the herd was exhausted and ready to mill. Then the weary animals were driven into corrals where the hunters could rope and bust them, after which they were sold to farmers.

Settlement was slow for many years, and almost all of this country was laid out in big cattle ranches, with houses and corrals built along the creeks. Great herds of cattle wandered far and wide, watering and finding shelter where they could.

At 105.9 *m.* is the northern junction with US 24 *(see Tour 2)*. Between this point and Halford, US 83 and US 24 are one route.

HALFORD, 107.9 *m.* (3,086 alt., 18 pop.), a rural trading center and shipping point, was founded as Vernier in 1887. When the railroad was built through the town one year later, the present name was adopted in honor of a railroad official.

OAKLEY, 126.5 *m.* (3,029 alt., 1,159 pop.) *(see Tour 3)*, is at the junction with US 40 *(see Tour 3)*.

At 147.8 *m.* is the junction with an improved road.

Left on this road to the junction with an improved road, 4 *m.;* R. on this road to the junction with another improved road, 6 *m.;* L. to another junction, 7 *m.;* R. to MONUMENT ROCKS, sometimes called the "Kansas Pyramids," 7.5 *m.,* in the valley of the Smoky Hill River. These chalk rocks rise with startling abruptness from the vast flatness of the High Plains. On an unmarked site a short distance southwest once stood an Army Post and a stage station of the Butterfield Overland Despatch, a line also known as the Smoky Hill route, which was established in the summer of 1865 by David A. Butterfield. Its route, 50 miles shorter than the Leavenworth-Fort Kearney road, extended southwest from Atchison through Grasshopper Falls *(see Tour 12)* and joined the Fort Leavenworth-Fort Riley military road at Indianola, a few miles north of Topeka. Between Junction City and Leavenworth the trail followed the valley of the Smoky Hill River. For a few months the new enterprise realized tremendous profits, but competition with Ben Holladay, millionaire freighting operator, soon proved too severe for Dave Butterfield's limited capital. Early in 1866 the company was on the verge of bankruptcy and Butterfield sold his equipment to Holladay, who abandoned the Smoky Hill route.

At the northern end of the group is the KANSAS SPHINX, one of the most unusual rock foundations in the State. Composed of chalk of the same geologic origin as the other rocks in this vicinity, it was thousands of years old when the Egyptian monument for which it was named was built. Its clear-cut, sphinx-like profile was carved by erosion.

ELKADER, 150.3 *m.* (3,029 alt., 7 pop.), is at the junction with an improved road.

Right on this road to the junction with an unimproved road, 5 *m.;* R. on this road to CHALK BLUFFS, 6 *m.,* a series of shallow canyons flanked by irregular bluffs of chalk and chalk shale. These formations cover an area of several hundred acres known often as the Gove County Badlands.

At 161.6 *m.* is (L) the SCOTT COUNTY STATE PARK *(cabin accommodations, scenic drives)*, one of the first of such parks to be set aside by the Kansas Forestry, Fish, and Game Commission. Comprising 1,200 acres of rugged country and 110-acre Lake McBride, the park lies between the flat High Plains and the shelved limestone walls of the Smoky Hill River valley.

In the park is a MONUMENT dedicated to the memory of H. L. Steel, and his wife, who owned the homestead on which the park lies. The monument stands on an eminence, reached by a flight of 144 steps. Nearby is the H. L. STEELE HOME, built with limestone from the surrounding hills, and now housing a MUSEUM *(open)*, exhibiting old furniture, curios, and an Indian flint collection. From the house is a splendid panorama of the surrounding hills and canyons.

Near the center of the park is a BUFFALO SANCTUARY, where a herd of nineteen animals are pastured on 200 acres of enclosed land. The buffalo were brought to the park in the summer of 1938 from a reservation near Garden City where they had been kept for several years. Continued drought burned the pastures at the reservation and feeding the great shaggy beasts soon became so expensive that the Forestry, Fish, and Game Commission prepared the new grazing area which is carpeted with a lush growth of native buffalo grass, and contains a number of water holes. In contrast with the perennial migrations of their ancestors who roamed the Kansas plains before they were virtually exterminated in the 1870's, this tiny herd made the 50-mile journey in motor trucks.

In the park are the RUINS OF EL QUARTELEJO, adobe stronghold of the Spanish and Picurie Indians in the early part of the eighteenth century. These ruins are believed to have been the first solid walls erected within what is now Kansas.

The Picurie, according to half-legendary accounts, originally inhabited the Taos region in New Mexico. Early in the seventeenth century they found the Spanish yoke unbearable and migrated to the plains of what is now western Kansas, establishing a pueblo approximately 150 Spanish leagues northeast of Santa Fe. From these directions it has been determined that the crumbled adobe walls in the valley of Beaver Creek are the ruins of the stronghold constructed by the fugitives.

The Picurie were civilized Indians, and they are believed to have lived a prosperous and peaceful life in this Kansas canyon. They planted fields of corn and irrigated them in dry seasons by diverting water from the Beaver. Within a few years they were discovered by a band of Spanish soldiers who persuaded them to return to their old home.

For a generation after the Spanish and the Picurie had departed, El Quartelejo was deserted, but one day a roving band of warlike Comanche rode into the canyon, found the shelter and moved into it. The Comanche were a migratory tribe who knew nothing of building or repairing these adobe structures. Consequently, the walls continued to crack and crumble under the constant attack of the elements.

At last, losing patience with the slow destructive processes of wind and rain, Nature destroyed the walls with a single blow, according to Indian legend. One summer night, as the Comanche encamped about El Quartelejo sat watching the moon rise over the rugged buttes, a storm rolled up from the southwest. Flashes of lightning darted across the sky and successive peals of thunder vibrated through the hills. Suddenly the valley was illuminated by a blinding flash and the walls of the pueblo crashed to the ground. The frightened Indians deserted the spot and as far as is known it has never been inhabited since that night.

At 168.7 *m.* is (R) CHRISTY LAKE *(restricted to members of the Baptist Church)*, part of a local Baptist assembly ground.

Right from Christy Lake on an improved road to BATTLE CANYON, 0.5 *m.*, sometimes called Squaw's Den, a rocky, eroded depression in the flat plains country.

BUFFALO PRESERVE, SCOTT COUNTY STATE PARK

Here the last Indian battle in Kansas was fought on September 27, 1878, between a detachment of the 19th Infantry from Fort Dodge under Lt. Col. William H. Lewis and the Cheyenne, who, led by Chief Dull Knife, had fled from their reservation in Indian Territory. After trailing the Cheyenne for several miles along Beaver Creek (then called Punished Woman's Fork), Colonel Lewis found them in the canyon, awaiting his attack. In the fight that followed Colonel Lewis was fatally wounded, a bullet severing the main artery in his thigh. Two soldiers were slightly wounded while carrying their dead commander from the field. The skirmish ended at nightfall and the Cheyenne continued their retreat. A dead warrior was found in the canyon. On the following day the Indians massacred nineteen settlers in Decatur County and crossed the Nebraska Line pursued by the soldiers, under Capt. Clarence Mauck of the 4th Cavalry, who had succeeded Colonel Lewis.

SCOTT CITY, 175.7 m. (2,971 alt., 1,544 pop.), is a comfortable-looking plains town with well-kept streets and homes, modern schools, and an abundance of shrubbery and trees irrigated with water from underground streams that have their source in the Rocky Mountains. These streams also supply water for successful irrigation projects in the surrounding countryside.

Cowboys scornfully dubbed the first farmers in this region "dry landers," but as great fields encroached more and more upon the range, cow-men were forced to move farther south and west.

1. Right from Scott City on paved State 96 to LEOTI (Ind., *prairie flower*), 24.1 *m*. (3,297 alt., 618 pop.), seat of Wichita County. Annually in September the Wichita County Fair is held in Leoti, which is the trade, educational, and amusement center of an extensive wheat and livestock area.

In 1885 a company from Garden City platted the townsite here in the exact geographical center of the county hoping to make it the county seat. William D. Weiler, a land speculator from Indiana, came to western Kansas to find most of the townsites already claimed. Not discouraged, he organized a company and founded a town three miles east of Leoti, naming it Coronado. With the organization of Wichita County in 1886, the two towns became bitter rivals for the county seat.

As usual, both factions resorted to extralegal measures. Gunmen were imported "to preserve order." From Dodge City the Coronado partisans brought a former sheriff, while Leoti sent to wild and woolly Wallace for a crew of "fun-loving" cowboys who terrorized all law-abiding citizens. Among the Leoti playboys was Charley Coulter, a professional badman. On the eve of the county seat election Coulter and six or seven other young men from Leoti loaded a case of beer into a rig and drove over to the rival town, where they announced that they could "lick anybody in Coronado." A burst of gunfire precipitated a pitched battle in the town's main street.

Every man in the Leoti party was hit by the withering fire of the Coronado men. Coulter and William Rains lay dead, and George Watkins was mortally wounded. According to local tradition, Coulter's trigger finger twitched for a half hour after his death. When the militia had restored order, fourteen Coronado men were arrested and tried at Garden City, but there were no convictions.

In the election a fortnight later Leoti received 822 votes, Coronado 349. Coronado claimed to have a majority of the legal votes and accused Leoti of stuffing the ballot boxes, but the election was declared legal and Leoti became the county seat. Two railroads, the Santa Fe and the Missouri Pacific, were building lines into Wichita County early in the year 1887. The county voted bonds and offered assistance to the first company to finish its line to Leoti. The Missouri Pacific won the race and the Santa Fe, which had reached the east boundary of the county, tore up its tracks as far back as Scott City. Coronado declined rapidly and, after a few years of hopeless struggle, passed out of existence. Today only a wheat elevator occupies the site.

2. Left on State 96 to DIGHTON, 24.6 *m*. (2,759 alt., 803 pop.), seat of Lane County, first named Watson for one of its founders, but incorporated in 1887 as Dighton, for Richard Dighton who platted additional ground for the village. In 1888 a boom swelled the population to 1,500. Real estate speculation ran high; a streetcar line was started; mills, factories, and elevators were projected. But by 1890 inflated values had collapsed, factories and mills disappeared, and the population dropped to less than 200. The old business district was deserted, and more modern structures were gradually built in another section.

Albert J. Beveridge, later United States Senator from Indiana, maintained a law office here in the 1890's.

Situated in a vast wheat-growing and stock-raising region, Dighton has a definitely rural character, but all streets are gravel-surfaced. Its light and water systems are municipally owned.

GARDEN CITY, 211 *m*. (2,830 alt., 6,121 pop.) *(see Tour 4)*, is at the junction with US 50 and US 50 N *(see Tour 4)*, and with US 50 S *(see Tour 4A)*.

At 212 *m*. is the junction with a dirt road.

Right on the dirt road to the GARDEN CITY EXPERIMENT STATION, 4.5 *m*., established in 1907. Since 1910 Federal studies of dry land agriculture and State experiments with irrigation, crop, and trees have been conducted here.

Near POINT OF ROCKS, 9.3 *m.*, according to tradition, lurked bands of Indians that preyed on pioneers. A sword, thought to have belonged to one of Coronado's soldiers, was found near here and is now in the State Historical Museum in Topeka.

US 83 crosses a TIME ZONE BOUNDARY, 229.5 *m.* South of this point Central Standard Time is used; watches of south-bound travelers should be set ahead one hour.

The IVANHOE SCHOOLHOUSE, at 233.5 *m.* (L), is all that remains of the town of Ivanhoe that boomed here in the early 1880's. On both sides of the highway are Santa Fe Trail markers.

At 240 *m.* is the northern junction with US 160 *(see Tour 6)*, which unites for a few miles with US 83.

At 246 *m.* on US 83-160 is the junction with State 45 *(see Tour 4B)*.

At 261 *m.* is the southern junction with US 160 *(see Tour 6)*.

LIBERAL, 279 *m.* (2,839 alt., 5,294 pop.) *(see Tour 5)*, is at the junction with US 54 *(see Tour 5)*.

At 283 *m.* US 83 crosses the Oklahoma Line, 9 miles north of Turpin, Okla. *(see OKLA., Tour 19)*.

‹‹‹‹‹‹‹‹‹‹‹‹‹‹‹‹‹☼›››››››››››››››››››››

Tour 9

(Columbus, Nebr.)—Concordia—Salina—Wichita—Wellington—(Enid, Okla.); US 81.
Nebraska Line to Oklahoma Line, 248.1 m.

Union Pacific R.R. parallels route between Salina and Mentor, and between Lindsborg and McPherson; Midland Valley Ry. between Wichita and Belle Plaine; Chicago, Rock Island & Pacific Ry. between Wichita and Wellington; Atchison, Topeka & Santa Fe Ry. between Belle Plaine and Wellington.
Paved roadbed. Open all year, except after occasional heavy blizzards.
Good accommodations in all larger towns.

A section of an international highway extending from Winnipeg to Mexico City, US 81 crosses the Blue Hills Uplands in the northern part of the State, gently rolling land cut by numerous small streams and sown to corn, wheat, and alfalfa. After winding through rough and rocky pasture land, it emerges on the Great Bend Prairie, center of the vast wheat belt, and, approaching the Oklahoma Line, follows the approximate route of the old Chisholm Cattle Trail, traces of which are still visible.

US 81 crosses the Nebraska Line, 0 *m.*, 115 miles south of Columbus, Nebr. *(see NEBR., Tour 3)*.

At 5.5 *m.* is the junction with a dirt road.

Right on this road which ascends a mesa to PIKE'S PAWNEE VILLAGE STATE PARK, 11 *m.* At or near this place on September 29, 1806, in a village of the Pawnee Republic, Zebulon M. Pike persuaded the Pawnee to raise the United States flag, an incident he describes in his journal:

Sept. 29th Held our grand council with the Pawnees, at which were present not less than 400 warriors, . . . I again reiterated the demand for the (Spanish) flag, adding that it was impossible for the nation to have two fathers; that they must either be the children of the Spaniards, or acknowledge their American father. After a silence of some time an old man rose, went to the door, took down the Spanish flag, brought it and laid it at my feet; he then received the American flag, and elevated it on the staff which had lately borne the standard of his Catholic Majesty. This gave great satisfaction to the Osage and Kansa, both of whom decidedly avow themselves to be under American protection. Perceiving that every face in the council was clouded with sorrow, as if some great national calamity were about to befall them, I took up the contested colors, and told them that as they had shown themselves dutiful children in acknowledging their great American father, I did not wish to embarrass them with the Spaniards, for it was the wish of the Americans that their red brethren should remain peaceably around their own fires, and not embroil themselves in any disputes between the white people; and that for fear the Spaniards might return there in force again, I returned them their flag, but with an injunction that it should never be hoisted again during our stay. At this there was a general shout of applause, and the charge was particularly attended to.

In the center of the mesa a 25-foot shaft, overlooking the Republican River, commemorates the Pike expedition. Every year (last week Sept.) a celebration is held here, during which Pawnee, brought from Oklahoma, assist in reenacting the flag-raising scene.

BELLEVILLE, 13 *m.* (1,514 alt., 2,383 pop.), built around the old-fashioned Republic County Courthouse, was founded in 1869 and named in honor of Arabelle Tutton, wife of one of the settlers. Since 1884 Belleville has been a railroad and trading center. In 1910 the town acquired its water, light, and power plants, and has operated them so profitably that no general taxes are levied. Rates compare favorably with those in communities served by privately owned utilities.

At the northern edge of town on US 81 is a PUBLIC PARK *(playgrounds, picnic grounds, swimming pool),* attractively landscaped with trees, shrubs, and flowers.

The annual North-Central Kansas Free Fair *(1st week in Sept.),* third largest in the State, features agricultural and livestock exhibits, horse and automobile races.

Belleville is at the junction with US 36 *(see Tour 1).*

At 22.2 *m.* is the junction with an improved road.

Left on this road to TALMO, 2 *m.* (1,362 alt., 106 pop.), a hamlet. Right from Talmo on a dirt road to the SEAPO SALT MARSH, 3.2 *m.,* covering 4,000 acres. In dry weather the water evaporates, leaving a thick salt crust that gleams in the sunlight. In early days the salt recovered by evaporation from the brine of this marsh was used for cooking; the brine, found at a depth of about 6 feet, averaged a bushel of pure salt to every 65 gallons.

At 23.5 *m.,* on the highest of a small range of hills (R), is a circle of stones pounded into the earth. This spot was used by the Indians as a lookout and signal point when the first white settlers came to Kansas. From the hilltop is a fine view of the broad valley and rolling upland, covered with well cultivated farms and grooved by rivers and winding creeks.

CONCORDIA, 33.7 m. (1,363 alt., 5,792 pop.), a railroad junction on the south bank of the Republican River, is the trade center of the surrounding dairying and farming country; it has several creameries and mills. J. M. Hageman selected the townsite about 1864 and at his own expense opened a road to Junction City. A town company was formed in 1869 and the settlement given the name Concordia, "in view of the harmony and unanimity" that marked the meeting at which the town was named seat of Cloud County. The settlement had a post office, a land office, a store, and a hotel. The hotel was pulled here by eleven yoke of oxen from its original site several miles to the west. In 1870 Concordia's first newspaper, the *Republican Valley Empire*, was established by Henry Buckingham. Late in 1872 a great fire swept through the town, and a large part had to be rebuilt from its foundations.

In the 1870's Boston Corbett *(see Tour 11)*, said by some to have been the slayer of John Wilkes Booth, President Lincoln's assassin, sought safety from enemies in a dugout on his claim a few miles to the southeast. He seldom appeared on Concordia's streets.

Concordia's FIRST HOUSE, a small frame structure at 100 Cedar St., was built by Hageman in 1866 or 1867. BROWN'S HILL, at the west end of 6th St., affords a fine view of the tree-shaded city and the rich agricultural valley. Especially noteworthy civic possessions are the RECREATION PARK *(band shell, swimming pool, tennis courts, playground)*, 10th and Washington Sts., and the CONCORDIA JUNIOR AND SENIOR HIGH SCHOOL BUILDING, 10th and Cedar Sts., which covers a city block. The school is of Georgian Colonial architecture and has a swimming pool, a large gymnasium, and an auditorium. The North-Central Kansas League Music Festival is held here each April.

At 48.9 m. is the junction with US 24 *(see Tour 2)*. Between this place and a point at 50.9 m. US 24 and US 81 are one route.

At 56 m. is the junction with State 41, paved.

Right on State 41 to DELPHOS, 3 m. (1,299 alt., 678 pop.), home of Mrs. Grace Bedell Billings, who died in 1936 at the age of 87. When a girl, she wrote Abraham Lincoln to suggest that he grow whiskers to conceal the thinness of his chin. Copies of her letter and of Lincoln's reply are preserved in a bank vault here. Mrs. Billings once refused $5,000 for the Lincoln letter and insured it for that sum.

MINNEAPOLIS, 67.5 m. (1,300 alt., 1,741 pop.), seat of Ottawa County, is a trading and shipping point for dairy products, stock, poultry, and grain raised in the fertile Solomon Valley. The town's name is Indian-Greek, combining Minne (Ind., *waters)* with polis (Gr., *city)*.

1. Right from Minneapolis on a zigzag improved road to ROCK CITY *(open)*, 3.5 m., a grotesquely eroded area of balanced rocks, toadstools, pyramids, spheres, castle-like structures, and other formations. As erosion continues to reveal more and more formations, old-timers around Minneapolis say that the rocks are "growing." An Indian legend relates that the Great Spirit rolled these immense stones here and told chiefs gathered from the four corners of the earth to drive the white men from the land. The Great Spirit said that when the winds had rolled these rocks

into the sea, and when the waves had lashed them into sand and had cast the grains again on the shore, the pale face would return to his home across the ocean.

2. Left from Minneapolis on an improved road to OTTAWA COUNTY STATE PARK *(cabins at nominal rent; band concerts, baseball games, swimming, fishing, boating)*, 6.5 *m.*, a game preserve and bird sanctuary in which the State Fish and Game Commission maintains a hatchery for quail and Chinese pheasants. This 711-acre park includes 150-acre Lake Goodwyn, formed by a large dam and fed by springs.

The highway crosses the Solomon River, 81.5 *m.*, into rolling prairie country watered by narrow creeks and occasionally broken by abrupt hills and ridges.

SALINA, 94.6 *m.* (1,220 alt., 20,155 pop.) *(see SALINA).*

Points of Interest: St. John's Military Academy, Wesleyan University, Marymount College, and others.

Salina is at the junction with US 40 *(see Tour 3).*

At 101.6 *m.* is the junction with an improved road.

Right on this road to the junction with another improved road, 3 *m.;* L. on this road is SALEMSBORG, 9 *m.* (1,500 alt., 14 pop.). Religious center of a Swedish farming community, this tiny crossroads settlement is dominated by the twin-towered Gothic SALEMSBORG LUTHERAN CHURCH, built in the 1920's of brick with limestone trim.

As originally planned, the church was to have one tower and a single portal. A wealthy parishioner of the older generation insisted that the inscription above the portal be in "the founding language of the church," saying that he would make no contribution to the building fund otherwise. But the younger generation, less familiar with Swedish, were equally insistent on an English inscription. A compromise was finally reached when they agreed to build two towers, each with a portal —one inscribed in Swedish, the other in English.

On nights when services are held in Swedish, lights gleam on the "Swedish" tower. When services are in English, the other tower is lighted and its chimes peal the anthems.

At 112.6 *m.* is the junction with an improved road.

Right on this road to CORONADO HEIGHTS *(picnic tables, ovens)*, 2 *m.*, one of the Smoky Hill (or Spanish) Buttes, just west of the Smoky Hill River valley. Coronado is reputed to have camped here on his search for Quivira *(see HISTORY).* Fragments of Spanish chain mail have been found nearby.

The Heights are the southernmost of a series of rugged buttes that rear above the level lowlands and extend to the northwest. Three or four miles to the west an unbroken ridge of similar height roughly parallels their course. Two or three of the higher buttes resemble gigantic prairie dog mounds. To the northwest, across Dry Creek, appears SOLDIER CAP MOUND (alt., 1,576 ft.), named for its resemblance to the headwear of Civil War soldiers.

On the crest of the Heights, a fairly level table covered with prairie grass, soapweed, and sagebrush, is a shelter house of sandstone boulders designed like an old fort. It was erected in 1936 by WPA. A serpentine highway constructed as a WPA project leads to the top of the Heights. To the south the church spires of Lindsborg rise above the trees. Stretching away to the northwest is a rough pastureland of prairie grass and deeply eroded gullies. At night the lights of six towns are visible.

LINDSBORG, 116 *m.* (1,332 alt., 2,016 pop.) *(see LINDSBORG).*

Points of Interest: Bethany College, Birger Sandzen's Studio, Swedish Pavilion, and others.

Left from Lindsborg on a dirt road to SHARP'S CREEK, 6 *m.*, the site of several unusual paleontological discoveries, including the skull of a giant sloth, the skull of an elephant, and numerous fossils.

At 128 *m.* is the junction with an improved road.

Right on this road to a SHELTER BELT NURSERY, 0.8 *m.*, a 40-acre tract on which the Federal Government is raising trees to be planted as windbreaks on the plains.

McPHERSON, 130.2 *m.* (1,480 alt., 6,147 pop.) *(see Tour 4)*, is at the junction with US 50 N *(see Tour 4)*.

South of McPherson oil derricks mark the northern edge of the central Kansas oil fields. One in every ten residents in this section earns his living from the oil industry.

MOUNDRIDGE, 144.9 *m.* (1,480 alt., 870 pop.), is at the junction with an improved road.

Right from Moundridge on this road to a SINK HOLE, 12 *m.*, as large as a city block. The depth of this water hole has never been determined (1938).

South of Moundridge the soil is a rich sandy loam, black and heavy in the river bottoms. The gently rolling country is watered by numerous streams. This region was settled largely by Mennonites *(see Tour 4)*, who left their homes in southern Russia in the middle 1870's to take up lands in central Kansas.

HESSTON, 152.4 *m.* (1,477 alt., 526 pop.), grew up on the homestead of Amos and A. L. Hess after the Missouri Pacific R.R. had been built through the territory in 1886.

HESSTON COLLEGE AND BIBLE SCHOOL (co-educational), a junior college with an enrollment of 160 (1938), was founded in 1908 by the Mennonite Church. The original college building, a frame structure built in 1909, is now used as a dormitory. A brick building completed in 1918 contains the present classrooms and administrative offices. From 1918 to 1927 the institution offered a four-year curriculum leading to the A.B. degree; lack of funds in recent years has made it necessary to discontinue many courses.

NEWTON, 160 *m.* (1,439 alt., 11,032 pop.) *(see NEWTON)*.

Points of Interest: Railroad shops, flour mills, Bethel College, and others.

Newton is at the junction with US 50 S *(see Tour 4A)*.

South of Newton bristling oil derricks and broad wheatfields, many a mile square, mark the level landscape.

The G. A. STEARNS BREEDING AND TRAINING FARM for harness horses, 172 *m.* (R), has a half-mile track. Every year during the first week of July, races sponsored by the Midwest Horse Racing Association are held here under floodlights.

At 174 *m.* is the junction with a paved road.

Right on this road is VALLEY CENTER, 2 *m.* (1,346 alt., 896 pop.); L. from Valley Center on a dirt road to CAMP BIDE-A-WEE, 4 *m.*, in an attractive wooded spot along the Little Arkansas River. The camp has a spacious lodge and is maintained by the Y.W.C.A. for the use of Camp Fire Girls, Girl Scouts, 4-H clubs, and conference groups of young people.

At 177 *m.* is the junction with an improved road.

Right on this road to the marked SITE OF THE LITTLE RIVER PEACE TREATY, 1 *m.*, concluded in 1865 between the United States Government and the Plains tribes. The valley at the time was inhabited by approximately 1,500 Indians, scattered between the mouth of Little River (in the present city of Wichita) and its source in central Kansas. The Government opened the valley to settlement by agreeing to pay the Indians seven cents an acre for their land and to transport them to Indian Territory. Black Kettle, later killed by Custer's men in the Battle of Washita, took a leading role in the negotiations. As early as 1601, Juan de Onate, Spanish explorer, found a settlement containing more than 1,200 lodges along the river here.

Traffic over US 81 between this point and Wichita is the heaviest in the State.

WICHITA, 185.5 *m.* (1,360 alt., 111,110 pop.) *(see WICHITA).*

Points of Interest: Wichita Art Museum, Sim Memorial Park, Municipal University, Friends University, United States Veterans Facility, and others.

Wichita is at the junction with US 54 *(see Tour 5).*

Between Wichita and the Oklahoma Line the highway follows in general the route of the old Chisholm Cattle Trail, celebrated in cowboy song and story. The exact route of the entire trail cannot be established, but traces of it occur along the way in the form of troughs winding across the country. Worn down by the hoofs of millions of half-wild Texas cattle driven along it to the railheads in Kansas, the trail was a bare, brown, dusty strip hundreds of miles long, lined with the bleaching bones of longhorns and cow ponies. Here and there a broken-down chuck wagon or a small mound marking the grave of some cowhand buried by his partners "on the lone prairie" gave evidence to the hardships of the journey.

By 1868 several cattle trails were well defined; they often followed older trails used by the great migratory herds of buffalo. The most renowned was first used by and later named for Jesse Chisholm (1806–1868), a half-breed Indian engaged in driving cattle through Indian Territory to frontier army posts. Chisholm, a scout, interpreter and trader, rescued from the Indians nine children whom he raised as members of his own family. He was reputed to speak fourteen Indian languages. In 1867 the trail ran as far north as Abilene *(see Tour 3),* the nearest railhead. With the building of the Santa Fe into Newton in 1871, that town became the terminus of the trail. The next year the railhead moved farther south to Wichita, which soon became a roaring cow town. But Wichita and Newton subsequently were cut off from their source of supply, for settlers rapidly took up land and fenced their farms. By 1880 the Chisholm Trail was closed to all but small herds, and the great cattle drives were diverted to Great Bend, Hays, Dodge City, and other towns to the west.

Cattle trails were necessarily wide, for herds had to be grazed along the way. When the annual drive was on, with some 300,000 head of cattle being moved to the railroad for shipment to market, it was often difficult for drovers in the rear to find pasturage without wandering far afield.

ALONG THE CHISHOLM TRAIL

The cattle were driven along the trail in herds of 2,500 to 3,000, usually under the command of a drover who had contracted with one or more ranchers to move their cattle to the railhead. An average-sized herd taxed to the utmost the skill, patience, and endurance of a trail crew composed of the drover, ten or twelve experienced cowhands, and a horse wrangler or two. Another member of the crew was the cook, known to the others as "the old woman," although his colorful and forceful speech was scarcely in character, especially when trying to persuade dead-tired cowboys to get up for breakfast at daybreak.

After breakfast the wranglers rounded up and brought in the "cavvie yard" or "remuda," as the herd of cow ponies was called. The cavvie yard consisted of 50 to 100 horses, for each cowboy had from five to eight mounts. He used his best pony—one that was gentle, sure-footed, and not easily excited—for night herding. He rotated the others in his "string," changing mounts twice a day.

The order of march was almost military; every man had his appointed station. The two most experienced cowhands rode at the front, one on each side, and pointed the herd. Other punchers rode behind them at regular intervals. The rear was brought up by green hands who were given the disagreeable and exhausting job of prodding along the "drags" —animals that could not keep pace because they were weak, footsore, or lame. A herd on the march would usually string out along the trail for a mile or two. A drive of 12 to 15 miles was a good day's work.

Late in the afternoon the drover or trail boss rode ahead, with the chuck wagon and cavvie yard behind him, to find a suitable camping ground for the night. As soon as one had been found, the cook, who had to know how to skin mules as well as flip a flapjack, unhitched his team, hobbled them and began preparations for supper. As half the crew ate, the other half tended the cattle. At dusk all helped to bed the herd, driving it into as small a space as possible by riding around and around it. Two cowboys were always on duty throughout the night, being relieved at appointed intervals. Those on guard circled the lowing cattle in opposite directions, occasionally soothing the restless or frightened animals by singing to them.

Before lying down on the prairie for the night, and wrapping himself up in blankets, every cowhand saddled and bridled his night horse, and either picketed him close by or went to sleep with the reins in his hand, so that he might be up and in his saddle instantly in case of a stampede. Stampedes were frequent, especially on stormy nights with heavy thunder and lightning. With the roar of a Niagara the herd would be off across the prairie, with all hands trying to reach the leaders and turn them until they came around in a large circle. Gradually the cattle were forced to mill in a smaller circle, and when the herd had at last been calmed it was carefully guarded on the spot for the remainder of the night. Next morning here was always a wide search for "strays," which sometimes were found as far as 40 miles off. Some drovers and trail bosses kept logs of their journeys, like the masters of whaling ships, and these prairie logs contain many passages such as this:

June 1   Stampede last night among 6 droves & a general mix up and loss of Beeves. Hunt Cattle again. Men all tired and want to leave. . . . Spent the day in separating Beeves & Hunting—Two men and Bunch Beeves lost—Many Men in trouble. Horses all give out & Men refused to do anything.

2nd. Hard rain & wind Storm   Beeves ran & had to be on Horse back all night. Awful night. wet all night   clear bright morning. Men still lost quit the Beeves & go to Hunting Men is the word—4 P.M. Found our men with Indian guide & 195 Beeves 14 miles from camp. Allmost starved not having a bite to eat for 60 hours   got to the camp about 12 M *Tired.*

On reaching Wichita, Dodge City, or other cow towns the herds were usually put out to pasture on the prairie in the environs and allowed to fatten on the juicy Kansas grasses before being sold. Although it was said of Texas cattle that they were tough to handle but tougher to eat, drovers usually found a ready market. Sometimes they sold their herds to local speculators or to agents sent out by slaughtering houses in the East. Occasionally the drover shipped the cattle on his own account, but all preferred to sell to Indian agents who were always in the market. Some 40,000 head of cattle were sold in 1874 to feed the Indians on the upper Missouri, according to Joseph G. McCoy, founder of Abilene, who explained why

CHANGING GUARD, A ROUND-UP SCENE IN THE 1890's

drovers and trail bosses eagerly sought such sales. The gross weight of the herd almost invariably fell below the net weight paid for. Herds bought one day would be stolen or mysteriously stampeded that night and be sold again to the same or another Indian agent the next day.

At 206.5 *m.* on US 81 is the junction with State 55, paved.

Left on State 55 to BELLE PLAINE, 3 *m.* (1,217 alt., 825 pop.), on the outskirts of which is the BARTLETT ARBORETUM *(small fee during tulip season, other times free),* consisting of 16 acres planted with more than 4,000 varieties of trees, shrubs, and plants. Thousands of visitors come to the arboretum every year, particularly in April when 200,000 tulips of every shade and hue are in bloom. Wild fowl nest along the banks of the stream that winds through the grounds. The arboretum—the result of 25 years of planning by Dr. W. E. Bartlett (1872–1937) —has an English rock garden, a Rocky Mountain section, a cactus section, a wild woods section, and a Japanese section. The "Primrose Path" leads past the "Wayside Cross," a towering rock, surrounded by all the varieties of trees native to the Holy Land that will grow here. The churches of the town unite on Easter morning for a sunrise prayer service at the foot of this rock.

WELLINGTON, 218 *m.* (1,189 alt., 7,405 pop.), seat of Sumner County, an old-fashioned plains town gradually assuming a modern aspect, lies along the valley of Slate Creek. Its low buildings and broad streets accentuate its spaciousness. Long a trading and railroad center, Wellington hummed with increased activity in the early 1930's with the development of oil fields in the vicinity. Sumner County produced 3,230,779 barrels of oil in 1936, placing it high among the production areas in Kansas.

Travelers along the Chisholm Trail often paused to rest their teams here in the valley of Slate Creek; many were so impressed by the beauty of the undulating prairie that they stayed and made their homes along its banks. Founded in 1871, Wellington had a strong rival for a time in Sumner City, a few miles to the northwest and already an important trail station for the wagon trains bound south from Wichita and the great cattle drives coming north from Texas.

Coveting this trade, the promoters of Wellington went to a point on the Chisholm Trail south of both towns and plowed a furrow through the turf to mark a new route for the trail. This furrow swung wide of Sumner City, passed through Wellington, and then arched back to the old trail. Wellington men then stationed themselves at the State line, and, when herdsmen inquired the way to Wichita, advised them to "follow the furrow." Thus Wellington prospered and became the county seat.

Together with other towns in southwestern Kansas, Wellington experienced a boom in the late 1880's; real estate was bought and sold at fabulous prices; the town claimed a population of 10,000. In 1892 a tornado struck here, doing great damage and killing a dozen persons. Although the general depression of the early 1890's was accompanied by an almost complete failure of crops in the region around Wellington, the town's banks endured the financial panic of 1893 without a failure, while scores of banks in more prosperous Kansas communities closed their doors.

Six blocks east of the business district on Harvey Ave. is COMMUNITY PARK *(playgrounds, tennis courts, croquet grounds, horseshoe courts, baseball and football fields, swimming pool),* an attractively landscaped 10-acre tract. At the western edge of town on US 160 is 160-acre ROOSEVELT PARK *(golf course, swimming pool, and playgrounds).*

Wellington is at the junction with US 160 *(see Tour 6).*

SOUTH HAVEN, 233.4 *m.* (1,218 alt., 442 pop.), surrounded by large fields of wheat, corn, and alfalfa, enjoyed a brief season of prosperity in September 1893 when hundreds of settlers came into the Cherokee Strip; thousands camped in or near the town while waiting for the free lands to be thrown open as homesteads.

South Haven is at the junction with US 166 *(see Tour 7).*

DRURY, 238.2 *m.* (1,084 alt., 50 pop.), has a WATER POWER GRISTMILL *(open on application),* one of the few still operating in Kansas. Built in 1882, this large weather-beaten wooden structure with a lower story of stone stands (L) near the highway on the western outskirts of town, just south of a dam on the Chikaskia River. Opposite the mill on the north side of the river is a small summer resort *(fishing, swimming, boating, dancing).*

CALDWELL, 245.7 *m.* (1,107 alt., 2,046 pop.), a substantial town named for Senator Alexander Caldwell of Leavenworth, draws trade from both Kansas and Oklahoma. Surrounded by scattered oil wells, it lies on an almost treeless plain.

Caldwell's first building was a weathered shack that had traveled far and wide over Sedgwick County. In the 1870's it stood on the Chisholm Trail and served as a saloon. As the last place where liquor could be bought on the road into Indian Territory, and as the first oasis for thirsty teamsters coming from the south. it was always crowded. In front hung a weather-beaten sign, with the name Last Chance Saloon painted on one side, and First Chance Saloon on the other.

Capt. Charles H. Stone, a member of the town company, built Caldwell's first store in 1871; on its opening day $711 worth of goods was sold over the counter. Many transactions were in gold coin.

The town grew slowly as the railheads for shipping Texas cattle moved southward from Abilene, first to Newton, then to Wichita. In 1880 the Santa Fe built a branch line from Wichita to Caldwell, and the settlement suddenly boomed. Caldwell was known as the "Border Queen" until 1889, when the Rock Island built south into Oklahoma. The booted, spurred, sombreroed cowboy, with money in pocket and a gun on hip, was king in the saloons and gambling houses, where many a minor disagreement ended in a burst of gunfire.

In those years great herds of cattle were loaded along a railroad spur just south of the town. Dust rose in clouds as the animals milled in the roughly constructed pens; their bellowing and the shouts of cowboys could be heard on Main Street above the general hubbub.

In the late 1880's an endless stream of freighters and soldiers, bound for forts in Indian Territory and Texas, followed the cattle trail and usually stopped at Caldwell for food and supplies. One city marshal after another took over the hazardous task of enforcing law and order, but few succeeded in stopping more than the most heinous offenses. Like other southern Kansas towns Caldwell had its greatest period of growth in the late 1880's. Almost all of its present business buildings were erected between 1883 and 1888.

In 1893 President Cleveland issued a proclamation admitting homesteaders to the lands of the Cherokee immediately south of the town. Early in September 1893, thousands of covered wagons converged on Caldwell to await the opening of the Cherokee Strip at noon on September 16. Caldwell could lodge only a small number. Thousands slept in their wagons or on the open prairie, and cooked their meals over campfires. The town's water supply was soon exhausted; water for 15,000 "boomers" had to be hauled by tank wagon and railroad car from sources farther north. Men, women, and children packed Caldwell's streets from early morning until late at night; merchants sold their wares much faster than they could replenish them from the East.

With the firing of a gun the Cherokee Run started. Homeseekers raced across the line and over the hills to the south, and Caldwell's streets were suddenly deserted. Several hundred stragglers, either unsuccessful in staking claims or disappointed in the land they gained, returned to Caldwell in the following weeks, but few remained long.

CHISHOLM STREET, the first east of Main, is believed to have been a section of the Chisholm Trail. In the Caldwell Stock Exchange Bank is a pair of cattle horns with a spread of 7 feet 2 inches, brought from southern Texas during the days of the great cattle drives.

On LOOKOUT MOUNTAIN, a red sandstone bluff frowning on Caldwell from near the Oklahoma Line, Coronado is said to have camped. On the crest of the bluff is the grave of a young Texas cowboy who met death in the Last (and First) Chance Saloon. He was buried here by a partner who would not allow him to rest in soil made odious to the South by association with John Brown.

At 248.1 *m.* US 81 crosses the Oklahoma Line, 51 miles north of Enid, Okla. *(see OKLA., Tour 11).* On the Line, about 300 yards (L) from US 81, a trough about 60 yards wide marks the place where the old Chisholm Trail crossed into Kansas from Indian Territory.

◄◄◄◄◄◄◄◄◄◄◄◄◄◄◄◄◄◄◄◄◄◄☿►►►►►►►►►►►►►►►►►►►►►

Tour 10

(Lincoln, Nebr.)—Marysville—Junction City—Eldorado—Arkansas City —(Oklahoma City, Okla.); US 77.
Nebraska Line to Oklahoma Line, 252.3 m.

Union Pacific R.R. parallels route between Nebraska Line and Randolph; Chicago, Rock Island & Pacific Ry. between Woodbine and Marion; `Atchison, Topeka & Santa Fe Ry. between Marion and Arkansas City.
Hotels and tourist accommodations in all larger towns.
Paved roadbed most of route, graveled for few short stretches; open all year.

US 77, following a somewhat irregular route, traverses rolling upland country in the northern part of the State and a region of broad level fields interspersed with thickly timbered ravines and low limestone ridges near Junction City.

South of Junction City it enters the Flint Hills, great ridges with gently sloping, grassy sides. Near Eldorado US 77 passes through a portion of the central Kansas oil fields and then descends gradually through a diversified farming country to the Arkansas River Valley and the Oklahoma Line.

US 77 crosses the Nebraska Line, 0 *m.,* 65 miles south of Lincoln, Nebr. *(see NEBR., Tour 2).*

MARYSVILLE, 13.2 *m.* (1,154 alt., 4,013 pop.), seat of Marshall County, was named for Mrs. Mary Marshall, wife of Frank J. Marshall, pioneer merchant, operator of Marshall's Ferry on the Blue River here, and proslavery candidate for Governor in 1857.

This region, now a prosperous grain, stock-raising and dairying area, was explored by the Fremont expedition in 1842, and settled largely by adventurers following a feeder of the Oregon Trail, which crossed the Blue here.

Richard F. Burton, journeying over the trail in 1860, recorded:

"Passing by Marysville . . . a county town which thrives by selling whisky to ruffians of all descriptions, we forded before sunset the 'Big Blue' a well-known tributary of the Kansas River. It is a pretty little stream, brisk and clear as crystal, about forty or fifty yards wide by two and a half feet deep at the ford. The soil is sandy and solid, but the banks are too precipitous to be pleasant when a very drunken driver hangs on by the lines of four very weary mules."

Of the vehicle he wrote:

"The mail is carried by a Concord Coach, a spring wagon . . . built to combine safety, strength, and lightness, without the slightest regard to appearances. The material is well-seasoned white oak . . . the color is sometimes green, more usually red, causing the antelopes to stand and stretch their large eyes whenever the vehicle comes in sight. . . . The whole bed is covered with stout osnaburg supported by stiff bars of whiteoak; there is a sun-shade or hood in front, where the driver sits, a curtain behind which can be raised or lowered at discretion, and four flaps on each side, either folded up or fastened down with hooks and eyes. . . . In front sits the driver, with usually a conductor or passenger by his side; a variety of packages, large and small, is stored away under his leather cushion . . . and in hot weather a bucket for watering the animals hangs over one of the lamps, whose companion is usually found wanting. The inside has either two or three benches fronting to the fore or placed vis-a-vis; they are movable and reversible, with leather cushions, and hinged padded backs; unstrapped and turned down, they convert the vehicle into a tolerable bed for two persons or two and a half. According to Cocker, the mail-bags should be safely stowed away under these seats, or if there be not room enough the passengers should perch themselves upon the correspondence; the jolly driver, however, is usually induced to cram the light literature between the wagon bed and the platform, or running-gear beneath, and thus, when ford-waters wash the hubs, the letters are pretty certain to endure ablution. . . ."

A forerunner of the 1938 pageboy bob is included in Burton's picture of the "ripper," or driver who ". . . emulates St. Anthony and the American aborigines in the length of his locks, whose ends are curled inward, with a fascinating sausage-like roll not unlike the Cockney 'aggrawator.' If a young hand, he is probably in the buckskin mania, which may pass into the squaw mania, a disease which knows no cure; the symptoms are, a leather coat and overalls to match, embroidered if possible, and finished along the arms and legs with fringes cut as long as possible, while a pair of gaudy moccasins, resplendent with red and blue porcelain beads, fits his feet tightly as silken hose. I have heard of coats worth $250, vest $100, and pants $150; indeed, the poorest of buckskin suits will cost $75, and if hard-worked it must be renewed every six months. The successful miner or gambler . . . will add $10 gold buttons to the attractions of his attire. The older hand prefers . . . a 'wamba' or roundabout, a red or rainbow-colored flannel over a check cotton shirt . . . when in riding gear, he wraps below each knee a fold of deer, antelope or cow skin, with edges scalloped where they fall over the feet, and gartered tightly against thorns and stirrup thongs. . . . Those who suffer from sore eyes wear huge green goggles, which give a crab-like air to the physiognomy, and those who cannot procure them line the circumorbital region with lampblack, which is supposed to act like the surma or kohl of the Orient. A broad leather belt supports on the right a revolver, generally Colt's Navy of medium size (when Indian fighting is expected, the large dragoon pistol is universally preferred), and on the left, in a plain black sheath, or sometimes in the more ornamental Spanish scabbard, is a buck-horn or ivory-handled bowie-knife. . . .

"If he trudges along an ox-team, he is a grim and surly man, who delights to startle your animals with a whip-crack, and disdains to return a salutation; if his charge be a muleteer's, you may expect more urbanity; he is then in the 'upper-crust' of teamsters; he knows it and demeans himself accordingly. He can do nothing without whisky, which he loves to call tarantula juice, strychnine, red-eye, corn juice, Jersey lightning, leg-stretcher, tangle-leg and many other hard and grotesque names; he chews tobacco like a horse, he becomes heavier on the shoulder or on the shyoot as, with the course of empire, he makes his way westward; and he frequently indulges in a spree which in these lands means four acts of drinking-bout, with a fifth of rough-and-tumble. Briefly, he is a post-wagon driver exaggerated."

A PONY EXPRESS STATION, 108 S. 8th St., is marked by a stone building that was used as a barn but is now (1938) remodeled and occupied by a produce company.

In the CITY PARK *(tennis courts, playgrounds, picnic grounds; weekly band concerts in summer)*, on US 77 at the south edge of town, is an Oregon Trail Marker.

Marysville is at the junction with US 36 *(see Tour 1)*.

Fossils of prehistoric animals, plants, and shell fish found in the limestone deposits around Marysville include a petrified tooth eight feet long, discovered in the Blue River just south of town. Sapphires, topazes, opals, agates, and jasper have also been found along the sand bars of the Blue River, though not in large enough quantities to make mining profitable.

At 19.2 *m.* (L) is the junction with an unimproved byroad which leads through a barbwire gate.

Left on this road, through a cow pasture and into a ravine, to ALCOVE SPRINGS, 1 *m.,* an overhanging shelf of rock in the bed of an usually dry brook that becomes a splashing waterfall after a heavy rain. An unfailing spring, below the rock shelf on the opposite hillside, flows at the rate of more than 500 gallons a minute, and forms a pool that is green, in summer, with watercress. The water flowing down the ravine fills wider pools where cattle drink, but in dry seasons sinks into the ground before it reaches the Blue River, about a quarter of a mile away. Alcove Springs was used as a camping place by travelers on the Oregon Trail.

On a grassy hill behind the springs a crude headstone marks the GRAVE OF MRS. SARAH KEYES, a member of the ill-fated Donner party. "Grandma" Keyes died and was buried here in May 1846, while the emigrants—over 90 persons traveling in 46 wagons—camped here. In October of that year the party became snowbound in the Sierra Nevadas where many of them died and the survivors subsisted on human flesh until their rescue the following April.

BLUE RAPIDS, 24.9 *m.* (1, 177 alt., 1,465 pop.), has a flour mill and a mill that ships gypsum, used in the manufacture of cement and plaster, to many points in the United States.

On the north edge of WATERVILLE, 30 *m.* (1,105 alt., 698 pop.), is IDLEWOOD STATE PARK *(picnic and playgrounds)*, with a small lake used only as a reservoir.

Right from Waterville on a dirt road to CAMP STEELWAY *(open)*, 6 *m.*, a favorite picnic spot. Indian relics found nearby have convinced some authorities that a form of civilization existed in this region several centuries ago.

At 57.3 *m.* is the northern junction with US 24 *(see Tour 2)*. Between this point and RILEY, 61.3 *m.* (1,108 alt., 431 pop.) US 77 and US 24 are one route.

JUNCTION CITY, 81 *m.* (1,077 alt., 7,407 pop.) *(see Tour 3)*, is at the junction with US 40 *(see Tour 3)*. Between this place and a point at 83 *m.* US 40 and US 77 are one route.

LOGAN GROVE (L), 82.6 *m.*, an attractive bit of timberland, is believed locally to be the site of one of the prehistoric Indian villages within the Quivira country explored by Coronado in 1541.

The STATUE OF AN INDIAN (L), 83.3 *m.*, scanning the eastern horizon, marks the burial place of some unusually large human bones found in 1884. It is said that one of the skulls, much larger than the average, contained back teeth three-fourths of an inch across. From the size of the bones it is estimated that one of the Indians was 6 feet 8 inches tall, the height of this concrete figure designed by C. G. Smith. In 1930 Potawatomi from the reservation near Mayetta *(see Tour 11)*, using the Indian tongue, dedicated it to the Four Winds.

HERINGTON, 110.5 *m.* (1,324 alt., 4,159 pop.), a railroad division point, serves as a shipping and shopping center for the surrounding farming and stock-raising area. Monroe D. Herington laid out the town early in the 1880's on 40 acres of his 2,000-acre ranch. By giving away land for homesteads and a right-of-way, he induced settlers and a railroad to come to his town.

The HERINGTON RANCH HOUSE *(private)*, 215 W. Main St., a low rambling frame structure topped with a belfry and surrounded by evergreens, was built in 1871 by the son of a wealthy Swiss family and purchased by Herington in 1880.

In the CITY PARK *(swimming pool)* is a tall sandstone shaft erected in 1904 as a MONUMENT TO FATHER PADILLA, the soldier-priest who explored this region with Coronado in 1541, and who, some believe, after returning in 1542, was slain by the tribe he sought to convert.

At Herington is the junction with US 50 N *(see Tour 4)*. Between this point and Marion, US 50 N and US 77 are one route.

At 119.9 *m.* is the junction with a graded road.

Right on this road to LOST SPRINGS, 1 *m.* (1,479 alt., 265 pop.), made conspicuous on an almost treeless prairie by a few oil wells—remnants of a boom in the early 1930's. In the city park is a Santa Fe Trail marker and adjacent to the depot is an old settlers' monument.

At 2.5 *m.* on this road, surrounded by huge old trees, is the spring about which the town was built. According to legend, the Kansa (Kaw) called the spring Nee-nee-oke-pi-yah, meaning *lost water,* and the Spaniards referred to it as Agua Perdida, which means the same thing. Some say the spring was destroyed by the Indians to discourage white settlement; others assert that a saloonkeeper destroyed it as an undesirable competitor. It is probable, however, that the town's name refers to the waters of the springs that disappear after flowing a short distance.

A marker designates the site of an old Army Post that was maintained on the Santa Fe Trail for protection against Indians. Close by was a trading post operated by Jack Costello, owner of the Lost Springs Ranch. Costello, a New Mexico cowboy, saddled his horse after the spring roundup in 1866 and started for Kansas City with a year's accumulated wages in his poke. It was Costello's intention to spend every penny in Kansas City saloons and dance halls. He stopped at Lost Springs Ranch, however, drank copiously at the trading-post bar, then sat down to a poker game. The next morning he awoke with a headache and a very hazy recollection of the previous night's play. As he was saddling his pony preparatory to resuming the journey to Kansas City, the proprietor came out and inquired, "Well, what are you going to do with the ranch?" Informed that he had won the ranch in the poker game, the amazed cowpuncher unpacked his blanket roll and moved in. He operated the ranch and trading post until 1868 when he sold the property and moved to Marion.

LINCOLNVILLE, 124.5 *m.* (1,423 alt., 270 pop.), founded as Peabody in the late 1860's on a site just west of the present Rock Island Ry. tracks, was an old Kansa (Kaw) trail. The establishment of the Lincolnville post office east of the tracks a few years later, caused such resentment that the office was moved from one side of the tracks to the other many times before the town was incorporated under the name of Lincolnville in 1910.

MARION, 136.9 *m.* (1,310 alt., 1,959 pop.), seat of Marion County, named for Revolutionary Gen. Francis Marion of South Carolina, is on the north bank of the Cottonwood River at its confluence with Mud Creek. It is a shipping point for the produce of the fertile river valley.

Marion was settled in 1860 by five Free-State families who moved to Kansas from Indiana because the proslavery environment in the latter State was offensive to them.

In the town's 20-acre CITY PARK *(playground and tennis courts),* a grassy shady site of natural timberland, the annual Marion County Fair is held (Oct.).

At 148.7 *m.* is the junction with US 50 S *(see Tour 4A)* which unites with US 77 into Florence.

FLORENCE, 149.9 *m.* (1,262 alt., 1,493 pop.), at the junction of Doyle Creek and the Cottonwood River, was platted in 1870 and named for Florence Crawford, daughter of S. J. Crawford, Governor of Kansas (1865–1868), and the wife of Arthur Capper, Governor (1915–1919).

Because of its hilly, protected site an Indian squaw predicted that no severe windstorm or tornado would ever damage Florence. None ever has (1938). Around Florence are stone quarries which have supplied the material for many of the town's buildings.

Oil wells visible along the highway south of Florence mark the northern edge of the central Kansas oil fields.

ELDORADO, 183.5 *m.* (1,285 alt., 10,311 pop.) *(see Tour 5),* is at the junction with US 54 *(see Tour 5).* Between this point and AUGUSTA, 200.8 *m.* (1,214 alt., 4,033 pop.) *(see Tour 5),* US 54 and US 77 are one route *(see Tour 5).*

WINFIELD, 233.3 *m.* (1,114 alt., 9,398 pop.), the modern-looking seat of Cowley County, serves as an arts center for smaller communities within a radius of 25 miles. It was founded by a townsite company organized in 1870 on land leased from Chief Chetopah for six dollars, and named for Winfield Scott, not the general who was commander in chief of the U. S. Army (1841–61) but a Civil War officer and Baptist missionary, who built the first church on the townsite. Incorporated in 1873, early in the 1880's it had a population of more than 2,000.

Winfield manufactures burners for natural gas and water coolers for oil fields, and ships wheat, corn, kafirs, sorgos, and alfalfa produced in the surrounding country. Old-timers remember its Chautauqua, one of the earliest in the State and in size second only to the mother Chautauqua in New York.

Winfield residents, the descendants of Germans and pioneer Americans, pay low taxes because the city receives income from municipally owned gas wells and a light and water plant. The 1938 levy was the second lowest in the State for cities of the second class. The sociology department of the University of Kansas recently (1938) decided that Winfield has the best environment in the State for rearing a family.

In the WINFIELD HIGH SCHOOL, 500 E. 9th Ave., are a number of original paintings, water colors, and lithographs, part of a definite program of acquisition.

The Cowley County Fair and the Winfield Race Meet are held here annually (*Aug.*).

ST. JOHN'S COLLEGE, NW. corner 7th Ave. and College St., housed in five buildings on a landscaped 8-acre campus, was founded in 1893 by John P. Baden to provide training for Lutheran ministers and for young people of both sexes. It is now a high school and junior college with an enrollment of 200. In the three-story ADMINISTRATION BUILDING, built of local limestone in collegiate Gothic style, is the HISTORICAL MUSEUM *(open during school hours)*. Its 5-acre athletic field, east of College St., is in an oil-producing area.

SOUTHWESTERN COLLEGE, NE. corner College St. and Warren Ave. (co-educational), founded in 1885, is maintained by the Kansas Conference of the Methodist Episcopal Church.

RICHARDSON HALL, completed in 1910, a three-story stone structure, with an imposing Ionic portico, is on the crest of a rocky hill. The college sponsors loan exhibitions of paintings and other objects of art and each spring presents Mendelssohn's oratorio *Elijah* with a chorus of 400 voices and a 60-piece orchestra.

Southwestern offers a course in art appreciation and confers degrees in liberal arts, fine arts, and science; the annual enrollment is approximately 500.

Oil wells on the campus contribute to the college income.

The WINFIELD CARNEGIE LIBRARY, SW. corner 10th and Millington Sts., a two-story red brick structure, contains 14,033 volumes (1938).

The KICKAPOO CORRAL, on the Walnut River at 19th St., a narrow strip of land in a hairpin bend of the stream, was once used by the

Kickapoo *(see Tour 11)* as a corral for their horses. At the entrance to the site is TUNNEL MILL, an abandoned gristmill built in pioneer days and so-called because a millrace tunneled under it. According to old accounts, the Kickapoo sought refuge in the corral from the Osage with whom they had broken a pledge of allegiance. The enraged Osage were unsuccessful in their attack until they crossed the river silently one stormy night and, taking their enemy by surprise, massacred the entire Kickapoo camp, with the exception of one man and one woman.

At the west end of Kickapoo Corral is the SITE OF KICKAPOO POND, the point where the Osage Trail crossed the Walnut River. Over the trail the tribe journeyed between their western hunting grounds and their villages along the Neosho, Verdigris, and Elk Rivers.

On the SITE OF CORONADO'S CAMP, at 8th St. and the Walnut River, now occupied by the Consolidated Flour Mills, it is believed the Spanish explorer and his band camped after crossing the Walnut River at Kickapoo Ford. A rusty piece of a sword and other broken implements of Spanish origin have been found on the site.

Winfield is at the junction with US 160 *(see Tour 6)*.

Left from Winfield on College St. is the STATE TRAINING SCHOOL *(grounds open; buildings open on application)*, 2.7 *m.*, for children and adults of subnormal mentality. On a 422-acre tract, the institution includes 13 major buildings, dairy and horse barns and poultry sheds. It was founded at Lawrence in 1881, moved to Winfield in 1883, and now (1938) houses approximately 1,200 inmates.

ARKANSAS CITY, 248.4 *m.* (1,075 alt., 13,946 pop.) *(see ARKANSAS CITY)*.

Points of Interest: Natural bridge, old Indian trails, Buffalo Bill Cody's campground, Arkansas City Fair.

Arkansas City is at the junction with US 166 *(see Tour 7)*.

The OKLAHOMA LINE, 252.3 *m.*, is marked by a granite MONUMENT TO THE HOMESTEADERS, 20,000 of whom started from this point in 1893 to settle in Oklahoma. US 77 crosses this line 131 miles north of Oklahoma City, Okla. *(see OKLA., Tour 10)*.

◄◄◄◄◄◄◄◄◄◄◄◄◄◄◄◄◄◄ ✿ ►►►►►►►►►►►►►►►►►►►

Tour 11

(Omaha, Nebr.)—Sabetha—Topeka—Yates Center—Independence—(Tulsa, Okla.); US 75.
Nebraska Line to Oklahoma Line, 233.9 m.

Chicago, Rock Island & Pacific Ry. parallels route between Holton and Topeka;
Missouri Pacific R.R. between Yates Center and Oklahoma Line.
Paved or graveled roadbed; open all year.
Adequate accommodations in all larger towns.

This route traverses two of the State's chief agricultural regions and, near the Oklahoma Line, crosses its earliest developed oil and gas belt.

US 75 crosses the Nebraska Line, 0 *m.*, 94 miles south of Omaha, Nebr., and traverses the orchard-clad hills of the Glacial Uplands between this point and Topeka.

SABETHA, 7 *m.* (1,300 alt., 2,332 pop.) *(see Tour 1)*, is at the junction with US 36 *(see Tour 1)*. Between this point and FAIRVIEW, 14.1 *m.* (1,240 alt., 367 pop.) *(see Tour 1)*, US 75 and US 36 are one route.

At 27.2 *m.* is the junction with a graded road.

Left on this road to the KICKAPOO RESERVATION (332 pop.), 0.5 *m.* In 1670 white men found the Kickapoo occupying lands near the Wisconsin and Fox Rivers. They lived on the Osage River in Missouri for some years, and then, by provision of the treaty of October 24, 1832, were assigned to a 76,537-acre reservation in Kansas. The present reservation consists of less than 6,500 acres.

Except when they participate in ancestral rituals—the New Year's Dance, Spring Dance, Corn Dance, and Harvest Dance *(1st week in Jan., Apr., July, and Oct. respectively)*—contemporary Kickapoo are not readily distinguished from the neighboring white farmers. The ceremonies are performed by men in native costumes on the TRIBAL DANCE GROUND *(visitors welcome; no noise or photographing during ceremonies)* near the entrance to the reservation. In inclement weather the ceremonies are held indoors. Most of the songs and symbolic dances were adopted by the Kickapoo from the Chippewa of Wisconsin. The drum, considered sacred, is always held so that it will face the rising sun.

Richard F. Burton found the Kickapoo living here in 1860 degraded by their association with white men. "They cultivate the soil," he wrote, "and rarely spend the winter in hunting buffalo upon the plains. Their reservation is twelve miles by twenty-four; as usual with land set apart for the savages, it is well watered and timbered, rich and fertile; it lies across the path and in the vicinity of civilization; consequently, the people are greatly demoralized. The men are addicted to intoxication, and the women to unchastity; both sexes and all ages are inveterate beggars, whose principal industry is horse-stealing. . . . They have well nigh cast off the Indian attire, and rejoice in the splendors of boiled and ruffled shirts, after the fashion of the whites. According to our host . . . when they first saw a crinoline, they pointed to the wearer and cried, 'There walks a wigwam.' "

Near NETAWAKA, 32.4 *m.* (1,149 alt., 229 pop.), a tiny village with a Lutheran parochial school, was a stage tavern on the route between Leavenworth and Topeka.

Of WALNUT CREEK, 38.6 *m.*, Burton wrote: "Our next obstacle was Walnut Creek, which we found, however, provided with a corduroy bridge; formerly it was a dangerous ford, rolling down heavy streams of melted snow, and then crossed by means of the 'bouco' or coracle, two hides sewed together, distended like a leather tub with willow rods, and poled or paddled. . . ."

Nearby is the SITE OF THE BATTLE OF THE SPURS. One of several accounts of this meeting relates that Deputy Marshal Wood, seeking the $3,000 reward for John Brown's capture, had pursued Brown and his party of about twenty fugitive slaves to this point.

High water in the creek caused Brown to halt at Fuller's cabin, about three miles north of Holton; when he learned that Wood had maneuvered into a position between him and the creek, he dispatched John Armstrong to Topeka for help. John Guthrie and sixteen men went to Brown's rescue.

"At four o'clock in the morning," Armstrong afterward wrote, "we were in Holton; and when we reached Dr. Fuller's cabin, Brown had the teams hitched and ready to go. Wood's party was some distance ahead and when we moved forward, they fell back to a stream known as Walnut or Straight Creek."

According to Guthrie, Wood had the larger party and "could have wiped us off the map." But neither side seemed eager to fight, for when Wood's men dug their spurs into their horses' flanks and galloped around the party on the east, Brown's men drove their wagons and horses into swollen Walnut Creek and scrambled up the north bank, heading for Nebraska. Hence the name, Battle of the Spurs.

In HOLTON, 42.5 m. (1,043 alt., 2,705 pop.), seat of Jackson County, is published the *Philatelic Weekly,* a stamp collectors' magazine.

Settled by Free-State men from Milwaukee, Holton in the 1850's and 1860's was a station on the Underground Railroad, then called Jim Lane's Trail. It is said that John Brown and Jim Lane escorted the first settlers to this site.

The SITE OF CAMPBELL UNIVERSITY, 9th and New York Sts., is now occupied by the Holton High School. The university was founded early in the 1880's and named for Allen Green Campbell, who donated the site and a substantial sum for an endowment. In 1903 the institution merged with Lane University, which was founded at Lecompton; in 1913 the school was moved to Kansas City.

The old bell mounted on a stone pedestal in front of the high school was used to summon Campbell University students to their classes.

At 50.1 m. is the junction with an improved road.

Right on this road to the 7,040-acre POTAWATOMI RESERVATION, 0.5 m. (1,013 pop.), the largest Indian reserve in Kansas. The tribe living here is called Potawatomi of the Prairie. They belong to the same linguistic stock as the Chippewa and the Ottawa who lived about the upper shores of Lake Huron. Their first agency was in western Missouri; thence they moved to Iowa; by treaty in 1837 they came to Kansas with the Chippewa, Ottawa, Potawatomi of the Wabash, and Potawatomi of Indiana. By 1862 most of the reservation land had been disposed of, but the Prairie band refused to accept land in severalty and were allowed to remain in Jackson County.

At 5 m. on this road is the 70-acre INDIAN FAIRGROUNDS. The Kack-Kack corporation, an Indian organization with 200 stockholders, sponsors the annual fair held here *(in July or Aug.; adm. 50¢)* to encourage the Indians in agricultural and craft pursuits. In addition to the exhibits of stock, preserves, rugs, homemade furniture, and fast horses, there are dances *(no photographing allowed during dances; tobacco and food welcomed by leader)* that attract hundreds of visitors. Performed around a slow-burning campfire, these include the ecstatic Dance of Victory and the solemn Dance of Death. Dressed in feather bonnets and beaded buckskin breechclouts, the Indians reproduce these ceremonials with great care. As in the Kickapoo ritual, the drums face the rising sun *(see INDIANS)*.

Unlike other Indians in Kansas, the Potawatomi have not lost all their identity through association with white men. Some of the elders refuse to give up their primitive mode of dress.

Although Kansas legalized the sale of 3.2 percent beer in 1937 by declaring it to be non-intoxicating, the Indian agents prohibited its sale to their wards. Tribal councils of the Sac, Fox, Iowa, and Kickapoo tribes voted to ask Congress to allow 3.2 percent beer on their reservations. The Potawatomi, however, asked and were permitted to refer the question to a popular vote. Only 103, of nearly 300 eligible, voted. A large majority of these were women. The sale of beer was defeated 80 to 23.

MAYETTA (L), 51.1 *m.* (1,189 alt., 294 pop.), a farmers' and Indians' trading center, is so close to Holton, the seat of Jackson County, that it has no need of a jail. Early in the 1900's, however, the citizens erected a little stone-and-concrete structure of one cell with a heavily barred window, and immediately sought and secured a prisoner—a tipsy squaw from the Potawatomi reservation. Next morning, when the constable brought breakfast to the squaw, he was dismayed to find her gone and a front wall of the jail wrecked. Days later a Potawatomi brave boasted that on hearing of the squaw's arrest he had tied his lariat to the bars of the cell window (which had not yet firmly set in the cement) and, mounting his pony, had pulled down the entire wall. Mayetta never attempted to have another jail.

At 70.3 *m.* is the junction with US 24 *(see Tour 3).*

TOPEKA, 73.2 *m.* (886 alt., 64,120 pop.) *(see TOPEKA).*

Points of Interest: Capitol building, Washburn College, Mulvane Art Museum, Kansas State Historical Library and Museum, Gage Park and Reinisch Rose Garden.

Topeka is at the junction with US 40 *(see Tour 3).*

South of Topeka the route is over the highland prairies of the Osage Plains—so named because they were inhabited by the Osage when white men first came to Kansas—following for a while the Cut-off Trail established by the United States Army as a link between the Oregon Trail in northern Kansas and the old Santa Fe Trail.

PAULINE, 79.2 *m.* (992 alt., 100 pop.), a trading point, is at the junction with an improved road.

Left on this road is LYONS CASTLE, 5 *m.,* built by Silas Lyons in the 1890's and occupied by him until his death a few years ago. Shaped like a cross, with stone walls and barred windows, the structure had a masonry well and several bake ovens in its center. According to legend, Lyons was preparing for the Armageddon which he thought would occur in the twentieth century.

At 91.5 *m.* is the junction with US 50 N *(see Tour 4).*

LYNDON, 102.2 *m.* (1,010 alt., 742 pop.), the seat of Osage County, was founded in 1869, just after most of the Sac and Fox had been removed to Oklahoma reservations. After the prosperity-bringing Santa Fe Ry. was routed through Osage City, Lyndon was able to survive on its county business and a small farm trade.

The modern limestone OSAGE COUNTY COURTHOUSE (L) on US 75 in the heart of town, contrasts sharply with the old business houses along Main Street.

Near Lyndon, certified seed corn is raised under the following conditions decreed by the Kansas Crop Improvement Association (organized in

1906 under the auspices of the State Agricultural College): (1) Varieties recommended by the State Experiment Stations must be planted. (2) The seed field must be 40 rods from any other corn field. (3) The field must be inspected by qualified inspectors from the Agricultural College. (4) The seed corn must be picked separately from other corn. (5) Seed must be inspected by authorized grain inspectors.

Between Lyndon and Burlington are larger pastures and fields of corn and hay. The latter, a native prairie grass once exported in great volume, is now used for feeding local dairy herds. This red sandy soil, unusual in eastern Kansas, was deposited by an ancient ocean.

At 117.8 m. is the junction with US 50 S *(see Tour 4A)*, which unites with US 75 for a few miles.

BURLINGTON, 135.6 m. (1,033 alt., 2,273 pop.), seat of Coffey County, is a prosperous-looking town centered around a courthouse and a long main street. Rock Creek, a tributary of the Neosho River, runs through the business district; in 1922 it overflowed and caused damage amounting to nearly $1,000,000. Since then the creek has been dredged out, straightened, and widened.

RUNT PARK *(open)*, one block north of the town's main street, occupies the back and side yard of a Burlington residence. In its center is a concrete figure of Runt, a diabetic dog once locally famous, in a characteristic pose at the corner of a miniature stone castle that is surrounded by a moat, a mirror lake, and concrete grotesqueries. King Alcohol, a concrete skeleton holding a whiskey bottle, and Eve, his first lady, being tempted by a wily concrete serpent, frown down upon Runt from behind.

This park was built by Marion Ellet "Most Easy" Budd, a printer employed by the Burlington *Republican* for many years before his death in 1934.

YATES CENTER, 166.7 m. (1,099 alt., 2,013 pop.) *(see Tour 5)*, is at the junction with US 54 *(see Tour 5)*.

South of Yates Center the series of low wooded hills is a spur of the Ozark Mountains.

At 168.9 m. (R) is the junction with an improved road.

Right on this road is the SITE OF SILVER CITY, 3 m. When, early in the 1850's, a substance found nearby was believed to be silver ore, hundreds of prospectors arrived. Mine shafts were sunk and promoters anticipated great wealth. Subsequent tests proved that the strata did not contain silver and the town faded away so completely that only the scars left on the hillside by the mine shafts now (1938) mark the spot.

BUFFALO, 171.1 m. (854 alt., 799 pop.), has one of the largest paving brick factories in the State. The plant also produces building tile.

At Buffalo is the junction with a dirt road.

Right on this road to the SITE OF OLD FORT BELMONT (R), 2 m., a military post and a stagecoach station until the middle 1860's. Near the site, though the exact spot is not known, are the graves of Hapo, Chief of the Osage, and his daughter who died while the tribe camped near the fort. Hapo, who fought for the North during the Civil War, journeyed to Leavenworth shortly after the Indian phase of the conflict had ended to seek President Lincoln's aid for his starving tribe. He died there before Lincoln could answer his request. Devoted tribesmen brought his body to lie here beside that of his daughter.

South of Buffalo many oil derricks are visible from the highway.

ALTOONA, 184.4 *m.* (878 alt., 839 pop.), a market town and shipping point on the Missouri Pacific R.R., is the home of General Mace Liverwurst, a Kansas Munchausen, whose adventures, reported in the weekly Altoona *Tribune,* by its editor, Austin V. Butcher, are widely quoted throughout eastern Kansas and western Missouri.

Right from Altoona on paved State 47 is FREDONIA, 10 *m.* (866 alt., 3,446 pop.), the seat of Wilson County. Fredonia was first called Twin Mounds for two rock-capped elevations that rise above the nearby valley of the Fall River. The present city, founded in 1868 and renamed for Fredonia, N. Y., won the county seat designation from Neodesha by allegedly voting many of the names on the tombstones in the village cemetery. Mail-order printing and the manufacture of cement, linseed oil, and brick and tile are the chief local industries. Fredonia has a $250,000 municipal light and power plant. It is the home town of Ben S. Paulen, ex-Governor of Kansas (1925–29); Thurlow Lieurance, Kansas composer and conductor *(see MUSIC),* also lived here.

NEODESHA (Ind., *meeting of the waters),* 194.8 *m.* (800 alt., 3,381 pop.), a refining center at the confluence of the Verdigris and Fall Rivers, is economically dependent on nearby oil fields that were opened in 1892. It is the home of a number of oilmen and retired farmers. Here in 1888 the reputed slayer of John Wilkes Booth, Sgt. Boston Corbett, was last seen a few days after he had escaped from the State Hospital for the insane at Topeka *(see TOPEKA).* The stolen pony on which he had fled was found in a local livery stable.

R. Thatcher, Neodesha superintendent of schools, had known Corbett when they both were confined at Andersonville prison during the Civil War. He wrote a letter to the Topeka *Capital,* three weeks after Corbett's escape, expressing indignation over the fact that Jefferson Davis was free while Lincoln's "avenger" was being hunted like a criminal. In the letter Thatcher admitted that Corbett had spent two nights in his home.

The WOODRING HOME *(private),* 1st and Wisconsin Sts., the home of Harry H. Woodring, ex-Governor of Kansas (1931–33) and Secretary of War in the second administration of President Franklin D. Roosevelt, is a two-story frame house with a spacious veranda. It is surrounded by a bluegrass lawn and shaded by large maple trees.

In 1933 Neodesha (Nee-o-desh-ay') was mispronounced by radio announcers throughout the country as they described to a shocked public the crash nearby of a plane carrying the Winnipeg Toilers, Canada's champion basketball team, who were returning home from a game with the Tulsa Oilers in Oklahoma. Six of the fourteen on board were killed instantly. The wreck occurred on March 31, the second anniversary of the air crash in which Knute Rockne was killed *(see Tour 4A).*

Right from Neodesha on a graveled road to LITTLE BEAR MOUND, 1 *m.,* and the GRAVE OF LITTLE BEAR *(see Tour 12),* the chief who led the Osage in the Rebel Creek Battle. This mound is a legendary Indian home, said by some of Neodesha's first settlers to have been occupied when they arrived here in the 1860's.

For years the Osage made pilgrimages to this mound and held ceremonies in memory of Little Bear. One year, old-timers say, they returned to find the grave open and the bones of the chief gone. Enraged, they began a war dance and were preparing to burn Neodesha when a doctor, taking a skeleton from his office, convinced the Indians that he had found the remains of their chief. What actually happened to Little Bear's bones is not known.

At 4.5 *m.* on the graveled road is DUNN DAM, a resort on the Fall River *(nominal rates; fishing, swimming, dance pavilion, outdoor fireplaces, bath houses, picnic tables).*

INDEPENDENCE, 210.3 *m.* (795 alt., 12,782 pop.), seat of Montgomery County, has a number of new store and office buildings, well-kept homes, broad lawns, and residential streets shaded by arched elms. The pioneer city of the southern Kansas oil fields, it is the headquarters of several nationally known oil companies and a group of independent concerns. Oil production in the Independence area reached more than 60,000 barrels in 1926, but the development of new fields here in the late 1930's may increase production.

Alfred M. Landon, independent oil operator, ex-Governor of Kansas (1933–1937), and Republican candidate for President in 1936, made his home in Independence until he was elected Governor. Independence was also the home of Martin Johnson (1895–1936) the explorer who, while operating a motion picture theater here, met and married Osa Leighty of Chanute. Together they produced motion pictures of explorations in Africa and elsewhere.

This area was formerly part of the Diminished Osage Reservation. In 1868 the Federal Government vetoed the Osage agreement to sell their 8 million acres to a railroad for less than twenty cents an acre. The transaction, if completed, would have been little short of outright theft.

In 1869 George A. Brown and a group from Oswego formed the Independent Town Company and obtained 640 acres from Chetopah, Chief of the Osage. On this they hurriedly constructed a cluster of huts by using poles and branches as framework, thatching this with hay, and weighing the structure to prevent it from being blown away. The settlement was nicknamed Haytown. In 1870 the entire Osage reservation was formally opened to settlers for $1.25 an acre. By the Drum Creek Treaty the Osage agreed to move to a reservation in Indian Territory (now Oklahoma), south of the Kansas Line.

Independence boomed after the discovery of natural gas here in 1881 and again in 1903 with the development of the first oil fields. By 1912 its population was more than 15,000, but the exhaustion of natural gas fields shortly afterward caused a decline.

Independence's RIVERSIDE PARK *(shelter houses, picnic conveniences, bathing beach, fishing pools),* is in the canyon-like valley of the Verdigris River.

"Neewollah" is celebrated annually *(Oct. 31)* in Independence with pageantry and mummery for the children, dances and a carnival for the adults.

At Independence is the junction with US 160 *(see Tour 6).* Between this point and 213.3 *m.* US 75 and US 160 are one route.

Near the Verdigris River, east of Independence, is the SITE OF THE REBEL CREEK BATTLE. On May 23, 1863, about 60 miles west of the Missouri Line, sixteen Confederate officers led by Col. Charles Harrison

A CCC CLASS, NEODESHA

and Col. Warner Lewis—a nephew of Meriwether Lewis of the Lewis and Clark expedition—were approached by a large band of Osage led by Chief Little Bear who asked their identity and the nature of their business. When the officers—who were on a recruiting trip for the Confederate Army and planned, according to some, to raid the gold camps in Colorado—spurred their horses, shots were exchanged. In the running fight that followed, an Indian and two officers were killed and Colonel Lewis was wounded.

At Rebel Creek, a tributary of the Verdigris, Capt. Park McClure, first postmaster of Denver, Colo., was knocked from his horse by an 18-year-old Osage medicine man, Gratah-noie. Colonel Harrison was shot and captured, and his heavy black beard "scalped" from his face.

The officers turned and raced for the Verdigris River, about a mile away. Unable to climb the steep bank on the opposite side they all turned downstream, except Colonel Lewis and John Rafferty who, under cover of the bank, crept upstream about a half mile and hid in the brush until nightfall. Without food and horses and in constant fear of capture, they made their way into Missouri. Soon after their arrival there Rafferty was killed, leaving Col. Warner Lewis as the sole Confederate survivor of the battle of Rebel Creek.

While Lewis and Rafferty were escaping, their comrades were pursued about 500 yards downstream to a sand bar, where they were all killed, scalped, and mutilated. The Osage reported the engagement to Major Doudna, in command of the Federal post at Humboldt. Taking a cavalry troop of fifty, he buried the dead Confederates on the sand bar. The bodies of Colonel Harrison and Captain McClure were interred where they had fallen at Rebel Creek.

Left from Independence on S. 10th St., a marked improved road, to the LEGION-VILLE PREVENTORIUM, 11 *m. (open on application),* maintained by the American Legion Auxiliary, the Kansas American Legion, and the Kansas Tuberculosis and Health Association to build up resistance in undernourished children against tuberculosis. The 388-acre farm, donated by Mr. and Mrs. D. A. Dabney as a memorial to their two sons, contains Legionville's three brick and stone buildings. In winter twenty children can be accommodated; in summer, fifty. They stay for periods of six weeks to three months.

When HAVANA, 229.6 *m.* (932 alt., 289 pop.), a hamlet of a few houses and two boxlike churches, was founded in 1869, its inhabitants proclaimed a ban against Negroes, planted cotton, and erected a cotton gin, which they claimed was "the northernmost cotton gin in the United States." Cotton raising soon proved a failure but Havana, now (1938) a farmers' trading village, still discriminates against the colored man; Negroes may purchase their supplies here but are warned not to remain overnight.

At 230.5 *m.* is the northern junction with US 166 *(see Tour 7).* Between this point and Caney US 75 and US 166 are one route.

Between Havana and Caney the route traverses a rolling, lightly wooded countryside from which the blue tops of timber-covered hills are visible in the distance (R). Large fields of sorghum lie adjacent to the highway.

In the early autumn, just before frost, the cane is cut and placed in mills. When horses, hitched to a long pole, are driven around the mill, its cylinders revolve, crushing the cane and allowing the juice to drain into tanks. The juice is then boiled down in great metal vats and converted into molasses. Skimmings are poured into barrels to mix with silage for cattle feed.

CANEY, 232.7 m. (737 alt., 2,794 pop.), a trim little town encircled by low wooded hills, was named for the canebrakes that grew nearby when the town was founded in 1871.

Long a trading point for Indian Territory (Oklahoma), Caney, like so many other towns in this region, experienced its first real boom early in the 1890's when the Mid-Continent oil fields were opened. By 1910 there were about 4,000 inhabitants. A subsequent slump in oil production caused the population to dwindle.

Caney was named in the headlines of the country's press in 1906 when a gas well at the outskirts of the town caught fire, and, despite the efforts of oil workers and engineers, burned continuously for six weeks. Railroads ran special trains from Chicago and New York City to accommodate those who wished to see the conflagration. According to residents of Caney a newspaper could be read by the light of the burning well eight miles away. The fire was finally smothered by a huge steel cap, constructed especially for that purpose.

At 233.9 m. US 75 crosses the Oklahoma Line, 78 miles north of Tulsa, Okla. (see OKLA., Tour 9).

◄◄◄◄◄◄◄◄◄◄◄◄◄◄◄◄◄◄◄☒►►►►►►►►►►►►►►►►►►►►►►

Tour 12

(St. Joseph, Mo.) — Atchison — Lawrence — Iola — Parsons — (Vinita, Okla.) ; US 59.
Missouri Line to Oklahoma Line, 232.5 m.

Atchison, Topeka & Santa Fe Ry. parallels route between Lawrence and Chanute; Missouri-Kansas-Texas R.R. between Chanute and Chetopa.
Paved roadbed entire route; open all year.
Adequate accommodations in all larger towns.

US 59 crosses the Missouri and Kansas Rivers in the north of the State, the Marais des Cygnes and Pottawatomie Rivers about midway, and crosses and recrosses the Neosho River three times near the State's southern border. The route is through wide valleys, interspersed with high rolling plateau land. The deep wooded ravines between Atchison and Garnett mark the real beginning of the prairie country. Eastward are the valleys of the Missouri, the Kansas, the Marais des Cygnes, the Neosho and other streams. Westward the terrain grows gradually more level until, in central Kansas, the actual prairie country begins.

US 59 crosses the Missouri River, 0 *m.*, the boundary between Missouri and Kansas, on the ATCHISON FREE BRIDGE, 23 miles southwest of St. Joseph, Mo. *(see MO., Tour 10A).* The bridge, a steel and concrete structure dedicated September 21, 1938, replaced the toll bridge constructed in 1875. Kansas and Missouri each paid one-fourth and the Federal Government one-half of the total construction cost of $650,000.

Steep wooded bluffs crowd close to the west bank and above the bridge the river makes a broad sweeping curve.

Atchison, 0.6 *m.* (795 alt., 13,024 pop.) *(see ATCHISON).*

Points of Interest: Rock Garden, Guerrier Hill, Lewis and Clark Monument, Lincoln Address Monument, St. Benedict's College, and others.

Atchison is at the junction with US 73 *(see Tour 12A).*

Right from Atchison on N. 3rd St. to the junction with a graveled road, 1.5 *m.*; R. on this road to INDEPENDENCE CREEK, 5.9 *m.* Nearby at the mouth of the stream, which has shifted its course in recent years, the Lewis and Clark expedition camped July 4, 1804, and named this creek in honor of the day. Their journal records that they dined on corn, fired a salute, and issued an extra gill of whiskey to each man. This was the first Fourth of July celebration in Kansas, fifty years before the Territory was organized *(see HISTORY).*

At 6.2 *m.* is DONIPHAN (866 alt., 140 pop.), remnant of a prosperous river town of the 1860's, grouped around a filling station and a general store. The town, named for Gen. Alexander Doniphan, Mexican War veteran, was platted in November 1854 by John and James Forman, Kentuckians, who joined a group of Missouri proslavery men in forming a town company.

In 1855 a band of fanatical abolitionists in Doniphan organized the Danite Society, a secret order that planned to murder every proslavery settler in the neighborhood. Pat Laughlin, a good-natured Irish tinsmith, joined the Danites, but, upon learning their purpose, publicly denounced them. Samuel Collins, Danite leader, angered by Laughlin's refusal to retract his charges, stabbed him with a hunting knife. Mike Lynch, a friend of the wounded man, shot and killed Collins. The Danites disbanded soon after the death of their leader.

Gen. James H. Lane and James Redpath, Free State leaders, founded the *Kansas Crusader of Freedom* at Doniphan in 1858. They later quarreled and publication was suspended.

Abraham Lincoln spoke briefly at Doniphan, December 2, 1859, when he stopped here on his way from Troy to Atchison.

Doniphan was Atchison's rival for the river trade in the 1860's and at one time had a population of 2,000, a steamboat landing, and a railroad. The bridging of the Missouri River at Atchison in 1875 gave that city rail connections with the East and hastened the decline of Doniphan. Its steamboat landing was soon deserted; the railroad was abandoned by the end of the century. Even the river has gradually shifted its channel eastward until Doniphan is now literally, as well as economically, stranded.

South and west of Atchison the road zigzags crazily and dips into each narrow valley only to climb still another hill. Slopes are steep and rocky, and ledges of yellow sandstone—their sharp contours softened in some places by overhanging moss and vines—line the creek banks. Most of the streams in this glacial terrain are narrow and trickle feebly through their spacious, rocky paths. Only after heavy rains do they flow bankfull.

Farmhouses in the region, many built in the 1890's, are frame structures adorned with cupolas and elaborate "gingerbread" work on eaves and porches. In the back yards, well platforms protected by canopies in the same ornate designs are visible from the roadside.

George Million, a Missourian who took a squatter's claim at the present site of Atchison in 1841, was the first white settler in this region. Million lived on the east bank of the river and made a living by cutting wood for the river steamers. In 1850 he began to operate a ferry near the townsite.

In 1844 Atchison County's first white farmer Paschal Pensoneau, a Frenchman, began to cultivate a few acres approximately nine miles south of the Atchison townsite. With his Kickapoo wife, Pensoneau operated a trading post here for several years. There was an Indian village at the mouth of nearly every creek that emptied into the Missouri in this area, and the French trappers had carried on a profitable fur trade in northeastern Kansas for many years before Pensoneau arrived.

South and west of CUMMINGS, 12.6 m. (980 alt., 76 pop.), the hills lose their ruggedness and become low rolling slopes. Apple, cherry, and peach orchards take the place of oak and maple thickets. Cider mills are plentiful, and along the roadside, in the fall, baskets of apples and jugs of amber cider are offered for sale by the farmers.

In NORTONVILLE, 19.5 m. (1,160 alt., 606 pop.), a railroad shipping center, founded in 1873, frequent fires have destroyed much of the business section, giving it a somewhat patchy appearance.

At 24.8 m. is the junction with State 4, paved.

Right on this road to VALLEY FALLS, 7 m. (960 alt., 1,238 pop.), a quiet shaded village west of the sluggish Delaware River. When founded as a Free State town in 1855 it was called Grasshopper Falls. In 1856 the new settlement was raided by "border ruffians," who greatly outnumbered the ablebodied men of the village. The latter fled on horseback, hoping the invaders would not harm the women and children left behind. The women and children were not molested, but the town was sacked and one of its main buildings burned.

At the eastern edge of Valley Falls just south of the bridge is the BUFFALO BILL TREE. One of the innumerable stories about Buffalo Bill Cody (1846-1917) related that he was tied to this oak by proslavery men and horsewhipped for making Free State speeches.

The OLD LUTHERAN CHURCH, corner of Phoebia and Elm Sts., was the first of that denomination west of the Mississippi. The building is constructed of walnut logs that were hauled from groves along the river and sawed at a mill of which Buffalo Bill's father is said to have been part owner. Shingles, clapboards, and laths were all split by hand. Other denominations often used the church while building their own places of worship. Members of the congregation erected a larger church in 1887 and the little walnut chapel is now (1938) used by Negroes.

Near the northeast edge of Valley Falls is the OLD PIAZZEK MILL, a huge sandstone structure. Built in 1878, the mill has been in operation ever since, except for a short period when work was suspended for lack of fuel.

On the unmarked SITE OF HICKORY POINT, 27.6 m., an extinct frontier town, a skirmish between proslavery and Free State men took place in 1856. Gen. Jim Lane, unaware that Governor Geary had ordered all armed forces to disband, raided the proslavery town of Ozawkie early in September 1856, and thence moved toward Hickory Point, where he had heard that a number of proslavery men were stationed. Finding them securely barricaded in a log building, he sent Colonel Harvey to Lawrence for the cannon "Sacramento." Shortly afterwards Lane learned of the disbanding order and started for Topeka, expecting to meet and head off the escort with the cannon.

However, the two groups failed to meet and Colonel Harvey returned to Hickory Point, set up the cannon and killed a proslavery man with its first ball. When several had been wounded on both sides, a truce was declared and, after partaking freely of whisky, the combatants decided to call off the fight.

Old "Sacramento" was captured in Mexico on December 22, 1846, in the battle of Brazito, when Col. Alexander W. Doniphan's men defeated Gen. Ponce de Leon's forces. After the war it was placed in an arsenal at Liberty, whence it was taken by Missourians who lost it to the Free Staters. It is now in Lawrence in Kansas University's museum.

According to some authorities, the Free State forces won a complete victory at Hickory Point and forced the surrender of 100 Kickapoo Rangers (proslavery militia). In either event, Free State leaders who took part in the battle were branded as rebels and warrants were issued for their arrest, although few of them were ever served.

OSKALOOSA, 35.1 m. (991 alt., 733 pop.), seat of Jefferson County, lies in a wooded vale, its tree-lined streets ending abruptly in farming country. Grocery, hardware, drug, and drygoods stores surround the Jefferson County Courthouse—a red brick building built in 1869.

Three blocks east of the courthouse a LOG CABIN (open), built by Daniel Briner in 1857, is the only one remaining of those built in this vicinity in the 1850's.

First settled in 1855, Oskaloosa was platted as a townsite in 1856 and established as a county seat in 1858 after a vehement contest with Valley Falls.

In 1860 Samuel Peppard of Oskaloosa built a "sailing wagon" which he claimed would go 15 miles an hour. The 350-pound vehicle was a cross between a spring wagon and a sailboat with a bed about three feet wide, eight feet long, and six inches deep mounted upon wooded wheels. A mast, with a sail nine by eleven feet, was raised over the front axle. The steering apparatus was attached to the front axle and resembled the reversed tiller of a boat.

After a few successful short trips, inventor Peppard and a crew of three set sail for Pikes Peak. They managed to get within 100 miles of Denver when a whirlwind struck them, wrecking the craft and injuring its crew. The sailing wagon was never rebuilt.

The Lazy Club, organized in Oskaloosa in the 1860's and revived at intervals since that time, disqualified members who lapsed in any way from their laziness. A Barlow knife was the prize ceremoniously awarded each year to the best loafer. In 1868, according to old accounts, the contest had narrowed down to two men, Tom Noble and Abe Sinnard. One day these two were reclining on a country road under a tree when the stagecoach, drawn by foaming horses, came rolling toward them. Noble watched apathetically as the coach came nearer and nearer, but finally

A POLITICAL DISCUSSION, OSKALOOSA

scrambled out of its path. Sinnard merely sat up, raised his hand, and motioned the startled driver to go around him. He won the knife.

The Oskaloosa *Independent* is the oldest weekly newspaper in Kansas. Since its founding in 1860 by John Wesley Roberts, a Free Stater from Ohio, the *Independent* has been edited and published every week by Roberts and his descendants.

South and west from Oskaloosa is the Kansas River bluff country. The low hills become higher toward the south until they are steep rocky slopes separated by narrow creek beds. In the spring these slopes are gay with sweet williams and yellow and blue violets. Feathery green ferns grow beneath the elm, oak, and maple trees that cover their sides.

The narrow gashes sliced by the roadbed from the summit of the hillsides reveal walls of rock, clay, and earth.

Broad level fields of grain and potatoes on both sides of the highway are broken occasionally by shallow muddy creeks. Houses huddle close to the ground like setting hens. A row of trees in the distance marks the course of the Kansas River.

Strange odors that sometimes permeate the atmosphere at about 43.5 *m.* originate at a stack of decaying hulls and vines near a PEA SHELLER, which is a center of activity from dawn until dark when the June pea crop is harvested. Farmers, who grow peas on contract for the Lawrence cannery *(see LAWRENCE),* load the vines on hayracks and wait their turns by the rapidly mounting stack. The sheller, a thrasher-like machine, is sheltered from the weather by a canopy of sheet iron.

At 43.8 *m.* is the northern junction with US 24 *(see Tour 3)*, which unites with US 59 between this point and 54 *m.*

At 56.1 *m.* is the northern junction with US 40 *(see Tour 3)*, which unites with US 59 between this point and Lawrence.

LAWRENCE, 58.3 *m.* (840 alt., 13,726 pop.) *(see LAWRENCE).*

Points of Interest: University of Kansas, Haskell Indian Institute, Spooner-Thayer Museum, Plymouth Church, and others.

Left from Lawrence on 13th St., paved, to OAK HILL CEMETERY (L), 1.1 *m.* In this cemetery are the GRAVES OF MANY VICTIMS OF QUANTRILL'S RAID *(see LAWRENCE).* Their bodies were removed from the old Pioneer Cemetery and reinterred shortly after this plot had been established in 1865. Also buried here are James H. Lane, U. S. Senator (1861–66); Charles Robinson, Governor (1861–62); Roscoe Stubbs, Governor (1909–13); and John P. Usher, Lincoln's Secretary of the Interior (1863–65).

Left from Lawrence on State 10 (23rd St.), paved, to FRANKLIN CEMETERY (L), 2.4 *m.*, on the site of a proslavery settlement that was Lawrence's early-day rival. The old burial ground is overgrown with underbrush and weeds and few of the inscriptions on the tombstones are legible. Franklin was a base of operations for proslavery forces during the period of border warfare. The Missourians built a blockhouse here to which they dragged their lone piece of artillery "Old Sacramento." Capt. Thomas Bickerton, a Free State leader with a company from Lawrence, laid siege to the blockhouse in August 1856. Finding it too strong to take by frontal attack, Bickerton's men drove a load of hay against the little fort and set fire to it, thereby smoking the defenders out. The Lawrence men took the cannon and used it two days later in the capture of Fort Titus *(see Tour 3).*

From 59.1 *m.* the red roofs and buff and white walls of the University of Kansas buildings atop Mount Oread are silhouetted against the northern horizon.

At 60.3 *m.* is the junction with an improved road.

Right on this road to PIONEER CEMETERY (L), 0.5 *m.*, called Oread Cemetery when it was established in the 1850's. Here is the GRAVE OF THOMAS W. BARBER, whose murder by proslavery forces in 1855, one of the last violent acts of the Wakarusa War, inspired John Greenleaf Whittier's poem, "The Burial of Barbour." The victims of Quantrill's raid were first interred here.

The Wakarusa Creek, 64 *m.*, a muddy low-banked stream, was the scene of the Wakarusa War *(see HISTORY).*

At 64.2 *m.* is the junction with an improved road.

Right on this road to 200-acre DOUGLAS COUNTY STATE LAKE, 13.1 *m.* *(boating, fishing, camping)*, in 424-acre DOUGLAS COUNTRY STATE PARK. The dam impounds water from Washington Creek, a tributary of the Wakarusa.

At 73.3 *m.* is the junction with US 50 *(see Tour 4).* Between this point and Ottawa US 59 and US 50S *(see Tour 4A)* are one route.

Immediately south of the junction of the two highways is a pasture gate (R).

Right through this gate on a winding byroad that crosses a pasture to HOLE IN THE ROCK, 0.5 *m.* The rock, about the size of a city lot, extends from the bank of a small stream. In its underside a cavern has been eroded by the current. In the top of the rock a hole four feet wide extends down thirty-five feet and is filled with water to within about five feet of the top. For years this was used by the settlers as a watering place when wells and streams in the vicinity were dry. Figures scratched in the soft sandstone indicate that it had served the same purpose for the

Indians. Among the thousands of names cut into the rock's sloping sides are many with dates in the 1850's.

Along the roadside are thickets of hickory, oak, and maple trees. In the grass-lands between patches of timber are hillsides from which all the soil has been washed, exposing the yellow sandstone.

At 77.3 *m.* is the junction with a rock road.

Right on this road is the SITE OF MINNEOLA, 3 *m.*, the former seat of Franklin County. Although it had been voted the Territorial capital over the veto of the Governor, it soon became known that several members of the legislature had a financial interest in the townsite and the more reputable members objected to meet-ing in Minneola. As a result of this "Minneola Scandal" the legislature that con-vened here March 23, 1858, adjourned to Lawrence on March 25.

At 79.1 *m.* is the junction with a crushed-rock road.

Right on this road to the junction with an improved road, 1 *m.;* R. here, through a gateway, to CALIFORNIA SPRINGS, 1.5 *m.*, whose clear cold waters gush from the top of a hill. Named by gold seekers in the 1840's, these springs were important as a stopping point for westbound travelers until the late 1880's. In the present cen-tury the many attempts to commercialize this spring water have met with only par-tial success. Water is dispensed free to farmers who haul it during dry seasons.

From a hilltop, 82.2 *m.*, the Marais des Cygnes River valley and the town of Ottawa spread out in a multicolored pattern. This spot, once part of the Ottawa Reservation, had been a signal point for the Ottawa, and before them the Sac, Fox, Osage, and Chippewa. In the Chippewa Hills, visible across the valley to the southwest, is another signal point.

OTTAWA, 86.3 *m.* (891 alt., 9,563 pop.) *(see OTTAWA)*.

Points of Interest: Ottawa University, Marais des Cygnes River Crossing, Tauy Jones Hall, and others.

Ottawa is at the southern junction with US 50S *(see Tour 4A)*.

1. Left from Ottawa on Wilson St. to the junction with an improved road, 2 *m.;* L. here 4.5 *m.* to the HOME OF TAUY JONES *(open),* a half-breed Indian born in Canada in 1807, who founded Ottawa University. This 14-room stone house, built in the 1860's, is of cut and faced limestone, two and one-half stories high, and has walls 34 inches thick. No nails were used in its construction; all the joists were fitted and pegged. The inside is finished in walnut and oak. Nearby was a much-used ford across Tauy Creek. A Government store, already established, was taken over by Tauy Jones in 1848. Beside it early in the 1850's Jones built a two-story hotel which became a Free State headquarters and was burned by proslavery men in 1856. The present stone house was also a headquarters for Free Staters in eastern Kansas.

At 3 *m.* on Wilson St. is the SITE OF THE OTTAWA BAPTIST MISSION (R), established by Jotham Meeker, printer and missionary in 1837. Here, with an old Seth Adams press, he got out the first book printed in Kansas, a textbook for Indians. A copy of Meeker's *Delaware First Book* and several others printed at the Baptist Mission are now owned by the Kansas State Historical Society at Topeka.

A short distance north of the road at this point is the OTTAWA INDIAN BURIAL GROUNDS, its stones and monuments visible in the uncut grass. The GRAVE OF JOTHAM MEEKER and that of his wife, Eleanor D. Meeker, are marked by a double monument in a stone enclosure. Just north of these the GRAVE OF JOHN T. (TAUY) JONES and that of his wife, Jane Kelly Jones, are marked with a monument.

On the west side of the cemetery, several rows of Indian graves are covered with unmarked stones. The GRAVE OF COMPEHAU, chief of the Ottawa, has a slab carved with a quiver, a drawn bow, and a tomahawk. Near this is the GRAVE OF ELIZA J. WIND, the child of an Ottawa woman and a French-Canadian who took his daughter to Canada when he grew tired of living with his Indian wife in Kansas. The mother followed them, stole the child, and returned with her to the reservation. There she permanently crippled the girl, believing that if she were deformed her father would not want her. Eliza grew to womanhood in Ottawa and married Judge James Wind, one of the original trustees of Ottawa University.

2. Left from Ottawa on 9th St., an improved road, is the CHIPPEWA BURIAL GROUND (R), 6 *m.*, in a grove of cedar trees on the slope of a grassy hill above the Marais des Cygnes River. The graves of chiefs and their families for the most part are completely covered with great slabs of red sandstone 14 inches thick. Many of the stones are elaborately carved with what are believed to be legends of the tribe. One headstone, placed here in the 1920's, bears a naval insignia and marks the grave of a Chippewa youth who had served in the United States Navy. Many Chippewa still live in the hills that surround the cemetery.

At 90.3 *m.* is the junction with an improved road.

Left on this road to an OLD WELL (L), 6 *m.*, marking the site of the Wayside Inn in the former town of Mount Vernon which was a stopping place on the early road from Leavenworth to Indian Territory. The well has been used since 1850.

At 94.8 *m.* is the junction (L) with the Osawatomie Road *(see Tour 12B).*

US 59 crosses the Pottawatomie River, 105 *m.*, on the NORTH FORK BRIDGE, the loftiest highway bridge in Kansas (1938). This steel and concrete structure is 79 feet above water level.

GARNETT, 110.8 *m.* (1,047 alt., 2,768 pop.), on a plateau above the wooded valleys of three streams, is the seat of Anderson County. It was founded in 1856 and named for William Garnett, president of the town company. Around the courthouse are a number of limestone-block store buildings with iron doorsteps, and window sills guarded by spiked iron railings whose sharp points have discouraged loafers for more than half a century.

BRUNS HALL *(private),* corner of 6th Ave. and Cedar St., built in 1857, is the oldest building standing in Garnett. In its back yard is a spring, around which the settlers built their first cabins. Even during years of severe drought this spring has never been dry.

The approximate SITE OF THE OLD ANDERSON COUNTY JAIL, built in 1864, is marked by a bandstand in the public square.

When Houdini, then just beginning his career as an "escapist," was stranded here in 1897 with a little troupe of performers, he offered to break out of the jail. While the sheriff, after locking Houdini in the strongest cell, was explaining to the crowd why it was impossible for his prisoner to get free, Houdini, smiling broadly, walked out of the jail. The "escape" attracted so many customers to the show that the performers were able to pay their hotel bill and leave town.

On the north limits of Garnett is the ANDERSON COUNTY STATE PARK, a 243-acre wooded area *(picnic- and playgrounds),* owned by the city of Garnett, with a 50-acre lake *(swimming, boating, fishing).*

1. Left from Garnett on US 169, improved, to a point just north of the town of GREELEY, 10 *m.* (1,040 alt., 504 pop.), whence WADSWORTH MOUND (L) is visible from the highway. This flat-topped elevation, 150 feet high and more than 300 feet long, overlooks the Marais des Cygnes Valley. It was used as a look-

out by the Indians and later by John Brown who sometimes stayed in James Townsley's cabin at the foot of the mound.

2. Right from Garnett on State 31, improved, is the Pottawatomie River, **8.5** *m.*
At approximately **0.2** *m.* L. of the road at this point is the SITE WHERE JOHN C.
FREMONT CROSSED THE POTTAWATOMIE on his expedition to the Pacific in 1848.
The record of this part of their journey in Anderson County, as told later by two
members of the expedition, constitutes the only known detailed record of the trip
in existence. A small iron cooking pot which was unearthed at the Pottawatomie
Crossing substantiates their story. According to these accounts, members of the
party saw and killed more buffalo immediately west of here than in any other place
along the route.

At 12 *m.* on this road is the junction with another improved road; L. on this are
GIANT ANT HILLS, **13.5** *m.,* two feet high and six to eight feet in diameter,
made by black ants.

3. Right from Garnett on 7th St., paved, are BUFFALO WALLOWS (R and L),
8 *m.,* and thousands of small ANT HILLS covered with grass.

South of Garnett US 59 winds through oil fields where pump jacks are
operated by pull rods from central power plants. Production is low in this
region and water is pumped into certain wells to force the oil into others
(see Tour 7).

At 112.4 *m.* is the junction with an improved road.

Right on this road to an OLD FRAME CHURCH, **6** *m.,* on the SITE OF CENTRAL
CITY, a boom town of pre-Civil War days. George W. Cooper, founder of the
town, sold lots to easterners by means of lithographs showing steamboats plying up
and down the Pottawatomie River, busy wharves along the water front, and streets
teeming with traffic. For years purchasers journeyed to Central City only to learn
that they had been swindled.

Central City later became a trading post for Indians, freight wagoners, soldiers,
and pioneers on the road from Leavenworth to the Indian Territory. But travel on
the road decreased in the 1870's and when the railroad avoided it by approximately
nine miles the town was finished. A farmhouse (L), rebuilt from the old hotel,
another farmhouse (R), the foundation of the old store (L), the church, and the
wreck of the parsonage (R) are all that remain.

US 59 crosses the 6,500-acre underground STORAGE BASIN OF THE
CITIES SERVICE OIL AND GAS CO., 120.6 *m.,* concealed beneath prairie
hayfields. This was a producing gas field until the wells became practically
exhausted and the pressure dropped from 200 to 17 pounds. Gas from the
high-pressure fields of western Kansas and Oklahoma is pumped into
these exhausted wells—which tap the gas-bearing sand pockets at a depth
of 600 to 700 feet—thus building up a reserve supply during the summer
to be turned into the mains in the winter.

COLONY, 128.1 *m.* (1,127 alt., 596 pop.), is an Ozark Ridge, an
elevation dividing the waters of the Missouri and the Arkansas Rivers.
Founded as Divide, the town's name was changed to Colony in 1872 by
settlers from Indiana.

The former HOME OF GENERAL FUNSTON *(private),* 134.3 *m.* (R),
is a frame farmhouse built in 1859. It is one and one-half stories high,
and seven rooms have been added at different times. Frederick Funston
(1865–1917) attended the University of Kansas, became a newspaper reporter, served as a botanist on the Government's Death Valley expedition,
and explored Alaska for the U. S. Department of Agriculture to report
on the flora. Funston was made a brigadier general for his services in the

Philippines, which included capturing Aguinaldo and swimming the River Pompanga at Calumpit, Luzon, under heavy fire to establish the rope-drawn ferry by which the United States troops crossed.

A large cottonwood tree in the back yard was planted by Fred Funston when he was six years old. A preacher, disapproving of its being planted on Sunday, predicted that the tree would never grow. The house is occupied (1938) by J. B. Funston, a brother of the general.

At 135.1 *m.* is the junction with State 57, graveled.

Right on this road, on the east bank of the Neosho River, is NEOSHO FALLS, 8 *m.* (973 alt., 462 pop.), named for the falls created by the settlers' first dam. Though only a village, late in the 1870's the community invited President Hayes, then on a tour through the Middle West, to make an address. Believing Neosho Falls to be a bustling young metropolis, Hayes accepted. When he arrived here with Mrs. Hayes and Gen. W. T. Sherman, the President was somewhat perturbed to find that he was to speak at a homecoming in a town of less than 500 population, but he delivered the address.

IOLA, 139.7 *m.* (957 alt., 7,160 pop.) *(see Tour 5)*, is at the junction with US 54 *(see Tour 5)*.

BASSETT, 141.6 *m.* (984 alt., 194 pop.), is populated by employees of the Lehigh Portland Cement Co. The LEHIGH PORTLAND CEMENT COMPANY'S PLANT *(open)*, is visible (L) from the highway.

OLD STONY LONESOME, 145.5 *m.*, the country schoolhouse in which Funston taught in his youth, has been preserved as a memorial to the explorer and soldier.

HUMBOLDT, 149.9 *m.* (961 alt., 2,558 pop.), named for Baron von Humboldt by its German founders who came to the region in 1857, was for years a supply point serving the territory between the Neosho and the Arkansas Rivers. Its steam sawmill furnished walnut beams for countless houses in the region. Humboldt, invaded and burned by rebels in 1861, raided twice by bushwhackers and devastated by grasshoppers, drought, and another fire, was stunted till after the Civil War, when it began to grow rapidly. Today farming in the fertile region along the Neosho River, the manufacture of cement, and the distribution of oil contribute to its prosperity. Attesting to Humboldt's industry, clouds of white dust from the cement plant settle on nearby telephone wires, where, moistened by dew, they form a cement coating sometimes an inch in diameter.

South of Humboldt US 59 follows the east bank of the Neosho, which is hidden from the highway but indicated by a zigzag line of trees (R).

A cluster of farm buildings (R) mark the SITE OF THE VEGETARIAN COLONY, 154.6 *m.*, established in the spring of 1856 by a group of almost 100 easterners who were attracted by promoters' advertisements. They experienced endless hardships. Stoves, utensils, and farm implements were inadequate; food was scarce; and when the summer was well advanced clouds of mosquitoes from the river bottoms made life almost unbearable. The spring, which the colonists had believed to be inexhaustible, went dry and the few pumpkins and melons they had been able to raise in the dry prairie soil were stolen by bands of Indians. The colony lasted less than a year.

CHANUTE, 160 *m.* (942 alt., 10,277 pop.), was named for Octave Chanute, a young railroad engineer who later was active in the development of aviation. Substantially built, with many new buildings and business houses, Chanute is a railroad center in the heart of a rich agricultural district. The successful operation of municipally owned public utilities has made Chanute tax free, and provided funds for an elaborate civic improvement program.

The KANSAS ROOM of the CHANUTE PUBLIC LIBRARY has a large collection of books by Kansas authors and works on Kansas history.

The CITY PARK *(tennis courts, playgrounds, subsurface-lighted swimming pool)*, is on the eastern limits of town.

Chanute is the former home of Thurlow Lieurance. musician and composer *(see MUSIC)*.

Railroad machine shops and roundhouses are visible (R) on the southern edge of Chanute.

Just southwest of the city is the MARTIN JOHNSON AIRPORT, named for the African explorer and photographer of wild game. Johnson is buried in Chanute, the former home of his wife, Osa Leighty Johnson.

A monument marks the SITE OF NEOSHO MISSION (L), 172.5 *m.,* founded in 1824 by the Reverend Benton Pixley and Samuel Bright. This was the first mission in Kansas and is believed to have been the scene of the first agricultural work carried on by white men within the present boundaries of the State. After Pixley and his family had endured many hardships, hostile Indians forced him to abandon his venture in 1829.

In a country churchyard (R), 173.6 *m.,* is a granite monument commemorating the SITE OF THE CANVILL TRADING POST founded nearby in the 1840's. Here in 1865 the Osage negotiated their Withdrawal Treaty, under the terms of which the Indians moved from the banks of the Neosho to the banks of the Elk and Verdigris Rivers, a few miles farther west.

A trial of four horse thieves conducted by the Osage in 1857 at the Canville Trading Post was described to F. T. Morrison of Chanute by Capt. Samuel Stewart, who "came to this vicinity with the vegetarian colony" and served as interpreter at the trial. "The prisoners were placed in a log house and guarded during the night. Next morning Chief Little Bear *(see Tour 11)*, was on hand to preside at the trial. The Chief at once made a ruling that in compliance with the Osage unwritten law, a jury of twelve men should hear the evidence and pass upon the guilt or innocence of the four accused horse thieves. Six of the jurors were to be half-bloods and six full-bloods. . . . After the hearing, which consumed half a day, the jury retired, under the blackjack trees now standing in the town of Shaw, Kan., and arrived at the following verdict: 'That if the four accused would tell all they know about the organization of horse thieves and give the names of those implicated, that their lives would be spared and they would be liberated after each had half of his head shaved and one ear cut off, and that they should leave the territory of Kansas in five days.'

"In the meantime Chief White Hair, with his wise men, had come from his home near St. Paul and as he took precedence over Chief Little Bear, he ordered, adjudged and decreed '. . . that if the accused men would tell all they knew about the horse thieves, they would be liberated and half of their head shaved,' and philosophizing said: 'If we cut off an ear it will always brand them as thieves, while if we cut off half their hair it will grow out again and will give them a chance to make good and become useful men again.' His word was law and this was the penalty.

"The Indians had questioned the accused separately and three of them told the same story and all they knew about the horse-stealing organization, and gave the names of all those implicated in stealing. Chief White Hair appointed Captain Stewart and three other white men to serve the five days' notice on all parties implicated by the three men in stealing, and as soon as the accused were liberated the notices were served on ten men and in five days all of them had left the country, which put an end to horse stealing for the time being."

ERIE, 179.5 m. (880 alt., 1,184 pop.), although little more than one-tenth the size of Chanute, is the seat of Neosho County. A station on two railroad lines, it is a shipping point for oil and farm products.

Left from Erie on State 67, improved, is ST. PAUL, 7 m. (886 alt., 800 pop.), formerly called Osage Mission.

At the southwest corner of St. Paul is the SAINT FRANCIS CHURCH AND MONASTERY, built in 1871, an outgrowth of an early Jesuit mission established here before 1850. Townspeople claim that the first mission on the present site of St. Paul was established in the 1820's and old records in possession of Saint Francis Church tend to confirm that theory. Government records, however, set the date at 1847. Saint Francis Church is built of natural gray stone and its interior is finished in native walnut. A light has burned continuously on its altar since 1871. The monastery is directly behind the church, and the buildings are surrounded with trees planted by the early Jesuit missionaries.

Large trees line St. Paul's streets. The houses, set far back from the sidewalks, are partly hidden by shrubbery. Black-robed monks, stained-glass windows brilliant in the sun's rays, and tolling church bells make Saint Paul seem an Old World village.

US 59 crosses the Neosho River, 181.4 m., on an old-type steel bridge. At its south end is an earthen fill topped with concrete to protect the highway from floodwaters that frequently cover the adjacent lowlands. Leaving the valley a few miles farther south, the route enters rolling farm country.

At 192 m. is the junction with an improved road.

Left on this road is the NEOSHO COUNTY STATE PARK, 6 m., McKINLEY LAKE (swimming, boating, fishing), principal attraction of the park, has an area of 100 acres. Visible in the Neosho Valley at the north of the park is Big Island, largest island in Kansas. It consists of 4,000 acres of rich farmland, encircled by the Neosho River.

PARSONS, 197.3 m. (896 alt., 14,903 pop.) (see Tour 6), is at the junction with US 160 (see Tour 6).

ALTAMONT, 207.7 m. (907 alt., 598 pop.), a rural trading and shipping point founded in 1875, is so named because it lies on an elevation. The center of a prosperous farming region, Altamont is the headquarters of the Labette County Farm Bureau, an office generally found in county seat towns. The LABETTE COUNTY COMMUNITY HIGH SCHOOL, in a two-story brick building near the center of town, was one of the first county high schools in Kansas. Many residents of Labette County objected so strenuously to its establishment in 1892 by a special act of the State legislature that a suit was filed to test the validity of the tax levy for its support. While the suit was pending, school was conducted in rented rooms and its teachers served without pay. The district court upheld the validity of the tax levy and the school was moved into its own building in 1895. It is now (1938) recognized as one of the most progressive secondary schools in Kansas. Extra-curricular activities—notably its band concerts and dramatic performances—have attracted attention outside the community and influenced the interests, manners, and customs not only of its 300 students but of their friends and families as well.

Southeast of Altamont US 59 drops into a wooded valley crossed by many streams. Corn, wheat, oats, and melons are grown extensively here.

OSWEGO, 219.6 m. (912 alt., 845 pop.), on the west bank of the Neosho, formerly known as Little Town, has plain, unadorned buildings and comfortable-looking frame houses. The OSWEGO TOWN WELL, corner of 4th and Union Sts., marks the site of a trading post established here early in the 1840's by John Mathews, pioneer trader. The first permanent settlers arrived at the Oswego townsite in 1865. Soon after the town had been founded D. M. Clover, in filing a petition for operating a ferry across the river, listed the following rates:

"4-horse mule or ox team and wagon	75¢
2-horse mule or ox team	50¢
2-horse buggy or carriage	50¢
1-horse and buggy	40¢
man on horseback	25¢
loose cattle, mules or horses	10¢
hogs and sheep	5¢
footman	10¢"

Clover offered special rates for combinations, and dogs accompanied by their masters were allowed to ride free of charge.

RIVERSIDE PARK (playgrounds, swimming pool, zoo, picnic grounds) is on the banks of the Neosho in the northeast corner of town.

CHETOPA, 229.4 m. (826 alt., 1,344 pop.), built on a site once occupied by an Osage village, was named for Chetopah, an Osage war chief. Although intelligent and powerful, Chetopah, because of some Indian superstition, was allowed to lead his tribe only when it fought an enemy.

Chetopa was founded in 1857 but was burned to the ground during the Civil War by Union soldiers who believed that the townspeople were Southern sympathizers. The original settlers returned after the war and rebuilt the town.

Chetopa is at the junction with US 166 (see Tour 7).

At 232.5 m. US 59 crosses the OKLAHOMA LINE, 27 miles north of Vinita, Okla. (see OKLA., Tour 15).

◄◄◄◄◄◄◄◄◄◄◄◄◄◄◄◄◄◄◄◄◄◄ ☼ ►►►►►►►►►►►►►►►►►►►►►►

Tour 12A

(Falls City, Nebr.)—Hiawatha—Atchison—Leavenworth—Victory Junction—Kansas City—(Kansas City, Mo.); US 73.
Nebraska Line to Kansas City, 107.2 m.

Missouri Pacific R.R. parallels route between Nebraska Line and Atchison; Chicago, Burlington & Quincy R.R. between Atchison and Leavenworth.
North half of route is improved road; south half is paved; open all year.
Good accommodations in county seat towns.

US 73 traverses an agricultural region where corn grows in abundance and the rainfall is often plentiful when the rest of the plains country is tortured and sun baked. The gently rounded hills are covered with timber and apple orchards. Missourians and Iowans, repelled by the arid plains to the west, settled here or returned to their native States.

Near Atchison the tawny clay bluffs of the Missouri River appear, the route twists through abrupt hills where farmers find it necessary to "grub out" tree spouts as well as weeds.

Near Victory Junction the terrain is gently rolling; the timber decreases and the wheat and corn fields are larger.

US 73 crosses the Nebraska Line, 0 *m.*, 5 miles south of Falls City, Nebr. *(see NEBR., Tour 1).*

RESERVE, 3 *m.* (905 alt., 197 pop.), dominated by a two-story red brick schoolhouse and a water tower, was founded as a railroad boom town in 1881. Prior to that the only building on this site was a log cabin that belonged to Thomas Hart, who came to this section of Kansas in 1856. The Hart cabin was a sort of halfway house for freighters going from St. Joseph, Mo., to Nebraska City, Nebr., and Mrs. Hart, called "Aunty Nancy," was noted throughout what was then the Wild West for her hospitality. On cold winter nights she kept a lighted candle in her window to guide travelers.

In 1896 the little village was demolished by a tornado that killed five persons.

Right from Reserve on an unimproved road is PADONIA, 4 *m.* (937 alt., 104 pop.), where settlers organized a court in 1855 and convicted two of their neighbors of selling whisky to the Indians. Although the accused men were not present at the trial, they were sentenced to a fine of $20 and banishment from the Territory. Destruction of the liquor was ordered. Court adjourned to the home of the convicted men for the purpose of enforcing the sentence, but after its members had sampled the whisky they declared it too good to be wasted. The fine was collected and divided among the members of the court but the sentence of banishment was withdrawn.

At 5 *m.* (L) is the SAC AND FOX RESERVATION (126 pop.). As these Indians have abandoned almost all of their ancestral folk rituals, costumes, and beliefs, there is little to distinguish them from white men.

The Sac *(yellow earth people)* and the Fox *(red earth people),* two of the Algonquian tribes, when first encountered by white men in the 1640's, were living in Wisconsin where they had migrated from eastern Michigan. Father Allouez in 1667 describes the Sac (or Sauk) as very warlike. "He was told that if they or the Foxes found a person in an isolated place they would kill him, especially if he were a Frenchman, for they could not endure the sight of the whiskers of the European."

When the Sac fled in 1733 after killing the younger Sieur De Villiers who had tried to force them to surrender some Fox fugitives, the Governor of Canada gave orders to attack any Sac and Fox that remained. This resulted in the close federation of the two tribes and their moving to Iowa. Apparently their manners had improved by 1773–1775 when Peter Pond wrote:

"These People are Cald Saukeas. Thay are of a Good sise and Well Disposed—Les Inclind to tricks and Bad manners than thare Nighbers. Thay will take of the traders Goods on Creadit in the fall for thare youse. In Winter and Except for Axedant thay Pay the Deapt Verey Well for Indians I mite hafe sade Inlitend or Sivelised Indans which are in General made worse by the Operation. Thare amusements are Singing, Dancing, Smokeing, Matcheis, Gaming, Feasting, Drinking, Playing the Slite of Hand, Hunting and thay are famas in Mageack. . . . Thay are Not Verey Gellas of thare Women. In General the Women find meanes to Grattafy them Selves without Consent of the Men."

In 1837 the Sac and Fox ceded their Iowa lands and accepted a tract in Kansas. Here they lived peacefully till about 1858 when most of the Fox—fearing punishment for killing a number of Plains Indians while they were on a buffalo hunt and angered because the Sac, in their absence, had made a treaty with the Government disposing of much of their land —returned to Iowa. In 1867 the Sac exchanged their Kansas land for a tract in Indian Territory and the few remaining members of the two tribes were placed on this much smaller reservation. (Their combined area in Kansas and Nebraska is only 894 acres.)

HIAWATHA, 13 *m.* (1,095 alt., 3,302 pop.) *(see Tour 1),* is at the junction with US 36 *(see Tour 1).*

LAKE HIAWATHA *(boating, fishing),* 16 *m.* (R), is surrounded by shrubbery and trees.

Around the landscaped shore line of 170-acre MISSION LAKE *(boating, fishing, picnicking),* 25.5 *m.* (L), are 17 miles of scenic drives. In 1924 this lake, costing approximately $250,000, was created as a water supply for Horton, by damming Mission Creek. Fireworks are displayed at night over the water during the annual Fourth of July celebration held by the citizens of Horton.

In the spring of 1925, torrential rains swelled the new lake to such a point that the dam was threatened and Horton was in danger of being inundated. Throughout an entire night citizens of Horton, aided by farmers from the surrounding country, worked on the dikes, bolstering the crumbling dam with sand bags while the population prepared to flee to higher ground west of the city. But the dam held, the rains ceased and the lake dropped to its normal level. Later the spillway was enlarged and has since been adequate for all emergencies.

HORTON, 26 m. (1,015 alt., 4,049 pop.), a tree-shaded town with well-kept lawns and neat appearing homes, was founded in 1886 by a townsite company which was a subsidiary of the railroad that built through here and established shops that are still Horton's biggest industrial unit. The town was named for Judge Horton, an early settler. An old opera house and a three-story red brick hotel, both built shortly after the town had been founded, still dominate its sky line.

The most important annual event in Horton is the Tri-County Fair, held here *(first week in Sept.)* by Brown, Atchison, and Jackson Counties.

At 32.5 m. is the junction with an improved road.

Right on this road is the ATCHISON COUNTY LAKE *(fishing, boating, picnic grounds)*, 1.5 m., covering 120 acres.
At 5 m. on the improved road is KENNEKUK (973 alt., 75 pop.), a minute settlement named for Kennekuk, a Kickapoo chief, who is said to be buried nearby.

ATCHISON, 54 m. (795 alt., 13,024 pop.) *(see ATCHISON)*.

Points of Interest: Guerrier Hill, Rock Garden, Lewis and Clark Monument, Lincoln Address Monument, St. Benedict's College, and others.

Atchison is at the junction with US 59 *(see Tour 12)*.

Between Atchison and Leavenworth, US 73 follows the general route of the old Leavenworth to Fort Laramie military road.

At 68 m. is the junction with a graded road.

Left on this road is KICKAPOO, 5 m. (799 alt., 50 pop.), a small nondescript community. One mile north, in the Missouri River, is COW ISLAND. Maj. H. S. Long stopped his steamboat here in 1819 to impress the 150 Kansa summoned to the island for a scolding by the Indian agent. The natives, astonished by the boat— which had a bow carved to resemble a serpent's head with a mouth through which smoke was forced—and pleased by the distribution of presents, agreed to cease molesting white men.
Many years ago the shifting of the river channel attached Cow Island to the Missouri shore although it is still (1938), politically, part of Atchison County, Kans. Children living on this 2,500-acre tract have their tuition paid by the county so that they may attend school in Iatan, Mo., and approximately 15 voters of the "island" must travel more than 12 miles and cross the free bridge to vote and pay taxes.

CODY HILL, 72 m., one of the longest hills in Leavenworth County, has at its south base the FOUNDATION OF BUFFALO BILL'S LOG CABIN described as an early home of Buffalo Bill Cody. A house nearby is believed to mark the SITE OF ISAAC CODY'S TAVERN. Isaac was Buffalo Bill's father. Between the cabin and the tavern sites is the OLD CODY WELL— still in good condition—that is said to have furnished water for the Cody family and their guests.

At 76.5 m. is the junction with State 92, paved, which leads (L) into Fort Leavenworth *(see LEAVENWORTH)*.

LEAVENWORTH, 78 m. (760 alt., 17,466 pop.) *(see LEAVEN-WORTH)*.

Points of Interest: Fort Leavenworth, Planters' House, Abernathy Furniture Factory, Cathedral of the Immaculate Conception, Parker Amusement Company, and others.

At 81.9 *m.* (L) is the UNITED STATES VETERANS ADMINISTRATION FACILITY *(grounds open; buildings open on application)*, familiarly known as the Soldiers' Home. There are 68 buildings on 644 acres of natural woodland that stretches away to the river valley on the east, including a chapel, barracks, post office, theater, library, messhall, laundry, greenhouses, shops, and the HOSPITAL *(open on application)*, a four-story functional-type structure of brick, completed in 1934. Disabled veterans of all wars are admitted to the hospital and home. There were approximately 1,500 inmates in 1938.

A huge FLORAL GLOBE near the entrance has the various continents delineated by the contrasting colors of the plants, some of which grow almost upside down. It is the work of ex-soldiers in the home.

ST. MARY'S COLLEGE *(open on application)*, 82 *m.* (R), a Roman Catholic boarding school for girls, was founded in 1860 by the Sisters of Charity. A semicircular drive leads past six buildings on a wooded 160-acre campus. The ADMINISTRATION BUILDING, a five-story brick structure of modern design, was completed in 1934. It contains classrooms, dormitory facilities, a gymnasium, and a swimming pool. St. Mary's offers accredited high school and college courses and degrees in liberal arts and fine arts.

LANSING, 84 *m.* (800 alt., 988 pop.), often mistaken for a suburb of Leavenworth, has developed as a result of the STATE PENITENTIARY and the INDUSTRIAL FARM FOR WOMEN *(to visit, apply at warden's office near main entrance)*.

The prisoners mine coal that underlies State property here. This is one of the few places in Kansas where deep-shaft coal mining is still carried on. It is preferred to strip mining, because the former method requires more labor and less machinery. Inmates of the Lansing prison make about 4 million pounds of binding twine a year and also small rings, bracelets, and other trinkets which are sold to visitors.

VICTORY JUNCTION, 92 *m.* (950 alt., 50 pop.) *(see Tour 3)*, is at the junction with US 40 *(see Tour 3)*. Between this point and Kansas City, 107.2 *m.*, US 73 and US 40 are one route *(see Tour 3)*.

⋘⋘⋘⋘⋘⋘⋘⋘⋘⋘⋘⋘☿⋙⋙⋙⋙⋙⋙⋙⋙⋙⋙⋙⋙

Tour 12B

Junction with US 59—Osawatomie; 17 m., Osawatomie Rd.

This route crosses a diversified agricultural area in the heaviest rain-belt in Kansas where corn, wheat, hay, apples, and pears are grown. It is the region associated with John Brown, the Free State leader, whose hanging at Charlestown, Va., now Charles Town, W. Va., in 1859 for "treason, murder and inciting slaves to rebel" was the inspiration for "John Brown's Body," the marching song of the Union forces during the Civil War.

Brown, born in Connecticut in 1800, moved to Ohio when he was a boy. There he became an abolitionist and kept the Richmond station of the Underground Railroad. Five of his sons moved to Kansas in 1855 to homestead land and work for Kansas' entrance into the Union in the Free State column. Their father followed them a year later in a wagon loaded with the guns they had requested.

After the proslavery forces had attacked Lawrence *(see LAWRENCE)*, Brown became a leader of the Free State men in the Wakarusa War *(see HISTORY)*. He retaliated with the murder of five proslavery men and attempted to prevent the burning of Osawatomie.

In 1859 he and his few followers captured the U. S. arsenal at Harpers Ferry and seized control of the town. But the Negroes failed to flock to his command as he had anticipated and old Brown—wounded and with half his men killed—was captured by U. S. marines led by Robert E. Lee. His serenity and sincerity during his trial and execution did much to make John Brown a hero and martyr to the abolitionists.

This route branches east from its junction with US 59 *(see Tour 12)*, 0 *m.*, at a point 8.5 miles south of Ottawa *(see OTTAWA)*.

A picnic ground *(open)*, 0.8 *m.* (R), has old shade trees, a swimming hole, and firewood.

At 9 *m.* is the junction with a graveled road.

Right on this road is the junction with a dirt road, 3.5 *m.;* R. 0.8 *m.* on the dirt road, in a timbered pasture about 20 rods (R) from the road, are the GRAVES OF JAMES P. DOYLE AND HIS SONS, William and Drury, who, with William Sherman and Allen Wilkinson, were the victims of the Potawatomie massacre, led by John Brown on the night of May 24, 1856 *(see HISTORY)*. The graves, marked with flat engraved limestone slabs, are covered with tangled masses of brush and the fallen limbs of trees. The SITE OF THE DOYLE HOME is about 400 yards northeast of the graves on the north side of Mosquito Creek at Flat Rocks, a solid-rock-bottom ford.

Southeast from the junction with the dirt road is LANE, 4.8 *m.* (950 alt., 291 pop.), a rural trading center, named for Gen. James H. Lane *(see HISTORY)*, military and political leader of the Free State forces and United States Senator from

JOHN BROWN'S CABIN, OSAWATOMIE

Kansas (1861–66). Settled in 1855 by New England abolitionists, Lane was a center of Free State activity during the early struggles.

A MONUMENT TO FREDERICK BROWN, 16 *m.*, a son of John Brown,
is (L) of limestone about five feet high. Approximately 200 yards southeast of this slab is the SITE WHERE FREDERICK BROWN WAS SHOT on
the morning of August 30, 1856, by the Reverend Martin White prior to
the Battle of Osawatomie.

About 200 feet northwest of the monument is the FOUNDATION OF
THE JOHN BROWN CABIN, built by the Reverend Charles Adair, a
brother-in-law of John Brown. The cabin is now in John Brown Park at
Osawatomie. The old well, filled with rock, and the broad limestone door-
step are near the house now on the site. A tall pine tree nearby and some
lilac bushes were planted in 1854 by the Adairs.

OSAWATOMIE, 17 *m.* (853 alt., 4,440 pop.), on the Marais des
Cygnes River, was founded in 1855, and is said to have been named for
the two Indian tribes living in the vicinity—the Osage and the Potawatomi. While there are many old buildings, both in the business and residential sections, most of these have been modernized. Osawatomie's income is derived from serving the neighboring farmers and from the
Missouri Pacific R.R. shops which employ from 600 to 1,000 men.

In the JOHN BROWN BATTLEGROUND MEMORIAL PARK *(picnic grounds,
playgrounds, athletic field, swimming pool)*, west end of Main St., is (R)
a life-size bronze STATUE OF JOHN BROWN, by George Fite Waters.

On the highest elevation in the park the JOHN BROWN CABIN *(open)*,
approached by winding walks and drives, is protected by a glassed and
roofed enclosure. Flowers and vines grow around the cabin which has a

main room, shed kitchen, and loft and contains many relics, some of which belonged to John Brown.

When Theodore Roosevelt dedicated this park in 1910, he outlined the policies of the new Progressive wing of the Republican Party. Some critics protested that the name of John Brown had received too little mention, but the local papers ignored this and emphasized that Roosevelt, like Brown, was militantly taking up the cause of an oppressed people in championing the less privileged class against the influence and power of the special interests.

There are several versions of the Battle of Osawatomie. Jason Brown, a son of John Brown, said that 400 pro-slavery men, under Gen. John W. Reid, started on August 29 from Kansas City to raid and burn Osawatomie. Hearing of this, John Brown and fifteen others, who were 30 miles away, rushed to the vicinity to recruit men for the town's defense. Both parties arrived at about the same time. Brown and his band of thirty camped just west of the Adair homestead and Reid camped just north of Osawatomie. On the morning of August 30 Reid advanced, and the defenders opened fire from their cover in the timber around Pottawatomie Creek. Many of Reid's men fell and the rest, breaking in disorder, had to be clubbed into line again. When Reid opened fire with cannon and continued his advance, Brown's men retreated across the Marais des Cygnes, but their casualties were few. Reid's losses were heavy—seventy killed or wounded.

Another account is that of Col. F. J. Snyder, of Reid's forces, who says: "The engagement did not last three hours; and to call it a battle is ludicrous. I knew nothing of the strength or losses of the John Brown forces, but we had few wounded and none killed."

Judge James Hale, of Lexington, Mo., a lieutenant with the proslavery party, said that troops under the command of General Reid advanced on the morning of August 30 and encountered three of John Brown's pickets—Frederick Brown, George Partridge, and Theron Powers. These pickets were shot by Reid's men. He, too, reports none of Reid's forces killed and few wounded.

General Reid's report admits the burning of Osawatomie after the retreat of Brown's forces, but says that it was contrary to his orders.

The JOHN BROWN MEMORIAL, 9th and Main Sts., is a shaft of Vermont marble about 11 feet high, above the GRAVES OF FREDERICK BROWN, DAVID GARRISON, GEORGE PARTRIDGE, THERON POWERS, AND CHARLES KAISER. Kaiser is thought to have been shot after he had been taken prisoner by the proslavery forces; his body was never recovered. This memorial, carved and erected by Hanway Brothers of Lane, was dedicated August 30, 1877, by John J. Ingalls, United States Senator (1873-91).

The OSAWATOMIE STATE HOSPITAL FOR THE INSANE *(grounds open; buildings by application),* on the northern edge of Osawatomie, is on a long low hill overlooking the Marais des Cygnes River. The original site, given to the State in the 1860's by Charles Adair, a nephew of John Brown, has been enlarged until the present (1938) area is more than 800 acres. A flight of terraced stone steps leads to the hill where the ten institutional buildings are surrounded by fine old trees, shrubbery, flowers, and winding drives.

Night ball games are held here during the summer on the lighted grounds. In the winter the 250 employees have weekly dances and picture shows.

On the institution farm are stock and hay barns, crop fields, orchards, and gardens, storehouses and greenhouses. The dairy herd numbers 250 registered Holsteins. Many of the 1,500 patients are allowed to work in the fields, shops, and barns, and at domestic occupations.

Left from Osawatomie on US 169, paved, to PAOLA, 11 *m.* (857 alt., 3,762 pop.), seat of Miami County. The town, established in 1855, was named for Baptiste Peoria, one of the founders. For about a year it was known as Peoria Village, but the name was later corrupted to Paola.

In 1860 prospectors digging with a pick and shovel near Paola found oil at a depth of 275 feet. This was the first oil well west of the Mississippi. However, oil in commercial quantities was not discovered in Kansas till 1889, when a well was sunk six miles east of Paola. In 1884 gas from a field developed a few miles from the town was piped here and Paola's homes and streets were the first in the State to be lighted with natural gas.

Paola depends largely upon the farm trade and a few small industries, including a creamery that manufactures butter. The URSULINE ACADEMY, east end of Wea St., is a boarding school for young women conducted by the Ursuline Sisters in four brick buildings on a small, attractively landscaped campus. It is an accredited school, has an average enrollment of 125 students, and offers high school and junior college courses.

In WALLACE PARK *(swimming pool, tennis courts, playground, athletic field),* south end of Walnut St., a 55-acre recreation center, shaded by large elm and walnut trees, is an attractive rose garden. Paola was the boyhood home of Henry Salem Hubbell (1870–   ), one of the three Kansas artists elected to the National Academy of Design.

◄◄◄◄◄◄◄◄◄◄◄◄◄◄◄◄◄◄◄☼►►►►►►►►►►►►►►►►►►►►►►

Tour 13

(Kansas City, Mo.)—Fort Scott—Pittsburg—Columbus—(Muskogee, Okla.); US 60.
Missouri Line to Oklahoma Line, 162.1 m.

St. Louis & San Francisco R.R. parallels route between Pleasanton and Fort Scott; Missouri Pacific R.R. between Fort Scott and Arma.
Paved roadbed except for a short graveled stretch between Pittsburg and the Oklahoma Line; open all year.
Good accommodations in all larger towns.

US 69—following the approximate route of the military road surveyed in 1837 between Fort Leavenworth and Fort Coffey on the Arkansas River in what is now Oklahoma—crosses country that ranges from the productive farms, attractive suburban homes, and wooded streams south of Kansas City to the bleak chert hills near the Oklahoma Line. Around Fort Scott is prosperous dairying country, Pittsburg is surrounded by bituminous coal fields, while Treece is within the Tri-State lead- and zinc-mining area. Much of this region was the scene of border warfare in the 1850's and early 1860's in which it was plundered by guerrillas and ruffians who stole from both sides.

US 69, following Southwest Boulevard in Kansas City, Mo., crosses the Missouri Line, 0 *m.*, approximately 2 miles southwest of the Union Station in Kansas City, Mo. *(see MO. Tour 17).*

At 4.7 *m.* is the junction with US 50 *(see Tour 4).* Between this point and 5 *m.* US 69 and US 50 are one route.

South of the junction with US 50 is a suburban residential district of attractive homes and broad landscaped lawns.

The KANSAS PORT OF ENTRY for trucks, 13 *m.*, is a filling station and garage at which truck drivers entering the State are required to stop, declare their cargoes, and pay revenue *(see TRANSPORTATION).*

STANLEY, 21 *m.* (975 alt., 200 pop.), is a neat roadside community named for Henry M. Stanley, the explorer who in 1871 found the Scottish missionary, David Livingstone, in Africa.

At 23 *m.* is the junction with a private dirt road.

Right on this road is the BLACK BOB LAKE, 0.3 *m. (nominal rates for cabins, boats, swimming, fishing, horseback riding),* named for a band of Shawnee who once owned land here.

West of Stanley are many Osage orange hedges. Bows made from these trees, called bois d'arc (Fr., *bow tree*) by French explorers, gave the Osage great hunting and fighting power. As late as 1840 a prairie Indian would trade a horse and blanket to an Osage for enough of this wood to make a bow. A weapon made of such material lasted a lifetime and could bring down the largest buffalo—a feat otherwise accomplishable only by a lance thrust.

The trees have waxy green leaves like those of orange trees and bear orange-like seed balls. When cut and trimmed they make a square hedge, densely leaved and so thorny that neither man nor beast can penetrate it. Uncut, the trees grow 20 to 25 feet high.

To encourage the planting of Osage orange trees, the State in 1867 offered a cash bonus of $2 for every four rods of hedge planted and sustained for five years. The seeds grow readily from nursery plantation, and in the 1870's hard-pressed settlers of eastern Kansas planted miles of "fence" without buying posts or wire.

Because their rapid growth and sharp thorns make trimming a difficult task, hundreds of miles of these hedges have been pulled up in recent years, burned for firewood, and replaced with barbwire fences.

The wood of the Osage orange tree is extremely hard and a beautiful canary yellow, but is unsuitable for furniture because it splits as it dries. Used as fence posts, however, its immunity to decay makes it very satisfactory. As a fuel it gives a quick clean fire with heat as intense as that of anthracite coal.

LOUISBURG, 38 *m.* (1,032 alt., 616 pop.), was founded by Colonel Sims and David Perry in 1867. When they came here to establish a town this site was part of a 10-square-mile reservation for four confederated Indian tribes—the Kaskaskia, the Peoria, the Wea, and the Piankishaw—and the only link with civilization was the narrow winding Ozark Trail that led from Fort Leavenworth in the north to the Ozark Mountains in the southeast.

The town, originally called Little St. Louis, was renamed at the request of the Post Office Department to avoid confusion with the Missouri city. In 1870 Anthony Cott, an Indian, built the first hotel.

In 1872, the year the railroad was built through the vicinity, Doyle and Sims bought land west of the main street. In 1873 they bought 100 acres to the north of the railroad. A mill and a store were established north of the tracks, and so violent a rivalry developed between the inhabitants of the new addition and those of the old site south of the tracks, that the settlement was nicknamed "Bloody Corners."

In 1880, after several capitalists had offered to open a bank in Louisburg if the two factions would unite, harmony was restored and two years later the village was incorporated.

At 57 *m.* is the junction with State 35, paved.

Right on State 35, beside a schoolhouse, is a junction with a dirt road, 1 *m.* Left on this road is SILVER MOUND, 1.5 *m.,* similar to other wooded mounds that rise so abruptly from the plain in this section except for the pseudo-silver mine at its crest. *(Snakes, cactus, thorny bushes, cave-ins make ascent dangerous.)* The shaft of this mine was dug years ago by a band of Osage who believed there was silver here. It was once so deep that the bottom could not be seen from the surface of the mound, but it has become filled with rock and debris and is now hardly more than 50 feet deep. When the sun is high overhead dozens of snakes are visible in the bottom of the pit basking in the light.

Just inside a cemetery gate (R), 64.5 *m.,* is the MARAIS DES CYGNES MASSACRE MONUMENT, a tall slender granite shaft. On May 19, 1858, Capt. Charles Hamelton with 50 Missourians appeared unexpectedly in the vicinity of Trading Post and began seizing Free State men, some of whom were planting corn. Eleven captives were taken into a ravine near the Missouri Line north of Trading Post, lined up against a bluff, and shot. At the first volley all went down—five killed, five wounded, and one untouched.

News of this massacre inflamed the abolitionists of Massachusetts and was the subject of John Greenleaf Whittier's "Le Marais du Cygne."

Two years later the Free Soil men, who had grown stronger in Linn County, took vengeance on the proslavery advocates. On November 12, 1860, Russell Hinds was seized and hanged by an organized mob under the command of C. R. Jennison. James Marshall reported that Hinds had been tried by a jury of twelve men and hanged for man stealing under the Mosaic law in Exodus, XXI, 16: "And he that stealeth a man and selleth him . . . shall surely be put to death." Hinds had returned a fugitive slave to his master and received a reward.

TRADING POST, 65 *m.* (862 alt., 100 pop.), a scattering of modest homes strung out on both sides of the highway, was a thriving town in the days of border warfare; as early as 1839 Michael Gireau established a trading post here.

According to local tradition Gen. Winfield Scott, commander in chief of the U.S. Army (1841–61), built a fort and stockade here in 1842. However, the general's biographers fail to mention the incident and his recorded activities during that year as well as his high rank make the story highly improbable.

Parallels, an open letter written by John Brown as propaganda, was dated Trading Post, January 1859.

There is a legend that the Marias Des Cygnes River, which is crossed at the south edge of Trading Post, was named by Evangeline, the heroine of Henry Longfellow's poem. Evangeline was abandoned by the British near the Canadian boundary; she and her companions came down the Great Lakes, the Illinois River, the Mississippi, and then up the Missouri to this, the Osage. While seeking a place in which to settle, they were guided by Osage Indians to the Indian village at the headwaters of the stream.

In this village Evangeline heard Sona tell the Indian children the legend of Osa, a young Potawatomi princess who was loved by Coman, a young war chief of a hostile tribe. Osa's father forbade their marriage and warned Coman to leave the camp or be killed.

Osa's tribe accompanied Coman to the banks of the river, which was at flood, and helped him launch his canoe. Suddenly Osa leaped in the boat with Coman who paddled swiftly away but in the middle of the turbulent stream the waves upset them and they sank. As the remorseful father and his horrified people gazed on the scene, two great white swans arose from the waters and swam away.

After hearing this sad story, tears filled Evangeline's eyes. Grieving for her own lover, she wandered into the woods and up a hill. From the top she saw the green valley with the shimmering stream winding through the marshlands and, spreading out her arms to its beauty, cried, "C'est le marais des cygnes!" *(This is the marsh of the swans).* Her French friends, who had followed the unhappy girl, ever afterward called the Osage River the Marais des Cygnes.

PLEASANTON, 72 *m.* (862 alt., 1,214 pop.), was founded in July 1869 and named for General Pleasanton who defeated the Confederates here in the only decisive battle fought on Kansas soil during the Civil War.

The Pleasanton High School, 2 blocks R. of the highway, is on a butte called Round Mound, the SITE OF THE BATTLE OF ROUND MOUND.

When General Price, the Confederate officer, was retreating after the Battle of Westport, the Federal forces began firing as soon as they had reached the Marais des Cygnes River, thus forcing Price to give battle. On Round Mound General Pleasanton stationed a battery of seven howitzers that shelled the Confederate battle line—drawn up two miles to the south

—till the Confederates retired and entered Missouri near Fort Scott. James Dunlavy, a 16-year-old recruit, writing to his father in Iowa on October 29, 1864, four days after the battle, gave the following account of his part in this engagement: "I got lost from Company D and fell in with Company C and had fired several shots when I saw men in Union uniforms to my right and started towards them. They were running and I later learned they were Rebels dressed in Federal uniforms. General Marmaduke saw me shooting at the "butternuts" and mistook me for a Rebel (as he had dressed many in our uniforms), and he came toward me cursing me for shooting at him. I saw my advantage, held my fire, and let hir gallop up to me before levelling my carbine at his breast. I told him to ￼urrender, and he handed me his pistol breach-end first, saying: "I surrender myself a prisoner of war." He told me his name and wanted to go to General Pleasanton. I didn't know his location and took him to General Curtis, who thanked me and told me to keep the revolver. Since then nearly all the officers have congratulated me, saying they are satisfied with me as a soldier."

On the eastern edge of town is LAKE PLEASANTON and a landscaped recreation park *(shelter houses, ball ground with floodlights, golf course)*. The lake is the source of the Pleasanton water supply.

At 74 *m.* is the junction with State 52, paved.

Right on this road is MOUND CITY, 5 *m.* (888 alt., 655 pop.), seat of Linn County. Mound City was founded in 1857 and named for Sugar Mound, an early landmark east of the city. It defeated Paris in a county seat contest but was unable to obtain the county records until John T. Snoddy of Mound City, and 50 men armed with rifles, trained a small cannon on the courthouse at Paris. Although the "army" had neither powder nor shot for their cannon, the Paris officials were intimidated and produced the hidden records from under a bed. Shortly after this "battle" Paris ceased to exist.

During the Civil War a wagonload of women armed with hatchets drove into Mound City from a nearby village. Joined by a group of local women, they demolished Mound City's saloon so completely that none took its place for many years.

The annual Linn County fair is held at Mound City (Sept.).

On his farm five miles northwest of Mound City, James Montgomery, the Free State leader, maintained a fort. Here David Sibbet met John Brown and here Brown is said to have planned the Harpers Ferry raid. Sibbet later told of spending the night at Montgomery's house, where he insisted on sleeping in the loft so that the Montgomerys could use their bedroom; but his host, pointing to bullet holes in the wall and bed which had been made in an attempt to murder him, said that it was unsafe for anyone to sleep in the room.

FORT SCOTT, 96 *m.* (800 alt., 10,763 pop.) *(see FORT SCOTT).*

Points of Interest: Old military barracks, historical museum, Fort Blair, Carroll Plaza, Market Square, home of Eugene Ware.

Fort Scott is at the junction with US 54 *(see Tour 5).*

In ARMA, 119 *m.* (934 alt., 2,004 pop.), a coal-mining town spread over a large area, many of the residents have been thrown out of work during the past few years by the substitution of strip mining for deep-shaft mining *(see Tour 6, Introduction to Section a.).*

South of Arma, thick coal deposits are visible in roadside embankments that were cut in building the highway.

FRANKLIN, 120 *m.* (900 alt., 1,683 pop.), is a mining town even more attenuated than Arma. A large part of the population in Franklin—as in all the towns between Arma and Pittsburg—is made up of Italians.

At the south edge of Franklin is the junction with State 57, paved.

Right on State 57 is GIRARD, 7 *m.* (993 alt., 2,442 pop.), seat of Crawford County. This quiet little town of old buildings was named for Stephen Girard, the Philadelphia merchant, banker, and philanthropist of pre-Civil War days.

The *Appeal to Reason,* a Socialist weekly paper, was founded here by J. A. Wayland in the 1890's. Its boasted circulation of half a million was achieved by selling bundle orders to enthusiastic partisans and enlisting them in subscription-getting brigades. Wayland had made a fortune in a real estate boom in Amarillo, Tex., and wished to devote his money to the abolition of the private ownership of land. He later leased the paper to Fred Warren. During President Taft's administration, Warren printed an article describing degenerate practices in the Federal penitentiary at Leavenworth; for this he was convicted for sending obscene matter through the mails and sentenced to the Federal prison he had criticized. "When they get me in there," he told readers of the *Appeal,* "they will practice on my body these same abominations until they kill me." He said that President Taft, acting as the tool of capitalism, was sacrificing him in order to silence the *Appeal to Reason.* The President pardoned him.

Propagandizing with ardent zeal, sometimes shrewdly, sometimes disingenuously, the paper was never without a crusade on its hands. It backed many an issue that has since won popular acceptance through enactment of social and labor legislation. Highly sensational in method, it exerted considerable influence at its peak, particularly in midwest and southwestern towns and rural districts, being influential in running up a vote of over 900,000 for Eugene V. Debs, Socialist candidate for President, in 1912. Through promoting "encampments"—a sort of Socialist Chautauqua—it combined campaigning with the sale of "sub cards" and in this way occasionally pushed its circulation near the million mark.

The businessmen of this conservative Republican town once said in defense of the Socialist weekly, "Their printing and mailing plant is the largest industry in town, and no disturbances here or anywhere else have resulted from its publication." In 1922, when the paper ceased publication, its current editor and owner, E. Haldeman-Julius, who had married the daughter of Girard's leading banker, began publishing abridged editions of the classics at five cents a copy and achieved, through these "Little Blue Books," one of the greatest outputs in American publishing history.

The CRAWFORD COUNTY STATE PARK *(campground, ovens, tables, zoo),* 123 *m.,* one of the most attractive sites in the State, is the result of strip mining. Rain filled the canyons left by the shovels; trees and other vegetation grew on the mountains of dirt heaped beside them; and in 1926 the State landscaped the area, stocked it with game and fish, and built a system of roads.

At 123.5 *m.* is the northern junction with US 160 *(see Tour 6)* which unites with US 69 a short distance.

Near Pittsburg the dumps and pits of abandoned strip mines border both sides of the highway. Fruit or nut trees grow on some of the mounds; many have been leveled and returned to pasture land. The pits, water-filled, are from 5 to 50 feet deep and are used for fishing and swimming holes. *(Unimproved pits are open; for those fenced and stocked with fish, a 25¢ fee includes rent of boat.)*

PITTSBURG, 127 *m.* (932 alt., 18,145 pop.), the coal metropolis of Kansas, was founded in the 1870's as a mining camp and named for the Pennsylvania city. Pittsburg's soot-producing industries are confined to the

TRANSPORTING STEAM SHOVELS FOR STRIP MINING

outskirts; the town, built along a long clean main street with attractive well-kept homes and few slums, resembles a prosperous trading center.

Ten years after Robert Lanyon had established a zinc smelter here in 1878, importing zinc from the mines a few miles south and utilizing Pittsburg's cheap fuel, the town became the leading zinc-smelting center of the United States.

The introduction in recent years of surface mining and the substitution of gas for coal as an industrial fuel have caused a severe local depression as is the case in other coal-mining towns of the State.

In the fall of 1919 a general strike for a 60-percent increase in pay, a 6-hour day, and a 5-day week—to meet the increased cost of living and relieve post-war unemployment—was called in the bituminous coal fields by the United Mine Workers. Although the Armistice had been signed a year before and the war regulation of coal prices had been withdrawn, President Wilson declared that the union's action was a violation of its wartime agreement not to strike and therefore unlawful, as the treaty of peace had not yet been signed. John L. Lewis announced that the union would fight producers but not the Government and agreed to accept the decision of a three-man commission; the commission later granted the miners a slight increase in pay.

Meanwhile, Henry Allen, then Governor of Kansas, called for volunteers to prevent a fuel shortage. About 1,000 men, many of them college students, were sent to Pittsburg where, protected by the militia, they operated the strip mines.

As a result of this strike the Governor also called a special session of the legislature to create the Court of Industrial Relations, designed to settle all disputes in industries affecting the public welfare (see INDUSTRY, COMMERCE AND LABOR).

The KANSAS STATE TEACHERS' COLLEGE, 17th St. and S. Broadway, is a State-maintained, co-educational institution. It was founded in 1903 as a school for manual-training teachers, largely through the efforts of R. S. Russ, superintendent of the Pittsburg city schools, and the first executive head of the training school. In 1913 the name was changed by legislative act from the Kansas Manual Training Normal School to its present name.

Among the fourteen buildings on the 55-acre landscaped campus is the administration building, RUSS HALL, a three-story brick and limestone structure of classic design, erected in 1907. PORTER LIBRARY (open 8 a.m.–9 p.m., schooldays) of similar design and construction, houses a MUSEUM (open) that contains geological and paleontological specimens, Indian artifacts, and a collection of insects and stuffed animals.

For a brief period after the United States had entered the World War the college campus was a military camp; here Batteries C and D of the 1st Kansas Field Artillery Regiment (later the 130th Field Artillery) were mustered into service.

The college now offers a four-year course and degrees in education, liberal arts, and fine arts. Enrollment in 1937 was 1,202.

LINCOLN PARK (swimming, golf, picnic grounds), on the northwest edge of town and SCHLANGER PARK (playgrounds, picnic grounds) on the east edge of town, are attractive recreation centers.

In the backyard of the WILLIAM M. LINDSAY HOME, 916 W. 4th St., is a petrified stump, found west of Pittsburg. An area, believed to be approximately 5 miles across and between 20 and 30 miles long, lying at the edge of the coal-mining district is known to contain other specimens of petrified wood, none of which appears above the surface of the ground. When Lindsay reported the discovery of his stump in 1936 a Pittsburg newspaper editor remarked, "Mr. Lindsay has been stumping this district for a long time. He has now got a stump that will not crack nor crumble under him." A few weeks later Lindsay was elected Lieutenant Governor.

Pittsburg is at the southern junction with US 160 (see Tour 6).

Left from Pittsburg on 20th St., graveled, is the KANSAS STATE QUAIL HATCHERY (open), 2.75 m. Twenty-nine of its 320 acres are occupied by incubators, brooder houses, and pens. The remaining 291 acres are planted in walnut, hickory, and pecan trees. About 250 pairs of quail are kept for brood stock and approximately 4,000 birds are shipped each year to deputy game wardens to replenish wild flocks in Kansas. A few partridges, prairie chickens, and other birds are also raised here.

COURTHOUSE, COLUMBUS

COLUMBUS, 149 *m.* (893 alt., 3,235 pop.), built around the Cherokee County Courthouse, has broad tree-lined streets, neat stores, attractive
houses, and several small manufacturing firms. Grazing, fruit growing,
and truck gardening are the principal sources of income in this region.

As early as 1868 Columbus was known as "the center" and in December of that year L. N. Lee opened a general store on the townsite. In 1871
a town of thirty-six blocks was organized and named Columbus by A. V.
Peters, a settler from Ohio. The discovery of a well of water having curative properties was widely advertised and brought many settlers.

The MAUDE NORTH MEMORIAL HOSPITAL, 22 N. Kansas Ave., a two-
story frame building of Georgian Colonial design, was built in 1886 as a
residence for R. A. Long (1850–1934), Kansas City lumber merchant
who founded Longview, Wash. Long married a Columbus girl, Ella M.
Wilson. The property was later acquired by Colonel Norton who donated
it to the city in 1918 as a memorial to his daughter, who was drowned in
the Spring River east of Columbus in 1915.

A tornado ripped through Columbus shortly before noon on March 30,
1938, killing 12 persons and injuring more than 200 as it spread devastation over an urban area nearly a mile and a half wide. Two schools were
damaged and approximately 200 houses were destroyed. Scores of school
children narrowly escaped serious injury when the top floor of the High-

land School collapsed. Townspeople worked furiously in the rain and hail that followed the tornado to rescue the children from the damaged building.

Martial law was declared; the injured and homeless were cared for by the American Red Cross. Workers from a nearby CCC camp at Chetopa, members of the State Highway Patrol, and scores of WPA workers aided local officers in patrolling streets and clearing away wreckage. Property damage was estimated at $500,000.

The tornado that struck Columbus was one of several which, at about the same hour, spread death and destruction over wide areas in southern Kansas, Missouri, Oklahoma, Arkansas, and Illinois.

At 159 *m.* is the junction with US 166 *(see Tour 7)*. On the southeast corner of this junction, locally called Four Corners, is a PORT OF ENTRY where cargoes of interstate transport trucks are inspected and taxed *(see TRANSPORTATION)*.

TREECE, 161 *m.* (880 alt., 749 pop.), a mining town, is surrounded by huge chert or "chat" piles, around which wind crooked graveled streets. Children attend school within the shadow of these white mounds—the residue from the lead and zinc mines—and, for lack of a better place, play on their dusty slopes after school hours.

In 1935 employees of the lead companies here, seeking recognition of their Union of Mine, Mill, and Smelter Workers, were locked out by employers who created and recognized a company union *(see COMMERCE, INDUSTRY AND LABOR)*. Alfred M. Landon, then Governor of Kansas, sent troops to protect the men who replaced the strikers. To prevent violence, the chat piles around Treece were lighted for three weeks with strings of electric lights.

Even today the animosity between union and non-union workers divides the town into two parts; the union men live on one side of Main St., and the non-union men in a section on the other side called Scabtown.

A Government survey in 1929 showed that 21.3 percent of the workers in this region were afflicted with silicosis and that 43 percent of the men working where the dust hazard was greatest ultimately contract the disease. The symptoms of silicosis are similar to those of tuberculosis and death is caused by the formation of scar tissue on the lungs. No cure for silicosis has yet (1938) been found. According to a later survey, conducted by the Kansas State Board of Health, about one-third of the children living in the mining region between Treece and Picher, Okla., have tuberculosis, induced by the abundance of silica dust in the air.

At 162.1 *m.* US 69 crosses the Oklahoma Line 95 miles north of Muskogee, Okla. *(see Okla. Tour 8)*.

PART IV

Appendices

Chronology

<table>
<tr><td>1540</td><td>Francis Vasquez de Coronado begins search for "Seven Cities of Cibola."</td></tr>
<tr><td>1541</td><td>Coronado expedition enters Quivira (Kansas), reaching a point near present site of Junction City.</td></tr>
<tr><td>1542</td><td>Fray Juan de Padilla returns as missionary to Quivira; murdered by Indians.</td></tr>
<tr><td>1673</td><td>Father Jacques Marquette and Louis Joliet explore Mississippi River from the Wisconsin to the Arkansas River.</td></tr>
<tr><td>1682</td><td>Rene-Robert Cavelier, Sieur de La Salle, follows the Mississippi from Illinois River to its mouth. France claims region drained by the Mississippi and its tributaries; named "Louisiana" by La Salle.</td></tr>
<tr><td>1719</td><td>Charles Claude du Tisné explores upper Louisiana; visits Osage villages near mouth of Osage River; crosses northeast corner of Kansas to Pawnee on Republican River.</td></tr>
<tr><td>1720</td><td>Lieutenant General Villazur's Spanish "caravan" defeated by Pawnee Indians. French left in undisputed possession of Platte region.</td></tr>
<tr><td>1722</td><td>French erect Fort Orleans near mouth of Osage River under command of Etienne Venyard, Sieur de Bourgmont.</td></tr>
<tr><td>1724</td><td>Bourgmont ascends Missouri River to Kansa villages; traverses Kansas to Rocky Mountains.</td></tr>
<tr><td>1725</td><td>Fort Orleans destroyed by Kansa. French terminate official activities in upper Louisiana.</td></tr>
<tr><td>1762</td><td>All French territory west of Mississippi River is ceded to Spain.</td></tr>
<tr><td>1764</td><td>Pierre Laclede Luguest and Auguste and Pierre Chouteau, French fur traders, establish headquarters at St. Louis. Development of Kansas fur trade begins.</td></tr>
<tr><td>1800</td><td>By the treaty of San Ildefonso (confirmed by the treaty of Madrid in 1801) Louisiana west of the Mississippi is retroceded to France.</td></tr>
<tr><td>1803</td><td>Napoleon sells all of Louisiana to United States.</td></tr>
<tr><td>1804</td><td>March 26. Kansas region becomes part of District of Louisiana, under control of Indiana Territory.
Lewis and Clark expedition lands at mouth of Kansas River, June 26; reaches stream in Doniphan County, July 4, naming it Independence Creek.</td></tr>
<tr><td>1805</td><td>March 3. District of Louisiana becomes the Territory of Louisiana, independent of Indiana Territory.</td></tr>
<tr><td>1806</td><td>June 24. Zebulon M. Pike leaves St. Louis on second exploratory expedition.
August 5. Lewis and Clark return to mouth of Kansas River with first reliable information on western country.
September 29. Captain Pike replaces Spanish flag with United States flag in Pawnee Indian village (now Pike's Pawnee Village State Park).</td></tr>
</table>

1807   Manuel Lisa, Spanish fur trader, establishes trading stations about head-
       waters of Missouri River.

1808   Auguste and Pierre Chouteau join Manuel Lisa in organizing Missouri
       Fur Company; a chain of trading posts throughout western country
       results.

1812   June 4. Territory of Missouri is created from the Territory of Louisiana;
       remainder of Territory left without law or official identification.
       Missouri Fur Company dissolves and is succeeded by American Fur Com-
       pany which concentrates in Kansas.

1819   August 10. Maj. Stephen H. Long's scientific expedition introduces the
       first steamboat, *Western Engineer,* to Kansas waters.

1820   Two Presbyterian missions established for the Osage; the Union on
       Neosho River and the Harmony on Marais des Cygnes.
       March 6. Missouri Compromise is signed by President Monroe, admitting
       Missouri as slave State, but providing that all future States west of the
       Mississippi and north of 36° 30′ shall be free.

1821   Captain William Becknell establishes route of Santa Fe Trail.

1823   Boundary between Missouri and Kansas is definitely fixed.

1824   Rev. Isaac McCoy proposes that Indians be removed to western reserva-
       tion; Daniel Webster describes Kansas as worthless area.

1825   By treaties the Osage, Kansa, and Shawnee give up part of their lands to
       make way for eastern emigrant tribes.
       Congress authorizes survey of Santa Fe Trail. Federal Government makes
       treaty with Cheyenne for right-of-way privileges.

1827   Col. Henry H. Leavenworth selects site of military post which bears his
       name.
       Government sends Daniel Morgan Boone to teach agriculture to Indians.
       Boone locates on land in what is now Jefferson County.

1828   August 22. Napoleon Boone is first white child born in Kansas region.

1829   Rev. Thomas Johnson establishes Methodist mission for Shawnee, near
       present site of Turner.
       Delaware Indians moved to Kansas.

1832   Kickapoo, Potawatomi, Kaskaskia, Peoria, Wea, and Piankeshaw Indian
       reservations established in Kansas.

1833   Rev. Jotham Meeker brings first printing press to Shawnee Baptist Mis-
       sion; two years later publishes first Kansas newspaper, the *Shawnee Sun.*
       Westport (now Kansas City, Mo.) becomes a depot on Santa Fe Trail.

1834   June 20. All territory west of the Mississippi, not included in States of
       Missouri and Louisiana or in Arkansas Territory, is set off as "Indian
       country" by Congress.

1836   Sauk, Fox, and Iowa Indians migrate to Kansas.

1837   Ottawa Baptist Mission (now Ottawa University) founded by Rev.
       Jotham Meeker.

1840   Miami Indians moved to Kansas.

1842   Fort Scott founded. Lieut. John C. Frémont, with Kit Carson as guide, ex-
       plores Kansas and Platte Rivers. Several later expeditions.

1843   Wyandot Indians settle on reservation in eastern Kansas; establish city of
       Wyandot (Kansas City, Kansas).

First group of Oregon emigrants (900) set out from Elm Grove, Kansas. (Larger groups pass through Kansas in 1844 and 1845).

1844 First move to organize Kansas into a Territory is made at Uniontown by Missourians.

1846 Mormons migrating to Salt Lake region cross Kansas plains in large numbers.

Mexican War begins. Gen. Stephen W. Kearny marches from Fort Leavenworth to California.

1847 August. The Mormon battalion starts from Fort Leavenworth for Mexican War service.

1848 February 2. Treaty of Guadelupe-Hidalgo ends Mexican War.

October. Frémont organizes fourth expedition westward across Kansas, in search of practical overland route to California. His published account increases interest in the West.

1849 California gold rush brings 90,000 people over Kansas trails.

1850 Government builds military road from Fort Leavenworth to Fort Kearney. Overland stagecoach with passenger and mail service to Pacific coast is introduced.

Coal found near present site of Pittsburg (Kansas) is dug by settlers for their own use.

1853 Fort Riley is established by Major Ogden.

July 23. Wyandot Indians organize Kansas-Nebraska into Provisional Territory and elect delegate to 33rd Congress. Congress fails to recognize the act and delegate.

1854 Congress debates (January to May) Kansas-Nebraska Bill. President Pierce (May 31) signs bill creating two Territories, divided on the 40th parallel of latitude. Pro-slavery emigrants cross Missouri border into Kansas (June); and anti-slavery groups come from New England.

May. 2,0000,00 acres of Delaware and Shawnee land made available to whites, by public auction and preemption.

Towns of Leavenworth (June), Atchison and Lawrence (July) are laid out and organized.

August 11. Masons organize first lodge in Kansas, the Grove Lodge, at Wyandotte.

October 15. First Congregational Church in Kansas founded in Lawrence.

November 29. Pro-slavery element dominates election of delegate (Gen. John W. Whitfield) to Congress.

December 5. Topeka founded.

1855 Kansas population estimated at 8,601.

February. Five sons of John Brown settle near Osawatomie.

March 30. Armed Missourians dominate election of so-called "Bogus Legislature."

April. Doctor Robinson sends an order to Eli Thayer for 100 Sharp's rifles, which became known as "Beecher's Bibles."

June 5. Free State Convention is held at Lawrence; adjourned till June 25, when Convention declares "In reply to threats of war . . . our answer is: 'We are ready'."

July 2. "Bogus Legislature" meets at Pawnee; pro-slavery members gain control and adjourn, July 16, to Shawnee Mission. Expelled Free State legislators meet at Lawrence. Governor Reeder declares Shawnee Mission Legislature illegal.

July 27. Shawnee Mission Legislature asks President Pierce to remove Governor Reeder. U. S. Court rules that Shawnee session is regular. July 28. President removes Governor Reeder.

August 8. Le Compton, near Lawrence, is selected as permanent seat of government. Wilson Shannon, Democrat, is appointed Governor.

August 14. Free State Convention at Lawrence calls for election of delegates to draw up a State constitution.

September 5. Free Staters, at Big Springs, nominate Reeder as delegate to Congress. Organize Free State Party.

October 3. Law and Order Society organized by pro-slavery men at Leavenworth.

October. Pro-slavery party elects J. W. Whitfield delegate to Congress. Free State electors, at separate election, choose A. H. Reeder as delegate.

October 23–November 11. Free State constitutional convention at Topeka adopts constitution and asks Congress to admit Kansas as Free State.

November 14. Pro-slavery convention at Leavenworth repudiates Reeder.

November 21. Charles W. Dow, a Free State man is killed near Lawrence by Franklin M. Coleman, a pro-slavery man. The so-called "Wakarusa War" results.

December 1. Siege of Lawrence begins. It lasts a week; Governor Shannon asks for U. S. troops. John Brown and his four sons arrive armed in Lawrence. Governor Shannon pacifies warring factions.

December 15. Free State constitution is adopted. Pro-slavery group at Leavenworth destroy ballot-box and office of Free State newspaper.

1856   January 15. Territorial election held. Free State Party also holds election. President Pierce supports legality of Territorial election, and denounces Free State Topeka convention as insurrectionary.

February 4. J. W. Whitfield is sworn in as Territorial delegate to Congress. A. H. Reeder (Free State delegate) contests election.

February 16. Secretary of War Marcy places Federal troops in Kansas at disposal of Governor Shannon.

March 4-15. Free State legislature convenes at Topeka. Senator Lewis Cass, of Michigan, presents Free State constitution to Senate.

April 18. Congressional committee arrives at Lawrence to investigate Whitfield-Reeder election.

May 5. A grand jury (Douglass County) indicts leaders of Free State government, on charge of treason.

May 21. Pro-slavery men, heavily armed, close in on Lawrence; town is sacked.

May 31. U. S. Marshal Henry Pate arrests two of Brown's sons at Osawatomie on charge of murder.

June 2–5. Battle of Black Jack. Free-staters, under John Brown, capture sheriff and 28 men. Governor Shannon orders use of U. S. troops to disperse all unauthorized armed bands. Colonel Sumner, with U. S. troops, overtakes Brown party, with pro-slavery prisoners. Brown agrees to disband.

June 23. Clashes continue; John Brown selects party for a "private expedition." Both sides become uncontrollable.

June 26. Galusha A. Grow introduces bill in Congress to admit Kansas under Topeka (Free State) constitution. Bill fails in Senate.

July 2. Congressional investigating committee sustains charge that legislature of Kansas was illegal. (Both Whitfield and Reeder are refused as delegates to Congress.)

August 2. Governor Shannon resigns, and John W. Geary is appointed.
August 7. James H. Lane enters Kansas with his "Army of the North"—
600 immigrants from New England.
August-September. David R. Atchison is elected commander-in-chief of
"The Army of Law and Order in Kansas," a pro-slavery force of 500-
1100 men. Law and Order army attacks Osawatomie. John Brown, and 40
Free Staters defend it, but have to retreat. Town burned. Force of 300
from Lawrence, under Lane, drive Law and Order band over Missouri
border. Governor prevails upon pro-slavery forces gathered in Lawrence
to disband.
December 5. Congress reconsiders Whitfield-Reeder case, and seats Whitfield as delegate from Kansas.

1857   January. Free State legislature memorializes Congress to admit Kansas as
a State under Topeka constitution. (Makes similar appeal in June.)
February 13. Territorial Legislature adjourns. Enacts a new code of laws.
February. Townsite of Emporia located.
March-May. Free State men protest against proposed election for dele-
gates to a new constitutional convention.
April 10. Robert James Walker is appointed Governor.
June 15. Free Staters refrain from voting in convention election. Votes
cast almost entirely pro-slavery.
July-August. Free Staters convene at Topeka, and reaffirm adherence to
Topeka constitution. Free State election polls 7,257 for and 24 against
constitution.
October 19–November 3. Pro-slavery men convene at Lecompton and
frame constitution, a clause of which provides that the "rights of property in slaves now in the Territory shall in no manner be interfered with";
another clause forbids any amendments in constitution, if ratified, until
1864.
November 27. Free State mass meeting at Leavenworth repudiates recent
Lecompton constitution.
December 21. Lecompton constitution before people, who were to vote
merely "For the constitution *with* slavery," or "For the constitution *without* slavery." Vote "with slavery" 6,143; "without slavery" 569. Free
Staters refused to vote.

1858   January. Kansas State Library founded.
January 4. Lecompton constitution, *as a whole,* is before people, and is
rejected (10,226 to 138). Pro-slavery element refuse to vote. President
Buchanan (February 2) recommends Congress to admit Kansas under
Lecompton constitution.
March 4. Topeka (Free State) legislature holds last session; no quorum.
March 23. U. S. Senate agrees to President's recommendation, lower
house disagrees (April 1), and refuses to act until a constitution ratified
by popular vote is submitted. Popular vote (May 18) adopts another
constitution, the Leavenworth, but Congress declines to accept it. Pro-
slavery band attack Free Staters near Trading Post on the Marais des
Cygnes River (May 19). Five killed. A modified Lecompton constitution
is rejected by the people (August 2).
May 21. Pike's Peak expedition leaves Lawrence.
October. Baker University established at Palmyra (Baldwin).
November 19. Samuel Medary appointed Governor.
December 20. John Brown and his men raid in Missouri, liberate 14
slaves, and bring them into Kansas.

1859   February 7. Scientific and Historical Society of Kansas chartered.
        May. Horace Greeley visits Kansas. Republican Party convention held at
        Osawatomie.
        July 5. Constitutional convention opens at Wyandotte. Completes new
        constitution (July 29), which prohibits slavery. Constitution ratified by
        voters (October 4), 10,421 to 5,530.
        November 8. First Territorial election, under Wyandotte constitution,
        gives Republicans majority in legislature.
        December 1. Abraham Lincoln tours Kansas; speaks at Atchison, Troy
        and Leavenworth.
        Fort Larned is built.

1860   Population 107,206.
        February 11. Legislature abolishes slavery in Kansas, over-riding veto by
        governor. Wyandotte constitution laid before Congress.
        February 29. Bill to admit Kansas as a State is sponsored in U. S. Senate
        by Seward, and in House (March 29) by Grow. Not carried.
        March–April. Marysville and Elwood Railroad completed between Elwood
        and Wathena.
        April. Pony Express established.
        Drought makes crop almost total failure; 30,000 settlers leave Kansas.
        Baptists organize Ottawa University.
        First oil well west of the Mississippi is dug near Paola.

1861   Last Territorial legislature opens (January 7) at Lecompton, and closes
        (February 2) at Lawrence.
        January 29. Kansas, under Wyandotte constitution, is admitted into the
        Union as the 34th State.
        February 9. First State Governor, Dr. Charles Robinson, inaugurated.
        March 26. First State legislature convenes at Topeka (adjourns June 4).
        April 4. First U. S. Senators from Kansas, James H. Lane and Samuel C.
        Pomeroy, are elected.
        April 15. President Lincoln issues call for 75,000 volunteers.
        May 21. Great Seal of Kansas adopted.
        June 3–20. First and Second Regiments of Volunteer Infantry mustered
        into service.
        July 18. First daily overland coach, from Sacramento, Calif., reaches St.
        Joseph, Mo., having taken seventeen days.
        August 10. Kansas regiments at Battle of Wilson's Creek, which saves
        Missouri for Union.
        November 5. Topeka chosen as permanent State capital.
        University of Lawrence becomes Lawrence University of Kansas, under
        Episcopal auspices.
        State temperance society holds its first meeting.

1862   June 24. Ottawa Indians in Kansas become U. S. citizens; heads of fam-
        ilies to receive 160 acres of land.
        Congress, by provisions of Morrill Act, grants Kansas 90,000 acres, to
        found an agricultural college.
        October 17. William Clarke Quantrill, Confederate guerrilla, raids Shaw-
        neetown.

1863   January 12. Inauguration of Thomas Carney as Governor.
        February 16. Manhattan is chosen as site for Kansas State College of
        Agriculture and Applied Science.
        March 3. Congress provides for removal of all Indians from Kansas.

May–October. Fight between Osage Indians and Confederate soldiers near Independence. Quantrill's guerrillas sack and burn Lawrence, killing about 150 citizens; massacre cavalry escort of General Blunt at Baxter Springs. Legislature selects Lawrence as site of State university.

1864   January 30. Wagon train of coal from Fort Scott arrives at Leavenworth.
April. Indians begin attacks on Kansas frontier settlements. Raids continue for several months.
October 24. Gen. Stirling Price invades Kansas in Linn County. Defeated at Mine Creek, Price retreats into Missouri.
Legislature authorizes establishment of an asylum for the blind in Wyandotte County.

1865   Civil War ends. Kansas contributed 20,097 men to Union Army.
April 23. Kansas observes day of fasting and prayer, mourning the martyred President.
May. State census: white 127,270; Negro 12,527; Indian 382.
September. Osage Indians sell to United States tract 30 by 50 miles square and cede strip 20 miles wide, partly in Kansas.
Kansas State Normal School established at Emporia.
Lincoln College (now Washburn) founded at Topeka.

1866   January. To foster railroad construction, State legislature authorizes sale of 500,000 acres of State land.
Construction begins on east wing of the State Capitol.
February. Deaf and dumb asylum established at Olathe.
July 11. U. S. Senator James H. Lane dies.
Settlements on White Rock River and at Lake Sibley attacked by Indians.
September 12. State university at Lawrence opened.
September. Grasshoppers over-run northern Kansas; are worse the following spring.

1867   Treaties made for removal of Sauk and Fox, Ottawa, Miami and Wyandot Indians to Indian Territory. Indian village of 300 lodges on Pawnee Fork destroyed by troops under Gen. W. S. Hancock. Cheyenne, Arapahoe, and Kiowa Indians attack Kansas border settlements and engineering parties on the Kansas Pacific R.R. Eighteenth Kansas Volunteer Cavalry, raised to protect the frontier from Indian attacks, mustered into service. Medicine Lodge Peace Treaty (October 28) negotiated with five Plains tribes. Joseph G. McCoy brings first herd of Texas longhorn cattle to Kansas plains. Abilene becomes terminus of Chisholm Trail.
November 5. Voters reject plan to amend Constitution by striking out words "white" and "male."
Lucy Stone and Susan B. Anthony stump Kansas for women's suffrage.
Legislature ratifies Fourteenth Amendment to the U. S. Constitution.

1868   February 10. William Allen White born in Emporia.
Wichita surveyed and platted.
September 1. Kansas Natural History Society, later the Academy of Science, organized at Topeka.
October 20. Nineteenth Kansas Volunteer Cavalry mustered in for Indian War. Regiment joins General Sheridan on the North Canadian River November 28.

1869   January 11. Inauguration of James M. Harvey as Governor.
February 4. Women's Suffrage convention held at Topeka.
April 10. Eight million acres of "Osage Diminished Reserve" opened for white settlement.

April 18. Nineteenth Kansas Regiment mustered out at Fort Hays.
May 3. Site of Kansas City surveyed.
May. Sioux and Cheyenne raid northwestern Kansas.
December 25. East wing of the State Capitol at Topeka occupied for the first time.

1870   Population 364,399.
January 19. Kansas ratifies Fifteenth Amendment to U. S. Constitution.
July. Wichita incorporated as a village.
September 10. Treaty concluded with Osage Indians for purchase of the "Osage Diminished Reserve."
Legislature provides for a State normal school at Leavenworth.
Willard-Murphy temperance movement sweeps the State.

1872   January 1. Henry King and James W. Steele begin publication of *Kansas Magazine.*
April. First grange lodge in Kansas organized at Hiawatha.
July 15. Congress authorizes removal of Osage Indians from Kansas to Indian Territory.
August 26. Town of Hutchinson incorporated.
First meat shipped in refrigerator cars leaves Salina over the Union Pacific.

1873   January. Thomas A. Osborn, Governor; and John J. Ingalls, U. S. Senator.
Mennonite immigration to Kansas from Russia begins.
Women's Crusade conducts saloon-smashing campaign.
September 8. Rich deposits of lead discovered near Baxter Springs.

1874   July–August. Plague of grasshoppers.
August 1. Compulsory education act becomes effective.
September. 1,500 Mennonite immigrants from Russia arrive in Topeka, buy 100,000 acres of land, and introduce "Turkey Red" wheat to America.
September 10-11. State Temperance Convention meets at Topeka and starts movement that results in prohibition for Kansas.
September 15. Legislature meets to provide relief to sufferers from grasshopper plague.

1875   May. Serious damage to crops by grasshoppers reported.
December. Kansas State Historical Society organized.
August 20. Kansas flour (30,000 pounds) shipped from Arkansas City by flatboat down Arkansas River.

1876   March 4. State legislature abolishes color distinction from Kansas laws.
Lead and zinc deposits discovered in Cherokee County.
October. Kansas apples are awarded gold medal at Philadelphia Centennial Exposition.

1877   January. George T. Anthony, Governor.
August 30. John Brown monument dedicated at Osawatomie.

1878   Santa Fe Railway workers strike. Governor calls out militia.
Last Cheyenne raid in western Kansas.

1878–79 Negroes from former slave States arrive in great numbers. 40,000 reach Kansas by end of 1880.

1879   January. John P. St.John, Governor.
Industrial School for Boys founded at Topeka.
Prohibition amendment passed by Legislature.

1880   Population 996,096.
November. Prohibition amendment ratified by voters.

1881   Last cattle drive made to Dodge City. Homesteaders begin to populate western Kansas.
       Bureau of labor established.
       Bethany College founded by Swedish Lutherans at Lindsborg; organizes Oratorio Society (1882) and presents first Messiah Festival.
       September 14. Farmers' Alliance meets at Topeka.

1882   Well near Paola produces natural gas in great quantities.
       College of Emporia established by Presbyterian Church.
       First Mennonite school in Kansas established at Halstead.

1883   January. George W. Glick, Governor.
       March. Board of railroad commissioners appointed.
       Edgar Watson Howe publishes his *Story of a Country Town*.

1884   July 4. Bull fight at Dodge City, said to be only one ever held in the U. S.
       September 2. Prohibition Party in Kansas organized.
       Haskell Institute, school for Indians, established at Lawrence by U. S. Government.
       Special session of legislature deals with foot-and-mouth disease afflicting Kansas cattle. Livestock sanitary commission created by legislature.
       Women's State Suffrage Association organized.

1885   Population (State census) 1,268,562.
       Legislature creates State board of health.
       Kansas Wesleyan University (Salina) chartered.
       Peak of "great boom" period.

1886   Municipalities of Kansas City, Armourdale, Armstrong, and Wyandotte consolidated and named Kansas City.
       Blizzard destroys herds; impoverishes cattlemen, and ends their "open range" war with farmers.
       National Guard organized under the 1885 militia law.

1887   February 15. Kansas women are granted right to vote in school affairs.
       Lutherans establish Midland College at Atchison; Mennonites establish Bethel College at Newton.
       Rock salt discovered near Hutchinson while drilling for gas.
       Legislature authorizes county high schools; passes act to redeem railroad bonds.
       Severe drought brings about collapse of agricultural "boom."

1889   U. S. Government gives old Fort Dodge military reservation to Kansas for a State soldiers' home (opened 1890).
       Kansas produces record-breaking corn crop, 273 million bushels.
       Manufacture of beet sugar begins in Kansas.
       First county high school in the U. S. established at Chapman.
       Legislature passes eight-hour law.

1890   Population 1,428,108.
       November. Populist Party wins national seats; "Sockless Jerry" Simpson elected to House, and William A. Peffer to Senate.

1891   June 23. Col. Sam Wood, pioneer Free Stater, is shot in county-seat fight in Stevens County.

1892   September 15. Fairmount College at Wichita opened as Fairmount Institute.
       October 5. The Dalton gang attempts a bank robbery at Coffeyville; Bob and Emmitt Dalton and two others of the gang are slain.

November. L. D. Lewelling, Populist, is elected Governor.

1893 January–February. Both Populists and Republicans claim the speakership of the house of representatives at Topeka. Republicans take possession of house by force. Peace agreement signed after Governor calls out State militia. Kansas Supreme Court rules the Republican house is the legally elected body.

Thousands start from Caldwell and Arkansas City in race for lands in the Cherokee Strip.

1894 November 6. Constitutional amendment giving full suffrage to women is defeated.

Many companies organized to develop Kansas oil and gas fields. Board of irrigation created.

1895 May. Topeka Industrial and Educational Institute, for Negro children, is opened.

December 25. Natural gas discovered near Iola in quantities sufficient for manufacturing purposes.

1896 April 25. Cyclone destroys lives and property in Clay, Cloud, and Washington Counties.

November. Populists elect their second Governor, John W. Leedy.

School textbook commission established.

1898 Spanish-American War. Kansas sends four regiments.

November 6. Republicans gain control of the State.

Quakers found Garfield University (later Friends University) at Wichita.

1899 March 4. Traveling libraries established.

Legislature provides for State hospital for epileptics (located at Parsons in 1902).

1900 Population 1,470,495.

Carry Nation starts crusade against saloons.

1901 March 23. Brig. Gen. Frederick Funston, a Kansan, captures Aguinaldo, leader of Philippines insurrection.

1902 Fort Hays Kansas State College founded.

1903 Kansas State Teacher's College established at Pittsburgh as Manual Training School.

Helium discovered at Dexter.

State Capitol at Topeka completed.

Kansas River overflows, causing immense property damage.

1905 Anti-discrimination law passed, compelling uniform oil prices.

1907 State tax commission created.

1909 State free employment bureau established.

1910 Population 1,690,949.

August. John Brown Memorial Park at Osawatomie dedicated by Theodore Roosevelt.

1911 Legislature provides for new hospital for the insane at Larned.

Carry Nation dies at Leavenworth.

1912 Kansas votes complete suffrage for women.

1913 State school commission created.

1914 June 24. Statue of Gov. Glick placed in Statuary Hall, National Capitol, Washington, D. C.

Large oil field discovered in Butler County.

Arthur Capper elected Governor, first native Kansan to hold the office.

1915 Industrial welfare commission created.

1916 Kansas National Guard sent to Mexican border.

1917 Camp Funston, World War training camp, established on Fort Riley reservation.
State highway commission created.

1918 End of World War. 80,261 in war service from Kansas.
Henry J. Allen elected Governor, and Arthur Capper, former Governor, elected U. S. Senator (reelected 1924, 1930 and 1936).

1919 Coal strikes cause fuel shortage menace; volunteer workers operate mines protected by National Guard.

1920 Court of Industrial Relations created to control strikes and fix minimum wages. Governor Allen and Samuel Gompers, president of American Federation of Labor, debate about court in New York City.

1923 U. S. Supreme Court decides in test case that statute which created the Court of Industrial Relations is unconstitutional.
State bonus of $25,000,000 paid to Kansas ex-service men.

1924 Ku Klux Klan issue becomes leading factor in State; William Allen White independent candidate for governor on anti-Klan platform.

1925 Court of Industrial Relations abolished.
Forestry, fish and game commission organized; lake-building program begins in Neosho County.
Public service commission created.

1927 First gas well drilled at Hugoton, Stevens County, opens large field in southwestern part of State.

1928 Charles Curtis, U. S. Senator from Kansas, is elected Vice President of United States (died in Washington, D. C., 1936).

1929 Government survey shows 25 percent of mine workers in vicinity of Treece, Cherokee County, afflicted with silicosis.

1930 Population 1,880,999.
Harry H. Woodring elected Governor; he becomes Secretary of War September 25, 1936.

1931 Record Kansas wheat crop of 240 million bushels.

1932 Alfred M. Landon elected Governor.

1933 "Pay-as-you-go" policy adopted for State by passage of Cash Basis Law.

1934 Governor Landon reelected.

1934-35 Dust storm sweeps Kansas and adjoining States, arousing interest in soil conservation legislation.

1936 November. Governor Landon is unsuccessful Republican candidate for President of the United States; vote for Landon aggregated 16,679,583. Kansas elects a Democrat, Walter A. Huxman, as Governor.
New oil fields developed in western Kansas.

1937 Manufacture and sale in Kansas of 3.2 percent beer is legalized.
Depression affects school finances. Legislature creates a State aid fund to help elementary schools.
Two percent sales tax is adopted.
John Steuart Curry is commissioned to paint murals in Kansas State Capitol.

1938   March 30. Tornado at Columbus, Cherokee County, fatally injures 12
persons.
November. Republicans recapture Kansas. Governor Walter A. Huxman
is defeated by Payne Ratner, and U. S. Senator George McGill by Clyde
Reed.

Bibliography

GENERAL INFORMATION

Kansas Facts; a Year Book of the State. Topeka, Kansas. Facts Pub. Co., 1928–33. 6 v. illus., plates, maps, diagrs.

Kansas Yearbook. Topeka, Capper Printing Co., Kansas. State Chamber of Commerce, 1938. 396 p. illus., tables, charts.

U. S. Dept. of Commerce. Bureau of the Census. Fifteenth Census of the United States: 1930. Population Bulletin. First Series. *Kansas. Number and Distribution of Inhabitants.* Washington, Govt. Print. Off., 1930. 31 p. map, tables.

DESCRIPTION AND TRAVEL

Cobb, Irvin S. *Kansas.* With illus. by John T. McCutcheon. New York, George H. Doran Co., 1924. 61 p. front., plates. (Cobb's America Guyed Books.)

Simpich, Frederick. "Speaking of Kansas." *National Geographic Magazine,* Aug. 1937, v. 72:135-182.

White, William Allen. "Kansas, a Puritan Survival." (In Gruening, Ernest, ed. *These United States.* 1st series. New York, Boni & Liveright, 1923. p. 1-12.)

Winans, George W. *Kansas.* New York, Macmillan, 1902. 47 p. illus., maps. (Tarr and McMurry Geographies. Supplementary vol.)

GEOLOGY AND PALEONTOLOGY

Abell, Letha. "Kansas Fossils." *Aerend,* Winter 1934, v. 5:44-52.

Bass, N. W. *Geologic Investigations in Western Kansas, with Special Reference to Oil and Gas Possibilities.* Prepared in co-operation with U. S. Geological Survey. Lawrence, Kan., B. P. Walker, State Printer, 1926. 96 p. illus., maps, diagrs. Kansas. State Geological Survey. Bulletin 11.)

Sternberg, Charles H. *The Life of a Fossil Hunter.* With int. by Henry Fairfield Osborn. New York, H. Holt & Co., 1909. 286 p. front., plates, ports., facsims. (Am. Nature Series. Group 4. Working with Nature.)

Williston, S. W. "The Geology of Kansas." (In Heilprin, Angelo. *The Earth and Its Story.* New York, Silver, Burdett & Co., 1899. p. 269-288.)

PLANT AND ANIMAL LIFE

Bartholomew, Elam. *The Fungous Flora of Kansas.* Topeka, Kansas State Printing Plant, 1927. 46 p. (Kansas State Agricultural College. Agricultural Experiment Station.)

Black, J. D. "Mammals of Kansas." (In Kansas. State Board of Agriculture. *Thirtieth Biennial Report.* Topeka, 1936. p. 166-217.)

Goss, N. S. *History of the Birds of Kansas.* Illustrating 529 birds. Topeka, G. W. Crane & Co., 1891. 692 p.

Kansas. State Board of Agriculture. "Trees in Kansas." (In *Quarterly Report,* 1928. v. 47, no. 186-A.)

Smyth, Bernard B. *Plants and Flowers of Kansas.* Topeka, Geo. W. Crane & Co., 1900. 118 p. (Twentieth Century Classics and School Readings, no. 9.)

CONSERVATION AND NATURAL RESOURCES

Coburn, Foster Dwight. *Kansas and Her Resources.* 80th thousand. Chicago, Passenger Dept., Atchison, Topeka & Santa Fe Railway Co., 1902. 69 p. front., illus.

Kansas. State Planning Board. *Water, Its Use and Control in Kansas*. Topeka, 1936. 28 p. illus., tables. Prepared by Kenneth D. Grimes.
Kansas. University. Geological Survey. *Mineral Resources Circulars*. Lawrence, 1928 to date.

ARCHEOLOGY AND INDIANS

Abel, Annie Heloise. *Indian Reservations in Kansas and the Extinguishment of Their Title*. Read before Kansas State Historical Society, Dec. 2, 1902. Topeka, 1903. 38 p. plan (M. A. thesis, Univ. of Kansas.)
Basket, James Newton. "Prehistoric Kansas. A Study of the Route of Coronado between the Rio Grande and Missouri Rivers." (In *Collections of the Kansas State Historical Society, 1911–12*. Topeka, 1912. v. 12, p. 219-252.)
Campbell, C. E. "Down among the Red Men." (In *Collections of the Kansas State Historical Society, 1926–28*. Topeka, 1928. v. 17, p. 623-691.)
Connelley, William Elsey. "Notes on the Early Indian Occupancy of the Great Plains." (In *Collections of the Kansas State Historical Society, 1915–1918*. Topeka, 1918. v. 14, p. 438-470.)
Green, Charles Ransley. *Early Days in Kansas. In Keokuk's Time on the Kansas Reservation. . . .* Charles R. Green, Historian and Publisher. Olathe, Kan., 1913. 101 p. front. (diagr.), plates, ports. (Green's Historical Series.)
Jones, Paul A. *Quivira*. Wichita, McCormick-Armstrong, 1929. 182 p. front., illus.
Morehouse, George P. *The Kansa, or Kaw Indians, & Their History, & the Story of Padilla*. Topeka, State Print. Off., 1908. 52 p. illus., plates, port. (Read before the Kansas State Historical Society. Repr. from *Kansas Historical Collections*, v. 10.)
Ross, Mrs. Edith Connelley. *The Old Shawnee Mission, the Pioneer Institution of Christian Civilization in the West*. Written by Mrs. Edith Connelley Ross for the Shawnee Mission Memorial Foundation. Topeka, State Printing Plant, 1928. 28 p. front. (port.), illus., plan.
Spencer, Claudius B. "The Lansing Man." *Christian Advocate*, Feb. 4, 1903, v. 47: 138-141.
Wedel, Waldo Rudolph. *An Introduction to Pawnee Archeology*. Washington, Govt. Print. Off., 1936. 122 p. plates, maps. (Smithsonian Institution. Bureau of Am. Ethnology. Bulletin 112.) Bibl.
Whiteford, G. L. *Prehistoric Indian Excavations in Saline County, Kansas*. Saline, Consolidated Printing & Stationery Co., 1937. 16 p. illus.
Zimmerman, Mark E. "The Ground-house Indians and Stone-cist Grave Builders of Kansas and Nebraska." (In *Collections of the Kansas State Historical Society*. Topeka, 1918. v. 14, p. 471-487.)
———. "The Pawnee Americans." (In *Collections of the Kansas State Historical Society, 1923–1925*. Topeka, 1925. v. 16, p. 463-475.)

HISTORY

Arnold, Anna E. *A History of Kansas*. Topeka, State of Kansas, B. P. Walker, State Printer, 1931. 262 p. front., illus., ports. First pub. 1914.
Asbury, Herbert. *Carry Nation*. New York, A. A. Knopf, 1929. 307 p. illus., plates, ports.
Becker, Carl. "Public Archives of Kansas." (In American Historical Assn. *Annual Report . . . for the Year 1904*. Washington, 1905. p. 597-601.)
Beecher, Henry Ward. *Defence of Kansas*. Washington, Buell & Blanchard, Printers, 1856. 8 p.
Blackmar, Frank W., ed. *Kansas; a Cyclopedia of State History, Embracing Events, Institutions, Industries, Counties, Cities, Towns, Prominent Persons, etc.* With supplemental vol. devoted to selected personal history and reminiscence. Chicago, Standard Pub. Co., 1912. 3 v. in 4. front., illus., ports.
Brown, G. W. *The Truth at Last. History Corrected. Reminiscences of Old John Brown . . .* Rockford, Ill., Stereotyped and printed by A. E. Smith, 1880. 80 p. front. (port.), illus.

Connelley, William E. *History of Kansas, State & People, Kansas at the First Quarter Post of the Twentieth Century.* With Kansas biography by special staff of writers. Chicago, New York, American Historical Society, 1928. 5 v. front., illus., ports., maps.
———. *Ingalls of Kansas; a Character Study.* Topeka, The Author, 1909. 234 p. front. (port.).
———. *James Henry Lane, the "Grim Chieftain" of Kansas.* Topeka, Crane & Co., 1899. 126 p. (Twentieth Century Classics and School Readings. v. 1, no. 2.)
———. *John Brown.* Topeka, Crane & Co., 1900. 426 p. front. (map).
———. *Kansas Territorial Governors.* 144 p. Topeka, Crane & Co., 1900. (Twentieth Century Classics and School Readings. v. 1, no. 8.)
———. *Wild Bill and His Era; the Life & Adventures of James Butler Hickok.* With int. by Charles Moreau Harger. New York. Press of the Pioneers, 1933. 229 p. plates, ports.
Crawford, Samuel J. *Kansas in the Sixties.* Chicago, McClurg, 1911. 441 p. front., ports. An autobiography. The author was governor of Kansas 1865–68, and colonel of the 19th Kansas cavalry, 1868–69.
Cutler, William G. *History of the State of Kansas* . . . With biographical sketches and portraits. Chicago, A. T. Andreas, 1883. 1,616 p. front. (map), illus., ports., plan.
Giles, F. W. *Thirty Years in Topeka; a Historical Sketch.* Topeka, G. W. Crane & Co., 1886. 411 p.
Harris, Frank. *My Reminiscences as a Cowboy.* Illus. by William Gropper. New York, C. Boni, 1930. 217 p. plates. (Paper books.)
Hinton, Richard J. *John Brown and His Men; with Some Account of the Roads They Traveled to Reach Harper's Ferry.* New York, Funk & Wagnalls Co., 1894. 752 p. front. (port.), illus. (American Reformers; ed. by C. Martyn.)
Howe, E. W. *Plain People.* New York, Dodd, Mead & Co., 1929. 317 p. front. (port.). Howe's autobiography.
Inman, Henry. *The Old Santa Fe Trail; the Story of a Great Highway.* With full-page plates by Frederick Remington. Topeka, Crane & Co., 1916. 493 p. front. (port.). First pub. 1897.
Ise, John. *Sod and Stubble; the Story of a Kansas Homestead.* Illus. by Howard Simon. New York, Wilson-Erickson, 1936. 326 p. front., plates, ports. Describes the early struggles of the author's parents.
Isely, Bliss, and W. M. Richards. *Four Centuries in Kansas; Unit Studies.* Wichita, Atlanta, etc., McCormick-Mathers Co., 1936. 344 p. illus., maps. Bibl.
Kansas State Historical Society. *Biennial Report* . . . Topeka, 1879 to date.
———. Collections of the Kansas State Historical Society . . . Topeka, 1881 to date.
———. *Publications.* Topeka, Kansas State Printing Plant, 1886–1920. 2 v.
Miller, Wallace E. *The Peopling of Kansas* . . . Columbus, O., Press of F. J. Heer, 1906. 134 p. tables.
Merrill, O. N. *True History of the Kansas Wars, and Their Origin, Progress and Incidents; with Statements concerning the Murders of Dow, Barber, Doyle and Others* . . . Illus. with colored engravings. Cincinnati, J. R. Telfer, 1856. 54 p.
Nation, Mrs. Carry A. *The Use and Need of the Life of Carry A. Nation, Written by Herself.* Rev. ed. Ten thousand copies . . . Topeka, F. M. Steves & Sons, 1908. 396 p. front. (port.) illus.
Phillips, William. *The Conquest of Kansas, by Missouri and Her Allies.* A History of the Troubles in Kansas, from the Passage of the Organic Act until the Close of July, 1856. Boston, Phillips, Sampson & Co., 1856. 414 p.
Prentis, Noble L. *A History of Kansas.* Ed. & rev. by Henrietta V. Race. Topeka, C. Prentis, 1909. 403 p. front., illus., ports.
Ray, P. Orman. "The Genesis of the Kansas-Nebraska Act." (In American Historical Association. *Annual Report* . . . *for the Year 1914.* Washington, 1916. v. 1, p. 259-280.)
Robinson, Charles. *The Kansas Conflict.* New York, Harper, 1892. 487 p. Robinson was the first Governor of Kansas.

Robinson, Sara T. D. *Kansas; Its Interior and Exterior Life.* Including a Full View
of Its Settlement, Political History, Social Life, Climate, Soil, Productions, Scen-
ery, etc. 10th ed. Lawrence, Journal Pub. Co., 1899. 438 p. front. (port.), plates.
1st ed. 1856.
Spring, Leverett W. *Kansas; the Prelude to the War for the Union.* Boston, New
York, Houghton Mifflin & Co., 1885. 334 p. front. (map).
Thayer, Eli. *A History of the Kansas Crusade, Its Friends and Its Foes.* With int.
by the Reverend Edward Everett Hale. New York, Harper, 1889. 294 p.
Villard, Oswald Garrison. *John Brown, a Biography, 1800–1859.* Garden City,
Doubleday, Doran & Co., 1929. 738 p. front., plates, ports., map, facsims. Bibl.
First pub. 1910.
White, William Allen. *Masks in a Pageant.* New York, Macmillan, 1928. 507 p.
front., illus., map, plates, ports. Reminiscences of Croker, Platt, Mark Hanna,
Grover Cleveland, McKinley, Theodore Roosevelt, Woodrow Wilson, Harding,
Coolidge, etc.
———. *A Puritan in Babylon; the Story of Calvin Coolidge.* New York, Macmil-
lan, 1938. 460 p. illus., ports. Revision of biography pub. 1925.
———. *Woodrow Wilson, the Man, His Times & His Task.* Boston and New
York, Houghton Mifflin & Co., 1924. 527 p. front., plates, ports.
Wilder, D. W. *The Annals of Kansas.* New edition covering years 1541–1885. To-
peka, T. D. Thacher, 1886. 1,196 p. front. (port.) 1st ed. 1875.

POLITICS AND GOVERNMENT

Bates, Frank Greene. *Civics of Kansas.* Rev. by I. Victor Iles. Boston, New York,
etc., Ginn & Co., 1914. 93 p.
Douglas, Stephen Arnold. *Speech of Hon. S. A. Douglas, of Illinois, against the
Admission of Kansas under the Lecompton Constitution.* Del. in the U. S. Senate,
March 22, 1858. 32 p.
James, J. A., and A. H. Sanford. *Our Government, Local, State, and National.*
(Kansas ed.) New York, Scribner, 1907. 216 p. Includes "The Government of
Kansas," by George W. Winans. (24 p.)
Kansas Governor. *Under the Statehouse Dome. Our State Government.* Radio
Speeches of Gov. Harry H. Woodring, Broadcast from His Desk in the Capitol
at Topeka, July to Sept. 1932 . . . Topeka, 1932. 216 p. tables.
Kansas. Legislative Council. Research Department. *Cost of Government in Kansas,
Five Fiscal Years.* Total and Per Capita Cost—State and Local—Covering Fiscal
Years 1929, 1932, 1933, 1934, 1935. Topeka, 1935. 2 l. incl. tables. Mimeo-
graphed.
Palmer, Frederick. *This Man Landon; the Record & Career of Governor Alfred M.
Landon of Kansas.* New York, Dodd, Mead & Co., 1936. 245 p. front. (port.).
Price, Ralph R. *Kansas and Her Government.* A Supplement to Munro and Ozane's
Social Civics. New York, Macmillan, 1925. 117 p.
Sumner, Charles. "Crime against Kansas." From his speech in the Senate, May 19,
1856. Boston, 1897. (Old South leaflets. Gen. ser. no. 83.)

AGRICULTURE

Capper, Arthur. *The Agricultural Bloc.* New York, Harcourt, Brace & Co., 1922.
171 p. (The Farmer's Bookshelf, ed. by K. L. Butterfield.)
Kansas State Board of Agriculture. *Reports.* Topeka, 1873 to date.
McCormick, Fannie. *A Kansas Farm; or, The Promised Land.* New York, J. B.
Alden, 1892. 163 p. front. (port.), plates.
McCoy, Joseph G. *Historic Sketches of the Cattle Trade of the West and South-
west.* Kansas City, Mo., Ramsey, Millett & Hudson, 1874. 427 p. illus. Repr. by
Rare Book Shop, Washington, D. C. 1932.
U. S. Dept. of Commerce. Bureau of the Census. *U. S. Census of Agriculture:
1935. Statistics for Counties and a Summary for the United States: Farms, Farm
Acreage and Value, and Selected Livestock and Crops.* Washington, Govt. Print.
Off., 1936. 951 p. Volume 1. Kansas statistics: p. 349-375.

INDUSTRY, COMMERCE, AND LABOR

Allen, Henry J. *The Party of the Third Part; the Story of the Kansas Industrial Relations Court.* New York and London, Harper, 1921. 283 p. Allen was Governor of Kansas from 1919 to 1923.

Capper, Arthur. *Kansas' Greatest Need: Industrial Development.* Address by Gov. Arthur Capper before the Chamber of Commerce, Pittsburg, Kansas, March 31, 1916. Topeka, 1916. 8 p.

Gagliardo, Domenico. "The Gompers-Allen Debate on the Kansas Industrial Court." (In *Kansas Historical Quarterly* [continuing *Kansas Historical Collections*]. Topeka, 1934. v. 3, p. 385-395.)

———. "A History of Kansas Child-Labor Legislation." (In *Kansas Historical Quarterly* [continuing *Kansas Historical Collections*]. Topeka, 1932. v. 1, p. 379-401.)

———. *Labor Legislation in Kansas* . . . Lawrence, Kansas University School of Business, 1931. 63 p. (Part of Ph. D. thesis, University of Chicago. Repr. from Kansas Studies in Business, no. 14.)

Huggins, William L. *Labor and Democracy.* New York, Macmillan, 1922. 213 p. This work is mainly concerned with the Kansas Industrial Act and its workings.

Kansas Bankers Association. *The Story of Banking in Kansas, Commemorating the Fiftieth Anniversary of the Organization of the Kansas Bankers Association, 1887–1937* . . . Topeka, H. M. Ives & Sons, Printers, 1937. 103 p. front., illus. (map), ports.

Kansas Business. Special issue devoted to advancement of industry in Kansas. Topeka, Kansas Business, Oct. 1937. 31 p. illus.

Kansas Commission of Labor and Industry. *Directory of Kansas Manufacturers. 1932.* Issued in cooperation with Kansas Chamber of Commerce. Topeka, Kansas State Printing Plant, B. P. Walker, State Printer, 1932. 209 p.

Kansas Commission of Labor and Industry. *Kansas Factories and Workshops, 1935.* Comp. by G. E. Blakeley, Commissioner of Labor. Topeka, Kansas State Printing Plant, W. C. Austin, State Printer, 1936. 116 p.

Progress in Kansas . . . Official pub. Kansas Chamber of Commerce. Monthly. Topeka, 1934 to date.

U. S. Department of Commerce. Bureau of the Census. Fifteenth Census of the United States. *Manufactures:* Prepared under supervision of Eugene F. Hartley, Chief Statistician for Manufactures. Washington, Govt. Print. Off., 1922. 31 p. tables.

Walker, Perley F. *Industrial Development of Kansas.* Topeka, Kansas State Printing Plant, B. P. Walker, Printer, 1922. 55 p. maps, tables, diagrs., atlas. (Bulletin of Univ. of Kansas. v. 23, no. 12.)

TRANSPORTATION

Kansas State Highway Commission. *Biennial Reports.* Topeka, 1919 to date. plates, tables, diagrs., charts.

Monahan, Deane. *The Arkansas Valley and Its Great Railway, together with Maps, Engravings, Tables, etc.* Topeka, Kansas Magazine Pub. Co., 1873. 22 p. plates, map. Repr. from the *Kansas Magazine.*

RACIAL ELEMENTS

Clark, Carroll D., and Roy L. Roberts. *People of Kansas; a Demographic and Sociological Study.* With foreword by William Allen White. Topeka, 1936. 272 p. illus., diagrs. (A publication of the Kansas State Planning Board.)

EDUCATION

Barr, Elizabeth N. "History of Kansas Colleges." (In Connelley, William E. *A Standard History of Kansas and Kansans.* Chicago, New York, Lewis Pub. Co., 1918. v. 2. p. 1,015-1,070.)

Kansas Dept. of Education. *Unit Program in Social Studies.* Sept. 1934 and Sept. 1935. Authorized and issued by W. T. Markham, State Supt. of Public Instructions. Topeka, Kansas State Printing Plant, W. C. Austin, State Printer, 1934–35. 2 v. illus., tables.

Kansas Dept. of Public Instruction. *Annual and Biennial Reports.* Topeka, etc., 1862 to date.

Milstead, Bertha. "Beginnings of Education in Kansas." *Aerend,* Winter 1931, v. 3:30-32.

RELIGION

Fisher, Rev. H. D. *The Gun and the Gospel; Early Kansas and Chaplain Fisher.* Chicago and New York, Medical Century Co., 1897. 344 p. front., plates, ports.

Hobbs, Wilson. "The Friends' Establishment in Kansas Territory." (In *Transactions of the Kansas State Historical Society, 1903–1904.* Topeka, 1904. v. 8, p. 250-271.)

Lutz, J. J. "The Methodist Missions among the Indian Tribes in Kansas." (In *Transactions of the Kansas State Historical Society, 1905–1906.* Topeka, 1906. v. 9, p. 160-235.)

McGonigle, James A. "Catholic Missions among the Indians in Kansas." (In *Transactions of the Kansas State Historical Society, 1905–1906.* Topeka, 1906. v. 9, p. 153-159.)

Shaw, Rev. James. *Early Reminiscences of Pioneer Life in Kansas.* With introduction by Rev. A. H. Tevis. Atchison Haskell Printing Co., 1886. 238 p. front. (port.)

Youngman, Rev. W. E. *Gleanings from Western Prairies.* Cambridge, Jones & Piggott, 1882. 214 p. diagr. Describes ranch life in Neosho County, Kansas; also tells of the Jesuit mission to the Osage Indians in that county.

SOCIAL AGENCIES

Kansas Conference of Social Work. *Hand book of Kansas Social Resources; Health, Education and Social Welfare.* Addresses, Abstracts and Committee Reports of the Kansas State Council for Health, Education and Welfare, and the Kansas Conference of Social Work. Topeka, Kansas State Printing Plant, B. P. Walker, State Printer, 1932. 302 p. illus.

LITERATURE AND JOURNALISM

Barker, Nettie Garner. *Kansas Women in Literature.* Kansas City, Kan., S. I. Meseraull & Son, Printers, 1915. 40 p. ports.

Callahan, James P. "Kansas in the American Novel and Short Story." (In *Collections of the Kansas State Historical Society, 1926–1928.* Topeka, 1928. v. 17, p. 139-188. With bibliography.)

Carruth, William Herbert, comp. *Kansas in Literature.* Topeka, Crane & Co., 1900. 2 v. (Twentieth Century Classics and School Readings. v. 1, nos. 5-6.) Vol. 1 contains poetry, preceded by a historical sketch of Kansas literature and followed by a bibliography. Vol. 2 contains prose selections.

Collister, Ida, comp. *A Kansas Calendar of Sentiments by Kansas Writers.* Topeka, Crane & Co., 1915. 54 l.

Hesser, C. E., comp. *"A Bokay of Wild Daisies" Home Grown and Full Blown; the Kind that Grows in and around La Cygne, Kansas.* A little Book of Native Verse, by the Natives and Near Natives. Kansas City, Mo., Printed by Punton Bros. Pub. Co., 1915. 90 p.

Howe, E. W. *Country Town Sayings; a Collection of Paragraphs from the Atchison Globe.* Topeka, Crane & Co., 1911. 298 p.

———. *Ventures in Common Sense.* New York, A. A. Knopf, 1919. 273 p. Made up chiefly of extracts from *E. W. Howe's Monthly.* (The Free Lance Books, II; ed. with introductions by H. L. Mencken.)

Kansas Magazine. v. 1-4, pub. monthly in Topeka, Jan. 1872–Oct. 1873. v. 1-6, pub. monthly in Wichita, Jan. 1909–Jan. 1912. v. 1 to date, pub. annually in Manhattan, Kansas State College Press.

Kansas State Historical Society. *History of Kansas Newspapers.* A History of the Newspapers and Magazines Published in Kansas from the Organization of Kansas Territory, 1854, to Jan. 1, 1916 . . . Topeka, Kansas State Printing Plant, 1916. 320 p. front., illus.

McMurtrie, Douglas C., and Albert H. Allen. *Gotham Meeker, Pioneer Printer of Kansas.* With a bibl. of the known issues of the Baptist mission press at Shawanoe, Stockbridge, and Ottawa, 1834–1854. Chicago, Eyncourt Press, 1930. 169 p. front. (port.), facsims.

Wattles, Willard, comp. *Sunflowers, a Book of Kansas Poems.* Chicago, McClurg, 1916. 208 p. A well edited anthology, reprinting poems by John J. Ingalls, William Herbert Carruth, Eugene F. Ware, Harry Kemp, etc.

White, William Allen. *Forty Years on Main Street.* Comp. by Russell H. Fitzgibbon from the columns of the Emporia *Gazette;* foreword by Frank C. Clough. New York, Toronto, Farrar & Rhinehart, 1937. 409 p. front., plates, ports., facsim.

ART

Reinbach, Edna. "Kansas Art and Artists." (In *Collections of the Kansas State Historical Society, 1926–1928.* Topeka, 1928. v. 17, p. 571-585.)

ARCHITECTURE

Wichers, H. E. *Designs for Kansas Farm Homes.* Manhattan, The College, 1929. 105 p. illus. (incl. plans.) (Kansas State Agricultural College Bulletin. v. 13, no. 10.) Bibl.

Whittemore, Margaret. *Sketchbook of Kansas Landmarks.* Illus. by the author. 2d ed. Topeka, The College Press, 1937. 125 p. illus.

MUSIC

Reinbach, Edna, comp. *Music & Musicians in Kansas.* Topeka, Kansas State Historical Society, 1930. 51 p. Bibl.

SPORTS AND RECREATION

Kansas State Fish and Game Warden *Bulletins* and *Reports.* Topeka, 1910 to date.

Index